Burning Dow

Mother, daughter, maid, South Africa, 1988. Copyright © 1997 Rosalind Solomon.

Burning Down the House

Recycling Domesticity

edited by
Rosemary Marangoly George

Routledge
Taylor & Francis Group

LONDON AND NEW YORK

First published 1998 by Westview Press

Published 2018 by Routledge
52 Vanderbilt Avenue, New York, NY 10017
2 Park Square, Milton Park, Abingdon, Oxon OX14 4RN

Routledge is an imprint of the Taylor & Francis Group, an informa business

Library of Congress Cataloging-in-Publication Data
Burning down the house : recycling domesticity / edited by Rosemary
   Marangoly George.
      p. cm.
   Includes bibliographical references and index.
   ISBN 0-8133-3425-X (hardcover)
   1. Family.   2. Home.   3. Sex role.   I. George, Rosemary
Marangoly.
HQ518.B85   1998
306.85—dc21   98-9570
                                                            CIP

ISBN 13: 978-0-367-00991-5 (hbk)
ISBN 13: 978-0-367-15978-8 (pbk)

Contents

Acknowledgments

My greatest debt is to the exceptional scholars who have contributed their work to this collection of essays on domesticity in a global context. Together they have shaped a thoughtful and thought-provoking reassessment of what domesticity signifies in several geographic and disciplinary locations at the close of this century. This book has been a while in the making, and I would especially like to thank the contributors for their immense patience during the publication process. Laura Parsons, my editor at Westview, has been most helpful in bringing this project to completion. I would like to thank Laura for her deep commitment to this book, for her forthrightness, and for her resourcefulness. The labor of others in the editorial and production teams at Westview/HarperCollins is also gratefully acknowledged. I would especially like to thank Kathleen Christensen for her outstanding copyediting work on this project. Permission to reprint Nancy Armstrong's essay from the *Yale Journal of Criticism* and Rosemary Marangoly George's article from *Cultural Critique* is gratefully acknowledged. Rosalind Solomon kindly gave us permission to use her powerful photograph as the frontispiece of this book. It is a telling essay in its own right. I wish to thank several of the contributors, who made helpful suggestions on editing such a volume: John Lowney, Nancy Armstrong, Aparajita Sagar, and Ann duCille. I would especially like to thank Michael Ryan for his enthusiasm for and critical input into this project at its various stages. And finally, I would like to thank S. G. Badrinath, whose constant support allows me the luxury of questioning the comforts of conventional domestic arrangements.

Rosemary Marangoly George

Chapter One

Recycling: Long Routes to and from Domestic Fixes

ROSEMARY MARANGOLY GEORGE

These [houses] are now good only to be thrown away like old food cans.
—Theodore Adorno[1]

My immediate and somewhat flippant response to Adorno's used-can dilemma is to urge recycling. In the west, recycling has become one of the prime late-twentieth-century means of responding to an overwhelming sense of a steady decline in the quality of (domestic) life. The recycling passion that has now gripped the United States is a result of the growing consciousness of the enormity of the amount of natural resources needed to sustain the high order of domestic consumption and to maintain the "basic" comforts of the average middle-class American home.[2] But champions of recycling seem nowadays to promise not just a world with renewed resources for future generations but also an unscathed domesticity to match. What is promised to future generations as a by-product of responsible recycling (smart use of planetary resources) is *continued* domestic pleasures of an order currently enjoyed only in select circles—pleasures such as wood-burning fires, limitless biodegradable cleaning supplies, and recreational fishing. In a metaphorical sense, recycling has become the solution to the problem of dealing with a concept, domesticity, that still supplies inordinate amounts of pleasure even after its organizing logic has gone awry.

The pleasures of the domestic are so deeply entrenched as to seem "natural"—necessary to our physical and mental well-being, regardless of the unsavory specifics or the labor involved in setting up these "comfort zones." Witold Rybczynski, the author of the popular 1988 book *Home: A Short History of an Idea*, asserts: "Domestic well-being is a fundamental human need that is deeply rooted in us, and that must be satisfied."[3] There is a general aura of wholesomeness about the domestic that is never abandoned, even when specific domestic arrangements are discarded. Patriarchal notions of the family and the home are seen as coterminous and in sharp decline the world over. Of course, those on the conservative right in the United States who lament the demise of the patriarchal nuclear family also mourn the loss of the pleasures of the domestic, which, in their view, cannot exist outside the working father–homemaking mother–2.0 children formula.[4] However, most liberal and left social and cultural commentators who dismiss such rigid conceptions of the family *also* remain firmly committed to a recycled form of "family values," except that the version they espouse does not use the same formula for "family" as does the right's version.[5] What such "alternative lifestyle" domestic arrangements *rescue* from traditional scenarios is precisely this sense of private comfort, safety, and exclusiveness. This rescue, more often than not, results in a nostalgically recycled domesticity that allows for a continued enjoyment of domestic pleasures without questioning or dismantling domesticity's founding assumptions.

The domestic, perhaps more than other modern institutions, has been recycled and reinvented in the last few decades. Much of this recycling aims for alterations in domestic forms and practices to better satisfy current demand without examining the social and gender inequalities that buttress domesticity. Since the mid–nineteenth century, domestic reform has been among the top priorities of most modern liberal social movements, such as liberal feminism. The constant reworking of domestic arrangements is an index of the success of these movements as much as an indication of the limits of liberalism. Liberal feminism has transformed our understanding of the domestic, but even as the institution is recycled in more gender-equitable ways, what gets deflected is the responsibility of addressing the other complexities that shape this arena—for instance, the economic and racial connections that hold domestic sites adjacent and yet unequal within a national or global framework.

The recycling that I advocate in this introduction and that is supported by the chapters that follow attempts to be responsive to these complexities.[6] I argue that recycling in this new sense is more than just a rescue operation or a salvaging of domestic pleasures that feeds on nostalgia and selective memory of old domestic grandeur. On the contrary, narratives and practices that responsibly recycle domesticity perform two tasks: first, they effect transformations that are attentive to the materials and the debris of past domestic edifices. Second, in being attentive to the material and historical factors that have enabled domesticity to flourish, such recycling narratives make the domestic a site from which countertheorizations about seemingly "larger" and unrelated institutions and ideologies can be produced. Thus domesticity can be understood, paradoxically, as both the site where the rescue and the retreat into an apolitical private sphere can be endlessly embroidered upon as well as a site from which social organizations can be rendered visible and open to critique. Many of the chapters in this collection study the ways in which domestic arrangements continue to be remade in both of these directions. The chapters examine how this recycling operates in the refiguring of institutions such as the family and in the redrawing of neighborhoods, of nations, of literary genres, and of other cultural artifacts. But most importantly this collection works to stretch our understanding of the territory covered by terms such as *recycling, the domestic,* and *domesticity.* How do we define *domesticity* in the late twentieth century?

The standard connotations of terms such as *the domestic* and *domesticity* were described by Karen Tranberg Hansen in her introduction to *African Encounters with Domesticity*: "To define it [domesticity] is to describe a set of ideas that over the course of nineteenth century western history have associated women with family, domestic values, and home, and took for granted a hierarchical distribution of power favoring men."[7] What is remarkable is how this "set of ideas" and practices has become globally hegemonic as a result of colonial and capitalist expansion and modernization, albeit not without contestation from other, local domestic ideologies.[8] In the late twentieth century, domesticity can be understood as a universal phenomenon just as imprecisely and yet accurately as patriarchy can be understood to be a staple feature of social organization all over the globe today. It is also necessary to note the distinctions among the terms *household, family,* and *the domestic,* if only to comprehend their conflation in our usage of these terms.[9] *The domestic* implies spatial arrangements in which certain practices of reproduction (children as well as certain modes of production) are situated. As a primary site at which modernity is manufactured and made manifest, the domestic serves as a regulative norm that refigures conceptions of the family from a largely temporal organization of kinship into a spatially manifest entity. The domestic with all its material and metaphysical accoutrements bridges the distance between seemingly public issues and the private concerns of families. Today, domesticity is fabricated with local variations across national borders and social classes. Class, race, and geographic location place heavy inflections on domesticity, and yet, like love, childhood, and death, the domestic is seen to transcend all specifics or rather to blur distinctions in the warm glow of its splendor.

The analyses of domesticity in this book are considerations of more than just the private home and homemaking practices. *Burning Down the*

House views domesticity through multiple frames until the domestic expands to bear on all social arrangements. Not only is domesticity understood as a manifestation of larger national and imperial projects, but it is also employed as a means of critiquing these unwieldy ideological structures from within. Since the inquiries in this book consider political, social, and historical implications of the domestic, they take longer routes to domesticity than the reader may be used to from other scholarly writing on the topic. This introduction, in turn, does not draw all the diverse chapters together under a grand narrative on domesticity but introduces the reader to the paradoxes and juxtapositions that render tight universalizations on domesticity wholly inadequate, even as suggestive connections are made between narratives on homemaking (and house breaking) in a global context.

New readings of domesticity that are attentive to its complex politics are emerging in several disparate academic discussions—for instance, those on the entanglement of the domestic within nationalist discourses and in recent (feminist) economic analyses of the home in the context of industrial "homework." Domesticity, in those discussions, has ideological functions that do not stop at constructions of the private lives of individuals, of home, and of family. Such analyses begin with the understanding that to bring home the hierarchies of gender, class, race, and religion is to render these hierarchies logical, viable, and seemingly natural. Researchers such as Jeanne Boydston and Alice Kessler-Harris see the impact of domesticity on wage and labor issues, which were hitherto understood to be purely market driven.[10] In her study of women's labor history in the west and the reliance on domestic ideologies to buttress capitalist expansion, Eileen Boris noted that a home/work split was an essential component of industrialization. She wrote: "Sometimes conceived of as separate spheres, other times expressed as private/public, reproduction/production, community/shop floor, and always seen as male/female, the home/work split pulls apart what in various concrete historical circumstances not only co-exists but defines boundaries that overlap, indeed, construct each other."[11]

In the preceding quote, taken from her review of recent studies in women's labor history, Boris has succinctly analyzed the home/work dichotomy that until recently formed the basis of the scholarly writing on domesticity in disciplines as diverse as literary criticism and architectural design. Other scholars have recently reworked the conventional links made between private homes and nations,[12] between domesticity and empire,[13] between home country and new land in the context of diaspora,[14] and of course, between domesticity and gender.[15]

The close association between women and the domestic arena is of such long standing that it is sometimes perceived as a natural affinity that draws the two together. Yet as Karen Tranberg Hansen reminds us: "The domestic is not everywhere nor exclusively organized by gender, but also by class and race relations, and gender relations are not only or even primarily negotiated across a politico-jural/domestic divide. Both women and men live in households and society, so rather than assuming that gender and the domestic encompass each other, we should ask questions about their changing interrelationship."[16] Much of the feminist work that has attempted to pry apart the almost automatic association of one gender with domesticity has unfortunately ultimately served to reinforce the easy association of women with issues of housework, house decoration, child care, and so forth. Of course, this association in people's minds only mirrors the domestic arrangements that we see around us, in which women are usually expected to and do take on the burden of maintaining domesticity.[17] A quick corrective to this order of things is provided by research on the colonizers' domestic arrangements in colonial Africa, which shows domestic work in White households to be one of the earliest and most common forms of wage labor that African *men* engaged in.[18] European colonizers were agreeable to having their cooking, child care, and laundry needs met by male African servants; such skills were perhaps understood to be learned skills rather than innate gender attributes. Clearly, the power dynamic that operates in deciding who does the housework is not always nor everywhere determined solely by gender. Work by Hansen and others demonstrates how the ready availability of household help in Africa and other parts of the world has resulted in *some* upper-class, middle-class, and even working-class African, Indian subcontinental, Asian, and Middle Eastern women having identities that are not thoroughly subsumed by their domestic duties. They have the luxury of occupying a supervisory relationship to child care and other forms of household labor, and yet this in itself is no guarantee of feminist emancipation.[19] We can no longer look exclusively at the domestic arena for explications of gender issues or expect gender analyses to generate all that we need to know about domestication projects.

The Domestic on the Domestic

Our reflections on our damaged domesticity must include sites like that represented by the Rosalind Solomon photograph that serves as a frontispiece for this book. This stunning photograph was taken in the 1980s in South Africa in the last years of apartheid.[20] The serene mother and daughter are framed by the accoutrements of modern middle-class domesticity—the TV, the elaborate coverings draped over the table, the bow-dotted framed paintings on the wall, the framed family photographs, and of course, the maid on her knees. To say that the servant is the stumbling block in this picture is to be delicate. The Black woman should serve as the stumbling block to several projects on display in the picture—modernity, feminism, domesticity, the family, the joyous mother-daughter bond, the sense of an apolitical private sphere. And yet it seems as if none of this dissonance is apparent to the housewife or her daughter. What Rosalind Solomon has caught so unflinchingly is the necessity of the servant's presence to complete the mistress's proud display of herself as an established, prosperous, fulfilled woman. The Black woman's facial expression refuses easy interpretations, but it is clear that this photographic event is not experienced in a similar fashion by all three subjects.

As in the urban collages created by the U.S. painter Kerry James Marshall, the undeniable pleasures of the domestic are ironically acknowledged in Solomon's photograph, even as their material basis is exposed.[21] Do recycled modes of domesticity radically alter or simply reproduce the dynamics represented in this family portrait? What are the virtues of domesticity when viewed by "the domestic" on her knees? Putting domestic comfort and "family" on display (as this photograph does so powerfully) requires both women to adopt unequal but complementary positions; only then is the work of homemaking complete.

What Solomon's photograph makes explicit is precisely what is rendered invisible in the usual nostalgia-streaked sentimental representations of domesticity. What is unusual about this photograph is the blunt representation of the economic, racial, and gender arrangements that need to be in place on a national and often international footing before respectable homemaking is successfully achieved. Needless to say, this situation is not unique to middle-class homemaking in South Africa. And yet the more typical representation is like the cover illustration of a special edition of *The Economist* (September 9 to 15, 1995) on the decline of the family (see Figure 1.1). This cover photograph, set in the "family values" fifties, pictured a White father at the center of the frame reading to his attentive family members, who have dutifully arranged themselves around him. The popularity of this roseate yet clearly patriarchal view of past domestic arrangements is echoed in a March 1996 letter to the editor of *Time* magazine:

> Well, let's see. Thirty years ago, the average dad could support his family with just one job, Mom could raise the kids if she chose to, a young person could jump right out of high school or college into a job, the person best qualified got the job, there was less crime, our morals had not yet decayed, and there was less sex and violence on TV or in the movies. So what's happened? Too many people coming into our country and too many jobs leaving.[22]

In fact, this letter might well serve as a caption for *The Economist*'s cover photo, for both are equally representative of a culturally selective amne-

The disappearing family

FIGURE 1.1   *The Disappearing Family*

sia in which people remember only a certain slice of domestic life divorced from the lives of Other Americans. In concrete ways, the family wage that this "average dad" brought home was predicated on the depressed wages of these other Americans.[23] However, nostalgia cuts a clean path from ideal past to the present and disregards the debris and costs accumulated along the way. The sentimental and selective remembrance of the fifties in the west is mainly contrived by the skillful use of black-and-white still photography buttressed by a selective set of statistics. Solomon's photograph cannily dispels any residual sentimentalism attached to "black-and-white" family portraits.

Whatever the specifics, what is common to any household is the labor of reproducing itself. Noting that "the product of labor of housework was the household itself," Jeanne Boydston defines this labor as "an evolving array of requirements, some stable and long-term, some arising from the contingencies of the moment, founded on the material and psychosocial need of its members."[24] Boydston's analysis, while directed at nineteenth-century households, rings true for domestic arrangements in the present.

The question that remains is who does this housework and at what costs? In *Domesticity and Dirt: Housewives and Domestic Servants in the US, 1920–1945*, Phyllis Palmer exposes the centrality of domestic servants to American models of perfect domesticity well into the mid–twentieth century.[25] Interestingly, in the final chapter of *Domesticity and Dirt*, Palmer obliquely suggests that the "problem with no name" (à la Betty Friedan) that beset so many White middle-class women at the end of the fifties arose in part because the era of ample cheap domestic labor came to an end as women of color who had tackled much of the domestic dirt found other employment avenues open to them. Studies show that in recent years, career women in the west are increasingly turning to domestic help, provided mainly by immigrants (both legal and undocumented) and other women of color, in order to juggle the tasks of maintaining both career and the high standards of child care and home maintenance expected from today's woman.[26] In the nonwestern parts of the globe, given the uneven nature of economic development, the use and exploitation of servants in domestic projects in which they are marginal has been the unbroken norm from premodern times to the present.[27] Perhaps Adorno was right—some kinds of domesticity need to be laid to rest. Yet this cannot be done without acknowledging the organizing power and pleasures of the domestic in its many manifestations. Furthermore, narratives that attempt to deconstruct the pleasures of the domestic do not automatically put to an end such pleasurable spaces and experiences. And this is what motivates further discussion.

Of Kitchen Tables

In a curiously ambivalent essay titled "Domestication," published in 1995, the literary and cultural critic Rachel Bowlby noted the ways in which feminist and other deconstructive scholarship has set up "domestication" as the opposite of "radical theorization."[28] Domestication, Bowlby notes, "refers generally to processes of simplification, assimilation and distortion—any or all of these—to which the theory in question falls victim or which it is powerless to resist."[29] Moving swiftly between metaphoric uses, such as the domestication of theories, and actual domestic fixes, Bowlby suggests that domestication is usually understood as the "reintegration or re-assimilation into the dominant culture, accompanied by the loss of . . . critical impetus."[30] What remains ambiguous in the essay is the degree of Bowlby's own agreement with this use of domestication as a negative metaphor, one that is "in need of no further analysis, [and] implies simply binary oppositions and two-stage stories, whereby something initially natural, spontaneous or subversive gets pushed into a conformity or homogeneity that deprives it of whatever made it different."[31] Assessing the importance of domesticity (both real and metaphoric) to feminist theory, Bowlby writes:

> Just as feminists are sure that the "domestication" of feminist theories is to be regretted, so the rejection of domesticity has seemed a principal, if not *the* principal, tenet of feminist demands for freedom. The home figures as the place where the woman is confined, and from which she must be emancipated in order for her to gain access to a world outside that is masculine but only contingently so, and which offers possibilities of personal and social achievement that are not available within its limited sphere.
>
> In various forms this representation could be said to run right through the western tradition of feminist writing from the past two hundred years—including in different ways Mary Wollstonecraft, Simone de Beauvoir, Betty Friedan, and at many points Virginia Woolf.[32]

We need to ask ourselves which feminisms and which feminists are left out of "the Western tradition of feminist writing from the past two hundred years" if, in 1995, such a tradition ends with Virginia Woolf and completely ignores the many feminists who have not experienced or written out of this dire opposition between domestication and radical theory.

If, for instance, we were to stop and consider the name chosen by the founders of the Kitchen Table Press, we would immediately be presented with a feminism that sees the very radical potential of domesticity and no incongruity in harnessing the wisdom and labor of this homely location onto their feminist practices. Writing in 1985 of the invisibility of Black lesbian writers due to the fact that they are usually overlooked by mainstream publishers, Barbara Smith stressed the contribution that small feminist presses such as Kitchen Table Press, of which she is a cofounder, have made in getting such works out to readers.[33] Similarly, in her 1986 essay titled "No More Buried Lives," Barbara Christian writes, "Despite the fact that Walker received the Pulitzer for *The Color Purple* and Naylor the American Book Award for *The Women of Brewster Place*, I doubt if *Home Girls*, an anthology of Black feminist and lesbian writing that was published by Kitchen Table Press, would have been published by a mainstream publishing company."[34] Here, alternative theorizations of race, of sexuality, of economics, of nation, and of gender are symbolically signaled (by the sign *kitchen table*) as produced from within the domestic arena. The kitchen table becomes a site that is rendered serviceable in this radical usage because it is recognized as constituted by and therefore hospitable to such discussions on the so-called larger issues. The list of groundbreaking projects nurtured and published by Kitchen Table Press is truly impressive. Its publications include *Home Girls: A Black Feminist Anthology*, edited by Barbara Smith, 1983; *Cuentos: Stories by Latinas*, edited by Alma Gómez, Cherríe Moraga, and Mariana Romo-Camona,

1983; and *This Bridge Called My Back,* edited by Cherríe Moraga and Gloria Anzaldúa, 1983. It would be impossible to label any part of the Kitchen Table enterprise as simple, tame domestication in the Bowlby sense, even as the press's name acknowledges an unglamorous domestic location as the focal point of undoubtedly radical energies. Projects such as the Kitchen Table Press recast domesticity as a launching pad for radical reflections on material conditions rather than a location that serves as a refuge from the same.

In a telling anecdote, Bowlby recounts how she decided to write her article on domestication the very week that she acquired a kitchen table:

> I suggested the topic of domestication and then noticed that this happened in the week when I unexpectedly acquired a kitchen table, having always thought that the room wasn't big enough to take one. My pleasure at the transformation of this domestic space was both mitigated and reinforced by the events of the following two weeks, when I went to Paris—a place where I like to think I feel at home—and had my wallet snatched, twice within the space of one week. For the first time, I felt a strong sense of urban paranoia, if that is the phrase, huddling inside the cozy familiar interior of the place where I was staying, wondering how I was going to write this paper on, of all things, domestication.[35]

Here, domesticity provided for Bowlby a safe haven against a menacing world, and her retreat into domestic coziness seemed to reverse the direction that she saw feminist activism as charting—the escape from the home. Yet in this anecdote more than elsewhere in her essay, Bowlby exposed her reliance on a domestic ideology that maintains a home/world split—a reliance that belied her best attempts at deconstructive readings of domestication.

Yet another reading of the kitchen table is provided by the researchers who analyze the use of the home as a workplace.[36] Such "homework" is not the unpaid domestic labor required in most homes but the poorly paid labor performed in the home and mainly by women for industrial manufacturers and contractors. In this context, kitchen tables are workbenches where entire families or at least the women and children assemble items of domestic and industrial use for which these individuals are paid by the piece. Indeed, the growing trend toward locating production within the "private" home is presented by employers and homeworkers as a means of extending the comforts of home life to one's work arrangements, thus once again erasing the significance of household labor as well as ironically celebrating the "privacy" of the home in the very act that invades this privacy.[37] Homework is championed by some women, who view it as a less restrictive and often even a creative work option compared with what they can find outside the home. Others insist that accepting homework is a recognition of their vulnerability in the marketplace. Research shows that homework carries both exploitative and liberating potential and thus underlines the paradoxical nature of the domestic scene. My intention in setting up these various kitchen tables next to each other is primarily to demonstrate that there are as many approaches to domesticity and domestication (even within western feminist theory) as there are different practices. So when Bowlby said in response to a trend she traced from John Ruskin's 1865 lectures onward, "Here, domestication runs its complete course," she was, of course, speaking not only of one kind of western rhetorical trajectory but also of one kind of narrative on domestication.[38]

Long Routes to Domesticity

Outside a handful of books that examine specific aspects of domesticity, few cross-disciplinary conversations have taken place on the ways in which social institutions such as homes and families were and continue to be refashioned from the late nineteenth century to the present. This book makes possible a multifaceted reading of domesticity in contemporary cultures through its deliberate juxtaposition of chapters that deal with different sociocultural domestic practices and that are written from different academic locations. All the disciplines represented in this volume (literary studies, cultural studies, history, architecture, geography, media studies, queer studies, and film studies) have their own takes on the domestic arena and usually get to pursue this topic more or less unhindered by what *domesticity* signifies in other disciplines. In this volume, however, the placement of chapters facilitates a certain amount of "leakage" and mixing, practices that enhance and enrich all the chapters as well as the usual "readerly" interaction with such a multiauthor book. The disciplinary location that many essays in this collection approach is cultural studies, and consequently, most of the essays are written within postmodern/postcolonial feminist and/or Marxist theoretical frames. Considerations of race, nationhood, history, gender, sexuality, and class are central to most of the contributions and yet are differently nuanced, mainly because of the variant ways in which different disciplines and individual writers engage with such issues. The domestic is an arena in which complex ideological negotiations are conducted to make the transition from past social practices in the process of meeting the pressures of the present. In the narratives and practices of domesticity that the chapters of this book analyze, the trauma of such transformation is absorbed (imperfectly at times) and the domestic is reissued in a usable format or, in rare cases, abandoned altogether.

Individual chapters engage the formation and impact of domestic and related practices in Canada, England, Egypt, Greece, India, Ireland, and the United States. Although this book is global in its considerations, the nation most thoroughly traversed is the United States. The chapters in this book on United States–centered domesticity invite us to confront the gaps and erasures in most United States–based academic and mainstream accounts of domesticity. Those chapters perform the important task of exposing the racialized and gendered logic of U.S. domesticity even as they demonstrate how such logic is rendered invisible. The chapters record oppositional constructions of home and family, expose the racism of American nostalgia for the good old days, and place U.S. concerns within larger maps. Together, the chapters of this book deconstruct the heteronormative singularity of visions conjured up by terms like *the home, the domestic arena,* and even *domestication.*

Notions of the domestic have been integral to academic discourse in several disciplines: architecture and design, anthropology, sociology, economics, philosophy, psychoanalysis, and most crucially, literary and cultural criticism. Much of the scholarly writing in literary and cultural texts attends to the domestic when working through the "domestic fiction" genre or when considering women's writing. Perhaps the most intense examination of the domestic has been performed under the aegis of cross-disciplinary women's studies. Yet gender, as I argued previously and as the chapters that follow demonstrate, is not a location that is everywhere subsumed by the domestic. The chapters in this book take a longer and more complex route to destinations that may not always look like the domestic that we are used to—in disciplinary discourses as much as in our geographical and historical location.

Given that so much of the scholarly and most evocative writing on domesticity is produced in the context of literary and other cultural texts, it is only appropriate that this is the discipline most represented in this book. The so-called literary essays in this collection together reshape the disciplinary practices of defining and theorizing the domestic in discussions of literary representations and genres. Chapters by Nancy Armstrong, Rosemary Marangoly George, David Lloyd, John Lowney, Amie Parry, Aparajita Sagar, and Siobhan Somerville consider literary texts in a primary or secondary fashion but arrive at the domestic in contestation and collaboration with nationalism, national nostalgia, wars, ideals of femininity, racial stereotypes, urban layouts, imperialism, modernity, and so forth. None of the discussions remain purely literary or purely domestic—that is, of course, granting that either purity is or was available at any point for our indulgence.

The chapters of this book fall into four capacious and overlapping sections organized not by the genre of the objects of study (film, literary text, home design, neighborhoods, material cultures, and so forth) or by geography, but rather by commonalties in the central foci of the chapters.

Thus, chapters in the section titled "On the Road: Nations, Empires, Texts, Homes" consider the national and transnational implications of home economics in several related contexts: in the formation of U.S. sentimental fiction, in the writing of colonial homemakers, in literary modernisms on both sides of the Atlantic, and in cross-cultural sighting and citing of sexuality. Nancy Armstrong's chapter studies the sentimental novel as it travels from England to the United States. Her chapter addresses the ideological tasks entailed in "becoming American" and in establishing the American domestic arena in the literary context. I (Rosemary Marangoly George) note the ways in which the writing of British homemakers in the empire recast in imperial and military terms both the domestic domain and their status as mistress of the house. More interesting is these women's assertions that empire building and maintenance was no more than housekeeping on a grand scale, thus complicating the gendered division of labor and revealing the proximity of certain feminisms with imperialism.

In her chapter on modernism and domesticity, Amie Parry contrasts the formal structure of English modernism with that in the United States through an examination of spatial categories in both strands of modernism. Domestic spaces in Gertrude Stein's *Tender Buttons* and *Lectures in America* and colonial spaces in Joseph Conrad's *Lord Jim* are discussed in terms of the differences between U.S. and European imperial practices. Gayatri Gopinath's central concern in her chapter is to engage with the vexing question of how to read sexuality across national and cultural locations. Gopinath reads the Indian subcontinental writer Ismat Chughtai's 1941 short story "The Quilt" as an exemplary account of sexuality that escapes existing theorizations of "lesbian" subjectivity. Chughtai's narrative is held in juxtaposition with Susan Seizer's 1995 account of an anthropological field trip to India that records the dissonance produced in her self-identification as U.S. lesbian by her Indian encounters (with domestic servants and other Indian women with whom she shared intimate spaces).

The second section, titled "DomestiCity: Redrawing Urban Space," presents chapters that examine how "domestic" ideologies shape the public arena so decisively as to dissolve the exclusive association of domesticity with private domains. Dayana Salazar writes of the architectural and cultural impact of the 1923 signing by Greece and Turkey of the Lausanne Treaty, which called for the compulsory exchange of Orthodox Christians living in Asia Minor and Muslims living in what was then Greek territory. This chapter explores the emerging expression of refugee architectural identity in Dekaokto, a refugee neighborhood built by the Greek government in Kaválla, a northern Aegean port. Salazar focuses on the ways in which the traces of a Turkish, "oriental," Ottoman-influenced past emerge in the Greek present, especially in contemporary domestic architectural style, and then explains how this recreated group memory clashes with the Greek national project of a "classic" (read western or European) revival officially adopted and promoted by the Greek state in its public architecture. In his chapter, David Lloyd traces the genealogy of the stereotype of the drunken Irishman and the representation of the same in James Joyce's short story "Counterparts." Alcohol and the pub, Lloyd argues, serve as ambiguous markers of national and masculine identity, just as religion and the feminine seem to share territory in Ireland. In working through these fixities of gender and of space demarcations that create a concomitant racial and sexual hierarchy, Lloyd demonstrates the usefulness of strict categories to British colonial powers and the altered shapes they take up in Irish nationalist discourses.

Working with Nawal El-Saadawi's fiction and other writing on Middle Eastern cultures, Aparajita Sagar analyzes the treatment of gendered spaces such as bodies, veils, homes, and urban public arenas to demonstrate the ways in which, in the texts, the dangers of all these spaces collapse into each other and blur the ferociously policed distinctions between the home and the street as well as between the sexes. Katharyne Mitchell's chapter explores the convergence of economic and cultural forces in the creation of a new urban landscape in Vancouver, British Columbia. In a period of "fast" capital, hegemonic assumptions about the home and the neighborhood are contested and reworked by a variety of different actors. Using the "Monster House" as a condensation point for numerous intersecting processes, Mitchell examines the ways in which local resistance to global forces becomes deeply imbricated in a racial and cultural discourse.

"Nostalgia, Modernity, and Other Domestic Fictions," the third section of this book, draws attention to domestic notions that have held the entire United States in their grip. Kimberly Wallace Sanders illustrates how the figure of Aunt Jemima functioned in the United States in the post–Civil War era and into the mid–twentieth century as a medium by which a conservative ideology of domesticity established the normative "American Home." Sanders exposes the "plantation life" rhetoric that was marshaled to tacitly lament the end of institutions such as slavery. The use of the Aunt Jemima figure in the first half of the twentieth century harnessed a national nostalgia that required African American women to be pushed back into the past even as the modern domestic pleasures epitomized by "instant" pancakes were celebrated. Working with the recent critical attention paid to the marriage convention in nineteenth-century African American literature, Siobhan Somerville suggests that in Pauline Hopkins's *Contending Forces*, lesbian desire is wedged between marriage and sexuality in ways unaccounted for in current scholarship. Under this new rubric, heterosexual marriage was only one of the ways (and reasons) to play house. The pleasures of other contending domesticities are, Somerville argues, discretely tucked away in the corners of the house—its basement, its attic, and of course, its closets.

Looking at U.S. domestic cultural texts produced a century later, John Lowney reads recent "war" novels written by Bobbie Anne Mason and Jayne Anne Phillips to argue that in the hands of these women writers, the novel about war becomes indistinguishable from domestic fiction. Lowney argues that these writers achieve more than innovative inclusions of female protagonists in what is usually understood to be a masculine literary and social arena. Instead, these Vietnam War novels alter a genre that Hemingway, among others, had carved out as a masculine, antidomestic space. Moving to a consideration of the status of women in the late 1990s, Ann duCille examines the media's recent categorization and racialization of U.S. women as "Black welfare queens" and "White feminists." Conservative rhetoric represents women as corrupted by feminism, lured from domesticity by jobs, or coddled at home by the welfare system; in short, women in these representations are demonized as the new public enemy number one of the nation-state. What national constructions of the domestic, of maternity and femininity, feminism and careerism, race and ethnicity, duCille asks, are conjured up in scenarios like those provided by Hollywood cinema and popular TV shows? Together, the chapters in this section illuminate aspects of domestic projects (domestic fictions, if you like) that are not central to other commentaries on U.S. domesticity: the indispensability of the figure of the slave in reconstructing a glorious past; homosexual homemaking; the impact of international aggression on reassessments of home and homesickness; and "the good mother" fixations as the century comes to a close.

The four chapters in the final section of this book, titled "Bringing Down the House: Dreaming, Revising, Burning," together discover the seamy side of domestic arrangements and of cherished domestic icons. K. Srilata maps the intricacies of the domestic consumption of concepts such as "romantic love" in contemporary India to argue that "tradition" and "modernity" are constructed upon each other. Through her reading of popular Indian women's magazines and other discourses, K. Srilata demonstrates the ways in which polarized ideological formations, such as family/feminism, marriage/romance, and caste/class, are gathered into articulations of "good/bad" Indian tradition and "good/bad" modernity. Susan Sánchez Casal looks at the conflicting processes by which Latinas and Latinos in the United States claim "home" at the national level, within their own communities, within academia, and within their varying shades of skin. Ultimately, the paper asks and answers crucial questions about "who is at home" in multiculturalism. Chandan Reddy examines the ways in which the very notions of family and the domestic are refurbished in the living arrangements documented in *Paris Is Burning,* Jenny Livingston's film about Black and Latino voguers in New York City. In the course of this examination, Reddy reads the history of "the American family" to argue that voguing, the balls, the matriarchies, and other everyday practices in this community challenge us to rethink what passes for reality and what has always passed for family. Finally, Maurizia Boscagli reads British filmmaker Ken Loach's *Riff Raff* (1990) not just as a commentary on the bleak scenario of unemployment and working-class uprootedness in post-Thatcherite England but as a social denunciation centered around the problematic concept of "home." The film centers around the lives of construction workers in London working to build a house that will never be home to them. Boscagli argues that home in *Riff Raff* can be represented only citationally, as a displaced quotation of an impossible, nonexistent real thing—that is, a catachresis. In this section, houses are for burning—however divergent the political motivations for such fires may be.

In Conclusion

Stephen Jay Gould has rightly remarked that "much can be learned . . . from the underbelly of traditional scholarship." This volume is intended as a forum that, having brought together writers from different academic and geographical locations, will hopefully provide opportunities for such learning to disparate readers. The book surveys the rhetoric and practices of domestication in contemporary cultures. It also examines the consequences and costs of homemaking in various geographic and textual locations in recent times. The domestic is read as a site where massive negotiations between often competing ideological pressures are undertaken and then processed into viable, even pleasurable, experiences of domestication. Most crucially, the chapters powerfully demonstrate the myriad ways in which analyses of domesticity itself can be used to critique the racialized and gendered logic of nationalist and imperialist modernity from the late nineteenth century onward. This cross-disciplinary conversation on the pleasures, the terrors, and the disciplines of the domestic has been carried out mainly on the "underbelly of traditional scholarship." Hence, the essays look into kitchen cupboards, into closets, at film, at changing neighborhoods, and at national obsessions with domestic affairs. Our collective plan is that this book serve as one of the sites at which this conversation on the domestic continues to turn over, reveal its underbelly, and be recycled.

Notes

I would like to thank David Lloyd and Chandan Reddy for their illuminating comments on various aspects of domesticity, many of which I have incorporated into this chapter. I am also grateful to John Lowney, Amie Parry, Liza Nelligan, Aparajita Sagar, and Michael Ryan for reading drafts of this chapter and commenting generously on specific issues.

1. From "Refuge for the Homeless," *Minima Moralia: Reflections from a Damaged Life*, Trans. E. F. N. Jephcott (London: New Left Books, 1974), pp. 38–39. In this essay, Theodore Adorno declares that "the house is past." He goes on to elaborate, in moving terms, the impossibility of "feeling at home" after the bombing of European cities, after the labor and concentration camps, and after the development of technology.

2. If we look outside affluent notions of recycling, we see different yet equally intermeshed associations of used domestic materials and the establishment of new domesticities. Putting together a home from the scraps and rags of past domestic settings is no new concept; in some parts of the globe, it provides a livelihood for entire families over several generations. See, for example, "Waste Picking as a Survival Strategy for Women in Indian Cities," Marijk Huysman, *Environment and Urbanization*, Vol. 6, No. 2 (October 1994), pp. 155–174; "Recycling in Bogota: Developing a Culture for Urban Sustainability," Margarita Pacheco, *Environment and Urbanization*, Vol. 4, No. 2 (October 1992), pp. 74–79. The internationally best known example is perhaps Smokey Mountain in Manila—a garbage dump that supported a large community that settled on the dump, building homes out of discarded materials and earning a living scavenging for usable and recyclable items: plastic, paper, wood, and old food cans. This community of squatters established what became an urban neighborhood called Tondo until they were moved to a less central, semiurban location as part of a Manila beautification program sponsored by the Marcos government.

3. Witold Rybczynski, *Home: A Short History of an Idea* (London: Longman, 1988), p. 217. The term *comfort zone* in the previous sentence is taken from Rybczynski's work.

4. It is necessary to note that this generic family is almost always pictured in the 1950s and always as Caucasian. See, for instance, the discussion in the next section of this chapter on the cover illustration of the September 9–15, 1995, issue of *The Economist*. Liberal, wishful projections into American (U.S.) families *in the future* might just picture them as Black or Hispanic. See Chandan Reddy's chapter in this book for more on the racial and class makeup of the representative American family.

5. "Family" seems to be an unendingly stretchable concept; perhaps this flexibility is precisely why it has lasted so long. Popular accounts of the family seem to forget the fact that the modern family as we know it has a historical beginning that dates from our not-so-distant past. See Philip Aries, *Centuries of Childhood: A Social History of Family Life* (New York: Random House, 1962) for a history of "the family" in the west. Also see *Rethinking the Family*, Ed. Barrie Thorne and Marilyn Yalom (New York: Longman, 1982), especially the essay by Rayna Rapp, "Family

and Class in Contemporary America: Notes Toward an Understanding of Ideology," in which she demonstrates the distance between ideal notions of the family and the reality of household organizations. In this collection see Chandan Reddy's discussion of *Paris Is Burning*.

6. I continue to use the notion of recycled domesticity (albeit responsibly recycled), if only to acknowledge the insidious and overt power of the domestic arrangements in place in any given location. Hence, while in the interests of clarity, I should probably mark the analytical goals of this collection with a different word, I continue to use the notion of "recycled domesticity" to acknowledge the pull of the ideologies manifest in auratic terms such as *home, family*, and so on.

7. Karen Tranberg Hansen, *African Encounters with Domesticity* (New Brunswick, N.J.: Rutgers University Press, 1992), p. 1. Also see Nancy Armstrong, *Desire and Domestic Fiction: A Political History of the Novel* (New York: Oxford University Press, 1987) for a detailed analysis of the extensive purview of the domestic in the context of the western novel.

8. For more detailed analysis of the vexed relationship between modernity and domesticity, see the argument developed by Dipesh Chakrabarty over two essays: "Postcoloniality and the Artifice of History: Who Speaks for 'Indian' Pasts?' *Representations*, Vol. 37 (Winter 1990), pp. 1–26 and "The Difference-Deferral of (A) Colonial Modernity: Public Debates on Domesticity in British Bengal," *History Workshop Journal*, Vol. 36 (1993), pp. 1–34. In this book see the articles by David Lloyd and K. Srilata for analyses of the colonial and other transnational negotiations between competing and often complementary domestic ideologies in the context of modernity.

9. See, for example, Elizabeth Fox-Genovese's extensive research on southern plantation *households* (slaves, servants, masters, mistresses, legitimate and illegitimate children) for an elaboration of the distinctions among *household, family*, and *the domestic* in this specific instance. *Within the Plantation Household: Black and White Women of the Old South* (Chapel Hill: University of North Carolina Press, 1988). Also see the chapter by Nancy Armstrong in this book.

10. Jeanne Boydston, *Home and Work: Housework, Wages and the Ideology of Labor in the Early Republic* (New York: Oxford University Press, 1990) and Alice Kessler-Harris, *A Woman's Wage: Historical Meanings and Social Consequence*, (Lexington: University of Kentucky Press, 1990).

11. Eileen Boris, "Beyond Dichotomy: Recent Books in North American Women's Labor History," *Journal of Women's History*, Vol. 4, No. 3 (Winter 1993), p. 163.

12. There is a vast amount of recent multidisciplinary writing on this and related issues. See, for instance, new readings of nationalism, of Third World feminism, of American frontier homemaking, and of immigration. The work done by Mary Layoun, Maria Mies, Benedict Anderson, Partha Chatterjee, Kumkum Sangari and Sudesh Vaid, Barbara Harlow, Adrienne Rich, Lisa Lowe, Caren Kaplan, and Inderpal Grewal is representative of the numerous books and articles that explore similar links. Almost all the chapters in this book elaborate on this theme.

13. See work by Timothy Mitchell, Jenny Sharpe, Margaret Strobel, Antoinette Burton, Vyon Ware, Vincente Rapheal, Anne McClintock, and Dipesh Chakrabarty. In this book see the chapters by Amie Parry, David Lloyd, and Rosemary Marangoly George.

14. See the recent writing by Paul Gilroy and Stuart Hall and other multidisciplinary writing on migrant labor and other global movements of people. In this book see the chapters by Chandan Reddy, Maurizia Boscagli, Dayana Salazar, Katharyne Mitchell, and Gayatri Gopinath.

15. Almost all the chapters in this book contribute to discussions on the proximity of domesticity and gender issues. Also see the important essays written in the mideighties by Adrienne Rich, Hortense Spillers, Minnie Bruce Pratt, Chandra Talpade Mohanty, and Biddy Martin. For discussions on homosexuality and domesticity in this book, see the chapters by Gopinath, Parry, Reddy, and Somerville.

16. Karen Tranberg Hansen, *African Encounters with Domesticity*, pp. 16–17.

17. Mary Tong, director of the Support Committee for Maquiladora Workers, based in San Diego, reporting on her conversations with maquiladora women workers in Tijuana, noted that the women were very clear about why the management of the many multinational companies in the region preferred to hire female rather than male workers. Those workers' theory was simply that management counted on women workers taking their domestic responsibility to feed and clothe their children more seriously than male workers did and therefore calculated that women workers would put up with more before they felt compelled to quit a low-paying, unsafe, or otherwise exploitative job.

18. Karen Tranberg Hansen, *African Encounters with Domesticity*, p. 17.

19. See Maria Mies, *Patriarchy and Accumulation on a World Scale: The New International Division of Labor* (London: Zed Books, 1986) for an incisive account of what she calls the disastrous privilege of middle-class domesticity for third world women.

20. I wish to thank Rosalind Solomon for permission to use this photograph.

21. See, for instance, Kerry James Marshall's painting *Many Mansions*, on display at the Chicago Art Institute. In *Many Mansions*, Marshall celebrates the domestic comforts that are wrought out of urban housing projects, even as he protests the constraints of low-income housing in the United States. I would like to thank Ashley Cross for bringing this painter's work to my attention.

22. From a letter to the editor by Larry V. Hawbaker, *Time*, March 18, 1996, p. 24.

23. See Chandan Reddy's chapter in this book for more on the family wage and the ways in which the narrative of patriarchy that provides for all is predicated on the fundamental relations of inequality, exploitation, and appropriation (of both labor and property). Also note that Hawbaker's not uncommon logic leads him to conclude that it is the fact that "too many people [come] into our country" that causes "the American family" to break up.

24. Jeanne Boydston, *Home and Work*, pp. 125–126.

25. Phyllis Palmer, *Domesticity and Dirt: Housewives and Domestic Servants in the US, 1920–1945* (Philadelphia: Temple University Press, 1989).

26. In Britain, for example, over the ten-year period from 1985 to 1995, domestic service has been the fastest-growing category of domestic spending (*The Economist*, December 14, 1996, p. 56). Most of this new domestic labor force (mainly young immigrants/foreigners and otherwise unemployed elderly) services middle-class, double-income families on a part-time basis.

27. See Cynthia Enloe, "'Just like One of the Family': Domestic Servants in World Politics," in *Bananas, Beaches and Bases: Making Feminist Sense of International*

Politics (Berkeley: University of California Press, 1990). Enloe notes that there are entire countries (Sri Lanka and the Philippines, for example) whose economic stability in the 1980s and 1990s is largely dependent on female migrant labor— women who are contracted to work, mainly as domestic maids, in Europe and the Middle East (p. 186). Also see Nilita Vachani's remarkable documentary film, *When Mother Comes Home for Christmas* (The Greek Film Centre and Filmsixteen, 1995), which records a Sri Lankan domestic worker's life as a housemaid in a suburb outside Athens, Greece, and her Christmas visit to her children and family in Sri Lanka after a period of eight years abroad.

28. Rachel Bowlby, "Domestication," in *Feminism Beside Itself*, Eds. Diane Elam and Robyn Wiegman (New York: Routledge, 1995), pp. 71–92.

29. Rachel Bowlby, "Domestication," p. 73.

30. Rachel Bowlby, "Domestication," p. 74.

31. Rachel Bowlby, "Domestication," p. 89.

32. Rachel Bowlby, "Domestication," pp. 77–78.

33. See Barbara Smith, "The Truth That Never Hurts: Black Lesbians in Fiction in the 1980s," in *Third World Women and the Politics of Feminism*, Eds. Chandra Talpade Mohanty, Ann Russo, and Lourdes Torres (Bloomington: Indiana University Press, 1991), pp. 101–129.

34. "No More Buried Lives: The Theme of Lesbianism in Audre Lorde's *Zami*, Gloria Naylor's *The Women of Brewster Place*, Ntozake Shange's *Sassafras, Cypress, and Indigo*, and Alice Walker's *The Color Purple*," in *Black Feminist Criticism: Perspectives on Black Women Writers* (New York: Pergamon Press, 1986), p. 188.

35. Rachel Bowlby, "Domestication," p. 72.

36. See *Homework: Historical and Contemporary Perspectives on Paid Labor at Home*, Eds. Eileen Boris and Cynthia R. Daniels (Chicago: University of Illinois Press, 1989) and *The Informal Economy: Studies in Advanced and Less Developed Countries*, Eds. Alejandro Portes, Manuel Castells, and Lauren Benton (Baltimore: Johns Hopkins University Press, 1989). Also see Eileen Boris, *Home to Work: Motherhood and the Politics of Industrial Homework in the United States* (Cambridge: Cambridge University Press, 1994).

37. In this book, see Ann duCille's critique of U.S. domestic diva Martha Stewart's tips on setting up the "home office."

38. Rachel Bowlby, "Domestication," p. 83.

Part One

On the Road: Nations, Empires, Texts, Homes

Chapter Two

Why Daughters Die: The Racial Logic of American Sentimentalism

NANCY ARMSTRONG

Slowly but surely, over the past ten years or so, scholars of English literary history have grown accustomed to the idea that sentimental literature—as exemplified by the novels of Samuel Richardson—systematically rewrote the sexual practices and domestic lives of English people. Scholarship also concedes that the English family so written took on a recognizably modern character. For at least fifty years, furthermore, American literary historians have credited Richardson for the brand of sentimental fiction that became so popular during the second half of the eighteenth century on this side of the Atlantic. Indeed, he provides the most obvious link between English authors and readers and their American counterparts. For the sake of argument, let us assume that in order to reproduce their way of life in the colonies, it was necessary for successive generations of English men and women to change the way they conducted sexual relationships as well as the households they made and maintained together. In undergoing these changes, it could then be said, the daily lives of these same English men and women became American. Might we not conclude that sentimental fiction must have changed as well—and changed in a way we must call American?

But scholars rarely so much as glanced in the direction of the sentimental tradition when it came to distinguishing fiction that speaks for English culture on this side of the Atlantic. To understand why the same subject matter that earned Richardson a central place in English literary history should have caused his American counterparts to be excluded out of hand, one can simply turn to the 1917 *Cambridge History of American Literature*. The editors of this history justify their literary preferences by mounting an argument against the anglophilia they attribute to previous editors. They condemn their predecessors for preserving a Restoration comedy and rejecting Bradford's *History of Plymouth*, for prizing a didactic poem in heroic couplets and despising the work of Jonathan Edwards, for relishing the letters of "some third rate English poet" and finding "no gusto" in the correspondence of Benjamin Franklin, or for sending a student to the novels of William Godwin and never directing him to *The Federalist*.[1] The editors of the *Cambridge History* claim that their inclusion of early American writers will "enlarge the spirit of American literary criticism and render it more energetic and masculine."[2] According to the logic laid out in their preface, the kind of masculinity that characterized our colonial forebears simultaneously placed a literary work within an English tradition of letters and identified that work as American. Within this classification system, popular writing could be called literary if it displayed certain traits of masculinity, and feminine writing would be tolerated—even applauded—when it exhibited signs of English literariness. Richardson's novels generally fell into this second category.

Published in 1941, F. O. Matthiessen's *American Renaissance* may have appeared more evenhanded than the *Cambridge History*. But Matthiessen allowed his favorite authors to do the work of gendering American literature, and they were hardly evenhanded. Nathaniel Hawthorne, for one, made this well-known and oft-quoted equation between women writers and sentimental fiction in the United States: "America is now wholly given over to a damned mob of scribbling women, and I should have no chance of success while the public taste is occupied with their trash—and should be ashamed of myself if I did succeed."[3] Given the sour grapes informing this statement, one has to ask why Matthiessen accepted Hawthorne's view so readily in formulating his account of American literature. More to the point, when Leslie Fiedler came up with his own definition of the great American novel in the 1950s, what could have possessed him to reproduce the same sexual logic? Perhaps most surprising of all is the fact that here we are almost forty years and many scholarly books later, and his *Love and Death in the American Novel* remains one of the most influential studies of the American novel.

This essay is part of a larger project that considers what happened to British sentimentalism when it came to this country. In addressing the problem of how to remain English in North America, the gendered logic of sentimental fiction, or how to get the right man together with the right woman on a permanent basis, had to address the problem of race, or how to distinguish those within the diasporic community from those whose inclusion would cancel out its English identity.[4] In order to explain how, why, and to what effect fiction simultaneously forged and suppressed this link between gender and race, I will turn first to the literary critical debates surrounding Harriet Beecher Stowe's *Uncle Tom's Cabin*. We can observe the historical relationship between gender and race as it generates certain predictable conflicts among various readings of this novel. To show that such conflicts indeed reenact a much earlier cultural logic—a peculiar relationship between gender and race that shapes Stowe's narrative as well—I will turn back to a tradition of colonial writing where these categories first began to stand in for and displace one another as the terms of American identity. In conclusion, I want to investigate the remarkable coincidence between our sudden willingness to call these categories into question and the emergence of an ethnic literature that uses gender to rethink the means by which we all acquire racial identities in the United States.

I. American Sentimentalism

Let us turn, then, to the critical tug-of-war between gender and race that identified Harriet Beecher Stowe's novel, *Uncle Tom's Cabin*, as the place where one goes to say what makes fiction American. In his epic attempt to answer this question, Fiedler assumes that ours is an exceptionally masculine nation. He also assumes that both women authors and popular writers drew upon a Richardsonian prototype in which a woman armed only with passionate virtue and the ability to verbalize it either converts her seducer or otherwise dispels all attempts at seduction. But he gives these commonplaces his own ingenious twist in articulating them one to the other. From the gendered definition of American culture as boy and sentimental fiction as girl, he concludes that "in popular fiction produced in America by and for females, the seduction fable comes chiefly to stand for the war between the sexes and the defeat of the seducer."[5] How on earth can we think of a novel as a work of American literature if, as Fiedler says, it entails "the emasculation of American men"?[6] To show how sentimental conventions could indeed prevent a masculine narrative from developing, he demonstrates how the collapse of those conventions allows such a narrative to unfold. This inverse thinking guides his reading of Harriet Beecher Stowe's *Uncle Tom's Cabin*.

He argued that Stowe made an important exception to the sentimental rule when she substituted a little girl for the traditional sentimental heroine. This way, she not only made it impossible to tell a story in which the heroine defeats her seducer, she also made it possible for us to read a novel written by, for, and about women as a major American novel. Before I explain how Fiedler gave Harriet Beecher Stowe's novel this foothold in a canon defined by the works of Nathaniel Hawthorne, Herman Melville, and Mark Twain, let us recall her famous description of the death of the child-heroine, Eva:

> The large blue eyes unclosed,—a smile passed over her face;—she tried to raise her head, and to speak.
> "Do you know me, Eva?"
> "Dear papa," said the child, with a last effort throwing her arms about his neck. In a moment they dropped again; and, as St. Clare raised his head, he saw a spasm of mortal agony pass over the face,—she struggled for breath and threw up her little hands.
> "O God, this is dreadful!" he said, turning away in agony, and wringing Tom's hand, scarce conscious what he was doing. "O Tom, my boy, it is killing me!"
> Tom had his master's hands between his own; and, with tears streaming down his dark cheeks, looked up for help where he had always been used to look.
> "Pray that this may be cut short!" said St. Clare,—"this wrings my heart."
> "O, bless the Lord! it's over,—it's over, dear Master!" said Tom; "look at her."[7]

In view of the fact that little Eva's death leaves her father sitting on her bed holding hands with another man, the scene appears to support Fiedler's argument that what Stowe kills off in her famous deathbed scene is nothing less than the heterosexual seduction plot and thus the sentimental novel itself. The moment Eva expires, various struggles on the part of women to reform men and incorporate them in a harmonious household indeed collapse, and there ensues a struggle between a good white man and a bad white man for possession of the black man's body. Wherever fiction manages to push the romance between men and women to the side, Fiedler insists, the reader will confront this romance between men of different races, which indelibly marks a work of fiction as American. Nor is this homoerotic narrative actually a romance between two different men, in his view, but a fantasy in which the Anglo-American comes to understand his identity as such in relation to an invented or spectoral black or red man. Pursuing this line of argument, he can read Stowe's sentimental narrative as a classic tale of the white man's confrontation with his own dark nature in the wilds of America—in this case, the infernal landscape of the antebellum South.

When he used Stowe's novel to demonstrate how sentimental fiction suppressed the interracial romance that distinguishes our major novels, however, Fiedler inadvertently gave the sentimental novel a kind of importance that could not be taken back. He also exposed the masculine basis for canonicity to scrutiny it would not be able to endure. What ensued several decades after he published his epic study of the American novel was a series of revisionary readings that reopened the whole question of what American fiction is, given what it does. In 1977, Ann Douglas linked sentimental fiction with what she called the feminization of American culture. She argued that as cause and symptom of America's feminization, sentimentalism "inevitably guaranteed, not simply the loss of the finest values contained in Calvinism, but the continuation of male hegemony in various guises."[8] In contrast with Fiedler, she saw sentimental fiction as doubly deleterious. Moreover, she blamed those effects, not on the fact of its association with women writers, but on its instrumental role in the emergence of the middlebrow, and the death of Eva provides the case in point: "Stowe's infantile heroine anticipates that exaltation of the average which is the trademark of mass culture."[9]

In 1985, Jane Tompkins rose up in defense of sentimental women writers. She argued that their desire to feminize American culture had nothing to do either with emasculating men or with feeding the banal appetites of a new mass readership. Rather, it aimed at socializing a murderously unjust society. She read the death of little Eva accordingly: as "a brilliant redaction of the culture's favorite story about itself—the story of salvation through motherly love."[10] This reading succeeded in revitalizing some of the very material that Fiedler had regarded as a symptom of sentimental writing's unliterariness and declared excessive, especially the protracted account of the gathering of the household—old and young, slave and master, male and female—around the child's deathbed. Rather than affirm or condemn the institution of slavery, in Tompkins's view, Stowe designed the deathbed scene to engender a revolution at the level of the individual heart, as it enabled readers to imagine a society held together by the superglue of family feeling. By doing so, the deathbed scene made readers experience a wrenching discrepancy between the sensational design and the social organization of *Uncle Tom's Cabin*, which would have promoted, however indirectly, an abolitionist agenda. Tompkins's stress on the gendered character of this strategy is clearly an effort to counter the familiar charges that sentimental writers used emotionalism to quiet the troubled political conscience of the United States and to offer the victims of slavery the compensation of a Christian afterlife.[11] She does not believe their fiction dished up a false idealism as the solution to the problem of social injustice. Quite the contrary, she contends, "the sentimental novelists made their bid for power by positing the kingdom of heaven on earth as a world over which women exercise ultimate control"; if readers once understood the cultural politics of such fiction in these terms, we should now judge it accordingly.[12]

We owe Tompkins an enormous debt for disputing the century-and-a-half old claim that American culture is truly and exceptionally masculine. By identifying a tradition of writing that was feminine as well as American, however, she raised a thornier problem than the one she appeared to resolve. She established a feminist framework for classifying sentimental fiction, but she did so without seriously challenging the masculinist criteria for a work of literature. She did not contest the assumption that great literature was boy literature; she simply argued that girl literature was just as political but in a different way.[13] And from her claim that sentimental fiction was equal to but different from the great American novels, another proposition followed. When she insisted that American literary history had to account for the work of women as well as men, Tompkins also implied that once it did, once literary scholarship and criticism had added feminine writing to the masculine tradition of letters, we could account for everyone—those who wrote with literary authority and those who wrote without it. Only by assuming that all people are either men or women could she place women writers in a sacrificial position rather like the one in which Stowe put little Eva: the fact of Stowe's exclusion from the literary canon provides the basis on which such women writers can represent all those who suffered exclusion at the hands of bad male institutions. This gendered logic brands Tompkins's feminist reading of *Uncle Tom's Cabin* a sentimental one.

Eight years have passed since her book first appeared, and we have seen a protracted debate over the politics of sentimentalism.[14] It is fair to say that anyone taking part in this debate who claims authority on the basis of exclusion has reproduced the sentimentalism of sentimental fiction.[15] Hortense Spillers appears to offer a notable exception among the post-Tompkins rereadings of Stowe. In an essay entitled "Changing the Letter," she identifies cultural information that is neither masculine nor feminine according to the criteria established by previous readers of *Uncle Tom's Cabin*. And, she says, "because there is [this cultural] 'noise' in the discursive field of this novel, and a path to radical social revision has not been properly cleared, . . . the work *metaphorizes* the very dilemma of *reading* and *living* that Afro-American readers . . . have palpably *felt* for over a century about *Uncle Tom's Cabin*."[16] For Spillers, the little slave girl Topsy personifies the illegible core of American culture. She provides what Spillers calls "an anti-energy for the captive woman"—presumably all those things that a woman could neither feel, nor think, nor say, nor do if she were to be considered Christian, female, and American.[17] The same logic that governs Topsy's behavior also saw to it that, of all the racist statements in her novel, Stowe gave Eva what Spillers takes to be the most outrageous of them all. When Eva and her father first cross paths with Tom, Stowe's tiny heroine delivers the words that leapt off the page and seized hold of Spillers. Learning that Tom has been taken from his family to be shipped downriver and sold as a slave, Eva makes this request of her father: "You have money enough, I know. *I want him.*" In Spillers's view, the fact that Stowe chose a child rather than a sexually mature young woman to make this statement was no coincidence. Only by assuring us of her early death could she allow Eva to express, as she does on more than this one striking occasion, what Spillers characterizes as "her daring and impermissible desire" for Tom.[18]

In place of a masculine or feminine reading of race, Spillers has given us a racially inflected reading of gender. As she explains, the little white girl stands in for "the symptoms of a disturbed female sexuality that American women of Stowe's era could neither articulate nor cancel."[19] Thus the novel uses Eva as a kind of fetish that allows readers both to acknowledge and to deny white female desire for whatever it was that black men embodied for white Americans. Spillers concludes that Stowe has brought the child and the object of her illegible desire, Tom, into the discursive field of the novel in order to kill them both off. Yet because she locates the meaning of these figures on a psychological terrain, gender assumes precedence over race in the course of her reading, and she ultimately defeats her own purpose. Once the black woman's sexuality becomes the white woman's neurosis, we do not think to ask why the social reproduction of some families depends on turning others into objects who could be traded without consideration of their family bonds and attachment to a place. There is no question that by revealing a darkly sensationalist flipside to the rhetoric of family feeling, Spillers's Topsy-oriented reading of Stowe's novel challenges feminist sentimentalism. But the moment she turns the hard facts of love and death into figures of white subjectivity, her reading begins to resemble Fiedler's psychocultural scenario, with a white woman substituting for the white man of the interracial romance. And like his antisentimentalism, her argument fails to dispel the power of conventions that make us think about the sexuality of slavery as an emotional problem.

II. Creolization

I have no interest in establishing which of these readings of Eva's death is morally, politically, aesthetically, or historically best. But I am extremely interested in exactly how this scribbling woman migrated to the center of critical attention during the second half of the twentieth century and why the operations of sexual desire in this particular novel continue to provide such an important way of identifying what is American about American fiction. Fiedler defined canonical fiction in a way that explicitly located racial conflict out of doors, in the masculine sphere. Tompkins as much as concedes his point that when women dominate social relations, a family template snaps into place, converting virtually everyone into parents, children, or—depending on their race and gender—both. Spillers fails to overturn the gendered division of cultural labor whereby differences between men define racial relations and similarities among women put us all in families. In fact, however, an argument can be made that the very differences most visibly distinguishing our culture were based on access to the means of social reproduction, that is to say, access that was given or taken away right there in the home. I want to go back into the colonial period now and demonstrate in what sense the American family was a racial formation from the start.

For nearly a century American literary criticism and scholarship has taken it for granted that sentimental fiction began in England and then came over to this country on the boat with Richardson's stories of seduction. This section of my essay will explain why we must rethink this long-standing assumption if we are going to understand the power of Stowe's sentimental logic. Consider the case of Susanna Rowson's *Charlotte Temple*. Though first written and published in England, it remains one of our most eligible candidates for the first American novel. The heroine commits the very error that Richardson's *Clarissa* told her to avoid: "What risks may poor giddy girls run when they throw themselves out of protection of their natural friends, and into the wide, wide world?"[20] Tossing both her virtue and the chance of a good marriage to the wind, Charlotte runs off to the colonies with a military man. Of course, she comes to a bad end. Mercifully, however, her misfortunes consume little more than two hundred pages. And were this all of poor *Charlotte Temple*, there would be no disputing those critics who read her as a bad imitation of Richardson's *Clarissa*. In *Clarissa*, a virtuous but desirable young woman manages to stave off many ingenious attempts at seduction, but only by preferring death to dishonor can she ultimately retain the status of a heroine.

In varying this pattern, Rowson becomes a contender for the first American novelist. Just before she dies, Charlotte's father arrives in America to forgive his daughter. Grief-stricken, he decides to take her daughter—his granddaughter—back home to England. Of this fortunate substitution, the novel has these words to say: "After the first tumult of grief subsided, Mrs. Temple gave up the chief of her time to her grandchild, and as she grew up and improved, began to fancy she again possessed Charlotte."[21] The household made of father, mother, and granddaughter may reproduce the structure of the original family made of father, mother, and daughter. But father and granddaughter in fact come from quite different nations. Thus we might pose the problem of being English in America in terms of this question: are you English because you are born of English parents, or are you English because your household is based on the English model? The mission of such a sentimental novel as *Charlotte Temple* is to conceal the gap that emerged between the household and the family in the New World by representing the one as a perfect substitute for the other.

To understand what happened when English sentimentalism took up this particular ideological task, we need to take a new look at colonial American culture. In one of the earliest examples of a specifically colonial genre, an Englishwoman named Mary Rowlandson described the trials she endured as an Indian captive. Embodied in this solitary woman, as I have argued elsewhere, English culture itself seemed to be under assault.[22] As it was cast in a defensive position, however, that culture acquired a form of legitimation peculiarly suited for the colonial situation. English men had to conquer native American men for the sake of English women and their children; colonialism was both a paternal and a patriotic obligation. It is only reasonable to assume that readers who accepted this logic would feel a sense of resolution once Rowlandson was securely in her husband's house and had arranged to buy back both her son and her sister's son from their captors. Indeed, as far as Cotton Mather was concerned, her captivity was over and done with at that moment. His *Magnalia Christi Americana* (1702) tells Rowlandson's story from the husband's point of view: her captivity tested his faith, and her return demonstrated that his faith was stronger than the evils she endured. In telling her own story, however, Rowlandson places a peculiar stress on her daughter's return. The narrator's separation from and reunion with this child mark the beginning and end of her trials in the wilderness, and the family does not become a whole family again until the daughter is restored to them. It is in these marvelous terms that Rowlandson describes the daughter's return: "Thus she traveled three days together, not knowing whither she was going, having nothing to eat or drink but water and green hirtleberries. At last they came into Providence where she was kindly entertained by several of that town. The Indians often said that I should never have her [back for] under twenty pounds. But now the Lord hath brought her in upon free cost and given her to me the second time."[23]

Why call this kind of attention to the daughter's return? Although Rowlandson was clearly obsessed by her need to keep in touch with both God and Boston during her trial in the wilderness, she also felt obliged to frame this experience with the loss and restoration of her daughter. In contrast with the difficulty of recording her emotional life in exile, the task of explaining the relationship between her fate and that of her daughter evidently required very little effort. That we cannot account for what appears to be an almost obligatory link between these divergent plots tells us precisely where our own brand of common sense differs from that which Rowlandson could count on from her readers. Let us try to imagine what importance they might have attached to the daughter's fate.

Whenever marriage outside a group threatens that group's ties to the country of its origin, daughters tend to become problematic. There is no question that North America provided such a situation. English people had to develop new courtship practices and marriage rules if they were going to remain English on this side of the Atlantic. Being in the colonies kept them from marrying in the same place and within the same group as their parents had. But since only birth guaranteed the continuity of the English family back in England, any other basis for constituting a household necessarily called into question the English identity of those who had to live by modified cultural rules. Although the very word "creole" inevitably carries connotations of racial impurity for modern readers, this was anything but true for those colonial Europeans to whom the term referred. A creole family distinguished itself and preserved its status as such by marrying only members of the same immigrant or diasporic group.[24] In the early seventeenth century, the English word referred to someone born and naturalized in the Americas but born of pure European or African blood. While "creole" implies that the original may have undergone substantial modifications in the New World, it does not, as the *Oxford English Dictionary* points out, carry any "connotation of colour," much less suggest a mixture of the two. The racialized sense of the term seems to have emerged during the nineteenth century and in American English.

Recognizing that the very concept of Anglo-America contains this contradiction, we can begin to account for the peculiar way in which our fiction deals with daughters. The miraculous return of Rowlandson's daughter is necessary to ensure that she remain her father's. According to narrative tradition, it makes all the difference that he never buys her back from the Indians; if she is truly his, then he is the only one entitled to offer her in exchange. The exclusive nature of the patriarchal prerogative is what makes it possible for Englishness to descend from him to her and through her into the family of another Englishman, thereby preserving the Englishness of the colonial community. When an object is conspicuously removed or somehow manages to remove itself from such a system of exchange, according to anthropologist Annette Weiner, it operates as the special kind of fetish she calls an "inalienable possession."[25] This kind of object is so valuable to the identity of the group that it can neither be taken nor traded away without threatening that group's identity. Daughters who are thus invested with the power of culture-bearers die—often willfully—when they leave the family. Thus we may find them returning through death to their fathers' homes, as Richardson's Clarissa does, or else reborn through their daughters, as in the case of Charlotte Temple. In both novels, the daughter ultimately proves to be the true one when she cannot live outside the family.

The omnipresent anxiety about losing one's English identity gives us reason to believe that this story of the daughter's magical return was written and read with another narrative possibility in mind: a story about going native and starting up a whole new family in the wilderness. Mary Jemison's account of her life among the Senecas, transcribed from her oral testimony in 1823, is such a story. She represents the recessive type of colonial heroine, the daughter who never returned, because she was miraculously chosen to survive among the Indians. Operating according to a different cultural logic than Rowlandson's, Jemison's mother leaves her with these parting words: "Alas, my dear! my heart bleeds at the thoughts of what awaits you; but, if you leave us, remember my child your own name, and the name of your mother and father. Be careful and not forget your English tongue. If you shall have an opportunity, don't try to escape; for if you do they will find and destroy you."[26] Heeding this practical advice, Jemison allows herself to be adopted into a Senecan family, marries, and produces a number of children, all the while helping other captives to survive as she did. She takes particular pride in creating a household under these adverse circumstances: "I live in my own house, and on my own land, with my youngest daughter Polly, who is married to George Chongo, and has three children."[27] Jemison's reward is one that eighteenth-century readers were likely to have considered more appropriate for men than women. She has become the head of a household at the expense of her femininity, and her daughter has married outside the Anglo community, which sets the Jemison family forever apart from "the rich and respectable people, principally from New England," who were beginning "to inhabit the whole country around her."[28] Her ability to reproduce an English household without an English husband distinguishes the members of that household from the creole families who had perpetuated their English identity patrilineally. Although such assimilation flies in the face of sentimental convention, Mary Jemison is nevertheless the heroine of her tale, which consequently exists in direct contradiction with the sentimental paradigm.

The commonplace that men want their daughters pure obviously conceals some questions that we must address with a bit more care if we are going to understand the various narrative traditions contending for the authority to read the death of little Eva: in what sense might our national identity have actually depended on the sexual behavior of young English women? how can English identity remain the same when it has to be reproduced outside of England? under these circumstances, isn't the difference between authentic and imitation Englishness destined to collapse? To address these questions, we need to think of the two different captivity narratives I have just described as offering two different theories of social reproduction. According to one, transmission of English culture occurs through the patrilineal family. In this case, the English family is virtually the same thing as English culture in that both depend on the descendants of an English family marrying with their kind. Such a culture abhors a mixture. It prefers a dead daughter to an ethnically impure one. According to the Jemison model, however, English culture is reproduced within the household, and there is nothing pure about it. That is precisely its virtue. No matter who makes up this household or where they come from, it can incorporate, imitate, reenact, parody, or otherwise replicate whatever appears to be most English about the English family. Such a household produces a family peculiar to the settler colonies.[29]

In just a paragraph or two, I will try to suggest how these two different ways of constituting national identity came together in Eva's bedroom, creating the basis for competing interpretations, inflected by race or gender, of her death. Stowe asks us to think of the two daughters Eva and Topsy "as representatives of the two extremes of society" (244). Next she asks us to translate these social positions directly into race: "There stood the representatives of their races. The Saxon, born of ages of cultivation, command, education, physical and moral eminence; the African, born of ages of oppression, submission, ignorance, toil, and vice" (244). As Hortense Spillers was again the first to note, however, Stowe challenges this absolute difference between black and white whenever she reveals the playfully sensual character of Eva's affection for Tom. In a scene that anticipates the spectacle of her deathbed, she engages Topsy in an exchange that empties the slave girl of her animating spirit and replaces her illegible—presumably African—elements with the language of English sentimentality. To Eva's claim that "people can love you, if you are black, Topsy. Miss Ophelia would love you, if you were good," Topsy responds with a "short, blunt laugh that was her common mode of expressing incredulity" (280). By shifting the terms of her emotional appeal from race to gender, however, Eva comes up with entirely different results. To her second injunction, that "I love you, because you haven't had any father, or mother, or friends;—because you've been a poor abused child! I love you, and I want you to be good. I am unwell, Topsy," her student responds with the correct gush of feeling: "large, bright drops rolled heavily down, one by one, and fell on the little white hand. Yes, in that moment," declares the narrator, "a ray of real belief, a ray of heavenly love, had penetrated the darkness of her heathen soul!" (280–81). The moral of this transformation is a simple one: Topsy has to be infused with Eva's sentimentality before she can become a member of the household. But the exchange of interiorities between the two girls has another effect as well. It accelerates Eva's decline.[30] As she pours her emotions into Topsy, all Africanness passes from the white girl's body, and sensuality is only the pleasure she takes in anticipating her departure from that body.

If Stowe's enormous popularity with readers is any indication, then Eva's extravagantly sentimental death indeed establishes her status as an "inalienable possession," a literary figure whose meaning could not be touched by the social-historical environment of slavery. This decontextualization of the refined and emotionally sensitive woman, I am arguing, is the whole purpose served by the sentimental elements in the novel.[31] A similar form of idealization, paradoxically, provides Stowe with the way of dealing with the problem posed by Topsy. As the narrator explains, "the child rapidly grew in grace and in favor with the family and neighborhood. At the age of womanhood, she has, by her own request, been baptized and taken into the church; and showed so much intelligence, activity, and zeal, and desire to do good in the world, that she was at last recommended, and approved, as a missionary to one of the stations in Africa" (432–33). In some respects, Topsy fulfills the narrative logic of assimilation and lives out the story of the daughter who goes native. However, Stowe ultimately refused to allow that story to emerge.

Her peculiar way of blanching Topsy ultimately works according to the logic guiding the return of Mary Rowlandson's daughter. Topsy is, in a manner of speaking, held captive by an alien culture, and her removal from the exchange of women therefore provides a way of preserving her African-American identity. To be sure, the sentimental tradition allows Topsy, in contrast with Rowlandson, virtually no cultural identity to preserve—no mother, no father, no known relatives at all. Her captors' blood already courses through her veins, and her African heritage has been reduced to an inarticulate force that spasmodically animates her little body. Her options as a daughter are just not the same as those available to sentimental heroines. Even so, the novel's commitment to a sentimental resolution—the return of a daughter that restores the family to its original wholeness—prevents her from starting up her own household as Mary Jemison did. Stowe starts off by promising Topsy a way out of captivity through assimilation, but she changes her mind as soon as Topsy matures and sends her back to Africa. Let us imagine black people making English families there, Stowe seems to say. This way of playing out the narrative of the true daughter subordinates all other sexual practices to a brand of English domesticity, which in turn exists—through Topsy—in the relation of a copy to the pure original.

III. Multiculturalism

I have gone back into the colonial period in order to suggest what historical task the sentimental tradition performs in *Uncle Tom's Cabin*. It consolidates within an imaginary household what were in fact several warring nations. The colonial experience generated mutually exclusive versions of that household, which created a contradiction within the English sentimental tradition as it was transported to and consumed in the United States. It is not the woman who resists seduction that receives the full charge of sentimental value in American literature so much as the daughter who cannot exist outside her original household. Given Stowe's historical moment and access to the sentimental tradition, we should not be at all surprised to find this conflict organizing her novel. What still remains a puzzle is why we have begun to rethink the sentimental tradition only now.

If Stowe has given me a perspective from which to reconstruct that tradition all the way back to Rowlandson and Jemison, then Toni Morrison's *Beloved* is a large part of the reason why. Morrison's novel is surely the most self-conscious literary examination we have to date of the dead daughter's centrality in American culture. As the title suggests, this novel also situates itself squarely within the tradition of sentimental fiction. The name "Beloved" is affixed to the tombstone of a child slain lest she fall into the hands of her mother's captors. The murder simply literalizes the slave's social death. Her fabulous reappearance as a grown woman, complete with the scar recording that moment long ago when her baby throat was slit, transforms what was social nonbeing into a positive cultural category, the more potent for its having a purely fictional basis that defies our legal, scientific, and even psychoanalytic definitions of the body. Since it was produced by the uncanny traces of a story canceled out, we might think of this position as the vantage point that Morrison felt she required in order to explain American culture more fully to itself. Because she figured out how to do so in a way that met with instant recognition both within and outside academic circles, her novel announces a new epoch in the history of American sentimentalism.

By resurrecting the story of the daughter who returned miraculously undefiled, Morrison invokes a third narrative tradition, commonly known as the slave narrative. She follows Harriet Jacobs's example as she revises the slave narrative to reveal the contradiction between family and household concealed within the sentimental tradition. Within a decade after the publication of *Uncle Tom's Cabin*, Jacobs's autobiographical *Incidents in the Life of a Slave Girl* (1861) had already challenged Stowe's sentimental description of the two little girls. Her point was to demonstrate how black and white become virtually inseparable—positive and negative versions of the same story—within the sentimental tradition. Jacobs recalls how she "once saw two beautiful children playing together. One was a fair white child; the other was her slave, *and also her sister*. When I saw them embracing each other, and heard their joyous laughter, I turned sadly away from the sight. I forsaw the inevitable blight that would soon fall on the little slave's heart."[32] By "blight" she means both the compulsory labor that supports her sister's leisure and the compulsory sex that allows her owners to reproduce that labor in and through her children. Jacobs proceeds to demonstrate that Stowe's novel might be read as a record of the struggle to possess the means of social reproduction. She suggests that the outcome of the struggle would distinguish those few for whom family and household are virtually the same from those who are torn between the two—torn from one family in order to serve another, and so compelled to substitute another household for what had been their family. This difference between household and family is what gives the ending of her narrative its peculiar shape: "I and my children are free! We are as free from the power of slaveholders as are the white people of the north; and though that, according to my ideas is not saying a great deal, it is a vast improvement on my condition. The dream of my life is not yet realized. I do not sit with my children in a home of my own."[33]

At stake in her need to close the gap between family and household is something more fundamental, I believe, than property ownership or the privilege of gathering her loved ones around her, although there is certainly evidence enough for both interpretations. At stake is the ability to reproduce herself socially and culturally in reproducing herself biologically. By refusing to describe her household as a family at every juncture, Jacobs provides us with what might be called a descriptive theory of the struggle that occurred within the creole household, a struggle that history and fiction have conspired to make us understand as a transaction strictly between men. In place of a family, her narrative produces a social unit that has been so systematically ruptured, polluted, and dismembered that rupture, pollution, and dismemberment become its identifying traits. Yet in challenging the sentimental equation of household and family, she never questions the sentimental definition of the family that American culture kept her from having. In making cultural reproduction contingent on biological reproduction, she also makes it depend on the patriarchal prerogative to own the daughter's body. To reproduce herself—indeed, to have a self—Jacobs has to keep her daughter pure. Upon taking possession of her children consequently depends her power to write a happy ending.[34] Toni Morrison decided it was time to reverse this equation.

Before I was halfway through *Beloved*, I knew—as a lot of other readers evidently did—that it would be classified as a great novel within just a year or two. An African-American woman had written a great American novel, and she knew exactly what she was doing when she did it. Where Leslie Fiedler thought he was getting to the heart of racial conflict by getting rid of sentimental conventions, Morrison used those conventions to stage the very relationship that so indelibly marks our fiction. In her view, the struggle between English and African America was not played out in the forests of New England, or on the Mississippi River, or on some Western plain. It took place within the sanctuary of the creole household, and to the extent that it did and indeed still does so, that struggle identifies certain works of fiction as distinctively our own. The sentimental character of a household complete unto itself—a world, what is more, with a woman displaying English refinement at its center—once depended on the compulsory labor of another people. The reproduction of this household required compulsory control of their reproductive labor as well, and that control—like Sethe's milk—was wrested from them time and time again. It might be said that these practices of denying African Americans the means to their social reproduction passed into history along with slavery.

But just because the biological means of reproduction have been restored to one along with the ownership of her body, the cultural means do not necessarily become available. This is the problem Morrison explores in her heroine's troubled relation to a past that takes the form of a slave narrative. She agrees with Jacobs that not even a dead daughter could be a pure one. Since her captor was her father—if not in biological fact, then by virtue of his power to exchange her body—the slave girl lacked a home and father that met the sentimental criteria. There was nowhere to go and no one to remove her from the system of exchange. The pure daughter's narrative was never a good way to tell her story, Morrison must have concluded, when she brought Beloved back to life. In doing so, she exposes the sentimental options—"Give me purity or give me death!"—as a fantasy that could materialize only for members of an elite minority. In contrast with Jacobs, however, she does not go to all the trouble of exposing this narrative as such a fantasy and then rest content with championing the underdog and so declare herself the author of a minor literature. For this would leave the fiction of ruling-class purity intact. Morrison demonstrates in no uncertain terms that the author who wants to challenge the hegemonic daughter's narrative must put the tradition of the slave narrative securely in the past as well.

As the pure daughter—who suddenly shows up as a full-grown woman dressed in white—Beloved is not simply one more example of the daughter's return but a gloriously violent disembodiment of the ruling idea that cultural identity depends on remaining true to one's biological origins. The novel rejects this basis for identity. It also insists at the end of its account of what happens to the pure daughter when she is entrapped within a slave's narrative that "It was not a story to pass on."[35] Why remember a family that never really did exist, if that memory exists at the expense of the immediate household composed, as it is, of part individuals, ghosts, and hybrid types held together within a framework of historical antagonisms?[36] When the novel brings the pure daughter back to life and kills her off a second time, the recessive story of American identity emerges, one whose traces can be detected in the story of the defiled slave girl as well as in that of the pure daughter who has been removed from the system of exchange. *Beloved* cuts the sentimental heroine free from the double bind in which colonial captivity narratives had placed her three centuries ago; the story of the daughter who can never return to her culture of origins because she has gone American gains ascendancy not only over the slave's narrative but over the fantasy of household autonomy and cultural purity as well. The emergence of this other kind of daughter represents a turning point in the novel: "Somebody had to be saved, but unless Denver got work, there would be no one to save, no one to come home to, and no Denver either. It was a new thought, having a self to look out for and preserve."[37] Denver's decision "to do the necessary" and go native brings us to a turning point in the history of American fiction as well.

To say that Morrison rejects the options offered her by the literary tradition does not go very far, however, toward explaining how her novel manages to elude the category of a minor literature: what possibilities in the Jemison story of assimilation does she mine in order to define *Beloved* as a classic in its time? She exploits the gap between family and household, first of all, in order to grant priority to the home. It takes a household to make a family, rather than the other way around. Once Morrison grants this kind of firstness to the household, she can proceed to define the mother and not the father as the origin of the family, as she does first with Baby Suggs and then with Sethe. What matters is one's ability to constitute a self within the material givens of the moment, no matter how hostile are those givens to the very existence of such a self. Moreover, in giving body to the idea that we acquire our identities in relation to those individuals who surround us, not through patrilineal continuity with a past that intrudes upon the present in the form of a furiously infantile ghost, the novel presents a more radical challenge to American identity politics.

It can be argued that in re-membering Beloved, Sethe recaptures the reproductive prerogative: she and not "schoolmaster," her owner, is surely the origin of this strange new life form. When she seizes hold of her reproductive labor, however, it is not the power to reproduce herself biologically that she acquires; she obviously had that all along. In post–Civil War America, Morrison's novel argues, cultural reproduction is what determines whether you are fully American or not. Whether or not she can close the gap between household and family and provide the kind of ending that Jacobs could not imagine for herself has everything to do with how Morrison's heroine decides to tell her story. Indeed, insofar as Beloved's existence seems to depend upon the telling of that story, it can be argued that Beloved is not so much Sethe's daughter as her story: "It [telling her story] became a way to feed her. Just as Denver discovered and relied on the delightful effect sweet things had on Beloved, Sethe learned the profound satisfaction Beloved got from storytelling. It amazed Sethe (as much as it pleased Beloved) because every mention of her past life hurt. Everything in it was painful or lost. She had agreed without saying so that it was unspeakable."[38]

What if her survival does require her to bury entire chunks of the past because they make the present feel palpably so lacking? What if the group's ability to endure under hostile historical circumstances does force it to incorporate new elements? How can this make it any less itself, and would incorporation into such an altered body really entail a loss of cultural identity? Morrison answers these questions with a resounding no when she refuses to leave Sethe, Denver, and Paul D in the curiously neither-nor position where Mary Jemison wound up her story. In contrast, Sethe's narrative concludes by opening up another set of possibilities, what with Paul D wanting "to put his story next to hers" and Denver perhaps going off to Oberlin.[39] Morrison scoops up what remains of "Sweet Home," puts it at the center of the cultural stage, and dares us to suggest that this is not in fact an American family. By shifting the weight of representing American identity from the biological family onto such a mixed, mangled, and yet fiercely knit group, she argues that our identities depend not so much on what bodies we reproduce but on the reproduction of a community that was entirely fictional to begin with.

The rise of feminism is clearly responsible for focusing critical attention on sentimental writing. But even given the ground that feminist theory has cleared for rethinking the American literary tradition, I seriously doubt I would have seized upon the figure of the daughter as a way of retelling the story of our cultural origins in terms of this conflict between family and household were it not for the work of contemporary women novelists. Indeed, since sometime in the 1980s, we have been witnessing an explosion of fiction by women subordinated to men in groups that have been marginalized by American culture.[40] With significant frequency, these authors write as daughters confronting a dilemma that recalls the situation of Englishwomen captured by native Americans: should they remain their fathers' daughters at any cost or mix into an alien nation and remake their mothers' households according to new rules? Separation, as we saw in the captivity narratives of Rowlandson and Jemison, is what turns the homeland into a self-contained organic unit capable of perpetuating itself through marriage. The absolute refusal to go native—in whatever form proscribed—is what allows such a unit the illusion of remaining what it had been originally. In diaspora, this set of relationships eventually lives only in the memory of the dead, as preserved in sentimental fiction.

Morrison, I am suggesting, is not the only one to pick up the story of assimilation. What she does is to articulate this moment of multiculturalism to the moment of Stowe, in turn clearing an intellectual-historical pathway for us back to the writing of colonial women. Her novel manages to define a position from which she could both understand the sentimental tradition in new terms and make a telling literary intervention. She used that tradition to portray racial identity as a process, or textual production, rather than a state of being, or condition of the body: who you are depends not on who your father was and where you came from but on how you reproduce yourself in others and on how you tell your story. To relocate the source of identity from family to household, she changes the means of social reproduction from those measures that ensure continuity with the past (in other words, biology) to those that allow assimilation to occur (or cultural transformation). This inversion of the relationship between original and copy might be said to make the difference between racial identity and what we call ethnicity.

As the agonistic character of her narrative suggests, this is no easy difference to traverse.[41] The move from race to ethnicity requires Morrison to renounce not only blood along with the patriarchal prerogative, but also the legacy of forced miscegenation. Either basis for cultural identity marks the body of the African-American woman as the special victim of Anglo-American history and the privileged site of our fiction's sentimental investment. The marvel is that in using Sethe's story to represent that of all diasporic Americans—and all Americans consequently as diasporic—Morrison manages to maintain the irreducibility of race. It clearly remains for her the category people occupy in this country when they can no longer call themselves English or African or Irish or Chinese or Mexican; race comes with the hyphen that hooks any and all such designations of national origin into the differential system of American identities.[42] The African-American experience exemplifies this process of racialization. As Barbara Field has argued, "Race is neither the reflex of primordial attitudes nor a tragically recurring central theme. It became the ideology medium through which Americans confronted questions of sovereignty and power because the enslavement of Africans and their descendants constituted a massive exception to the rules of sovereignty and power that were increasingly taken for granted."[43] The slave's narrative therefore represents with maximum clarity how terrible it feels to occupy the position of racial otherness. *Beloved*, however, points out that the racialization of identity could not occur without the sentimental tradition. The racial claims of that tradition are what the novel challenges in challenging the essentialism of the daughter's narrative.

What happens to the sentimental novel when it no longer provides the means for reproducing a lost or otherwise unattainable English original? What happens to the sentimental novel when it authorizes the hybrid formation that traditionally positioned racially marked groups in a peripheral relationship to the Anglo core of American culture? Reading *Beloved* requires just such a radical shift in the sentimental reader's affective investment. Morrison's replacement of the pure daughter with an assimilated one amounts to an inversion of insider and outsider, or core and periphery, if you will. She makes us see how essential sentimental fiction has been in reproducing an American brand of Englishness, or what she elsewhere calls "the whiteness of the literary imagination."[44] Indeed, she makes us ask if cultural origins in this country can *ever* be much more or less than fiction. Isn't this precisely what happened to English culture when women tried to reproduce an English home in New England and then reproduced that reproduction in written accounts of their captivities? From the beginning—provided we are willing to understand our origins in these terms—a distinctively American identity emerged in relation to an English core, a core that was in turn written from a vantage point outside of and in a peripheral relation to it. *Beloved* simply reveals, better perhaps than any other narrative, the degree to which American fiction is an effort to deal with a rupture between people and their home and homeland and not the continuous development of a European tradition. In this essay, I have tried to suggest how the tradition of American fiction might begin to look from such a vantage point.

Notes

The Yale Journal of Criticism, volume 7, number 2, © 1994 by Yale University. Published by Blackwell Publishers, 238 Main Street, Cambridge, MA 02142, and 108 Cowley Road, Oxford, OX4 1JF, UK.

1. William Peterfield Trent, et al., eds. *The Cambridge History of American Literature, Colonial and Revolutionary Literature, Early National Literature: Part I* (New York: G. P. Putnam's Sons, 1917), x.

2. Trent, *Cambridge History*, 1:x.

3. F. O. Matthiessen, *American Renaissance: Art and Expression in the Age of Emerson and Whitman* (New York: Oxford University Press, 1941), x–xi.

4. Doris Sommer has explained how nineteenth-century Latin American novels combined gender with racial proscriptions "to solve the problem of establishing the white man's legitimacy in the New World." "Without a proper genealogy to root them in the Land," she reasons, "the creoles had at least to establish conjugal and then paternity rights, making a *generative* rather than a *genealogical* claim. They had to win America's heart and body so that the fathers could found her and reproduce themselves as cultivated men." See *Foundational Fictions: The National Romances of Latin America* (Berkeley: University of California Press, 1991), 15.

5. Leslie Fiedler, *Love and Death in the American Novel* ([1960] New York: Avon, 1992), 89.

6. Fiedler, *Love and Death*, 89.

7. Harriet Beecher Stowe, *Uncle Tom's Cabin* (New York: Bantam, 1981), 294. All references in the text are to this edition and will be cited by page number.

8. Ann Douglas, *The Feminization of American Culture* ([1977] New York: Avon, 1978), 13.

9. Douglas, *Feminization of American Culture*, 2.

10. Jane Tompkins, *Sensational Designs: The Cultural Work of American Fiction, 1790–1860* (New York: Oxford University Press, 1985), 125.

11. In his 1949 essay "Everybody's Protest Novel," James Baldwin offers a memorable indictment of *Uncle Tom's Cabin*. Infuriated at the novel's power to make readers feel good about feeling bad about the atrocities committed in the name of slavery, he condemns the entire genre along with *Uncle Tom*: "The 'protest' novel, so far from being disturbing, is an accepted and comforting aspect of the American scene, ramifying that framework to be so necessary. Whatever unsettling questions are raised are evanescent, titillating, remote, for this has nothing to do with us, it is safely ensconced in the social arena, where, indeed, it has nothing to do with anyone, so that finally we receive a very definite thrill of virtue from the fact that we are reading such a book at all. This report from the pit reassures us of its reality and its darkness and of our own salvation; and 'As long as such books are being published,' an American liberal once said to me, 'everything will be all right.'" In *The Price of the Ticket: Collected Nonfiction, 1948–1985* (New York: St. Martin's, 1985), 31.

12. Tompkins, *Sensational Designs*, 141.

13. Tompkins argues that "the jeremiad throws light on *Uncle Tom's Cabin* because Stowe's novel was political in exactly the same way the jeremiad was" (*Sensational Designs*, 140).

14. See, for example, *The Culture of Sentiment: Race, Gender, and Sentimentality in Nineteenth-Century America*, ed. Shirley Samuels (New York: Oxford University Press, 1992). Laura Wexler provides an important perspective on the Tompkins-Douglas debate in "Tender Violence: Literary Eavesdropping, Domestic Fiction, and Educational Reform," *The Yale Journal of Criticism* 5.1 (Fall 1991): 151–87.

15. In *Sentimental Modernism: Women Writers and the Revolution of the Word* (Bloomington: Indiana University Press, 1991), 3–5, Suzanne Clark suggests as much by arguing that, while she praises Stowe for the sentimental rhetoric Douglas deplored in *Uncle Tom's Cabin*, Tompkins refuses to see the sentimental element in the very writers who are preferred by Matthiessen, Fiedler, and Douglas. It is as if sentimental fiction has to be the subordinated tradition in order for her feminism to rescue it from critical scorn and obscurity.

16. Hortense Spillers, "Changing the Letter: The Yokes, The Jokes of Discourse, or Mrs. Stowe, Mr. Reed," in *Slavery and the Literary Imagination*, eds. Deborah E. McDowell and Arnold Rampersad (Baltimore: The Johns Hopkins University Press, 1989), 35.

17. Spillers, "Changing the Letter," 35.

18. Spillers, "Changing the Letter," 44.

19. Spillers, "Changing the Letter," 44.

20. Samuel Richardson, *Clarissa, or the History of a Young Lady*, ed. Angus Ross (London: Penguin, 1985), 1005.

21. Susanna Rowson, *Charlotte Temple* (New York: Oxford University Press, 1986), 118.

22. Nancy Armstrong and Leonard Tennenhouse, *The Imaginary Puritan: Literature, Intellectual Labor, and the Origins of Personal Life* (Berkeley: University of California Press, 1992), 196–216.

23. Alden T. Vaughn and Edward W. Clark, eds., *Puritans Among the Indians: Accounts of Captivity and Redemption, 1676–1724* (Cambridge, Mass.: Harvard University Press, 1981), 73.

24. See, for example, Benedict Anderson, *Imagined Communities: Reflections on the Origin and Spread of Nationalism* (London: Verso, 1991), 41 n1.

25. Annette Weiner, *Inalienable Possessions: The Paradox of Keeping-While-Giving* (Berkeley: University of California Press, 1992).

26. James E. Seaver, *A Narrative of the Life of Mrs. Mary Jemison*, ed. June Namias (Norman: University of Oklahoma Press, 1992), 69.

27. Seaver, *A Narrative of the Life of Mrs. Mary Jemison*, 158.

28. Seaver, *A Narrative of the Life of Mrs. Mary Jemison*, 54.

29. Karen Kupperman, *Providence Island, 1630–1641* (Cambridge: Cambridge University Press, 1993), makes clear that in order for an English colony to succeed, colonists had to have a share in the profits and enjoy ownership of the land, to exercise local control of the military, and to help determine local expenditures and hence have a voice in taxation. But the single most important element was the presence of women. She writes, "Colonial promoters were aware . . . that women were crucial to the long-term success of any English colony." They brought "essential skills of food production" and preparation as well as "clothing production and maintenance," and their presence promised stability and the possibility of social reproduction. She quotes one Virginia planter, "it is not known whether man or woman be more necessary" for the success of the colonial project (158).

30. I am arguing that sentimentality behaves in this scene much as Philip Fisher says it generally does in Stowe: "Sentimentality, by its experimental extension of humanity to prisoners, slaves, madmen, children, and animals, exactly reverses the process of slavery itself which has at its core the withdrawal of human status from a part of humanity." See *Hard Facts: Setting and Form in the American Novel* (New York: Oxford University Press, 1985), 100. But I am also arguing that the narrative logic by which suffering humanizes the slave is immediately short-circuited in the case of Topsy, so that any humanity she displays has its source in Eva's suffering. That Topsy's humanity keeps her both from being integrated into the white community and from beginning a family of her own within the boundaries of the United States tells us that humanity so-called cannot move across racial lines in Stowe's imagination, at least not when that humanity is housed in the body of a sexually mature woman.

31. Of course, this decontextualization is anything but political, as Lauren Berlant has explained: "In a world where the abstraction of woman from women, of Sambo from African Americans, is both a sign and cause of American disenfranchisement, we can see at least that this mode of abstracting discourse within the female culture industry promotes consciousness as opposed to action, mind and memory versus politics, as a way of naming and containing female excess. It produces as a commodity for women a form of identification whose power derives from its apparent natural superiority to social practice and public exchange." See "The Female Woman: Fanny Fern and the Form of Sentiment," in *The Culture of Sentiment*, 278–79.

32. Harriet A. Jacobs, *Incidents in the Life of a Slave Girl: Written by Herself*, ed. Jean Fagan Yellin (Cambridge, Mass.: Harvard University Press, 1987), 29.

33. Jacobs, *Incidents in the Life*, 513.

34. There is abundant evidence to suggest that Jacobs's efforts to purchase freedom for herself and her children were repeated in her efforts to publish her auto-

biographical account of this struggle. In both instances, she was rescued by white women whose sympathy for her as a woman did not make them extend to her the same rights on which they based their own identity as women: the rights to reproduce themselves in both children and books. That these women put as many obstructions in her path as they removed is evident whenever Jacobs writes to or hears from one of them about the condition of her daughter. Her correspondence also reveals that she had to write her book in secret and only when she could steal a moment from caring for the Willis children, that she trusted only her daughter Louisa to transcribe the manuscript, and that were it not for a string of fortunate events she would never have seen the book in print, much less have been able to purchase the stereotype plates from her publisher. These details of her life indicate that Jacobs understood the power of literary self-reproduction in the most literal way. See Yellin's introduction and the correspondence in the appendix included in her edition of *Incidents in the Life of a Slave Girl: Written by Herself.*

35. Toni Morrison, *Beloved* (New York: Alfred A. Knopf, 1987), 274–75.

36. Postcolonial theory offers a number of valuable insights into the meaning of such a formation under the term of "hybridity," among which Homi Bhabha's is the most succinct: "Hybridity is the sign of the productivity of colonial power, its shifting forces and fixities; it is the name for the strategic reversal of the process of domination through disavowal (that is, the identity of authority). Hybridity is the revelation of the assumption of colonial identity through the repetition of discriminatory identity effects. It displays the necessary deformation and displacement of all sites of discrimination and domination." See "Signs Taken for Wonders: Questions of Ambivalence and Authority Under a Tree Outside Delhi, May 1817," in *Race, Writing, Difference,* ed. Henry Louis Gates, Jr. (Chicago: University of Chicago Press, 1985), 173.

37. Morrison, *Beloved*, 252.

38. Morrison, *Beloved*, 58.

39. Morrison, *Beloved*, 273.

40. One need only think of the outpouring of novels and short stories by such writers as Paule Marshall, Jamaica Kincaid, Julia Alvarez, Cristina García, Maxine Hong Kingston, Linda Ty-Wagner, Bharati Mukherjee, Sandra Cisneros, Cynthia Kodahata, Judith Ortiz-Cofer, Jessica Hagedorn to name but a few.

41. The conflict necessarily entailed in taking up this position is apparent throughout black feminist theory and criticism that takes some of its interpretive strategies from poststructuralism. This statement from the conclusion of Ann duCille's recent book eloquently illustrates the dilemma: "My own project would prove me a fraud, I'm afraid, if in the eleventh hour of this study I were to debunk entirely the notion of tradition and canon or to advocate the complete abandonment of cultural mooring and racial markers. I do want to suggest, however, that black literary studies must put its practice where its theory is. Critics and theorists of African American literature must conceptualize race, class, culture, and experience, as well as traditions and canons, in terms far less natural, absolute, linear, and homogeneous than we have in the past." *The Coupling Convention: Sex, Text, and Tradition in Black Women's Fiction* (New York: Oxford University Press, 1993), 148.

42. In "Cultural Identity and Diaspora," Stuart Hall argues that ruptures and discontinuities, perhaps even more so than a single and continuous experience or

identity, constitute the uniqueness of the African presence in the Americas: "Cultural identity, in this second sense, is a matter of 'becoming' as well as 'being.' It belongs to the future as much as to the past. It is not something which already exists, transcending place, time, history and culture. Cultural identities come from somewhere, have histories. But, like everything which is historical, they undergo constant transformation. Far from being fixed in some essentialized past, they are subject to the continuous 'play' of history, culture and power. Far from being grounded in a mere 'recovery' of the past, which is waiting to be found, and which, when found, will secure our sense of ourselves into eternity, identities are the names we give to the different ways we are positioned by, and position ourselves within, the narratives of the past." In *Identity: Community, Culture, Difference*, ed. Jonathan Rutherford (London: Lawrence and Wishart, 1990), 225. See also, Michael Omi and Howard Winant, *Racial Formation in the United States: From the 1960s to the 1990s* (New York: Routledge, 1994) and Howard Winant, *Racial Conditions: Politics, Theory, Comparisons* (Minneapolis: University of Minnesota Press, 1994), especially 157–170.

43. Barbara J. Fields, "Race and Ideology in American History," in *Region, Race, and Reconstruction: Essays in Honor of C. Vann Woodward*, ed. J. Morgan Kousser and James M. McPherson (New York: Oxford University Press, 1982), 168.

44. Toni Morrison, *Playing in the Dark: Whiteness and the Literary Imagination* (Cambridge, Mass.: Harvard University Press, 1992).

Chapter Three

Homes in the Empire, Empires in the Home

ROSEMARY MARANGOLY GEORGE

Don't return male stares . . . it is considered a come-on. Turning away haughtily and draping your shawl over your head will have the desired effect. . . . [I]f you get the uncomfortable feeling that he's encroaching on your space, chances are he is. A firm request to keep away—use your best memsahib tone—may help.
—Crowther et al., "Facts for Visitors: Women Travelers,"
Lonely Planet Travel Survival Kit: India

Whatever their differences, women shared the experience of having been denied access to an authoritative self as women.
—Elizabeth Fox-Genovese

In juxtaposing the above two quotations, my intention is to draw attention to the codes of authorization that are available to some women in some situations. The self as "memsahib" is a role that is as readily available to white women tourists today as it was to white women colonists yesterday. The two citations also disclose the marks of ruling ideologies on the social constructions of gender: for the Englishwoman in the empire, colonialism provided an "authoritative self" whose vestiges can be traced even in a travel tip from the 1990s. What are the implications of these historical continuities?

In "Deterritorializations: The Rewriting of Home and Exile in Western Feminist Discourse," Caren Kaplan articulates the recent emphasis on the politics of location in some first world feminisms. Working within and against the constructs of Deleuze and Guattari's theory of "deterritorialization," which she interprets as the "moment of alienation and exile in language and literature," Kaplan attempts to describe "a new terrain, a new location, in feminist politics" (197).[1]

This deterritorialization or "becoming minor" requires that:

> We must leave home, as it were, since our homes are often the sites of racism, sexism, and other damaging social practices. Where we come to locate ourselves in terms of our specific histories and differences must be a place with room for what can be salvaged from the past and what can be made new. (Kaplan 194–95)

As Western feminists begin to formulate the ways in which leaving home is a necessary first step in the attempt to practice "not imperialism but nomadism" (Kaplan's phrase), it would be profitable to turn to historic instances when Western women have actually left home and set up house in alien territory and grappled with manipulating an alien language. Englishwomen in the British empire in the late nineteenth/early twentieth century serve as a useful and recent example of such excursions outside the home. Of course, this is not a randomly chosen example. Rather, this essay will try to demonstrate that the sojourn of Englishwomen in the empire writes a crucial chapter in the history of the formations that we today know as Western feminism. Given this earlier "travel" in Western women's history, one which was also represented by the women involved as "alienation and exile," Kaplan's call for "nomadism" becomes impossible to bring into practice. What the call for such counter-travel does do is to bring to the surface the very structures of both imperialism and/or tourism that are so deeply entrenched in Western gestures of leaving home. The history of race and gender in the West make problematic any contemporary excursions into Other territories whose echoes of earlier similar gestures are wished away.[2] In this context, Kaplan's suggestion that we use "what can be salvaged from the past" necessitates a return to this period in the past of Western feminism.[3]

This essay will argue that the colonial occupation of the Indian subcontinent[4] established one of the primary arenas in which the Englishwoman first achieved the kind of authoritative self associated with the modern female subject. It is in the colonies that nineteenth- and early-twentieth-century Englishwomen become "the full individual" that Fox-Genovese sees as the desired goal of feminism in capitalist societies (26). This authoritative self was defined against a racial Other in encounters that were located in space that was paradoxically domestic as well as public: the English home in the colonies.

Examining several popular novels and home management guides written by and about Englishwomen in the Indian empire, this essay assesses the impact of imperialism on issues pertinent to Englishwomen's emancipation in this period. In these texts, the British empire was represented as an arena in which Englishwomen had hard tasks to perform and where the quality of that performance could buttress or jeopardize the imperial project. There was an assumption that the successful running of the empire required the womanly skills of household management. Most importantly, the imperial occupation of India allowed for the prescription of the domestic as the most fulfilling arena in which a modern female subject could operate. Hence, while in England in this period this prescription was being vociferously challenged by feminists, the colonies provided a contemporary situation in which housework and home management were valuable national contributions and celebrated as such by Englishwomen.

In *Desire and Domestic Fiction,* a study of novels and conduct books from eighteenth-century England, Nancy Armstrong has argued that "the modern individual was first and foremost a female" (66). Reading similar English texts written in the Indian empire in the early twentieth century, I will argue that the modern individual woman was first and foremost an imperialist.

Imperialism and the Authoritative Englishwomen

Our understanding of the status of female political and personal authority in this period is largely based on recent studies on the women's suffrage movement. Writing on the emergence of this movement in England, Ellen Carol DuBois explains that since the "independent, virtuous citizen was entirely male in conception, . . . the labor of women, like that of servants, [was] obscured by (though necessary to) the appearance of men's independence."[5] As a result, women's political contributions were thought to be indirectly but adequately represented through their husbands, fathers, or brothers. The demand for women's direct political participation as articulated by the suffragettes was firmly resisted and ridiculed.

In "Imperialism and Motherhood" Anna Davin notes that the word "citizen," in the days when women did not vote, referred exclusively to men (26). Women's only avenue for patriotic contributions to the wellbeing of the nation and empire was via motherhood. The quality of motherhood was seen as directly affecting the quality of the "future citizens" (read "male children")—which in turn determined the vigor of the imperial race. The establishment of English homes in the colonies increased the avenues through which Englishwomen could directly contribute to the national enterprise of imperialism as well as earn recognition for their labor. And such contributions were rarely in the conventional category of "motherhood." In fact, most English mothers in the colonies sent their children back to England for schooling while themselves remaining behind with their husbands. Hence, while motherhood was deemed the most important and fulfilling role for women in England, Englishwomen imperialists stoically bore their separation from their children and earned praise for a maternal stance that was in other circumstances greeted with the highest censure.

In *"Am I That Name?": Feminism and the Category of "Women" in History*, Denise Riley notes that it is the classification according to gender, "and here the critical gender is female," that keeps "women" from becoming "human"—from achieving the status of "truly sexually democratic humanism."[6] It is significant that most feminist commentary on European women in the nineteenth and early twentieth centuries does not consider the impact of imperialism on issues of authoritative selfhood and the move from "woman" to "human."[7] Yet, as Gayatri Spivak astutely states in "Three Women's Texts and a Critique of Imperialism":

> what is at stake, for feminist individualism in the age of imperialism, is precisely the makings of human beings, the constitution and "interpellation" of the subject not only as individual but as "individualist." . . . As the female individualist, not-quite/not-male, articulates herself in shifting relationship to what is at stake, the "native female" as such (within discourse, as a signified) is excluded from any share in this emerging norm. (176–77)

Spivak's account of female individualism makes imperialism a central feature of the making of the white female subject in nineteenth-century texts. Colonial occupation allowed for the continued evolution of this domestic female subject even as it seemed to disrupt the ideological and material requirements for domesticity. With the establishment of the English home outside England, there was a physical repositioning of the hitherto private into what had been considered the most public of realms—the British empire. The domestic, on which the effects of capital had been naturalized and neutralized over decades of industrial and imperial expansion, was now being reconstituted outside England. This process of reconstitution, which began with the advent of imperial women to the colonies, resulted in a dramatic refiguration of England as home country and of women as [national] subjects.[8] Consider the epigraph which sets the tenor of Maud Diver's popular conduct and home management guide, *The Englishwoman in India*:

> What would India be without England, and what would the British Empire be without Englishwomen? To these women are due gratitude not only of their country but of the civilized world. Fearlessly the woman of British birth looks in the eye of danger. Faithfully and with willing sacrifice she upholds the standard of the King-Emperor—the standard of culture and of service to humanity.[9]

The imperial enterprise gives "of British birth" its significance in this instance. Of course the terms "faithful," "willing sacrifice," "culture," and "service" were commonly used in descriptions of women's contribution, but only in the context of the domestic world. The colonies offered a legitimate "public domesticity" to late-Victorian and early-twentieth-century Englishwomen that required the most imaginative skills of the homemaker and yet held out the promise of inclusion in (masculine) public life.

Writing on the construction of the category "woman" in this period in England, Denise Riley coins the term the "social sphere" in order to refer to a feminized area of operation which extended even into public space but which was in opposition to the "political" (masculine) sphere. Working within the "social" realm, women "became both agents and objects of reform in unprecedented ways," but these divisions also kept "women's issues" out of politics (Riley 51). The "social" sphere "provided the chances for some women to enter upon the work of restoring other, more damaged, women to a newly conceived sphere of grace" (49). Spivak extends this analysis by considering the impact of such restoration on the female colonial subject. Working with Brontë's *Jane Eyre* she asserts that the novel can be read as "an allegory of the general epistemic violence of imperialism, the construction of a self-immolating colonial subject for the glorification of the social mission of the colonizer" ("Three Women's Texts" 185). Colonialism extended the scope of the "social" and allowed women to advocate and practice social reform quite untouched by any acknowledgement of the violence of imperialism. Hence, as later sections of this essay will demonstrate, the glorification of the Englishwoman as a "full individual" was daily reestablished by the encounters with Indian women who could then be represented as such "self-immolating" female colonial subjects.

Ellen Carol DuBois claims that the significance of the women's suffrage movement rested precisely on the "fact that it bypassed women's oppression within the family, or private sphere, and demanded instead her admission to citizenship, and through it admission to the public arena" ("The Radicalism of the Woman Suffrage Movement" 128). Elsewhere she argues that "suffragette militancy literally took women out of the parlour and into the streets" ("Woman Suffrage and the Left" 37). This bypassing of the private sphere, according to DuBois, made the movement a prime target for repression and ridicule. In contrast, the colonial space and its discourses offered a private sphere to the white woman that was unmistakably public and yet palatable to a patriarchal, imperial society in ways that the "new woman"/suffragist demands were not.

In the colonies, the circumstances in which the ceremonies of public and private were played out were vastly different from those in the home country. The distinctions between public and private, while they were maintained, repeatedly broke down and had constantly to be redrawn. Consider briefly the setting up of households in camps, when military and/or administrative work at borders required that officers live at the very outposts of empire for years on end. At camp, flimsy partitions were used to create the necessary aura of privacy, of separation between home and work. There was also the popular view that all of one's stay in India was an extended camping trip (undertaken for sport or military purposes or both). In their letters, diaries, and conduct books, housewives applauded themselves for their own and their servants' inventiveness in producing a semblance of domestic order out of the most meager resources.

Conventionally, the only link that has been made between English-women and British imperialism is their status as consumers of the material benefits of this enterprise. This assessment is in keeping with discussions of subject status that are based entirely on the degree of economic participation in the chain of production. For instance, Fox-Genovese writes that "for women, their relative exclusion from [the] process of commodification went hand-in-hand with their exclusion from full individualism" (26). The Englishwomen in the Indian empire, however, were not merely decorating house and self but managing "base camp." In this context, the work done by Englishwomen, even when it was what had hitherto been defined as "house-keeping," was recognized as valuable labor. Hence, one could argue that given the value placed upon their contributions to the imperial cause, the Englishwomen in the colonies were further along the route to "full individualism" than women back home—even those struggling to win the right to vote. The novels and home management books that the imperial enterprise engendered were deeply concerned with the capacity of the Englishwoman to use and abuse this opportunity to function as contributing national subjects alongside the Englishman.

Making the Memsahib

From about the mid-nineteenth century there was a vast amount of literature, fictional and otherwise, written on English life in the Indian subcontinent. A great number of these texts were written by Englishwomen, who had spent varying amounts of time in the colony themselves. Their audience was their fellow imperialists of both genders, at "home" and in the empire. The avowed aim of many of these "lady romancers," as Benita Parry calls them, was to draw attention to the role played by English-women in the imperial endeavor (6). Novels and home management guidebooks written in the late nineteenth and early twentieth century, by Maud Diver, Flora Steel, Alice Perrin, and so on, created a new and self-proclaimedly "modern" female figure: the energetic, strong, benevolent partner in the imperial mission. In the course of these texts, these female colonizers fare much better than the "New Woman" whose sense of self is informed by the "feminist" notions in circulation in contemporary Europe and America. In this literature, England is represented as the originary and ultimate destination of the narrative journey. And needless to say, whether one is a character in the novel or an implied reader of it, one needs to be "of British birth" to travel the whole route.

Hence, "whiteness" and "Englishness" in the discourse of Empire, and again especially in its fiction, take on a power that only masculinity and/or capital could command in the Western world at the time. And this results in a radical re-presentation of the heroine of such fiction as desirable not just in terms of the literary conventions which require that she be young and physically attractive, but because she is white and English. Consider the terms in which the reader is introduced to Honor, the English heroine of Maud Diver's 1914 novel, *Captain Desmond V. C.*:

> In the clear light the girl's beauty took on a new distinctness, a new living charm. The upward-sweeping mass of her hair showed the softness of bronze, save where the sun had burnished it to copper. Breadth of brow, and the strong moulding of her nose and chin, suggested powers rather befitting a man than a woman. But in the eyes and lips the woman triumphed—eyes blue-grey under very straight brows, and lips that even in repose preserved a rebellious tendency to lift at the corners. From her father, and a long line of fighting ancestors, Honor had gotten the large build of a large nature; the notable lift of her head; and the hot blood, coupled with endurance, that stamps the race current coin across the world (6).[10]

Here and elsewhere in the novel, Honor is described as the optimal genetic flowering of her race. She falls in love with her eugenic equal, Captain Theo Desmond. His wife Evelyn, who is described at the outset as "a mere slip of womanhood," is presented as the epitome of everything a memsahib cannot afford to be (*CD* 15). The plot details the ways in which Honor tries to make a true memsahib out of the flighty Evelyn. In the climax of the novel, Evelyn is shot and killed by "rebel natives" from the hill region that Desmond and his regiment were in the process of "subduing." Honor leaves for England. Desmond, who for some time before Evelyn's death has been in love with Honor, spends a year in mourning and traveling through Europe. He meets Honor in England, and they acknowledge their love for each other.

This novel illustrates the two levels at which the role of "Englishwoman as buttress to empire" operated: the first, which was overtly stressed by the fiction writers, was that of the managers of "base camp," helpmates and partners in the imperial enterprise. The second level is the more covertly articulated use of the white woman's presence in the colonies as a rationalization for the "necessity" of the violent repression of colonized peoples. *Captain Desmond V. C.* illustrates the complex use that is made of the Englishwoman as pawn and player in the machinations of empire. Honor, as "player," is the efficient memsahib, and Evelyn is the "pawn" whose death at the hands of the Afridis is used to justify the "punitive expeditions" that Desmond periodically undertakes over the course of the narrative.[11]

In 1917, Maud Diver published *Unconquered: A Romance*,[12] a novel set in contemporary England, touching the same ideological registers as her novels set in India. The novel begins on the eve of the First World War. Sir Mark Stuart Forsyth, a Scottish aristocrat who is the hero of the novel, falls in love with the entirely unsuitable Bel Alison. Bel Alison, whose lack of a masculine last name is significant, is a woman of the world; "modern," shallow, sexy, she has been an actress, writer, and feminist, among other fleeting vocations. Her devoted companion is the staunch feminist "Harry," whose lesbianism is represented as a lightly veiled monstrosity. Mark's mother and mainstay, Helen Forsyth, who is central in the novel, is the gracious, strong woman of (noble) character. Helen dislikes Bel and would rather Mark marry their common friend, the kind and gentle Sheila Melrose, who is also well born and well bred. When war breaks out, Mark enlists to fight. Helen and Sheila cheer him on in contrast with the pacifist Bel who begs him not to enlist. Mark is declared first lost and then killed in action. However, he returns home after a period of convalescence in a convent in France. Because he is partially paralyzed Bel deserts him. She goes on to become an anti-war/feminist crusader. Sheila's steadfast adoration finally pays off when she gets her man, albeit physically much damaged.

Like her novels set in India, Diver's *Unconquered* reads in part like a conduct book that is full of exhortations to "true womanliness" and "true manhood." Diver's characters serve as illustrations of the best and the worst of the two genders. It is interesting to examine her discourse on women and the etiquette of their movements within and between public and/or private space. Much emphasis is placed on the fact that Bel has no home and no parents. Her past is indeterminate and somehow more eventful than is deemed proper; she has lived in many homes with relatives, with friends, with "Harry" (whose love for her is "like a man's"), and the gossip is that she had even gone away with a married man for a weekend. She has lived abroad in indeterminate circumstances—in the United States, in India, on the continent—and, much like the prototypical rake, has seduced hapless lovers, leaving behind her several broken hearts.

Helen Forsyth, the hero's mother, is the female character most valorized by the text. Helen translates poetry, but her main passion is the revival of English arts and crafts through a revival of "home industries." One needs to read Diver's novels set in India to appreciate how this portrait of the cultured, benevolent lady of the manor is transferred to the Indian setting and democratized in the sense that it is made available to all Englishwomen in the colony. In India, one need not be an aristocrat or be married to one, nor have an estate—a husband with an official post, servants, and a modest compound around one's house are the only prerequisites for playing the grand lady. Helen Forsyth's "true life" is centered well within her (feudal, yet refinished with "unlimited light and air") ancestral home. The narrator maintains that:

> the world's most strenuous workers found in her home atmosphere, a refreshment and inspiration worth some sacrifice of activity to preserve in an age of wholesale experiment in life, and art and religion. They might rate her for living in a backwater; but, as their intimacy grew, they realised that she was more vitally in touch than themselves with the world's greater issues; that her uneventful days were rich in experience, informed by a central purpose and an unshaken faith in certain abiding truths . . . (UR 39–40)

This paean to domesticity on a grand scale is greatly enhanced when it is located in the colonies. Here, the alien nature of the terrain makes it a challenge for the most "restless" of women.

In *Unconquered*, when the war starts, the women characters have the option of playing a visible public role. The contours of this role are always defined in terms of serving as supports to their men in wartime. Diver's novels suggest that everyday events in the lives of Englishwomen living in India call for Helen Forsyth's and Sheila Melrose's wartime capacity to "rise to the occasion" and manage homes, houseguests, and servants as adroitly as they nurse dying soldiers on the battlefront, ride, drive, shoot, and give and take orders.

The parallels between the women in *Captain Desmond V. C.* and *Unconquered* are instructive. It is consistent with the differences between Honor/Sheila and Evelyn/Bel that the women who have authorial approval see the men's work of quelling enemies of the empire and nation as crucial, whereas both Evelyn and Bel are passivists who keep urging the men to leave off fighting. Like Sheila in *Unconquered*, Honor expects Desmond to continue with the Frontier regiment even after he is wounded in a skirmish. To restrain men from the manly work of Empire and nation is to hamper them. And in this discourse only "the native" needs restraint. Consider the following exchange between Desmond and Evelyn where he explains to her that a "punitive expedition" against the Afridis is imminent and necessary:

"The Frontier's been abnormally quiet these many months. It will do us all good to have a taste of real work for a change."

"Do you mean . . . will there be much . . . fighting?"

"Well—The Afridis don't take a blow sitting down. We have to burn their crops you see; blow up their towers; enforce heavy fines, and generally knock it into their heads that they can't defy the Indian Government with impunity. Yes; it means fighting—severe or otherwise, according to their pleasure."

"Pleasure!—It sounds simply horrible; and you—I believe you're *glad* to go!"

"Well, my dear, what else would you have?" (217–18)

This passage is among the many that mark Evelyn's wifely inadequacies. That no irony is intended in Desmond's account of burning the "enemy's" crops, and so on, or in his definition of "a taste of real work" is clear from one notable plot detail: it is at this point in the novel that Honor, who has been witness to the above exchange between husband and wife, discovers that she is in love with Desmond.

It is the inroads that Desmond's work makes into her private sphere that Evelyn most resents. The time and space marked home, which she expects to share exclusively with her husband, are invaded by his colleagues' use of their home as an extension of the workplace and of work hours. Honor's position on this complaint that Evelyn constantly voices is exactly that which is advised in the section on housekeeping and hostessing in Diver's nonfictional guide, *The Englishwoman in India*.[13] In a chapter titled "Hostess and Housekeeper," Diver writes, "Every Anglo-Indian wife is of necessity a hostess also in her own degree. . . . [W]hatever her natural inclination, she must needs accept the fact that her house, and all that therein is, belongs in a large measure, to her neighbour also" (*EI* 48–49).

The contrast between Honor and Evelyn could be rewritten as a list of "dos and don'ts" for potential memsahibs. It is no surprise that some of the best-known home management guides were written by women who had already written several novels. Of these, the most popular one was written by Flora Anne Steel (who was also a prolific writer of fiction) and Grace Gardiner, entitled *The Complete Indian Housekeeper and Cook* with a lengthy subtitle: *Giving the Duties of Mistress and Servants, the General Management of the House, and Practical Recipes for Cooking in all its Branches*. This book's popularity can be gauged by the fact that it was revised and reprinted more than a dozen times between 1888 and 1917.[14]

In the introductory chapter to this guide, the authors write:

Here [in India], as there [in England], the end and object is not merely personal comfort, but the formation of a home—that unit of civilization where father and children, master and servant, employer and employed, can learn their several duties. When all is said and done also, herein lies the natural outlet for most of the talents peculiar to women. It is the fashion nowadays to undervalue the art of making a home; to deem it simplicity and easiness itself. But this is a mistake, for the proper administration of even a small household needs both brain and heart. (*CIH* 7)

Hence, setting up home in the Empire, because of the many challenges involved, once again made the "art of making a home," an occupation worthy of a woman with "brain and heart." Furthermore, in the Empire, the need for constant creation of such "civilization" was urgently felt. Novel after novel suggests that it is the daily construction of the home country as the location of the colonizer's racial and moral identity and as the legitimization of the colonizer's national subjecthood that made possible the carrying out of the work of Empire. And, as Diver and others were quick to point out, it was on the home, this "unit of civilization," that the reputation of the entire civilizing project (as imperialism was often perceived to be) rested.[15] Thus Diver cautions, "the individual man and woman may still, in their degree, help to defer or hasten a catastrophe that only a policy of power—just, yet unflinching power—can remotely hope to avert (*EI* 87–88). Needless to say, Diver's advocated methods of home management are based on a similar "policy of power—just, yet unflinching power." And the administration of this power was assigned to the memsahib.

Household Management: Discipline and Punish

If the Englishwoman recognizes herself and is recognized as national subject only outside the national boundaries, then she becomes "of the master race" only in the presence of "the native" who will hail her as "memsahib" (literally, "Madame boss"). The home is the primary, and often the only, site where such encounters between white women and those of the colonized races took place.

In the absence of her children, the Englishwoman sets out to discipline the "natives" in her compound—and we are repeatedly assured that these persons are no more than children requiring discipline. With her home and compound as her domain, the Englishwoman's challenge, her duty even, is to keep this strange and unmanageable territory under control. Her triumph is to replicate the empire on a domestic scale—a benevolent, much supervised terrain where discipline and punishment is meted out with an unwavering hand. As with the Empire, the territory of the home is already secured for the English occupant. Thus the Englishwoman does not have to keep house as much as supervise the keeping of her house. A direct parallel can be drawn to Desmond's work in *Captain Desmond V. C.*, which entails not the conquest of new territory but the maintenance of law and order. The English home in the colony thus represents itself as the Empire in miniature. Diver writes:

> In fine, if a woman wills to keep house successfully in India, she must possess before all things a large tolerance and a keen sense of justice, rare feminine virtues both, even in these days. She must train her mind to look upon petty falsehoods, thefts, and uncleanliness not as heinous offenses, but as

troublesome propensities, to be quietly checked. Swift should she be also to recognize the trustworthy man, and to trust him liberally . . . (*EI* 70)

The language is that of statecraft and high diplomacy. The housewife is to aspire to the role of the politically astute leader who holds the reins of the Empire in her hands, adept at knowing when to let them go slack and when to tighten the grip. Since these are "rare feminine virtues," only exceptional women can "man" the turbulent colonial house.

What is even more interesting and unexpected in this discourse is the representation of the Empire as no more than an expanded version of the domestic arena. Steel and Gardiner write: "We do not wish to advocate an unholy haughtiness; but an Indian house hold can no more be governed peacefully, without dignity and prestige, than an Indian Empire" (*CIH* 9). Time and time again, the colonial discourse, especially the texts written by women, represent the management of Empire as essentially "home management" on a larger scale. There are doors to be locked; corners to be periodically dusted; rooms to be fumigated and made free of pests; children (i.e., "natives") to be doctored, educated, clothed, and disciplined; accounts to be kept; boundaries redrawn and fences mended.

Housekeeping in the colonies is often represented as a military/imperial campaign. Writing of the need to follow a simple accounting system and a written inventory of food supplies, Steel and Gardiner note, "life in India always partakes of the nature of a great campaign" (*CIH* 21). Hence, the daily supervision of servants is presented as "an inspection parade" which "should begin immediately after breakfast, or as near ten o'clock as circumstances will allow" (*CIH* 8).

At the heart of all advice and every tip that this text offers is the attempt to inculcate the proper deportment of rulers—for the mistress rules alongside the master. Hence the first chapter of the Steel and Gardiner guide, "Duties of the Mistress," presents the domestic realm in terms of duties, rules, rewards, and punishment:

The first duty of a mistress is, of course, to be able to give intelligible orders to her servants; therefore it is necessary she should learn to speak Hindustani. . . .

The next duty is obviously to insist on her orders being carried out. . . . "How is this to be done?" . . . The secret lies in making rules and keeping to them. The Indian servant is a child in everything but age. . . . [F]irst faults should never go unpunished.

But it will be asked, How are we to punish our servants when we have no hold on their minds or bodies?—when cutting their pay is illegal, and few, if any, have any sense of shame.

The answer is obvious. Make a hold. (*CIH* 3–4)

Citing their "own experience," the authors then go on to describe a system of fines and rewards that circumvent the rules that they themselves are subject to, even as they devise punishments for servants who break the rules! The trick is to engage servants at the lowest rate possible and then offer some extra as "buksheesh" conditional on good service. As an example of another "kindly and reasonable device" to control "the obstinate cases" as well as "to show what absolute children Indian servants are," Steel and Gardiner suggest the forced administration of castor oil "on the ground that there must be some physical cause for inability to learn or to remember" (*CIH* 4).

> This is considered a great joke, and exposes the offender to much ridicule from his fellow-servants; so much so that the words, "Mem Sahib tum ko zuroor kaster ile pila dena hoga" (The Mem Sahib will have to give you castor oil), is often heard in the mouths of the upper servants when new-comers give trouble. In short, without kindly and reasonable devices of this kind, the usual complaint of a want of hold over servants must remain true until they are educated into some sense of duty. (*CIH* 3–4)[16]

Such selections from the first three pages in the text are enough to understand the force with which Steel and Gardiner meet the object of their text—described in passing in the very first footnote, which is a quick justification for their use of phonetic spellings: "The object of this book being to enable a person who is absolutely unacquainted with India, its languages and people, to begin housekeeping at once, the authors have decided on adhering throughout to purely phonetic spellings" (*CIH* 2, n.1). Since the essence of housekeeping is the learning of imperial privilege, it is logical that this is the lesson that every chapter reinforces. Hence, as the above-quoted footnote indicates, even the scattered citations from the languages or cultures of the Indians are represented only as means of improving the memsahib's "hold" on the native. In her novels Diver presents language acquisition as an intellectual pursuit unique to the colonial situation. Honor marvels at Desmond's dedication to his work when she sees him struggling to improve his Persian language skills before he takes the administrative exam that would get him his promotion in the services. It follows then that she is eager to master various Indian languages whereas Evelyn is bored with the entire enterprise. Honor's knowledge of "the native language" is yet another charming indication of the overwhelming compatibility between her and Desmond. The mysterious, romantic, even spiritual (given that Desmond is a married man for most of the novel) bond between them rests on a bedrock of a shared imperial ideology—both proudly take up the burden of being English in the Indian Empire. And as "good" imperialists, their first task is the mastery of the language. In the context of colonialism, the language of imperial control and discipline is primarily the imperial languages—namely, English or French. "Native" language acquisition is represented in popular imperial discourses as motivated by an unpolitical, often purely aesthetic/linguistic, interest in an alien culture. However, in her home management guide, Maud Diver bluntly advocates the acquisition of the relevant "native" language by Englishwomen for the sole reason of administering power. She writes: "Surely, no sight could be more pitiful and ludicrous than that of a woman who has given place to wrath, and is powerless to put it into words; nor can such an one [sic] ever hope to keep a retinue of a dozen servants under control" (*EI* 71). No house, these management guides repeatedly insist, runs smoothly on its own accord. And yet, as with the Empire, the image that is conveyed must be one of ease of authority. The ultimate aim of house management as advocated in these guides is to erase the signs of supervision and struggle from the surface. Thus Diver writes:

> for experience shows that the most successful housekeepers and hostesses are not found among the women whose minds, tongues and feet run incessantly upon household matters, but among those who—by hidden method and management—give a surface impression of large leisure, and of a mind free to give its undivided attention to the subject or the individual of the moment. (*EI* 54–55)

That Lady Helen Forsyth's leisure and radiant benevolence in *Unconquered* is born of centuries of class privilege is part of the ideological underpinnings of the culture that the novelist glosses over. However, in her guide to colonial India, Diver can clearly and repeatedly advocate that "a surface impression of large leisure" be secured "by hidden method and management." Imperial privileges, unlike those privileges created by class divisions in England, are unproblematically presented as available for all English subjects in the colonies.[17]

Diver's conduct book was written for English audiences in the attempt to introduce them to the travails of the Englishwomen in India, and thus to alter Kipling's and other writers' renditions of these women as "idle, frivolous and luxury-loving" (*EI* 5). "Circumstance," according to Diver, "is, after all, the supreme test of character, and India tests a woman's character to the utmost" (*EI* 23). In these difficult circumstances, "constant, personal supervision," writes Diver, is "the one weapon that can never fail" (*EI* 35). The panoptic principle as a means of household management was widely advocated by these writers and it is not surprising to learn that this device was designed for the purposes of colonial surveillance and was first used on the borders between Europe and the Ottoman Empire and then in colonial India (see Mitchell 35). Sophisticated supervision, of course, also requires that the memsahib "learn not to see all that comes in the ways of her eyes; for with natives, as with children, the art of not seeing, practiced sparingly and judiciously, will go far to preserve domestic peace" (*EI* 71). The language here is not, as we might at first think, of nursery rules but once again of state management. In the Empire, indigenous populations were often represented as "unruly" children, a move that rendered juvenile the acts and aspirations of such peoples while also erasing the serious, meditated nature of their resistance. Managing a home and managing the Empire were ultimately part of the same project.

Supervision also included the regulation of the private life of servants. Steel and Gardiner place this job under the category of the "minor duties" of a mistress. There is no doubt in the minds of these writers that privacy is not a concern in Indian homes. Diver writes that this is so because "man, in his undeveloped state, [is] untroubled by a senseless passion for privacy" (*EI* 131). In the interest of keeping "bazaar" illnesses and indecencies out of the household, Steel and Gardiner advocate that all servants be compelled to live in the compound. But this, they add,

> is no reason why they should turn *your domain* into a caravanserai for their relations to the third and fourth generation. As a rule, it is well to draw a very sharp line in this respect, and if it be possible to draw it on the other side of mother-in-law, so much the better for peace and quietness. (*CIH* 4; emphasis added)

Hence, Englishwomen who want to "begin housekeeping at once" are here instructed to delineate, with "very sharp" lines, the familial bonds that they would find acceptable in their compound. Not surprisingly, the Western nuclear family structure is the one deemed appropriate. The local practice of married couples living with their families is represented in this instance through the figure of the quarrelsome mother-in-law. Furthermore, Steel and Gardiner add, the mistress should enquire every day if there is any illness in the compound and "as often as possible—once or twice a week at least—she should go a regular inspection round the compound, not forgetting the stables, fowl-houses, & co." (*CIH* 4). In the final instance then, the servants are no more than livestock requiring inspection.

Indian homes, if, as Diver puts it, "by courtesy they may be so called," are dim, lightless, segregated quarters that can be lighted up only by the introduction of Western practices (*EI* 131). In the place of homes, these writers find "dwellings" that are ramshackle huts, palaces that are disproportionately large, or simply "ruins" inhabited by people. Hence the "native" as manifest in the representation of his/her home is either a "lack" or in "excess." Hence, differences in class, region, religion, and even architectural style are erased as Indian domestic arrangements are rated solely on the basis of their degree of Westernization.

My Indian Family: A Story of East and West Within an Indian Home, a
novel in the form of a diary set in the 1930s, written by Hilda Wernher, a
Scandinavian based in England, examines the intricacies of life in an Indian household.[18] The narrator and central protagonist is a middle-aged
European woman who moves to India and into a Muslim household
when her daughter Mary Ann marries Rashid, an Indian research scientist whom she met in England. The blurb on the book jacket of *My Indian
Family* quotes from a *New York Times* review of the novel: "It is like a small
window opened in the great haunted house of India to let in the sunshine
and fresh air of Western comprehension."[19] The narrator presents herself
as a blend of "Western comprehension" with a sympathetic appreciation
of things Indian.

And yet, despite this effort to understand specific nuances of Indian
domestic/social arrangements, there is in *My Indian Family* the inevitable
final rejection of most of it. The only solution is to "let in the sunshine and
fresh air of Western comprehension," and the only enlightened Indians
(and Indian homes) are those amenable to these changes. Once again we
have the lamenting of the lack of privacy in Indian homes, accompanied
by an inability to recognize Indian interpretations of privacy. The boundaries between the spaces assigned to two sexes, those which separate
adults from children and the sahibs from the servants, are recognized and
valorized only if they draw on contemporary European concepts of privacy. Hence the narrator finds unacceptable the Indian practice of children sharing beds or of entire families sleeping in courtyards in the
hottest months of the year.

English women writers repeatedly insist that the only way of changing
this sorry state of affairs in the Indian home is to work on the Indian
woman. And yet there was no suggestion that any role but the purely domestic could fulfill the potential in Indian women. Diver writes:

> The advanced woman of the West is apt to conclude overhastily that the nar-
> row, hidden life of her Eastern sister, with its lack of freedom, its limited
> scope for self-development and individual action, must needs constitute her
> a mere lay figure in the scheme of things; a being wholly incapable of influ-
> encing the larger issues of life; whereas a more intimate knowledge of facts
> would reveal to her the truth that, from that same hidden corner, and by the
> natural primal power of her sex, the Eastern woman moulds the national
> character far more effectively than she ever could hope to do from the plat-
> form or the hustings. (*EI* 100–01)

Here then we have another example of the ideological continuance between the conservative view on the role of women in England and in her
colonies. Thus, because of the "natural primal power of her sex," the Indian woman (like any other woman) is most powerful when she operates

from her home. The problem that needs to be eliminated is the fact that "the Eastern sister" is confined to a hidden corner instead of having the entire house as her territory. This is where the Englishwoman has to step in to introduce her to her rightful dominion and of course to point out to her that aspiring to any larger or more public space (perhaps of national dimensions as in the freedom struggle movement) was futile. What must be noted, if only in passing, is that from the late nineteenth century onwards, contemporary Indian women who were accepted as role models or at least well known, led very public lives as active participants in various social reform movements as well as in the national independence movement.[20]

"Our Eastern Sisters": The White Woman's Burden

In the discourses of empire, there were very few if indeed any moments when alliances between genders overshadowed racial solidarity. When overtures made by white women toward establishing such alliances with Indian women failed, the conclusion reached was that Indian women themselves resisted self-improvement and liberation from the social tyrannies they were subject to. In *My Indian Family*, the narrator relates how she tries, unsuccessfully, to instill the "ladies first" principle at a formal tea party with her Indian guests—a Mr. Jarwarkar and his two unnamed wives. What is specially noteworthy in narratives such as this is how smoothly the knowledge of the Other is transformed into a means of dismissal of cultural differences:

> True, we know that a Hindu woman considers it correct to serve her lord first and that, somehow, all Orientals have similar customs. But this is our house. We can stage an object lesson in different treatment of women, by serving tea in Western fashion. . . . Both ladies refuse, both motion me unashamedly to take the first cup to their joint lord. I remain adamant, saying that "West in," ladies come first. Mary Ann seconds me; Rashid says to the ceiling—he can't address ladies directly—that it is high time things were altered in this country. Mr. Jarwarkar, an educated man, laughs and says he'd like to try the new regime for once. But it's no use. Burri bai [the elder wife], seeing that I don't give in, rises, takes the cup from my hand and presents it ceremoniously to her unfaithful lord, thus carrying out to the letter the Code of Manu, as far as the conduct of wives is concerned. The same procedure is repeated over each dish. Man comes first. Again India has won the day. (*MIF* 55–56)

The narrator's self-confidence is clearly demonstrated in this passage. What escapes her "Other"-wise careful reasoning is the fact that "ladies first" does not dramatically alter the gender inequalities present in a scenario where "man comes first." The encounter between white women and Indian women, in either's home, once again serves to underline the assumption of superiority that the Englishwoman has of her status as woman.[21] Thus despite the occasional reference to Indian women as "our Eastern sisters," there is no substantial alliance possible between the two groups of women. In this context, "again India has won the day" reverberates with the narrator's resignation at her failure to instill an English sense of female worth in her Indian guests.

As English writers (of both genders) were quick to note, the white woman's status in society was the norm, the yardstick by which "native" lack was measured.[22] Perhaps it is consequent that while in Europe at the time some women were struggling to win the right to vote, in the Indian empire there was a comfortable belief that the white women's emancipation was a completed project—one only had to look at "native" women to know so. A chapter entitled "Eastern Womanhood" in Diver's *The Englishwoman in India* ends with:

> In these days, too, when education behind the Purdah seems tending towards an ultimate lifting of the veil, it lies with the Englishwoman in India to prove, by the simplicity and uprightness of her own way of life, that a woman, being free in all things, may yet refrain from using her liberty as a cloak of vanity and folly; that tender womanliness and self-effacement may, and do, go hand in hand with an unrestricted outlook upon the world at large; a fact that Orientals—the women no less than the men—are singularly slow to believe. (88–89)

The contemporary white woman (circa early twentieth century) is emancipated and has achieved all that there is to achieve in terms of gender equality or self-development. Clearly, the right to vote is not what gender equality is measured by, for it is without this liberty that Diver finds her fellow countrywomen "free in all things."

In her guidebook, Diver repeatedly suggests that the ordinary Englishwoman in India has the responsibility of her Eastern sisters in her hands:

> Every mistress of a house has, within her compound, some scope for work in this direction. True she has only one female servant, but every man in her service is certain to possess a wife and family. For celibacy is an outcome of civilization, and the Hindu and Mohommadan have yet to discover its advantages. By means of this patriarchal system, then, any Englishwoman can find material ready to her hand, should curiosity or sympathy prompt her to take an active interest in the joys and sorrows of those sister-women whom chance has brought together within her gates. (*EI* 77–78)

"Curiosity," "sympathy," and "love" are all equally legitimate reasons to work one's designs on this "material ready to her hand."[23] Projects like the *Female Medical Aid Fund* started by Lady Dufferin allowed English-women entry into areas and events in Indian homes that would otherwise have remained unknown to them.[24] Writing of the "foyer social," a government-sponsored educational and social welfare program for urban African women in Belgian Africa between 1946 and 1960, Nancy Rose Hunt details the many ways in which the program provided European women with the means and materials with which to reshape the domestic arrangements of the African women living in the colonial city of Usumbura, Ruanda-Urundi (present-day Bujumbura, Burundi). The "house visit" part of the program gave European social workers physical access to the students' private lives and an opportunity to inspect, correct, and applaud all signs of emulation of European domestic ideology.

Nor was this practice of inspection of the homes of one's "lesser sisters" confined to the colonies. From the late nineteenth century onward, in cities in England and France, a concerted effort was made by local authorities and women's volunteer groups to curb infant mortality rates and generally to improve the quality of the imperial race by monitoring the domestic life of the urban working-class population. A vital part of this supervision was carried out by "lady health visitors" who inspected working-class homes, dispensing disinfection powder and hints to mothers on feeding, clothing, schooling of children, on dirt and on "the evils of bad smells," as well as urging, "on all possible occasions, the importance of cleanliness, thrift and temperance."[25]

In the Indian colony, the practice of demarcating domestic and public space between the genders through the use of the purdah especially frustrated the Englishwoman's attempts at reform. Any resistance on the part of Indian women to such schemes was interpreted as the "evil result" of their "innate ideas and customs" (*EI* 96–98). Hence, writing on the Dufferin Fund, Diver concludes:

> Yet despite all that money, tact, and stringent regulations could achieve, high-caste Zenana women have shown no disposition to avail themselves freely of the medical skill placed at their disposal; possibly because female life is of no great value in the East. (*EI* 98)

Diver's conclusion implies that because female life is of no great value, Zenana women do not attempt to save themselves from death. Perhaps their faith in alternative methods of healing was stronger than their trust in the Dufferin Fund, but this is not how Diver chooses to read the situation.

Conclusion

Writing about city planning in colonial Egypt, and the colonialists' apparent need to fix boundaries, to create order by differentiating interior from exterior, abd so on, Timothy Mitchell unintentionally provides us with an articulation of the project of the colonial novel as written by these women writers:

> The world is set up before an observing subject as though it were the picture of something. . . . It follows that the appearance of order is at the same time an order of appearance, a hierarchy. The world appears to the observer as a relationship between picture and reality, the one present but secondary, a mere representation, the other only represented, but prior, more original, more real. This order of appearance can be called the hierarchy of truth. (60)

Mitchell's "picture" is that which is suggested by the "Egypt" exhibits at world exhibitions in Paris and other Western metropoles in the mid- to late nineteenth century. Travelers from Europe to Egypt expected, according to Mitchell, to walk from the exhibit to the truth "behind" it. The truths that they recognized in Egypt, then, would be those which corresponded to the "preview" provided by the exhibit in Europe. One could argue that the novels and guidebooks by these women writers were similarly constructed and consumed. They were written and read as representations of the truth about British India and as such became self-fulfilling prophecies. The "preview" that the books provided thus becomes identical to the reality inhabited and represented by writers. For the author to have visited India did not necessarily add to or subtract from the quality or success of the novels she wrote—hence the phenomenon of writers like Ethel Dell, who wrote several very successful novels set in British India, the most famous being *The Lamp in the Desert*, without having left England.[26]

What is remarkable about these novels and handbooks is the confidence of the female authorial voice. The ideological proximity of the imperial romance novel and of the imperial home management guides constructs "the Englishwoman"—a female subject who is firmly anchored as a "full individual" through her racial privileges. Hence, despite the dislocation (geographic and linguistic) that these women experienced, their written texts represent a coherent, unified bourgeois subjecthood.[27] These texts serve to translate the discomfort of dislocation into a means of self-aggrandizement even as they record the Englishwoman speaking an alien language in an alien terrain. A rudimentary grasp of the "native" language (often just the imperative mode) is all the linguistic equipment one needs to be marked as "White." Similarly, in these imperial romances, non-English characters are marked by a curious inability to master the English language or at least the correct British accent—a lack which is indicative of their less than whole subject status.[28]

If, in the late nineteenth and early twentieth centuries, women writers in England (Virginia Woolf, for example) saw literary, aesthetic, and even political distance between themselves and an easy understanding of the self within a community, such contradictions were erased in the colonies.

In the colonies, "not belonging" was one's only avenue to unified and autonomous subject status. Being white and English was what marked the imperialist as the fortunate outsider. And as such, it was a status shared equally by Englishmen and -women and was therefore erased as a possible site of gender struggle.

Despite the fact that the English imperialists in India often represented themselves as exiled from their homeland, it is hard to justify the use of the term "exile" in this context today. Yet, "Gender, Colonialism, and Exile: Flora Anne Steel and Sara Jeanette Duncan in India," an article by Rebecca Saunders, explores this instance of what she sees as "women writing in exile."[29] Exile is not the same as manning one's post in the empire. The twentieth century has presented us with so many harrowing instances of exile that is experienced as extreme homelessness, refugee status in detention camps, constant fear of expulsion, and so on, that Saunders's application of the term here comes across as very facile. And yet this term is unproblematically used in contemporary scholarship to describe the situation of Western women who are away from home. In 1987 Helen Callaway published an ethnographic study of colonial women entitled *Gender, Culture and Empire: European Women in Colonial Nigeria;* her self-proclaimed agenda was to reverse the negative representation (in literature and scholarship) of these women who despite being "doubly alien" in the colonies were made to bear more than their fair share of the blame for the excesses of empire.

I have tried to demonstrate that it was because of the autonomy afforded by their dislocation that the written texts by "lady romancers" displayed a self-confident female subject not possible in the history and literature of Englishwomen in the England of that time.[30] In 1929, when Virginia Woolf wrote her impassioned feminist manifesto calling for "a room of one's own," she needed only to have looked over to the everyday discourses inscribed by her countrywomen in the Empire. By 1929 the English wife in the colonies had enjoyed decades of greater political participation and greater personal authority than feminists and women modernists of the time in England. The memsahib was a British citizen long before England's laws caught up with her.[31]

Notes

I would like to dedicate this essay to the memory of Roger B. Henkle (1935–1991). For their comments at various stages in the writing of this essay, I would like to thank Neil Lazarus, Ellen Rooney, Nancy Armstrong, Roddey Reid, Vince Rafael, and Molly Sholes.

1. See Gilles Deleuze and Félix Guattari, 17.

2. Recent scholarship such as *The Wages of Whiteness: Race and the Making of the American Working Class* by David R. Roediger and *Woman of the Klan: Racism and Gender in the 1920s* by Kathleen M. Blee examines gender and race in the United States in the late nineteenth century and early twentieth century. Both Roediger's and Blee's studies of the construction of whiteness in American culture suggest that "becoming White" is articulated via discourses that refuse all affiliations with the African Americans who also occupy the physical and imaginary landscape of America at the time. In the British context, Vron Ware's study of the construction of white womanhood, *Beyond the Pale: White Women, Racism, and History*, provides the most comprehensive and thought-provoking analysis of the ideological power of whiteness.

3. Kaplan's essay is an exceptionally nuanced example of recent feminist texts that try to formulate ways of rectifying the flaws in 1970s and early 1980s white feminism by advocating that white women move outside the comfort zone of their relative privilege. While this stance does enhance one's understanding of what/who was left out of early decades of feminist theorizing and praxis, my contention is that such travel has a prior parallel in the advent of benevolent imperial women on the colonies. I will argue that this prior moment of travel had as far-reaching implications for feminism at that time as our contemporary, feminist "nomads" might have on the future of Western feminism.

4. The "Indian subcontinent" includes contemporary Pakistan, India, Bangladesh, and parts of Afghanistan. The East India Company was in the area from as early as the sixteenth century. With the mutiny/revolt of 1857, control of the area passed from the company to the British crown. In 1947, colonial India was partitioned into two independent countries—Pakistan and India. In 1971, East Pakistan declared its independence and became Bangladesh.

5. Ellen Carol DuBois, "Woman Suffrage and the Left: An International Socialist-Feminist Perspective," 24. Here DuBois argues against the accepted reading of woman's suffrage movements as conservative Faustian bargains made at the cost of other political freedoms for all women. She maintains that in the 1890–1920 period, women's suffrage was a "left" or "militant" demand that "reflected the existence and vigor of both the socialist and feminist movements" (23). See, also by DuBois, "The Radicalism of the Woman Suffrage Movement: Notes Toward the Reconstruction of Nineteenth-Century Feminism."

6. "There is, as we have repeatedly learned, no fluent trajectory from feminism to a truly sexually democratic humanism; there is no easy passage from 'women' to 'humanity'" (Riley 17).

7. For instance, despite focusing on the issue of Englishwomen's authority (in the period between 1890 and 1920) in the context of women's rights, the vote, the debate on public and private spheres, etc., Ellen Carol DuBois does not mention imperialism or the establishment of homes in the colonies. Carole Pateman's otherwise comprehensive study of the public/private debate is also silent on the issue of imperialism. See Pateman, "Critiques of the Public/Private Dichotomy." The exceptions invariably focus directly on imperialism as is the case with the earlier cited article by Davin, "Imperialism and Motherhood." In this context, Vron Ware's "Britannia's Other Daughters: Feminism in the Age of Imperialism" (*Beyond the Pale*, 119–66) is remarkable for its insistence that "feminist ideology and

practice were shaped by the social, economic and political forces of imperialism to a far greater extent than has been acknowledged" (119). The course that Ware's argument takes is substantially different from the one that I outline in this essay. Ware examines the potential in Englishwomen to participate in "the political emancipation of the colonies" in the course of their feminist activism for and alongside Indian women. My concern is with how the colonies participated in the political emancipation of Englishwomen.

8. In the seventeenth and eighteenth centuries Englishwomen were sent by the shipload, in what were called "fishing fleets," to search for husbands in India. Such arrangements were made by the East India Company for whom these men worked. Margaret MacMillan writes: "The cargo, divided into 'gentlewomen' and 'others,' were given one set of clothes each and were supported for a year—quite long enough, it was thought, for them to find themselves husbands" (17). The journey took as long as six months. The invention of steam power and the opening of the Suez Canal in 1869 helped shorten the trip to about four weeks. This, as well as the establishment of large administrative and military institutions that accompanied all colonial governments, increased the number of English women who travelled to India in the capacity of wife, sister, fiancée, daughter, and missionary. Yet, throughout the British rule in India, European men outnumbered European women three to one. In 1881 when the first India-wide census was taken, there were 145,000 Europeans out of a total population of 250,000,000. In 1921 there were 165,000 Europeans. Half of these Europeans lived in the cities and larger towns, especially in Calcutta and Bombay. When the British capital was moved from Calcutta to Delhi in 1911, the English population in that city mushroomed. Karachi (in present-day Pakistan) and Madras were other cities with sizable white populations in the early decades of this century (MacMillan 42). Also see Patricia Barr, *In Praise of the Women of Victorian India;* Marian Fowler, *Below the Peacock Fan: First Ladies of the Raj.*

9. This epigraph is attributed to Count Jon Konigsmark, *Die Englanders in India.* Benita Parry's biographical note on Maud Diver tells us that she was born in 1867 in India (79). Daughter of a colonel in the Indian Army, she married Lieutenant Colonel Diver when he was a subaltern in the Indian Army. At 29, she settled in England and began writing her many novels on the British in India.

10. In 1914, Diver published a revised version of *Captain Desmond V. C.* that was to become a first in a series of novels set on the northwest border region of the Indian empire. *Captain Desmond V. C.* will be cited hereafter in the text as *CD.*

11. In the British empire, the threat of violence enacted by the "black" male on the "white" female was constructed via prohibitory laws and restrictions on both parties. In the discourse of Empire, this violence was always represented as sexual and illegitimate, unlike the representation of relationships between white men and colonized women, which was coded in terms of love and marriage between a subordinate wife and a masterful husband. Not surprisingly, the enterprise of imperialism was often similarly represented (see Theresa Hubel, "'The Bride of His Country': Love, Marriage, and the Imperialist Paradox in the Indian Fiction of Sara Jeanette Duncan and Rudyard Kipling"). Laws such as the White Woman's Protection Ordinance (Papua, New Guinea 1926) brought into legislation the death penalty for rape and attempted rape of white women by indigenous men

(Strobel 5–6). At the time of its passage, Strobel writes, no white women had been raped in Papua. And yet such a harsh law was considered quite necessary. Desmond's brutal "punitive expeditions" operate on the same logic of setting up the punishment and administering it before the crime can be committed.

12. Cited hereafter in the text as *UR*.

13. Hereafter cited in the text as *EI*.

14. This work will hereafter be cited in the text as *CIH*. It is interesting to read quite a different assessment of Flora Anne Steel and of this text as represented in Strobel's text: "A famous and indefatigable British woman from the late nineteenth century, Flora Annie Steel, coauthored the indispensable *Complete Indian Housekeeper and Cook*. Married at twenty to an officer in the Indian Civil Service, she took advantage of the relative isolation of his posting to learn several vernacular languages and dialects and accompany him on his inspection tours. In addition to compiling the hints that comprise her book, she designed the town hall where she lived, wrote on the oppression of small landowners by usurers, served as a semi-official school inspector in the Punjab, and worked for Indian women's education" (8). To Strobel, Steel represents a positive and therefore "heartening" figure but one who is, "unfortunately," an exceptional aberration on all counts. I try to argue that Steel helped to contruct the exemplar figure of the competent memsahib both through her written exhortations and through her personal self-fashioning.

15. Other writers in the discourse of Empire reiterate this point. For instance, George Newman, author of *Infant Mortality* (1906) and the first Chief Medical Officer of Health to the Board of Education (1907), believed that homes were the vital core of a nation and that the British empire depended "not upon dominions and territory alone, but upon men, not markets alone, but upon homes" (qtd. in Davin 31).

16. The sentence in "Kitchen Hindi" exhibits the usual distortions of tense, gender, and syntax. What is especially noteworthy is that the writers represent Indian servants as not having mastery of their own language. On the other hand, one could read this casual insertion of "the native language" as an authorial demonstration of cultural familiarity and ease that is quite oblivious of linguistic errors.

17. Contemporary Western feminist scholars who write on Englishwomen in the Empire usually stress the many ways in which the class division in England was carried over and even inflated in its purchase over daily life. Hence Strobel, Fowler, MacMillan, and Barr spend much effort in understanding and explaining the details of the rules of precedence that governed the social interactions of the British in the colonies. They list the many seemingly insignificant markers that made clear the class and rank hierarchy within any assembled group of British citizens. To break precedence or "dastur" (a favorite Hindi word among colonists) as in ignoring rank while seating one's guests at dinner was to violently shake the established order of imperial hierarchy. Yet the overwhelming superiority of the Englishwoman on the lowest rung of the precedence ladder to any and all Indian men and women is not brought into this analysis. Not that this very obvious fact of the life of the female colonist is ignored by contemporary scholars but that such issues of white women's authority over the colonized are dealt with as if it were an entirely different and unrelated concern.

18. Cited hereafter in the text as *MIF*.

19. This metaphor of letting English light into dark Indian homes is popular with several writers of colonial texts. Writing about the Lady Dufferin medical aid scheme (the details about which are discussed later in this essay), Diver says: "its ultimate aim is to roll away the stones from before the darkened doors; to flood the dim, cobwebbed corners of India's homes with the life-giving light of healing truth and love" (*EI* 102).

20. For more information on the activities of prominent Indian women in the political and social spheres, see Kumari Jayawardena, *Feminism and Nationalism in the Third World*, especially the sections called "Agitation by Women" and "Women in Political Action" in the chapter entitled "Women, Social Reform and Nationalism in India," 73–109. Diver's *The Englishwoman In India* contains a second, shorter section that follows the one entitled "The Englishwoman in India." This second section, entitled "Pioneer Women of India," contains short chapters on Pundita Ramabai, Dr. Anandabai Joshee, Maharani of Kuch Behar, and Cornelia Sarabji, all of whom had broken out of the conventional role prescribed to Indian women. While Diver praises these women, she repeatedly stresses that they were exceptions, and she concludes, albeit regretfully, that most of their lives and efforts were futile. The early deaths and chronic illnesses of these women are taken by Diver as proof of the fact that Indian women could not bear the mental and physical demands that leading a public life in their own country would demand from them.

21. See Gayatri Chakravorty Spivak, "French Feminism in an International Frame." Spivak writes, "[I]n order to learn enough about Third World women and to develop a different readership, the immense heterogeneity of the field must be appreciated, and the First World feminist must learn to stop feeling privileged as a woman" (136). In the conclusion to the same essay, Spivak writes that her emphasis on heterogeneity, discontinuity, and topology may not "necessarily escape the inbuilt colonialism of First World feminism toward the third. It might, one hopes, promote a sense of our common yet history-specific lot" (153). This passage from *My Indian Family* demonstrates that "wanting to learn enough" or even having this knowledge about third world women does not necessarily challenge this inbuilt colonialism. The European woman imperialist very often possessed a minute knowledge of her racial Others and of the "immense heterogeneity of the field." The narrator of this novel proudly and repeatedly displays her easy understanding of the cultural differences between Indians from various parts of India, of different religions, castes, class backgrounds, etc. Yet it is this very knowledge that supports her overarching knowledge of her superiority as a white woman.

22. During the recent Persian Gulf War, in Western commentaries on the status of Saudi women, the assessments were always defined by two factors: the veil and the prohibition to drive. The American woman soldier stationed in the desert was, in contrast, a manifestation of U.S. gender equality haven, and her emancipation was measured in her all-but-equal opportunity to kill and die for her government.

23. I would like to draw attention to the statement on celibacy. The oddity of this particular comment arises from the fact that it is inserted in a text on household management. The household is premised on marriage and procreation—the

very opposite of celibacy. Yet, I don't think there is any ironic or unconscious aligning of "Christian" alongside "Hindu and Mohommadan" when celibacy is at issue. Do we read irony in the very next statement, which begins, "by means of this patriarchal system"? Again I do not think that Diver means to suggest that we read the English household arrangement as implicated in the term "this patriarchal system." If there is so much as the slightest doubt that there is, in this passage, some acknowledgment of commonalities between the English domestic arrangements and those of the "patriarchal system" of "the Hindu and Mohommadan," then the use of the word "chance" in the last sentence should lay such a suspicion to rest.

24. The Marchioness of Dufferin, wife of the British Viceroy (highest government official) in India in the 1880s, started the *Female Medical Aid Fund*, also called the Dufferin Fund, to provide medical tuition for women in India (English and Indian) and thereby provide women and children in India with medical care that was administered solely by women.

25. From the duties for four lady health visitors appointed by the Birmington county council in 1899, published in *Public Health* (qtd. in Davin 37). See Davin's article for an in-depth analysis of the ramifications of empire on the domestic life of the Englishwoman in England in the late nineteenth and early twentieth centuries. For more on women and social work in this period, see Julia R. Parker, *Women and Welfare: Ten Victorian Women in Public Social Service*; A. F. Young and E. T. Aston, *British Social Work in the Nineteenth Century*; Angela Burdett-Coutts, ed., *Woman's Mission: A Series of Congress Papers on the Philanthropic Work of Women, by Eminent Writers*; Kathleen J. Heasman, *Evangelicals in Action: An Appraisal of Their Social Work in the Victorian Era*.

26. Dell's biographer notes that she got her information about India from other India-writers, among them Kipling and Diver, and from *The Illustrated London News*. See Penelope Dell, *Nettie and Sissie: The Biography of Ethel M. Dell and Her Sister Ella*, 69, 97.

27. In thinking through this final section of my essay, I was influenced by a discussion of Ghassan Khanafani's *Men in the Sun* in Mary Layoun's "Deserts of Memory," 177–208.

28. Thus, in *Captain Desmond V. C.*, the Kresneys' lack of the correct English accent is metonymic of their "taint of mixed blood." Consider the following passage from the novel: "Miss Kresney's insistence on the consonants and the final vowels was more marked than her brother's; for although three-fourths of the blood in her veins was English, very few of her intimate associates could make so proud a boast without perjurying their souls: and there are few things more infectious than tricks of speech" (84).

29. Diver (in 1909) among others refers to the Englishwomen in India as exiles (*EI* 33). Suzanne Howe (in 1949) calls them "ladies in exile" (*Novels of Empire* 43).

30. In these texts by Englishwomen, the representations of India, of Indians, and of the English in India owed much to the prevailing dominant ideology of imperialism, but these texts also shaped this ideology especially as available to us in its literary fiction. Hence, one could argue that later novels, such as *Burmese Days* (1934), and to a certain extent, *A Passage to India* (1925), essentially follow the same romance plot in the same Indian setting with the same race and gender dynamics and ideo-

logical stances, though written by better-known (canonical, male) writers. For instance, traces of Evelyn, the unhappy heroine of *Captain Desmond V. C.*, can be found in Elizabeth Lackersteen, the heroine of *Burmese Days*. Mrs. Moore figures abound in the novels of these women writers. Her mystical link with India and its people, made famous in Forster's novel, would already be familiar to readers of the imperial novel through their acquaintance with fictional middle-aged women who are central to the plot, such as Lady Helen Forsyth in *Unconquered*. If we are to give over to these writers, or "lady romancers" as Parry chose to call them, their proper literary terrain, then we would have to read Orwell and Forster as writers in the Imperial Romance tradition or, alternately, read Diver and others as practitioners of the realist/naturalist school.

31. See the excellent study by WING (Women for Immigration and Nationality Group) entitled *Worlds Apart: Women Under Immigration and Nationality Law*, ed. Jacqueline Bhabha et al., for a detailed historical discussion of the vexed status of white Englishwomen as national citizens under the law.

Works Cited

Armstrong, Nancy. *Desire and Domestic Fiction: A Political History of the Novel*. New York: Oxford UP, 1987.

Barr, Patricia. *The Memsahibs: The Women of Victorian India*. London: Secker and Warburg, 1976.

Bhabha, Jacqueline, Francesca Klug, and Sue Shutter. *Worlds Apart: Women Under Immigration and Nationality Law*. London: Pluto Press, 1985.

Blee, Kathleen M. *Woman of the Klan: Racism and Gender in the 1920s*. Berkeley: U of California P, 1991.

Burdett-Coutts, Angela, ed. *Woman's Mission: A Series of Congress Papers on the Philanthropic Work of Women, by Eminent Writers*. London: Samson Low, Marston, 1893.

Callaway, Helen. "Women in 'A Man's World.'" *Gender, Culture, and Empire: European Women in Colonial Nigeria*. Urbana: U of Illinois P, 1987. 3–29.

Crowther, Geoff, Tony Wheeler, and Raj. *Lonely Planet Travel Survival Kit: India*. New York: Lonely Planet, 1990.

Davin, Anna. "Imperialism and Motherhood." *History Workshop* 5 (1978): 9–65.

Deleuze, Gilles, and Félix Guattari. *Kafka: Towards a Minor Literature*. Trans. Dana Polan. Minneapolis: U of Minnesota P, 1986.

Dell, Penelope. *Nettie and Sissie: The Biography of Ethel M. Dell and Her Sister Ella*. London: Hamilton, 1977.

Diver, Maud. *The Englishwoman in India*. London: Blackwood, 1909. [*EI*]

_____. *Captain Desmond V. C.* New York: Grosset and Dunlap, 1914.

_____. *Unconquered: A Romance*. London: Putnam's, 1917. [*UR*]

DuBois, Ellen Carol. "The Radicalism of the Woman Suffrage Movement: Notes Toward the Reconstruction of Nineteenth-Century Feminism." *Feminism and Equality*. Ed. Anne Phillips. New York: New York UP, 1987. 127–38.

_____. "Woman Suffrage and the Left: An International Socialist-Feminist Perspective." *New Left Review* 186 (1991): 20–45.

Fowler, Marian. *Below the Peacock Fan: First Ladies of the Raj.* London: Penguin, 1988.

Fox-Genovese, Elizabeth. "Placing Women's History in History." *New Left Review* 133 (1982): 5–29.

Heasman, Kathleen J. *Evangelicals in Action: An Appraisal of Their Social Work in the Victorian Era.* London: G. Bles, 1962.

Howe, Suzanne. *Novels of Empire.* [1949]. New York: Kraus, 1971.

Hubel, Theresa. "'The Bride of His Country': Love, Marriage, and the Imperialist Paradox in the Indian Fiction of Sara Jeanette Duncan and Rudyard Kipling." *Ariel* 221.1 (1990): 3–19.

Hunt, Nancy Rose. "Domesticity and Colonialism in Belgian Africa: Usumbura's Foyer Social, 1946–1960." *Signs* 15.3 (1990): 447–74.

Jayawardena, Kumari. *Feminism and Nationalism in the Third World.* London: Zed, 1986.

Kaplan, Caren. "Deterritorializations: The Rewriting of Home and Exile in Western Feminist Discourse." *Cultural Critique* 6 (Spring 1987): 187–98.

Layoun, Mary. "Deserts of Memory." *Travels of a Genre: The Modern Novel and Ideology.* Princeton: Princeton UP, 1990. 77–208.

MacMillan, Margaret. *Women of the Raj.* New York: Thames and Hudson, 1988.

Mitchell, Timothy. *Colonizing Egypt.* New York: Cambridge UP, 1988.

Parker, Julia R. *Woman and Welfare: Ten Victorian Women in Public Social Service.* New York: St. Martin's P, 1989.

Parry, Benita. *Delusions and Discoveries: Studies on India in the British Imagination.* Berkeley: U of California P, 1972.

Pateman, Carole. "Critiques of the Public/Private Dichotomy." *Feminism and Equality.* Ed. Anne Phillips. New York: New York UP, 1987. 103–26.

Riley, Denise. *"Am I That Name?": Feminism and the Category of "Women" in History.* Minneapolis: U of Minnesota P, 1988.

Roediger, David R. *The Wages of Whiteness: Race and the Making of the American Working Class.* London: Verso, 1991.

Saunders, Rebecca. "Gender, Colonialism, and Exile: Flora Anne Steel and Sara Jeanette Duncan in India." *Women's Writing in Exile.* Ed. Mary Lynn Broe and Angela Ingram. Chapel Hill: U of North Carolina P, 1989. 304–24.

Spivak, Gayatri Chakravorty. "French Feminism in an International Frame." *In Other Worlds: Essays in Cultural Politics.* New York: Routledge, 1988. 134–53.

———. "Three Women's Texts and a Critique of Imperialism." *The Feminist Reader: Essays in Gender and the Politics of Literary Criticism.* Ed. Catherine Belsey and Jane Moore. New York: Blackwell, 1989. 175–96, 237–40.

Steel, Flora Anne, and Grace Gardiner. *The Complete Indian Housekeeper and Cook: Giving the Duties of Mistress and Servants, the General Management of the House, and Practical Recipes for Cooking in all its Branches.* London: Heinemann, 1904. [*CIH*]

Strobel, Margaret. *European Women and the Second British Empire.* Bloomington: Indiana UP, 1991.

Ware, Vron. *Beyond the Pale: White Women, Racism, and History.* New York: Verso, 1992.

Wernher, Hilda. *My Indian Family: A Story of East and West Within an Indian Home.* New York: John Day, 1945. [*MIF*]

Young, A. F., and E. T. Aston. *British Social Work in the Nineteenth Century.* London: Humanities P, 1956.

Chapter Four

Modernism and Domesticity: From Conrad's Eastern Road to Stein's Empty Spaces in the Home

AMIE PARRY

It is natural that a woman should be one to do the literary thinking of this epoch.
—**Gertrude Stein,** *The Geographical History of America*

Gertrude Stein's extensive writings on literature constantly put pressure on the categorical structures of identity, including sexual and gender identity. This pressure on the categorical is crucial to Stein's critical engagement with the space and time of modernity. It thereby opens up the possibility of rethinking the epistemological crisis characteristic of literary modernism in relation to both the spatial and temporal contours of (colonial) modernity and the crisis of representation engendered by lesbian desire. The interrelatedness of these apparently divergent epistemological critiques is evidenced in the links that we find throughout Stein's work between "woman" and the modernity, literary or otherwise, of the twentieth century in the United States, a period that Stein also referred to as that of "the cinema and series production" and that she sees as distinct from European and British modernities. By contrasting the formal structure of English modernism with that of U.S. modernism, this paper explores the complex and often contradictory relationship between an "American" modernity and the categories of woman and domesticity in Stein's work.

Because of the relationship of the domestic sphere to racial discourse in the United States, an examination of the category of woman is central to the task of reading any of Stein's texts in terms of the particular formation of colonial modernity that structures U.S. modernism. The function of woman in relation to domesticity, then, plays a double role in this paper. First of all, it is in Stein's treatment of the category of woman that we can read her most radical critiques of the bourgeois individual/literary character (as a stable identity characterized by depth and development over time) along the lines of gender and sexuality. Second, in contradistinction to her critique of gender identities, Stein's formulation of domesticity as the site of woman's erotic pleasure is also the vehicle through which individuality (as a gesture of containment and exclusivity) subtly reconfigures itself in precisely the same narratives that produce the notions of (White) womanhood that come under scrutiny in Stein's work.

With this function of woman and domesticity in mind, this paper explores the spatial categories that serve as the setting for Stein's critiques of sexual and gender norms in *Lectures in America* and *Tender Buttons*. In these texts, spatial categories constitute the sites in which knowledge is produced amidst the broader epistemological crisis out of which literary modernism emerges. This crisis is clearly evidenced in works of modern poetry, such as *Tender Buttons*, that are characterized by a lack of narrative structure and a corresponding collapse of the spatial divisions that organize modern experience on a daily, lived basis. I discuss this in more detail later; here it is important to observe that because literary modernism is, partially, a response to the breakdown of the imaginative mappings that support colonial discourses, it can be read as a crucial remapping and recategorizing of the spaces in which modernity is experienced. In these two texts, such spatial categories include the home, "America," and a more abstract spatial construct that Stein defines as a space filled with movement and that she metaphorizes as a movie screen in *Lectures in America*. Although such interrelationships are often overlooked, these spatializations and the knowledge about sexuality and gender produced through them are crucial factors in the persisting and newly emerging imperialistic epistemologies that structure early-twentieth-century notions of domesticity as well as the boundaries of "America."

First, however, I discuss the relationship between domesticity and imperial expansion in Joseph Conrad's *Lord Jim* and Virginia Woolf's *The Voyage Out*. In these two British texts, "the road" functions as a spatial category through which important meanings about the nation are articulated; as we shall see, the road or sea voyage as a literary trope is emblematic of a colonialism in which empire is configured through an inside/outside or metropolis/colony model, a model that is significantly different from that of U.S. imperialism, in which a pre–World War II U.S. empire is more effectively configured in the self-contained, interiorized space of the "home."

To understand how domesticity functions to support both colonial expansion and the cultural and political apparatuses of the racial state, it is necessary to outline the ways in which the metaphor of the home enables the nation to take on its significational force. In his article "DissemiNation," Homi Bhabha argued that the idea of nation begins with an important "forgetting" of "the violence involved in establishing the nation's writ."[1] The violence that Bhabha referred to is colonial violence, the forgetting of which is largely made possible by national "narrations": narratives that pedagogically and performatively produce the nation and its subjects by attempting to locate difference outside national boundaries, thereby establishing the discursive terms for the definitional, but always contradictory, opposition between civilized western cultures and their primitivized colonial others. These narrations facilitate the activity of "forgetting" by locating the colonized space outside of western history through what Johannes Fabian termed "the denial of coevalness." Fabian used this term to describe how the colonized country is conceptualized as a timeless, unchanging, and "primitive" other that occupies a radically different space outside of western history.[2] Although this relegation of colonial locations to primitive time can never be seamlessly achieved, it is important to recognize that as the home becomes a metaphor for the nation, this primitive space seems to hover threateningly at the margins of the nation, and the consequential need to protect the White woman and the domestic sphere adds a heroic dimension to imperialist conquests. This gendered aspect of the heroics of colonial domination is often overlooked; however, it is as central to this type of narration as is the conceptualization of a primitivized colonial subject who needs to be civilized through contact with the west.

By primitivizing these subjects and representing the colonized space as barbaric, these narrations also dehumanize the colonized subjects so that the violence that accompanies colonialism is unimportant (and forgettable), a necessary evil in the larger, imperial project of bringing "sweetness and light"[3] to barbarous lands and reaping enormous profits, both economically and ideologically, in the process. This ideological erasure of the violence of colonialism, however, is difficult to achieve precisely because such violence is so fundamental to any imperial conquest. For this reason, the erasure or displacement of violence must be deployed at all levels of "narration" involved in writing the nation. This paper, before dealing exclusively with Stein, considers ways this forgetting has been accomplished in English literature and analyzes what can be termed two different literary colonialisms (that is, those of England and the United States) by examining the relationship between the form of Joseph Conrad's novel *Lord Jim*, which can be read as a narrative "road" that marks the impossibility of the boundaries of the British empire, and the way U.S. modernism's poetic object functions to displace the colonial violence taking place *within* national/geographical boundaries. Although in both cases the boundaries of the nation are often represented in literature through the metaphor of the home, the possible forms the figuration of the nation can take on and the fraught sites of intersection between nation and empire are significantly different.

On the Colonial Road: Lord Jim and Mrs. Dalloway

In Fredric Jameson's article "Modernism and Imperialism," he showed the erasure of imperialism in modernist texts to be the "something missing" in modernism, the cause of the "privation which can never be restored or made whole" (51) that distinguishes modernism historically rather than purely aesthetically from other literary periods.[4] Jameson argued that the colonial reality, the setting for so much English history, is "structurally occluded" from representation in high modernism and can never be sutured back onto the metropolis. This structural occlusion of the colonial reality from the literary text is what necessitates the radical sense of incompleteness characteristic of modernism. In the same article, Jameson described a particularly modernist configuration of meaning located within a "textual game" (55) that is no longer symbolic but is also not quite not symbolic, which he referred to as a "hesitation" within textual signification and which he discussed at length using the example of Forster's description of the "Great North Road" in *Howard's End*. Jameson points out that in Forster's text this road is "suggestive of infinity"; however, as the novel progresses, the meaning of infinity itself "grows less and less evident" (54). He then argues that what infinity ultimately signifies in Forster's novel is not an essential truth or idea but a "new grey placelessness" that Forster cannot name (except in the displacement of "Howard's End") but that Jameson identifies as imperialism.[5] In this way, Jameson names the historical fact of imperialism as the "something missing" that causes the radical incompleteness that distinguishes what he names as high modernism from other literary genres. Jameson's argument is crucial to any historically astute understanding of modernism; however, a closer look at a more popular form of modernism, the seavoyage novel, reveals that a similar logic controls the representational possibilities in this discursive arena as well. This observation modifies Jameson's thesis in two ways. First, in the sea-voyage novel, it is not so much the general fact of imperialism but rather English responsibility for its foundational violence that cannot be brought into the representational framework. I discuss this point in more detail later, but for now it is important to note that English responsibility for the violence of imperialism rather than the general fact of imperialism, in turn, indicates that the clear distinction between high modernism and other modernisms can be maintained only at the expense of neglecting to account for the many generic forms that are possible within a "modernist" representational framework.

Jameson's thesis, however, has far-reaching ramifications for theorizations of narrativity. If, as Jameson argues, the "road" as infinity/empire is emblematic of the stylistic incompleteness or significational gap of modernism, then the whole project of narration is, when set within modernism, fraught with a foundational inconsistency at the level of theme (the novel as a journey to self-discovery, mastery of self and others, and so on) and formal structure (a narration based on a stable, linear temporality of development and progress). In this sense, Jameson's (and Forster's) "road" is an effective vehicle for both masking *and* articulating this discrepancy and thus for participating in what Jameson has termed the "hesitation" that is modernism. The image of a road or especially of a sea voyage in a modern text can signify several important tropes of modernity (and nationhood within modernity): economic development and expansion, the temporal progress of culture into a more and more civilized way of life, and spatially, the heroic progress of culture in its civilizing movement across most of the nonwestern world. However, at the same time, the road in its necessary relation to the colonies also makes visible or at least suggests the instability of the very national boundaries that it brings into narration. In other words, the place to which such roads within modernist texts cannot lead, because of modernism's formational structural occlusion, is precisely a representation of the violence at the road's "end"; however, it is this violence that inscribes the boundaries of nations and secures national identities. Thus the problematics of inscribing the nation according to a thematic or structural road (that is, the novel) lie in the fact that this road constantly threatens to slip into the unrepresentable space of colonial violence, bringing with it the unwitting protagonist in his or her journey toward (self) mastery and (national) identity. And once placed at the scene of this violence, this self-mastery threatens to expose itself as attained only through the domination and subjugation of men and women of other races (and when the protagonist is also male, the women of his own race), and national identity becomes a subjectivity of "sameness" that threatens to include the other in the terms of its own humanist definition but is "stabilized" as essentially different through precisely the same violence.

Because of the importance of this narrative "road" to formulations of national identity, framing this discussion of domesticity and imperialism with a brief analysis of Joseph Conrad's sea-voyage novel *Lord Jim* demonstrates not only the different narrative functions that each genre serves but also the surprising amount of shared ground between the adventure novel and domestic literature. Most importantly, what is at stake in making this shared ground apparent is the necessity of recognizing the centrality of ideological formulations of womanhood and domesticity, as well as masculinity and adventure, to the narratives of progress that underlie colonial modernity.

In "Modernism and Imperialism" and in his lengthy discussion of Conrad's *Lord Jim* from *The Political Unconscious*,[6] Jameson drew a clear distinction between high modernism, of which genre Forster's novel would be an early, prototypical example, and the more popular adventure novel, which, Jameson asserted in the more recent article, using the example of Conrad, "draws on more archaic storytelling forms" (44). Indeed, important distinctions between the genres of high modernism and the adventure or sea-voyage novel should be recognized. At the same time, however, it is equally important to account for the way in which Conrad's adventure novel can be considered as prototypically modern as Forster's, even according to Jameson's description of that modernism, if it is not the more general colonial reality that we discover to be structurally occluded from modernist representation but, more specifically, colonial violence. As we will see, it is the Englishman's guilt and responsibility for this violence that constitutes the "truth" that is endlessly deferred in Conrad's novel, both in its content (we can never know for certain the truth of the past event through its recollection or representation) and in form (the impossibility of closure even at the sentence level).

In *Lord Jim*,[7] colonial space and the west's imperialistic violence are in fact represented, but they are represented in a way that constantly attempts to defer or deny the reality of and responsibility for the disruption and exploitation of cultures and the bloodshed and deaths of the "natives" themselves. This violence is deferred, after the incident on the *Patna*, into an ultimately futile attempt to salvage the heroics and romance of the imperial protagonist in his journeys[8] and, by extension, the ever onward movement of colonial domination itself. This deferral of responsibility or guilt is most apparent in Marlow's narration of the trial scenes and takes the form of a complicated and multilayered critique of the possibility of uncovering the truth of the event. For example, the description of Jim's "leap" (perhaps it is better described as a "Fall" with a capital *F*) off the presumably doomed ship onto the lifeboat is understood as tragic not because of the incriminating truth of his abandonment of 800 Muslim pilgrims (for whom the crew had not prepared enough lifeboats in case of an emergency), but because Jim had abandoned his chance to be a hero. At the same time, however, the philosophical understanding of the truth or righteousness of heroism itself is constantly called into question in the trial scenes, which cannot avoid incriminating "all of us."

The rest of the novel chronicles Jim's flight from this disgrace, which follows him across more and more remote colonial locations as he looks for a place where he can finally regain his status as a White master. And once in Patusan, his legitimate "lordship" (which he paradoxically can only achieve in the extreme anonymity afforded by Patusan's particular geography) is secured by his killing of a Malay native: "He [Jim] found himself calm, appeased, without rancor, without uneasiness, as if the death of that man had atoned for everything" (224). Here Conrad, in a series of complex logical maneuvers, managed to have this killing function textually according to a logic not of guilt but of atonement, even as the need for atonement attests to the criminality of the act. But most importantly, this logic, that endless displacement of the death of the native into the politically "neutral" aesthetic structures of heroism and romance, never quite works; thus, we have Conrad's dense and convoluted style, which moves laboriously toward a truth that can never be found out in its entirety. In fact, the search for truth, instead of structuring the novel along a model of linear progression toward a goal, instead seems to take on the structural form of a thematic leap that in its long, repetitive narrations takes Conrad further and further from the desired disclosures of any ideational *whys* (205) that could answer questions posed by the very form of the novel about the nature of identity and destiny.

In addition to examining the form of Conrad's novel and how that form participates in the "forgetting" of imperial violence, one must also consider the importance of the trope of memory that constitutes one of the novel's underlying themes. In Marlow's narration, the idea of memory is associated directly with the act of storytelling. The fallibility of Marlow's gaze in always seeing Jim only "through a mist" or "under a cloud" suggests a narrator ultimately incapable of "knowing" the subject of his story, thus shrouding memory (and storytelling) in an essential mystery; Marlow often interrupts his story with comments such as "I was confronted again with the unanswerable why of Jim's fate" (205). Most importantly, memory as enigma is located in a specific moment within a larger conception of memory that includes two prior temporalities: one located in a distant, antiquated past still fully accessible to memory and characterized by what Conrad calls "assurance," and a more recent prior moment, perhaps the emerging past of modernity, where that assurance has been called into question.[9] In the context of this novel, the divide between these two temporalities is the moment of a denied, deferred, or subjugated recognition of not only the fundamental "untrustworthiness" of British leadership and heroism, but more sinisterly, the English sub-ject's constitutive criminality.[10]

If what causes the emergence of a sense of modernity within the tempo-ralities of the English novel is in fact this (denied or displaced) recogni-tion, then the modernist story loses utterly the "assurance" of its goal and becomes a kind of "immobility" in which causes of events and human ac-tions are never illuminated and no goals are ever reached. In this sense the novel itself inhabits the same immobility that Conrad often described as a silent, almost transcendental pause before death, which, for example, the *Patna* inhabits before it "sinks." This "immobility," moreover, res-onates with Jameson's concept of "hesitation," which he described in "Modernism and Imperialism" as "modernism itself" (55). And it is ex-actly this immobility that underlies the displaced terror and guilt that structures this narration of British colonialism. Such terror and guilt func-tion at two levels of meaning: at the surface level is a thematic fear of dis-covering that "we" are not heroic and therefore not worthy of carrying the "White man's burden," and at a more cryptic level of textual nuance is a pervasive fear of discovering the actual violence that constitutes the truth of our laws. Because of the displaced guilt that structures the unique temporality of modernism, the modernist can never "go home," because, as Marlow says, "the return entails a clear conscience." Instead, "he" is immobilized, so to speak, on the gaping, obscure, and disorienting "East-ern roadstead" that Conrad described, in his preface, as the place where he first envisioned Jim, who is persistently claimed as "one of us" but who is forever exiled from the "commonplace" English countryside (vii).

Thus, it is important to read the character of the Englishman or En-glishwoman abroad as central even to configurations of national identity "at home" during the colonial period. In this sense, the "road" or sea voy-age becomes an important vehicle through which not only the adventurer but also the domestic subject is figured. Just as the adventurer is figured in relation to "home" and the nation, so too is the domestic subject not only envisioned in relation to a wilderness that hovers at the edges of the home and the nation, but also at times placed not at home but in a foreign setting that usually functions to underscore the domestic subject's domes-ticity and femininity. In fact, in the latter case, the relationship between domesticity and an imperialist subjecthood and national identity be-comes especially apparent. An example of this is Virginia Woolf's charac-ter Mrs. Dalloway as she makes an early appearance in Woolf's first novel, *The Voyage Out*, saying to her husband in the cabin of a ship off the coast of England (later to sail to South America):

> "D'you know, Dick, I can't help thinking of England," said his wife medita-tively, leaning her head against his chest. "Being on this ship seems to make it

so much more vivid—what it really means to be English. One thinks of all we've done, and our navies, and the people in India and Africa, and how we've gone on century after century, sending our boys out from little country villages—and of men like you, Dick, and it makes one feel as if one couldn't bear *not* to be English! Think of the light burning over the House, Dick! When I stood on deck just now I seemed to see it. It's what one means by London."[11]

In the word *House* in this passage, there is a telling slippage between concepts of "home" and the political center of the nation and the empire and, in the implicit reference to a lighthouse, the nation's geographical/ natural boundaries; in all cases the "light" of rationality shines as a beacon of domestic well-being and the fullness of national life in the metropolis. This slippage is further emphasized by the fact that these words are spoken by Mrs. Dalloway, who was to become one of the most famous domestic subjects of English literature. Following Rosemary George's statement that the modern bourgeois individual is not only a woman but also an imperialist,[12] the rest of this paper is concerned with the relationship between domesticity and empire, but in the United States and its empire rather than in Britain or its colonies. Moreover, although Fredric Jameson does not make these connections explicitly in his article, the importance of the relationship between the domestic sphere and the imperialist subject in U.S. modernism is also suggested by the fact that in his reading of *Howard's End*, he acknowledges almost parenthetically (in a long, final endnote) that the text that first prompted his thoughts on the relationship between modernism and imperialism was *Lectures in America* by Gertrude Stein.

Domesticity and the Empty Spaces of U.S. Modernity

The home the rich and self-made merchant makes to hold his family and himself is always like the city where his fortune has been made. In London, it is like that rich and endless, dark and gloomy place, in Paris it is filled with pleasant toys, cheery light and made of gilded decoration and white paint and in New York it is neither gloomy nor yet joyous but like a large and splendid canvas completely painted over but painted full of empty spaces.
—**Gertrude Stein, "The Making of Americans"**[13]

Four years after *Lord Jim* was first published in 1899, Gertrude Stein was working on her first draft of *The Making of Americans*, from which the previous quote is taken. I would like to use this quote as a point of departure into a discussion of two of Stein's works, *Lectures in America* (1935) and *Tender Buttons* (1914), because it makes explicit the contrast between the different strategies of the erasure of imperial violence in the writing of the nation in English and U.S. modernisms. Just as Stein's description of the London home as "rich and endless, dark and gloomy" is evocative of the Conradian road, her description of the New York home as a "large and splendid canvas" that is "completely painted over but painted full of empty spaces" suggests a different figuration of the nation and the empire and of literary form, one that is predicated on a self-contained, yet "empty," bounded space. This difference must be understood in relation to the extent to which the United States' multiple imperialistic histories are distinct from those of England and Europe and the fact that these historical distinctions have been distorted into a premise for false understandings of the United States as uniquely nonimperialistic.

Although the United States did not exert its force in much formal colonialism during the first half of this century, its history is implicitly one of imperialistic conquest: American independence from English rule did not free the young country from the logic of colonialism. On the contrary, the country's economic stability was dependent on a large population of African slaves who provided the plantations of the South with free labor. Moreover, the growth of the country was founded upon massive appropriation of land and the genocide of Native American peoples in an imperialistic movement across the continent.

By the time Stein was writing this draft of *The Making of Americans*, the United States had been developing a new foreign policy of "expansionism." Although imperialist ventures in Asia were dominated by Britain, France, Germany, and Japan, by the turn of the century, the United States had annexed Hawaii, Guam, Samoa, and the Philippines. At the same time, U.S. hegemony was also exerted forcefully in Latin America. This was especially true around the first three decades of the twentieth century, when U.S. imperialism took the form of annexation of Puerto Rico in 1898 and political and economic control (rather than formal colonialism) in Mexico, Cuba, Haiti, the Dominican Republic, Honduras, and Nicaragua.

These histories suggest that the displacement of imperial violence works differently in U.S. modernism than it does in British and European modernism as a result of the different geographical boundaries of the U.S. imperial project. U.S. hegemony in Latin America was not considered to form an "empire" analogous to European presence in Asia and Africa, perhaps because there were fewer formal colonies and perhaps, less obviously, because Latin America had long been considered "America's backyard," a conceptualization made possible by the combination of its geographical proximity and the long history of justifying annexations of land from indigenous peoples across the continent as a natural consequence of "manifest destiny." Moreover, the long tradition of slavery, the genocide of Native Americans, and persisting forms of racial injustice and discrimination, for example, all occurred to a larger extent on the same continent as the "metropolis," and the United States did not recognize its own imperial expansion into Asia until after World War II, even as it exerted its military power forcefully in the Philippines. This imperial violence takes place to a significant extent "at home," then, in the doubled sense of on this continent (and in the "backyard" of Latin America) as well as in the slave owner's household and in the White bourgeois household that employs non-White servants. For this reason, the displacement of imperial violence is articulated not as much through the problematics of a narrative road, but through what Stein as early as 1903 identified as "empty spaces" within the "home" itself.

The "splendid canvas completely painted over but painted full of empty spaces" that Stein described in the quote opening this section is a modernist, palimpsested canvas, among whose layers the foundational violence that has been largely "painted over" threatens to show through. In response to this threat, which haunts the modernist writer from the margins of his or her text, those "empty spaces," rather than being filled with images of the social and political realities that make the bourgeois home possible, are filled with the highly aestheticized modernist object. It is precisely the "painting over" of those empty spaces, then, that functions in the U.S. modernist text as the erasure of both the imperial violence itself and any sense of First World guilt or responsibility for it, by providing a "blank" ground or perceptual field that allows for the emergence of the importance of the modernist object, which must always be presented as "the thing itself."[14]

Unlike the texts of many of her contemporaries, however, Stein's contain another layer of complexity with regard to the presentation of objects and events in writing because of the significant extent to which her work must also deal with the problem of how to represent experiences of lesbian desire. As such, these experiences have no access to what Judith Butler described as the (in this case, heterosexual) epistemological system legitimated as "reality" and thus cannot be incorporated into a structure of knowledge in which a prior reality is expressed in textual representations.[15] With this problem in mind, one should read Stein's insistence on what has been termed a presentational rather than a representational strategy, which complicates the notion of a one-way relationship between referent and representation and which assigns the textual object as "authentic" an existence as the nontextual one, as a strategy that challenges ontological normativity and instead opens up the possibility of a performative relationship to gender and sexuality. In other words, this challenge to representation contests gender and sexuality norms without figuring the lesbian as an identity that can be represented. Catherine

Stimpson's discussion of how Stein "forgot" about the existence of her first novel can be read as an interesting example of the problematics of lesbian representation. In "The Mind, the Body, and Gertrude Stein,"[16] Stimpson described how the story lines from *Q.E.D.*, an early text that was more explicitly about (autobiographical) erotic friendships between women, were later encoded into conventional heterosexual plots in "Melanctha" and *The Making of Americans*. She then went on to describe how *Q.E.D.*'s own existence as a separate text was entirely forgotten until it was rediscovered and published, significantly enough, under the title *Things as They Are*.

However, I do not argue here that (as Stimpson seems to suggest) the earlier novel is a more direct, uninhibited, and authentic representation of "lesbian experience." On the contrary, Stein's "forgetting" of the earlier manuscript is an indication of the very complexity of the relationship between lesbian social and sexual practices and those that are legitimated as the heterosexual real. Read in this light, her works that follow *Q.E.D.*—most notably *Tender Buttons*—can be read as a more thorough exploration of possible ways in which to write about sexual experience that contests heterosexual norms because *Tender Buttons* takes as its subject both the sexual and social practices themselves *and* their complex, contestatory relationship to the real. When one reads for the erotic in Stein's texts, then, the relationship between sexuality and knowledge becomes particularly crucial, thus signaling the importance of reading her characteristically modern preoccupation with the textual (re)presentation of the object as what might now be considered a postmodern critique of epistemology in the broadest sense of the term. Her concern with the categorical (man/woman as well as many other binaries and lists), her critique of "fullness" in characters, and her lack of plot development, all of which seem to open up a kind of textual emptiness, must also be read in this light.

It is precisely these types of empty spaces, of course, that signify the beginnings of a modernist aesthetic that is founded upon a radical instability of meaning. These spaces can be read as the absence of meaning or its indeterminacy or as the lack of a coherent metanarrative in the literary text that is coextensive with the breakdown of the developmental, teleological narratives that support imperialist conquests and that in the first decades of the twentieth century began to be threatened by early stirrings of nationalism in the colonies, as Kumkum Sangari argued in her article "The Politics of the Possible."[17] This textual emptiness, then, does not serve a purely aesthetic function; rather, it registers those events that, according to Butler's formulation, have no access to reality within modernist epistemologies and therefore are excluded from the representational framework. The exclusionary nature of modern epistemological systems covers a broad range of topics; the most relevant for our under-

standing of Stein's "empty spaces" are lesbian sexuality and the imperialist violence that consolidates "America" as a national entity. These two
exclusions are far from parallel, however, and their absences exert different influences on the significational functions of the formal structures of
modernism. This distinction is most apparent in the fact that not only
Stein but a notable number of modernist writers have attempted, however indirectly, to "represent" sexual relationships between women.[18] In
contrast to such attempts in the realm of lesbian sexuality, when the colonial scene is represented, it is represented in a way that either omits its violence and brutality or presents this violence as unimportant and forgettable. Both exclusions are structural, but they are differently structured;
they produce different types of textual emptinesses and pose nonequiva-
lent challenges to the epistemological fullness of other literary genres. For
example, when considered in relation to colonial discourse, the importance of the unmediated presentation of the object for Ezra Pound (and
the later modernists who were influenced by his theories on the relationship between the subjectivity of the poet and the poetic object) and, in a
more complicated way, the importance of the highly abstract object in
Gertrude Stein's "portraits" suggest that these objects compensate for the
modernist emptiness that is brought about by its epistemological impasse
by being framed against its multiple representational gaps. To take this
logic a step further, these objects acquire their meaning as "the thing itself" precisely because they are set within a conceptual space and time
that is radically empty. Their status as modernist fragments, then, derives
from their having broken off from the fullness of meaning produced by
teleology as metanarrative, and at the same time, these objects as fragments mask the relationship of the history that they occlude to modernism's constitutive emptinesses. In this sense, not only does the formal
structure of modernism articulate the breakdown of the teleological narratives that support imperialist expansion, but it also creates possibilities
for replacing that metanarrative with new (nonteleological) methods of
forgetting the violence of colonial histories. When Stein's objects are considered in light of the problematics of lesbian representation, however,
the poetic object has a double function in relation to a modernist emptiness: it articulates the representational crisis engendered by lesbian desire
as well as masks the absence of a representational possibility.

In "The Politics of the Possible," Kumkum Sangari pointed out an important difference between the postmodern (and modern) crisis of meaning in the west and "the inscription of the marvelous in the real" (217) in
the novels of Gabriel García Márquez: the "cultural simultaneity" caused
by foreign domination in areas that have experienced colonialism is significantly different from the "cultural synchronicity" of the west, which is
a result of the breakdown of a teleological model of time as a rational

process of evolution and progress. An important aspect of this difference for Sangari lies in the fact that whereas the western version of the dissemination of teleologically based meaning into a chaotic "synchronicity" can easily propel its writers into an apolitical posture, the Latin American "cultural simultaneity," in its articulation of a heterogeneity that includes effects of colonialism but is not contained by them, does not produce the same preoccupation with a highly aestheticized and often self-consciously apolitical textuality. This, is not to say, however, that one version of modernism is more "political" than the other, but that politics circulate differently in each type of modernism.

This difference can perhaps account for the way in which the oppositional potential of the early modernists in the west is often to some extent swept back into what is usually read as an apolitical aesthetic. As I suggested previously, however, this modernist aesthetic serves an important ideological function within colonial discourses. In this analysis, then, it is important to read modernism's characteristic lack of narrative cohesiveness, linear story lines, and "developed" characters as not only the sites where teleological meaning breaks down, which itself is certainly a valid reading, but also and simultaneously the sites where national narratives subtly reassert themselves in, for example, the reaffirmation of the lifestyle and values of the bourgeois individual. The breakdown of developmental narratives and the reconfiguration of certain aspects of those narratives can perhaps best be explored in the genre of poetry, a genre often overlooked in this connection precisely because of its lack of narrative form. I suggest here not only that poetry is as crucial to the narrations of nations as is the novel, but also that poetry is particularly productive in locating those narratives' ambivalences, precisely because of its lack of narrative and because its brevity demands that individual words and phrases take on multiple, and at times contradictory, meanings, as is the case in *Tender Buttons*. Before turning to that series of prose poems, however, I first consider how some of these ambivalences make an earlier appearance in the novel *The Making of Americans*, a novel that, in its last chapter, marks the relationship between the breakdown of narrative form and the contradictions involved in the construction of national identity.

Although it may appear that these conceptual absences or "empty spaces" are not employed in the narration of *The Making of Americans*,[19] which is long and not at all "empty," in that it contains a large number of characters, events, and so on, I argue that the novel's narrative technique of repetition functions to defy the fullness of narrative development. In this early novel, phrases and sentences are often repeated, sometimes in exactly the same words, and this repetition is emphasized by introductory phrases such as "I have said that" and "As I was saying." Here is an example from the first chapter of the novel:

Yes, Julia looked much like her mother. That fair good-looking prosperous woman had stamped her image on each one of her children, and with her eldest, Julia, the stamp went deep, far deeper than just for the fair good-looking exterior. (13)

I have said that a strong family likeness bound all three children firmly to their mother. That fair good-looking prosperous woman had stamped her image on each one of her children, but only with the eldest Julia was the stamp deep, deeper than for the fair good-looking exterior. (17)

Here, repetition not only hampers the narrative temporal flow, but also emphasizes a thematic repetition: Julia's resemblance to her mother. The concept of "resemblance" is, in Stein's later essays, developed into a sophisticated critique of what she terms the "oneness" of the textual object or extratextual subject (which is also referred to as the individuality of the human subjects of her "portraits"), the beginnings of which are apparent in this novel in paradoxical statements such as "Every one then is an *individual* being. Every one then is *like many others* always living, there are many ways of thinking of every one, this is now a description of all of them. There must then be a whole history of each one of them. There must now be a *description of all repeating*" (212, emphasis mine).

In such descriptions of individuality as part of a process of resembling and repeating, Stein is perhaps writing against the usual fullness of protagonist characters (representations of "individual beings") that, in the Victorian or realist novel, develop over the course of the story line and are fundamentally distinct from other characters. Because of this lack of character development, the differences between characters in this novel have been read as differences between "types" rather than "individuals."[20] In this way, both the structural repetition and the theme of resemblance function to heighten similarities between characters, and this essential resemblance reaches its climax (perhaps best described as an anticlimax) in the closing chapter about the death of one character, which is discussed, at length, in terms of how "any one" will eventually become a "dead one," thus homogenizing or equalizing all characters in death. Most importantly, it is this closing section on "dead ones" that definitively marks the death of the "character" in the repetition of its absence and opens up another textual "emptiness" of the type discussed previously.

If, as Jo-Anna Isaak has argued, Stein's "entire work can be seen as an attempt to circumvent the end, the closure which is implied in the capitulation to the 'Law of the Father,'"[21] then this final death of the character must be read not as an ultimate closure but as an absence that "completes" the text only by ending it with a pervasive sense of emptiness. Although this technique must be appreciated as a defiant and innovative departure from narrative structures based on character development and linear story lines, in this case by having a dead male character stand in for what Isaak refers to as the "Law of the Father," it also provides Stein with philosophical grounds for the exclusionary nature of her portrait of the "making of America." By exclusionary nature, I refer to how Stein writes in this novel and in later expository prose that she was attempting in *The Making of Americans* to describe all the people that have ever lived in the United States, yet the novel centers on the story of two German immigrant families, the Dehnings and the Herslands.

In *"The Making of Americans* as an Ethnic Text," from her book *Pocahontas's Daughters*,[22] Mary V. Dearborn provides a detailed analysis of the ways in which *The Making of Americans* is a quintessential immigrant and ethic novel. Dearborn's reading is particularly illuminating to the extent that it demonstrates the necessity of reading this text as a forerunner of a genre for which notions of "Americanness," generation, and continuity/discontinuity are central themes. However, by considering the novel exclusively as an ethnic text, Dearborn loses sight of the ways in which the construction of Whiteness is central to the writing of this German immigrant ethnicity and to the "Americanness" that it defines and is defined by. For example, in Stein's attempt at an all-inclusive representation, the exclusion of depictions of the exploitation of the largely racialized labor forces (upon which the progress of the generic "American" family rests) is justified in the logic controlling the sentence that opens the last chapter, generically entitled "A History of a Family's Progress." The sentence reads: "Any one has come to be a dead one" (395). The logic of representation here is one in which heterogeneity (everyone) becomes "any one" in the form of a homogeneous, abstracted (and dead) White body. Most importantly, the unusual strategy of universalization, this dead White body, can be read as a stand-in for or displacement of the real deaths that take place in order that the European immigrant family make its "progress."

The opening paragraph continues: "Any one has not come to be such a one to be a dead one. Many who are living have not yet come to be a dead one. Many who were living have come to be a dead one. Any one has come not to be a dead one. Any one has come to be a dead one" (395). The repetition of this generic "one" here serves to "paint over" textual spaces that otherwise could be inhabited by more traditional characters and their fates (the usual ending for a novel). At the same time this aesthetic "blankness" functions as the kind of empty perceptual field that is also characteristic of modern poetry, within which the modernist poetic object can be presented as "the thing itself" or, according to Stein's terminology, an autonomous "entity."[23]

The form and function of this "empty space within the home" become clearer and more developed in Stein's collection of expository prose entitled *Lectures in America*,[24] in which a similar concept is expressed through the metaphor of a movie screen in "Portraits and Repetition," which echoes the earlier image of a "splendid canvas." Stein's first step toward formulating this idea, however, is worked out in the opening essay of this collection, which consists of a detailed and complex answer to the question that serves as its title: "What Is English Literature?"

In this essay, Stein suggested that nineteenth-century English literature is composed of phrases rather than sentences or paragraphs and that its primary function is to explain the relationship between England's "inside," or daily life on the island, and its "outside," which she defines as everything England "owns." As she began to consider this relationship, she wrote:

> As I say what happened was that the daily island life was more a daily island life than ever. If it had not been it would have been lost in their owning everything and if it had been lost in their owning everything they would naturally have then ceased to own everything. Anybody can understand that. They needed to be completely within their island life in order to own everything outside. (36)
>
> And now how do phrases come to be phrases and not sentences, that is the thing to know. Because in the nineteenth century it does. . . . As they owned everything outside, outside and inside had to be told something about all this owning, otherwise they might not remember all this owning and so there was invented explaining and that made nineteenth-century English literature what it is. (40)

In the first of these quotes, Stein demonstrated how "daily life" functions in English literature to "explain" and reinforce the notion of a (national) "inside," thus preventing the very existence of an "outside" subsumed within English ownership from challenging the stability of the boundaries of national geography and identity. Stein did not speculate on exactly how a national literature preoccupied with its internal affairs during a period of expansive imperialism manages to "explain" this inside/outside relationship; however, we can assume that such literature serves as an explanation and defense of imperialism, in accord with Matthew Arnold's thesis, by describing the daily life of the English as the most cultured and refined of all human communities.

Perhaps the most puzzling aspect of Stein's argument is her statement that English literature of this period consists of phrases, which she said are characterized by incompleteness, rather than complete sentences or paragraphs. Grammatically, in the transition from a clause to a phrase, what is often lost is the subject. So in delineating the boundaries of the inside in a literature based on phrases, the subject is perhaps already lost or displaced into its definitional outside. Earlier in the same essay, Stein described a sense of "incompleteness" that is necessarily caused by the insularity of English life, since there is an entire outside that is also part of the English experience of this time but is not "brought inside" or represented in the literature. This outside, moreover, cannot be represented, because literature reinforces notions of the inside precisely by excluding the outside from representation: "As they owned everything outside and brought none of this inside they naturally were no longer interested in choosing complete things" (34). Stein often wrote that a paragraph (which contains a complete idea and, importantly for Stein, its "emotion") is itself a complete thing and is useful in representing complete things, adding at one point in the essay that if a thing is complete, "it does not need explanation" (43). The "incompleteness" of England itself, then, is what accounts for Stein's observation that its literature is written according to an aesthetic of partial, explanatory phrases. This phrasal incompleteness perhaps articulates both the lack of recognition of the nation's definitional outside and the (threatened) loss of the national subject in that outside realm.

In this essay, Stein attributed the same reason for what she considers an incompleteness in nineteenth-century English literature that Jameson attributed to the radical incompleteness of English modernism: the incommensurable distance between the colonies and the metropolis, the outside and the inside, causing what Jameson calls a significational gap or incompleteness in the high modernist text, whose very structure is formed by the impossibility of representing the colonial reality. Stein apparently sees this incompleteness as already existing in the style (rather than the structure) of earlier, Victorian novels; thus Stein's model, when considered alongside Jameson's, allows us to see a degree of continuity between the two periods, rather than considering modernism, as it is usually described, as a radical break from past literatures.

According to Stein's thesis, a literature of phrases was appropriate only while England was "certain" in owning everything, and she went on to say that in the twentieth century, literature began to be written in paragraphs (48). Moreover, she argued that U.S. literature is most distinctively a literature of paragraphs: "The English have not gone on with this thing but we have in American literature" (49). In this way, Stein arrogantly located all modernism written in English within a specifically "American" context; to do so was appropriate to her geographical conception of the United States as a "whole thing" contained entirely on one continent and not dispersed, like England, across the globe in imperial conquests. This self-containment makes "American literature" particularly well suited to the paragraph, which is useful in describing a "whole thing."

Now we have apparently come full circle, moving from a discussion of modernism as a radical structural incompleteness to a depiction of "whole things." If, however, such incompleteness is a result of a particular configuration of western imperialism, then it follows that U.S. modernism adheres to what Stein terms a logic of whole things to the extent that U.S. imperialism was established with an internal slave economy and an expansionist movement across a single continent. This is not to say that American modernism is not characterized by a radical incompleteness, but rather that its particular lack of totality is not structured according to the same inside/outside model. In this context, Stein's notion of a literature characterized by "self-containment" (the paragraph) gains a new significance because it is precisely within a national inside that the representational crisis of colonial discourse is contained, and I argue later that it is in precisely this sense that the "paragraphs" that constitute *Tender Buttons* should be read. Before moving on to that text, however, we must first consider how this notion of "self-containment" produces a particular formulation of "the American thing."

In the closing pages of "The Gradual Making of the Making of Americans," Stein describes "the American thing" as existing within a "space of time" and characterized by "combination" and movement:

> It is singularly a sense for combination within a conception of the existence of a given space of time that makes the American thing the American thing, and the sense of this space of time must be the *within* the whole thing as well as in the *completed* whole thing. . . . [I] am always trying to tell this thing that a space of time is a natural thing for an American to always have inside them as something in which they are continuously moving. Think of anything, of cowboys, of movies, of detective stories, of anybody who goes anywhere or stays at home and you will realize that it is something strictly American to conceive a space of time that is filled with moving. (160–61, emphasis mine)

Perhaps the most important metaphor for understanding this "space of time" is that of the movie, since Stein also referred to the period in which she wrote as "the period of the cinema and series production" (177). The two movements suggested here, the cowboy's movement within the boundaries of a continental frontier and the detective's movement across a space delineated by the epistemological boundaries of what can be discovered as the truth, are both contained within the larger temporal metaphor of the movie screen. It is the movie screen that allows for such "contained movement" (that is, the movement of time contained within the film), and in its essential blankness and strictly demarcated boundaries, it serves as the "space in time" within which the "object" (as a single isolated thing or a series of such things) can be foregrounded in a kind of cinematic movement that allows it to "escape its frame" (86) while still being "contained within the whole thing."

This object, of course, is also itself the "whole thing" that is capable of representing "American" experience, and *Tender Buttons* can be read as a "series" of such objects. This declaration of independence from (and even usurpation of) the cultural dominance of English literature, however, is achieved through its own strategy of literary colonization. Stein relegates every "American" experience that cannot be written as a White, bourgeois one to the margins of her texts that purport to tell a story about all U.S. inhabitants, and in "Melanctha," she appropriates Black English Vernacular as a "linguistic utopia that is a domain not colonized by England"[25] in a story that repeatedly reaffirms an absolute distinction between "Negroes" and Whites and the "natural" superiority of the White race. At the level of characterization, as A. L. Nielson points out, although Stein's "Negro" characters in "Melanctha" are sympathetic in comparison with those of other White writers of the same period, "Stein's sympathy is the sympathy of romantic racism, and it is this that marks it as the signpost of modernism's discourse on the nonwhite" (21).[26]

But how might such textual colonization work in *Tender Buttons*,[27] which contains no characters, not to mention dialogue? Instead, this text is made up in the first two sections (entitled "Objects" and "Food") of a series of brief prose poems, written in Stein's most difficult, experimental style, which describe, in the first section, a series of objects and, in the second section, a series of food items. And the final section, entitled "Rooms," is composed of one long and equally difficult prose poem. To answer the question, one must remember that the collection of "paragraphs" in *Tender Buttons* collectively describes a "home." Susan E. Hawkins has pointed out Stein's contribution to rewriting the domestic sphere within the larger effort of creating a women's literature. After a complicated analysis of Stein's syntactic experiments in *Tender Buttons*, Hawkins wrote: "Is there anything *else* going on in *Tender Buttons* besides innovative technique and radical syntactic experimentation? And the answer is, yes; at a very comprehensible level Stein reveals to us, in an extraordinary way, the house we live in every day" (123).[28]

As Hawkins points out, Stein's experimental refiguring of the home should be acknowledged as important to the feminist project of rewriting domesticity. Along these lines, Stein's most significant contribution is the way in which the home in *Tender Buttons* is no longer the site of the daily lived experience of compulsory heterosexuality but instead is transformed into the scene of what Elizabeth Freeman has termed an "erotic syntax" of lesbian desire. In "Queer Syntactic Strategy, Body Performance, and the Dialect of Lesbian Couplehood in Gertrude Stein,"[29] Freeman describes Stein's interest in the categorical and in lists as a way to examine "the structure of taxonomy itself" and the relationship of taxonomy to the new sexual identities that served as objects of knowledge for scientific discourse in the late nineteenth century. In an argument that is too complex to summarize adequately here, Freeman goes on to read the "objects" in *Tender Buttons* as, among other things, "nouns" that do not quite function as nouns and therefore signal the link for Stein between grammar, not lexicon, and sexuality: "By moving away from an erotic *lexicon* towards an erotic *syntax, Tender Buttons* abandons the static, the monumental, synecdochal quality of the noun which 'identifies' for the pulsions and rhythms of a syntax which 'performs'" (5). In this way, Freeman provides a detailed analysis of the way Stein's objects, food, and rooms reappropriate the setting for the heterosexual family into an erotic of lesbian couplehood that extends into the (Parisian Left Bank) lesbian community, which is in the process of developing its own public sphere.

The problems with Stein's conception of the home are apparent not in the allusion to a lesbian community as Freeman describes it, but in the "we" that appears in Hawkins's analysis of this new "home." In a move typical of an identity-based feminism, Hawkins assumes that an unproblematic "we" can represent a women's literary movement. Unlike Hawkins, Stein does problematize the notion of women's identity and experience by thematizing the relationship between lesbian social/sexual practice and the heterosexual real that excludes nonheterosexual experience in order to function as the legitimated site of referentiality for knowledge produced about sexuality. However, by situating a critique of heterosexual norms within the domestic sphere without critiquing the other ideological functions of the home, Stein subtly reconfigures this "we" in her text. With this problem in mind, in addition to reading the text as an innovative critique of heterosexual formulations of domesticity, I would also like to account for how *Tender Buttons* is structured by what can be termed a pre–World War II U.S. colonial discourse that transforms the inside/outside model of English imperialism into an internal, contained, and domestic configuration of empire. To read *Tender Buttons* in this way is to ask what other functions Stein's paragraphs perform in their presentation of a series of complete American things—things that "paint over" the historically empty modernist present with the depiction of household objects, food, and rooms.

The motif of "spreading" or "widening," which begins in the first prose poem and continues throughout the three sections, suggests the kind of "movement" in the textual presentation of objects that Stein later, in *Lectures in America*, described as the movement that allows an object (as the "American thing") to simultaneously be a self-contained thing *and* an aesthetic object that escapes a static and reductive "framing." This movement, however, is apparently a strictly *intra*textual one, and its implicit challenge to ideological and hierarchical classifications of objects (or human subjects) is also highly linguistic. Even the rewriting of the home as one sphere of woman's power and pleasure and the nuanced critique of gender norms are presented quite explicitly as linguistic projects and as language games. The most obvious examples of this linguistic play are the lines "The sister was not a mister. Was this a surprise. It was" (65), and "Who is a man" (67). However, because Stein's concepts of identity and resemblance complicate the relationship between the work of art and its referent, it is important to read the apparent aestheticization of this critique of gender norms mapped out by heterosexuality not as a failure of a potentially politically charged project, but rather as the *presentation* of alternative gender formations. Most importantly, this presentation is not a *re*presentation of something "real," prior, and extratextual, but rather it is an "entity" in itself with a significational force that is as "real" as anything outside the text.

It is helpful here to consider *Tender Buttons* as an example of what Jo-Anna Isaac termed Stein's "presentational" style, which Isaac opposes to Joyce, whose interest in neologisms makes him difficult but still "representational": "Stein was interested in the presentational rather than the representational in language. . . . Stein's writing derives its meaning from nothing external to the writing, but from her realization of what she presents in, rather than suggests by, her words."[30] Although Stein does not use these particular terms, examples of this distinction between presentation and representation can be found in her own expository writings. In the chapter entitled "Portraits and Repetition" in *Lectures in America*, Stein explicitly complicates notions of referentiality in art by arguing that the value of a work of art lies not in its "resemblance" to a referent, but in its own aesthetic existence, which should be as independent as possible from the referent (188–89). And underlying her definition of *composition* in "Composition and Explanation"[31] is an implicit parallel between texts and things: Both are examples of "composition." In other words, the textual object does not have a less authentic existence than the actual one. This textual, presentational world may in fact be, for Stein, one location where it becomes possible to create a realm beyond that of "proper names" and norms, where gender identity is freed up from biological determination and where an improper gender identification does not entail a loss of "completeness."

To understand both the complex textual meaning of the objects in *Tender Buttons* and, just as importantly in my analysis, how they also function ideologically to produce an aestheticized absence of meaning, one needs to undertake not a close reading of the description of each object in its relation to the other objects, but a brief analysis of Stein's textual "frames," within which her objects repeatedly "spread" or "widen."

Stein begins the first series ("Objects") with a prose poem entitled "A CARAFE, THAT IS A BLIND GLASS." Of course, the image is of a container; however, the suggested containment is complicated by the last line of the poem, which reads, "The difference is spreading" (9). *Tender Buttons* thus begins with an example of how Stein's "nonsensical" style allows her objects to escape the boundaries of the "proper" (name, norm, and so on) while it also accommodates the presentation of a complete thing. Her new experimental language, then, is itself a frame, a complicated strategy of containment within which objects continually move within their "space of time," and as becomes clear in the last section, this language is also the "home" containing the "rooms" that constitute the text. In *Tender Buttons*, then, language itself is what the home or domesticity has been rewritten into; the poems written in this new, self-contained language are not representations of actual objects, food, and rooms as much as they are themselves presentations of textual objects, food, and rooms. If, in *Tender Buttons*, the bourgeois home can be said to be aestheticized, this aestheticization is not a simple retreat from everyday experience but a textual form of that experience. In other words, Stein's aestheticization is, ironically, a result of her refusal of representational meaning, a refusal that, in the case of *Tender Buttons*, results in a nonreferential presentation of everyday objects. Again, it is in this sense that her rewriting of the home and the gendered identities that might inhabit it should not be considered a limited project that does not extend beyond the textual realm; rather, the textual should be considered as a real and compellingly articulate aspect of the social. However, this shared ground between the work of art and the referent, according to which both have the status of "compositions," has other implications as well; this apparent absence of meaning serves an ideological purpose that is different from a critique of gender norms and that subtly restores its referentiality. As her language "widens" and "spreads" over any possible realities other than the textual ones it creates, Stein successfully "paints over" any links between this "home" and the conditions of exploitation and violence that bring about the conditions of its (textual and extratextual) existence. Thus, "the house we live in every day" is "reveal[ed] to us" as a nonreferential, completely aestheticized object that functions, paradoxically, to reassure "us" of its sanctity and exclusive claims to referentiality.

In articulating this nonreferentiality, which is necessarily and continually fraught with history, *Tender Buttons* becomes the quintessential western modernist text. This is not to say, however, that *Tender Buttons* is exemplary of a universalized modernism whose tenets are developed and defined in the west and then "exported" to the rest of the world as criteria for literary and artistic achievement. On the contrary, to see it as emblematic of the increasingly globalizing historical configurations that structure canonical modernist texts in the first world is to suggest that the notion of modernism itself, to the extent that it has been defined within the parameters of White, first world epistemes, needs to be fundamentally rethought, and as Dipesh Chakrabarty has argued in the context of European historiography, provincialized.[32]

That *Tender Buttons* becomes emblematic of the fraught relationship between western modernism and history happens not simply in spite of Stein's critique of hegemonic gender norms, but rather because of its setting within the home. The critique itself, ironically, also supports the colonial narratives that produce certain notions of the domestic sphere, even as it suggests the breakdown of the colonial narratives of progress and development. It is important to recognize that feminist and sexuality-based critiques of domesticity, such as the one that Stein provides, are especially relevant to all areas of cultural criticism because the home is so often the site of multiple deployments of patriarchal and heterosexual oppression. However, because in the United States the home is also the site of capitalist and imperialist exploitation, such critiques must also account for the ways in which, within this context of domesticity, a feminized Whiteness is defined in opposition to the racialized domestic labor that also inhabits the home. Although Stein provides a salient critique of the domestic in her early writings, that critique does not consider how the subjugation of women within the domestic sphere not only occurs within patriarchal and heterosexist structures of power but is also significantly linked to the reproduction of labor relations that are a colonial legacy of racialized exploitation. In other words, by critiquing conventional notions of domesticity through sexuality (by eroticizing the home as a setting for lesbian desire) and gender (by freeing up gender identity from biological determinism) but not through the axes of race and labor, Stein's new version of domesticity reinvests itself in the narratives of bourgeois individuality that inform the very notions of womanhood and identity that her texts consistently call into question.

This is not to say that writing that is not set within the home necessarily avoids this problem; rather, it is to suggest that Victorian and modern versions of domesticity as they circulate within domestic literature and other literary genres are consonant with formulations of bourgeois individuality that rest on a logic of containment that marks off the boundaries of inside and outside, self and other, knowable and unknowable terrains. In the context of U.S. colonialism, the contradictory nature of these boundaries is suggested in the problematics of a self-contained configuration of empire according to which the nation/home contains its definitional "outside" within its own boundaries. The home, as presented in *Tender Buttons*, is a particularly resonant metaphor for this type of containment, which refers on the one hand to the boundaries of "America" and on the other hand to First World, bourgeois individuality itself, which, in this sense, is also significantly feminized.

Notes

Portions of this paper were written with the support of a Fulbright grant and a fellowship from the University of California Humanities Research Institute; I would like to thank these institutions for their support. I would also like to thank the friends, colleagues, and teachers who read versions of this paper and offered comments essential to bringing it into its present form: Michael Davidson, Lisa Lowe, Wai-lim Yip, Masao Miyoshi, Chandan Reddy, Kim Dillon, Elizabeth Freeman, and Michael Lin. Lastly, I owe the greatest debt to Rosemary George, without whose many illuminating suggestions and encouragement, this paper would not have come to completion.

1. From *Nation and Narration*, also edited by Homi Bhabha (London: Routledge Press, 1990), 310.

2. *Time and the Other: How Anthropology Makes Its Object* (New York: Columbia University Press, 1983).

3. This phrase is taken from Matthew Arnold's *Culture and Anarchy*; it is the title of the first chapter, which attempts to justify British imperialism by defining English culture as unique in consisting of "sweetness and light": "He who works for sweetness and light united, works to make reason and the light of God prevail. . . . The sweetness and light of the few must be imperfect until the raw and unkindled masses of humanity are touched with sweetness and light" (69).

4. From *Nationalism, Colonialism and Literature*, by Terry Eagleton, Fredric Jameson, and Edward W. Said (Minneapolis: University of Minnesota Press, 1990), 43–66.

5. *The Political Unconscious* contains a chapter entitled "Romance and Reification: Plot Construction and Ideological Closure in Joseph Conrad," in which Jameson discussed Conrad's use of heroism as a theme, stating that "in the midst of capitalism . . . such a theme must mean something else" (217). In his analysis of the novel, the "sea" and the sea voyage are read as the "absent work place" (the place of labor that would be absent in "high modernist" texts). My reading of the same novel takes on a different focus than his earlier reading does in that I am looking at the effects of the representation of this labor pool/market located in the nonwest on texts produced and read in the metropolis. My central question is not the larger one of how this text can be read in the context of western imperialism and capitalism but, more specifically, how do its representations of the nonwest and an Englishman's adventures in it function in the larger cultural narrative of English national identity and justifications for its large-scale colonial dominance.

6. In *The Political Unconscious*, Jameson referred to Conrad as an emerging modernist and did not assign his works the canonical status of "high modernism."

7. New York: Signet, 1961.

8. Marlow at one point interrupts his story to remind his listeners: "Remember this is a love story I am telling you now" (221).

9. The past that is characterized by assurance is placed *before* the Patna's mysterious event occurs. In fact, the chapter in which this event occurs begins: "A marvelous stillness pervaded the world, and the stars, together with the serenity of their rays, seemed to shed upon the earth the assurance of everlasting security. . . . The propeller turned without a check, as though its beat had been part of the scheme of a safe universe. . . . Jim on the bridge was penetrated by the great certitude of unbounded safety and peace that could only be read on the silent aspect of nature like the certitude of fostering love upon the placid tenderness of a mother's face" (19). This "marvelous stillness" and its corresponding psychic "assurance" ends abruptly with the unexplained "bump," and in marked contrast to

the previous passages, the closing paragraph reads: "What had happened? . . .
Had the earth been checked in her course? They could not understand; and suddenly the calm sea, the sky without a cloud, appeared formidably insecure in their
immobility, as if poised on the brow of yawning destruction" (26).

10. For example, on page 56 Brierly exclaims to Marlow, "We are trusted. Do
you understand?—Trusted! Frankly, I don't care a snap for all the pilgrims that
ever came out of Asia, but a decent man would not have behaved like this. . . . We
aren't an organized body of men, and the only thing that holds us together is just
the name for that kind of decency. Such an affair destroys one's confidence."

11. London: Hogarth Press, 1957; 53.

12. In "Home in the Empire, Empire in the Home" (*Cultural Critique* 26, Winter
1993–94), George demonstrated the ways in which a protofeminist and nationalist
individuality for women first appears in colonial writings on English womanhood and domesticity produced in India.

13. *Fenhurst, Q.E.D., and Other Early Writings* (New York: Liveright, 1983), 160.
This collection of early writings contains the previously unpublished 1903 first
draft of the first five chapters of *The Making of Americans* (finished in 1908 but not
published until 1925).

14. Robert Duncan's 1967 introduction to *Bending the Bow* contains an interesting variation on just such a "field," whose relationship to military and economic
domination of the nonwestern world has by this time, in this case in light of the
Vietnam War, become explicit.

15. This formulation of reality as a form of fantasy legitimated as such for ideological purposes is from Judith Butler's essay "The Force of Fantasy: Feminism,
Maplethorpe, and Discursive Excess" (*Differences* 2[2], Summer 1990).

16. *Critical Inquiry* 3 (1977): 491–506.

17. In *The Nature and Context of Minority Discourse*, ed. Abdul R. JanMohamed
and David Lloyd (New York: Oxford University Press, 1990), 216–245.

18. In *Are Girls Necessary? Lesbian Writing and Modern Histories* (New York:
Routledge, 1996), Julie Abraham demonstrates how as lesbian writing began to be
written about, "the 'lesbian novel' was overidentified with literary realism" (23),
thereby causing the extensiveness of lesbian writing to be routinely overlooked:
"Prolific writers such as Virginia Woolf, Gertrude Stein, Willa Cather, Amy Low-
ell, Janet Flanner, H. D., Vita Sackville-West, and so on, who nevertheless did not
produce lesbian novels, can be seen as having been silenced only if the lesbian
novel is understood as *the* lesbian text. The gap between the multitude of lesbian
writers and the comparative paucity of lesbian novels produced by respected or
even identifiable writers, then only reinforces a reading of lesbians as silenced.
This insistence on the silencing of lesbians either renders invisible most of what I
have called lesbian writing, or at best relegates this work to secondary status as
unauthentic or opaque—coded" (24).

19. New York: Harcourt, Brace and Co., 1934.

20. Jane L. Walker argues in "History as Repetition: 'The Making of Americans'" that unlike the characters in realist narratives, who are both "unique individuals and at the same time representatives of social types," Stein's characters
are written according to a "typological system [that] emphasizes identities and ignores particularizing differences of social and historical circumstances" (180).

This article appears in *Gertrude Stein*, ed. Harold Bloom (New York: Chelsea House Publishers, 1986).

21. Jo-Anna Isaak, "The Revolutionary Power of a Woman's Laughter," in *Gertrude Stein Advanced: An Anthology of Criticism*, ed. Richard Kostelanetz (Jefferson, N.C.: Macfarland and Co., 1990).

22. New York: Oxford University Press, 1986.

23. For my understanding of Stein's complicated use of identity/entity, I am indebted to Michael Davidson for his chapter on Stein entitled "The Romance of Materiality: Gertrude Stein and the Aesthetic" in his book *Palimptexts: Modern Poetry and the Material World* (Berkeley: University of California Press, 1997).

24. Boston: Beacon Press, 1935.

25. Charles Bernstein, "Professing Stein/Stein Professing" (*Poetics Journal* 9, June 1991), 50. In this brief article, Bernstein attempts to rescue Stein from accusations of racism in A. L. Nielson's *Reading Race: White American Poets and the Racial Discourse in the Twentieth Century*; Bernstein thus never acknowledges that Stein's use of B.E.V. is itself an act of literary colonialism.

26. *Reading Race: White American Poets and the Racial Discourse in the Twentieth Century* (Athens: University of Georgia Press, 1988). In the introduction to this book, Nielson discusses "Melanctha" at some length as the precursor of White modernist texts that contain Black characters (see pages 21–28).

27. Los Angeles: Sun and Moon Press.

28. Susan E. Hawkins, "Sneak Previews: Stein's Syntax in *Tender Buttons*," in *Gertrude Stein and the Making of Modern Literature*, ed. Shirley Neuman and Ira B. Nadel (Boston: Northeastern University Press, 1988), 123.

29. From *Queerly Phrased*, ed. Anna Livia and Kira Hall (Oxford: Oxford University Press, 1996).

30. Jo-Anna Isaac, "The Revolutionary Power of a Woman's Laughter," 28.

31. This essay appears in *Selected Writings of Gertrude Stein*, ed. Carl Van Vechten (New York: Vintage Books, 1990), 515–523.

32. Chakrabarty demonstrates the importance of provincializing European historiographic accounts of modernity in his article "Postcoloniality and the Artifice of History: Who Speaks for the Indian Pasts" (Representations 37, Winter 1990), 1–26.

Chapter Five

Homo-Economics: Queer Sexualities in a Transnational Frame

GAYATRI GOPINATH

In her 1941 short story "The Quilt,"[1] Urdu writer Ismat Chughtai depicts the curious relationship between a sequestered wife and her female maidservant in an upper-class Muslim household, as observed by the young girl who narrates the tale. Every night, the girl is alternately fascinated and alarmed by the energetic contortions of the two women under the quilt; curious sounds and smells emanate from there. The quilt becomes the organizing metaphor of the story, and its shifting surfaces suggest the mobile relations of erotic pleasures that Chughtai weaves throughout the text. Chughtai's quilt—and the patchwork effects of multiple desires that it represents—provides a useful site upon which to engage with the vexed question of how to read alterior sexuality across national and cultural locations.[2] Anthropologist Rosalind Morris, in her essay on gender and sexuality in Thailand, warns against the "homogenization of differences that emerges when . . . [particular] forms of alterior sexual identity are considered in fetishism's vacuum, independent of the culturally specific sex/gender systems from which they emerge."[3] Taking Morris's cautionary observation as a necessary point of departure—and keeping in mind the dangers and difficulties of juxtaposing two texts that speak to what appear to be radically different genealogies and historical contexts—I here read "The Quilt" against and through a piece of contemporary reflexive feminist anthropology, written by Susan Seizer and published in 1995 in the pages of *Public Culture*.[4] In so doing, I seek to foreground the structures of looking, seeing, and being seen at work in the formation of colonial and postcolonial sexual subjectivities, and the centrality of the figure of the gendered subaltern to such formations. I hope, in the process, to make clear the mechanisms by which current discourses around the formation of "lesbian" or queer subjectivity—even those that are avowedly feminist and antiracist—can rely upon and function in the service of familiar colonial strategies of subjectification. I end with a brief look at what can be termed queer South Asian diasporic cultural practices that undercut globalizing discourses of sexuality and that instead offer up a more enabling formulation of transnational processes of sexual subjectification.

Chughtai's text puts forth a particular conceptualization of female homoerotic pleasure that exceeds and escapes existing theorizations of "lesbian" subjectivity.[5] "The Quilt" must be understood not as a representative "lesbian" narrative but through the very structures set up by the story itself; these demand that female homoeroticism be located as simply one form of desire within a web of multiple, competing desires that are in turn embedded in different economies of work and pleasure. In particular, Chughtai's respacialization of female homoerotic desire through tropes of concealment and visibility, secrecy and disclosure, challenges dominant (and often universalizing) paradigms of same-sex desire. To cite just one of the many instances of this universalizing tendency within queer theory, Eve Sedgwick, in her tremendously influential work *Epistemology of the Closet*, claims the closet as "the defining structure for gay oppression in this century," thereby disregarding other possible epistemic categories or tropes of spacialization that may exist outside, or indeed within, a Euro-American context.[6] Conversely, Chughtai's work demands a consideration of those bodies and spaces that fall outside the rigid narrative configurations constructed by such sweeping theoretical gestures and instead opens up a potentially generative site of alternative narratives and significations of female homoerotic desire.

Reterritorialized Desire

Chughtai's "Quilt" is set within the confines of the household of a wealthy landowner (the Nawab) and his wife (the Begum) and is narrated by an adult who tells the story through the eyes of her childhood self. As a young girl, she has been "deposited" in the Begum's home by her mother in the hopes that this sojourn will initiate her into proper feminine behavior, given that she has a penchant for fighting with the boys rather than "collecting admirers" as her older sisters do (7). The adult narrator frames the story as a remembered childhood instance of both fear and fascination, in which the Begum's quilt—"imprinted on [her]

memory like a blacksmith's brand" (7)—embodies the scene of her own
ambivalent sexual awakening and desire for the Begum. Memory in the
text works not to evoke a narrative of nostalgia, one that imagines
"home" as a site of subjective wholeness or originary, heterosexual identity; rather, the narrator remembers the domestic arena experienced by
her childhood self as an apparent site for the inculcation of gender-
normative behavior as well as of complicated, nonnormative arrangements of pleasures and desires. This antinostalgic narrative radically
destabilizes conceptions of the domestic as a site of compulsory heterosexuality, while the partial knowledge afforded by the child gaze (one
that is unable to fully grasp the meanings of the scenes that it witnesses)
allows Chughtai to simultaneously resist articulating these arrangements
of desires within prescribed frameworks as "lesbian" or "homosexual."

It quickly becomes evident that the question of space, territoriality, and
access is critical to the narrative framing of the story, as well as to the articulation of the desiring subject, whether male or female. The Nawab, we
are told, has a curious "hobby" of "keep[ing] an open house for students;
young, fair and slim-waisted boys, whose expenses [are] born entirely by
him," and whose "slim waists, fair ankles and gossamer shirts" torture
the Begum as she glimpses them through "the chinks in the drawing-
room doors"(8). The Begum witnesses this scene of pleasure, commerce,
and desire, but she is absolutely shut out of its circuits of exchange—
predicated as they are on the consumption and circulation of food,
money, and labor—and is thus rendered valueless within its terms: "Who
knows when Begum Jan started living? Did her life begin . . . from the
time she realised that the household revolved around the boy-students,
and that all the delicacies produced in the kitchen were meant solely for
their palates?"(8). The introduction of the female servant Rabbo into the
narrative, however, shifts the spatial focus of the story away from the
Nawab's drawing room and this partially glimpsed scene of an eroticized
(male) homosociality to one that centers upon the zenana (the women's
quarters in "traditional" Muslim households) and, in particular, the space
beneath the Begum's quilt.

It is Rabbo's entrance into her life that allows the Begum to finally
"start living," in that it marks her entry into an alternative homosocial
economy of desire that functions parallel to the dominant desiring economy of the household within which the Nawab and the boys operate. The
money-food-pleasure nexus that frames the scene of male-male desire
also marks the relation between the two women but signifies differently
within the context of an eroticized female homosociality. Denied access to
the "real," material resources of the household, the Begum and Rabbo
generate their own, drawing sustenance and nourishment from the work
that their bodies do in the production of pleasure. Indeed, their erotic

pleasure is insistently figured in the text in terms of food and the satiation of hunger: "Rabbo came to [the Begum's] rescue just as she was starting to go under. Suddenly her emaciated body began to fill out. Her cheeks became rosy; beauty, as it were, glowed through every pore! It was a special oil massage that brought about the change in Begum Jan"(9). Here and elsewhere, the text reveals an intense preoccupation with touch, smell, and the enumeration of body parts (lips, eyes, skin, waist, thighs, hands, ankles) as each becomes libidinally invested through Rabbo's relentless massaging of the Begum's body; hence, the narrative refuses to conceptualize the desired and desiring body as a highly localized and conscribed site of libidinal investment. Instead, the story configures female desire and pleasure as an infinitely productive and transformative activity that generates and is generated by the literal and metaphoric production and consumption of food. The child narrator, for instance, describes the activity under the quilt in the terms available to her as "the sounds of a cat slobbering in the saucer"(13) and later comments: "Smack, gush, slobber—someone was enjoying a feast. Suddenly I understood what was going on! Begum Jan had not eaten a thing all day and Rabbo, the witch, was a known glutton. They were polishing off some goodies under the quilt for sure"(19). Indeed, Rabbo's touch becomes for the Begum "the fulfillment of life's essential need—in a way, more important than the basic necessities required to stay alive"(10). Female desire, then, is predicated upon a survival economy of work and pleasure as intermingled.

While it would be tempting to read the representation of female same-sex eroticism within the text as a paradigm of "lesbian" desire, such a categorization shuts down precisely what is most useful about Chughtai's story. The text resists positing the scene of desire between women as a privileged or purely enabling site outside the hegemonic workings of the household and militates against an easy recuperation of any such space of undiluted resistance or subversion. For instance, as references to the "gluttony" of Rabbo and the Begum make clear, Chughtai evokes female homoerotic desire not only through images of satiation but through those of insatiability, greed, and excess as well. The space beneath the quilt, functioning as it does as a site of nonreproductive pleasure—one that has no use value within a heterosexual economy of desire—can be figured only in terms of overindulgence and waste. Furthermore, the narrator locates the scene of female homoerotic sexuality within a conflicted relation of pleasure, desire, and disgust, in which she finds herself simultaneously attracted to and repulsed by the physicality she witnesses between Rabbo and the Begum. The narrator's ambivalence to such physicality is underscored by her repeated evocations of decay and nausea[7] and is most apparent in her reaction to the Begum's advances: Tahira Naqvi's translation has the narrator "nauseated" by the Begum's touch (16), whereas Susie Tharu and K. Lalitha's reading of the same line describes the narrator as "driven to distraction" by "the warmth of [the Begum's] body."[8] While the text in these instances references dominant configurations of female sexuality,[9] its representation of female homoerotic desire is not reducible to nor fully contained by such framings. Instead Chughtai posits an eroticized female homosociality that functions within multiple discourses and that contains numerous, often contradictory significations. The erotic circuits within which Rabbo, the Begum, and the girl narrator circulate are marked by radically uneven positions of power, both generational and economic. There are similarly uneven eroticized male homosocial economies in the text; indeed, in the narrative's mapping out of intersecting trajectories of erotic pleasures between men and boys, women and women, women and girls, and masters and servants, desiring relations are always infused and crosscut by other economies of power. Women as desiring subjects constantly shift in and out of multiply and hierarchically coded gendered, generational, and class positions, so that the text refuses to allow particular configurations of desire to settle into stable structures of sexual identity.[10]

The servant Rabbo figures the text's resistance to conflating sexual practices with identity, for it is through her that Chughtai is able to rework the category of female subalternity in terms of space, gendered agency, masculinity, and desire. Chughtai complicates the notion of domestic labor, desire, and servitude in her refusal to map out unambiguous relations of exploitation and domination within the household. The figure of the female servant occupies a privileged space of indeterminacy within the gendered and class-marked economy of the household—a location that allows subalternity to be conceptualized beyond mere functionality or instrumentality. Whereas the Begum occupies spaces that are more and more limited as the narrative progresses—from the "prison" of the house at large to the "closed doors" of her "sanctum" to the territory beneath the quilt—Rabbo is granted tremendous mobility and access to the various classed and gendered spaces of the house. In addition, her ability to leave the confines of the house—as she does when she visits her errant son—contrasts sharply with the Begum's increasingly constricted spatial existence. Indeed, with her ability to transgress spatial boundaries, Rabbo becomes the purveyor of both bodily and psychic knowledge, effecting miraculous transformations upon the Begum's body as well as relieving her of periodic "fits" of hysteria.

Rabbo's spatial, social, and sexual mobility makes her an object of both envy and anxiety within the household; she is repeatedly referred to as a "witch," as possessing unsettling powers that are beyond the understanding of the girl narrator and the other members of the household (11).

Indeed, if "possession" implies both the ownership of property as well as the taking over or inhabiting of another body, Rabbo—in a reversal of the typical mistress-servant relation—can be seen as "possessing" the Begum. This reversal is most evident in the Begum's monstrous metamorphosis as she advances upon the narrator, in which the Begum appears "possessed" (16), while the "claustrophobic blackness" of the room, the darkening of her "upper lip" and "deep eyes," bring to mind earlier descriptions of Rabbo as "black . . . like burnt iron ore"(11). The startling conflation of the "white" body of the Begum with Rabbo's "black" one within this scene of female homoerotic desire can be read not so much as a reinscription of dominant models of "lesbian" sexuality as predicated on narcissistic identification (where, as Valerie Traub has pointed out, "identification with" is conflated with "desire for"[11]); rather, it reads as a textual imperative toward an adequate theorization of female homoerotic desire as functioning within a visually coded economy of class difference.

Significantly, this scene also underscores the ways in which the text militates against reading Rabbo as the "real lesbian" in the story, despite familiar dominant discursive productions that locate the "truth" of sexual, class, and gender difference and transgression upon particular, designated bodies.[12] For example, the masculinity that characterizes Rabbo and signifies her obvious transgression of a classed and gendered ambit of femininity is not solely locatable on her dark, "solidly packed" body but marks the various scenes of women as desiring subjects. Chughtai masculinizes her female characters when and where they desire or are desired; the Begum's overt masculinity in this scene, as she turns her "arduous heat" upon the child narrator, echoes earlier passages in which the narrator describes the Begum's face—with its downy upper lip and "temples covered with long hair"—as transformed under her own "adoring gaze" into "that of a young boy"(10).[13] Chughtai thus resists reading female homoerotic desire only upon certain bodies and in certain instances; instead, desiring subjects within the story occupy multiple locations within a structure of visuality that renders desire visible by means of specific markers of class and gender. At the same time, the inscription of such markers upon the bodies of the Begum and Rabbo speaks to Chughtai's investment, in this instance, in a hegemonic logic of visibility that demands that bodily surfaces be intelligible in particular ways. That female desiring agency can signify and be signified only by means of exterior bodily transformations that work within a visual register of class and gender difference undercuts, to a certain extent, the destabilizing effects of the text's representation of desire as always mutable, unfixed, and mobile.

Just as the text refuses to locate desire solely upon particular bodies—and hence avoids reifying desires into identity structures—it also refuses to privilege particular sites as the "proper" locations of the practice of such desire. Shifting critical scrutiny away from the space beneath the quilt to the quilt itself suggests the possibility of a reterritorialized desire that exceeds the master narrative of "the closet" as a way of theorizing alterior sexuality. The quilt can be read not so much as a concealing device beneath which the "truth" or visual "proof" of sex and desire lie, but rather as a kind of mediating and constantly shifting surface that negotiates and marks the border between different economies and organizations of erotic pleasure. The quilt—as a surface area suspended between that which is "hidden" and that which is "visible"—calls these categories into question and suggests the impossibility of viewing the spaces they connote as discrete territories. Instead, a more complicated relation between inside and outside, secrecy and disclosure, and visibility and invisibility is suggested by the discursive function of the quilt in the narrative. The text on one level seems to privilege what D. A. Miller termed the "will-to-see"[14] in the girl narrator's insistent attempts to (quite literally) bring to light the curious goings-on beneath the quilt. Indeed, the narrative is propelled by this scopic drive, this desire for "proof," and the promise of eventual revelation of the "truth" beneath the quilt. The story's final scene, in which the narrator does catch a glimpse of what lies beneath the quilt, causes the abrupt shutting down of the narrative:

> Once again the quilt started billowing. I tried to lie still, but it was now assuming such weird shapes that I could not contain myself. . . . In the dark I groped for the switch. The elephant somersaulted beneath the quilt and dug in. During the somersault, its corner was lifted one foot above the bed. Allah! I dove headlong into my sheets! What I saw when the quilt was lifted, I will never tell anyone, not even if they give me a lakh of rupees. (19)

This sudden blankness, effected by the narrator's refusal (and inability) to disclose what she sees, defers and thwarts the will-to-know that the narrative produces and the scopic satisfaction that it promises but fails to deliver. The ultimate refusal to enunciate with which the story ends may initially appear as a capitulation to the "prohibition on a certain naming"[15] and the denial of entry of "lesbian" sexuality into the realm of representation—an apparent consignment to unspeakability of female homoerotic sex and desire. I argue, however, that the failure to name the activity under the quilt speaks, rather, to the impossibility of containing the erotic configurations within the text through a strategy of "naming," of making "sayable" that which must first be produced as visible. Instead of marking "lesbian" sexuality as spectral or unspeakable, the girl's silence encapsulates the text's refusal to grant this space beneath the quilt privileged status as the paradigmatic site of "lesbian" sexuality; the very notion that the "truth" of sex can be revealed or spoken is evoked, only to be overturned. Female homoerotic pleasure within the text quite simply exceeds the enclosed space beneath the quilt, just as it does the structures of visibility and visuality that the text references. Rather, it saturates all points of the text, eluding location within the ocular field through its manifestation as oral and aural in the sensations, sounds, and smells with which the narrative is infused. The sight beheld by the narrator, as well as her subsequent failure to disclose, then, become merely incidental; there is no "secret" that can possibly be revealed, spoken, or withheld given the continuous eruptions of multiple desires that permeate the text.

The quilt, then, represents a textured and layered form of sexuality that resists solidifying into structures of identity. Same-sex desires and practices in the text produce quilted effects, rather than identity effects, as Chughtai maps out multiple, uneven erotic relations that are simultaneously stitched into and undermine dominant circuits of pleasure and commerce. Chughtai's refusal to privilege either the sight or the site of same-sex desire means that the text resists being rendered intelligible within dominant narratives of "lesbian" sexuality. Indeed, as I have thus far sought to make clear, reading the text through such dominant configurations of pleasure, identity, and visibility only obscures Chughtai's contestation of precisely those hegemonic formulations.

"At Home I Am a Lesbian"

I now turn to a moment in contemporary lesbian and gay scholarship that is symptomatic of the dangers and representational violences involved in rendering particular sexualities intelligible through dominant structures of visuality and identity. A growing body of work in transnational cultural studies, and anthropology in particular, attempts to think through the translatability and mutability of sexual subjectivities as they traverse national and cultural borders.[16] It is worth taking a closer look at such work, as it is becoming an important site of queer theorizing within a transnational and cross-cultural frame. In recent years, valuable collections that speak to "the reflexive turn" in anthropology have sought to make visible the traditionally unmarked position of the ethnographer by situating his or her erotic subjectivity in "the field."[17] As Don Kulick, the coeditor of one such collection, pointed out, the deflection of the anthropological gaze onto the sexual subjectivity of ethnographer can serve to redress the ways in which "anthropology has always trafficked in the sexuality of the people we study," where "sex—their sex, the sex of 'the Other'—has always constituted one of the gaudiest exhibits in the anthropological sideshow" (2–3). Much of the current reflexive anthropological work on sexuality importantly complicates conventional notions of the "self" in ethnographic texts and highlights the limits of universalizing discourses of sexuality. For instance, in an essay on her painful and plea-surable sexual involvement with a person she termed "an-Other lesbian" during her fieldwork in West Sumatra, Indonesia, Evelyn Blackwood elo-quently narrated her struggles to recreate a familiar "lesbian" identity for herself in "the field."[18] Blackwood detailed the ways in which she im-poses on Dayan, her Indonesian lover, a model of "lesbianism" predi-cated upon "American lesbian feminist" principles of egalitarianism and gender neutrality. Her attempts to situate Dayan within a lesbian feminist framework as another "woman who loves women" are consistently thwarted by Dayan's own self-identification as *cowok*, which Blackwood explains is the Indonesian slang term for the masculine partner in a les-bian couple (62). Blackwood concluded:

> As an American in Indonesia, I felt strongly the loss of my lesbian identity.
> Thinking I had found it again with Dayan, I attempted to reconstruct that
> identity in a way that resonated with my own familiar categories. I wanted
> my relationship to be safe, to be home. . . . But while I persisted in defining
> our relationship and providing the categories, it refused to be simply "les-
> bian." . . . I was forced to examine our differences and recognize my privi-
> lege in relation to her. (70–71)

Throughout the narrative, Blackwood usefully critiques her quest to find sameness where difference (in terms of sexual and gender identifica-tions, class, and racial hierarchies) is constantly at work. However, what remains curiously inert in Blackwood's text is the notion of what it means to be a "lesbian" at "home"; while Blackwood is painfully aware of how her lesbian feminist identity as construed "back home" ceases to be func-tional in "the field," she offers no sense of how the very space of "home" may also be the locus of radical difference and multiple articulations of "lesbian" sexualities. When "Other" gender and sexual identifications are located firmly in "the field," "home" remains the site of a remarkably sta-ble, homogeneous "lesbian" identity characterized by sameness and egal-itarianism.

A similar evocation of "home" as a fixed site of a transparent "lesbian" identity against which erotic configurations in "the field" are read also emerges in another piece of feminist reflexive anthropology, an essay by Susan Seizer entitled "Paradoxes of Visibility in the Field: Rites of Queer Passage in Anthropology." In focusing on Seizer's essay, I hope to point to the ways in which particular forms of queer anthropological reflexivity may serve to solidify the very structures of power that they seek to desta-bilize. Seizer's article explores the author's own problematic relation to "being a lesbian" engaged in fieldwork in a non-Euro-American setting and is one of the few that importantly takes up a South Asian (specifically South Indian) location for a confrontation between different erotic economies. Granted an award by the Association for Feminist Anthropology, Seizer's text is useful in offering up a model of contemporary feminist anthropology, in that the author, like Blackwood, is involved in the valuable project of foregrounding the positionality of the ethnographer and the particular burdens attached to lesbian and gay bodies that travel. However, the essay also enacts the kind of reading of female homoeroticism that Chughtai's text resists, in that it seeks to locate the absence or presence of alterior sexuality through the gaze of a hegemonic subjectivity that Seizer codes as "lesbian." The implications of such a gesture are particularly significant and deserve critical scrutiny given the increasing globalization of a lesbian and gay movement.[19] Anthropologist Martin Manalansan, for instance, detailed the problematic nature of an "international" lesbian and gay movement as one that involves an "authentic nativist search for primordial 'gay and lesbian' phenomena [through] the imposition of international egalitarianism"(2). Manalansan also pointed out the implicit progress narrative that structures globalizing "gay" ideologies, in which "all same-sex phenomena are placed within a developmental and teleological matrix that ends with western "gay" sexuality"(4). Clearly such a trend toward the consolidation of a "pan-cultural/pan-global"(4) sexual subjectivity ignores both the particularities of local sexual economies and the complicated navigation of diasporic and transnational circuits of ideological exchange and influence undertaken by "local" sexual subjects.

It is within this context of the circulation and contestation of global "gay and lesbian" identities that Seizer's essay must be placed. The article takes the form of a personal narrative that lays bare the fictions and biases of a White American lesbian ethnographer doing fieldwork in the South Indian state of Tamil Nadu and as such seems to run counter to precisely these homogenizing discourses of alterior sexualities. In a lengthy introductory passage, for instance, Seizer constituted her readership as follows: "Firstly, I assume the reader is consciously antiracist, and aware of the racism of the colonial project and its legacy for present-day relations between first-world travelers and residents of postcolonial societies. Secondly, that s/he is fundamentally feminist with a belief in multiple feminisms" (75). Seizer's constitution of the reader—and by extension of the essay itself—as "fundamentally feminist" and "antiracist" effectively forecloses a critique that would seek to question the taking for granted of such a position. Despite (or perhaps enabled by) such an "assumption," the essay functions instead as the reaffirmation of a "lesbian" subjectivity, one that demands the return of the gaze from the racialized other—in this case a female domestic worker—in order to realize and reconfirm its own dominance. Whereas Chughtai's text insists on a scrupulous attention to "local," highly particular logics and organizations of multiple pleasures and desires, Seizer refuses to grant any such specificity or signifying power to the erotic configurations within "the field" that she details.

Such a refusal is particularly evident in Seizer's (mis)reading of the relation of the female homosociality she witnesses to female homoerotic practices and the possible subject positions from which they may emanate. For instance, early on in her essay Seizer evocatively details the world of female homosociality that she observes and participates in during her stay with a working-class family in the city of Madurai. She finds herself "moving in tandem," as she puts it, with the other women of the family, as they include her in the daily intimacies of dressing, sleeping, cooking, and touching (78). Seizer goes on to explain that while she finds much affectionate love in this context, "sexual desire, lust, love" is utterly absent from it. She states: "A gauze of memory surrounded me like a mnemonic wrap, always repeating the same message: 'At home I am a lesbian; these practices mean something very different there.' But no one else heard this nagging refrain"(78). As in Blackwood's text, the nostalgically constructed site of "home" becomes for Seizer the locus of a "lesbian" identity that is granted a homogeneous stability and coherence, an epistemological certainty against which she is unable to gauge or read the erotic as it plays out within this "other" site. Instead, Seizer attributes to the "female homosocial life" she experiences in Madurai both a pervasive "sensuality" and an utter lack of nonheterosexual desire (81). By stabilizing the meaning of "lesbian" as it exists "at home," Seizer is able to state, upon having the opportunity to have sex with her partner for the first time in India: "From what I could tell, women never had their clothes off in India. We were the only two women I knew who ever had their clothes off, let alone had them off together, in naked union"(85). Both literally and discursively, that which lies outside Seizer's own epistemological field of vision simply fails to signify; whether "at home" or in "the field," female same-sex erotic practices and subjectivities are assumed to exist solely in the form in which Seizer knows them. Chughtai's quilt appears to cover up the "truth" of sex between women, but pleasure and desire infuse the text in myriad locations and forms; Seizer, on the other hand, privileges the sight and site of "lesbian" sex—two women, naked on a bed, behind the closed doors of a room—as the only "proper" expression and location of female same-sex desire. The category of "lesbian"—which is continuously exceeded by Chughtai's text as well as by the multiple meanings and articulations of female same-sex desire that shadow Seizer's space of "home"—remains for Seizer the standard against which other forms of female homoerotic expression always fall short.

Seizer's characterization of female homosociality in "the field" (delimited to an urban household in Madurai) as "tamely sensuous" stands in marked contrast to Chughtai's rendering of the complicated and wild desiring relations between women in a seemingly "traditional" zenana. As Geeta Patel argues, in locating female homoeroticism within the confines of the zenana and not as that which occurs "elsewhere," Chughtai both "queries and queers the arena of 'the domestic,'" while challenging the symbolic function of women as bearers of inviolate tradition within nationalist narratives (13–14).[20] Chughtai's configuration of female desiring subjects also troubles dominant representations of Muslim women as generic, chaste, and oppressed, as immured in the home and lost to the living. Female interactions within the zenana of "The Quilt" instead produce a particular relation between female homosociality and female homoerotic practices, one that "denaturalize[s] the apparently necessary slide from marriage into heterosexuality."[21] In contrast, Seizer's inability to step outside the anthropological parameters of "the field" that she witnesses (whether that of the household in Madurai or her subsequent house-sitting stint in Madras) leaves intact the linkages between heterosexuality and "the domestic" that Chughtai's narrative interrogates.

Seizer's adherence to what Manalansan terms "the teleological matrix that ends with western 'gay' [or 'lesbian'] sexuality" is all the more surprising given that her essay attempts to narrate "the disintegration of . . . U.S. lesbian identities"(73) that she and her partner experience during her two years of fieldwork. The essay's narrative trajectory is thus one that seeks to chart Seizer's progressive disinvestment in dominant mechanisms of visuality through which a specifically White, western lesbian subjectivity comes into being and is kept in place. Quotes from Bronislaw Malinowski, David Maybury-Lewis, and Claude Lévi-Strauss frame each section of the essay and appear to serve as an ironic metacommentary on Seizer's own vexed relation to the problematic positionality of the ethnographer in "the field," particularly when faced, as she is, with the paradoxical and unsettling situation of her hypervisibility as "White" and "foreign" and her simultaneous invisibility as "lesbian" and "leftist." As the narrative progresses, however, it becomes increasingly apparent that the real paradox of Seizer's essay lies elsewhere. Even while the essay takes as its object of critical scrutiny Seizer's own positionality as an "unwilling dominatrix" trapped within the discursive productions of power of the postcolony, the narrative itself works to replicate these very relations of power, domination, and control through a continued investment in particular structures of visuality. As I shall discuss, the text's self-referentiality and self-parody do not succeed in rescuing it from reiterating the very mechanisms of subjectification that it seeks to both foreground and interrogate. Seizer ends her piece by stating that "Kate and I realized that we had quite unceremoniously dumped the idea of maintaining our treasured public dyke identity in Tamil Nadu. . . . We fit in and stuck out differently in this other system of differences, which we gradually came to appreciate"(99). If indeed Seizer resituates herself as a sexual subject at the narrative's end, the question such a movement poses is this: At whose expense is Seizer able to arrive at her appreciation of "this other system of differences"? Who bears the costs of this "rite of passage," and ultimately, is there anything particularly "queer" about it?[22]

The answers to these questions are hinted at in the failed irony that marks Seizer's text—a failure to trouble the conventions of her overdetermined status as White, first world ethnographer in "the field"—and that is most evident in her rendering of the figure of the female servant and the uses to which this figure is put in the narrative structure of the essay.

The central, epiphanic moment around which the narrative revolves concerns a servant named Angela, who works for the owners of the roomy, middle-class Madras home where Seizer and her partner are house-sitting and who has been overtly hostile to the friendly overtures of the two White women. One morning, Angela walks in on Seizer and her partner as they are having sex. Later Angela tells a neighbor that she believes the activity that the two women were involved in behind the closed doors of the bedroom is that of "minting money." This statement of Angela's—multiply translated and relayed from Angela through the neighbor to Seizer to the reader—is taken up by Seizer as a provocative commentary on what she terms the "recreation of . . . lesbian selves" in which she and her partner were engaged when Angela interrupted them. Seizer states:

> Angela was the only one who got it. She was the only person who knew how valuable Kate and I were to each other. She gave us the translation into local currency that we'd been looking for, horrifying as it was. We'd never found a way to explain how much we mattered to each other, because relations between women don't rate by themselves. . . . Nothing we did together was important enough for anyone to even remark on. Except Angela. She saw what we were doing as something serious. Criminal even. . . . Her take on us was strangely familiar, resonating as it did with the ways we learned to see ourselves at home. (92–93)

Once again, Seizer problematically invests the term *lesbian* with an easy homogeneity, as it signifies "at home"—the fantasied site of a normative "lesbian" identity—while simultaneously enacting an abrupt foreclosure of other possible narrativizations of "what Angela saw." Seizer seizes upon Angela's comment as a productive metaphor for the act of "lesbian" self-construction as it occurs within global circuits of power and capital but states that she is "convinced that Angela's description of our private activities . . . was not intentionally metaphoric"(95). Such a move is eerily reminiscent of colonial discursive framings of colonized subjectivity, in that Seizer denies to Angela the power of metaphoricity and intentionality that she so readily claims for herself. Seizer's repeated insistence on what and how Angela sees, what and how Angela "imagines," is precisely what animates the narrative and frames it in such a way as to curtail the possibility of Angela possessing an agency that exceeds Seizer's own discursive and narrative field of vision. Such a figuring of Angela is at odds with Chughtai's more nuanced formulation of female subalternity and domestic labor in terms of shifting, mobile positions of power that exceed mere fixity and instrumentality. That figuring of Angela also undercuts the apparent irony with which Seizer prefaces the section with a quote from David Maybury-Lewis, who comments on his fieldwork in Brazil: "I had to admit to myself that the Indians had got on my nerves. . . . Who could blame them for their begging and their truculence, for their hypocrisy and their deceit? . . . Still, that did not make them any easier to live with"(84). Given Seizer's use of "native" female subjectivity in the passage, the quote fails to function as wry commentary on her own positionality in relation to "her" Indians (as opposed to Maybury-Lewis's Indians) and instead reenacts the historical homogenization of racial and cultural difference that occurs under the sign of "Indian."

The incident with Angela is all the more significant within the context of the various trajectories of looking and being seen already mapped out by the narrative. Seizer traces the ways in which her badges of first world alterity—her lesbianism and progressive politics—fail to signify as anything other than foreignness and Whiteness within a particular class dynamic in India. In front of the gaze of "women of servant status," she is irreducibly other; all that is legible is the whiteness of her skin as the primary marker of racial, cultural, and class difference. She states: "We were other, but not for reasons we were used to. We were odd, but not as a statement we'd chosen to make. We were not people to engage with, but to stare at"(87). Seizer is forced into the uncomfortable position of having to relinquish agency in determining her legibility as spectacle or how her spectacular self-presentation is read.[23] While the narrative ostensibly traces Seizer's progressive acceptance of her unintelligibility as "lesbian" away from "home," the incident with Angela forestalls just such a trajectory and instead is critical in Seizer's reconstitution and reinstatement as a legible "lesbian" subject in an other site. Angela's "sulky, suspicious gaze"(86)[24] becomes wholly instrumental in allowing Seizer to once again render visible her own sexual subject position, in that Angela functions as unwilling interpellator who speaks the "truth" of Seizer's lesbianism, placing it as she apparently does within the context of late-capitalist systems pleasure and commerce. Within the logic of the essay, then, the "field" that Angela inhabits is one in which she cannot be read as a worker (where she may have numerous other houses to attend to, a possibility never allowed for by Seizer); rather, Angela's primary activity is seen to be that of spying on the two White women. While in Chughtai's text the domestic arena is refigured in terms of converging economies of work and pleasure, labor in the domestic space that Seizer occupies is elided, to be replaced by Angela's activity as spy and witness.

The functionality of the servant gaze in Seizer's narrative raises and leaves uninterrogated critical questions around the discursive production of sexual subjectivities within postcolonial regimes of visibility. What kind of seeing is permitted? When and by whom? Who has the power to demand to be looked at, to be visible, to read and be read? Clearly not Angela. Instead, she operates in Seizer's imaginary at the level of stereotype, in Homi Bhabha's sense of the word—as the pivot around which Seizer as subject turns to return to a point of total identification.[25] Yet Angela, in a sense, also speaks to the productive "ambivalence" of the stereotype that Bhabha so usefully articulates, operating as a product and production of "the demand for the Negro that the Negro disrupts" (82). Just as she refuses throughout the narrative to be contained by Seizer's disciplinary and regulatory tactics, crossing thresholds and opening closed doors at will, she embodies the "threatened return of the look" that is always embedded within stereotype. Her gaze can be read not solely as that which is called forth and harnessed to conjure Seizer's "lesbian" self into being, but as one that refuses to privilege the "primal scene" of "lesbian" sex as speaking the truth of sexual subjectification in the postcolony and "at home" and instead produces its own set of generative narratives that exceed the discursive and representational boundaries of Seizer's text. Hence, Angela's description of the (not necessarily sexual) activities of the two women as "minting money" echoes Chughtai's strategy of disarticulation in "The Quilt," which ends with the girl narrator stating, "What I saw when the quilt was lifted, I will never tell anyone, not even if they give me a lakh of rupees"(19). The narrator refuses to exchange her recently acquired "knowledge" for money precisely because there is no "truth" to tell; sex is enmeshed in the circulation and consumption of money, food, pleasure, and labor but not—as is the case in Seizer's text— in an economy of visibility, of disclosure and exposure within which "lesbian" identity takes shape. Similarly, Angela's phrase is interesting not because it comments on the scene of "lesbian" sex, as Seizer's reading presumes, but because it fails to replicate the logic of the essay that grants this site/sight its status as privileged signifier.

Diasporic Sexualities

I have focused in such detail on the particular fault lines and fissures of Seizer's text because it provides a useful example of contemporary queer criticism that is profoundly implicated in, and contributes to, the same totalizing discourses around sexuality that it seeks to interrogate. Indeed, it is precisely those narratives that escape intelligibility, representation, or containment within the structures of visuality set in place by Seizer's essay that are opened up by a text such as Chughtai's. Clearly, however, I have not meant to frame "The Quilt" as either a representative or purely redemptive counterhegemonic text that can be placed in absolute opposition to Seizer's article; for Chughtai, desire is hardly utopian but rather is a contradictory and contestatory site of relations of pleasure, work, exploitation, and domination. In positioning Chughtai's narrative as an interlocutory text to Seizer's, I hope to have gestured toward the ways in which even seemingly radical contemporary critical discourses around alterior sexualities are enabled by and work within hegemonic tropes of power and pleasure. What is needed, then, is a more nuanced understanding of the traffic and travel of competing systems of desire in a transnational frame and of how colonial structures of knowing and seeing remain in place within a discourse of an "international" lesbian and gay movement. The necessity for such a theorization becomes all the more apparent when considering, for example, the recent attempt by San Francisco–based organizations to bring an "international" lesbian and gay film festival to Bombay, New Delhi, and Calcutta.[26] The festival was to be funded with the proceeds of what was termed a "queer tour" of India. The brochure advertising the tour promised the following for the intrepid "gay or lesbian traveler" who "want[s] to visit places which are off the beaten track":

> We will visit huge cities and small towns, great monuments and little-known temples. We will drift down the Ganges by night and swim in the Bay of Bengal. We will dine in the shadow of Delhi's Jama Masjid and marvel at the Taj. But most important of all, we will learn about homosexuality in India. From ancient traditions to modern lives. Through the eyes of activists, hijras, and other Indian lesbians and gay men.[27]

The tour and festival exemplify the ways in which globalizing "gay and lesbian" ideologies can be explicitly predicated on orientalist[28] traditions of travel as they play out within a postcolonial context.

I end by offering up a moment of postcolonial and diasporic sexual subjectification that maps an alternative and perhaps more enabling trajectory of travel and movement. I do so while working against a purely celebratory model of diaspora and with an awareness of the ways in which particular notions of diaspora have relied upon gender, class, nationalist, and religious hierarchies.[29] Nevertheless, the dismissal of emerging articulations of diasporic sexualities as simplistic or hopelessly misogynist, classist, essentialist, or Hindu nationalist misses the complexities and multiple, simultaneous significations of such articulations. For instance, in a critique of the 1993 South Asian gay and lesbian anthology *Lotus of Another Color*, Dennis Altman claims that "some homosexuals of Asian origin living in the west seem to make no distinction between their situation and that of people back home."[30] Altman thereby subscribes to and reiterates a conventional construction of diaspora as referencing fixed points of departure and arrival between "home" and "the west" and ignores the challenge posed to precisely such a notion by the intricate web of geographic and political movements and affiliations enacted by queer diasporic South Asians. While it is obviously essential to point out the complicity of queer diasporic practices and subjectivities with hegemonic nationalist and patriarchal structures, such practices are always multivalenced and continue to constitute the cultural site upon which, as Lisa Lowe phrases it, "individuals and collectivities struggle and remember, and in that difficult remembering, imagine and practice both subject and community differently."[31]

An instance of the potentialities of these practices and the subjectivities to which they give rise is evident in a reading of the hit song "Choli Ke Peeche," which was staged in the vastly popular 1993 Hindi movie *Kalnayak* as a scene in which two women (Madhuri Dixit and Nina Gupta) are ostensibly singing and dancing for the male hero of the film (Sanjay Dutt). The song is enacted as a highly eroticized duet between the two women, in which the possibility of female homoerotic desire is both suggested and apparently foreclosed: The women never share the same frame, and the camera repeatedly interrupts their dance sequence by cutting from shots of their bodies to Dutt as he looks on appreciatively. As such, Dutt's spectatorial pleasure and admiring gaze seem to orchestrate the erotic circuits of the scene, yet we can also read the scene as setting up a structure of female homosociality, in which, following Eve Sedgwick's formulation of erotic triangles, female homoerotic desire between Dixit and Gupta is routed and made intelligible through a triangulated relation to the male hero.[32] Such a reading foregrounds the ways in which the conventional heterosexual and gendered staging of the scene is exceeded by the shifting eroticized relations of power between the three characters. As the song progresses, for instance, Dutt's authority as privileged spectator is consistently undercut: Rather than embodying a virile and potent masculinity, he appears oddly ineffectual, offering Dixit money only to have her throw it back in his face and then grab it away when he least expects it. Not only does the sexual availability of the two women elude Dutt's monetary control, but it spins out of his spectatorial control as well. The song's chorus, repeated suggestively by the gyrating heroines, translates from Hindi as "What's under your *choli* (blouse)? What's under your *chuniri* (scarf)?" Evoking Chughtai's use of the quilt, these questions initially seem to reference a sexual economy of secrecy and disclosure, a promise of the truth of sex that lies underneath the *chuniri* and the *choli*, waiting to be uncovered. However, as with Chughtai's text, the song also refuses to grant the listener/viewer scopic satisfaction and ends by answering its repeated question with the line "My heart is in my blouse, underneath my *chuniri*, and I'll give it to you, my lover, my love." This apparently anticlimactic ending again echoes Chughtai's text, in that it gestures to an economy of desire and pleasure that exceeds fixed framings of sexuality within dominant regimes of visibility. By the scene's end, Dutt is reduced to cupping his hand behind his ear in the hopes of catching the song's final phrase, while Dixit disappears behind a screen.

The eruption of nonnormative erotic and gender configurations within sites of extreme heteronormativity that can be read in *Kalnayak* is rendered remarkably explicit in another recent Hindi film (also starring Dixit), *Hum Aapke Hain Koun*. The film's main musical number takes place during a women-only celebration of a marriage and an upcoming birth. Into this space of female homosociality enters a woman cross-dressed as the film's male hero, in a white suit identical to his, who proceeds to dance suggestively with Dixit and other women. What follows is an elaborate dance sequence in which the cross-dressed woman and Dixit engage in a teasing, sexualized exchange that parodies the trappings of conventional middle-class Hindu family arrangements (marriage, heterosexuality, domesticity, motherhood). Their performance brings to the fore the female homoeroticism hinted at in *Kalnayak*; as in "The Quilt," female same-sex pleasure and desire—in Patel's apt phrase—"queries and queers" the site of home and marriage and its fantasies of middle-class domestic respectability. It is precisely this emergence of queer desire at the interstices of heterosexuality and colliding class, caste, gender, and sexual ideologies—so apparent in Chughtai's story—that queer diasporic cultural practices seize upon and put into circulation; the song "Choli Ke Peeche," for instance, has become a staple at parties and in drag performances within South Asian queer spaces in multiple diasporic locations. Indeed, the intersecting trajectories of exchange and influence, affiliation and affect,[33] among queer diasporic sites that can be charted through the use of such popular cultural artifacts by queer diasporic South Asians are utterly unintelligible in the imaginary landscape of a text such as Seizer's. Clearly the "queer diaspora" that is called into existence by such cultural practices is far from a transcendent or egalitarian liberatory space; rather it is one marked by multiple power hierarchies, the "scattered hegemonies" against and through which the category of sexuality in the context of transnational cultures must be read.[34] It is only by considering these diasporic trajectories of movement and their intersections with various hegemonies that an adequate theorization of alterior sexual subjectification within postcolonial regimes of visibility and identity can take place.

Notes

I have benefited tremendously from the constant enthusiasm and support of Judith Halberstam throughout the writing of this essay; I thank her for countless conversations and editorial insights. I am also grateful to Geeta Patel for sharing her work with me and am especially indebted to Rosalind Morris and Rosemary George for their generous comments and suggestions, many of which I have incorporated here.

1. Ismat Chughtai, *The Quilt and Other Stories*, trans. Tahira Naqvi and Syeda Hameed (New Delhi, India: Kali for Women Press, 1992).
2. I use the term *alterior* to suggest a range of nonheteronormative practices and desires that may not necessarily coalesce around categories of identity.
3. Rosalind Morris, "Three Sexes and Four Sexualities: Redressing the Discourses of Gender and Sexuality in Contemporary Thailand," *Positions* 2 no. 2 (Spring 1994), p. 16.
4. Susan Seizer, "Paradoxes of Visibility in the Field: Rites of Queer Passage in Anthropology," *Public Culture* 8 no. 1 (1995), pp. 73–100.
5. Theorists such as Teresa de Lauretis and Judith Butler, even while arguing against the immutability of epistemic categories such as "lesbian," still see such categories as embedded within particular identity structures in the west and take as their implicit (or explicit) starting points a Euro-American desiring subject.
6. Eve Kosofsky Sedgwick, *Epistemology of the Closet* (Berkeley: University of California Press, 1990), p. 71. Of course, Sedgwick deliberately limits her field of inquiry to Euro-American texts and makes claims only about these. Nevertheless, Sedgwick's formulation of "the closet" and concurrent tropes of silence and invisibility have become totalizing narratives in theorizing queer existence. Little attention has been paid to the different tropes of spacialization at work among differently raced lesbian and gay subjects within, say, a U.S. context. Anthropologist Martin Manalansan, for instance, has argued that notions of "coming out" and "the closet" are inadequate in narrativizing queer identity among gay Filipino men both in New York City and in the Philippines, where sexuality is always refracted through experiences of immigration. See Martin Manalansan, "In the Shadows of Stonewall: Examining Gay/Lesbian Transnational Politics and the Diasporic Dilemma," *GLQ* 2 (1995), pp. 1–14.
7. For instance, the narrator comments, "I can say that if someone touched me continuously like this, I would certainly rot," and later, "Imagining the friction caused by this prolonged rubbing made me slightly sick"(11).
8. See Susie Tharu and K. Lalitha, eds., *Women Writing in India, Volume II: The Twentieth Century* (New York: The Feminist Press, 1993), p. 135.
9. As Elizabeth Grosz and others have argued, psychoanalytic discourse as articulated by Freud and Lacan has thought of "desire, like female sexuality itself, as an absence, lack, or hole, an abyss seeking to be engulfed, stuffed to satisfaction." See Grosz, "Refiguring Lesbian Desire," in *The Lesbian Postmodern*, ed. Laura Doane (New York: Columbia University Press, 1994), p. 71.
10. As Geeta Patel comments, "The women in ['The Quilt'] do not 'become' lesbians even though they engage in physical activities with each other. This form of

not being a lesbian . . . raises the question about where (in what national/cultural/historical sites) performance needs to be located in order for it to produce 'identity.'" See Geeta Patel, "Homely Housewives Run Amok: Lesbians in Marital Fixes," unpublished essay, p. 10.

11. See Valerie Traub, "Ambiguities of Lesbian Viewing Pleasure: The (Dis)articulations of *Black Widow*," in *Body Guards: The Cultural Politics of Ambiguity*, eds. Julia Epstein and Kristina Straub (New York: Routledge, 1991), p. 311.

12. A number of theorists have explored the linkages in Euro-American medico-moral and other discourses between various paradigmatic figures of female sexual transgression, such as the prostitute, the "lesbian" or female invert, and the working-class female. See, for example, Judith Walkowitz's *The City of Dreadful Delight: Narratives of Sexual Danger in Late-Victorian London* (Chicago: University of Chicago Press, 1992).

13. The way in which this masculinization of desiring female subjects in the text may intersect with western sexological discourse on Indian female sexuality remains to be further examined. Havelock Ellis, for instance, noted that sex between women, which he deemed particularly prevalent in India, is practiced by women endowed with the penetrative power of enlarged clitorises. See Havelock Ellis, *Studies in the Psychology of Sex* (New York: Random House, 1908), p. 208.

14. D. A. Miller, "Anal Rope," in *Inside/Out: Lesbian Theories, Gay Theories*, ed. Diana Fuss (New York: Routledge, 1991), p. 130.

15. Judith Butler, *Bodies That Matter: On the Discursive Limits of "Sex"* (New York, Routledge, 1993), p. 162.

16. A few recent examples of transnational and cross-cultural work on sexuality include *Out in the Field: Reflections of Lesbian and Gay Anthropologists*, eds. Ellen Lewin and William Leap (Urbana: University of Illinois Press, 1996); *Taboo: Sex, Identity and Erotic Subjectivity in Anthropological Fieldwork*, eds. Don Kulick and Margaret Willson (New York: Routledge, 1995); Katie King, "Local and Global: AIDS Activism and Feminist Theory," *Camera Obscura* 28 (1992), pp. 79–98.

17. See Don Kulick, "Introduction: The Sexual Life of Anthropologists: Erotic Subjectivity and Ethnographic Work," in Kulick and Willson, pp. 1–28.

18. See Evelyn Blackwood, "Falling in Love with An-Other Lesbian: Reflections on Identity in Fieldwork." In Kulick and Willson, pp. 51–75.

19. This is witnessed, for instance, in the 1994 Stonewall anniversary march, which was couched as an international human rights initiative, as well as in the burgeoning number of international lesbian and gay human rights groups.

20. Partha Chatterjee, for instance, argues that the anticolonial nationalist elite of preindependence India created an "inner" sphere as its hegemonic space, one that existed outside the workings of the colonial state. The figure of the woman came to embody this space of an essential, immovable "Indian" identity or tradition. See Chatterjee, *The Nation and Its Fragments* (Princeton: Princeton University Press, 1993), p. 133. Patel holds that Chughtai's critique of the notion of women as desexualized and static markers of "tradition" had much to do with the charges of obscenity leveled against "The Quilt" upon its publication.

21. Patel, p. 7.

22. I mean "queer" here to denote, as Judith Halberstam phrases it, "a postmodern, postidentity politics focused on but not limited to sexual minorities." See

Judith Halberstam, "Imagined Violence/Queer Violence: Representation, Rage and Resistance," *Social Text* 37 (1993), p. 196.

23. Seizer's discomfort here echoes the writings of Euro-American women in the turn-of-the-century colonial Philippines, which Vicente Rafael critiques. Rafael describes the ways in which those writings depict the scrutinizing gazes of the natives as making White women's bodies strange and uncanny, "irresistible objects of native curiosity." By reversing their sense of displacement back onto native bodies, American women turn native bodies into "objects that occasion the emergence of a White female agency capable of representing itself amid the dislocating forces of imperial history." See Vicente Rafael, "Colonial Domesticity: White Women and United States Rule in the Philippines," *American Literature* 67 no. 4 (1995), pp. 639–666.

24. Such a rendering of Angela as sulky, sullen, suspicious, and truculent—as both infantile and vaguely threatening—resonates with stock descriptions of "native" servants within colonial discourse. See Rafael, pp. 656–657.

25. See Homi Bhabha, "The Other Question: Stereotype, Discrimination and the Discourse of Colonialism," in *The Location of Culture* (New York: Routledge, 1994), p. 76.

26. The organizers of "India: The Queer View," as the 1994 festival and tour were dubbed, were Trikone (a South Asian lesbian and gay organization), the International Lesbian and Gay Human Rights Commission, and Frameline.

27. "India: The Queer View" brochure, 1994.

28. I use *orientalist* in Edward Said's sense of the term, as referring to an enumerative, homogenizing, and managing discourse of "occidental representations . . . which both constitute the Orient as Other to the Occident, and appropriate the domain of the Orient by speaking for it." See Lisa Lowe, *Critical Terrains: French and British Orientalisms* (Ithaca: Cornell University Press, 1991), p. 3.

29. See, for example, Gayatri Gopinath, "'Bombay, U.K., Yuba City': Bhangra Music and the Engendering of Diaspora," *Diaspora* 4 no. 3 (1995), pp. 303–322; Amarpal K. Dhaliwal, "Reading Diaspora: Self-Representational Practices and the Politics of Representation," *Socialist Review* 24 no.4 (1994), pp. 13–44; Stefan Helmreich, "Kinship, Nation, and Paul Gilroy's Concept of Diaspora," *Diaspora* 2 no. 2 (1992): 243–249.

30. Dennis Altman, "Rupture or Continuity? The Internationalisation of Gay Identities," *Social Text*, 48 (Fall 1996), p. 90.

31. Lisa Lowe, *Immigrant Acts: On Asian American Cultural Politics* (Durham, North Carolina: Duke University Press, 1996), p. 3.

32. See Eve Kosofsky Sedgwick, *Between Men: English Literature and Male Homosocial Desire* (New York: Columbia University Press, 1985), pp. 21–27.

33. I borrow these terms from Paul Gilroy, *The Black Atlantic: Modernity and Double Consciousness* (Cambridge, Mass.: Harvard University Press, 1993), p. 16.

34. See Inderpal Grewal and Caren Kaplan, "Introduction: Transnational Feminist Practices and the Questions of Postmodernity," in *Scattered Hegemonies: Postmodernity and Transnational Feminist Practices* (Minneapolis: University of Minnesota Press, 1994), pp. 17–19.

Works Cited

Altman, Dennis. "Rupture or Continuity? The Internationalisation of Gay Identities." *Social Text* 48 (Fall 1996), pp. 77–94.

Bhabha, Homi. *The Location of Culture.* New York: Routledge, 1994.

Blackwood, Evelyn. "Falling in Love with An-Other Lesbian: Reflections on Identity in Fieldwork." In Don Kulick and Margaret Willson, eds. *Taboo: Sex, Identity and Erotic Subjectivity in Anthropological Fieldwork*, pp. 51–75. New York: Routledge, 1995.

Butler, Judith. *Bodies That Matter: On the Discursive Limits of "Sex."* New York: Routledge, 1993.

Chatterjee, Partha. *The Nation and Its Fragments.* Princeton: Princeton University Press, 1993.

Chughtai, Ismat. *The Quilt and Other Stories.* Translated by Tahira Naqvi and Syeda Hameed. New Delhi, India: Kali for Women Press, 1992.

Ellis, Havelock. *Studies in the Psychology of Sex.* New York: Random House, 1908.

Gilroy, Paul. *The Black Atlantic: Modernity and Double Consciousness.* Cambridge, Mass.: Harvard University Press, 1993.

Grewal, Inderpal and Caren Kaplan, eds. *Scattered Hegemonies: Postmodernity and Transnational Feminist Practices.* Minneapolis: University of Minnesota Press, 1994.

Grosz, Elizabeth. "Refiguring Lesbian Desire." In Laura Doane, ed. *The Lesbian Postmodern*, pp. 67–84. New York: Columbia University Press, 1994.

Halberstam, Judith. "Imagined Violence/Queer Violence: Representation, Rage and Resistance." *Social Text* 37 (1993): 193–207.

Kulick, Don, and Margaret Willson, eds. *Taboo: Sex, Identity and Erotic Subjectivity in Anthropological Fieldwork.* New York: Routledge, 1995.

Lowe, Lisa. *Critical Terrains: French and British Orientalisms.* Ithaca: Cornell University Press, 1991.

_____. *Immigrant Acts: On Asian American Cultural Politics.* Durham, N.C.: Duke University Press, 1996.

Manalansan, Martin. "In the Shadows of Stonewall: Examining Gay/Lesbian Transnational Politics and the Diasporic Dilemma." *GLQ* 2 (1995): 1–14.

Miller, D. A. "Anal Rope." In Diana Fuss, ed. *Inside/Out: Lesbian Theories, Gay Theories*, pp. 119–141. New York: Routledge, 1991.

Morris, Rosalind. "Three Sexes and Four Sexualities: Redressing the Discourses of Gender and Sexuality in Contemporary Thailand." *Positions* 2(2) (1994): 15–43.

Patel, Geeta. "Homely Housewives Run Amok: Lesbians in Marital Fixes." Unpublished essay, 1995.

Rafael, Vicente. "Colonial Domesticity: White Women and United States Rule in the Philippines." *American Literature* 67(4) (1995): 639–666.

Sedgwick, Eve. *Between Men: English Literature and Male Homosocial Desire.* New York: Columbia University Press, 1995.

_____. *Epistemology of the Closet.* Berkeley: University of California Press, 1990.

Seizer, Susan. "Paradoxes of Visibility in the Field: Rites of Queer Passage." *Public Culture* 8(1) (1995): 73–100.

Tharu, Susie, and K. Lalitha, eds. *Women Writing in India, Volume II: The Twentieth Century*. New York: The Feminist Press, 1993.

Traub, Valerie. "The Ambiguities of 'Lesbian' Viewing Pleasure: The (Dis)articulations of *Black Widow*." In Julia Epstein and Kristina Straub, eds. *Body Guards: The Cultural Politics of Gender Ambiguity*, pp. 305–328. New York: Routledge, 1993.

Part Two

DomestiCity: Redrawing Urban Space

Chapter Six

Reconstructed Identity: Spatial Change and Adaptation in a Greek-Macedonian Refugee Neighborhood

DAYANA SALAZAR

In 1923 Greece was flooded with a million and a half refugees from Asia Minor, increasing the country's population by one-third and transforming a multireligious, multiracial, multilingual society into an exclusively Greek Christian Orthodox one.[1]

The presence of refugees in mainland Greece was the unfortunate result of competing Turkish and Greek nationalist and expansionist policies during the first two decades of the twentieth century. Under the auspices of the Allied powers, the young Greek and Turkish states signed the Lausanne Treaty, calling for the compulsory exchange of their populations using faith as sole indicator of nationality.[2] These events were to end 3,000 years of Greek life in Asia Minor, resulting not in a repatriation but rather in a deportation into exile of Orthodox Christian Turks to Greece and of Muslim Greeks to Turkey.[3]

The refugees were thrown into the midst of the national image-building endeavors common in the Balkans and the Near East during the nineteenth and early twentieth centuries. Young states were zealously engaged in promoting symbols and artifacts designed to invest these countries with distinctive identities, different from those of their neighbors and the old Ottoman guardian, thereby manufacturing a sense of legitimacy for otherwise fluid and arbitrary national boundaries.

Nations as imagined communities "are to be distinguished, not by their falsity/genuineness, but by the *style* in which they are imagined" (emphasis added).[4] Since there is no such thing as a delivered national presence, but a *re-presence* or a *representation*, we must look at the message's *style* and method of dispersion, rather than its correctness or its fidelity to some "great original."[5] The representation of a national identity relies upon institutions, traditions, conventions, and codes of understanding for its transmission. The language and style of the national message thus gain a heightened importance, since only those who speak that language well and understand its style are fully welcomed into the imagined community.[6] To comprehend the style of Greek nationalism, we need to examine closely the method used to propagate a proposed national culture in the form of its invented tradition.

An imagined community, as a concept, exists through the tacit implication of its opposite, a "natural community," and their respective styles of representation therefore need to be understood through a similar juxtaposition: If a new tradition is used to represent the invented national culture, then custom corresponds to a living collective memory.[7]

The construction of buildings and cities (along with music, literature, theater, and the arts in general) has traditionally been used as a vehicle to represent and propagate a national conscience.[8] I examine here Architecture (with a capital *A*) and building (with a lowercase *b*) as modes of self-representation. The former corresponds to the "high culture" of building, created and promulgated from the national center by a professional design elite, trained and conversant in the neoclassic European architectural tradition.[9] The latter is embodied in vernacular building traditions that are tried and refined locally for centuries.

Nations as political units are designed and presented as "homogeneous" entities, each one a group of people sharing a common history, common values, and a common culture as defined by the ruling elite. The few commonalities between constituent groups are therefore stressed and differences suppressed in pursuit of a national facade. In an attempt to create a national high culture and purge all "foreign"—read Turkish or oriental—influences, the cultural heritage of Asia Minor Greeks was actively repressed by the central government in Athens. The diversity of the Ottoman Empire was thus sacrificed to the altar of national ethnic and cultural homogeneity.

In an attempt to uncover the identity of those who were assumedly being represented in the Greek national building program, we must examine closely the refugee experience. Assimilation, in reality, did not occur as smoothly as envisioned and promulgated from the national center. Instead, refugees *(heterochthons)* as well as natives *(autochthons)* perpetuated a perception of belonging to dissimilar, and perhaps even incompatible, social groups.[10]

The feeling of enmity toward Turkey was not gratuitous but was rather the planned result of continued exposure to political propaganda disseminated through the media and of an educational system preaching a narrow nationalistic view of history. Turkey, as the modern heir of the Ottoman Empire, became the living symbol of oppression of the Greek nation, stagnation, and corruption of Greece's superior national identity—an identity defined in opposition to the Other's image. Turkey, for the Greeks, embodied their collective enemy, the "Other." As a consequence of the prevalent anti-Turkish sentiment, the refugees' cultural baggage was condemned to remain a subculture.[11] Hence, refugees were relegated to the margins of the Greek social, economic, political, and educational systems.[12]

Despite this official antagonism, urban refugee culture was created and re-created uninterruptedly throughout decades of hostility and discrimination. By examining the refugee experience, I intend to document the quiet voice of resistance, the challenge of a "high," or national, culture from the margins, by the "low," or local, culture, as found in the living testimony of the domestic and neighborhood space emerging from the compact social fabric of the urban refugees from Asia Minor.

I trace high culture through the neoclassic or classic revival—read European or western—national program officially adopted and promoted by the Greek state in public architecture and urbanism. Evidence of refugee "low culture" is to be found in the living testimony of the residential space of the refugee neighborhood of Dekaokto and in its adaptation to the regional urban space and building conventions.

Dekaokto was built by the Greek government as part of the refugee settlement effort in the northern Aegean port of Kaválla. Kaválla, the second largest city in Greek Macedonia after Thessaloníki, has an extraordinary tradition of diversity and is a prime indicator of the demographic impact of the population exchange in Greece.[13] Ever since the refugees occupied Dekaokto, neighborhood space has been gradually appropriated and modified to fit a group memory in an attempt to re-create the life left behind in Asia Minor.

Dekaokto presents an ideal opportunity for a case study of this opposition, since underneath years of alterations, its basic fabric has remained essentially legible, allowing us to trace the degree of change versus the degree of permanence in this setting compared with the radical transformation of neighborhoods all over Greece. Change and permanence in Dekaokto are manifestations of a search for an identity rooted far away in time and place, and its result is the creative adaptation of neighborhood and domestic space to the needs of the community. Change in Dekaokto emerges from the need for a balance between "continuity and breaks in continuity, between tradition and transformation."[14]

Dekaokto emerged from a single particular historic and political event, and its process of transformation illustrates a group's search for identity through the control of its physical space, in opposition to a strong central government's attempt to impose its own pattern. From Dekaokto's experience, we learn that the search for a sense of community and communal identity follows a road of its own—parallel to, independent of, and even opposed to that of the search for a national high culture. Dekaokto's search proved to be more pervasive and adaptable than the national cultural program promoted by the state.

The Neoclassic Universalist Program

Most of the nations emerging from the disintegrating Ottoman Empire during the nineteenth and early twentieth centuries developed their own versions of local versus universalizing (namely westernizing) trends. In Greece, two competing nationalist programs claimed to represent the true essence of the Greek nation but ultimately were manipulated to perpetuate or secure their respective champion elite's power.[15]

National consciousness as envisioned originally by a cultural elite infects and affects last the popular masses—and subcultures such as the urban refugees from Asia Minor.[16] The Greek intellectual elite chose to advocate the ancient Greek classical tradition as the style of representation of the new nation, seeking to identify it closely with the west and warmly welcoming nineteenth-century European ideology.[17] The European facade finally won the contest. In a world divided in two, east and west, Greece sought to associate itself with Europe.[18] All things western represented order, reason, cleanliness, liberty, science, humanism, nationalism, power—in other words, the superiority of the descendants of the Greeks. On the other hand, the Orient was represented as the "Other"—irrational, immature, picturesque, exotic, and strange—and above all as the locus of oppression of the Greek nation. The young Greek state and its ruling elite chose to sever the indelible immediate and remote historical ties with the eastern and southern Mediterranean in pursuit of a more recently manufactured association with the north.[19]

And what was more appropriate to represent western ideals than neoclassicism? In Greece the language and the image of neoclassicism were appropriated as an "iconographical bridge" that provided an apparent historical continuum with ancient Greece, thus giving a sense of validity to the claim to fatherland and culture.[20] Neoclassicism moved in promptly to displace traditional architectural forms. Regional building typologies and all forms of popular expression labeled Turkish by the state authorities were openly discouraged and replaced with western models.[21] Traditional building methods continued to be used only on the periphery of the state, while in the cities ideological and cultural pressures led to the introduction, the dissemination, and ultimately the triumph of neoclassicism.[22]

Neoclassicism fitted neatly within the hellenizing plans of the newly created Greek kingdom, promoted officially by its first monarch, Otto, who called himself "King of the Hellenes"—in reference to the ancient empire—rather than "King of Greece."[23]

Thus, the logical choice for representing the Greek national heritage was Greek Revival architecture, a branch of European neoclassicism already in vogue in all the major European capitals.[24] Revivalists advocated the faithful reproduction of ancient Greek architectural language, orders—Doric, Ionic, and Corinthian—and ornamental motifs in contemporary construction. They were concerned with the restoration of strict proportions, symmetry, balance, and the coherence of abstract design. They advocated pure geometrical forms emphasizing volumetric clarity and the sparing application of ornament and insisted on tying together all the elements of a building with crowning entablatures (architraves, cornices, and friezes) and other devices. Clinging to discipline and rule, Greek Revival architecture may be the strictest of all versions of neoclassicism, generating buildings that are solid, severe, and rigid.

Neoclassic—or monumental—civic design language is found in the "noble planning" of infinite vistas, arrogantly oversized monuments, and an exaggerated sense of grandeur and scale. Centralized power, in fact, was the ideal; architecture and urbanism became its image and its symbol. This language was strategically applied to the highly visible public realm—along public spaces, in public buildings and monuments, and throughout the overall trace of main cities.

Gradually, Greece entered a growing competition of nationalist symbols and power, mirrored in the large-scale building and rebuilding of capital cities. In December 1834 Athens was chosen as the new capital over the more developed port of Salonika to the north—today's Thessaloníki. Salonika lost her natural position as capital of the Greek state because of the "oriental" flavor of the city, embodied in a large multiethnic population and built structures inherited from Ottoman times. When it became the national capital, Athens was just a township of a few thousand with a small church and a few solid Turkish houses in the Plaka, the foothills of the ancient Acropolis.[25] However, it was soon to be turned into a "Paris of the Levant."[26]

The reconstruction of Athens followed principles similar to those behind monumental civic design projects already well established in European capitals. The immediate model for all of these interventions was invariably Baron Georges-Eugène Haussmann's reconstruction of Paris with avenues and monuments lining the entire city, cutting across the tight medieval fabric of the city.

During Otto's reign (1833 to 1862), public administrative buildings, hospitals, schools, churches, private houses, and villas were erected around public squares and connected with Parisian-style boulevards. The road system that serves the center of the city today was shaped during that time period.

King Otto's royal palace was designed in an austere neo-Grecian style by his German father's principal architect, Friedrich von Gartner. The palace, which now houses the Greek Parliament, was for a long time the only impressive building in Athens.[27] The university, initially housed in a large mansion in Plaka, was built by a Danish architect in classical style. Mansions for the westernized elite and royal palaces for subsequent monarchs, such as the palace of Saint Michael and Saint George in Corfu, followed suit.

Refugee Housing

The construction of refugee housing itself was used as a vehicle for implementing the Greek nationalist program and as an opportunity to speed up the modernization of the Greek state. The antioriental, modernizing policy behind the refugee housing settlement was described by Pentzopoulos:

> The refugee quarters, with their neat, practical houses and their wide streets, contrasted vividly with the old neighborhoods dominated by the oriental-type dwellings. "It is no exaggeration to say," wrote Sir John Campbell [first vice chair of the Refugee Settlement Commission from 1924 to 1927], "that when visiting the refugee quarters in the majority of the towns in Macedonia and Thrace, one steps from the seventeenth to the twentieth century."[28]

To cope with the need to shelter masses of refugees, the Greek government applied a general scheme of urban settlement by building dwellings on the outskirts of the main cities, where job opportunities were greater.[29] Refugees were also relocated into the houses left behind by expatriated Muslims.

This policy placed a great deal of pressure on Athens, Piraiévs, Salonika, and Kaválla. As the center of the Greek tobacco industry, Kaválla attracted a floating population from throughout Greece, who flocked to the city in the hope of finding work, making it difficult for refugees to secure employment there.[30]

Housing needed to be provided for the refugees who, upon arrival in Kaválla, were settled in mass outdoor facilities and warehouses immediately surrounding the harbor area. Even though the shelters were considered temporary accommodations, most refugees remained in them for about six months and even up to a year.[31] Three refugee housing projects were built by the Greek government in what were the outskirts of Kaválla between 1926 and 1927: Dekaokto, Pentakosia, and Horafa.[32] From the beginning, these refugee neighborhoods became the locus of a subculture with strongly defined social boundaries.

Dekaokto is perched on mountainous terrain overlooking the Aegean Sea, two kilometers to the northwest of the city's central business district. It is clearly representative of a refugee settlement, distinctive from the homogenized fabric of the remainder of the city, where modernization has taken a heavy toll. Because of Dekaokto's topographical predominance on the northern hills of Kaválla, the neighborhood's tile-covered roofs are visible from afar, providing a contrast to the rest of the city, which is generally characterized by five- to six-story apartment buildings with metal and concrete balconies alongside their facades.

Three typical types of housing units were built originally in Dekaokto: types A, B, C1, and C1's two-story variation, C2 (Figure 6.1). These spartan structures follow a rigorous tripartite composition with a distinct base, body, and roof definition. The facade plane is arranged symmetrically alongside vertical axes. The overall mass of the house follows a strict geometric ratio formula for each of its composite parts. The pyramidal volume of the roof acts as a cornice of sorts, tying together all the subvolumes of the house. The closed planes, or solid walls, dominate over the openings, or voids, generating an enclosed, introspected volume with a nearly hermetic external "skin." The discipline and regular spacing of the narrow vertical fenestration pattern is interrupted only by the building's framing moldings, which are the only detail added to the essentially bare volume of the house. All of these features invest Dekaokto's original housing units with a distinctive neoclassic flavor, though the style was scaled down to fit the meager available resources and the state of emergency surrounding the birth of this neighborhood.

The trace of the settlement reflects a neoclassic language as well, with wide, straight streets surrounding rectangular building blocks. Axial roads cutting straight against steep slopes were laid out to celebrate a grand entrance to the neighborhood and to generate uninterrupted vistas terminating in public buildings. Open central areas perched on the rugged terrain were reserved with the hope they would be developed in time as the refugees settled. Consistent with the principles of monumental civic design, these central squares were intended to be used for public events, for the congregation of citizens to partake of public life and to glorify the state and its power.

The units built in Dekaokto provided shelter for approximately eight hundred families. Plots surrounding the original core and in between

134

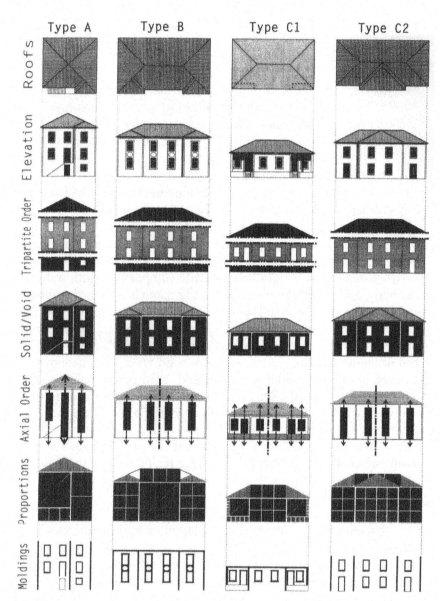

FIGURE 6.1   *Original House Types, Dekaokto*

blocks were left open and built individually only in years to come. Given the structure of refugee settlement efforts, most houses were not sold but rented to the settlers until recently. Even when the titles were straightened out and houses could be sold to the settlers, many simply refused to pay the nominal sum for their titles, since for most urban refugees these housing units constituted the only compensation for everything they had lost in the exodus.

Partly due to that legal entanglement of ownership patterns, only 11 percent of the original units have been entirely replaced with new structures (Figure 6.2, part i). Of the remaining 89 percent of the structures, 53 percent are practically the same as when they were built in the 1920s, and 36 percent have undergone some change, ranging from minor window alterations (Figure 6.2, part k) to two-story cement-and-metal verandas wrapped around the entire length of the facade (Figure 6.2, part c). Hence, most of the original houses and the urban fabric of Dekaokto have remained essentially identifiable even after over thirty years of small-scale modifications. Dekaokto's private realm, the housing environment, remains recognizable through decades of transformation.

In Search of an "Open" State Through Adaptation

Ever since their arrival, residents of Dekaokto have been modifying their houses in search of a sense of "openness" as well as increased functional space. Initially, overcrowding was the main driving force behind these changes. Several families were assigned to live in one unit, sharing the kitchen and sanitary facilities. A family of as many as eight to ten people was given one room to live in. The situation remained practically unchanged for over twenty years until the mid-fifties, when a number of refugee families were given land in the suburb of Kalamitsa, one kilometer to the west of Dekaokto.[33]

As in most of Greece, the dowry system adds to the need for space in refugee neighborhoods, placing social pressure on parents to provide independent living quarters for their marrying daughters.[34] Usually, the only way to accomplish this is by subdividing and expanding the family house, which in many instances is the family's most valuable asset. The inflated value of the dwellings has its roots in the endemic housing shortages and soaring land values in major urban centers all over Greece ever since the population exchange of 1923. Until the mid-1970s, land speculation and the construction sector, especially housing, were the main force behind urban growth in Greece.[35]

Population density and the dowry system placed tremendous pressure on the residents to expand their original units, further entangling the already complex landownership patterns in the neighborhood. Rooms sprout on

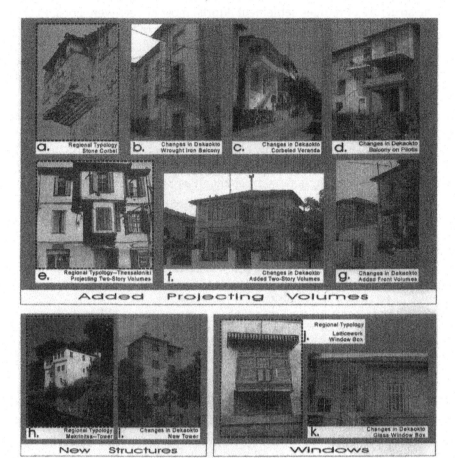

FIGURE 6.2 *Changes and the Sahnisin, Dekaokto*

second stories all throughout Dekaokto (Figure 6.2, part f), and added sheds encroach onto the street and the backyards in the interior of the blocks (Figure 6.2, part g) to satisfy a need to expand the interior space of the houses.

However, mere functional need leaves unexplained an aspect of these changes: a sense of individual and collective identity that the original, state-built units were incapable of fulfilling. "Some newcomers had been dissatisfied with their state-erected dwellings; their stereotyped and plain architecture had insulted the exiles' sense of individualism and beauty."[36]

In the midst of the disintegration of their old lives and finding themselves in a foreign, hostile land, the refugees turned to their memories of an idealized life in the lost paradise of Asia Minor as a means to reconstruct their fragmented social structures.

The refugees needed to re-create the old home in a myriad of ways, through their neighborhood space and life, their domestic architecture, their music, their dance, their social and religious rituals, their literature, and so on. This re-creation served as a bridge to a severed way of life and provided a vehicle for establishing a sense of continuity amidst the chaos of resettlement. Among all these types of re-creation, the spatial reconstruction of the neighborhood played a capital role in the establishment of connections to the new land. As a form of self-representation, this re-creation lay on the most visible public areas of the neighborhood, its streets, and extended to the interface between the private interior space of the house and the neighborhood street—the house's facade and the space immediately in front of it.

This reconstruction was modeled after neighborhood life in the *mahalles*, the different ethnic quarters in the Ottoman Empire. Refugee neighborhoods, places, streets, and landmark buildings were named after neighborhoods, places, streets, and buildings in the Asia Minor homeland in an attempt to reestablish a familiar geography based on common points of reference.[37]

Today's refugee neighborhoods, the legacy of the *mahalles*, are structured around a series of symbolic oppositions. These "open" and "closed" states are described in detail by Reneé Hirschon in *Heirs of the Greek Catastrophe*, a study of refugee social structures in Piraiévs. "Open" is a "positive, inclusive state, denoting a communal mode of orientation, open interaction, sociability, new life, continuity, luck, light, and the divine realm," and "closed" is a negative state denoting "exclusive bonds and closure, isolation, confinement, deprivation." We find instances of these symbolic orientations in verbal metaphors: Young girls are encouraged to "marry and open a house," and the house is "closed" when sons die or men are absent. These symbolic orientations extend to the perception of other physical spaces as well. For example, rural Greek villages were thought of as inward looking ("closed"), and in contrast, Asia Minor towns were centers of contact, exchange, and variety ("open" to the world).[38]

The "open" and "closed" states are reflected spatially in the nested public and private realms of the neighborhood and their corresponding gendered boundaries. At the core we find the private "closed" space of the home, the ultimate female realm, with strongly confined boundaries. Enveloping the home we find a zone of transition, its interface and point of contact with the world of the neighborhood; it is here where we find the most significant modifications to the houses, since the structure's original hermetic facade plane could not support the required flexible, permeable boundary. Adjacent to the transitional zone, neighborhood space is "open" to everyone, male and female, young and old, in its streets and niches. The neighborhood's boundaries with the public realm outside the community are fluid yet ambiguous: "open" for men and "closed" for women. And finally, beyond the neighborhood lies the public space "open" to the world beyond the neighborhood, an exclusively male realm.

Residents have adapted their individual houses for reasons that go beyond a practical search for space. Through residents' choice of forms, locations, proportions, and materials, Dekaokto's houses have been brought closer, step by step, to the regional vernacular typology of the *sahnisin,* or corbeled architecture.

The *sahnisin* employs mostly wooden or stone bracket supports (Figure 6.2, part a) that allow upper rooms to take a functional rectangular shape and that increase the floor area to a maximum in often irregular urban sites. The room itself is often extended over the street or the garden on consoles or corbels and sometimes even on columns, or *pilotis.* As a result, streets are lined with upper rooms jutting out under wide eaves to create shade and rows of windows projecting as if "hungry for the view and for fresh air."[39]

Different sources attribute the origins and the "creative ownership" of the domestic building typology of the *sahnisin* to different nations, including Greece, Turkey, Bulgaria, and the former republic of Yugoslavia, according to the personal affiliations of the author.[40] This suggests that the typology itself transcends arbitrary national territorial boundaries and therefore that its application still carries meaning to a variety of builders and users who perpetuate this building tradition across borders. It is unlikely, nevertheless, that the prototype of the *sahnisin* lies with the origins of the Ottoman Empire, since private property and the sense of a home were not particularly pursued by the Ottomans or the nomadic Selçuks before them; the real home of the sultan and his *vezirs* was a tent.[41]

It is likely, though, that the *sahnisin* developed to its height during Byzantine times and was then adopted and adapted via the Ottoman *konak,* an urban multistoried house. The typical Byzantine house was narrow and tall, two or three stories in height, with the upper stories always projecting farther than the ground floor and supported by wooden corbels or brackets. These projections also resulted in the extensive use of bay windows—a feature that was widely repeated later in houses of the Ottoman period. In the stone houses of the Phanar, the usual curved wooden bracketed support takes the form of a stone corbel that has been cut in curves (Figure 6.2, part a).[42]

Most of the houses were built by groups of traveling builders (*bouloukia* or *isnafs*). The members of those mason's guilds came from mountainous and usually poor areas, such as western Macedonia, northern Epirus, Langadia, and Kárpathos. Highly mobile, these craftsmen became familiar with the architecture of the different regions of the empire. They were in charge of continuing and disseminating a collective building tradition throughout the Ottoman Empire. Hence, the typology of the *sahnisin* and its construction methods are found throughout the Balkans and Greece just as much as in Anatolia.[43]

The millenary existence of the *sahnisin* was abruptly interrupted after independence and the installation of the first Greek kingdom. Urban legislation imposed by the Bavarian rule of Otto I prohibited the creation of these regional architectural forms. The Bavarian law was soon followed by town-planning legislation that precluded cantilevered and other regional architectural forms and actively favored the language of neoclassicism.[44]

After its near extinction throughout urban Greece, the *sahnisin* resurfaced in unexpected ways in Dekaokto. However, instead of taking form exclusively as a traditional wooden or stone structure, the *sahnisin* has been constructed of materials that are more readily available in the construction industry: glass, reinforced concrete, cement, and metal (Figure 6.2, parts b, c, and d). The inherent limitations and characteristics of these materials and their respective construction systems result in creative adaptations of the traditional typology.[45]

Throughout Dekaokto we find volumes projecting onto the street, extending the interiors of the houses out into the neighborhood space. Keeping with the spirit of the *sahnisin*, these structures have been placed almost exclusively on the upper levels of the original houses. Balconies, verandas, and entire rooms are supported with reinforced concrete or wrought iron brackets that resemble closely in form and function the traditional wooden and stone corbels of the *sahnisin*. We also find cement columns, or *pilotis*, supporting the larger of these added volumes (Figure 6.2, part d).

Height is added to houses as well, resulting in cement towers with a strongly dominant vertical proportion (Figure 6.2, part i). The fortresslike quality of those towers is clearly reminiscent of Byzantine masonry structures and of vernacular typologies throughout northern rural Greece (Figure 6.2, part h).

The original houses' rigid and introverted fenestration pattern has also been subject to change. The narrow, vertical proportion of the windows has been enlarged and widened substantially. The sense of enclosed yet permeable interior spaces supported by the regional wood latticework—*musharrabiehs*—and window boxes (Figure 6.2, part j) has been achieved in Dekaokto using glass and metal screens instead (Figure 6.2, part k).

In addition to the optimization of floor space, these added projecting rooms, enlarged windows, and window boxes offer many other amenities to the women who spend most of their time in the houses: They provide a sense of openness that the original houses denied, they better capture the abundant Mediterranean sunlight, and most important, they enable the housewives to monitor the life of the street below. In sum, they are the "open eyes" of the house and its link with the world of the neighborhood, the public extension of a very private home.

The interior of the house itself is not open for outside scrutiny; only on rare occasions, and under controlled conditions, does the house open up to visitors: in the case of a death or a wedding in the family. Therefore the skin of the house and its extension into the street of the neighborhood serve as the interface between the two states and realms of neighborhood life: closed and open, public and private. The sense of neighborhood space involves first an outdoor area potentially rich in social contacts, and the buildings are subordinated to it.[46] Neighborhood space does not intersect interior space. In keeping with this fundamental dichotomy between interior space (a sanctuary, an exclusive realm normally restricted to the family) and exterior space (the public face of the dwelling), maintenance of the exterior appearance of the home and the space immediately surrounding it is a crucial area of competence.

Gendered Neighborhood Space

The gendered dichotomy of public and private realms created by the separation of men and women by activity and locale is a fundamental ordering principle in Greek life even today. In the mornings, the urban neighborhood is the locus of domestic female social life, with housewives busily going about their daily chores and housework, exchanging tidbits of food and coffee in front of their houses, hanging out the laundry, or shopping for groceries at the local store. Most of the women do not engage in paid work and are economically dependent on the male members of the household. Labor outside of the house is not actively sought by women, who usually think of that type of work as auxiliary and temporary. Even when outside jobs are necessary—mostly so women can contribute to their own dowries—work in nearby locations is preferred, so the usually young and single women are under the supervision of older female relatives and acquaintances. Work and daily social life patterns are chosen carefully so as not to threaten the husband's, or to a lesser extent, the father's (vulnerable) pride. Older men are proud of the fact that few wives have ever worked outside the familial household.

The rigid boundary between public domain and home neighborhood is still a reality for Greek women. A woman's sense of place is restricted to her private domain of home-as-workplace and its immediate neighborhood, by a multitude of family obligations and accepted practices.[47]

The morning activities emphasize the house, which is a "closed" territory in the overall context of social life. Housewives do not by rule invite neighbors or acquaintances to enter, in avoidance of uncalled-for criticism of their housekeeping practices, since housekeeping is a matter of competition. However, while the dwelling itself is closed to outside scrutiny, the house's public face and the care that the housewife takes on the space in front of it take on heightened importance in the neighborhood's social life.

The neighborhood "opens up" to everyone during afternoon gatherings, which usually start after 5 P.M. and continue throughout the evening, until midnight. Women gather outside to chat or to sit in groups, crocheting or knitting. They usually sit sideways to the street, enabling them to interact with passersby without appearing to involve themselves too directly. Children play on side streets, and men set up tables there to play backgammon or cards. During these gatherings, groups are oriented outward, toward the street, and the social and spatial division between house and outside world is transcended. Social life occurs on the street, on the interface between the house and the public areas; chairs are pulled out to the street to initiate and support social interaction. Thanks to a moderate climate, this outdoor social interaction continues throughout most of the year, and Greeks find it frustrating to stay indoors, even in the winter.

Chairs and stools are among the "essential objects" brought out to the pavement. They help bridge the separation between secluded inner areas and visible outer areas and contribute to creating a sense of place. The universal chair is a sturdy straight-backed one, found all over provincial Greece. The pavement thus becomes an extension of the home in full public view; the house "opens up" to the street, and its boundaries stretch outward. This transitional area in front of the house, neither entirely public nor fully private but somewhere in between, creates a spatial link promoting neighborliness.

The neighborhood's open social interaction takes place in informal, irregular spaces: streets, corners, and the interstices between houses. Hence, squares and other such places are not needed. The public realm is structured as a fluid, flexible system of paths and edges rather than a series of neatly laid interconnected places, as in Haussmann's urban design tradition. The public realm is shaped to maximize social contact.[48]

It is not surprising that in refugee neighborhoods, the European concept of the square—either grand or small—was never fully adopted. In Dekaokto, the space for squares and gathering plazas connected with wide, straight streets, in accordance with the principles of monumental civic design, was provided. But despite efforts to impose a rational geometric grid on Dekaokto's rugged terrain, these grandiose plans never materialized, and the neighborhood space evolved following closely the Ottoman model of the *meydan*, or open space, with the street as its locus of social interaction. In reality, these planned spaces were ignored and neglected, and they remain undeveloped even today. Social life takes place in the space of the neighborhood street and the important extension of the house into the street.

The Ottoman *meydan* was usually irregular and "untidy," since, whenever provided, it was meant either as an encampment for caravans or as a sports field, rather than as a stage for social interaction or for the display of centralized power.[49] The bulk of social and neighborhood life took place on the irregular street pattern of the *mahalles*. This irregular pattern, dating back to Byzantine days, was perpetuated by Islamic law during Ottoman times, when the *mahalles* followed an organic development around religious cores (mosques, churches, and synagogues). Islamic law placed private property rights above public property rights, allowing encroachment upon the public way so long as it did not interfere with the rights of others.[50]

While the neighborhood public space welcomes all ages and genders during its "open" time in the afternoon, the male realm tends to operate always in an exclusionary fashion. Male social life is usually centered in the coffeehouse *(kafenio)*, beyond the house and the neighborhood and consequently beyond the reach of the female realm.

Kafenia are the present-day legacy of the hashish-smoking dens, or *tekés*, of the beginning of the century, where *manges*, or *rembetes*, gathered to listen to *rembetika*, the music of the underworld. The *mangas*, a potent image of masculinity, emerged out of the refugee experience as a challenge to middle-class respectability.[51]

Refugees, living on the edge of Greek society and segregated by language and customs from the bulk of the Greek population, were attracted to the *tekés*, to which they were accustomed in Turkey. Women did not venture into this exclusively male realm unless they were the women of the *manges* or the *rembetika* singers themselves (women did not play musical instruments other than the tambourine), out of fear of being labeled "loose women." In a *teké* one could find "men with fine moustaches . . . sitting on rush-bottomed chairs, playing with their amber worry-beads and talking of the difficulty of finding a job, or of their lost houses and lands in Turkey."[52]

Tekés have long been extinct. During the Metaxas dictatorship (1936 to 1941), prohibition and persecution forced most of the *tekés* to close. Gradually, the *kafenio* became the stage for male interaction around a cup of Turkish coffee, with political debate, competitive talk, singing, storytelling, and card games replacing hashish smoking and *zeibekiko* dancing.

The Modern Universalist Tradition

The *mahalles*, with their closed and open orientations as well as their gendered practices as determinants of social exchange patterns, had a lasting influence on refugee neighborhood life. Life throughout all Greek urban neighborhoods followed a similar path. Its traces, however, have been obliterated by the construction boom, land speculation, and the radical change residential areas have experienced since the 1970s.

After the fall of neoclassic architecture, it was soon replaced with the other great universalist tradition, international style, which, coupled with the construction boom of the 1960s and 1970s, extended one more layer of sameness throughout urban Greece. Modern architecture became the ultimate stateless person, with its language replicated all over the globe.[53] The traditional fabric of the city has since been replaced with five- to six-story apartment buildings. The principles of the modern movement were given free reign with the new general building code in the 1980s. The maximum use of every inch of a site has been the main generative force behind thousands of apartment blocks that replaced the old, lower-density building stock in Greek cities, Kaválla included.

The search for communal identity through the domestic and neighborhood space has taken place largely without intervention from "technocrats"—planners, architects, and engineers—and in many cases in spite of their intervention. Representatives of the state government are deeply distrusted throughout Greece, a legacy from Ottoman and more recent military junta times. Communities throughout Greece are fiercely self-reliant, banking mostly on their own collective and individual resources.[54]

The historical reasons for this widespread mistrust of centralized government among the refugees are clearly exposed by Pentzopoulos:

> The rather tolerant authority of the Ottoman Empire and the autonomy granted to the various heterogeneous elements had given the opportunity to the subjected races to develop an almost independent way of life. The unredeemed Hellenes, proud of their culture, cognizant of their nationality, devoted to their customs and traditions, were organized into close, compact groups. They elected their chiefs among the respected elders, they worshipped in churches they had built, they were educated in schools they financed. The Greek community was the social framework within which every activity took place. One could almost characterize the system as one of local government or of self-administration. To these persons, the highly centralized state, the omnipotent bureaucracy of the capital which controlled every aspect of life ... was a foreign concept which their idiosyncrasy instinctively rejected.[55]

This centralized power the refugees so distrusted attempted to impose a way of life concordant with its own view of a Greek national image—an image that in most cases ran counter to the self-image created and re-created by the uprooted population.

National identity as represented by its building activity is used as an attempt to demonstrate evidence of cultural uniqueness, unity, and homogeneity. Nationhood is not easily represented, though. While its rhetoric promulgates unity and homogeneity, the symbols that represent the nation are in reality chosen by a cultural elite. A close look under the blanket thrown over an apparently homogeneous society demonstrates that states are seldom, if ever, culturally unified, and national identity rarely represents a clearly bounded group to which all citizens may claim membership. Whether neoclassic or modern, universal standards and a dominant grand tradition cannot replace the meaning that local urbanism and customary building practices carry throughout their communities.

Greek national identity was forged oppositionally; the new buildings and neighborhoods were seen as a welcome alternative to the old quarters of the Ottoman regime. But if Greece as a nation chose to "forget" its oriental identity, its refugees did not comply obediently with the national amnesia. Greece tried to repress and even deny its eastern identity as the darker side of itself. The refugees, a thorn in the side of the nationalist program, continually reminded the state that the scorned "Orient" was an integral part of the Greek psyche.

Experiences such as those faced by Dekaokto's refugees will continue haunting us as long as groups of people are driven from their homelands because of religious convictions, ethnicity, or any other pretext used to uproot entire populations. We are reminded that the force that binds together different groups is no longer strong enough to make them abandon a "communal" identity in favor of the "acquired" identity of the nation-state.[56] Not far from Greece, the states of the former Yugoslav republic are emerging from a tragic debacle that rings heavily of the events of the 1920s. Like the Greco-Turkish war, the Yugoslav debacle is rooted in state-provoked manipulation of religious and ethnic hatred in the service of nationalist claims that can only engender widespread destruction.

Notes

1. For an extended discussion of the years following the population exchange, see Dimitri Pentzopoulos, *The Balkan Exchange of Minorities and Its Impact upon Greece* (Paris: Mouton and Co., 1962); Charles Eddy, *Greece and the Greek Refugees* (London: George Allen and Unwin, 1931); and Elie Kedourie, ed., *Nationalism in Asia and Africa* (New York: World Publishing Co., 1970).

2. The nations that emerged in the Balkans and the Middle East in the nineteenth and early twentieth centuries emerged largely along the ethnoreligious, social, and economic lines established under the Ottoman Empire. See Richard Clogg, *A Concise History of Greece* (Cambridge: Cambridge University Press, 1992) and Kemal Karpat, *An Inquiry into the Social Foundations of Nationalism in the Ottoman State* (Princeton, N.J.: Center of International Studies, 1973).

3. This unprecedented exchange experiment gave moral and official backing to massive deportations and even mass extermination of entire ethnic communities

in eastern and western Europe from then on. It became a model for dealing with the so-called ethnic minority problem. During World War I, the modern Turkish state followed an extreme version of that policy to exterminate its Armenian population (Vahakn N. Dadrian, "A Theoretical Model of Genocide, with Particular Reference to the Armenian Case," *Sociologia-Internationalis* 14 [1976]: 99–126).

4. See Benedict Anderson, *Imagined Communities: Reflections on the Origin and Spread of Nationalism* (London: Verso Editions, 1983), 15. I adopt Anderson's proposition of nations as imagined political communities, recognizing that nationalist ideology, rather than emerging spontaneously as a result of a few commonly shared traits (language, race, religion, history, territory), is manufactured and then instilled "through the mass media, the educational system, administrative regulations, and so forth."

5. Edward Said, *Orientalism* (New York: Pantheon Books, 1978), 21.

6. Ernest Gellner, *Nations and Nationalism* (Oxford: Basil Blackwell, 1983), 127.

7. Eric Hobsbawm and Terence Ranger, eds., *The Invention of Tradition* (Cambridge: Cambridge University Press, 1983).

8. Nezar AlSayyad, ed., *Forms of Dominance: On the Architecture and Urbanism of the Colonial Enterprise* (Aldershot, England: Avebury, 1992).

9. I refer here to Ernest Gellner's definition of high cultures as "standardized, literacy- and education-based systems of communication" (*Nations and Nationalism*, 54–55).

10. Dimitri Pentzopoulos evokes the voice of the nation in his account of the refugees' "lack of assimilation," revealing a sense of disappointment on the part of the Greek state when the expatriates refused to shed an inherited millenary culture to comply in an orderly way with a national, homogenizing pan-Hellenic plan. Furthermore, Pentzopoulos argues that the refugees did not assimilate into the mainstream native culture because of their "refugee consciousness," or their desire to return to their previous lives and settlements as reflected in their idiosyncrasy. In one word, their "Turkishness" (*The Balkan Exchange*, 108–109, 202).

11. Reneé Hirschon, *Heirs of the Greek Catastrophe: The Social Life of Asia Minor Refugees in Piraeus* (Oxford: Clarendon Press, 1989), 12.

12. The newcomers were not successfully absorbed by the Greek economic structure, driving a great majority of exiles into poverty, destitution, and desperation (Pentzopoulous, *The Balkan Exchange*, 211).

13. The population exchange had its strongest impact on the northern Greek region of Macedonia, where refugees comprised 45 percent of the total number of inhabitants (Pentzopoulos, *The Balkan Exchange*, 183). The city of Kaválla, for instance, was under Ottoman rule as late as 1912, and the Turkish influence is tangible even today. In 1912, 29 percent of Kaválla's population was "Greek," 69 percent Muslim (Turkish ethnic), and 2 percent "miscellaneous"—Jews (mostly Ladino-speaking Sephardic Jews), Vlachs, and Albanians. In 1926—three years after the Lausanne convention—Kaválla's population was entirely "Greek," and more than half were refugees from Asia Minor (Eddy, *Greece*, 193).

14. Robert Jay Lifton, "A Conversation with Robert Jay Lifton," interview by Marilyn Berlin, *Utne Reader* 70 (1995): 62–70.

15. These competing programs were the purist and the demoticist, the former claiming to be the representative of the classical Greek tradition, the latter claim-

ing to be defending the Greek masses and their popular language. They mirrored the existence of two cultural elites: the local ruling class and the diaspora bourgeoisie. The former are the Phanariots, a small but influential group of Greeks in positions of power in the highest reaches of the Ottoman state, named after the Phanar, or Lighthouse quarter of Constantinople, where the Ecumenical Patriarchate is situated. The latter are the sons of Greek merchants, who enjoyed a relatively privileged free-trade structure in the Ottoman Empire, gradually becoming the capitalist Christian middle class. For further reading on this period of Greek history, see Mary N. Layoun, *Travels of a Genre: The Modern Novel and Ideology* (Princeton, N.J.: Princeton University Press, 1990); Karpat, *An Inquiry*; and Clogg, *A Concise History*.

16. Eric Hobsbawm, *Nations and Nationalism Since 1780: Programme, Myth, Reality* (New York: Cambridge University Press, 1990), 12.

17. Wealthy young Greeks studied in the universities of western Europe. They came in contact with the ideas of the Enlightenment, the French Revolution, and romantic nationalism and were made aware of Europe's infatuation with ancient Greek civilization and language (Clogg, *A Concise History*, 27).

18. A world conveniently classified by orientalism, "a political vision of reality whose structure promoted the difference between the familiar (Europe, the west, "us"), and the strange (the Orient, the east, "them")" (Said, *Orientalism*, 43).

19. Greece's decision to associate itself with the west via a common Aryan past has not been unequivocal. Given its geographic location and history, Greece was just as easily classified by nineteenth-century "orientalists"—namely, European and American expert scholars of the "Orient"—as part of the east. In the 1892 International Congress of Orientalists held in London, the geographic boundaries of the east were established as "stretching through Egypt over Africa, and into Europe over Turkey and *Greece*" (emphasis added) (Timothy Mitchell, *Colonising Egypt* [Cambridge: Cambridge University Press, 1988], 165).

This alignment stems from the dominant, European view of ancient Greek history, in which Greece is presented as the cradle of western civilization. That position is based mainly on the "Aryan Model" of western history developed during the nineteenth century. The Aryan Model promulgates that an invasion from the north overwhelmed the local "Aegean" or "Pre-Hellenic" culture. Greek civilization is thus seen as the result of the mixture of the Indo-European-speaking conquerors and their indigenous subjects, and therefore all of its cultural production is accredited to a basically White race. The model advocating the Nordic influence on ancient Greece, and therefore on western society and thought, has been challenged in rigorous scholarly works such as *Black Athena: The Afroasiatic Roots of Classical Civilization*, vol. 1, by Martin Bernal (New Brunswick, N.J.: Rutgers University Press, 1987). Bernal exposes the "Ancient Model," whereby the influence of North Africa and the eastern Mediterranean on Greece is acknowledged (121).

20. Lawrence Vale, "Designing National Identity: Post Colonial Capitols as Intercultural Dilemmas," in AlSayyad, ed., *Forms of Dominance*.

21. Nic C. Moutsopoulos, *L'Encorbellement Architectural 'Le Sahnisin': Contribution à L'étude de la Maison Grecque* (Thessaloníki: Société D'études Macédoniennes, 1988), 390.

22. Charalambos Bouras, "The Approach to Vernacular Architecture," in *Greek Traditional Architecture*, vol. 1: *Eastern Aegean, Sporades, Ionian Islands*, ed. Dimitri Philippides (Athens: Melissa Publishing House, 1983).

23. Layoun, *Travels*, 29–30.

24. Other forms of representation followed a similar trend in the quest for identity. In music, for instance, it took the form of a return to "the science of harmony," with nationalist lyrics that had long been "stunted by mixing their songs with the *primitive chants of the Turks*" (emphasis added) (George Chaconas, *Adamantios Korais: A Study in Greek Nationalism* [New York: Columbia University Press, 1942], 72).

25. Athens's population was estimated at between 4,000 and 12,000 (Douglas Dakin, *The Unification of Greece: 1770–1923* [London: Ernest Benn, 1972], 94).

26. Istanbul and Cairo underwent the same "modernizing" process. In Istanbul, the regulations enforced through the Tanzimat called for "the creation of an efficient street network, monumental public squares, regular street façades, and a uniform urban fabric." In Cairo, the face-lift of the capital required "the opening up of main streets and new arteries, the creation of squares and open places, the planting of trees, the surfacing of roads" to be lined with "European façades." For a detailed discussion of these two cities' urban development during the nineteenth and early twentieth centuries, see Zeynep Çelik, *The Remaking of Istanbul: A Portrait of an Ottoman City in the Nineteenth-Century* (Seattle: University of Washington Press, 1986) and Mitchell, *Colonising Egypt*.

27. Hugh Montgomery-Massingberd, *Royal Palaces of Europe* (New York: Viking Press, 1983).

28. Pentzopoulos, *The Balkan Exchange*, 115.

29. Pentzopoulos, *The Balkan Exchange*, 12.

30. In 1928 the Refugee Settlement Commission estimated that as many as 30 percent of all tobacco workers in Greece were located in Kaválla (Eddy, *Greece*, 193).

31. Michael Romanos and Linda Brott, eds., "A Development Plan for the Neighborhood of Pentakosia" (Summer Program in Greece, School of Planning, University of Cincinnati, 1989, photocopy), 17.

32. Dayana Salazar, "Design Parameters for the Transformation of Dekaokto: A Refugee Neighborhood in Kavala" (master's thesis, University of Cincinnati, 1990), 13.

33. Romanos and Brott, "A Development Plan," 18.

34. A dowry is usually provided in the form of the daughter's share of familial inheritance. In urban settings a house or, more exactly, separate living quarters are the bride's family contribution. See Stephen Salamone, *In the Shadow of the Holy Mountain: The Genesis of a Rural Greek Community and Its Refugee Heritage* (Boulder: East European Monographs, 1987).

35. Greece held the 1971 world record for new housing construction (17.7 houses per 1,000 people) followed by Sweden (13.7), Japan (11.9), and Denmark (10.1). In Greece, this tendency toward investing in houses and land reflects a perceived lack of long-term social security among the working classes (Vithleem Hastaoglou, Costis Hadjimichalis, Nicos Kalogirou, and Nicos Papamichos, "Urbanisation, Crisis and Urban Policy in Greece," *Antipode* 19 [1987]: 154–177).

36. Pentzopoulos, *The Balkan Exchange*, 228.

37. In *The Collective Memory*, Maurice Halbwachs explains the importance of a common geography in restoring a sense of community among an uprooted group of people:

> The group not only transforms the space into which it has been inserted, but also yields and adapts to its physical surroundings. It becomes enclosed within the framework it has built. The group's image of its external milieu and its stable relationships with this environment becomes paramount in the idea it forms of itself. . . . Although one may think otherwise, the reason members of a group remain united, even after scattering and finding nothing in their new physical surroundings to recall the home they have left, is that they think of the old home and its layout. (New York: Harper Colophon Books, 1980), 130–131.

38. Jane K. Cowan, *Dance and the Body Politic in Northern Greece* (Princeton, N.J.: Princeton University Press, 1990) and Hirschon, *Heirs of the Greek Catastrophe*.

39. Burton Berry, "The Development of the Bracket Support in Turkish Domestic Architecture in Istanbul," *Ars Islamica* 5 (1938): 273–282, and Godfrey Goodwin, *A History of Ottoman Architecture* (New York: Thames and Hudson, 1987).

40. Consider, for instance, G. Arbaliev, *National Traditions in Architecture* (Sofia, Bulgaria: Teckhnika, 1982); B. Chipan, "Contemporary Architecture in Macedonia," *Macedonian Review*, Yugoslavia, 13 (1983): 86–92; Georgios A. Megas, *The Greek House, Its Evolution and Its Relation to the Houses of the Other Balkan Peoples* (Athens: Ministry of Reconstruction, 1951); Moutsopoulos, *L'Encorbellement*; and J. Patterson, "Some Nineteenth- and Twentieth-Century House Types of Thrace," *Revue Roumaine D'Histoire de L'Art*, Romania, 9 (1972): 89–93.

41. Goodwin, *A History of Ottoman Architecture*, 429.

42. Berry, "The Development of the Bracket Support," 280.

43. Bouras, "The Approach to Vernacular Architecture"; Godfrey Goodwin, "Ottoman Architecture in the Balkans," *Art and Archaeology Research Papers*, AARP (December 1976): 55–59; and Moutsopoulos, *L'Encorbellement*.

44. Moutsopoulos, *L'Encorbellement*, 390.

45. Figure 6.2 illustrates the most common types of alterations to Dekaokto's original houses in reference to the regional typology they follow closely. The regional precedents are emphasized with a dashed-line frame.

46. S. G. Thakurdesai, "Sense of Place in Greek Anonymous Architecture," *Ekistics* 204 (1972): 334–340.

47. Dina Vaiou, "Gender Divisions in Urban Space: Beyond the Rigidity of Dualist Classifications," *Antipode* 24 (1992): 247–262.

48. Denis Jesson, "Domain and Definition: The Model of the Greek Littoral Village," *Ekistics* 265 (1977): 313–318.

49. Goodwin, *A History of Ottoman Architecture*, 452.

50. See Çelik, *The Remaking of Istanbul*.

51. Through the fusion of Anatolian musical traditions and those of the mainland, the refugees created a unique new type of music called *rembetika*. *Rembetika* music was originally the province of the "Other," the refugee. For further reading on *rembetika*, see Gail Holst, *Road to Rembetika, Music of a Greek Subculture: Songs of Love, Sorrow and Hashish* (Athens: Denise Harvey and Co., 1975) and Dimitri

Monos, "Rebetico, the Music of the Greek Urban Working Class," *International Journal of Politics, Culture and Society* 1 (1987): 111–119.

52. Holst, *Road to Rembetika*, 19.

53. One of the early proponents of the international style in Greece was the architect Dimitris Pikionis, who, like the early nationalist elite, had been educated in Europe. Pikionis promoted the ideas of modern art and the principles of the modern movement to take the place of the by then discredited neoclassic movement (Anastasia Dimitracopoulou, "Dimitris Pikionis [1887–1968]: Pioneer Greek Modernist," *Architectural Association Quarterly* 13 [1982]: 59–68).

54. The planning profession in Greece originated in 1923, with the main objective of ridding the cities in the territories recently liberated of their Turkish/oriental appearance. Its efforts concentrated on the alignment of streets and the use of a rectangular grid in city plans. However, since then, no one land use or master plan has ever been implemented. For further reading on Greek city planning, see A. P. Lagopoulos, "Greece," in *Planning in Europe: Urban and Regional Planning in the EEC*, ed. R. H. Williams (London: George Allen and Unwin, 1984); Lefteris Tsoulouvis, "Aspects of Statism and Planning in Greece," *International Journal of Urban and Regional Research* 11 [1987]: 500–521; Michael Herzfeld, *A Place in History: Social and Monumental Time in a Cretan Town* (Princeton, N.J.: Princeton University Press, 1991).

55. Pentzopoulos, *The Balkan Exchange*, 175.

56. Peter Sugar, "From Ethnicity to Nationalism and Back Again," in *Nationalism: Essays in Honor of Louis L. Snyder*, eds. Michael Palumbo and William O. Shanahan (Westport, Conn.: Greenwood Press, 1981).

Chapter Seven

Counterparts: Dubliners, *Masculinity, and Temperance Nationalism*

DAVID LLOYD

The man returned to the lower office and sat down again at his desk. He stared intently at the incomplete phrase: *In no case shall the said Bernard Bodley be* . . . and thought how strange it was that the last three words began with the same letter. The chief clerk began to hurry Miss Parker, saying she would never have the letters typed in time for the post. The man listened to the clicking of the machine for a few minutes and then set to work to finish his copy. But his head was not clear and his mind wandered away to the glare and rattle of the public house. It was a night for hot punches. He struggled on with his copy, but when the clock struck five he had still fourteen pages to write. Blast it! He longed to bring his fist down on something violently. He was so enraged that he wrote *Bernard Bernard* instead of *Bernard Bodley* and had to begin again on a clean sheet.

He felt strong enough to clear out the whole office single-handed. His body ached to do something, to rush out and revel in violence. All the indignities of his life enraged him. . . . Could he ask the cashier privately for an advance? No, the cashier was no good, no damn good: he wouldn't give an advance. . . . He knew where he would meet the boys: Leonard and O'Halloran and Nosey Flynn. The barometer of his emotional nature was set for a spell of riot.[1]

In this brief scene from the story "Counterparts," James Joyce draws out the complex rhythms of alienated labor in early-twentieth-century Dublin, linking the repetitive functions performed by the legal clerk Farrington with his sense of humiliation, frustration, and rage. Male rage and violence at the conditions of work in an office with which, apparently, Farrington's very bodily frame is at odds are counterpoised with the heterotopic site of the public house, with its odors and sensations and the prospect of homosocial conviviality. In the larger course of the story, Farrington indulges in a brief witticism at the expense of the Northern Irish head of the clearly British firm and consequently is further humiliated by having to make public apology. Later, in the pub, as the story is retold and circulated, the humiliation is erased, and the scene becomes one in which Farrington figures as momentary hero. But as the evening progresses, Farrington is again humiliated, this time by an English actor whom the "boys" meet. The actor sponges off them and then defeats Farrington in an arm-wrestling contest; both Farrington's own honor and the "national honour" he is jocularly called on to defend are tarnished. Returning home raging, his money spent, his watch pawned, his thirst unslaked, he finds the house dark, his dinner cold, and his wife out at chapel. The story concludes with him savagely beating his son, who pleads for mercy with the promise that he will "say a *Hail Mary*" for his father.

This spare and desolate story, together with many others in *Dubliners*, is bitterly diagnostic of the paralysis of Irish men in colonial Ireland, of their alienation and anomie, which, so often, are counterpointed by drinking. As is so much of Joyce's work, the story is also profoundly suggestive of the disposition and practices of gendered social spaces in early-twentieth-century Dublin—spaces of work, leisure, domesticity, and religion. As much as anything, it is indicative of the troubled nature of the intersections of these spaces, of their antagonism and contradictory formations. In what follows, I situate "Counterparts" in relation to the gradual and complex emergence of modernity in late-nineteenth- and early-twentieth-century Ireland and to the sites of "countermodernity" that seem simultaneously to be engendered. In particular, I follow the story's suggestions in an exploration of the forms in which Irish masculinity was deliberately and programmatically reconstituted by Irish nationalist movements at this moment and of the recalcitrance that the performance of masculinity in popular culture presented to such projects. Since this chapter is a small and early part of an ongoing project on the transformation of bodily practices in the modernization of Ireland and on the survival of "nonmodern" forms of cultural difference, I will from the outset make no apology for the speculative nature of the argument at many points. Much remains to be done by way of producing a "gender history" of Irish social spaces and their refiguration within nationalist as well as colonial projects of modernization. What I hope to do here is suggest the singularity and unevenness of the ways in which Irish culture enters modernity and the complexity of the historiographic project that we require in order to grasp the implications of such singularity.

The problematic status of the nationalist project of modernization is in evidence in Ireland, just as it is in evidence in the case of most third world nationalisms. This problematic nature is evident both in relation to the philosophical foundations of modernity from which nationalism largely derives and in relation to the cultural formations of the colonized society as these emerge in time with, but yet athwart, modernity. The problematic nature of nationalist projects has been more fully elaborated elsewhere and can be summarized briefly here. Nationalism is deeply informed, and yet simultaneously judged lacking or "secondary," by the twin concepts of autonomy and originality, which furnish the regulative norms for virtually every level of the modern *socius:* for the individual, for culture, as this emerges as a separate or distinct sphere, and in turn for each of the increasingly differentiated social spaces of civil society. In its drive to produce or capture the modern state, the nationalist project in its turn must pass by way of the reproduction of such autonomous entities. At the same time, the legitimacy of the call for independent national statehood must be founded in the establishment of the cultural difference of the nation or people, a difference necessarily derived from the traditions of the people that are distinct from those of the dominant or colonial culture. In this way, the claim to autonomous statehood is founded in the originality of national identity, but in an identity whose configurations derive from the elements of society that have, in some sense, survived the inroads of colonial modernity, that are the formations of nonmodernity. Nationalism proceeds, furthermore, by the direct politicization of cultural institutions: Whereas in dominant societies, aesthetic culture functions discretely to form subjects for the state, insurgent nationalism charges culture with political significance. Culture cannot be either disinterested or autonomous but is openly subordinated to the political projects of the nationalist movement.

But nationalism's relation to tradition is no less refractive and problematic. For what, through a rigorous process of selection, canonization, and fetishization, gets called "tradition" in relation to modernity emerges as such in the very recalcitrance of popular practices to colonial modernity. These practices prove to be no less recalcitrant to nationalism insofar as it is itself devoted to modernization as the very condition of state formation. In particular, popular practices tend to be resistant to the cultural disciplines that seek to forge the formal citizen-subjects of political modernity that the nation-state requires to constitute its people. Accordingly, in its drive to produce subjects to be citizens of the nation that has yet to come into being, nationalism seeks to refine its own version of national culture out of the heterogeneity of popular cultural practices, modernizing and regulating what survives in the form of cultural difference. This is understood, of course, as an attempt to overcome the damage inflicted by colonialism; it is the function of national culture to produce national subjects as empowered agents against the heteronomy and the paralysis of the colonized culture and to restore the wholeness of a fragmented society. In this respect, the function of the icons selected as representative of tradition—whether national heroes or aestheticized natural or artifactual objects—is not merely inspirational. They are symbols that, by virtue of their participation in the original and—in its occluded depths—the continuous life of the people, represent the virtual nation that has yet to be realized. Around these symbols the aesthetic formation of the citizen-subject takes place. Tradition becomes, in this refined form, the means by which the nation accedes to modernity. But tradition itself, as Frantz Fanon vigorously argued in *The Wretched of the Earth*, thus becomes the paradoxical enemy of the popular culture wherein the cultural difference of the colonized persists in its embedded resistances, its unevennesses, and its perpetual transformative adaptations.[2] It is this problematic and doubled relation to its own modernity and traditionalism that makes nationalism, in Partha Chatterjee's memorable phrase, at once "a different discourse, yet one that is dominated by another."[3]

A principal means by which nationalist movements declare their cultural distinctiveness from the dominant power and engage in the refinement of popular culture is manifest in a certain "transvaluation of values" undertaken generally in the early stages of anticolonial mobilization. This transvaluation involves the inversion of stereotypes by which the colonizer has marked as inferior the signs of the colonized's cultural difference. Thus, for example, within Irish cultural nationalism, the notion of Irish factionalism, based in an inveterate attachment to clan or family rather than to the abstract forms of law and state, becomes the sign of an indomitable resistance and of a spirit of loyalty capable of attachment to the nation. It forms, no less, the foundations of a masculinity that would be transformed and disciplined through institutions ranging from sports to paramilitary movements. The famous quality of "sentimentality" is recast as the foundation for piety and for an empathetic moral identification with the oppressed, while even the stereotype of a racially determined backwardness becomes the sign of a distaste for mechanical English modes of modernity and the grounds for an alternative conception of the modern. It is important to emphasize this point, since it is rarely the case, even with such ardent defenders of Gaelic tradition as Douglas Hyde, that Irish nationalists seek to go against the current of history; it is an alternative modernity rather than the restoration of old forms that nationalists seek, even as they appeal to traditions. The transvaluation of the stereotype at once recognizes it as a form of knowledge, predicated on the apprehension of a difference, and converts its meaning in relation to the possibility for modernization. A Celticist nationalism engages in a revalorization of social or cultural traits whose material conditions of possibility it in fact seeks to eradicate.

But in certain cases, both reversal and eradication are attended by peculiar difficulties. This is evidently the case with that most common and perdurable of stereotypes of the Irish, our propensity for drink and drunkenness. The reasons for the difficulty that nationalism found in dealing with the possibility that drinking represented an ingrained ethnic trait are at once logical and cultural. Logically, it is difficult to conceive of a *reversal* of intemperance—though its eradication was all too readily advocated—because, though in different forms, drinking is the effect of a prior cause, whether that cause be considered, as we shall see, colonialism or ethnic predisposition. Unlike sentimentality, it is not an essential characteristic whose valence only is in question; it is a metonym for Irishness that can be disavowed, suppressed, or denied but not inverted or transvalued. Even when attempts were made to convert the phenomenon of drinking into a perversion of native "hospitality," drinking remained an ever-possible effect of that trait, not its obverse; as Weathers, the English actor in "Counterparts," slyly remarks, "The hospitality was too Irish" (90). Culturally, drinking practices remain a critical site for the performance of Irish masculinity and ethnicity, an actuality so embedded that any national movement that attempted to overlook this phenomenon would be obliged to disavow a profoundly significant popular mode of articulation of cultural difference. As I shall suggest, it is in the attempt to transform the terms of Irish masculinity, rather than to transvalue the stereotype, that nationalism backhandedly acknowledges the significance of this cultural trait while at the same time necessarily suppressing the countermodern implications of drinking practices themselves. But this may be because of a third difficulty that attaches to nationalism's relation to drinking, which is that drinking itself may be seen as an allegorical figure for nationalism itself. That is, like nationalism, drinking represents the imbrication of resistance with dependence: As a practice that refuses the values of the colonial economy, values of labor, regularity, and thrift, in favor of an alternative mode of homosociality, drinking resists the incorporation of the colonized culture into the colonial enterprise; as a practice that entails debt as well as psychic dependence, drinking is at once the cause and effect of an individual and national lack of autonomy. It is, to paraphrase Partha Chatterjee, a practice of difference, but a dependent one.

I take up this line of argument again momentarily. But the acknowledgment that drinking practices constitute a mode for the performance of masculinity raises a second stereotype that proved difficult for nationalists to reverse: the famous "femininity" of the Celt. The notion of an essentially feminine Celtic nature emerges in the writings of philologists and ethnographers in the nineteenth century and receives its clearest and most widely disseminated formulation in Matthew Arnold's *On the Study of Celtic Literature* (1867): "The sensibility of the Celtic nature, its nervous exaltation, have something feminine in them, and the Celt is thus peculiarly disposed to feel the spell of the feminine idiosyncrasy; he has an affinity to it; he is not far from its secret."[4]

But it is important to note that the stereotype of the feminine Celtic nature is constituted within a matrix of stereotypes that intersects, on the one hand, with a corresponding set of stereotypes about the "feminine idiosyncrasy" and, on the other, with the set of stereotypes that constitute the "ungovernable and turbulent" Irish as the proper objects of Anglo-Saxon discipline within the Empire. The femininity of the Celt is a function of his "receptivity," of a certain more or less passive submission to impulse, whether the impulse of unreflective personal inclination or the impulse of external influence of nature or society. It is the very foundation of Celtic sensibility, and Arnold's only wish is "that he [the Celt] had been more master of it" (85). The lack of self-mastery makes possible the convergence of apparently incompatible stereotypes, of feminine sensibility with the violent turbulence that, especially in the proliferating caricatures of simian Irish terrorists that stemmed from the Fenian campaigns of the 1860s, dominated popular images of the Irish in late-nineteenth-century England.[5] An unmastered sentimentality founds the political servility of the Celt no less than his aesthetic hypersensitivity:

> The Celt, undisciplinable, anarchical, and turbulent by nature, but out of affection and admiration giving himself body and soul to some leader, that is not a promising political temperament, it is just the opposite of the Anglo-Saxon temperament, disciplinable and steadily obedient within certain limits, but retaining an inalienable part of freedom and self-dependence. (86)

The Celt's "unpromising political temperament" requires its complement in Anglo-Saxon rule, just as, within the gradually consolidating domestic ideology of Victorian Britain, woman's private sentimental morality required regulation by male civic virtues.[6]

For an Irish nationalism seeking to restore a sense of agency to a colonized people, femininity is a no less unpromising stereotype to confront than is intemperance. Rather than a transvaluation, however, this stereotype requires eradication through a series of projects that are directed at the reconstitution of Irish masculinity. I use the term *reconstitution* advisedly, to suggest that what is at stake here is not merely assertions of Irish manliness in denial of the stereotype but a more or less systematic attempt to reproduce in Ireland a modern division of gendered social spheres within which the image of a masculine civic or public sphere could be reframed in opposition to a privatized feminine space.[7] The nationalist modernization of Ireland is inseparable from its project of mas-

culinization of Irish public culture and the regulation of a feminine domestic space, a project, as I shall suggest, that to a large extent runs
against the grain of both cultural and material popular practices. This is
so because nationalism at once accepts the colonial stereotype of "turbulent" Irish masculinity and seeks to respond by transforming Irish masculinity into "governable" forms that would found an independent state
formation.

In the first place, there seems little doubt that we are dealing here with
the emergence of something new in Irish culture. The apparent self-evi-
dence of the assumption that masculinity is properly defined and differentiated in opposition to femininity was by no means predominant earlier in the century. For Young Ireland nationalists in the 1840s,
"manliness" as an ethical and political disposition of the subject was
properly opposed not to womanliness but to slavery as the ultimate index
of subjection. The autonomy of the politically free citizen and nation was
opposed to the absolute instantiation of heteronomy, the slave. Thus
Thomas Davis, in an essay entitled "The Young Men of Ireland," addresses the problems of moral corruption in a colonized society:

A Frenchman, M. De Beaumont . . . has discussed the character of our People
. . . and he has discussed it with severity and beauty. He has attributed the
"dark vices" of the Irishman to that part of him which is the making of Englishmen—to that part of him which is a slave. If he be improvident and
careless, it was because there was no use of accumulation under the eyes of
English avarice; if he be "ireful" and vindictive, it is because "six hundred
years of hereditary slavery, physical suffering, and moral oppression, have
vitiated his blood and tainted his habits." . . . The vices of Irishmen are of
English culture; their virtues are of the homegrowth of the heart—the nation's heart—"that recess where tyranny has vainly endeavoured to force an
entrance; which has remained free from every stain; that part which holds
his religion and his charities."[8]

A series of oppositions structures this passage: between slavery and
moral manliness, between "English culture" and Irish nature, between
the alien and tyrannical rule of the colonizer and the besieged
home/body of the Irishman, between the healthy and the "vitiated"
body. What now seems surprisingly undeveloped is an opposition between a distinctly feminine space for Irish culture that is to be protected
or liberated by manly resistance. On the contrary, despite the implicit
feminization of the inviolate "recess" that resists the invader, the Irishman is himself the site of division between a contingent outer world that
is subject to slavery and an intimate and essential inner world in which
the moral constitution of manliness itself is preserved. The project of
Young Ireland is, in a sense, to expand that inner space in order to take

back the "part" that is enslaved, to make the slave moral that he might be free. We can perhaps throw the distinctiveness of this formulation into greater relief by comparison with Partha Chatterjee's discussion of "the nationalist resolution of the woman question" in Bengal. There, in the context of the material domination of British colonialism, a discourse emerges that asserts the superiority of Indian *spiritual* values while acknowledging the *material* superiority of English civilization. While Indian men are obliged to function in the public world of the British Raj, the feminized domestic space is constructed as that of the preservation and reproduction of inviolate Indian spiritual values.[9] Clearly, Davis's formulations place the division rather within the Irish male body and psyche, at most foreshadowing the divide between the feminine domestic and the male public spheres, which, as we shall see, in any case emerge in Ireland in ways different from those Chatterjee suggests to be the case for Bengal.

By the turn of the century, however, a fundamental shift has taken place in nationalist discourse such that a major component of its rhetoric involves the proper distribution of opposed male and female spaces and practices, a distribution that is, as is well known, finally enshrined in the constitution of 1937. The conditions leading to this shift are numerous, but I can cite several relevant ones here. First is no doubt the simple fact of the abolition of slavery, which made unavailable the common analogy between the conditions of the slave in the southern states of the United States and those of the Irish poor. Second, the emergence into prominence in the second part of the nineteenth century of a powerful Victorian discourse on domestic ideology was made possible by the productivity of British capitalism and the extension of the middle-class domain of the private family home among the skilled working classes. This ideology doubtless provides the model with which a modernizing nationalism seeks to compete. Third, the intervention of a new racial discourse on the Irish, which asserts their femininity as part of the set of characteristics that makes them incapable of self-government, demands a response in the form of a remasculinization of the Irish public sphere.

We can identify two distinct but interlocked modes of response to the feminization of the Irish during this period. The first can be seen as a celebration of those elements of Irish culture that could be identified in certain ways as feminine. In general, the stereotype of femininity attaches to those survivals of a Gaelic culture that are now seen as the domain of folk or peasant society. As is well known, the Irish Literary Revival and the Gaelic League's project to restore the Irish language were predicated on a massive effort to collect, catalog, disseminate, and refunction Irish folklore. This project required the translation of oral cultural elements into the forms of a print culture and in powerful if inadmissible ways foregrounds the opposition between the modernity of the collectors and their public and the premodernity of the folk. But the gathering and rationalization of a body of materials that includes fairy and folk tales, superstition and rural religious practices, and records of medical and other lore is shadowed equally by an implicitly gendered division. It is not for nothing that, although many of the storytellers and informants were men, the figure of the old woman as repository and transmitter of folk culture dominates the folkloric imaginary. The space of the Irish peasantry is at once premodern and feminine; in its conversion and refinement into a coherent body of tradition, it is subject to the labor of modernizing nationalist men. At the same time, the tone of the collector is elegiac; these are the records of a dying civilization that nationalism itself has displaced, even though that cannot be acknowledged. In the new dispensation, the feminine oral tradition has been absorbed into the foundations of a virile Irish modernity. Yeats's famous distinction between the moon of folk culture and the sun of an aristocratic literary culture is only the most notable expression of such an attitude.[10]

This ambiguous celebration of the "feminine" elements of Irish folk culture is thus both counterpointed by and contained within a vigorous project aimed at the reconstitution of Irish masculinity. Given the current context, wherein it is all too often assumed that anticolonial violence stems from the aberrant "hypermasculinity" of the Republican "physical force" tradition, it is important to register that it is not only within the tradition that lays claim to the right to take up arms that this project of re-masculinization is expressed. Not only in the paramilitary organizations that found legitimation in the traditions of the United Irishmen, Young Ireland, and the Fenians but in a whole range of closely articulated civil and paramilitary organizations, institutions, and practices, did this project emerge. Paramilitary displays constituted only one mode in a larger effort to recapture the public sphere as the site for the performance of Irish masculinity, and they belong accordingly in the context of linked endeavors that seek to redefine the public sphere in relation to the production and protection of a distinctive Irish private or domestic sphere. Paramilitary disciplinary formations are linked, similarly, to the attempt to transform the "turbulent" Irish male body, whose habits are the end result of colonialism, into a disciplined and moral *laboring* as well as fighting body on whose productivity the future prosperity of the nation must be predicated. These political and economic projects are triangulated and, at the moment of the turn of the century, explicitly linked with the cultural projects that found expression in the literary revival, the national theater, and the Gaelic League. The emergent institutions of cultural nationalism are no less concerned with the production of a new Irish masculinity and have at their core the project of organizing Irish political desire around feminized symbols of the nation that become the object of a heterosexual male devotion. There is, as I argue more fully later, a profound connection between the symbolist poetic mode, no less present in Patrick Pearse than in the Yeats of circa 1904, and the transformation and regulation of social space that a modernizing nationalism requires.

The projects of this modernizing nationalism meet in every domain a deep material and cultural resistance. The desire to produce an Ireland whose foundations lay in a feminine domestic space was at best utopic in a country where a large proportion of the most exploited workforce was female, both in the industrialized and semi-industrialized cities of Belfast and Dublin and in rural areas, where much female labor was unpaid and unacknowledged. That desire was equally utopic in a country where urban centers had a constantly acknowledged and drastic shortage of dwellings, leaving whole families to inhabit single rooms in Dublin's notorious tenements, and where in rural society the stem family system continued to predominate over any emerging nuclear family unit. That desire also came up against an increasingly organized social resistance to the new post-Famine patterns of both industrial and agrarian labor, especially in the form of a syndicalist labor movement whose agenda was by no means always congruent with or subordinated to nationalist mobilization and which forged its own version of engagement with capitalist modernity. These struggles and resistances, of course, produce the contestatory field within which Irish nationalism takes its shape. But another mode of resistance to official nationalism, which I term recalcitrance, has less to do either with the difficulties of material conditions in the colony or with alternative modes of organization and far more to do with cultural practices that are at once embedded in the popular imaginary and incompatible with nationalist canons of tradition and moral citizenship. They are problematic, as I have already suggested, precisely because they represent, alongside nationalism, significant sites for the performance of cultural difference that cannot simply be erased or disavowed.

In what follows, then, I focus on the cultural significance of drinking in Ireland and its rendering within nationalism as a problem of intemperance. The focus is not on what we would now call alcoholism, though that is ineradicably one aspect of an anomic culture within which dependence itself constitutes a form of resistance to incorporation by antipathetic social norms. I want rather to approach drinking practices more widely as they are embedded within a whole matrix of behaviors that are the recalcitrant effects of modernity. That is to say, Irish drinking is not to be seen as the residue of premodern, preindustrial practices, or as in any simple way congruent with, for example, working-class drinking in modern industrial societies, but rather as itself transformed and reconstituted in relation to an emergent modernity as an element of unincorporated cultural difference.

Let us proceed by way of a brief history of temperance movements in nineteenth-century Ireland. Prior to the 1830s, temperance work was principally undertaken by dissenting Protestants, whose campaigns were largely conducted against intemperance as an individual matter and without reference to the larger social conditions that might have contributed to excessive drinking in Ireland. In fact, on the contrary, their views tended rather to assume that the reputed turbulence of Irish society derived from intemperance rather than to understand that both drinking and unrest might stem from social conditions. In this connection, it is perhaps important to note that the evil was primarily understood as binge drinking, occasional excessive drinking at fairs or other social gatherings, rather than habitual drinking. Binge drinking was seen as the effective cause of riot and faction fighting, and it was generally assumed that the poverty of the Irish lower classes made habitual drinking impracticable. The problems caused by intemperance were thus associated with what might be called a "spasmodic" theory of social violence, whereby the poor Irish are understood to be reactive and effectively passive in relation to their conditions. We will see shortly how this understanding of intemperance seems to have shifted by the end of the century.

The first mass movement for temperance was instigated by the Capuchin Father Mathew in the 1830s and 1840s. This movement, which for the first time drew mass Catholic support, was nonetheless largely in accord with Protestant assumptions that the control of intemperance was a means to regulate and diminish social disorder. Father Mathew's work continued to emphasize individual reform rather than any genetic connection between intemperance and larger social ills. That connection was, however, directly made by the Young Ireland movement, which endorsed Father Mathew's campaign but did seek, in correspondence with its larger analysis of Irish society as a product of British rule, to connect the regulation of intemperance with its roots in the social and economic conditions of the Irish poor.[11] The abortive uprising of 1848 and the effective dissolution of Young Ireland interrupted the development of this understanding of intemperance, which was not to find full force till the end of the century.

By the 1880s and the 1890s, a new convergence had become possible between the Irish Catholic church, the resurgent nationalist movement, and the cause of temperance. The increasingly unchallenged authority of the church, which may be seen to have gradually emerged as a kind of shadow civil society in nineteenth-century Ireland, made it possible for priests to articulate an ever more uncompromisingly nationalist position, one that supplanted an earlier sense of institutional dependence on the British state. The concern of the church with combating intemperance and with the general moral reform of the Irish accordingly coincided with a new political militancy. Within this new formation, an earlier concern with individual reform was linked to a vigorous rejection of English stereotypes of an essentially bibulous Irish race and an uncompromising attribution of intemperance to the effects of British rule:

> How many Englishmen ever reflect that England is responsible for [the] intemperance of the Irish? Our Celtic ancestors were a very temperate people before the English landed on our shores. . . . It was only after they had lost their independence that this vice broke out among the Irish; and when we take into consideration all that they suffered from English tyranny during the last seven hundred years, can we be astonished that they turned to drink?[12]

Intemperance is thus no longer to be seen as the symptom of an internal racial organization already given to modes of dependence that fit it only for the external discipline of British rule, but as a synecdoche for the larger effects of that rule on the Irish body and the Irish psyche. Colonialism is a kind of intoxication of which intemperance is one among many effects. Accordingly, intemperance and political dependence are seen to be in a reversible relation, such that the eradication of intemperance leads to the eradication of British rule and vice versa. Hence emerges the celebrated slogan "Ireland sober, Ireland free." In this respect, we may note again the difference from what Chatterjee analyzes in the Bengali context. In Ireland, the assumption is that the Irish body and spirit are indeed both already contaminated by the effects of British rule, so that private no less than public life requires "detoxification," a process that Douglas Hyde in another context termed "deanglicisation."[13]

Accordingly, the work of temperance nationalism becomes inseparable from the production and dissemination of a vigorous domestic ideology that seeks to establish the well-regulated feminized home as the counterpart to a reformed masculine labor as the foundation of a reformed and independent nation-state. Typical in its pedagogical insistence is the Reverend J. Halpin's *Father Mathew Reader on Temperance and Hygiene*, a text intended for school use, which makes explicit the connections between the reform of men for public duties, the feminine sphere of the domestic, and the home as foundation for society:

> For the homes make up the nation; and as are the homes, so will be the nation itself. Whatever wrecks the home wrecks the nation as well. . . . Now, what destroys the home more surely and more quickly than intemperance? (7)
>
> If intemperance unfits man for the discharge of his duties, how much more truly does it unfit woman for hers? What is to become of her home and her domestic duties—the care of her children, for instance, in the exercise of which so much depends for society itself as well as for the family? As the nation depends on the homes, the homes depend on the mothers that reign there. (14–15)

> All women can, each in her own sphere, give good example. . . . We must
> be very practical here. In the first place our Irish women are blamed for their
> cookery, or rather for their ignorance of cookery. And it is said that a better
> knowledge of that "lost art" would half solve our drink question in Ireland.
>   Closely connected with this subject is another of hardly less importance.
> We have seen the woman as a cook; let us next see her as a druggist. (20–21)
>   Yet more than all this may woman do for temperance. She can make the
> home attractive and sanitary, and even beautiful; yes, beautiful, for even the
> humblest and poorest home may be made beautiful and attractive in its way
> and measure, and all that a home should be, by a tidy thrifty and intelligent
> woman. . . . Well, there is a rivalry between the home and the public-house;
> and if the home is to prevail it must have something attractive about it;
> something better than disorder and dirt, untidy children and an ill-tempered
> wife. (22–23)[14]

Halpin's linked concerns not merely with temperance but with the inculcation of "domestic economics," with hygiene, cookery, and medical
knowledge, mark this and texts like it as part of a larger project of modernization that, in its desire to regulate the feminine domestic sphere, establishes domestic economy as a foundation for the national or political
economy. It is not so much a discourse about the repression of an evil,
drunkenness, as it is about the reconstitution of the social formation and
the establishment of the domestic sphere as the counterpart to an invigo-
rated masculine public sphere of economic and political labor.

Inasmuch as "there is a rivalry between the home and the public-
house," we can understand the public house to be no less a rival to the
public sphere. It constitutes a third term whose very name marks its ambiguous location. It is a rival to the home in providing an alternative
space for male conviviality, leisure, and community, one not yet subordinated to the regulations of private domesticity and accordingly "public."
At the same time, it rivals the public sphere insofar as it constitutes a
space for the dissemination of news and rumor, for the performance of a
heterogeneous popular culture, and indeed, for the organization and dissemination of dissent, sedition, and resistance. But it is no less a recalcitrant space, the site of practices that by their very nature rather than by
necessary intent are out of kilter with the modern disciplinary projects.
As a site that is irrevocably a product of modernity in its spatial and temporal demarcations and regulations, in its relation to the increasingly disciplined rhythms of work and leisure, it is nonetheless a site that pre-
serves and transforms according to its own spaces and rhythms
long-standing popular practices that will not be incorporated by discipline: treating, or the round system; oral performance of song, story, and
rumor; and conversation itself, which becomes increasingly a value in a
society ever more subject to the individuation and alienation of the

worker within the system of production.[15] The public house may be seen as a crucial site of countermodernity.

In this respect, then, the pub is no less a rival than might be otherwise believed to the linked set of national institutions that came into being alongside and in relation to temperance nationalism and often under the auspices of the same figures: the Gaelic Athletic Association, the Gaelic League, the Irish Literary movement and the National Theatre, and the various paramilitary movements. At the same time as such institutions often expressly seek to provide an alternative to drinking as the predominant form of male recreation, they seek to produce a public sphere cleansed of the intoxicating influence of English culture and commodities. As Archbishop Croke, first patron of the Gaelic Athletic Association, put it: "England's accents, the vicious literature, her music, her dances, and her manifold mannerisms . . . [are] not racy of the soil, but rather alien, on the contrary to it, as are for the most part, the men and women who first imported and still continue to patronise them."[16]

Yet it is clear that these various institutions sought equally and no less importantly to constitute an alternative, nationalist civil society alongside the institutions of the colonial state, in the anticipation of an independent national state with its own civic institutions. Their function is not only to propagandize and disseminate nationalist ideology; it is also to produce *formally* a counterhegemonic set of articulated but autonomous spheres that perform the modernizing functions of education, recreation, political organization, and opinion formation and through which the national citizen is formed.

The public house not only rivals such institutions, then, it troubles their intents. It is a site of the performance of a profoundly heterogeneous popular culture, one inflected, as the "Sirens" chapter of *Ulysses* alone might suggest, by Italian opera, English music hall, nationalist balladry, gossip, irreverence, and humor, all of which is intrinsically recalcitrant to nationalist refinement. At the same time, the pub is, even in its demarcation as a distinct space, internally resistant to differentiation; it is a crucial site not only for the mixing of cultural elements but for the intersection of functions: leisure and work, politics and religion, literature and orality, public life and a kind of domesticity. It is the locus of cultural differences with which nationalism must intersect but that it cannot fully incorporate.

Nationalism, as we have seen, requires the establishment of cultural difference from the colonial power to legitimate its own claims to statehood, but the cultural difference it requires must, to fit with its modernizing drives, be a difference contained and refined into the canonized forms of tradition. The civil institutions of national modernity work off but also against the grain of popular cultural practices through which the heterogeneous, unrefined, and recalcitrant modes of cultural difference are continually constituted and transformed. What is intended is not the ideal form of pure and originary difference toward which an extreme traditionalist and separatist nationalism might tend; it is rather that mode of constant differentiation, refraction, and refunctioning that occurs in the encounter between the evolving institutions of colonial modernity and the adaptive spaces of the colonized culture. What determines cultural difference is not its externality to modernity or the persistence of a premodern irrationality, but rather the mutually constitutive relation between the modern and the countermodern. The temporal structure within which the colonized culture emerges in its difference is not that of a movement from an origin that is interrupted by and then assimilated into a more developed, more powerful state, or that of the recuperation of an authentic and ultimately unbroken tradition within the revivalist logic of nationalism. It is rather the structure of the eddy by which Walter Benjamin redefines the processes of origination: "Origin [*Ursprung*], although an entirely historical category, has, nevertheless, nothing to do with genesis [*Entstehung*]. The term *origin* is not intended to describe the process by which the existent came into being, but rather to describe that which emerges from the process of becoming and disappearance. Origin is an eddy in the stream of becoming, and in its current it swallows the material involved in the process of genesis."[17]

The cultural forms of the colonized do not simply disappear; in the turbulence of the encounter with colonization, they become something other that at once retains the traces of the violence of that encounter, preserving it in the very form of a persistent damage, and yet survives. Survival in this sense is a mode of adaptation that is often more resistant to than acquiescent in domination, a "living on" that is not about the preservation or fetishization of past forms but nonetheless refuses incorporation. This unevenly distributed relation of damage and survival forges the recalcitrant grain of cultural difference.

We can situate Irish drinking as one element in a matrix of such historically shifting cultural differences, differences of practice and social form that prove unincorporable by either colonial or nationalist modernity and that remain accordingly ungathered by history, as a kind of dross or irregularity of which neither sense nor use can be made. The problematic status of Irish drinking has over and over again to do with what seems to the modernized eye the improper confusion of spaces and practices. One instance of this is evident within the arguments for licensing and regulation of drinking to separate work time from leisure or drinking time and to end such practices as paying workers in public houses. This was, as Rosenzweig points out, the ubiquitous concern of industrial societies, but it may be that the uneven penetration of rationalized capitalist modes of labor in Ireland permitted the persistence of mixing labor and pleasure to a greater degree than elsewhere.[18] Similarly, particularly in rural districts, the overlap between public and domestic drinking, between the shebeen and the private dwelling, and the persistence of customs like the wake and the *ceilidh* (a formal or informal festival of music, storytelling, and dance) spelled a culture spatialized not only in ways different from those that were coming to be regulated by state law and religious dictate, but in ways increasingly seen to be improper. These spaces of popular drinking were clearly not gendered and indeed could involve whole communities; there is little to suggest the homosociality of drinking practices, at least prior to the Famine. At the same time, these were spaces often regarded as giving material expression to the fluctuations of Irish "sentimentality": wakes, in particular, which had always been suspected by English observers, were the object of increasing censure by the Catholic church as the century progressed, not least because of their improper display and mixing of lament and keening, laughter, social criticism, and satiric, often impious, invective, all under the influence of drinking.[19]

What each of these instances figures is the persistence and complexity of a culture of orality, in the fullest sense, alongside, inflecting, and inflected by a modern state and print culture. What *orality* here signifies is not so much the modes of transmission of a nonliterate society—it would be hard to point to any moment at which Gaelic culture was not already chirographic at the least, and nineteenth-century Ireland was saturated with writing—as the modes of sociality and bodily practice.[20] Indeed, it would perhaps not be entirely fanciful to suggest that the persistence of forms of orality in Irish culture represents the sublimation and survival of the nonnucleated settlements of pre-Famine Ireland, whose patterns and social relations furnish a material map of contiguity rather than differentiation, a map that underlies like a palimpsest the actual and psychic landscapes of modernized Ireland.[21] What disturbs the modernizing mentality is the confusion of spaces, emotions, and functions that are signified in Irish orality. The improperly differentiated functions of the mouth and the tongue are the indices of that disturbing cultural difference—mouths that imbibe drink and utter sedition, nonsense, lament, and palaver are the figure for an absence of distinction and for the borderless contiguity of social and psychic or emotional spaces. Looseness of the tongue makes of it an insubordinate and virtually separable autonomous organ, one that is closely associated in "Counterparts" with the recalcitrance and pleasures of the drinker: "Almost before he was aware of it, his tongue had found a felicitous moment" (87). "He had made a proper fool of himself this time. Could he not keep his tongue in his cheek?" (88). "The bar was full of men and loud with the noise of tongues and glasses" (90).

Within the emergent modernity of Dublin in the early 1900s, the pubs that Farrington repairs to constitute heterotopic sites within which drinking is articulated with a whole set of other cultural practices that functions as an Irish mode of countermodernity. It is precisely this fact that makes the public house an alternative space for homosocial conviviality that operates outside the norms and rhythms of alienated labor or the hierarchies of the work space that impinge on Farrington's daily life—outside, but nonetheless constrained and defined in relation to those rhythms and norms as a transgressive negation. The public house as alternative space is already defined by licensing hours as a space of leisure that no longer intersects with the rhythms of work. The consumption of alcohol during the day has become marked as the sign of indiscipline and anomie; its pleasures are tainted and secretive. The public house, with its traditions of treating and oral exchange, abuts the theater that has become marked as the domain of English incursions and commodification. The figure of Weathers condenses that displacement and contamination of Irish male pleasure by its rivalrous counterpart, and the English actor's victory over Farrington is doubly humiliating, expressing not only a breach in his performance of masculinity but his inferiority within a colonial hierarchy and the consequent endangerment of his spaces of pleasure. Within the unforgiving laws of commodity exchange, drinking is only notionally a space of reciprocity; defiant of the logic of the cash nexus as a cultural survival, such as treating may be, modernity makes of it an accumulation of debt. Pawning his timepiece to subvent the evening's drinking, as if in revolt against the clock that has marked his entrapment, Farrington nonetheless ends his evening penurious and on the edge of a fatal economic dependence that matches as it is produced by his alcoholic dependence. His outlet is to bring home the violence he could not express at work; the story concludes with a violence that, for all its vigor, is no less paralyzed insofar as it is issueless and doubtless the source of its own repetition, generation after generation.

Read in this way, "Counterparts" stages drinking as a dangerous and unstable instance of damage and survival within and athwart the terrain of modernity. To be sure, drinking represents the recalcitrance of an Irish orality against the alienating rhythms of labor, against the regulation and division of time and space characteristic of modernity. It is no less opposed in this to the domestic than to the work spaces of modernity and is by no means the site of a sentimental celebration of hearth and home against economic rationality and calculation that structures domestic ideology as a function of capitalist modernity. Yet its containment within the spaces of modernity makes of it the locus of a damaged masculinity, predicated on the recalcitrance of an anomie that constantly swallows up any articulation of resistance that might emerge there. Shot through with the paralysis of anomie, drinking repeats, at the level of the individual, the violent colonial apparatus of humiliation, with its system of economic and cultural dependence. In this, I have already suggested, drinking is, as Joyce clearly grasped it, the shadowy figure of nationalism's own articulation of resistance and dependence: Drink, not temperance, is nationalism's counterpart.[22] The ceaseless movement that arises between the popular practices that make up cultural difference and the nationalism that seeks to contain them plays itself out on the field of a masculinity in reconstitution, a masculinity that is at once the uncertain vehicle and the product of nationalism itself.

Notes

1. James Joyce, "Counterparts," in *Dubliners*, intro. Terence Brown (New York: Penguin Books, 1992), p. 86.

2. Since the literature on nationalism from which I have drawn here is so voluminous, let me cite those sources from which I have drawn most closely: Frantz Fanon, *The Wretched of the Earth*, trans. Constance Farrington (New York: Grove Press, 1968), esp. pp. 223–224; Partha Chatterjee, *Nationalism and the Colonial World: A Derivative Discourse?* (London: Zed Books, 1986); Luke Gibbons, "Identity Without a Centre: Allegory, History and Irish Nationalism," and, indeed, the whole book in which Gibbons's essay is collected, *Transformations in Irish Culture*, Critical Conditions: Field Day Essays, no. 2 (Cork, Ireland: Cork University Press, 1996), pp. 134–137. My own explorations of the discrepancies between official nationalism and popular culture are in *Anomalous States: Irish Writing and the Post-Colonial Moment* (Dublin: Lilliput Press, and Durham, N.C.: Duke University Press, 1993).

3. Chatterjee, *Nationalism and the Colonial World*, p. 42.

4. Matthew Arnold, *On the Study of Celtic Literature*, in *On the Study of Celtic Literature and Other Essays*, intro. Ernest Rhys (London: Dent, 1910), p. 86.

5. On the Victorian representation of the Celt, see L. P. Curtis, *Anglo-Saxons and Celts: A Study of Anti-Irish Prejudice in Victorian England* (Bridgeport, Conn.: Conference on British Studies at the University of Bridgeport, 1968) and *Apes and Angels: The Irishman in Victorian Caricature* (Washington, D.C.: Smithsonian Press, 1971).

6. Indeed, Arnold's aesthetic appreciation of the sentimentality of the Celt, which finds expression in the propensity to elegiac poetry lamenting the Celts' perpetual defeats, finds a precise correlative in John Ruskin's highly popular text on male and female dispositions, *Sesame and Lilies*, in which he puts forth that one of woman's principal functions is to mourn: "She is to extend the limits of her sympathy . . . to the contemporary calamity, which, were it but rightly mourned by her, would recur no more hereafter." See John Ruskin, *Sesame and Lilies*, in *Works*, eds. E. T. Cook and Alexander Wedderburn (London: George Allen, 1905), vol. 18, p. 126.

7. I use the term also by analogy with Kumkum Sangari and Sudesh Vaid's conception of the "reconstitution of patriarchies" that takes place continually both under the British Raj and in the context of Indian nationalism. See their introduc-

tion to *Recasting Women: Essays in Colonial History* (New Delhi, India: Kali for Women, 1989), pp. 1, 25, and passim.

8. Thomas Osborne Davis, "The Young Men of Ireland," *The Nation*, July 15, 1843, p. 32.

9. Partha Chatterjee, "The Nationalist Resolution of the Woman Question," in Sangari and Vaid, eds., *Recasting Women*, pp. 232–253.

10. See W. B. Yeats, "Gods and Fighting Men," in *Explorations* (New York: Macmillan, 1962), pp. 24–26. Marjorie Howes has explored in detail the ways in which Yeats responded to the Arnoldian stereotype by setting his own masculinity over against the femininity of folk culture (unpublished book manuscript, forthcoming). I have discussed Douglas Hyde's need to refine and purify the Irish songs he collected to produce a coherent sense of the Irish "spirit" in "Adulteration and the Nation," *Anomalous States*, pp. 101–104.

11. Elizabeth Malcolm remarks:

> The Young Irelanders took up and supported his [Father Mathew's] call for self-discipline, thrift and education, but as only one part of a much broader movement. To them major political reform was essential; teetotalism of itself was not adequate to achieve the desired ends. Only when Irishmen substantially controlled their own government would the country's problems be solved. The Young Ireland programme for political reform and social advancement shows all the hallmarks of a modernising urban radicalism, but at the same time it highlights the very limited and simplistic nature of Father Mathew's philosophy.

See *"Ireland Sober, Ireland Free": Drink and Temperance in Nineteenth Century Ireland* (Dublin: Gill and Macmillan, 1986), p. 147. I have drawn extensively on Malcolm's work for this essay. For a briefer but no less valuable overview of temperance work in that period, see her "Temperance and Irish Nationalism," in *Ireland Under the Union: Varieties of Tension*, F. S. L. Lyons and R. A. J. Hawkins (Oxford: Clarendon, 1980), pp. 69–114.

12. Father C. J. Herlihy, *The Celt Above the Saxon* (1904), cited in Luke Gibbons, "Race Against Time: Racial Discourse and Irish History," *Oxford Literary Review* 13 (1991), p. 103. On the emergence and spread of such views in temperance nationalism, see Malcolm, "Temperance and Irish Nationalism," pp. 101–108.

13. See Douglas Hyde's influential essay "The Necessity for Deanglicising Ireland," in *Language, Lore and Lyrics: Essays and Lectures*, ed. Breandán Ó Conaire (Blackrock: Irish Academic Press, 1986), pp. 153–170.

14. Reverend J. Halpin, P. P., *The Father Mathew Reader on Temperance and Hygiene* (Dublin: M. H. Gill, 1907).

15. Surprisingly, little historical or anthropological work has been done on the Irish pub or on Irish drinking practices. But for a suggestive analysis of the cultural significance of the pub, or saloon, that has considerable insight to offer on Irish practices despite examining the context of Massachusetts, see Roy Rosenzweig, "The Rise of the Saloon," in *Rethinking Popular Culture: Contemporary Perspectives in Cultural Studies*, eds. Chandra Mukerji and Michael Schudson (Berkeley: University of California Press, 1991), pp. 121–156.

16. Quoted in Kevin Rockett, "Disguising Dependence: Separatism and Foreign Mass Culture," *Circa 49* (January/February 1990), pp. 20–25.

17. Walter Benjamin, *The Origin of German Tragic Drama*, trans. John Osborne, intro. George Steiner (London: Verso, 1985), p. 45.

18. See Rosenzweig, "Rise of the Saloon," pp. 121–126.

19. I have discussed this more fully in "The Memory of Hunger," in *Irish Hunger*, ed. Tom Hayden (Boulder: Roberts Rinehart, 1997).

20. On the imbrication at any historical moment, and especially in modernity, of past and emergent modes of cultural transmission and practice, see Donald Lowe, *History of Bourgeois Perception* (Chicago: University of Chicago Press, 1982), pp. 14–16.

21. On the pre-Famine landscape and the social forms of the rural Irish poor, see Kevin Whelan, "Pre- and Post-Famine Landscape Change," in *The Great Irish Famine*, ed. Cathal Poirteir (Cork and Dublin: Mercier Press, 1995), pp. 19–33.

22. This is perhaps also allegorized in the fate of Jimmy in the story "After the Race," whose attempt to emulate the representatives of more powerful modern nations—England, France, and the United States—leads him into drunkenness and enormous gambling debts.

Chapter Eight

Repetition and Unhousing in Nawal El-Saadawi

APARAJITA SAGAR

Efforts to link the production of gendered subjects and the production of space have often focused on the house and ideologies of the domestic. Third world feminists and U.S. minority feminists in particular have called attention to the house and home as spaces to which women are assigned not just in imperial, patriarchal, and heterosexist discourses, but also in a variety of emancipatory struggles. A dramatic instance of the link between imperialism and the ideologies of the domestic is provided by Karen Hansen, who notes that one meaning of domestication is closely imbricated with cultural imperialism: Until 1964, the Oxford dictionary listed "to civilize" as one of the connotations of "to domesticate" (Hansen 3).

Meanwhile, the need to theorize women's agency has led to a shift from reading the home as the site of oppression to one that engenders unique feminist resistance and subversions. The slogan "personal is political" emerges from this reconceptualization, and it calls attention among other things to the resistance forged by women within the home and within privatized spheres in general.

I argue that this reclaiming of the home, without an ongoing attention to the ceaseless negotiation between the categories of home and the outside, brings its own dangers. Some of these are succinctly outlined by Diana Fuss, who warns that "a severe reduction of the political to the personal leads to a telescoping of goals, a limiting of revolutionary activity to the project of self-discovery and personal transformation. 'The personal is political' reprivatizes social experience" (Fuss 101). Whether the home is seen as the locus of unique terrors or unique subversive energies, the implicit projection of it as a contained and self-identical site remains problematic.

What need to be kept in sight, of course, are the discourses that mandate some sites as home and others as the outside and that obscure the unending and mutually constructive negotiations between both categories. Homes lie within the jurisdiction and the panoptic gaze of state apparatuses and are always already permeable by the outside. On the other hand, women often enter the outside and the public only after those spaces have been recast in terms of the domestic. For instance, the fiction of Algerian novelist Assia Djebar persistently calls attention to the fact that the veil remains the mandated home for the female body when it moves into the public sphere. In the context of Indian nationalism, Ketu Katrak, Kumkum Sangari, and Sudesh Vaid, among others, have noted how women entered the struggle only with the proviso that they bring with them the baggage of home and domesticity. In her study of Palestinian nationalism, Mary Layoun pointed to a similar reprivatization of women's agency. These important accounts of the persistence of domestic ideology in the public sphere have made it untenable to project home as a site that women are able to abandon even when thoroughly imbricated in the outside world. As untenable are the efforts to single out various gendered subject positions, male and female, the privileged and the subaltern, the modern and the premodern, as located autonomously either at home or the outside. As the work of Maria Mies and Cynthia Enloe has shown, the ability of privileged first world and third world women to be at ease in the public world, the outside, has required a global economy that relies on keeping subaltern women mired in first world and third world homes and sweatshops. This international division of labor not only unravels the distinction between home and the outside but also makes it impossible to project first world and third world subjectivities as autonomous of each other.

But this dissolution of boundaries is of course more often acknowledged than elaborated. My chapter turns to Nawal El-Saadawi, the Egyptian activist, cultural critic, and novelist, whose work offers a complex series of such elaborations. In particular, her textual strategy of repetition deconstructs oppositions such as those between home and the outside and questions the autonomy of any subjectivity. Accounting for the startling immediacy of her writing, this strategy is confined to Saadawi's fiction and is absent from her feminist cultural critiques, such as *The Hidden Face of Eve* and *My Travels Around the World*. In her early and relatively realist novels such as *God Dies by the Nile*, as well as in more recent and experimental works such as *The Fall of the Imam* and *The Circling Song*, one finds incessant repetitions of extended passages and scenes, many of which are frozen into stills and tableaus to be cited throughout the text. Some of these are scenes of rape, of clitoridectomy, of an army of men bounding the horizon as it marches in rank and file, always circling in on

itself, of the figure of a robed man approaching the supine, splayed body
of a woman while fingering a hard object through his pocket (knife, stick,
baton, penis), of an excised and mutilated female body haunted by a desire it cannot name, of a woman running and then transfixed, turned into
a statue, running again and again transfixed. These repetitions act as
hammer blows in the novels, marking moments in the text when the narrative itself freezes and the act of narrating becomes paralyzed.

Such scenes abound in all of Saadawi's fiction and keep the violence of
gender, class, patriarchy, and imperialism always in sight. Although it is
tempting simply to inventory their content, the spinning out of this content in the text is also of special interest. Through the narrative re-citation
of the scenes, the novels question the uniqueness, the autonomy, and the
selfsameness of subjectivity and of sites such as the home and the outside.

Although impossible to overlook, Saadawi's use of repetition has only
recently received attention in English-language criticism. Julia Emberley
suggests that repetitions and the "textual seriality of these scenes of
abuse" are indications of a psychological disorder caused in turn by political and material oppression; characters perceive the world as repetitious
because they themselves are "separated from an embodied experience of
a meaningful and accessible 'reality'" (65). In my view this explanation
does not go far enough, locking the strategy, as it does, within the realm
of character motivation and, even more problematically, pathologizing
Saadawi's characters (and, by extension, Egyptian subjectivities) as exceptionally cut off from "meaningful reality." Critics such as Fedwa
Malti-Douglas, Francoise Lionnet, and Peter Hitchcock, while touching
less directly on the strategy of repetition, still usefully examine it in the
context of intersubjectivity. In that process, they implicitly contest Emberley, who is troubled by what she sees as an elitist vanguardism in
Saadawi, one that abjects the subaltern. More persuasively, in my view,
Malti-Douglas, Lionnet, and Hitchcock suggest in various ways that in
Saadawi, subjectivity is moved from a closed to an intersubjective domain in which any abjecting is constantly kept in sight.

My chapter returns to that question of intersubjectivity but focuses on
the textual means through which it is achieved not in *Woman at Point Zero*,
the novel on which most western readers have focused, but rather in
works that have, with the exception of Malti-Douglas's recent study, received less Anglophone critical attention: *God Dies by the Nile*, *The Circling
Song*, and *The Fall of the Imam*. Disidentification and intersubjectivity in
these works put into question the autonomy of various gendered subject
positions, of various faces of oppression—for instance, religious ideology
and western imperialism—and of specific sites of exploitation and resistance, such as home and the outside. Saadawi's works disallow all effort
to see the home and even the body as spaces carrying minimal suggestion

of privacy and refuge and holding out possibilities of discrete resistance. In such a worldview, the prerequisite for any burning down of the house is a conclusive revolution in language and in the categories in which one thinks.

Repetition achieves complex effects in Saadawi's fiction. It acknowledges local and specific configurations of power, such as those of religion or domesticity, but also urges one to move beyond these and confront the banal and self-producing operations that span these configurations. Repetition leads to a critique of the closed subject, creating a space in which that subject is least at home and bringing to crisis powerful interpellating categories such as identity and gender. It calls attention to power's need to recycle itself and to certain forms of resistance made possible when power's need for continuity and recycling is recognized. This recognition, as *God Dies by the Nile* in particular demonstrates, is not easy, but it is the prerequisite for revolution. As a textual strategy that never stops disorienting the reader, repetition puts the reader in a zone in which subjectivity cannot easily be stabilized or foreclosed and in which one is least at home.

An example of Saadawi's focus on the network rather than on any isolated node of power comes in *The Fall of the Imam*. A gloss to the title of the novel is the repeatedly staged scene in which a vainglorious, immense, and posturing single figure, standing on the podium and making a speech on the Day of the Big Feast, is threatened by a voice in the crowd and then shot. The figure then falls slowly to the ground and is revealed to be the Imam, identified elsewhere in the novel as the single visible conduit for all patriarchal and neocolonial discourse in the state. Linking this recurring scene with the novel's title, one might assume that a certain Islam stands at the front of a systemic oppression. But the Imam and his Imamate are flanked and supported, literally held in place and in view, by four important state personages—the Chief of Security, the Great Writer, the Leader of the Lawful Opposition, and the Body Guard—most of whom are marked visibly by their ties to first world imperial structures. The Imam is threatened, is shot, and falls with regularity in the novel, and on each occasion, it is one or the other of these personages who actually steps in to take the fall: his face and body "melt . . . in no time, only to be replaced by another body with exactly the same rubber face which he was wont to wear over his own face so that he remained the living image of the Imam" (41).

Through this figuration, the novel suggests that the faces of the Imam and of Islam are rubbery and mobile. In all of Saadawi's fiction, religious ideology in general is shown to have a pliable face that can be worn by other systems, such as a continuing western imperialism with its ties to a neocolonial state.[1] In the episode just discussed, an archetypal scene is scored into the text—a scene that vigorously recruits bodies to occupy all temporarily vacated subject positions in its mise-en-scène. The specific oppression targeting women is not confined to religion or Islam, as western readers sometimes allege; it emerges from the network of power as a whole, not from any single node on that network.

The same narrative logic is enacted as the novels unravel the opposition between home and the outside. Power operates by establishing false distinctions, for instance, between Islam and western democracy, home and the outside. Lionnet's and Hitchcock's readings of *Women at Point Zero*, as I suggested earlier, emphasize the continuity of oppressions between the different subject positions to which women are assigned under imperialism and patriarchy—for instance, between the socially "diseased" prostitute who kills and the middle-class psychiatrist who fails (or loses the desire) to heal her.[2] *God Dies by the Nile* similarly dissolves the apparent distance between Fatheya—the wife of the religious leader, housebound and thus outside the reach of the mayor-god—and Zakeya and other subaltern women, whose bodies are more exposed to his gaze. In doing so, the novel effects an even more radical meditation on intersubjectivity and questions whether not just the privilege of class but even flesh and the body can provide a housing for the woman.

Fatheya is immured in the house and behind the veil by her husband, the religious leader of the village and one of the mayor-god's trusted underlings. Unlike the other village women, she is not under direct threat from the mayor-god. But Fatheya transgresses against her husband and the mayor by taking an abandoned and illegitimate child—by definition, a child of sin and, as it happens, the product of one of the mayor's rapes—into her home. On the mayor's instruction, the village becomes an avenging force. Fatheya is chased by the mob, cornered, unveiled, and finally, as skin is torn from her body, unfleshed. This unfleshing is also an unsexing, as is implied when another character, Sheikh Mathewali, appears after the mob has departed the scene. Mathewali is a mendicant healer and con artist, living outside the village and in the periphery of most human interaction, a man whom powerlessness and extreme want have reduced to the status of scavenger. One of the few sexual pleasures available to him is that of necrophilia, the extraction of the last sexual use from a body, for in the world of extreme deprivation in which Mathewali lives, nothing can be thrown away. But when he approaches Fatheya's mangled body, Mathewali is either moved or repelled into making an uncharacteristic gesture. He covers Fatheya's torn body with her torn veil, thus performing the parodic last rites for an unsexed body that is now nothing but refuse, that will yield no further value to the most determined scavenger. Even flesh cannot veil Fatheya; neither home nor the body isolate her from the mayor's governance.

Saadawi's insistence on the continuity between different subject positions to which women are assigned under patriarchy and imperialism may have a tactical value for present-day Egyptian feminism. As critics such as Soha Abdel Kader and Margot Badran have noted, the gains women made in the fifties and sixties (a period during which Saadawi herself founded a radical feminist organization and pioneered the move to bring sexual oppression from the private to the public sphere) are now being overturned. Abdel Kader notes that the backlash has led to "a call for 'retraditionalization'" and for "women's return to their 'proper' place within the home and within society as a whole" (137).[3] Similarly, Badran observes that in "the current popular Islamist discourse in Egypt, there is an essentializing of culture, an allocation to women of timeless attributes" (208); she adds that the roles to which women are being returned are primarily the domestic and familial.

Without direct allusion to this historicized feminist discourse, the Fatheya episode powerfully dismantles such oppositions by showing that women, whether or not they are protected by privilege or tradition, are not guaranteed a "proper" place at home or outside. Saadawi's fiction questions the tenability of distinctions that either single out specific manifestations of power (such as religion) or remain willfully blind to repeated processes of regulation and violence across supposedly discrete terrains such as the home and the outside, the public and the private. Repetition in her fiction makes possible emotive and powerful elaborations of the activist and public stances she has taken—for instance, in her address to the Arab Women's Solidarity Association (AWSA), the feminist organization she headed until its recent dissolution by the state. On this occasion, as on many others, Saadawi insisted that "freedom cannot be less than whole, that human life is not divided into the public and private, and that rights are acquired rather than bestowed" (quoted in Hitchcock 50).[4]

Moreover, in Saadawi, neither home nor the outside is a hermetic site requiring specific forms of exploitation and enabling discrete forms of resistance. In that, she departs conclusively from her Algerian contemporary Djebar. Djebar does not project the home in the western terms of the nuclear family either; instead, she calls attention to its continuity with such spaces as the harem and the veil. Like Saadawi, Djebar emphasizes a second continuity, that between the segregated, immured woman in the home of the veil and the modern unveiled woman who seeks to "trade" segregation for "an often fallacious face to face with men" ("Forbidden" 53). But unlike Saadawi's fiction, Djebar's nonallegorical and historically particularized writing presents the home and the veil as sites of specific forms of exploitation and resistance. Saadawi's reflections on the production of space and of gender more radically dismantle the opposition between home and the outside, the veiled and unveiled body, the private and the public spheres, the imprisoned and the free.

Repetition in Saadawi's fiction also brings about a disclosure of the processes by which power recycles itself. It enables an understanding also of resistance as that which intervenes in the recycling process to turn a particular vector of power upon itself, as though a clockwise movement were made to reverse direction. One of the most oppressive of these movements is that of gendering. Saadawi's attention to the strong links between material oppression and discursive violence leads her to examine the conceptual categories—such as individual identity and gender—through which meanings are fixed in language and through which subjects are interpellated and brought into the regime of ideologies.

Markers of sex and subsequently of gender are sex organs, fleshly appendages bestowed on the body at birth. But under conditions of brute poverty and the unrelenting extraction of the body's labor, especially sexual labor, the body can become ungendered and even unsexed. Hortense Spillers proposes a similar argument in "Mama's Baby, Papa's Maybe—An American Grammar Book": On slave ships, during the Middle Passage, the torn, mutilated, and flayed body of the slave sometimes became unfleshed—and thus rid of the most visible signs of gender or sex. In Saadawi, as the unfleshing of Fatheya and the repeated scenes of incessant rapes, castrations, and clitoridectomies show, the flesh is subject to intervention through pain, mutilation, and torture. In the brutally violent world of her allegories, the body is subject to the most radical of transformations through pain. Marks of sex therefore can always be mutilated, excised, torn off, as in the act of clitoridectomy; they can also be supplemented or substituted for by fetishized objects. Scenes of the unfleshing of male as well as female bodies are repeatedly figured in Saadawi's fiction, serving as a constant reminder of the constructedness and precariousness of sex.

God Dies by the Nile gives us the unforgettable image of Kafrawi, a man who labors in the fields from predawn to sunset, a monotonous, unending hard labor under a burning sun, so that his body becomes slippery and coated with blood, sweat, urine, and semen. Kafrawi can no longer feel the difference between these bodily fluids or between the emotional complexes connoted by each. If gender/sex is to be established partly on the basis of the fluids secreted by the human body, then that classificatory system is itself threatened by their confluence under extreme bodily strain.

Because sexing is not only an arbitrary act, but also a precarious one, identity and gender demand several repetitions, many re-citations. One of the most powerful instances of this process comes in *The Circling Song*. The novel focuses on Hamido and Hamida, twins born of "one embryo." Pregnant after a brutal rape, Hamida is put on a train to the city by her mother, who hopes her daughter might escape the wrath of her avenging father; the crime, that of getting raped, is the daughter's. In the next scene, Hamido is taken by his father to the same train the following day, given a knife, and told to find and kill Hamida, for "only blood can wash away shame" (17). In the act of searching for Hamida, Hamido finds himself retracing her steps—through various dark rooms where a series of robed male figures have raped Hamida, through other rooms where she has undergone clitoridectomy, through a "small dank spot before the kitchen sink" where she stood rooted for several hours at a time laboring as a household servant, and through brothels, where Hamida had finally won acclaim and celebrity in a new career as a prostitute (32). Gradually it becomes clear that the retracing will take its toll on Hamido. In his search for her, Hamido not only visits all the dark rooms, prisons, brothels, kitchens, and refuse bins that she has lived in, he eventually finds himself repeating her actions, undergoing the rapes and mutilations she underwent, and losing his "manly implement," becoming unfleshed, and becoming Hamida (43). Yet this move too is not conclusive, and the novel culminates in an incantation in which Hamido and Hamida exchange sexes back and forth in a dizzying and circling movement.

In the novel, men are often found fingering through their pockets a "sharp, hard implement, hanging down along the thigh" (30). The implement varies; it can be a knife, a stick, a baton. Those continually checking and rechecking its presence are looking not for sexual gratification alone but also for reassurance that they are still male. Hamido shares in this general anxiety. Why the paranoia? *The Circling Song* delineates a world in which gender is in need of constant confirmation, for it is frequently tested through such state apparatuses as the Department of Citizen Identification and Documentation. Hamido's own sexed identity is hostage to the crazy workings of this department. If most male figures in the novel are found repeatedly checking and rechecking their manly implements, the reason is their profound fear of losing their classification as male in the badly kept records of the department.

Given the unacknowledged but dangerous slipperiness of gender and identity, categories indispensable to the state's control of its citizens, it is not surprising that the department has an obsessive need to update its sorting list, to classify, reclassify, and classify again. The department maintains a gender-sorting list and conducts frequent unannounced examinations of masculinity. In these examinations, "the shrivelled and terror-stricken member" is measured with "finely calibrated scales" and the results recorded with a Parker Pen in a notebook reserved for this purpose (43). In such a world Hamido must always burden under the continual obligation to "establish that he [is] *not* a woman" (42)—that he is not in fact Hamida, his twin sister, born of the same embryo. It is in the state apparatus's compulsive need to recite that we can find an important axiom in Saadawi: the fact that gender is constructed and not natural must be hidden by those who need to keep that knowledge at bay. To obscure the knowledge of gender as construct, one must continually re-cite it as essence. For the Department of Citizen Identification and Documentation, the classifying of sex and gender in specific bodies necessarily leads to the business of reproducing sex and gender as conceptual categories.

A similar attention to discursive violence marks Saadawi's reflections on identity categories. In "Imitation and Gender Insubordination" Judith Butler writes, "Identity categories tend to be instruments of regulatory regimes, whether as the normalizing categories of oppressive structures, or as the rallying points for a liberatory contestation of that very oppression" (13–14).[5] In Saadawi's fiction, categories such as gender and the self are pried loose from the naturalizing rhetoric in which they have gained currency and are instead presented as ideological constructs through which subjects think their worlds. Her strategy of repetition in particular persistently tells us of the arbitrariness of identity categories masquerading in the regime of the natural and of common sense. Moreover, in her presentation of resistance, as well, Saadawi herself draws minimally on closed identity categories even when proposing "a liberatory contestation."

Reading Saadawi's novels in translation from the Arabic, most Anglophone critics such as I are not in a position to appreciate fully their play with language. But her strategy of repetition nonetheless gives us a glimpse of her strong interest in language as the terrain in which gender is constructed. In *The Circling Song*, Hamido's problem is compounded not only by the fact that gender and sex are subject to change as the body itself changes under torture and pain, but also by the fact that they exist in language, itself a slippery thing. The sorting lists of the Department of Citizen Identification and Documentation are often ridden with typographical errors; most entries are in adulterated and diluted ink. This error-prone system inevitably has horrific consequences for a character such as Hamido, who is under the continual obligation of proving that he is not Hamida, his twin sister, the woman. And if simple typos or slips of the pen can have such momentous consequences, this is because, as Saadawi tells us,

> in the Arabic language, even one point—a single dot—can completely change the essence of a word. Male becomes female because of a single dash or dot. Similarly, in Arabic, the difference between "husband" and "mule," or between "promise" and "scoundrel" is no more than a single dot placed over a single form, an addition which transforms one letter into another.[6] (CS 8)

Names are especially vulnerable, for a "single-letter feminine ending can turn a male name into a female name, so that Amin becomes Amina, Zuhayr turns into Zuhayra ... and Hamido becomes Hamida" (CS 42). The novel thus calls attention simultaneously to the great power of the gendering machine and its arbitrariness and vulnerability to error.

It is in its need to repeatedly stage its operations, to reproduce itself, that the power network becomes vulnerable. *The Circling Song* gives us a powerful instance of the ways in which power needs to recite its paradigms; the very arbitrariness and precariousness of sex and gender categories, for instance, necessitates that they be continually affirmed. It is in that need for compulsive recitation that the department (and state apparatuses in general, symbolized by the department) becomes vulnerable, and the possibility of revolution begins to surface.

Both *The Circling Song* and *The Fall of the Imam* hint at this possibility, which Saadawi explores more fully in *God Dies by the Nile*. Resistance is not presented in any of these novels as subversion—the undermining of power from within fixed parameters—as it is in the work of writers such as Djebar. Subversions might depend on viewing the structure to be subverted, the home for instance, as finite and bounded. In Saadawi's fiction, where there is no outside to the home and where home and the outside often abruptly metamorphose into each other, we glimpse not subversions but more rare and often forestalled possibilities of revolution.

One specific form of resistance, relevant in particular to gendering, involves misrecognition. Gender becomes precarious in *The Fall of the Imam* because the mirror stage is no longer a foundational moment in which the self falsely coheres, but a scene that is endlessly repeated, with the foundational concepts of the self brought into crisis with every restaging. In this novel, a marching column of men comes upon an army of ants, and the men snigger among themselves that ants are condemned to crawl upon their bellies because they have submitted to female rule, that of the queen ant. Yet as often happens in Saadawi's writing, these distinctions between the ants and the marching male army abruptly fall away, and the men find that

> their bodies had not been reclining nor standing nor sitting as they thought but crawling on their bellies, zigzagging from one side to the other unlike ants which tend to move in a straight line, pushing a way through themselves, making pits with their elbows in each other's bellies as they fought their way with hands and feet. . . . [They] could not get a glimpse of anything at all because the column extending to where the sky and earth met kept twisting like the spiral of a spring. (*Fall*, 78–79)

What fixes the human army in its tracks is a sudden obstacle: the figure of a naked female body, a body that is dead but that appears at different points in the novel to be running, to be transfixed into a statue, and to be running again. Though taking little note of this intrusion at first, the men are soon struck by a profound and disturbing memory of mutilations and suffering they themselves have undergone for the Imam/god. And a huge terror is born (the title of the chapter is "Collective Fear"): the dead woman's heart continues to beat, and the men realize that whatever they do, wherever they go, "she will see him," this body could "pass through anything, could see them wherever they went, yet remain invisible herself" (80). Saadawi's fiction often presents us with recurring scenes of characters standing before opaque mirrors; as the narrator of *The Circling Song* says, "The mirror is always at hand, positioned like another person standing between one and oneself" (11). The sighting of the marching men by the running female body has momentous consequences; her body now stands between them and the masculine identities they have laboriously constructed and upheld, returning their gaze and unpicking the fabric of their gendered male worlds. It is in this fashion that the alternatively running and transfixed body of the woman counteracts the speech issued by the Imam just before he falls; both moments are staged repeatedly in the novel, punctuating and stilling the narration.

Such scenes of misrecognition operate less in a realist space than in the hallucinatory and discursive domain in which Saadawi, as a practicing psychiatrist, is specially interested. As resistance, these moments call for a seismic shift in perception, a revolution in language and thought. This aspect of resistance is most fully elaborated in *God Dies by the Nile*, and it too originates in the trope of repetition. The novel conclusively demonstrates that if the categories through which power operates, such as those of gender and closed identity, are arbitrary, their brutality and power must still not be underestimated. Their unmasking is painful, tortured, and slow, as we discover in all of Saadawi's fiction, and particularly in this novel.

God Dies by the Nile tells of the protagonist Zakeya's unmasking of the fact, profoundly simple and subject to profound mystification, that if the mayor is god, then god is the mayor and vulnerable in his corporeality and mortality. What makes the mayor so powerful is that his mansion, figuratively the house of god, is elastic, endlessly expandable and mobile, capable of superimposing itself over the world. A tangible image for this process is the gates of the mayor's house, which set up uncrossable barriers between him and the villagers. The latter are expected to produce labor for the mayor-god's governance and bodies for his sexual satisfaction. The gates appear in the nightmares of several villagers. In repeated and vivid scenes, the novel plunges us from one character's nightmare into another's, and in each, the dreamer does not watch herself going toward or away from the gates, but instead sees the gates, "their iron bars like long black legs . . . advancing slowly" toward her (19).

In Saadawi's fiction, the boundaries of identity, of gender, resemble the gates of the mayor's house, not merely in the obduracy with which they enclose and demarcate entities, but also in their unsettling ability to move, to erupt into the consciousness of the wary and the unwary, and thus to actively imprison all that lies outside them. The question then is how might such an all-pervading power, that of god, be resisted. And once again power becomes vulnerable in its need to repeat itself.

It is the neocolonial/imperial state, embodied in the mayor, that compulsively needs to recite and repeat, to find more and more bodies to inhabit subject positions required for its mise-en-scène. In this novel, as in Saadawi's other stagings of oppression, it is the mise-en-scène that first comes into view; only then do we see individual bodies, male and female, take up their assigned positions on the stage. The subject position exists prior to the body that must inhabit it, and in Saadawi, body after body is made to inhabit the position in succession, or relay form. There is no respite. When the last sexual or other use value is extracted from the raped, mutilated body of the subaltern, that body must die. Another body must succeed it, taking up the vacated position in a scene of violence that is otherwise unchanged. Saadawi's fiction often gives us the image of a dense mass of human bodies, so dense as to form a sea of undifferentiated flesh, sweat, noise, urine, semen, and blood. Upon this sea from time to time a hand descends—the hand of the Imam or mayor—and plucks out one form from the mass, maneuvering it into the empty position on stage. The scene will continue to be played out, but it will always already be in need of repetition. And it is in its need for re-citation that the regime—the mayor's plot, for instance—becomes vulnerable so that the possibility of revolution takes root.

We know from the beginning of the novel that the mayor has a need to rape and exploit—to extract the maximum sexual and use value from the village that he rules absolutely. The refrain that the mayor is god is repeated by every villager who invokes his name, so much so that the appellation becomes automatic and unquestioned. The villagers know that the mayor is the government, and they know also that government comes from god and is good. As young girl after young girl in the village is pressed into service at the mayor's house, raped, impregnated, and made to disappear, he himself remains beyond the reach of the law. As god, he also remains above suspicion. But if the mayor appears invulnerable in his godhead, it is precisely this godhead that becomes his undoing.

The mayor is impelled and indeed defined by the need or desire to exploit, murder, and rape—in short, to extract the maximum use from the bodies over which he rules. Zakeya (a name that partly connotes "intelligence" or "thought"), a destitute peasant woman in the village, has two daughters, each of whom is made to assume her role in the mayor's plot, is forced in turn to work as a servant in the mayor's house, is raped and impregnated by the mayor, and then is surreptitiously removed from the scene. After being raped, the body of each must disappear, for it is impregnated by the mark of the mayor, which, when it becomes visible, must eventually betray his role in the plot. A man must be selected from among the villagers to account for the woman's disappearance and her rape. This man must in turn be murdered so that he cannot undermine the mayor's plot. A second man must then be charged with the murder. Because he operates in a finite space, that of the village, and soon runs out of bodies, the mayor too is under some constraints. Eventually, he chooses to cast all the parts in his plot from among Zakeya's family; her two daughters, her brother, and then her nephew are all made in turn to take the stage.

Zakeya knows that in the larger scheme of things it is god who has brought such intense suffering to her family, for reasons known only to him. But Zakeya, like other villagers, also knows that the mayor is god, a knowledge that for her, as for other villagers, operates in a fuzzy domain between figuration and literalization. As the mayor stages and restages his unchanging plot of oppression, casting first one then another of Zakeya's family members in the various roles, Zakeya recites numbly to herself the lesson that god is responsible for all that happens and is thus the mastermind of this particular plot as well. With each restaging of the mayor's plot, Zakeya finds herself mechanically repeating two lessons: god is responsible for her sufferings, and the mayor is god. With each repetition, her knowledge that the mayor is god moves from the figural to the literal. Not only is the mayor like god, but he is god.

This understanding can be contracted into a single sentence—"the mayor is god"—which is uttered in one version or the other, and with varying degrees of resignation and irony, by the villagers at various points in the novel. But if this sentence is recited over and over again and as numbly as Zakeya recites it, an interesting reversal in meaning becomes possible. And the entire narrative movement of the novel enacts this reversal, taking Zakeya past any domesticated or even ironic acceptance of the given sentence and into the uncharted terrain of reversed sentences and eventual revolution. The repetition of the sentence—the mayor is god the mayor is god the mayor is god—allows a second sentence to be heard behind the first, and that sentence is "God is the mayor." God is mortal, possessed of a body—that of the mayor—which, like other bodies and unlike any godhead, is mortal and subject to destruction. Since god is her oppressor, Zakeya's new knowledge of the mortality and corporeality of the source of oppression is earthshaking in its implications. The shift in understanding from "The mayor is god" to "God is the mayor" is momentous and revolutionary, and it marks the site of agency in the novel. Now bereft of all that she ever called her own, with nothing left to lose but her body, Zakeya, or intelligence and thought, kills god by killing the mayor. At the end of the novel, she is heard telling a casual acquaintance who is trembling before a vision of god that "god is dead, my child. I buried him by the Nile" (167). Zakeya's revolution in language and thought is made possible through repetition.

The original title of the book, *God Dies by the Nile,* was regarded as so blasphemous that, despite Saadawi's vehement objections, it was changed to what would best translate as *The Death of the Only Man on Earth.*[7] In that change what is lost is, of course, the complex interdependence the novel posits between revolution in language and political revolution.

In the foreword to her translation of *Woman at Point Zero,* Djebar pointed to other such revolutions in Saadawi; she reads this novel as being about the "birth of a word"—and the birth is momentous, starting a new tradition of Arab writing by women ("Firdaus" 372). Saadawi's strategy of repetition allows her to keep in sight the discursive paradigms underlying material oppression and violence; it also enables her to foreground the discourses that legitimate this violence. An interest in language and the production of meanings marked Saadawi's earlier, more realist fiction, and it is increasingly evident in her most recent and experimental work. In a 1986 interview, Saadawi said that she is increasingly troubled by the fact that "the Arabic language, like the English language, is very male-oriented" ("Reflections" 402). She sees her writing as "really trying to change the language" (402). "Now I have to experiment. Before, I didn't have the pleasure or the freedom to experiment with the language, to experiment with ideas" (404).

The outcome of such experiments has been the kinds of novel-allegories discussed previously, which, without always naming historical moments and topical events, nonetheless intervene strongly into present-day crises confronting third world and other feminisms. Through Saadawi's strategy of repetition, these allegories make it difficult for readers and characters to be housed in stable categories such as gender, identity, or the body. If domestication connotes ease and comfort, the ability to negotiate smoothly over known terrain, Saadawi's fiction counters this possibility, disallowing any glib and formalist processing of characters and scenes and controverting any impulse to be at home in the fiction.

Undoing the false opposition between the discursive and the material, Saadawi's fiction demonstrates that material resistance and revolution are effected through a revolution in language and in the conceptualizing of interpellating categories such as gender and identity. Her fiction constructs a space for agency and does so outside the bounds of closed, unitary, and selfsame notions of subjectivity. Her method is to take disparate identities and paradigms of oppression, strip them of the accidents of language that bestow a uniqueness upon them, and reconfigure them into a very few scenes that have the recitative power to arrest and paralyze narration itself. Yet even as the narrative comes to a halt, it marks the site of revolution, figuring agency as a complex discursive/material possibility, conceptualized in collective terms and outside the enclosure of stable and individuated identity.

Notes

I am grateful to Rosemary M. George, Nancy J. Peterson, and Marcia Stephenson for their thoughtful critiques of earlier versions of this chapter.

1. By thus positioning some repressive contemporary Islamic practices in the realm of ideology rather than essence, Saadawi is not attempting to minimize their power. She has observed that contemporary Arabic writers, including in particular men who share her progressive politics and in some cases even her Marxist-feminist orientation, have moderated their public critique of the distorted Islam proclaimed as state ideology—so much so, she notes, that many in this group now "start their works with the *bismillah* and end them with al-hamdulilla ar rahman, al rahim (Praise be to God, the Compassionate, the Merciful)" ("Reflections" 404). In such a climate she herself cannot but be considered seditious. Consequently, her works have been subjected to intense scrutiny and have been censored; they rarely find publishers in Egypt. She herself has been removed from public positions and has been imprisoned. The publishers of the Arabic original brought out *God Dies by the Nile* only after changing its title to *The Death of the Only Man on Earth*.

More recent manifestations of this persecution are noted by Hitchcock, who observes that Saadawi's opposition to the Gulf War and the genocide of Iraqis might have been responsible for the Egyptian government's banning of AWSA, the radical feminist organization that she founded and led. For a complex discussion of Saadawi's reception in Egypt and the Middle East, see Fedwa Malti-Douglas's invaluable recent study, *Men, Women, and God(s)*, especially pages 1 to 19.

2. Calling attention to the "erosion of distance between the authorial self and the narrating 'I' of Firdaus," Lionnet notes that they become "uncannily similar" (143). For Lionnet, such intersubjectivity puts into question the autonomous subject and offers a paradigm of a space for coalitional (but nonappropriative) links between women—for instance, between the third world subaltern and the western feminist. In his reading of the same novel, Hitchcock emphasizes that this intersubjectivity is distinct from formalist identification between reader and characters, for it inserts an alienation effect into the act of reading: Saadawi's framing serves "to distance or delay the most obvious forms of reader identification" and makes possible a focus on "subjectivity in a process of nonidentity and identification" (Hitchcock 35, 44). Alienation effects can of course be read as one kind of unhousing of the reader.

3. Abdel Kader's 1987 study notes that Egyptian women at present "enjoy extensive civil freedoms, occupy one-third of university seats, and hold one-quarter of professional jobs" (139). But these gains are rapidly being overturned. Some of the more drastic reversals are a "draft law" proposing that women working outside the home should "quit their jobs while retaining half their salaries" (137). Earlier reforms redressing wrongs done to women by divorce and custody laws were overturned, as was the constitutional law reserving thirty seats for women in the People's Assembly (138).

4. Hitchcock is quoting from "The Political Challenge Facing Arab Women at the End of the Twentieth-Century," in *Women in the Arab World*, ed. Nahid Toubia (London: Zed, 1988), 23.

5. Even when, for political action, she groups herself under the sign woman or lesbian, Butler says that "I would like to have it permanently unclear what precisely that sign signifies" (14). In my view, Saadawi's fiction also confers a useful and permanent unclarity on fixed identity categories, such as those of gender, while still impressing upon us their harshly regulative regimes. See Malti-Douglas for an excellent discussion of language in Saadawi and specifically of what she, invoking Butler, calls "gender malleability" in *The Circling Song* (86).

6. This particular imaging of identity as such is reminiscent of Spivak's observation in "Acting Bits/Identity Talk" on the Sanskrit and Latin roots of the word *identity*: "the Sanskrit *idam* or the Latin *idem*," usually taken to mean "same." But, Spivak adds, in both Sanskrit and Latin, the word does not translate as "'same' in the sense of one, but rather, same in the sense of multitudes or repetitions. Not in the sense of 'unique' or 'primordial,' but, rather, that which can be cited through many recitations" (774). Not the "undiminishing selfsame," for "as a pronoun it does not have even the dignity of the noun, and it is always enclitic or inclined towards the noun, always dependent on the proximity of a particular self, for *idam* must always remain monstrative, indexed" ("Acting" 774). Though it emerges from a different tradition from the Sanskritic or the Latinate, Saadawi's use of repetition points to the sense of identity as not the selfsame but the other in the self, as not unique, not primordial, but multitudinous. Her writing presents identity as recitable, as needing to be recited, to be inhabited by a succession of bodies.

7. Saadawi discusses this change in title in "Reflections of a Feminist," her 1986 interview with Fedwa Malti-Douglas and Allen Douglas.

Works Cited

Abdel Kader, Soha. *Egyptian Women in a Changing Society, 1899–1987*. Boulder: Lynne Rienner Publishers, 1987.

Badran, Margot. "Gender Activism: Feminists and Islamists in Egypt." In *Identity Politics and Women: Cultural Reassertions and Feminisms in International Perspective*. Ed. Valentine M. Moghadam. Boulder: Westview Press, 1994, 202–227.

Butler, Judith. "Imitation and Gender Insubordination." In *Inside/Out: Lesbian Theories, Gay Theories*. Ed. Diana Fuss. New York: Routledge, 1991, 13–31.

Djebar, Assia. "Firdaus: The Birth of a Word." In *Opening the Gates: A Century of Arab Women's Writing*. Eds. Miriam Cook and Margot Badran. Bloomington: Indiana University Press, 1990, 387–93.

_____. "Forbidden Sight, Interrupted Sound." *Discourse* 8 (1986–1987): 39–56.

Emberley, Julia. *Thresholds of Difference: Feminist Critique, Native Women's Writings, Postcolonial Theory*. Toronto: University of Toronto Press, 1993.

Fuss, Diana. *Essentially Speaking: Feminism, Nature, Difference*. New York: Routledge, 1989.

Hansen, Karen, ed. *African Encounters with Domesticity*. New Brunswick, N.J.: Rutgers University Press, 1992.

Hitchcock, Peter. *Dialogics of the Oppressed*. Minneapolis: University of Minnesota Press, 1993.

Katrak, Ketu. "Indian Nationalism, Gandhian 'Satyagraha,' and Representations of Female Sexuality." In *Nationalisms and Sexualities*. Eds. Andrew Parker et al. New York: Routledge, 1992, 395–406.

Layoun, Mary. "Telling Spaces: Palestinian Women and the Engendering of National Narratives." In *Nationalisms and Sexualities*. Eds. Andrew Parker et al. New York: Routledge, 1992, 407–423.

Lionnet, Francoise. *Postcolonial Representations: Women, Literature, Identity*. Ithaca: Cornell University Press, 1995.

Malti-Douglas, Fedwa. *Men, Women, and God(s): Nawal El-Saadawi and Arab Feminist Poetics*. Berkeley: University of California Press, 1995.

El-Saadawi, Nawal. *The Circling Song*. London: Zed Books, 1988.

_____. *The Fall of the Imam*. Trans. Sherif Hetata. London: Methuen (Minerva), 1988.

_____. *God Dies by the Nile*. Trans. Sherif Hetata. London: Zed Books, 1988 (1974).

_____. "Reflections of a Feminist." Interview with Fedwa Malti-Douglas and Allen Douglas. In *Opening the Gates*. Eds. Miriam Cooke and Margot Badran. Bloomington: Indiana University Press, 1990, 395–404.

Spillers, Hortense. "Mama's Baby, Papa's Maybe: An American Grammar Book." *Diacritics* 17, no. 2 (Summer 1987): 65–81.

Spivak, Gayatri. "Acting Bits, Identity Talk." *Critical Inquiry* 18, no. 4 (Summer 1992): 770–803.

Chapter Nine

Fast Capital, Race, Modernity, and the Monster House

KATHARYNE MITCHELL

At cocktail parties and conferences, on television documentaries and the front page of the daily newspapers, the word was out: the Monster had escaped and was running rampant through Vancouver's west-side neighborhoods. Studies were commissioned to document its history, vital statistics, and probable future, and neighborhood organizations were formed to curtail its path. Endless government and private reports detailed who was responsible and who was not responsible, who was to blame and who was not to blame. Politicians cut their campaign eyeteeth on it. The *Sunday Telegraph* in London did a story on it, as did several U.S. papers, the Hong Kong *South China Morning Post,* and even, in 1992, the *National Geographic.*[1] What was this thing that so galvanized a city and laid its soul bare to the world?

In the late 1980s, there was a tremendous movement of people and capital from Hong Kong to Vancouver, British Columbia.[2] The foreign-based purchase of residential property and the rapid influx of large numbers of wealthy Chinese immigrants into Vancouver's west-side neighborhoods disrupted many established notions of home, community, and way of life for older residents. The large, so-called monster houses that were constructed in these neighborhoods threatened the symbolic capital of this way of life, a set of beliefs and practices predicated largely on the values of a British Protestant elite. Shock effects from the changes reverberated nationally and internationally, exacerbating both the monument and the myth of the Monster House.

Many residents of these west-side neighborhoods linked the physical changes in the built environment with the arrival of the Hong Kong Chinese, and protest movements against change became imbricated in a racial discourse. Questions of architectural style, taste, landscape design, and neighborhood character were bound up with questions of race, racism, and cultural difference. Controlling the meanings of terms such as *race* and *racism* thus became an increasingly important form of ideological power, because these meanings influenced urban development, capital accumulation and circulation, and the international articulation of Chinese and Canadian capitalisms.

But how were struggles over house style related to definitions of race? And why were racial meanings interlocked with the movements of local and international "fast" capital?[3] Following the oil crisis and recession of the 1970s, new regimes of capitalist accumulation were marked by a "startling flexibility with respect to labour processes, labour markets, products, and patterns of consumption."[4] The new flexibility in cycles of production and consumption was facilitated by the widespread deregulation of financial systems and markets across the globe. An increasing lack of national control over finance has abetted the rapid movement of capital across international borders and enabled the simultaneous decentralization and consolidation of economic functions worldwide.[5]

As manufacturing plants relocated to areas heralding cheap labor and the opportunity for expansion into new markets, executive functions were increasingly consolidated in urban financial centers. Cities able to extend lines of control across national boundaries became strategic centers—new "global" cities—in the extension and coordination of integrated production complexes worldwide.[6] With the growing economic, political, social, and urban interlinkages, the world of modern capitalism is becoming both "a worldwide net of corporations and a global network of cities."[7]

Why are global networks and the internationalization of the economy important for an understanding of the politics of the home in Vancouver? The decentralization and consolidation of capitalist functions within an increasingly global economy were not spread evenly across space or by urban region, but tended to exacerbate preexisting unevennesses. The threat of massive devaluation of fixed capital interests in production plants and the loss of government support of the local real wage put a number of cities such as Vancouver in a precarious position. It became increasingly imperative to maintain a level of urban competence to fit into the new networked systems. Political and economic restructuring in the 1970s and 1980s thus forced urban areas to compete against each other in ever more bitter struggles to attract national and international capital investment and to assume a prominent position in the hierarchy of "global" cities. The new patterns of flexible accumulation dovetailed nicely with these competitive efforts, as interurban competition "opened spaces within which the new and more flexible labour processes could be more easily implanted."[8]

In this context, the effort to sell Vancouver as an attractive site for investment and consumption took place on many fronts and presaged major economic, social, and cultural upheavals for its urban residents. While municipal and provincial politicians did backward somersaults to attract foreign capital and to promote the city's "open for business" message, many long-term Vancouverites questioned the ramifications of these policies in their daily lives. The changes in house prices, architectural design, and neighborhood character were linked with the increasing economic and cultural globalization of the city. Resistance to the wider processes and dynamics of change became condensed in the battle over the architectural design of the house next door. Local resistance to global forces thus took shape and crystallized out in the struggle over the Monster House.

Owing to the immigration of many wealthy Chinese into west-side neighborhoods where Monster Houses were being constructed, the assertion of hegemonic racial definitions and appropriate tastes became crucial points of local resistance and contestation. The process of rapid physical, economic, and cultural change in the urban environment opened up previously implicit definitions of race, place, and home, rendering articulate, in both senses of the word,[9] the assumptions and categorizations employed in conceptions of neighborhood character and architectural style. It was thus through the reworking of Vancouver's built environment that these hegemonic assumptions first began to emerge openly; in the period of "fast" capitalism or "hyper" modernity, the naturalized, heretofore opaque connections between the economic and cultural capital of Vancouver's elite, White neighborhoods became increasingly transparent. The manner in which these questions of capital, race, culture, and taste appeared, intersected, and were manipulated in the Monster House saga is the subject of this chapter.

Dreaming of Monsters: Nostalgia as a Highway to Racism

> I could tell you how many steps make up the streets rising like stairways, and the degree of the arcades' curves, and what kind of zinc scales cover the roofs; but I already know this would be the same as telling you nothing. The city does not consist of this, but of relationships between the measurements of its space and the events of its past.[10]

Monster House is a term used for houses that are especially large in the context of Vancouver neighborhoods on the west side of the city. These neighborhoods include most of the area west of Oak Street, advancing toward the University Endowment Lands and bounded on the north and the south by English Bay and the Fraser River. The neighborhoods with the highest density of large new houses are in southwest Oakridge between Granville and Oak Streets and Forty-ninth and Fifty-seventh Streets. The most vociferous and highly publicized opposition to the Monster Houses, however, has come from the wealthier neighborhoods of Kerrisdale and Shaughnessy. I have drawn from these areas for my Vancouver-based interviews.[11]

Three basic forms or envelopes shape the generic Monster House, corresponding with the zoning regulations before 1986, the zoning revisions of April 1986, and the zoning revisions of April 1988. Features that many Monster Houses share include the following: a rectangular, usually symmetrical shape occupying the maximum allowed lot surface coverage and height and built to the maximum allowed square footage in size;[12] a large entranceway with double doors and two-story entrance hall; large, symmetrical unshuttered windows with occasional glass brick detailing; and external finishes that are often composed of brick or stone on the first story and stucco, vinyl, or cedar siding on the second. The interiors are spacious and plain, with an average of five to seven bedrooms and an equivalent number of bathrooms. The landscaping is often bounded by a stylized hedge or a fence (both of which are uncommon in Vancouver) and tends to be more formal and minimalist in the use of shrubbery and trees than traditional Vancouver yards are. Occasionally the entire yard is paved.

The Monster Houses vary in form and style from neighborhood to neighborhood, depending on the zoning laws that were in effect at the time of their construction. When I asked long-term residents to describe the Monster Houses, they often responded with some irritation and surprise: "Well, haven't you seen them?" The generalized image of the Monster House was so prevalent in the popular imagination that any particular description seemed somehow less (and yet also more) than warranted. Annie Humphreys, a leader in the organization Concerned Citizens for Affordable Housing (CCAH), drove me around her Kerrisdale neighborhood for over three hours, pointing out the numerous recent changes to the area. Her conversation wove together the abstract and the concrete, memory and desire. From sharp comments on an ugly architectural feature and poor-quality materials, she shifted instantaneously into nostalgia for the garden that had been displaced:

> This building up here, which is locally known as "The Fortress," has iron bars on every single window and every single doorway [1200 block of Forty-eighth Street]. If you go up the side of this smaller house alongside this one, you go through a tunnel, virtually, because they've overbuilt their fence. . . . This is a new one on the corner. It just goes on and on, and it's so ugly, because you get these columns at the front, these Greek columns which are two stories high. And it's a disaster [Montgomery and Forty-ninth]. These three houses in a row—there used to be such beautiful gardens here. People

prided themselves in their lawns and garden area. . . . Look at this one. It's gone. And they haven't done anything about that garden [Montgomery and Fiftieth]. . . . This whole block . . . this is where that prizewinning garden was. And this house here has the most rhododendrons I've ever seen in my life. And you know that that house is doomed.[13]

In 1988, the house next to Annie's had been demolished and a much larger one constructed in its place. At the time of construction, the effluent from the building materials ran onto her lawn, and the workers left garbage and building waste on her property. The noise during the construction period was horrendous. After the new building was constructed, it was so much larger than hers that it blocked the sunlight, and she felt that the new neighbors could look into her backyard from their second-story windows. She told me that she had written to city hall several times, describing the ubiquity of bulldozers and the unpleasant changes occurring in the neighborhood, but that nothing had been done.

Annie's anger about the Monster Houses and the demolition of low-rise apartment buildings in Kerrisdale spurred her to become an active member of CCAH. She was frequently interviewed by journalists and became a familiar spokesperson for the community. When I visited her in 1990, she gave me three large scrapbooks and several shoe boxes full of newspaper clippings about Monster Houses, apartment demolitions, and general neighborhood change. She had also collected articles on immigration, demographics, education, population statistics, and the Hong Kong Chinese. Members of other residential organizations had written her to ask advice about community organizing and to request and offer support, and these letters were also present among the files.

When I examined Annie's collection, two letters and a brochure from White supremacist organizations caught my eye. The brochure was from an organization called the British/European Immigration Aid Foundation and was headed with the saying "The *True* North, Strong and Free." The text began,

"This Foundation is based on and will build on patriotism. We need to be patriots. Deep down, we believe most of us are quietly proud of our British and European roots. We treasure more than we realize the common traditions, the shared values which form the very basis of our Canadian nationhood, the strong and abiding links of kinship. In the present immigration picture, the importance of these are being swept aside. For Canada's sake, they must be reaffirmed. . . . Patriotism, inspiration and united determination will do it. PRESERVE CANADA'S HERITAGE."

At the bottom of the brochure, Annie had written a telephone number for the organization and a meeting place, the "Kits Rec. Centre" (Kitsilano Recreation Centre), and date, June 26, 1989.

One of the two letters that was sent to Annie was from another White preservationist group, called The Spokesman. This pro-White group was more vociferous in its demands for an end to "multiracism" and the immigration of non-Whites. In the letter, the writers made it clear that the influx of other "racial groups" signaled the deterioration of "our way of living." At the bottom of this more virulently racist document, Annie had written "strange people!!"

Annie's response to the unsolicited letters and advertisements from White supremacist groups positions her on a complex spectrum of racist reaction to the changes in her neighborhood. For Annie, the aim to preserve Canadian "heritage" was significant enough to attend or think of attending a meeting emphasizing the curtailment of non-European immigration. At the same time, she found it strange when a group with the same basic agenda but using a much stronger language of racism apprised her of their organization's intents. Annie's feelings about the arrival of the Hong Kong Chinese were clearly mixed. Although she voiced sympathy with "the people that are coming from the Asian countries and feel very threatened by the communist system," she also felt that the dollars these people ostensibly wanted to get out of Hong Kong should not be used in her neighborhood. "Of course they wanted to get their dollars out. But let's get them to put their dollars where it ultimately benefits the country. And I can't see how people getting evicted from their homes is benefiting the country."

In her interviews with me, Annie clearly positioned herself as a community organizer and defender of the rights and values of the White, upper-middle-class women who were being evicted from their Kerrisdale walk-up apartments in the late 1980s. As a divorced professional musician, she identified with the plight of the elderly women whose apartments were being demolished to make way for twelve-story luxury condominiums. She portrayed her community activism against Monster Houses and unwanted demolitions as her primary role; her feelings about the underlying causes of these occurrences, that they were the result of a government sellout to Hong Kong investors, was secondary. Annie was wary of being labeled a racist and attempted to separate her work as a neighborhood activist from the "social" issue of the arrival of immigrants from Hong Kong. At the same time, her fear of loss of control and her desire to have "Canadians," rather than Chinese immigrants, retain authority over the use of residential urban space indicates the conflation of the two in her mind. She said:

> It isn't that we're against the people coming from Hong Kong, but . . . this is not a social issue. They're trying to make it into a social issue, and they point fingers at anybody who complains about this investment, and they say you're

racist. Racism is a social issue; it is not a financial issue. This is two different arguments we're dealing with here. We're talking about *our* country not having the control, or not willing to have the control, to put *our* population, the *Canadians*, in control of their own land. They are bartering our land in order to get all those billions of dollars from another country in investment to stimulate the economy, . . . and of course it makes the government look glowing in their balance sheet. And the city. Certainly they're going to benefit with higher taxes on all these million-dollar homes, and so it makes them look good. But I'm afraid that it hasn't had the results that they expected.

The concern about maintaining *Canadian* control manifests the belief that the people buying "all these million-dollar homes" are not, and cannot *be*, Canadian. Canadian land is being "bartered" by politicians who are selling its priceless heritage to stimulate the economy and improve the "balance sheet." Annie believes her views are not racist because racism "is a social issue" and because what she objects to is financial, the sellout of Canadian heritage for money. Her equation of Canadian heritage with British culture and Anglo people is so natural in her mind that she cannot understand the racist implications of maintaining heritage by keeping Chinese capitalists from investing in land and houses in the city.[14]

Annie's sincere, if misguided, efforts to separate the workings of capitalism and racism, however, are constantly thwarted by those to whom the interlocking of the two processes is advantageous. For some groups, *facing* capital—projecting it and maintaining it in the image of the other—furthers their own ideological purposes. Although Annie was careful to verbally position herself as an urban activist, her well-publicized role in the confrontation over the bulldozing of several apartment buildings in Kerrisdale caused some individuals and organizations to position her in a different manner. The White supremacist groups and individuals who sent her unsolicited mail linked her actions to protect the neighborhood and community from unwanted capitalist development with their own aims of exclusionary immigration and the fomentation of anti–Hong Kong Chinese sentiment. In her interviews with me, Annie made a point of declaring her stand to be one of opposing international capitalism and the negative effects that global real estate investment was having on her community. She did not want her struggle to be tarnished or undermined by people labeling her racist, regardless of her own internal feelings or dilemmas. She was not, however, able to deflect the desires of marginal groups, who perceived her as the perfect conduit for their messages of White supremacy.

The bitter struggle over the foregrounding of race in these neighborhood movements demonstrates the crucial role that race construction plays in the contemporary articulation of global capitalisms and international investment. The desire of neighborhood activists to keep race out of the Monster House controversy was met with the equally fierce desire of marginal groups to advance their causes in this public domain. Businesspeople and state representatives benefiting from international investment and real estate development eagerly pointed to the visible racism of these groups and loudly proclaimed all neighborhood slow-growth movements to be fundamentally racist in scope.[15]

In examining the manipulations of racism in this scenario, the social relations of power involved in the struggles over the meaning of the Monster House become apparent. Annie's own ambivalence elucidates the difficulties involved in determining agendas and makes the allegations of racism made against her organization impossible to completely refute. Meanwhile, the hegemonic construction of these meanings remains extremely important, as those who are able to control them may then acquire ideological control over a number of related processes. Particular sites of struggle have included questions of culture, architecture, aesthetics, heritage, taste, and lifestyle. How are neighborhood meanings experienced and articulated, and by whom? How is "race" imbued in questions of culture and in more general concerns about the loss of local control and community cohesion?

Aesthetic Articulations, Architecture, and Alibis

> I grew up in Shaughnessy, on Balfour Street, and have watched closely the changes happening within it. I am saddened and disgusted when I walk through it today to see so many of the trees and houses gone, only to be replaced by hideous monster houses!! . . . I talked to a construction worker who was working on one of these new atrocities they call a house. . . . He said, and I quote, "the house is a piece of shit and will probably be falling to pieces in ten years." So, is this what Shaughnessy is to become? We need assurances that the character of the neighborhood will be maintained![16]

> Asymmetrical power in the visual sense suggests capitalists' great ability to draw from a potential repertoire of images, to develop a succession of real and symbolic landscapes that define every historical period, including postmodernity. This reverses Jameson's dictum that architecture is important to postmodernity because it is the symbol of capitalism. Rather, architecture is important because it is the capital of symbolism.[17]

The architecture of the Monster House has had real repercussions for social relations and for actual material changes in west-side neighborhoods. At the same time, the struggles over architectural design, aesthetics, taste, and character have all served ideological purposes with equally "real" repercussions. In this context, the Monster House functions and must be understood on a number of levels: as a concrete form, a spatial system, and an object of value, but also as a sign and ideological symbol—an emblem of acute neighborhood transformation enmeshed in chronic and complex global processes.[18]

Aside from a discourse of loss that permeated most discussions of the Monster House and the demolitions of older buildings, a major concern expressed by White Kerrisdale and Shaughnessy residents related to architectural aesthetics. Without identifying specific features, older residents commented on the overall ugliness and inappropriateness of the new houses. Many felt that the homes were in bad taste, particularly for west-side neighborhoods. In an editorial entitled "Monster Houses: A Matter of Taste," one writer commented, "It's been said that some people's taste is all in their mouths. Those words must often come to the lips of passersby who behold the more bizarre examples of the monster houses inflicted on Vancouver. The neighbors use much stronger language."[19] Innumerable statements in the press, letters to the city council, and research reports reflected similar feelings of aesthetic disapproval. The most common remarks can be paraphrased: "They're lot-line monsters," "I just don't like them; they're ugly," "They're OK, but not in this neighborhood," "Ugly, box-like monsters," "You know; you've seen them. They just don't fit in."

One oft-told anecdote was of the doctor's wife who spray-painted "This Is An Ugly Home" on one of the new houses in her neighborhood. Another, more esoteric Monster House graffito asked in large, black, spray-painted letters, "Genius Loci?" *Genius loci?* is a Latin phrase that asks, Is the guardian spirit of the place in its rightful context? The phrase operates on a number of levels. *Genius,* from the Greek, refers to birth and in this context could be seen to question the nativity or indigenous nature of the Monster House. The use of *genius* could also function as an ironic play on the English usage, in effect questioning the architectural genius of the project. Finally, *genius* from the Greek is often employed in a metaphysical sense and, in the usage here, could be seen as a subtle attack on the material uses of the house by Hong Kong buyers as a site of profit rather than as a place of spirituality.[20]

In both of the previous examples, the power expressed and wielded by the graffiti artists is explicit. In the first example, the tacit assumption of the graffitist that her message of disdain would be acceptable to the White community is evident in the public nature of the act. Those who told me the anecdote were well aware of the woman's identity and related the story with some delight at the presumptuousness of her message and action. The smug assurance that the taste of other community residents was in accord with her own allowed the graffitist to express her opinion as a universal one. When she sprayed "This Is An Ugly Home" on the house, it was an act of mastery and control. In the second example, the arcane nature of the Latin phrase positioned the graffito at the level of "high" culture and highbrow taste. The elite knowledge necessary to unpack the meanings of the graffito was assumed as the norm for the other residents of the neighborhood in which it was displayed. The assumption of a shared esoteric taste allowed an in-joke to be spread among community residents yet implicitly excluded outsiders whose knowledge of the Greek and Latin languages and literary canons was presumed to be inadequate for an understanding of the phrase's many-layered references.

Anglo residents of west-side neighborhoods often utilized local elements and dynamics of spatial and architectural change to describe the unwelcome transformations of their communities. Rather than depicting a process of change that included social and economic ramifications, such as the introduction of wealthy Chinese people into the neighborhood, many residents focused their criticisms on relatively neutral problems, such as the poor architectural design of the new buildings. Some people pointed to the high level of waste and problems of disposal of razed building materials, while others referred to ecological concerns related to tree and shrubbery removal. A few discussed a fear of social breakdown occasioned by the new, "unneighborly" architectural styles.

Most of the people I spoke with perceived the houses as leeches on the landscape sucking up space and resources from the community. References to the people who inhabited the houses were rarely made. The houses themselves were the "evil" things that threatened the sanctity of hearth and home. The Monster House, in this usage, functions as what Spivak, in reference to Foucault's studies of the spaces of prisons, calls a "screen allegory."[21] Broader narratives are occluded through the concentration on a local, restricted plot. The expressed fear of waste, couched in the environmental lingo of pollution and disposal, serves as an alibi for the unexpressed and largely unconscious fear of the filth of the other.

When references to Monster House residents were made, the architecture itself was used as an alibi for lack of contact. Suzanne Barlow, a young home owner and homemaker in Kerrisdale, felt that the placement of the garage in the new Monster House next door was a crucial factor in her ensuing lack of contact with her new Chinese neighbors. She said in an interview:

> These big houses that they're putting up with very little backyard . . . it gives me a funny feeling because it's like they're putting barriers up. The garages would front here in the old style [she points to the backyard], if they had children, we would see them. But they get in their car, they open their garage door, and they go. And there's no mixing. When people cross your alley, you usually run into them because you're getting in or out of the car or taking your garbage out, but you don't get any of that. There's a wall. And that's kind of the nice thing people usually like about neighborhoods that's lost now.[22]

Although the spatial layout of the house, the garage, and the garden may indeed exacerbate social atomization, the idea that architectural design is responsible for social breakdown also operates like the screen formed by dream displacement discussed by Freud. In this kind of displacement, "acceptable representations" are created and substituted for "unacceptable wishes."[23] By placing the responsibility for the lack of contact and neighborliness on the house itself, attention is shifted away from more structural or institutional problems in social relations involving class or race. In this case, specific design features of the Monster House are criticized for causing a lack of contact between neighbors. These negative design features can then be cited as the more neutral rationale behind neighborhood anger and subsequent mobilization to curb the transformation of the houses and the neighborhood. The more fundamental problems of social and economic relations and histories can thus be successfully elided.[24]

The fear and anxiety expressed about the loss of neighborhood character and community also reflect a concern about loss of control. The meanings of community and neighborhood that were felt to be safe and secure were suddenly exposed as open for contestation. Minutely constructed borders that defined and distinguished the local from the global, in from out, taste from lack of taste, meaning from meaning, class from class, race from race, and us from them were no longer stable and impermeable. And the process responsible for these borderline transgressions was inherently difficult for Shaughnessy and Kerrisdale residents to criticize. For those who derived their authority and had long benefited from the dynamism and innovation of capitalist development, the sudden personal apprehension of its destructive side was confusing and painful. The neighborhood of Kerrisdale, which one resident spoke of as "rather fossilized" when he was a kid, was transformed before his very eyes. As the buildings fell, so did the presumption of an inherent stability of meanings.

With the destruction of older buildings and the creation of Monster Houses, previously fixed meanings in the landscape became unmoored. Many scholars have narrativized postmodern architecture by emphasizing the impermanence of meanings—the possibility of inversion, regeneration, and the recycling of signs and symbols that formerly were felt to be securely attached and immobile.[25] Others have linked these cultural manifestations with changes in the nature and processes of capitalism itself.[26] But the experience of creative destruction and its inscription on the landscape is an old story in Vancouver. In the specific context of Vancouver's west-side neighborhoods in the 1980s, the rapid integration of the local housing market into global real estate portfolios unquestionably had immense repercussions for the dislocation of formerly static meanings in the built environment. Yet in the longer-term view, demolitions, constructions, and urban redevelopment in the greater metropolitan area have followed the boom-bust swings of the economy with chilling regularity.[27] Although the acute sense of crisis and shock felt by many residents of rapidly changing west-side neighborhoods was real, the ultimate embeddedness of these changes within a broader, more chronic scenario is historically evident. What made the shock of the new different this time around?

Until the 1980s, large-scale foreign investment in Vancouver real estate occurred primarily in commercial, downtown properties. The investors themselves were invisible, and urban restructuring was blamed largely on progrowth politicians and the collusion between political and development interests.[28] With the acquisition of west-side residential property by Hong Kong Chinese in the 1980s, however, the sacred repository of cultural capital and symbolic stability, the home, was opened up as a site of investment for the first time. While these new spaces of consumption were busily administered to by an army of *enablers*,[29] the Chinese were targeted for marketing and for blame. Negative repercussions of capitalist creative destruction in the neighborhoods were linked with the pending loss of cultural meanings brought about by the entry of a different group. In this particular intersection of the local and the global, the acute experience of modernity was mediated not just by the reworking of capitalism on the landscape, but also by the reworking of the meanings of race and culture.

Local Heritage and the Hong Kong Transnational

"Invented tradition" is taken to mean a set of practices, normally governed by overtly or tacitly accepted rules and of a ritual or symbolic nature, which seek to inculcate certain values and norms of behavior by repetition, which automatically implies continuity with the past. In fact, where possible, they normally attempt to establish continuity with a suitable historic past.[30]

To understand how a concept of heritage, or invented tradition, is established and maintained in west-side neighborhoods, it is useful to examine the types of houses and landscape traditions of Kerrisdale and Shaughnessy prior to the 1980s. In both these neighborhoods, the predominance of detached, single-family houses has remained a central feature of the landscape. According to Deryck Holdsworth, Vancouverites of the early years saw themselves as part of a unique and distinctive urban setting, one with a high standard of living predicated largely on its open green spaces and single, detached houses. These relatively spacious "models of architectural style" were perceived as important alternatives to the tenements and flats common in European and East Coast cities; in the wealthier suburbs, such as Shaughnessy, they could even serve as a bucolic escape, a "foil for work in the industrial city."[31]

In 1976, the Vancouver metropolitan region was composed of more single detached dwellings than apartment units; nearly 56 percent of the region's housing was provided by detached houses and only 35 percent by apartment buildings.[32] The statistics for Kerrisdale and Shaughnessy show an even higher percentage of detached homes. In addition to low-density, single-family detached houses, west-side neighborhoods were also characterized by open, landscaped front yards with mature trees and hedges and by wide, grassy, and landscaped boulevards. English Cottage and California Bungalow were typical house styles for neighborhoods with a high proportion of middle-class and some working-class residents. These two styles and their many variations were derived from the Arts and Crafts movement popular in Britain and North America in the 1920s. The bungalows are typically one-story, wooden buildings with broad verandas, shingled siding, and informal indoor-outdoor plans. The cottages are stucco, with some half-timber trim. They are often decorated with a half-hip gable that suggests thatched roofing, with asphalt tiling around the eaves and small, eyelid dormers.[33]

Many other styles are evident in West Point Grey, Dunbar Heights, and Kerrisdale, but the 1920s bungalow and cottage are the most common basic forms for these areas. In Shaughnessy Heights, the restrictive measures enforced on lot divisions and house prices ensured that variation occurred only within a spectrum of extremely high-end designs and materials. The most common style for this area was the revival of the English Tudor manor, although other house forms are also evident.[34]

The use of British architectural and landscape symbols in Vancouver's west-side neighborhoods was deliberate. The Canadian Pacific Railroad, which owned most of Point Grey, intentionally modeled the elite subdivision of Shaughnessy Heights on the pastoral myths of the English countryside.[35] By claiming an ongoing, albeit transformed, English tradition in the new spaces of Vancouver, an easy, unhurried grandeur and an idyllic, preindustrial way of life gradually became recognized and incorporated as the symbols and codes of the new suburban elite of "British" Columbia. The appropriation and reworking of these symbols over time operated on an aesthetic level that enabled residents of these neighborhoods to feel pride of place, security, and well-being and, like the Shaughnessy graffiti artist, to assume a universal notion of appropriateness, of what fit in. Much of the anxiety of loss expressed in the late 1980s related not to the actual buildings or trees that were demolished, but to a more general fear of deprivation and dispossession of this way of life.

The angry letters about the built environment written to city hall between 1987 and 1991 include a vast litany of ambience words. Words such as *quality, character, heritage, tradition, neighborliness,* and *community* appear frequently. Many letter writers decried the loss of the "village atmosphere" or the "coziness" of the past; nearly all were angered at the destruction of the community's trees and gardens. At a public meeting in 1985, a spokesperson for the Shaughnessy Heights Property Owners Association (SHPOA) expressed anxiety about the burgeoning Monster Houses (then called Vancouver Specials and associated more with eastside neighborhoods) and urged rapid action on a first set of proposed regulations: "You get three or four of these in a couple of blocks," he explained, "and all of a sudden you have completely changed the character of a neighborhood." Executive secretary of the organization, Evelyn Mackay, said the "threat" of Vancouver Specials had shaken the confidence of Shaughnessy residents in their ability to preserve the character of their area. "This is a real threat to a neighborhood—to have these oversized houses suddenly spring up on a street which we thought was safe and secure forever," she remarked.[36]

These strongly felt sentiments, expressed in terms of heritage, character, and safety, involved more than the construction of Monster Houses, were not merely aesthetic concerns. These feelings of emotional loss were imbricated in profound economic and symbolic processes that involved the ability to reproduce a particular way of life. In the context of global restructuring and fast capital, this way of life was threatened by new economic and cultural disjunctures and by new types of political legitimacy. Most shockingly, this way of life was increasingly contested by new meanings of race and nation. All of these changes seemed to arrive via extralocal forces, via foreigners who threatened established patterns of meaning and dominant forms of ideology. Jane Samuels, a home owner in Shaughnessy, expressed her confusion and resistance to these outside, or nonlocal, forces in this way:

> It sounds reactionary, but I don't think I'm a reactionary person. And I realize that, and it's very frightening when you have to sort of start holding on to things. But when you see everything being destroyed and pretty soon it will be sort of treeless, you have the feeling . . . We live outside in this area, in this city. We don't live inside; it's not an indoor city. We're outside a lot. And people who are used to living in an apartment in Hong Kong don't realize that you can have more green space. It's an appreciation factor that you find out once you've lived here. It's sort of bigger than the way I'm talking. I'm talking in a very small way. I guess there is that large threat that the whole city is changing. . . . Maybe we don't want to make it that attractive [to outsiders] to make it that big. As you watch all these cities grow, you start saying, *why* do we want to get bigger. Why? What good does it do all the people who are living here now?[37]

In Jane's perception, a shady, pastoral, and unchanging landscape modeled on preindustrial England was rapidly being destroyed by the global, urbanizing tentacles of the new transnational. Wealthy Hong Kong capitalists used to "living in an apartment" reached into and transformed the very meanings of hearth and home. The experience of confusion and fear and the new forms of racism that this image induced influenced community articulations and representations of the Monster House. These representations were then used in many neighborhood campaigns for tighter zoning regulations and controls over urban design.[38] What were some of the embedded meanings of this landscape that were felt to be under attack, and why was a loss of local control over these meanings so threatening for many Anglo residents?

Monstrous Taste and Relations of Power

Tastes (that is, manifested preferences) are the practical affirmation of an inevitable difference. It is no accident that, when they have to be justified, they are asserted purely negatively, by the refusal of other tastes.[39]

For centuries the ownership of land in Britain was the surest basis of gaining and maintaining power in society. The power was invested not in the use of land for farming but in the social relations engendered through its ownership. The attraction and retention of tenants, who provided military and political support, allegiance, and rent money, were crucial for manifesting the type of wealthy and well-endowed establishment that could then attract money from the central government. Each landowner needed to manifest power to attract the social supports necessary to gain more power. In this process, the image of the house was key. Girouard writes:

> Land, however, was little use without one or more country houses on it. Land provided the fuel, a country house was the engine which made it effective. It achieved this in a number of ways. It was the headquarters from which land was administered and power organised. It was a show-case, in which to exhibit and entertain supporters and good connections. In early days it contained a potential fighting force. It was an image-maker, which projected an aura of glamour, mystery or success around its owner. It was visible evidence of his wealth. It showed his credentials—even if the credentials were sometimes faked. Trophies in the hall, coats of arms over the chimney-pieces, books in the library and temples in the park could suggest that he was discriminating, intelligent, bred to rule and brave.[40]

The natural landscape and the social harmony expressed by landscapers and philosophers of the eighteenth century served to naturalize the inequitable social relations of landowner and tenant that were part of British preindustrial and early industrial society.[41] That landscape and those expressions of social harmony also served as blinds for the true manner in which wealth was acquired and power maintained. The houses themselves were integral components of the continuation of these power relations and the ongoing maintenance of domination by a ruling elite. Housing and landscaping styles that were appropriated for Vancouver's west-side neighborhoods were part of webbed social processes and networks of power that both shaped and were shaped by these spatial relations. Although the symbols and meanings of house and garden were obviously transformed in their Canadian regeneration, they nevertheless embodied and retained some latent meanings and traditions as well.

In the case of west-side Vancouver neighborhoods such as Shaughnessy and Kerrisdale, much of the aesthetic dislike of the Monster House was associated with an attempt to preserve the distinction between the old and the new, between old money and new money. The symbols of the nineteenth-century British landscape were based on an idealized notion of the lifestyle of the eighteenth-century landed aristocracy. Part of the romanticized image of this preindustrial setting was also predicated on a disparagement of capitalism and industrialism and the new money and moneymakers involved in these processes.[42]

Although this antibourgeois sentiment faded somewhat in Vancouver, the dislike for new money and its threat to the established meanings of an older elite remain strong. The Monster Houses, which do not blend in and are brashly new and ostentatious in size and ornamentation, are identified with a nouveau riche display that is antithetical to the retiring and faded gentry image of old-money Vancouverites. Statistics from a market research report of 1987 show that, on average, 44.1 percent of Kerrisdale residents' total assets are tied up in their houses.[43] This differs sharply from the widely held image and representation of the new buyers of Kerrisdale houses, who are often reputed to arrive from Hong Kong with suitcases full of cash, which they then use to purchase houses outright. I was told an anecdote on three separate occasions about a Hong Kong Chinese buyer who flew to Vancouver from Hong Kong, was driven through west-side neighborhoods in a limousine, and then purchased several houses with cash.

Although the anecdote was told with different intentions by different people, it is clear that the public representation of the "typical" cash-rich Hong Kong Chinese buyer was acknowledged by many. Furthermore, the image of the brash, greedy, new-money buyers with unlimited funds and entirely liquid assets was inextricably linked to the recent house demolitions, the construction of the new Monster Houses, and the loss of neighborhood character. A mentality of greed and profit was seen as the evil characteristic of the nouveau riche, who were represented as caring little or nothing for Vancouver's vaunted traditions and heritage. The conflation of this new wealthy group with the Hong Kong Chinese immigrants was made explicit in several ways. One writer to the city council commented on a proposal to limit house size:

> My greatest concern, which is only briefly mentioned in the proposal, is that of "neighborhood character." . . . This is a charming section of Vancouver with beautiful tree lined streets and Georgian, Tudor or Colonial type architecture. However, this is changing with the influx of new people wanting to build these huge eyesores. . . . Let's act now before all of Vancouver becomes another Richmond.[44]

Richmond is a rapidly growing suburb that has a singularly high proportion of Chinese Canadian residents and has recently attracted many middle- and upper-middle-class immigrants from Hong Kong. Although Richmond has only recently become embroiled in the Monster House controversy, many extremely large houses have been constructed there in the past decade. In the letter, the writer attempts to separate the building activity in Richmond—which is explicitly linked to the "influx of new people" and implicitly linked to a specific group, the Hong Kong Chinese—from his or her own "charming section of Vancouver." He or she seeks to ban the negative and tasteless eyesores of the new people from the areas of Vancouver that are presumably still charming and attractive. The preference for a particular type of cultural consumption and lifestyle (owning a Georgian-, Tudor-, or Colonial-style house) is expressed as a manifestation of taste and culture unquestionably superior to other tastes (owning a Monster House). The expression of difference serves to legitimate and confirm social and cultural differences between the long-term Anglo residents and the nouveau riche Chinese interlopers and at the same time to legitimate and confirm the systems or structures that are implicated in the reproduction of these social differences. Bourdieu writes:

> For a habitus structured according to the very structures of the social world in which it functions, each property (a pattern of speech, a way of dressing, a bodily hexis, an educational title, a dwelling place, etc.) is perceived in its relation to other properties, therefore in its positional, distinctive value, and it is through this distinctive distance, this difference, this distinction, which is perceived only by the seasoned observer, that the homologous position of the bearer of this property in the space of social positions shows itself.[45]

The attempt to separate and distinguish old-money values, traditions, and neighborhoods from the culture and traditions of the new-money immigrants was made repeatedly in opinion pieces and letters to the editor in the local media. Often the traditional values that were being lost were equated with national identity, with what it meant to be Canadian. Although many people I spoke with expressed genuine concern about the loss of a Canadian way of life, using Canadian culture as the point of defense also functioned as an alibi for personal feelings and individual material gain. One person wrote in a letter to *Western News* in 1989: "Canadians see monster housing as an arrogant visible demonstration of the destruction of Canadian culture. Yes, we have a Canadian identity and Canadians should beware of persons who say we don't while they try to rebuild Canada in a different mould for their own purpose and profit."[46]

The reference to profit in the letter is a direct jab at the Hong Kong Chinese, who are widely represented as responsible for house price escalation as a result of using homes for speculation and profit rather than as places to live. Investing in tasteful or "high" culture in Vancouver society, which includes the home where one lives, secures profit yet does not have to be pursued as profit. Living in an established area such as Shaughnessy, purportedly because the character of the neighborhood feels right, allows the home owners to profess innocence of any cynical or mercenary motives such as profit yet establishes their fundamental connection to the underlying systems that generate it.[47]

Although the letter refers to the destruction of a national identity, the concern over social identity is implicit; profit-generating development in Vancouver's east-side neighborhoods and outlying areas is rarely contested, nor are those areas (which are far more economically and racially mixed) defended on the grounds of preserving heritage, tradition, or identity of any kind. The violence of the reaction against the aesthetic changes in Kerrisdale and Shaughnessy betrays the profound fear that the symbols of the established and dominant group are being eroded and, with them the chance of appropriating, and naturalizing the appropriation of, the rare rights and assets that are dependent upon one's position in social space as well as the distribution of those assets in geographical space.[48]

When other dominant class fragments, expressing differing patterns of cultural consumption and lifestyle, gain access to the formerly self-contained and bordered spaces of hegemony, they threaten the distinction of the original group by depreciating old meanings and by calling into question the legitimated "natural" association of real differences in economic relations with differences in taste. The average economic status of residents in west-side neighborhoods such as Kerrisdale and Shaughnessy is considerably higher than in average east-side or downtown neighborhoods.[49]

Part of the national and international alarm emanating from the Monster House constructions arose not just from the wealth, power, and prestige of most members of west-side communities, but also from the fact that many of the new people moving in were even wealthier, more powerful, and more prestigious Chinese immigrants from Hong Kong. The different meanings of "home" for that group were now backed by substantial material and cultural power. And for the first time, new interpretations of lifestyle and landscape threatened the hegemonic assumptions of the formerly dominant Anglo home owners. In the next section, I examine a few of the cultural differences involving Chinese geomancy that occurred between the long-term residents and some of the recent Hong Kong immigrants. Following that, I investigate how these incipient cultural differences were actively manipulated by local and international capitalists involved in Vancouver's urban development.

Feng Shui and Capitalist Revisions

Bob Iu, a young professional architect in a small, family real estate company, spoke of his differences with his father in the perception of development and architectural design. Bob was born in Hong Kong and studied in Canada at the University of Manitoba. He practiced as an architect in Vancouver for two and a half years and recently returned to Hong Kong to join the family business. When he worked on a family development project located in downtown Vancouver, he was confronted with traditional ideas of his father's regarding the importance of geomancy—ideas that Bob himself did not hold. In an interview at his office, he spoke about the ramification of these differences for the new project:

> My father went and looked at the *feng shui* of the place. When I look at the site, I evaluate it according it to floor space and relationship to area and facilities ... very academic. So we started designing the project ... then my father came in with the *feng shui* and influenced the positioning of the tower. The entrance to the building, he doesn't like it because he doesn't like ... I'll show you [he points to an architectural model]. In the model there, it's bounded by two streets, and basically the only entrance is from this side. And my father doesn't like it because it's facing west. And according to *feng shui*, it's not good. It had to face north. So what happened was we put in a stair towards the north so that you can actually come into the building from this side. . . . That's how the older generation influences us.[50]

For most people who believe in *feng shui*, any alterations to a landscape by human beings can cause disturbances that "may redound to influence, even control, the fortunes of those who intrude."[51] Careful attention to *qi* (cosmic energy or life breath) is crucial for ensuring that the landscape alteration is a positive one, ultimately beneficial for the health, well-being, and financial outlook of the person who is intervening or inhabiting a particular place. The siting of a new building, including the location of the entrance and the method of circulation, affects the flow of *qi* and is thus an important factor for *feng shui* followers to consider. North, south, east, and west have differing meanings and, depending on the local landscape features, can be considered positive or negative points of entrance, affecting whether there is a harmonious balance of yin and yang and an unhindered flow of *qi*.

Bob's father is typical of many elderly Hong Kong residents, whose belief in the importance of *feng shui* can have an impact on design and development and on choice of residence for themselves and their families.[52] Although many long-term, Anglo residents of Vancouver spoke with scorn and dislike of the mammoth double doors that became ubiquitous on the newly constructed Monster Houses in the late 1980s, by far the most controversial feature of *feng shui* in Kerrisdale and Shaughnessy was tree removal. In *feng shui* belief, trees are tied into *qi* in complex ways and can represent either good or bad luck, depending on their placement. If trees are poorly placed, directly in front of either the house entrance or windows (blocking *qi*), they are considered destructive and oppressive.[53] The removal of large trees on Monster House lots was a source of great anger in west-side neighborhoods and led to the formation of social movements specifically established to curtail tree removal in Granville and Kerrisdale.

The cultural beliefs of *some* immigrants about *feng shui* and about the desirability of spaciousness and the undesirability of garden maintenance affected the choice of *some* houses and neighborhoods. At the same time, developers, who were attuned to the slightest nuances of market behavior, reacted to perceived changes in demand by targeting specific houses and neighborhoods to build and sell to wealthy buyers from Hong Kong. In this interaction, timing was key, as early indications of changes in spatial and aesthetic demand were immediately captured and played out in the media and through informal informational networks, thereby greatly expanding and reworking the incipient cultural differences. As with Zukin's study of the interplay of forces in the conversion of loft buildings in Manhattan, supply did not *create* demand for Monster Houses.[54] But supply *reworked* demand, which itself was a complex mix of social and cultural needs at a given historical moment.

Jack Sherman, a Vancouver developer who owned a small company and had been involved in construction for thirty years, described mammoth changes in the development industry and in the type of buyer that he served in the 1980s. After the recession in the early 1980s, when some developers lost everything, the market remained steady for a few years. In late 1984 and 1985, "things started to move," and he began to invest in housing on Vancouver's west side. According to Jack, "All the action was on the west side, and 99 percent of it was triggered by foreign, mostly Hong Kong and Taiwan, investors. . . . For a few years, all of my clients were Chinese."[55]

Jack began to change his development and marketing practices "drastically," starting with a greater emphasis on size and a commitment to building to the maximum square footage per lot. Other changes that he instituted were an increase in the number of bathrooms, a greater emphasis on the entrance, which was now "usually out of marble," a larger kitchen, and a grander en suite master bedroom. When I asked Jack why he made these changes, he told me that he was responding to the demands of the Chinese buyers. According to the statistics of previous sales, it seemed that the houses with greater space and more bedrooms were selling better. Following the irrevocable logic of numbers, he thus "built to that demand." Jack reported that other development companies were reacting in the same way because "builders know each other, stick together, and share information."

Max Ng, a Vancouver developer who grew up in Hong Kong and commutes regularly between the two cities, iterated a similar viewpoint. He emphasized the role of the developer in determining what the average taste of the client was and then building to that taste. At the same time, he felt convinced that developers had accurately discerned the "Hong Kong Chinese taste," which could be generalized as one requiring lots of space. In response to a question about whether Hong Kong clients were demanding larger, newer houses or whether the developers were building and supplying larger houses (and creating demand for them), he said:

> Actually, the developer. Tailor-made for the customer. Depending on the taste of the customer. If you live in Hong Kong, if you grow up in Hong Kong, you know space is very important. You have to spend a lot of money . . . space is not for free. In Canada, space is free. So when an Asian moves to Vancouver, they like to have more space. Inside or outside. They would prefer to sacrifice the outside space so that they can have more inside space. So this is the need of the people.[56]

According to these developers, in the mid-1980s the different aesthetic tastes, spatial needs, and cultural style of Hong Kong clients influenced house design and the marketing of real estate in Vancouver's west-side neighborhoods. At the same time, both acknowledged the role of the developer in systematically elaborating on incipient cultural differences and in reacting to them in a manner calculated to derive maximum profit out of the venture. The cultural differences of some immigrants, such as belief in *feng shui* and dislike of gardening, were seized upon, fixed in place, and processed by the meaning machines of the development industry; the ongoing process of cultural negotiation and change involved in the transition of meanings and systems of belief from one geographical location to another was thus reified and rarified by those who were able to use this process for profit.

Nuanced, geographically and historically specific changes in demand, along with the elaboration and profit-generating utilization of these changes by developers, led to the creation of a new style of housing and landscaping and to a concerted effort at niche marketing targeted at a

specific clientele. Although in this case the production of housing did not
create demand, neither was demand an autonomous force operating to
push the market in a clearly defined direction. The creation of demand for
the new Monster House was an articulation of the differing tastes and
lifestyle of a new client group, the Hong Kong Chinese, with the assumption and expansion of this group's perceived tastes by developers—both
in Vancouver and Hong Kong. The impact of this joining had major ramifications for Vancouver's urban landscape in the late 1980s, owing to state
intervention in attracting foreign investment from Hong Kong as well as
to the particular conjuncture of local, national, and international capitalist
interests operating in the city at that time.

In late 1980s Vancouver, the articulation of capital interests and conflict
over local cultural meanings operated in a complex and shifting relationship. It was in the context of Vancouver's rapid integration into the global
economy that the hegemonic assumptions of race, taste, and place were
initially exposed and reworked. As new capitalist networks were formed,
older spatial meanings were transformed. For elite west-side residents,
the acute shock of modernity was experienced through this literal and fig-
urative loss of place.

In this context, the struggle over the meanings of landscape and the
home can be seen as struggles over the meaning of social and economic
organization and of society itself. Who am I? What is this place? And
what is my position in it? These questions are central to the experience of
modernity in Vancouver. In a period of fast capital, the threat of dislocation and fragmented cultural meanings is brought *home* to places that
were formerly protected from the ravages of creative destruction. The
Monster House controversy reflects this pending loss while at the same
time rendering articulate the racial and class assumptions upon which the
edifice of neighborhood "meaning" was built. For elite west-side residents, these global economic and cultural disjunctures both created and
reflected alien and uncertain landscapes that once were defined as home.

Notes

1. See, among others, Peter Taylor, "Hong Kong Yacht People Buy Up Vancouver," *Sunday Telegraph*, June 4, 1989; Moira Farrow, "Tomorrow Has Arrived in Today's Thriving Vancouver," *San Diego Union*, April 22, 1990; Andrew Malcolm,
"Where Minorities Find Riches and Resentment," *New York Times International*,
March 17, 1990; "Good Luck City," *National Geographic*, April 1992.

2. Between 1988 and 1990 there were 17,097 immigrant landings in Vancouver
from Hong Kong. Of this group, approximately one-third arrived under the entrepreneur and investor categories. (These immigration categories require a substantial investment in Canada as well as a large personal net worth. See Diana Lary,
"Regional Variations in Hong Kong Immigration," *Canada and Hong Kong Update*,

Fall 1991, p. 6.) Exact amounts of capital flow are difficult to estimate, but bankers and immigration consultants I interviewed in Hong Kong put the figure as high as 1 to 2 billion Canadian dollars flowing annually from Hong Kong to Vancouver in the late 1980s.

3. I use the expression *fast capital* to underscore both the rapidity of capital flow in the contemporary period of global restructuring and also the frequent separation of financial and productive operations. *Fast capital*, as it is used here, refers to financial or speculative capital rather than industrial capital.

4. David Harvey, "Flexible Accumulation Through Urbanization: Reflections on 'Post-Modernism' in the American City," *Antipode*, Vol. 19, No. 3, 1987, p. 260.

5. For a further discussion of the spatial effects of deregulation and privatization in the finance industry, see Nigel Thrift, "The Perils of the International Financial System," *Environment and Planning A*, Vol. 22, 1990, and Allan Leyshon and Nigel Thrift, "Liberalisation and Consolidation: The Single European Market and the Remaking of European Financial Capital," *Environment and Planning A*, Vol. 24, 1992.

6. Saskia Sassen, "New Trends in the Sociospatial Organization of the New York City Economy," in Beauregard (ed.), *Economic Restructuring and Political Response* (London: Sage, 1989).

7. Michael Peter Smith and Joe Feagin, *The Capitalist City: Global Restructuring and Community Politics* (Oxford: Basil Blackwell, 1987), p. 3.

8. Harvey, "Flexible Accumulation," p. 264.

9. See Stuart Hall, "Race Articulation and Societies Structured in Dominance," in UNESCO 1980.

10. Italo Calvino, *Invisible Cities*, trans. William Weaver (New York: Harcourt Brace Jovanovich, 1978).

11. Over eighty open-ended interviews were conducted in Vancouver and Hong Kong in 1990 and 1991. In this chapter I focus on the interviews conducted with long-term Anglo residents of west-side communities. The names of individuals have been changed to protect privacy.

12. The maximum height and square footage depend on the size of the lot and the time of house construction. The height limit was thirty-five feet before April 1986 and thirty feet after April 1988.

13. Interviews with "Annie" took place between October and December 1990. Bracketed sections of the previous quote refer to street locations in Vancouver.

14. See Paul Gilroy, *"There Ain't No Black in the Union Jack": The Cultural Politics of Race and Nation* (Chicago: University of Chicago Press, 1991).

15. For a comparison in Los Angeles, see Mike Davis, *City of Quartz: Excavating the Future in Los Angeles* (London: Verso, 1990).

16. Letter to Vancouver City Council, April 10, 1990.

17. Sharon Zukin, *Loft Living: Culture and Capital in Urban Change* (Baltimore, Md.: Johns Hopkins University Press, 1982).

18. Jon Goss, "The Built Environment and Social Theory: Towards an Architectural Geography," *Professional Geographer*, Vol. 40, No. 4, 1988.

19. Quoted in the *Courier*, April 2, 1990.

20. The phrase may also come from Book 5 of Virgil's *Aeneid*, in which he speaks of the "genius of the place" in reference to the individual and preexisting spirituality of particular places.

21. Gayatri C. Spivak, "Can the Subaltern Speak?" in C. Nelson and L. Grossberg (eds.), *Marxism and the Interpretation of Culture* (Chicago: University of Illinois Press, 1988), p. 291.

22. Interview, October 24, 1990.

23. Kaja Silverman, *The Subject of Semiotics* (New York: Oxford University Press, 1983), p. 61.

24. Kate Bristol discusses how architectural style was used as the scapegoat for the numerous problems associated with the Pruitt-Igoe public housing project in Saint Louis. By focusing on "bad design," people displaced and ignored problems of chronic racism, poverty, unequal access to resources, and general social and economic breakdown. See "The Pruitt-Igoe Myth," *Journal of Architectural Education*, Vol. 44, No. 3, May 1991.

25. See, for example, Charles Jencks, *The Language of Post-modern Architecture* (New York: Rizzoli, 1984) and Robert Venturi, *Complexity and Contradiction in Architecture* (New York: The Museum of Modern Art, 1983).

26. See Fredric Jameson, "Cognitive Mapping," in C. Nelson and L. Grossberg, *Marxism and the Interpretation of Culture* (Chicago: University of Illinois Press, 1988); "Postmodernism, or the Cultural Logic of Late Capitalism," *New Left Review*, Vol. 17, No. 1, 1984; David Harvey, *The Condition of Postmodernity: An Enquiry into the Origins of Cultural Change* (Oxford: Blackwell, 1989).

27. For a numbing portrait of urban transformation in Vancouver in the 1960s, see Donald Gutstein, *Vancouver Ltd.* (Toronto: James Lorimer and Co., 1975).

28. Gutstein, *Vancouver Ltd.*

29. The term is discussed in both Yves Dezelay, "The *Big Bang* and the Law: The Internationalization and Restructuration of the Legal Field," *Theory, Culture and Society*, Vol. 7, Nos. 2–3, June 1990, and Donald Gutstein, *The New Landlords: Asian Investment in Canadian Real Estate* (Victoria, British Columbia: Porcepic Books, 1990).

30. Eric Hobsbawm and Terence Ranger, *The Invention of Tradition* (Cambridge: Cambridge University Press, 1987), p. 1.

31. Deryck Holdsworth, "Cottages and Castles for Vancouver Home-Seekers," *B.C. Studies*, Nos. 69–70, 1986, p. 28.

32. See "Understanding Vancouver's Housing," *Vancouver's Housing: Housing Stock*, Housing Resource Documents, Planning Department, City of Vancouver, January 1979.

33. For detailed descriptions of these house styles and their architectural history in Vancouver, see Holdsworth, "Cottages and Castles," pp. 29–30, and *House and Home in Vancouver: The Emergence of a West Coast Urban Landscape, 1886–1929*, Ph.D. thesis, Department of Geography, University of British Columbia, 1981.

34. For more details on architectural style in Shaughnessy, see H. D. Kalman and J. H. Roaf, *Exploring Vancouver* (Vancouver: University of British Columbia Press, 1974), pp. 145–164.

35. James Duncan and Nancy Duncan, "A Cultural Analysis of Urban Residential Landscapes in North America: The Case of the Anglophile Elite," in J. Agnew, J. Mercer, and D. Sopher (eds.), *The City in Cultural Context* (Boston: Allen and Unwin, 1984), p. 270.

36. Quoted in the *Courier*, December 18, 1985, p. 7.

37. Interview, February 20, 1991.

38. The motivation to increase or tighten controls over landscape symbols is often formed in reaction to socioeconomic stress. See Lester Rowntree and Margaret Conkey, "Symbolism and the Cultural Landscape," *Annals of the American Association of Geographers*, Vol. 70, 1980, pp. 459–461, and Robert Hewison, *The Heritage Industry: Britain in a Climate of Decline* (London: Methuen, 1987).

39. Pierre Bourdieu, *Distinction: A Social Critique of the Judgement of Taste* (Cambridge, Mass.: Harvard University Press, 1984), p. 56.

40. Mark Girouard, *Life in the English Country House* (New York: Penguin Books, 1980), p. 3.

41. See John Berger for a similar analysis related to eighteenth-century painting. *Ways of Seeing* (London: British Broadcasting Corporation and Penguin Books, 1972).

42. Duncan and Duncan, p. 260; M. J. Weiner, *English Culture and the Decline of the Industrial Spirit* (Cambridge: Cambridge University Press, 1981).

43. "Assets and Indebtedness: Dollar Values," Forty-first and West Boulevard (Vancouver). Benchmark: Vancouver Census, Metropolitan Area, Compusearch Market and Social Research, October 29, 1987.

44. The quote is from a letter sent to Vancouver's Planning Department on March 5, regarding the RS–1 zoning proposal of 1988. The Planning Department received forty-two letters and briefs in February and March commenting on this proposal. Of those, 90 percent supported the general intent to limit house size. See *1988: RS–1 Proposals: Public Consultation and Submissions*, City of Vancouver Planning Department, 1988.

45. Pierre Bourdieu, *In Other Words: Essays Towards a Reflexive Sociology* (Palo Alto, Calif.: Stanford University Press, 1990), p. 113.

46. Letter to the Editor, *Western News*, July 26, 1989.

47. Bourdieu argues that legitimating culture as a second nature allows those with it to see themselves as disinterested and unblemished by any mercenary uses of culture. See *Distinction*, p. 86

48. Bourdieu, *Distinction*, p. 124.

49. Census statistics of 1986 show that the average annual family income for Kerrisdale residents was Can$76,451. The average family income for Shaughnessy residents was approximately Can$96,034. These figures are considerably higher than the average household incomes for other neighborhoods. See *Vancouver Local Areas 1986*, City of Vancouver Planning Department, June 1989.

50. Interview, April 16, 1991.

51. Ronald Knapp, *The Chinese House: Craft, Symbol, and the Folk Tradition* (Hong Kong: Oxford University Press, 1990), p. 54.

52. Although one source estimated that "four out of five Hong Kong–born Chinese follow *feng shui*," these kinds of numbers are not particularly helpful for my discussion here. *Feng shui* unquestionably plays a role in the architecture and landscape decisions of some Hong Kong people doing business or moving to Vancouver. More important, however, are the manipulation of this particular system of beliefs by developers and the perception of it by White residents. These types of cross-cultural articulations have had equal if not greater ramifications for house design, tree removal, and social harmony in Vancouver. The estimation is by Danny Chang of *Asian Homebuyers Digest*. Quoted in *Atlantic*, November 1991.

53. Sarah Rossbach, *Interior Design with Feng-Shui* (New York: E. P. Dutton, 1987), p. 51.

54. Zukin, *Loft Living*, p. 15.

55. Interview, June 5, 1991.

56. Interview, November 15, 1991.

Part Three

Nostalgia, Modernity, and Other Domestic Fictions

Chapter Ten

Dishing Up Dixie: Recycling the Old South in the Early-Twentieth-Century Domestic Ideal

KIMBERLY WALLACE SANDERS

The story of Aunt Jemima, whom we know as Pancake Queen,
Starts on an Old Plantation, in a charming Southern scene.
There folks grow sweet magnolias and cotton in the sun,
And life was filled with happiness and old-time Southern fun.[1]

In 1994 Grammy-award-winning singer Gladys Knight appeared in several television commercials advertising Aunt Jemima pancake mix and syrup. Knight was criticized for endorsing a product that has a stereotyped African American woman as its trademark. Knight insisted that the Aunt Jemima logo had been appropriately updated—her head scarf had been replaced by a modern curly hairstyle and pearl earrings—and was no longer offensive. *Emerge* magazine responded with a short editorial called "It's the Stereotype, Stupid."[2] A caricature of Knight accompanied the article, showing her dressed not as the more modern Aunt Jemima, but as the older stereotype in head scarf, kerchief, and an enormous smile. The caption reads "Nothing is wrong in the face of it, but a subtext lurks beneath the Aunt Jemima ads." Author Karen Grigsby Bates points out that although Quaker Oats gave Aunt Jemima a makeover, disturbing aspects of the company's continued use of the title "aunt" still remain. Bates writes:

The comforting mammy icon still beams from the box, albeit an updated one. Jemima's kerchief may be gone, but she still is offensive to many Blacks—especially women, who, after all, do most of the household shopping, and who, I suspect, would have a lot less of a problem with Gladys' endorsement of pancake mixes, et al., if the box was modified still further: Jemima's pancakes would work just fine without the whopping smile. . . . Betty Crocker doesn't have to flash her teeth.[3]

A subtext has always lurked beneath the Aunt Jemima advertisements. In my research on the promotional history of Aunt Jemima products, I found that one subtext in particular has been consistent since the early twentieth century.

As we see in the rhyme above, a romanticized antebellum plantation life has always been the backdrop of the trademark portrait of Aunt Jemima. In advertisements from the 1920s, the words "Old South," "Old Time," and "Plantation" appear again and again as an incantation invoking the spirit of antebellum America. The narratives promise "old time plantation flavor" that was once available only to "Aunt Jemima's master and his guests," since it was "a secret from the South before the Civil War, . . . a famous recipe celebrated in Dixieland." We learn that Aunt Jemima is Colonel Higbee's "old mammy cook" or "old nigger cook," whose incredible "fluffy plantation pancakes," with their "matchless plantation flavor," made the Rosewood household famous "among the plantations along the Mississippi River."[4]

This chapter explores the influence of antebellum romanticism on the construction of an early-twentieth-century domestic ideal. Southern idealism was projected and promoted by a national advertising campaign exploiting the symbols and language of the Old South as part of a national vocabulary. I argue that during the 1920s the Aunt Jemima Mills/Quaker Oats Company helped construct a national longing for the Old South and that its copywriters effectively transferred a romantic mythology of plantation fiction into the commercial and marketing arena.[5] An emerging definition of American domesticity was enriched and shaped by this fantasy through advertisements placed in popular women's magazines such as *Ladies Home Journal* and *Good Housekeeping*. Both *Ladies Home Journal* and the Aunt Jemima trademark emerged as cultural phenomena in the late nineteenth century; by 1900, *Ladies Home Journal* was the most widely advertised magazine in the country. It led the way in transforming the magazine industry by manipulating the expectations of its female, middle-class audience.[6] In Jennifer Scanlon's history of the *Ladies Home Journal* as "both an artifact and an industry" (8), she argues that the *Journal* developed and promoted "a domestic ideology that defined editors as experts, advertisers as prophets, and, most importantly, women as consumers" (3). This domestic ideology represented the home as a reflection of women's values, and these values were directly influenced by magazine advertising.

I next explore the origins of the Aunt Jemima trademark, which was introduced along with the famous pancakes at the 1893 Chicago World's Fair. This fair systematically excluded African Americans from most venues; one exception was the World Congress of Representative Women, at which several African American women spoke eloquently about racial tension and African American progress.[7] Their presence provided a significant contrast to the plantation nostalgia accompanying the Aunt Jemima phenomenon.

My overview of Aunt Jemima pancake advertisements reveals a dramatic shift from an original emphasis on the product's nutritional value to an emphasis on Aunt Jemima as an attractive emblem of revisionist history. For example, turn-of-the-century advertisements use drawings of Aunt Jemima's face as eye-catching details to attract readers to the new product's mix of prepared wheat, corn, and rice flour.[8] The drawings are crude and are probably meant to be comical. By the mid-1920s, Aunt Jemima's image and "autobiographical" accounts have become the centerpiece for promoting pancake and muffin mix.

Awakening a "National Memory"

They awaken childhood memories!
—**Aunt Jemima advertisement,** *Good Housekeeping,* **1928**

The "promise" of Aunt Jemima thus went much further than household convenience: her condensation of racial nostalgia, national memory, and progressive history was a symptomatic, if not important, vehicle for post–Civil War national consolidation.
—**Lauren Berlant[9]**

Cultural historian Lauren Berlant links Aunt Jemima with the establishment of an "American progressive modernism . . . and the introduction of advertising itself as an arm of American sovereignty."[10] I develop Berlant's point in this section, first by exploring the introduction of a "living" Aunt Jemima trademark within the context of the turn-of-the-century racism evident in every aspect of the 1893 World's Fair. Berlant wrote about the fair as a platform for innovation and technology: "A huge success, Aunt Jemima became associated with a line of new products that include the 'skyscraper, the long-distance telephone, the X-ray, the motion picture, the wireless telegraph, the automobile, the airplane and radium.' She herself was an example of state-of-the-art technologies. . . . She did not, however, contain the promise of further racial emancipation."[11]

In fact, Aunt Jemima's "promise" was a regression of race relations, since her character helped usher in a resurgence of the "happy slave" mythology of the antebellum South. Berlant misses a disturbing point; the Aunt Jemima trademark was hinged on a Black woman pretending to be a slave in 1893, so that its success revolved around the fantasy of returning a Black woman to slave labor. Aunt Jemima's "freedom" was negated in this role because it was essential for the character's persona to be a plantation slave, not a free woman employed as a domestic.

The first woman to play the Aunt Jemima character was Nancy Green, a former slave from Kentucky.[12] Green was a middle-age woman working as a cook and housekeeper for a prominent Chicago judge. After a series of auditions, she was hired to cook and serve pancakes from the new recipe at the fair. Green represented Aunt Jemima for the Davis Milling Company until she died in 1923.[13] Part of her act was to tell stories from her own early slave life, along with plantation tales written for her by a White southern sales representative. This combination of historic and mythic plantation lore was designed to induce the "historical amnesia necessary for confidence in the American future" (Berlant 122). That the amnesia occurred at the expense of African American progress was clearly not an issue for the Davis Milling Company.[14]

The racial nostalgia and national memory to which Berlant refers in the quote at the beginning of this section imply a nostalgia for a particular kind of racial interaction, a nostalgia for a certain "racial reality," as it were. For the Pearl Milling Company, that reality not only was one of Black servitude but was specific to the region, time, class, and setting of slavocracy. My point is that the nostalgia is not simply race specific, but specific to the plantation South. The nostalgia then reproduces and affirms the myth of benign slavery popularized in the late nineteenth century by southern authors Joel Chandler Harris and Thomas Nelson Page.

"Racial nostalgia" and "national memory" met and married at the exhibition where Nancy Green entertained crowds with stories about Aunt Jemima's slave "childhood" in New Orleans.[15] The concepts of racial nostalgia and national memory are easily expanded to raise questions about whether there was, in 1893, a national nostalgia for a common racial memory. The goal of this kind of advertising is to induce a memory by using familiar symbols: Aunt Jemima affirms a national memory of participation in slavery. The plantation kitchen serves as a universal symbol of slavocracy as a positive, enriching experience shared by White Americans in the North and the South.

That national memory and national nostalgia for slavocracy supplied a cross-national unity for the 1893 World's Fair. The southern ideal then displaced the national memory of secession hostilities and the destructive Civil War. National racial nostalgia became equal to a national memory— an invitation for Americans to remember a time when Aunt Jemima cooked for the national family. This induced or planted memory fueled Aunt Jemima popularity; her familiarity was constructed as a universal reality. Aunt Jemima became a national household product because of the suggestion that she awakened a national memory of southern domesticity.

The Aunt Jemima trademark was also meant to be integral to the budding concept of an American Dream. One year after the fair, the Pearl Milling Company introduced the Aunt Jemima paper-doll family, six dolls that could be cut out of the pancake box. Aunt Jemima is shown with her husband, Rastus—whose name was later changed to Uncle Mose to avoid confusion with the Cream of Wheat man.[16] Aunt Jemima and her husband appear with their four children, who are described as "comical pickaninnies." Their names reflect the fictional slave names of popular plantation literature: Abraham Lincoln, Dilsie, Zeb, and Dinah. The doll family is dressed in tattered clothing, and all of them are barefoot.[17]

The text accompanying the cutout dolls is more complex. The caption below the barefoot dolls reads, "Before the Receipt was sold" (*receipt* is an archaic form of the word *recipe*). Then an overlay of new, elegant clothing covers the dolls, and the caption beneath reads, "After the Receipt was sold." By assigning the Aunt Jemima family a rags-to-riches biography, the company placed them within the Horatio Alger tradition of American possibility. This was one of several successful efforts to integrate Aunt Jemima into the very fabric of American culture.

This fabrication of an African American woman's life stood in direct opposition to the lives of real African American women at the turn of the century. The Aunt Jemima character epitomized an African American woman embracing her slave experience at a historic moment when African American women and men were taking the first steps to establish themselves as full-fledged citizens. The struggle of African American women attempting to gain support from White women is reflected in the planning process of the 1893 World's Fair, where the Aunt Jemima trademark was introduced. In the next section I demonstrate how the trademark became an emblem of antebellum race relations opposing, and in many ways negating, the emergence of educated and economically stable African American women.

Stirring Up Trouble: African American Female Intelligentsia at the Columbian World's Fair

In the March 1921 issue of *Ladies Home Journal*, a full-page advertisement for pancake flour commemorated the 1893 World's Fair with an enormous illustration of Aunt Jemima mixing pancakes before a large crowd. The narrative begins with a conversation between Aunt Jemima and her "mulatto helper"; the plantation dialect could be from any Thomas Dixon novel: "'Lawzee, we ain't nevah gwine be able to make enuf pancakes fo'

all dem white folks,' sputtered Aunt Jemima to her mulatto helper. 'Pow'-
ful sight o' vis'ters yo' all's got t'day,' responded the girl."[18]

The text "documents" Aunt Jemima's popularity by assuring readers
that her pancake stand needed guards to keep the crowds from blocking
the display area. The overwhelming appeal of Nancy Green's act is best
understood within the context of alternative representations of African
American womanhood also present at that World's Fair.

During the summer of 1890 a group of White women serving as the
Board of Lady Managers for the Columbian Fair was besieged by two
African American women's organizations. The Woman's Columbian Association and the Women's Column Auxiliary Association wanted the
Lady Managers to address the absence of African Americans in the exhibition plans for the fair. Both organizations were composed of educated,
middle-class women who wanted the fair to reflect the success of post-
emancipation African America. The latter group was clearer about its demands; it wanted the Lady Mangers to recognize it as a supplemental
branch of the original board. The board had its hands full with White
southern and northern women attempting to work together on a project
"in spirit of national solidarity"; regional differences were proving to be
enough of a challenge. The suggestion that there should be close interaction with Black women was insulting enough for one "Southern Lady" to
publicly announce: "We will speak to Negroes and be kind to them as employees but we will not sit with them."[19]

The dispute continued for over a year. Eventually the two African American women's organizations joined forces with other Black women to take
their cause to Washington. Together they composed and circulated a petition outlining their charges of racism against the Board of Lady Managers:

> Shall the Negro woman of this country have a creditable display of their la-
> bor and skill at the World's Columbian Exposition? The Board of Lady Man-
> agers created by an act of congress, says no. . . . Shall five million Negro
> women allow a small number of white women to ignore them in this the
> greatest opportunity to manifest their talent and ability in this the greatest
> expression of the age?[20]

The Fair Commission responded by making several minor concessions.
An African American woman, Fannie Barrier Williams, was appointed by
the board "to help supervise the installation of all exhibitions in the
Woman's Building." The board also agreed to Williams's suggestion that
two African American clerks be appointed to solicit exhibitions of work
by African Americans. Another African American woman, Imogene
Howard, was appointed to the New York contingent of Lady Managers to
collect statistics on African American women's work and "provide an example of the progress they had made."[21]

Lastly, Hallie Q. Brown, also African American, was offered an unpaid position in the Department of Publicity and Promotion. Brown, a well-paid university administrator, was hesitant to give up her job and asked to be made member of the board instead. She wanted the money and authority to validate the needs of the Black women she represented. Mrs. Palmer, head of the Board of Lady Managers, was impressed with Brown's intelligence but refused to admit Brown to the board for fear of antagonizing the White southern women on the board. Palmer saw the board as a significant agent in promoting sectional reconciliation; she believed it was more important for White northern and southern women to unite on behalf of the fair than to work in partnership with African American women.

Where would African American women stand in this display of regional harmony? Evidently there was little room for outspoken Black feminists in this celebration of American progress. Yet we know that the fair did provide adequate space for and approval of Nancy Green, telling happy slave stories and serving pancakes as Aunt Jemima.

As well, when the fair opened, six African American women addressed the World Congress of Representative Women. Fannie Barrier Williams and Anna Julia Cooper both used the opportunity to address how young African American women working as domestics were being harassed and exploited by White men. Cooper was a graduate of Oberlin College and later served as principal of the renowned M Street/Dunbar High School in Washington, D.C. She had eloquently attacked the racism of White southern women directly in her book *A Voice from the South* (1892):

> The Black Woman has tried to understand the Southern woman's difficulties; to put herself in her place, and to be as fair, as charitable, and as free from prejudice in judging her antipathies, as she would have others in regard to her own. She has honestly weighed the apparently sincere excuse, "But you must remember that these people were once our slaves"; and that other, "But civility towards the Negroes will bring us on social equality with them."[22]

Cooper also successfully predicted the appeal of Aunt Jemima and the southern domestic ideal when she described the northern fascination with southern traditions: "One of the most singular facts about the unwritten history of this country is the consummate ability with which Southerners from the very beginning even up to the present day, dictated to and domineered over the brain and sinew of this nation."[23]

Cooper insisted that despite sectional tensions, northerners were infatuated with southern concepts of bloodlines and chivalry. Cooper's insight and foresight were almost a prophetic indication of the Aunt Jemima phenomenon. The fact that Green was a woman of working-class status and Cooper was a member of an emerging Black middle class places them at opposite ends of a spectrum detailing African American women's progress. Nancy Green represented a long-standing tradition of African American women working as domestics around the country, and Cooper represented the growing reality of African American sociopolitical and economic progress.

Anna Julia Cooper was among the three Black women who were invited to participate in the World Congress of Representative Women. Her colleagues were equally middle-class and accomplished: Fannie Barrier Williams was a graduate of the New England Conservatory and the first African American woman appointed to Chicago's library board, and Hallie Q. Brown was a teacher and administrator at Wilberforce College.

I believe that this group of women representing the nineteenth-century Black elite held elitist attitudes. We see this reflected in the attitude of fellow club woman[24] Ida B. Wells (who selected as chair of her women's club the wife of the "wealthiest man in Chicago" to assure the club's prestige) about another concession by fair officials: "Negro Day." Negro Day was a picnic sponsored by fair officials and open to African Americans, but it was held off the fairgrounds.

Like her fellow club women, Wells was disgusted by the way African Americans were excluded from mainstream fair activities. She supported the women's actions, giving their plight ample space in the pamphlet she compiled and distributed at the fair, "The Reason Why the Colored American Is Not Included in the World's Columbian Exposition." Instead of confronting fair authorities, Wells thought, it was more efficient to address the fair-goers themselves. "The Reason Why" chronicled recent violence against Black men and contained several brief biographies of eminent Black women, including poet Phillis Wheatley and sculptress Edmonia Lewis.

What is most intriguing is that when Wells made her disapproval public, she blamed the exposition officials for not making a more appropriate appeal to the middlebrow and for enticing the lower class with offers of free food.[25] I believe she articulated the feelings of many of the Black elite, who worried that an appeal to the masses would embarrass the group later designated by DuBois as "the talented tenth." According to Wells:

> The self respect of the race is sold for a mess of pottage and *the spectacle of the class of our race* who will come out on that excursion roaming around the grounds munching watermelon will do more to lower the race in the estimation of the world than anything else. The sight of the horde that would be attracted there by the dazzling prospect of plenty of free watermelon to eat will give our enemies all the illustration they wish as excuses for not treating the race with the equality of other citizens.[26] [emphasis mine]

I have no interest in denigrating Ida B. Wells; her career as premier anti-lynching crusader is beyond reproach. I know that Wells established the

Negro Fellows League in 1910 specifically to encourage Black professionals to support the underclass. Her remarks reveal Wells's desire for the fair to showcase the intellectual and cultural development of the race; for Ida B. Wells this did not include fueling the stereotype of the watermeloncrazed Negro. The fact is that Nancy Green belonged to "the class of our race" to which Wells referred. And although women like Anna Julia Cooper felt obligated to speak on behalf of domestic workers, I suspect they would not have invited Green to speak on her own behalf.

Negro Day turned out to be more popular than Wells anticipated; hundreds of African Americans attended, and Frederick Douglass delivered a rousing speech on the accomplishments of the race. Wells quickly rescinded her criticism of the picnic and apologized to Douglass for not supporting him.

We must not forget the question posed by the petition against the Board of Lady Managers: what was a creditable display of labor and skill for Black women in 1893? Was it six highbrow Black women—forerunners of the "New Negroes"—giving public speeches about the morality, progress, and worth of African American womanhood? What kind of Black woman could have a viable, visible role in the fair's show of regional unity as well as display of labor and skill? The African American woman who had, since the early nineteenth century, been the ultimate symbol of racial accord: the Black mammy, represented at the 1893 World's Fair as Aunt Jemima.

In this section I used the examples of the Chicago Black women's clubs and the quotes from Ida B. Wells to explore the elements of classism evident in the women's organizations. The classism serves to contextualize the polemics that African American women were forced to engage in because of subtle racial politics surrounding the fair's reunification theme and the more overt racism of the fair officials. The classism evident in the women's organizations is unfortunate but not uncommon. Although the clubs' motto, "Lifting As We Climb," was no doubt genuine, the clubs represented the growing Black elite who were struggling for recognition and power. This ideology of intellectual politics existed in direct opposition to the domestic- and labor-related participation of Nancy Green, hired to introduce the Aunt Jemima trademark.

So while Cooper, Williams, and Brown were stressing the morality and intellect of African American women, Nancy Green was playing a part in a post-Reconstruction fantasy. Would Nancy Green have been welcome to participate in the other women's program at the Woman's Building? Cooper, Williams, and Brown apparently felt quite capable of defending the morality of domestic workers without inviting one to join them on stage.

The 1893 World's Fair allowed the Davis Milling Company of Saint Joseph, Missouri, to promote an agenda of race relations less threatening than that of the African American women giving speeches at the Woman's Building. Aunt Jemima and her pancake recipe were reconciliation gifts from the South to the North; reunification meant they could now share her as a southern prize. As one 1924 advertisement exclaimed, "Now millions have this famous breakfast." Aunt Jemima's popularity in her role at the Columbian Exposition illustrates how her race and gender make her an ideal balm to heal Civil War wounds. Her instant acceptance indicates the appealing familiarity of the southern Black mammy image deeply embedded in the American consciousness.

Affirmation of this invented or revised history of Aunt Jemima takes on greater significance when compared with the resistance "real" Black women experienced in their efforts to discuss and celebrate their real histories. As a symbol of racial harmony, Aunt Jemima proved to be the preferred version of African American womanhood—an exultation of slavocracy nostalgia. Aunt Jemima's popularity directly relates to the belief that slavery cultivated innate qualities in African Americans; the notion that African Americans were natural servants further reinforced a racist ideology negating the reality of African American intellectualism.

Ironically, similar racist ideology was transferred into advertising Aunt Jemima products. It is equally important to evaluate the importance of redeeming the antebellum South in the ideology of early commercial advertising.

A Marketable Past

The owner, Colonel Higbee, a most kind and gracious host,
Served his guests fine dishes, though they liked his pancakes most.
Of course, the cook who made them—or so the legend goes—
Was good old Aunt Jemima, as our pretty picture shows.[27]

Beyond their primary role of attracting new consumers and selling products, advertisements present value systems framed by the constant reminder that we live in a vibrantly successful capitalist society. The illustrations and texts for Aunt Jemima Pancake Flour reveal covert and overt messages about the centrality of antebellum idealism in America's developing consumer culture.[28] The "pretty picture" of good-natured slave cooks, kind slave masters, and well-fed southern gentry was quickly accepted by northern and southern consumers. This poetic advertising was written primarily for middle-class White women whose contact with African Americans was largely limited to advertising icons like Uncle Ben, Rastus, and the Gold Dust Twins. These trademarks were equally as stereotypical as Aunt Jemima; however, they did not rely as heavily on a formulaic plantation setting.

The vignettes describing Aunt Jemima's "life" on the Higbee plantation were written by southern copywriter James Webb Young, whose version of plantation life echoed that of Joel Chandler Harris.[29] Young's imaginative narratives about Aunt Jemima were given credibility by this note appearing in many of the ads: "We are often asked, 'Are these stories of Aunt Jemima and her recipe really true?' They are based on documents found in the files of the earliest owner of the recipe. To what extent they are a mixture of truth, fiction and tradition, we do not know. The Quaker Oats Company, Chicago."[30]

Certainly other food companies capitalized on the romance of the Old South: smiling Uncle Ben sold rice, his fraternal twin Rastus, the Cream of Wheat chef, hawked breakfast cereal, and Maxwell House Coffee is named for a Nashville hotel "famous throughout the old South" as a favorite gathering place for "illustrious visitors to old Dixie."[31] One Cream of Wheat advertisement actually featured Robert E. Lee IV as an example of the cereal's appeal to American children as a product full of "much Southern Charm."[32]

Similar advertisements in domestic magazines encouraged women to believe that certain products would give them access to a special knowledge, a domestic wisdom that transformed ordinary women into exceptional housewives. At the root of promotions of plantation domesticity is a sophisticated plan to confirm the benign nature of slavocracy, capitalize on the appeal of "brown-hand service," and appeal to the female reader's desire for special traditional hints on how to improve her own domestic space.

T. J. Jackson Lears addressed this in his theory about the commercial appeal of a marketable past:

> As the ties to their own past attenuated, the urban bourgeoisie became more susceptible to the commodified version of the past served up in national advertisements. . . . Housewives among this group were most likely to respond to the nostalgia peddled by the Mennen company in "Aunt Belle's Comfort Letters" which began in *Good Housekeeping* in 1920. "Aunt Belle is a *real* person and that is her *real* name. She really understands babies."[33] [emphasis mine]

The Mennen Company capitalized on the American obsession with European sophistication by making Aunt Belle sound as if she might be a professional British nanny. In a similar manner, Aunt Jemima was created as an expert on the ideal southern breakfast. The Aunt Jemima persona exemplifies a commodified version of the past, one that negates the lives of thousands of historical slave women who cooked and served during their lives as bondwomen.

Innovation that was both modern and old-fashioned was a common strategy between 1900 and 1930, when advertisers still struggled to win

American confidence. T. J. Jackson Lears's essay on advertising strategies and the therapeutic ethos is helpful in explaining the move away from nutritional value and quality assurances: "By the early 1900s the most successful advertising agents were trying not only to attract attention but aggressively to shape consumer's desires . . . pointing advertising away from the product and towards its alleged effects, away from sober information and toward the therapeutic promise of a richer fuller life."[34]

Among the therapeutic strategies were promises of good health and medicinal properties and promises "that the product would contribute to the buyer's physical psyche or social well being, the threat was that his well being would be undermined if he failed to buy it" (Lears 18).

A special blend of flours became the "secret recipe" of Aunt Jemima Pancake Flour, yet the true uniqueness of the recipe might have been its blend of agrarian and industrialized idealism. The Davis Milling Company introduced the new mix of flours in the Agricultural Building at the World's Fair to emphasize the wholesome quality of a premixed, prepackaged product. Early advertisements announced that the pancake flour was a "specially prepared combination of wheat, corn and rice containing all the good qualities of those great food products."[35] Copywriters went to great lengths to convince potential consumers that factories could produce homemade results: "Between the mixing machines and the packaging room at the Aunt Jemima Mills, there's a kitchen. As the Flour mixture goes through, our cooks take some out, and every five minutes they make pancakes. This is to make doubly sure that we have retained in Aunt Jemima Pancake Flour the old-time Southern flavor."[36]

A kitchen between the packaging room and the mixing machines! Professional cooks mixing and frying pancakes every five minutes! Here the southern plantation meets the northern mill in a perfect marriage of progress and tradition.

By the mid-1920s Aunt Jemima advertising narratives by Young became longer and more sophisticated.[37] "How Aunt Jemima Saved the Colonel's Mustache and His Reputation as a Host" is a coming-of-age story for Jemima. As a young slave girl, Jemima is called upon to save the reputation of the Higbee household when guests arrived unexpectedly for breakfast. Her mother, Eliza (perhaps this is where Stowe's Eliza might have ended up had she not escaped to Canada)—the Big House cook—was ill, and this "test" provided Jemima with an opportunity to "rise to the occasion" and prove her domestic ability. After that breakfast, she was given the title "aunt," usually reserved for much older Black women, making Jemima a child prodigy among slave women.[38]

In the advertisements that followed, readers learn about a variety of incidents and adventures involving Aunt Jemima and her pancakes. Perhaps the most provocative is "An Old Southern Cook Whose Pancakes

Have a Romantic History," in which Aunt Jemima feeds hungry Confederate troops who are camped near her cabin.[39] By directly associating the character with the rebel troops instead of the Union army, the copywriter presents Aunt Jemima as a slave woman who is indisputably loyal to the South and to the slave system. I argue that as commercial markets recognized the power to shape a domestic ideal through advertisements, the plantation kitchen validated the South as a region with superior appreciation for good food and for the good life. Consider these lines from an advertisement with the headline "Why No Other Pancakes Can Have That Famous Aunt Jemima Flavor": "No one can match the Aunt Jemima Flavor. Even in the old time South, in the land of good cooks, that was generally admitted."[40]

Aunt Jemima repeats her rescue mission in "The Night the Emily Dunstan Burned," by making pancakes for passengers from a wrecked steamboat. In this installment of the Aunt Jemima legend, her maternal instincts are supposedly honored by the line "When us men went up [to her cabin] we found that a nigger mammy was a-motherin' 'em all. An angel could 'a' done no better."[41] Aunt Jemima's heroism was always directed toward saving southern Whites, making her one of the many loving and loyal mammy figures predating Margaret Mitchell's Mammy in *Gone with the Wind*. Like Scarlett's Mammy, Aunt Jemima is set apart from other fictional plantation slaves and therefore from any aspect of autonomous African American life. First Aunt Jemima belonged to Colonel Higbee, then she belonged to the rest of the country; she never belongs to others like her, or to herself.

A 1921 *Ladies Home Journal* printed the closing chapter of Aunt Jemima's years with the Higbee family on the back cover of the first issue of the year. In "Aunt Jemima Bids Goodbye to the Old Plantation," we learn that the loyal Aunt Jemima stayed on the Higbee plantation for twenty years after the Civil War. She left only when convinced that she should go to Missouri and oversee the production of Aunt Jemima Pancake Flour. Lest readers think that her move was based on some personal motive, the text assures us that the only reason Aunt Jemima left Louisiana was to provide pancakes for the collective American kitchen.

In a later advertisement the narrative's incremental refrain is almost poetic in extolling the quality of the mix:

A recipe that first won fame when good food meant even more than it does today—down South before the Civil War. A recipe that mammy cooks on many plantations tried in vain to equal. *A recipe that has been used and liked by more women than any other in the history of food.* While her master lived, so the story goes, Aunt Jemima refused to tell a soul the secret of the wonderful flavor in the tender pancakes she baked for him and his guests.[42] [emphasis mine]

As I pointed out earlier, this commodified past was served up first at the 1893 World's Fair when Nancy Green played the Aunt Jemima character. As late as 1953, the company currently known as Quaker Oats reminisced about Nancy Green's role as "Pancake Queen" of the 1893 World's Fair. An advertisement featuring Aunt Jemima and "Lovely Mrs. Schenk, Mrs. America of 1953" used the headline "Pancake Queen Tells Mrs. America About Her Newest Pancake Success." Beneath the headline, two women, one White and slender, one African American and buxom, stand in a red and white kitchen decorated to match Aunt Jemima's famous uniform: red and white checked dress, white scarf around her neck, white apron around her ample waist, and red, yellow, and white kerchief around her head. Mrs. America appears wearing her jeweled crown, so the reader will not miss the stark difference between the queen of pancakes and the queen of homemaking.[43]

One photograph shows the two women standing in a stiff semiembrace and is strangely similar to the racially specific Benneton ads that were popular and controversial in the 1980s. In another photograph Aunt Jemima stands in the background with an approving smile as Mrs. Schenk serves her husband breakfast. It is ironic that this scene is set in "Aunt Jemima's kitchen," since part of the ready-mix appeal was that buying and cooking these pancakes delivered Aunt Jemima into your kitchen with "that famous Old South goodness." This picture of domestic integration still relies on the appeal of the Old South, even on the eve of the civil rights movement.

While the logo of Aunt Jemima's face has been altered and updated through the years, the message accompanying that face is surprisingly consistent. From the 1928 advertisement proclaiming "They awaken childhood memories!" to a 1981 ad inquiring "Do you remember your first bite of an Aunt Jemima pancake?" we see how a nostalgic evocation of a historic past is manifested through the guise of childhood memories, thus providing an effective linkage of consumer to product through domestic patriotism.[44]

Harpers magazine recently published a volume of essays and editorials on the South at the turn of the century. In one essay the anonymous late-nineteenth-century author writes whimsically of the uniquely innate cooking skills of African Americans, and although he or she does not mention Aunt Jemima directly, all of the references (except gender) bring her to mind:

> The negroes are born cooks as other less favored beings are born poets. The African brute, guided by the superior intelligence of his Caucasian master, in the days of slavery in Louisiana, gradually evolved into an artist of the highest degree of excellence, and had without any conscious analysis of principles created an art of cooking for which he should be immortalized.[45]

The romantic Old South is immortalized in this passage with memories that do not remind us of sectional hostilities or the bloody destruction of war between the states, but of the warm and "artistic" generosity of America's favorite plantation cook.

Notes

1. Marilyn Kern-Foxworth, *Aunt Jemima, Uncle Ben and Rastus* (Westport, Conn.: Greenwood Press, 1994), 71.

2. Karen Grigsby Bates, "It's the Stereotype, Stupid," *Emerge* (December/January 1995): 67.

3. Bates, "It's the Stereotype," 67.

4. Excerpts from advertisements appearing in *The Saturday Evening Post* and the *Ladies Home Journal* between 1920 and 1925.

5. A brief history of the frequent name changes of the company behind the Aunt Jemima trademark is necessary here. Chris Rutt originated the Aunt Jemima trademark in 1889 while he owned the Pearl Milling Company. The company went bankrupt, and a few months later the same owners organized the Aunt Jemima Manufacturing Company. In 1890 the trademark was sold to the Davis Milling Company, which was renamed the Aunt Jemima Milling Company in 1914. In 1925 Aunt Jemima Milling Company was sold to the Quaker Oats Company. See Arthur Marquette, *Brands, Trademarks and Good Will* (New York: McGraw Hill, 1967).

6. On the linkage between women's magazines and emerging consumer culture, see Jennifer Scanlon, *Inarticulate Longings: The Ladies Home Journal, Gender, and the Promises of Consumer Culture* (New York: Routledge, 1996). According to Scanlon, "The LHJ of the early twentieth century was both an important purveyor of twentieth-century culture and an enormously successful business enterprise" (9).

7. On African American women participating in the 1893 World's Fair, see Hazel Carby, "Woman's Era," in *Reconstructing Womanhood* (New York: Oxford University Press, 1987); May Wright Sewell, *World's Congress of Representative Women* (Chicago: Rand McNally, 1894), 433–37, 697–711, 715–17, 718–29; and Ann Massa, "Black Women in 'The City,'" *Journal of American Studies*, Vol. 8 (December 1974): 320.

8. *Ladies Home Journal*, March 1896.

9. Lauren Berlant, "National Brands/National Body," in *Comparative American Identities: Race, Sex and Nationality in the Modern Text*, ed. Hortense Spillers (New York: Routledge, 1991), 122.

10. Berlant, "National Brands," 122.

11. Berlant, "National Brands," 122.

12. Six women officially represented Aunt Jemima from 1893 to 1964. For biographical information on these women, see Kern-Foxworth, *Aunt Jemima*, 66–70.

13. Kern-Foxworth, *Aunt Jemima*, 67.

14. According to Arthur Marquette, historian for the Quaker Oats Company, the real triumph of Aunt Jemima as an advertising symbol was her ability to obliterate boundaries between legend and history, or fiction and autobiography. When

he describes Green's performance at the fair, he writes, "The crowds loved the fantasy and many took it for gospel" (Marquette, *Brands*, 155).

15. Chris Rutt, one of the original owners of the Pearl Milling Company, adapted the trademark of a plump and smiling Black woman from a New Orleans blackface minstrel song and dance routine called "Old Aunt Jemima." On minstrelsy and the Aunt Jemima trademark, see Marilyn Kern-Foxworth, "Aunt Jemima," *Black Ethnic Collectibles*, Vol. 2, No. 5 (1989): 18–19, and Phil Patton, "Mammy: Her Life and Times," *American Heritage* (September 1993): 78.

16. Uncle Mose was first introduced as the butler on the Higbee plantation, where Jemima lived.

17. Joleen Robison, *Advertising Dolls: Identification and Value Guide* (Paducah, Ky.: Collector Books, 1980), 40–41.

18. *Ladies Home Journal*, March 1921, 86.

19. Jeanne Weiman, *The Fair Women* (Chicago: Academy Press, 1981), 104.

20. Ann Massa, "Black Women in the White City," *American Studies*, Vol. 8 (1989): 319.

21. Beverly Guy-Sheftall, *Daughters of Sorrow* (New York: Carlson, 1990), 172.

22. Anna Julia Cooper, *A Voice from the South* (New York: Oxford University Press, 1988), 100.

23. Cooper, *A Voice*, 101.

24. The Black women's club movement emerged on a national level in the 1890s as a manifestation of middle-class Black women's obligations to address the complexities of race and gender oppression. Black women were also prohibited from joining most White women's clubs during this time. See Barbara J. Harris, "Early Community Work of Black Club Women," *Journal of Negro History*, Vol. 59 (April 1974): 158–167 and Elizabeth L. Davis, *Lifting As They Climb: The National Association of Colored Women* (n.p.: National Association of Colored Women, 1933) for primary source material. See also Beverly Guy-Sheftall, *Daughters of Sorrow: Attitudes Toward Black Women, 1880-1920* (Brooklyn, N.Y.: Carlson Publishing, 1990), 24–28.

25. Whereas Wells was insulted by the patronizing implications of Negro Day, her coauthor Frederick Douglass insisted that it was a triumph for them, since all of the gains made by the race began with small concessions. Douglass was also the scheduled keynote speaker.

26. M. J. S. Mier and August Rudwick, "Black Man in the White City," *Phylon*, Vol. 26 (1965): 360.

27. Kern-Foxworth, *Aunt Jemima*, 71.

28. The advertisements evoke the southern aristocracy by listing the "names" of the families who were privy to Aunt Jemima's breakfasts at Rosewood: "From New Orleans, the Southwoods, the Carters and the Marshalls came frequently, for it wasn't so far up the river to Colonel Higbee's mansion. But folks came too from all over the South, even from far Virginia." *Ladies Home Journal*, February 1921, 165.

29. Marquette, *Brands*, 155.

30. "Do you know this secret of making lighter, fluffier pancakes?" *Good Housekeeping*, November 1927, p. 124.

31. *Ladies Home Journal*, January 1927, *Ladies Home Journal*, June 1925: "Throughout the old South, the Maxwell House was celebrated for its hospitality and for its delicious food."

32. *Good Housekeeping*, March 1931, 185. Slavery was a familiar reference point for cleaning products as well. Premier electric vacuum cleaner used this theme in a 1928 promotion: "My Premier Duplex freed me from the slavery of cleaning. I would rather let my Premier do my cleaning in an hour or so and then go out and enjoy myself than work like a slave all day and then go to bed all tired out like I used to." *Good Housekeeping*, May 1928, 183.

33. T. J. Jackson Lears, "From Salvation to Self-Realization," in *The Culture of Consumption*, eds. Richard W. Fox and T. J. Jackson Lears (New York: Pantheon, 1983).

34. Lears, "From Salvation," 18.

35. *Ladies Home Journal*, March 1896.

36. *Ladies Home Journal*, March 1924, 145.

37. Marquette, *Brands*, 155.

38. *The Saturday Evening Post*, circa 1920, 75.

39. *Pictorial Review*, November 1920.

40. *Ladies Home Journal*, March 1924, 145.

41. *Pictorial Review*, November 1920.

42. *Good Housekeeping*, September 1927.

43. My copy of the advertisement is missing publication information; however, the date is clear from the text of the advertisement.

44. *Good Housekeeping*, February 1929, 99, and Ellen McCracken, "The Codes of Overt Advertisements," *Decoding Women's Magazines* (New York: Saint Martin's Press, 1993), 97–105.

45. "Plantation Life," *The South: A Collection from Harpers Magazine* (New York: Gallery Books, 1990), 193.

Chapter Eleven

Domestic Renovations: The Marriage Plot, the Lodging House, and Lesbian Desire in Pauline Hopkins's Contending Forces

SIOBHAN SOMERVILLE

Recent feminist studies of African American women's literature have emphasized the important role of the domestic novel in late-nineteenth- and early-twentieth-century representations of African American women. Critics such as Hazel Carby, Claudia Tate, and Ann duCille have shown that African American women writers claimed the domestic novel as a medium for exploring and revising ideologies of true womanhood within the context of African American culture.[1] Countering dominant cultural stereotypes about Black women's sexuality, novelists such as Pauline Hopkins, Frances Harper, Emma Dunham Kelley, and Amelia Johnson appropriated and revised the conventions of domestic fiction as a way to imagine and affirm Black women's access to respectable womanhood.

Much of this important recent scholarship has focused on the marriage plot as one of the primary conventions of the domestic novel. Understood as a figural device, marriage functions in domestic fiction as a way not

only to represent the fulfillment of the domestic ideal, but also symbolically to resolve larger social conflicts. As Nancy Armstrong explained in
her study of the domestic novel and the history of sexuality: "The good
marriage concluding [domestic] fiction, . . . where characters achieve
prosperity without compromising their domestic virtue, could be used to
resolve another order of conflict, the conflict between an agrarian gentry
and urban industrialists, for one, or between labor and capital, for another."[2]

Critics of African American women's domestic fiction have demonstrated the importance of understanding the symbolic functions of the
marriage plot within the specific histories of African Americans in the
United States. Because state-recognized marriage was a right denied to
slaves, dominant cultural constructions of marriage do not adequately account for the political meanings of marriage within African American culture and history. As duCille has argued:

> Certifying the importance but not necessarily the traditional power dynam-
> ics of the institution of marriage, these [Black women] writers [of the 1890s]
> . . . used the convention of coupling to critique and reorder gender relations.
> Departing from the popular—though by no means unchallenged—portrait
> of the proper, submissive Victorian wife, they theorized utopian unions in
> which empowered black heroines achieve parity with the men they marry
> and actively participate in the public sphere, usually through social welfare
> and racial uplift work.[3]

Likewise, Claudia Tate has argued that marriage should be understood
as an emancipatory political symbol for African Americans in the post-
Reconstruction era: "For black people, the importance of marrying in the
private sphere of domestic affairs may have paralleled that of voting in
the public sphere."[4]

These critics' important analyses significantly reorient understandings
of the political and cultural work accomplished by African American
women's domestic novels at the turn of the century. Whereas some critics
have characterized these novels as texts that reinforced accommodation-
ist views, Carby, duCille, and Tate instead demonstrate the complex ways
in which the novels attempted to shape and participate in a range of
emancipatory political goals for African Americans.[5] Because the meanings of marriage may differ profoundly depending on historical and cultural contexts, it is impossible to equate late-nineteenth-century African
American women writers' emphasis on middle-class heroines and the
marriage plot with a necessarily conservative social or literary vision.

"What happens to the marriage tradition . . . when it is considered in the
context of a literature by and about American men and women who for
generations were denied the hegemonic, 'universal truth' of legal mar-

riage?" asks duCille.[6] By demonstrating that marriage rests within a history of entitlements based on race and one's status as "slave" or "free," and therefore by denaturalizing the narrative, cultural, and political meanings of marriage, scholarship such as duCille's also raises questions about other axes of difference through which entitlements to the marriage plot have been denied, particularly those of sexuality.[7] Although duCille uses the term *coupling convention*, "both to destabilize the customary dyadic relation between love and marriage and to displace the heterosexual presumption underpinning the Anglo-American romantic tradition,"[8] a great deal of work remains to be done on how the specific history of the emergence of "heterosexual" and "homosexual" identities in the late nineteenth and early twentieth centuries might inform and be informed by analyses of African American women's cultural production during that period. Although we know that African American lesbian and gay subcultures existed in urban centers by the 1920s in the United States, the meanings of same-sex erotic attachments within African American culture before that period remain generally unexplored.[9] Precisely because legal recognition of heterosexual marriage itself was a relatively new liberty for African Americans in the second half of the nineteenth century,[10] it seems particularly important to ask how the meanings attached to same-sex relationships may have been transformed during this period as well.

The dominant cultural status of erotic relationships between women in the nineteenth-century United States has been the subject of vigorous debate among feminist literary critics and historians of sexuality. Much of this scholarship (focused primarily upon White women) has accepted the notion of "romantic friendship," in which passionate (and often physical) attachments between women were seen as acceptable and not incompatible with marriage between men and women.[11] In a discussion of turn-of-the-century literary representations of lesbians, for instance, Lillian Faderman suggested that passionate relationships between women were fully compatible with constructions of respectable (White) womanhood. According to Faderman, "Popular magazine fiction, well into the twentieth century, could depict female-female love relationships with an openness that later became . . . impossible."[12] Recently this model has been challenged by scholars who have argued for a more complex understanding of erotic relationships between women before the twentieth century. In an insightful article on the representation of same-sex desire between women in popular fiction in the mid–nineteenth century, Marylynne Diggs has countered previous historiography by identifying "the emergence throughout the nineteenth century of a specific sexual identification built upon the pathologizing of erotic and exclusive relationships between women."[13] The emergence of a model of lesbian desire and identity was probably a gradual and uneven process, depending upon a number of factors, including, among others, region, class, education, and mobility. Scholars generally agree, however, that the last decade of the nineteenth century was a particularly volatile period in the public recognition of women's homoerotic/sexual attachments. Lisa Duggan, for instance, has shown that this decade was characterized by competing narratives about women's same-sex attachments. In her discussion of the highly publicized case of Alice Mitchell, who murdered her lover, Freda Ward, in 1892, Duggan identifies this incident as a site for "a new narrative-in-formation—a cultural marker of the emergence of a partially cross-gender-identified lesbian and her separation from and conflict with the family-based female world of the nineteenth century and . . . from the bourgeois values of sexual purity and motherhood."[14]

Viewed in relation to these shifts in the history of women's sexuality, then, the emphasis on marriage in post-Reconstruction novels by African American women raises questions about the position of women's homoerotic bonds in these texts. Are women's homoerotic bonds figured as compatible with the marriage plot in post-Reconstruction novels by African American women, or are they seen as a narrative alternative or threat to the conventions of heterosexual coupling? This article explores these questions by means of an analysis of Pauline Hopkins's novel *Contending Forces* (1900).[15] First, I explore how Hopkins reconfigures the traditionally privatized and feminized setting of the domestic novel and how that reconfiguration parallels her attempts to reshape the conventions of the domestic novel in the interest of African American women. Second, I show that, within these "renovated" conventions of the domestic novel, it is possible to see Hopkins's ambivalence toward women's homoerotic desires and the political meanings of these attachments. In *Contending Forces*, conflicting narratives of same-sex desire coexist and compete for narrative authority. On the one hand, Hopkins represents women's erotic friendships as crucial to the domestic sphere, marriage plot, and African American women's political advancement, and on the other hand, she draws upon a nascent model of lesbian desire as incompatible with respectable womanhood and the traditional narrative resolution of marriage in domestic fiction.

Renovating Domestic Space: Ma Smith's Lodging House

Set in Boston in 1896, the central narrative of *Contending Forces* takes place in an important variation of the conventional private household of domestic fiction, a lodging house owned and operated by "Ma" Smith and her two adult children, Dora and Will. Hopkins carefully outlines the history of the lodging house and the Smith family. Originally, the house was purchased by Henry Smith, the husband and father of the family, as the family's private residence. Upon his death, his wife inherited this "house in a respectable part of the South End of Boston, Mass, with a heavy mortgage upon it" (*CF*, 82). Importantly, the death of Henry Smith results in a gendered transferal of property ownership that becomes important for Hopkins's reconfiguration of the narrative possibilities within the novel.[16]

Hopkins's choice to set her novel in a lodging house revises one of the premises undergirding the tradition of domestic fiction. As Armstrong and others have argued, one function of domestic fiction was the production of the gendered split between public and private domains and, further, the detachment of sexuality from the political sphere. Armstrong notes that "as it became the woman's sphere, then, the household appeared to detach itself from the political world and to provide the complement and antidote to it. And in this way, novels helped to transform the household into what might be called the 'counterimage' of the modern marketplace, an apolitical realm of culture within the culture as a whole."[17]

Hopkins's choice to locate the central action of *Contending Forces* in a lodging house seems to expose the instability of the gendered split between marketplace and home. As Traci Reed Carroll has pointed out in her discussion of *Contending Forces* and commodity culture, "Rather than disaffect from American society and look to the past for utopian social models that escape commodification . . . Hopkins begins from the assumption of one's imbrication in systems of ownership and exchange."[18] The lodging house setting allows Hopkins to position her female characters in both public and private spheres; she depicts women who participate in the marketplace at the same time as they remain literally at home, aspiring to the ideals of the domestic heroine.

The lodging house is both residence and workplace for her primary female characters, and importantly, unlike traditional heroines of domestic fiction, none of the women who reside at 500 D Street relies primarily on male figures for her upkeep.[19] Mrs. Smith and her daughter, Dora, are the proprietors, the newcomer Sappho is a typist who works in her room, and two minor characters, Mrs. Ophelia Davis and Sarah Ann White, run a laundry on the ground floor of the house. In the collective space of the lodging house, the women's combined resources create possibilities for their financial autonomy. Yet working in the space of the lodging house also affords these women protection from the abuses of the marketplace. Importantly, Hopkins identifies racism as a primary danger for African American women in the marketplace, in addition to the presumed sexual dangers that threatened all women in the labor force. White and Davis, for instance, exclaim, "'Yas'm, I'm tired o' livin' in white folkses' kitchens. Yas'm, thar's lots o' talk 'bout servant gals not bein' as good as enybody else" (*CF*, 105). Likewise, Sappho works at home, in part because of the racist attitudes of her employers and fellow workers. When Dora remarks that she has heard that "it was very difficult for colored girls to find employment in offices" (*CF*, 127–128), Sappho acknowledges the racism and harassment that she has experienced: "The proprietor said, 'Yes; we want a stenographer, but we've no work for your kind.' However, that was preferable to the insulting familiarity which some men assumed. It was dreadful!" (*CF*, 128).

By situating these female characters in the lodging house, Hopkins deftly resolves contemporary questions about the status of African American women circulating in the labor market at the turn of the century. These concerns were voiced in 1914 by sociologist John Daniels, for instance, in his study of African Americans in Boston, *In Freedom's Birthplace*. Drawing upon federal census figures of 1900, the year in which *Contending Forces* was published, Daniels noted that 40 percent of African American women and girls in Boston worked for wages: "That such is the fact bears witness not only to a larger contingent of unmarried working-women, but also to the excessive proportion of wives, mothers, and daughters in Negro homes who, by the rigor of the demand for family support, are forced into labor beyond their own domestic responsibilities."[20] While the seeming "excessive proportion" of African American women in the labor market caused Daniels alarm in 1914, Hopkins in contrast suggests that paid employment afforded her female characters a sense of accomplishment and agency, in addition to financial stability. Commenting upon her work as a typist, for instance, Sappho remarks, "Generally speaking, I prefer it to most anything that I know of" (*CF*, 99). Likewise, in her duties as landlady of the lodging house, Dora is described as "a woman of ability and the best of managers, husbanding their small income to the best advantage" (*CF*, 85).

By portraying unmarried female characters who circulate in the labor force while still remaining identified with the domestic sphere, Hopkins to some extent resists dominant cultural constructions of women employed in turn-of-the-century urban centers. As historian Joanne Meyerowitz has demonstrated, this period saw widespread concern about increasing numbers of "women adrift," unmarried women who moved to urban centers to support themselves and who did not live as a part of a family.[21] Likewise, Hazel Carby has shown that the figure of the unmarried African American woman in urban centers became the target of "moral panics" in the early twentieth century. Although her discussion focuses on the 1920s, Carby notes that as early as 1905 a discourse was in place that began to pathologize urban unmarried Black women. She writes that "the movement of black women between rural and urban areas and between southern and northern cities generated a series of moral panics. One serious consequence was that the behavior of black female

migrants was characterized as sexually degenerate and, therefore, socially dangerous."[22] Carby notes that numerous reformers, both White
and African American, responded to the perceived threat of African
American women migrating to cities by creating various institutions
charged with their "protection," including organized homes. However
benevolent their intent, one effect of those institutions was, of course, the
surveillance of migrating Black women.[23]

The organized homes that Carby discusses were a response by reformers to a slightly earlier shift from boarding houses to lodging houses as
the primary accommodations for unmarried women in urban centers in
the late nineteenth century. Whereas boarding houses provided a room
and meals in a more familial arrangement, lodging houses provided only
rooms, thus tending toward less structured relationships among occupants. In *The Lodging House Problem in Boston*, a study focused on the
South End furnished-room district at the turn of the century, Albert Benedict Wolfe remarked that "something of the home element" usually characterized "old-time" boarding houses.[24] In contrast to lodging houses, according to Wolfe, in the boarding house,

> boarders knew each other, they met at table two or three times a day, and lin-
> gered a few moments in conversation after dinner in the evening. In summer
> they gathered on the front steps and piazzas, and in winter they often played
> euchre and whist in the landlady's parlor. Congenial temperaments had a
> chance to find each other. There was a public parlor in which guests were re-
> ceived, and, in a reputable boarding-house at least, a girl would not have
> thought of taking a gentleman caller to her own room. The landlady of the
> good boarding-house took something of a personal interest, even if remote,
> in her boarders, and they often found themselves becoming a part of the
> family even against their wills. There was a certain personal element in the
> relations between individuals; no one could be isolated and entirely shut up
> within himself.[25]

Wolfe's comments are particularly relevant for understanding the historical meanings of the lodging house at the time when Hopkins published *Contending Forces*. In 1900, Boston had a higher percentage of lodging houses than any other major American city and the highest
proportion of women workers living in boarding and lodging houses, approximately one-fourth of all employed women.[26] The rapid replacement
of boarding houses with lodging houses in Boston caused particular concern among reformers such as Wolfe, for whom the lodging house represented a breeding ground for wide-reaching evils:

> Nor is it too much to say that the lodging-house makes criminals. When a
> young man and a young woman are thrown together in illicit relations by the

very force and circumstances of lodging-house environment, and through the chain of events thus started, the girl becomes a suicide or the boy a murderer, the lodging-house must be held responsible for social dissolution.[27]

For Wolfe, who obviously invested wholeheartedly in nineteenth-century domestic ideologies, the narrative trajectory attached to the lodging house could be imagined only as tragic. Yet, importantly, and particularly for African American women, lodging houses were desirable compared with boarding houses or other domestic arrangements. As Meyerowitz has discussed, the lodging house was generally more practical for both African American women lodgers and African American landladies; because many African American "women adrift" were employed as service workers in private homes, restaurants, and hotels, they received their meals in the workplace and had no need for landladies to provide meals.[28]

Meyerowitz has also shown the importance of the lodging house as a site for unmarried working women's participation in redefining the meanings and parameters of female sexuality. According to Meyerowitz,

> By the early twentieth century, the furnished room districts of Chicago and other large cities were known as havens for women and men who chose to defy conventions. ... Women and men could live together outside of marriage or with members of their own sex in homosexual relationships. In many rooming houses, occasional or professional prostitutes could come and go without arousing concern of family or neighbors.[29]

Beyond the watchful eyes of parents, family, and longtime neighbors, unmarried female lodgers found unprecedented opportunities, if they chose, for new sexual, political, and cultural experiences within urban social networks. With this range of options, traditional prohibitions against extramarital sexuality seemed to be loosened. As Wolfe lamented, "One fact we may be sure of: the tendency of lodging-house life is to postpone both marriage and the intention to marry."[30]

Given contemporary cultural anxieties about the moral decline associated with lodging houses, Hopkins provides crucial details about the Smith lodging house to distinguish it as a positive institution within the African American community. Although it occupies a space between public and private, the lodging house nevertheless is imbued thoroughly with domestic ideals, resembling more the older-style boarding house described by Wolfe than the new, impersonal lodging house. Hopkins tells her reader that Mrs. Smith's house "contained respectable though unlettered people, who possessed kindly hearts and honesty of purpose in a greater degree than one generally finds in a lodging-house" (*CF*, 102). The character of the lodgers is crucial for the respectable reputation of the lodging house itself: "It was also whispered that to enjoy these privileges one must be 'pretty nice,' or as some expressed it: 'You've got to be high-toned to get in there'" (*CF*, 103). Rather than corrupting its inhabitants, Mrs. Smith's lodging house seems to exert upon its lodgers all the proper civilizing effects of home. Mrs. Smith regularly arranges gatherings in the evenings, with the explicit purpose of reforming her lodgers: "She argued, logically enough, that those who were inclined to stray from right paths would be influenced either in favor of upright conduct or shamed into an acceptance of the right" (*CF*, 102). "Ma" Smith has decidedly maternal ways of keeping her lodgers under her influence, providing "plenty of good homemade cake, sandwiches, hot chocolate, and on very special occasions, ice cream or sherbet" (*CF*, 103).

In turn-of-the-century descriptions, reformers and sociologists repeatedly emphasized the moral dangers posed by the lack of a parlor in most lodging houses. In the eyes of these observers, the absence of a parlor broke down social relationships and led to isolation and a sense of anonymity among lodgers. Frequently, reformers emphasized the sexual dangers posed by the lack of a parlor. As Wolfe alarmedly wrote, "Probably not one girl in a hundred who finds herself in a rooming-house would have thought while at home of receiving a gentleman caller in her bedroom. Yet ninety per cent of the women lodgers, if they associate with men at all, must either receive them in that way or loiter with them in the streets."[31] Hopkins responds to these contemporary characterizations of the lodging house by providing careful details of its interior spaces. She positions the parlor, for instance, as a significant setting for two crucial events in the novel. First, upon Sappho's arrival, Mrs. Smith and Dora arrange a reception in the parlor as part of Mrs. Smith's design to make sure "that her tenants might have a better opportunity of becoming acquainted with each other" (*CF*, 102). Likewise, later in the novel, in a chapter entitled "The Sewing Circle," the parlor serves as the site of political, economic, and social activism within the African American community in Boston, particularly for women.

At the same time as Hopkins portrays Ma Smith's lodging house as upholding and extending the civilizing influences of the middle-class home, she also distinguishes this version of domesticity from a traditional, father-headed household. In a scene in which Mrs. Smith narrates a story about her own upbringing, she first details the differences between the household equipment of the past and the present: whale-oil lamps versus kerosene, a hearth versus a stove, handmade versus manufactured carpets. The story then shifts into a tale about her father's surveillance of his daughters' sexuality. A hardworking man, her father usually slept after returning home in the evening, during which time his wife had permitted her daughters' suitors to visit the house. When the father discovers a young man in the house one evening, he dismisses him angrily: "'Young

man, if you have a home, go to it; this is no half-way house for the accom-
modation of young squirts'" (*CF*, 95). Mrs. Smith's nostalgic tale distinguishes her father's strictness from her own more relaxed standards for
visitors. Yet, in effect, the story establishes Mrs. Smith's own upbringing
as a virtuous daughter, protected by a patriarchal figure who imposes
strict boundaries between his daughters and the attentions of men, as
well as between public and private.

Hopkins's strategy of setting her narrative in the lodging house also locates the Smith family within contemporary hierarchies of social status
among African Americans. In his characterizations of lodging-house landladies, Wolfe described "two great classes of lodging-house keepers,—
those who care about what their lodgers do and are, and those who do not
care." Property ownership was a significant factor in making this distinction: "A considerable number of landladies own their dwellings, land and
all. In such cases the moral tone of the house is generally high."[32] Likewise,
according to Daniels, in 1900, boarding- and lodging-house keepers fell
into the most esteemed group of workers within Boston's African American population, those in professional or semiprofessional work (7.8 percent
of all African American men at work; 5.9 percent of all African American
women at work).[33] This group, according to Daniels, "represents the height
of the Negroes' industrial achievement;—namely, their rise into positions
of more or less complete proprietorship."[34] Interestingly, running a boarding or lodging house is listed by Daniels as the most frequent occupation of
professional and semiprofessional women. Thus Dora and Mrs. Smith, as
proprietors of the lodging house and, perhaps more significantly, as property owners, would be recognized as members of the professional or semiprofessional class.

Hopkins's strategy of locating her novel in a lodging house revises the
function of the bourgeois household in domestic fiction. The Smith lodging house appears to offer the best advantages of both the traditional domestic sphere and the marketplace. For its unmarried female inhabitants,
the lodging house provides the moral protection associated with the domestic sphere. At the same time, these characters have access to the economic advantages of the urban marketplace. While the lodging house
provides a space in which Hopkins can establish exemplars of respectable
African American womanhood, the very circulation of unmarried women
within the lodging house carries with it threats to these constructions of
respectability and to the novel's narrative progress toward marriage. In
the next two sections, I focus on the function of two pairs of females
within the novel. By looking at where Hopkins locates these couples in
the literal spaces of the lodging house, it is possible to see their ambiguous positions within Hopkins's novels and her attempts to construct
models of respectable womanhood.

Queer Talk and Bachelor Maids

The central action of *Contending Forces* begins with the entrance of Sappho Clark, a beautiful but mysterious stenographer who takes a room in the Smith lodging house. Later in the novel, we learn that Sappho, originally named Mabelle Beaubean, was abducted at the age of fourteen by her own uncle, raped, and then abandoned at a brothel. Hopkins positions the brothel as an antihousehold, a space that runs counter to all the ideals of domestic respectability. As Luke Sawyer, a faithful worker in the Beaubean household, narrates, "After *three weeks* of incessant searching we found her a prisoner in a house of the vilest character in the lowest portion of the city of New Orleans—a poor, ruined, half-crazed creature in which it was almost impossible to trace a resemblance to the beautiful pet of our household" (*CF*, 260). The "house of the vilest character" is the breeding ground for the "ruined creature[s]," in contrast to the production of "beautiful pet[s]" by proper bourgeois households.

Interestingly, as the Smiths anticipate Sappho's arrival, she circulates as the projection of their various desires and anxieties. Fascinated, Dora describes Sappho's physical irresistibility: "Talk about your beauties! my, but she's the prettiest creature I ever saw! I expect all the men in this house will be crazy over her" (*CF*, 89). Dora's brother Will responds by expressing his sexual anxiety about this unknown woman and his sister's fascination with her: "I'll bet you a new pair of Easter gloves that she's a rank old maid with false teeth, bald head, hair on her upper lip" (*CF*, 96). Invoking specifically masculine characteristics ("bald head, hair on her upper lip"), Will imagines a stereotype of grotesque female sexuality, a "rank old maid."

Sappho turns out to be anything but a rank old maid; when she finally arrives, she appears beautiful beyond question to Will and Dora alike. Hopkins describes a deep physical and emotional attraction between Dora and Sappho:

> After that evening the two girls were much together. Sappho's beauty appealed strongly to Dora's artistic nature; but hidden beneath the classic outlines of the face, the graceful symmetry of the form, and the dainty coloring of the skin, Dora's shrewd common sense and womanly intuition discovered a character of sterling worth—bold, strong and ennobling; while into Sappho's lonely self-suppressed life the energetic little Yankee girl swept like a healthful, strengthening breeze. Care was forgotten; there was new joy in living. (*CF*, 114)

Hopkins portrays Dora and Sappho's attachment as one of mutual and transformative desire.

A number of critics have remarked upon the significance of the choice of "Sappho" as the pseudonym for the protagonist of *Contending Forces*, suggesting that Hopkins's invocation of the ancient Greek poet resonated both with the feminist symbolism of this figure as well as the fragmentation that characterizes knowledge of the ancient Sappho's life and writing.[35] In a discussion of *Contending Forces* that generally criticizes Hopkins's focus on middle-class femininity, Houston Baker suggests an irony at work in Hopkins's choice of "Sappho." Her name, he argues, "does not refer textually to anomalous sexual proclivities, but only, one assumes, to a classical mastery of the word. Ironically, such mastery for a mulatto woman in nineteenth-century Boston does not yield an island poet, but a clerk typist."[36] In his ironic reading of Hopkins's allusion and his focus on poetic "mastery," Baker too quickly overlooks another significance of Hopkins's choice of this pseudonym for the central figure of her text. What Baker refers to as "anomalous sexual proclivities"—that is, Sappho's sexual attachments to other women—may indeed be relevant to Hopkins's portrayal of her heroine. In fact, critical discussions of Hopkins have tended to avoid an obvious cultural resonance of the pseudonym, its almost clichéd function as a marker of lesbian desire.[37] DuCille, for instance, writes that "the signal name change . . . is not from Mabelle Beaubean to Sappho Clark but from Sappho Clark to Mrs. William Smith" at the end of the novel.[38] DuCille explains that this shift marks "the text's and the race's 'declaration of independence' from impossible standards of womanhood and respectability."[39] Indeed, Hopkins radically transforms understandings of true womanhood, making it accessible to those whose history is inextricable from sexual violence. Yet it is important to keep in mind that the restoration of a respectable position for Mabelle/Sappho by means of the title "Mrs. William Smith" also suggests the erasure and containment of the implications of the pseudonym "*Sappho.*"

Hopkins's position toward the possibility of Dora and Sappho's mutual desire is contradictory, in keeping with the uneven historical emergence of lesbian identity at the turn of the century. She seems to oscillate between, on the one hand, the model of romantic friendship, with its unselfconscious representations of female attachments, and, on the other, that of emerging models of lesbian relationships, in which female homoeroticism is figured as unnatural and dangerous. Although Hopkins does not explicitly name lesbian desire per se, she does represent the intimacy between Dora and Sappho as potentially threatening, if not tragic. Dora herself treads cautiously at first in her friendship with Sappho: "She did not, as a rule, care much for girl friendships, holding that a close intimacy between two of the same sex was more than likely to end disastrously for one or the other" (CF, 98). This remarkably direct acknowledgment of same-sex desire, in all its threatening dimensions, suggests that Hopkins was aware of the growing tendency to view intimacy between women as potentially dangerous. As Lisa Duggan comments, during the 1890s "nearly all the newspaper stories [of women's erotic attachments] had tragic endings. They were stories of struggle and failure; they ended with violence or loss. . . . The suggestion of sexuality, however subtle or implicit, was generally paired with bloodletting. . . . The stories were thus structured to emphasize, ultimately, that no real love story was possible."[40]

Hopkins herself may have been familiar with these popular cultural representations of cases like that of Mitchell and Ward and may have recognized the corresponding difficulty of representing women's homoerotic bonds as unproblematic.[41] Hopkins nevertheless appears to raise the specter of dangerous lesbian desire only to deny it as a characterization of Dora and Sappho's relationship. In spite of her professed reluctance to engage in "girl friendships," Dora cannot resist her attraction to the new lodger: "Sappho Clark seemed to fill a long-felt want in her life, and she had from the first a perfect trust in the beautiful girl" (*CF,* 98).

As a means of fulfilling Dora's "long-felt want," and at the same time short-circuiting the inevitable "disastrous ending" of same-sex desire, Hopkins sets their most intimate scene in a carefully controlled space set apart from the main narrative, a household space of both containment and transgression, not coincidentally resembling what one might call "the closet." Ironically, in her depiction of homoerotic desire, Hopkins reconstructs the spatial separation between public and private domains that she had previously challenged by setting her novel in the semipublic, semiprivate lodging house. The central scene of this boundary making *within* the lodging house takes place when an overnight snowstorm makes it impossible for Sappho to leave the Smith lodging house to pick up her morning's work. Sappho "beg[s] Dora to pass the day with her and play 'company' like the children" (*CF,* 117). Dora and Sappho take advantage of their enforced isolation to construct an idyllic private enclosure within the lodging house: "By eleven o'clock they had locked the door of Sappho's room to keep out all intruders, had mended the fire until the little stove gave out a delicious warmth, and had drawn the window curtains close to keep out stray currents of air. Sappho's couch was drawn close beside the stove, while Dora's small person was most cosily bestowed in her favorite rockingchair" (*CF,* 117).

Hopkins's description of the scene suggests miniaturization and contraction, a characterization that diminishes the importance of the women's friendship, according to Mary Helen Washington.[42] Perhaps it is more accurate to see this miniaturization as a necessary aspect of the erotics between the two women, simultaneously containing and domesticating the desire that is being expressed. The women play "like the children" in a room where the "little stove" echoes Dora's "small person." Moreover, phrases like "delicious warmth," "mended," and "cosily bestowed" suggest specifically domestic comfort, while the repetition of "drawn close" suggests an increasing intimacy between the two women. "Locked" in, Dora and Sappho ironically are now "free" to explore their mutual desire in the privacy of a thoroughly feminized domestic space.

Within the context of literary representations of race and sexuality, the scene of Dora and Sappho "locked" pleasurably away has larger implications. The combination of the unspoken acknowledgment and literal marginalization of homoeroticism links *Contending Forces* to the "closet," a literary trope that Eve Sedgwick has identified as "the defining structure for gay oppression in this century."[43] A "skeleton in the closet" is "a private or concealed trouble in one's house or circumstances, ever present, and ever liable to come into view."[44] To be "in the closet" is to be palpably invisible in a structure of visibility, proximity, and knowledge. Although individuals may desire to be "in" or "out" of the closet, they can never fully control their status and so constantly renegotiate the boundary between "in" and "out" in a culture that simultaneously seeks out and erases lesbian and gay identity.

Hopkins may not express any literal physical desire between Sappho and Dora (nor does she describe any explicitly physical sexual contact, heterosexual or homosexual, anywhere in the novel), but this scene is loaded with sensuality, albeit of a specifically middle-class "flavor": "A service for two was set out in dainty china dishes, cream and sugar looking doubly tempting as it gleamed and glistened in the delicate ware. One plate was piled with thinly cut slices of bread and butter, another held slices of pink ham" (*CF*, 118). Hopkins's description suggests doubleness, not only through the literal "service for two" and "doubly tempting" cream and sugar, but also through syntax, balancing the alliterative adjectives "gleamed and glistened" and the parallel clauses "One plate, . . . another" (*CF*, 118). Similarly, Sappho herself is described in the same terms as the food. The sweets that "gleamed and glistened" mirror Sappho's body, itself described later in the same scene as "all rosy and sparkling."

Hopkins emphasizes the specifically oral pleasures in her descriptions of food in this scene. As the women complete their feast with cream pie and chocolate bonbons, Sappho teases Dora, "And your teeth, your beautiful white teeth, where will they be shortly if you persist in eating a pound of bonbons every day?" (*CF*, 120). Dora teases back, "I'll eat all the bonbons I want in spite of you, Sappho, and if you don't hurry I'll eat your slice of cream pie, too" (*CF*, 120). Hopkins giddily narrates, "At this dire threat there ensued a scramble for the pie, mingled with peals of merry laughter, until all rosy and sparkling, Sappho emerged from the fray with the dish containing her share of the dainty held high in the air" (*CF*, 120). Hopkins's flowery language—"dire," "ensued," "mingled," "peals," "merry," "fray," "dainty"—suggests the lighthearted and inconsequential diction of respectable drawing room conversation. This lan-

guage, stilted and feminized, reinforces the specifically bourgeois sensuality of the scene and its fetishization of color, especially pinks and
whites: "cream," "sugar," "bread and butter," "pink ham," "cream pie,"
and "beautiful white teeth." The emphasis on pinks and whites, of
course, has significance in relation to ideologies of purity and racialized
characterizations of women's bodies, particularly in the context of Hopkins's description of Sappho's own body as a combination of "queen rose
and lily in one" (*CF*, 107).

In this private space, the tea party enacts a displacement of Dora and
Sappho's desire, sensual satisfaction, and veiled sexual aggression. What
reinforces the homoerotic significance of this scene is the intimate conversation that follows it, an additional development and extension of the
women's oral pleasure. The scene shifts from gastronomic desire to a
more direct discussion and simultaneous evasion of the delicate subject of
sexual desire. Dora, who at this point in the novel is engaged to marry her
brother's best friend, raises her doubts about marriage: "I don't believe
there's enough sentiment in me to make love a great passion, such as we
read of in books. Do you believe marriage is the beautiful state it is
painted by writers?" (*CF*, 119). Later in the conversation, she reframes and
repeats her question, now importantly posing an alternative narrative to
the marriage plot. She earnestly asks Sappho, "'Do you ever mean to
marry, or are you going to pine in single blessedness on my hands and be
a bachelor-maid to the end?'" (*CF*, 121). Sappho's reply reinforces the ambiguity surrounding her sexuality: "'Well,' replied Sappho, with a comical
twist to her face, 'in the words of Unc' Gulliver, "I mote, an' then agin I
moten't"'" (*CF*, 121–22). The rest of their conversation reveals Dora's
vexed relationship to the marriage plot:

> "What troubles me is having a man bothering around. . . . I'm wondering if
> my love could stand the test."
> "That's queer talk for an engaged girl, with a fine, handsome fellow to
> court her. Why Dora, 'I'm s'prised at yer!'" laughed Sappho gaily.
> ". . . I dread to think of being tied to John for good and all; I know I'll be sick
> of him inside of a week. I do despair of ever being like other girls." (*CF*, 122)

This conversation reveals a great deal about Dora and Sappho's understanding of their own sexuality, as well as their relationship to each other. It
presents a potential obstacle to the expected heterosexual coupling of domestic fiction; the "queer talk" of "single blessedness" and "bachelor-
maids" threatens to denaturalize, if not disrupt, the conventional romance
narrative. Sappho is not willing to commit herself to any particular desire,
though her laughing and "comical twist" suggest that a certain anxiety sur-
rounds the subject of heterosexual marriage. Dora's despair stems not from
the absence of a potential husband, but from her difference from "other

girls," for whom heterosexual narratives seem effortless and unproblematic. In fact, when Sappho recites the traditional maxim of romantic love,
"A woman loves one man, and is true to him through all eternity," Dora responds, "That's just what makes me feel so *unsexed*" (*CF*, 122).

Dora's self-diagnosis of her indifference ripples with anxiety; because
her desire does not correspond to the conventional cultural narrative that
culminates in heterosexual marriage, Dora can define herself only by the
negation of desire. By using the word *unsex*, Dora locates herself at the
unspecified space between genders and outside of traditional romance.[45]
Dora also echoes the rhetoric of those who voiced more conservative
standards of gender for African American women in the late nineteenth
century. For example, in an editorial entitled "The Women Who Are
Loved Are Those Who Are Women," Julia Ringwood Coston, editor of
Ringwood's Journal of Fashion, expressed her concern about what she perceived as some women's sacrifice of femininity in their increasing aspirations for public careers. Coston recognized the need for African American
women's paid employment, claiming, "There is no good reason why a
woman should cease to be feminine because she is compelled to work."
Yet she criticized women who too eagerly sought public careers, particularly women writers, "who have thrown off the veil of modesty, and who,
in the name of reform, pose as martyrs, sacrificing themselves to a great
work." Coston characterized these women as unfeminine, asking, "But
what is to be done with an unsexed creature, a thing neither man nor
woman?"[46]

Hopkins's use of *unsex* resonates further within the growing discourse of
female homosexuality during this period. In his 1915 article on "Inversion
and Dreams," for example, the American sexologist James Kiernan included a 1910 report of a young woman who had engaged in both homosexual and heterosexual activity and who was troubled by dreams and fantasies in which she appeared as both male and female. Kiernan reported,
"This the patient regarded as abnormal, believing herself to be what she
called unsexed."[47] Like Kiernan's patient, Dora both acknowledges and resists her sexual indifference toward men. Yet in a less self-conscious moment, she readily takes up a position of active desire for Sappho: "Dora
gazed at her friend with admiration, and wished that she had a kodak, so
that she might catch just the expression that lighted her eyes and glowed in
a bright color upon her cheeks" (*CF*, 126). Dora's urge to capture Sappho's
beautiful image through the lens of a camera unambiguously positions her
as the bearer of an active gaze, a position that, as feminist film theorists
have demonstrated, significantly counters the culturally dominant configuration of women as objects of a sexualized male gaze.[48]

Within the context of the entire novel, this scene of closeted intimacies
has great implications for Dora, who here feels "the sincerity of the love

that had taken root in her heart for Sappho" (*CF*, 127). Eventually Dora does abandon her engagement to her initial fiancé, John Langley. Yet she does not completely abandon marriage; Dora marries Doctor Arthur Lewis, a promoter of industrial education, aligned with the historical figure of Booker T. Washington. Hopkins, however, makes clear Dora's ambivalence toward their marriage. When Doctor Lewis proposes, Dora rationalizes her decision: "No; she could not remain single; she would marry one whose manliness she could respect, if she did not love him. Love was another thing, with which, she told herself, she was done" (*CF*, 360–61). At the end of the novel, after Dora has married Lewis and had a child, her brother, Will, assesses her well-being: "If ever a doubt of Dora's happiness had troubled Will's thoughts, it was dispelled now that he saw her a contented young matron, her own individuality swallowed up in love for her husband and child. She had apparently forgotten that any other love had ever disturbed the peaceful current of her life" (*CF*, 389–90).

This description suggests the limits of the heterosexual resolution to Dora's narrative; she trades her "individuality" for the role of respectable matron.[49] Significantly, Dora's voice is also submerged; her thoughts and feelings are now mediated by her brother, rather than expressed in her own words. Likewise, by leaving its source unspecified, Hopkins offers the possibility that the "other love" that Dora had "forgotten" was for Sappho. Although Hopkins incorporates a heterosexual resolution to each woman's narrative, she also, however mutedly, suggests that marriage does not necessarily represent the complete fulfillment of their respective sexual or political desires.

Don't Go in the Basement: Closeted Narratives in the Marriage Plot

The literal space in which Dora and Sappho express their desire is analogous to its place in the narrative. The privatized, locked room keeps female homoeroticism out of the public spaces of the lodging houses and out of the way of the novel's public narrative of heterosexual coupling. Hopkins similarly positions female homoeroticism in the architecture of her plot through the minor (and ostensibly comic) characters Sarah Ann White and Ophelia Davis. These "two occupants of the basement rooms" (*CF*, 104) of the Smith lodging house literally inhabit the space below the main action of the novel.

Davis and White, as ex-slaves, embody a number of contradictions and anxieties about sexuality, class, respectability, and mobility within African American communities. As they explain, upon emancipation from slavery at the end of the Civil War, the two women decided to go north. Importantly, Hopkins points out that their desires are shaped primarily according to the ideals of domesticity and respectability. Hopkins writes,

As their ideas of life and living enlarged, and they saw the possibilities of enjoying some comfort in a home, they began to think of establishing themselves where they could realize this blessing, and finally hit upon the idea of
going into partnership in a laundry. After looking about them for a suitable
situation for such a project, their choice finally fell upon Mrs. Smith's house,
because of her known respectability, and because they could there come in
contact with brighter intellects than their own. (*CF*, 104)

White and Davis thus aspire to attach themselves to both the respectability symbolized by Mrs. Smith's lodging house and its status as a
semipublic space, in which they gain access to possibilities for mixing
with people from a range of class positions. Further, the Smiths' lodging
house allows the laundresses a site not only to realize their own class mobility, but also to profit from the class aspirations of other inhabitants of
Boston, a city that at the turn of the century was experiencing a rapid influx of African Americans migrating from the southern states, as well as
immigrants from Europe. According to Hopkins, "The two women engaged the rooms and prospered in their enterprise. The clothes under
their deft fingers seemed to gain an added prettiness. They became the
style; and no young bride on the Back Bay felt that she was complete unless 'The First-class New Orleans Laundry' placed the finishing polish on
the dainty lingerie of her wedding finery" (*CF*, 106).

Through language such as "engaged," "prospered," "deft," "finishing
polish," "dainty," and "finery," Hopkins emphasizes the gentility with
which Davis and White conduct their laundry trade. It is no coincidence
that the desire for upward mobility is also represented through the details
of "wedding finery," the wedding signifying for women a consolidation
of class and sexual aspirations, as critics of romance conventions have
pointed out.

Despite their subordinate position in both class and narrative status,
Davis and White represent potential disruptions to the narrative. First, because of their previous lives in the southern slave economy, they seem to
have access to knowledge that potentially threatens Sappho and the maintenance of her secret past. When they first meet Sappho, Davis and White
immediately recognize something extraordinary and uncannily familiar
about this beautiful young woman: "'Lord,' said Ophelia Davis to her
friend Sarah Ann, 'I haven't see anything look like thet chile since I lef'
home'" (*CF*, 107). Davis's partner confirms the uncanny familiarity of Sappho: "'That's the truth, 'Phelia,' replied Sarah Ann; 'that's somethin' God
made, honey; thar ain't nothin' like thet growed outside o' Loosyannie'"
(*CF*, 107). This scene flirts with the special kind of paranoid and privileged
knowledge that Sedgwick, in her discussion of the mechanisms of the
closet, associates with the phrase "It takes one to know one."[50] "'I knowed
it,' says White, '... Ol' New Orleans blood will tell on itself anywhere'"
(*CF*, 108). The belief that "blood will tell on itself" is, of course, a threat that

circulates through a belief in the physical legibility of race and that provides the suspense that structures novels of passing. In 1913, an anonymous writer published "Adventures of a Near-White," which summed up
the racial logic of "It takes one to know one": "I would take a chance with
a white man where I would not dare do so with a colored man. Inevitably
a colored man knows but usually keeps his mouth shut, aided by a generous tip."[51] Sappho successfully insulates herself from recognition among
the northerners who have no access to her past, but she risks exposure
among southerners such as Davis and White who are similarly mobile and
displaced. Although White's revelation about Sappho is her Louisiana upbringing, the scene nevertheless raises the possibility that Sappho's secret
past might betray her at any moment, in the audience of those who can de-
code "a story written on her face" (*CF*, 89).[52]

Davis and White are potentially threatening because they seem intimate
not only with Sappho's past life, but also with each other. Hopkins's narrative voice tends to expose and discipline Davis and White's physical and
verbal excesses, which mark the limits of middle-class sensibilities of self-
restraint and deference. At times Hopkins positions Davis and White's actions as parodies of genteel feminine manners. For instance, Hopkins describes Davis's singing in the parlor with a tone of ridicule: "With much
wheezing and puffing—for the singer was neither slender nor young—and
many would-be fascinating jumps and groans, presumed to be trills and
runs, she finished, to the relief of the company" (*CF*, 109). Yet she also characterizes Davis and White as a team throughout the novel, boosting each
other with encouragement and taking pride in each other's accomplishments. Hopkins situates White in the position of an admiring spectator:
"Her friend, Mrs. White, looked at [Davis] with great approval" (*CF*, 109).
White gives Davis unconditional and enthusiastic praise ("'That's out o'
sight, 'Phelia!'" [109]) and insists upon Davis getting recognition *as a
woman* for her public accomplishments. When Davis wins a competition at
the church fair, for instance, Hopkins writes, "And after that the pastor
could not forbear saying a few words about how good it was 'to dwell together in brotherly love.' Sister Sarah Ann White said 'the *brothers* had
nuthin' to do with it, it was Ophelia Davis an' nobody else'" (*CF*, 218, original emphasis). By constructing a comic role for Davis and White, Hopkins
is also able to voice an ironic critique of the public erasure of women at the
same time as she contains it within a comic portrayal of minor characters.

Hopkins sustains the relationship between Davis and White until the
very end of the novel, when she quickly and mechanically stages Davis's
engagement to marry a younger male inhabitant of the lodging house,
Tommy James. In a discussion of problematic aspects of *Contending Forces*,
Richard Yarborough writes that "the neat resolution of the intricate plot
may not sit well with modern readers weaned on psychological realism."[53] I would argue further that Hopkins recognized that leaving a fe-

male couple intact would be a potentially dangerous break in form from the marriage plot. Instead, she ends the novel according to the narrative limits that she had delineated earlier, preferring a narrative resolution that avoids the "disastrous" ending of "a close intimacy between two of the same sex" (*CF*, 98). Just as she provides Dora and Sappho with husbands by the end of the novel, Hopkins disrupts Davis and White's attachment by suddenly producing a fiancé for Davis.[54]

Dismantling the relationship between White and Davis, however, takes substantial narrative energy, an effort that ironically belies the intensity of their attachment. When Davis tells Ma Smith about her plans to marry a younger man, she constructs her new fiancé in terms parallel to her female companion:

> "Sarah Ann an' me'll have to part after I'm married, she's that jealous." . . .
>
> "Now that would be a pity, after you've been together so long," remarked [Ma Smith].
>
> "She's got to drop sayin' ticklish things to me. A 'ooman's got a right to git married, ain't she? . . . Mr. Jeemes says he knows the Lord sent me fer to be a helpmeet to him, an' I dassay he's right. Sarah Ann says my money's the 'helpmeet' he's after, an' somebody to cook good vittals to suit his pellet. But I know better; he's a godly man ef he ain't much to look at." (*CF*, 365–66)

In this conversation, Hopkins uses the voice of the absent Sarah Ann White to critique the subordinate role of women in marriage, in contrast to the relatively equitable arrangement between the two women. The scene ends with Davis's passion focused on White: "'Sarah Ann says I'm a mortalized ol' ijit, an' a insane mannyack, an' Jeemes knows what he's a-fishin' fer. She's insultin', mos' insultin'" (*CF*, 369). That Hopkins includes a split, however mechanical, between these two characters is evidence of their important place in the story. That the women's "breakup" involves jealousy and protectiveness is also evidence that she wanted in some way to express the passion existing between the women, in contrast to Davis's feelings about her fiancé, who "ain't much to look at." Like Dora, in her earlier lukewarm response to Doctor Arthur Lewis, Davis is compelled by cultural custom and narrative conventions to agree to marriage, in spite of her indifferent desire and her contrasting passionate attachment to her female companion.

"Who Spoke of Marriage?"

In one climactic scene of the novel, the blackmailing character, John Langley, mockingly questions Sappho's entitlement to marriage: "'Marriage!' exclaimed John, 'who spoke of marriage? Ambitious men do not marry women with stories like yours!'" In John's eyes, Sappho, as a victim of rape (through which she gave birth to a child), cannot claim the right to marry because she cannot claim literal sexual purity. By the conventional standards of true womanhood, Sappho seems destined for a tragic ending. As recent discussions of the novel have emphasized, however, Hopkins defies convention and refuses to cede Sappho's claim to true womanhood because of her status as a victim of sexual violence.[55] Instead, in the last pages of the book, Sappho becomes engaged to marry the virtuous hero Will Smith and seems destined for satisfaction in marriage: "Sappho was happy in contemplating the life of promise which was before her. Will was the noblest of men. [Her son] Alphonse was to him as his own child. United by love, chastened by sorrow and self-sacrifice, he and she planned to work together to bring joy to hearts crushed by despair (*CF,* 401). With this ending, Hopkins finds a way to resolve the seemingly irreconcilable facts of the history of African American women's sexual subjugation and their claims to the status of respectable womanhood.

Despite Hopkins's use of the conventional marriage plot to conclude *Contending Forces,* scenes of female homoeroticism assume an important position in structuring the narrative. Hopkins portrays female couples as potentially necessary sites for the expression of desire and identification, at the same time as she controls their threat to the overall trajectory of the heterosexual narrative. Hopkins contains these scenes of homoeroticism within the literally peripheral and subordinate spaces of the novel, the locked room where Dora and Sappho have their tea party and the basement apartment where Sarah Ann White and Ophelia Davis make their home and run their laundry business. Although the ostensible sexual secret that threatens to destroy Sappho's claim to respectable womanhood is her experience of being raped by a White man, it is also possible to see anxieties about lesbian desire structuring the narrative of *Contending Forces.* In fact, if we understand the rape of Mabelle Beaubean as a symbol of the historical negation of African American women's sexual agency, it could be argued that the figure of Sappho, precisely because of her association with lesbian desire, mediates Hopkins's attempts to imagine a narrative of African American women's subjectivity.

Hopkins's choice to locate this domestic novel in the spaces of the lodging house allows her to explore and revise the position of African American women within ideologies of domesticity, but it also raises perceived dangers about the public circulation of women. Through the lodging house, Hopkins rewrites a history of African American women's relationship to property and ownership. Her female characters revise African American women's historical and symbolic functions as property and domestic servants within a system of slavery and replace it with their position as property owners themselves. While the lodging house is this space of possibility, it is also one that Hopkins characterizes as potentially vulnerable to the very women who inhabit it. Ex-slaves such as Mrs. White and Mrs. Davis, as well as women with secret pasts, such as Sappho, carry symbolic associations with dangerous sexuality, including emerging constructions of lesbian desire. Their circulation within the lodging house parallels the circulation of new threats to constructions of genteel womanhood that Hopkins both validates and revises.

While Hopkins's renovations of the domestic novel in *Contending Forces* make it an enabling genre for her project of claiming respectability for African American women, it also poses risks to this goal. The female bonds that characterize the feminized household of the domestic novel and that once supported the marriage plot have a more ambiguous role as they circulate among women in the lodging house. In *Contending Forces* Hopkins reveals a profound ambivalence toward same-sex affection, at once recognizing its crucial role in fostering African American women's political gains while at the same time guarding against its emerging cultural associations with criminality and violence. In Hopkins's attempt to rewrite African American women's claims to domestic ideologies, lesbian desire sometimes functions as a new dangerous sexuality against which to define domesticated womanhood and, at other times, as a crucial supporting framework for the structure in which respectability resides.

Notes

1. See Hazel V. Carby, *Reconstructing Womanhood: The Emergence of the Afro-American Woman Novelist* (New York: Oxford University Press, 1987); Claudia Tate, *Domestic Allegories of Political Desire: The Black Heroine's Text at the Turn of the Century* (New York: Oxford University Press, 1992); and Ann duCille, *The Coupling Convention: Sex, Text, and Tradition in Black Women's Fiction* (New York: Oxford University Press, 1993).

2. Nancy Armstrong, *Desire and Domestic Fiction: A Political History of the Novel* (New York: Oxford University Press, 1987), 48.

3. DuCille, *Coupling Convention*, 31.

4. Tate, *Domestic Allegories*, 92.

5. See Houston Baker, *Workings of the Spirit: The Poetics of African-American Women's Writing* (Chicago: University of Chicago Press, 1991), 25.

6. DuCille, *Coupling Convention*, 3.

7. DuCille's question is highly relevant for our own historical moment, within the context of current efforts to legalize gay and lesbian marriage and the corresponding backlash against these efforts, perhaps most tellingly demonstrated by the proposed "Defense of Marriage Act," which would attempt to renaturalize the connection between legal marriage and heterosexuality.

8. DuCille, *Coupling Convention*, 14.

9. On African American lesbian identities and subcultures, see, for instance, Thadious M. Davis, *Nella Larsen, Novelist of the Harlem Renaissance: A Woman's Life Unveiled* (Baton Rouge: Louisiana State University Press, 1994), and Hazel Carby, "'It Jus Be's Dat Way Sometime': The Sexual Politics of Women's Blues," in *Un-*

equal Sisters: A Multicultural Reader in U.S. Women's History, ed. Ellen Carol DuBois and Vicki L. Ruiz (New York: Routledge, 1990), 238–249. On gay and lesbian communities in Harlem, see Eric Garber, "A Spectacle in Color: The Lesbian and Gay Subculture of Jazz Age Harlem," in *Hidden from History: Reclaiming the Gay and Lesbian Past,* eds. Martin Duberman, Martha Vicinus, and George Chauncey Jr. (New York: Meridian, 1989), 318–331, and George Chauncey, *Gay New York: Gender, Urban Culture, and the Making of the Gay Male World, 1890–1940* (New York: Basic Books, 1994).

10. The legal prohibition against marriage, of course, did not prevent slaves from marrying without legal recognition. As historians have shown, extralegal and religious ceremonies frequently formalized sexual and affectional unions between slaves. See Herbert Gutman, *The Black Family in Slavery and Freedom, 1750–1925* (New York: Pantheon, 1976).

11. See Carroll Smith-Rosenberg, "The Female World of Love and Ritual: Relations Between Women in Nineteenth-Century America," *Signs* 1 (Autumn 1975): 1–29.

12. Lillian Faderman, "Lesbian Magazine Fiction in the Early Twentieth Century," *Journal of Popular Culture* 11 (1978): 802.

13. Marylynne Diggs, "Romantic Friends or a 'Different Race of Creatures'?: The Representation of Lesbian Pathology in Nineteenth-Century America," *Feminist Studies* 21, no. 2 (Summer 1995): 321.

14. Lisa Duggan, "The Trials of Alice Mitchell: Sensationalism, Sexology, and the Lesbian Subject in Turn-of-the-Century America," *Signs* 18 (Summer 1993): 799.

15. Pauline E. Hopkins, *Contending Forces: A Romance Illustrative of Negro Life North and South* (1900), reprint with an introduction by Richard Yarborough (New York: Oxford University Press, 1988). Hereafter, this edition will be abbreviated as *CF*.

16. In *Domestic Allegories,* Tate comments upon the function and prevalence of widows in African American women's fiction at this time: "Indeed, widows are so numerous in black female post-Reconstruction fictions that they constitute not only a standard character type but also a popular tactic for transforming patricentric authority into matricentric influence" (162).

17. Armstrong, *Desire and Domestic Fiction,* 48.

18. Traci Reed Carroll, "Subjects of Consumption: Nineteenth Century African American Women Writers" (Ph.D. Dissertation, English, Northwestern University, 1992), 287.

19. Significantly, the only male figure in the Smith family, Will, works outside of the house, as a bellboy in "one of the fashionable hostelries of Boston" (*CF*, 84).

20. John Daniels, *In Freedom's Birthplace: A Study of the Boston Negroes* (Boston: Houghton Mifflin Company, 1914), 312.

21. Joanne Meyerowitz, *Women Adrift: Independent Wage Earners in Chicago, 1880–1930* (Chicago: University of Chicago Press, 1988).

22. Hazel Carby, "Policing the Black Woman's Body in an Urban Context," *Critical Inquiry* 18 (Summer 1992): 739.

23. Carby, "Policing," 741.

24. Albert Benedict Wolfe, *The Lodging House Problem in Boston* (Boston: Houghton, Mifflin and Co., 1906), 47.

25. Wolfe, *Lodging House Problem,* 47.

26. Lucile Eaves, *The Food of Working Women in Boston* (Boston: Wright and Potter, 1917), 66–67.

27. Wolfe, *Lodging House Problem*, 138.

28. Meyerowitz, *Women Adrift*, 73–74.

29. Meyerowitz, *Women Adrift*, 111–12.

30. Wolfe, *Lodging House Problem*, 151.

31. Wolfe, *Lodging House Problem*, 112.

32. Wolfe, *Lodging House Problem*, 64.

33. Daniels, *In Freedom's Birthplace*, 358–59.

34. Daniels, *In Freedom's Birthplace*, 357.

35. See, for instance, Elizabeth Ammons, *Conflicting Stories: American Women Writers at the Turn into the Twentieth Century* (New York: Oxford University Press, 1991), 80, and Tate, *Domestic Allegories*, 148–49.

36. Baker, *Workings of the Spirit*, 24.

37. Elaine Marks writes that "Sappho and her island Lesbos are omnipresent in literature about women loving women, whatever the gender or sexual preference of the writer and whether or not Sappho and her island are explicitly named" ("Lesbian Intertextuality," in *Homosexualities and French Literature*, eds. George Stambolian and Elaine Marks [Ithaca: Cornell University Press, 1978], 356). For a more detailed discussion of the significance of Sappho in the late nineteenth century and contemporary associations of Sappho with both lesbian and African American identity, see my article "Passing Through the Closet in the Fiction of Pauline E. Hopkins's *Contending Forces*," *American Literature*, special issue, "Unnatural Formations: Erotics in the Making of American Cultures" (March 1997).

Carla L. Peterson has suggested that Dora, more than Sappho, exhibits homoerotic desires: "Despite the names, the lesbian sensibility appears to belong to Dora rather than Sappho, whose heterosexual attraction to Will conforms nicely to the conventions of the romance." See "Unsettled Frontiers: Race, History, and Romance in Pauline Hopkins's *Contending Forces*," in *Famous Last Words: Changes in Gender and Narrative Closure*, ed. Alison Booth (Charlottesville: University of Virginia Press, 1993), 188.

38. DuCille, *Coupling Convention*, 43.

39. DuCille, *Coupling Convention*, 43.

40. Duggan, "Trials of Alice Mitchell," 808.

41. These newspaper reports occasionally referred to such relationships among African American women. Duggan includes an 1892 newspaper account of "an unnatural passion" between two African American women, a liaison that ended in attempted murder. See Duggan, "Trials of Alice Mitchell," 803–4.

42. Mary Helen Washington, *Invented Lives: Narratives of Black Women, 1860–1960* (New York: Doubleday, 1987), 81.

43. Eve Kosofsky Sedgwick, *Epistemology of the Closet* (Berkeley: University of California Press, 1990), 71.

44. *Oxford English Dictionary*.

45. The *Oxford English Dictionary* defines *unsex* as "to deprive or divest of sex, or of the typical qualities of one or other (esp. the female) sex."

46. Julia Ringwood Coston, "The Women Who Are Loved Are Those Who Are Women," *Ringwood's Journal of Fashion*, quoted in Tate, *Domestic Allegories*, 158–59.

Originally quoted in Monroe A. Majors, *Noted Negro Women: Their Triumphs and Activities* (1893; Reprint, Nashville, TN: Fisk University Library Negro Collection, 1971), 251.

47. James G. Kiernan, "Inversion and Dreams," *The Urologic and Cutaneous Review* 19 (June 1915): 352.

48. The classic formulation of this relationship is Laura Mulvey's "Visual Pleasure and Narrative Cinema," *Screen* 16 (1975): 6–18. Although this model has subsequently been critiqued and revised, it remains an important point of reference for theories of the gaze.

49. It also suggests a link to Sappho, who is described elsewhere in identical language. When Sappho sneaks out of the Smith boarding house after she has been blackmailed by John Langley, Hopkins writes, "A form attired in black, closely veiled . . . was *swallowed up* in the heart of the metropolis" (*CF*, 321–22, emphasis added).

50. Sedgwick, *Epistemology of the Closet.*

51. [Anonymous], "The Adventures of a Near-White," *The Independent* 75, no. 3376 (August 14, 1913): 375.

52. For an intriguing discussion of "passing in drag" as a particular type of literacy, see Amy Robinson, "It Takes One to Know One: Passing and Communities of Common Interest," *Critical Inquiry* 20 (Summer 1994): 715–36. Robinson argues that "'It takes one to know one' thus signifies a position that identifies a performance, not one that claims ontological knowledge of the identity of the performer" (722).

53. Yarborough, introduction to *Contending Forces*, xli.

54. Paterson has a more positive reading of this plot mechanism: "Ophelia and Tommy's marriage represents . . . a movement toward gender equality and the reconciliation of contending within the black community" ("Unsettled Frontiers," 194.)

55. See Carby, *Reconstructing Womanhood*; Tate, *Domestic Allegories*; and duCille, *Coupling Convention.*

Chapter Twelve

"Homesick for Those Memories": The Gendering of Historical Memory in Women's Narratives of the Vietnam War

JOHN LOWNEY

There's not a day goes by that I don't think about my buddies that didn't come back. . . . Sometimes I feel homesick for those memories.
—**Bobbie Ann Mason,** *In Country*

I miss M*A*S*H. I've been homesick for it since the series ended.
—**Mason,** *In Country*

In a novel full of unpredictable moments of displaced memory, *In Country*, a veteran of the Vietnam War named Hudson tells a tale of "homesickness" reminiscent of numerous American war narratives. What differentiates this tale of survivor guilt from that of other war narratives is the teller's peculiarly captive audience, Samantha (Sam) Hughes, the novel's seventeen-year-old protagonist, whose father died in Vietnam before her birth. Reflecting on his wartime experiences, Hudson explains that when he becomes "homesick for those memories" of Vietnam, he has to leave town on his dirt bike to "go out and bump around in that woods behind the fairgrounds. I just let the memories come. It's like being back with them. It's kind of pleasant, really. But you have to go someplace like that, off to the Bottom, or out on a dirt bike trail. You can't stay in town and afford to think about what happened."[1]

His impulse when "homesick" is, paradoxically, to leave "home" on a solitary ritualistic quest to be united with the imagined community of his remembered "buddies." The cost of such memories is too much to "afford" within the domestic confines of the town: "You have to go" to the masculine space of the wilderness. In this economy of memory, the exchange of "I" ("just let the memories come") for "you" ("can't stay in town") is at once the survivor's offering of solidarity with his dead "buddy's" daughter and an unconscious universalizing of his response to war trauma.

In Country, like so many Vietnam War narratives, is a novel of "homesickness"—sickness at home, sickness for home. Home is where the memories are located, but home is always somewhere other. For the "homesick" war veteran, the memory of masculine collectivity on the war front supplants any domestic associations of family or home country, especially because his memories of Vietnam do not correspond with the subsequent perceptions of his experience by those "in town." Is this longing for a more clearly defined sense of home symptomatic of the veteran's—and the nation's—"post-Vietnam syndrome": the repression of the returned, followed by the return of the repressed?[2] Or is this "homesickness" more generally symptomatic of postmodernity, what Fredric Jameson characterizes as our amnesiac age of "nostalgia" for a meaningful connection of past to present?[3] As so many moments of *In Country's* mass mediated world suggest, homesickness manifests itself nostalgically in fleeting idealized images of domestic security, images that situate home in opposition to invisible but threatening others, that conflate the presumed inviolability of home country with the always elusive desire for "normal" family life. Such images themselves are often all that makes the home cohere. "'I miss M*A*S*H. I've been homesick for it since the series ended,'" says Sam's Uncle Emmett, the father/brother/"pal" with whom she lives, an unemployed Vietnam War veteran who wears a skirt, as Corporal Klinger did. When her high school boyfriend, Lonnie, so rationally explains that *M*A*S*H* had to end because "'they couldn't fight the Korean War forever'" (33), their immediate impulse is to head for the swamp "named for a notorious outlaw" (34), Cawood's Pond, the legendary wilderness on the edge of town. If they can't fight the Korean War forever, can they fight the Vietnam War forever? The return of the repressed—again and again? Or the return of the repressed endlessly deferred—the repeated return to the woods, the swamp, the Gulf? An end-less series of reruns.

In a novel that begins and ends on a road farther from "home" than Sam had ever been, but where "everything seems more real than it has ever been" (7), the departure from "home" for a road or wilderness "more real" seems as natural for Sam as it seems for the idealized veteran she wants to know, the father she never knew, the uncle she hardly knows, and the boyfriend she wants to know no longer. But how differentiated is *her* understanding of the Vietnam War from their collective memory? To what extent does *In Country* simply recuperate the hegemonic masculine collective memory of war? To what extent, that is, does it reaffirm the bi-nary opposition of the "foreign" war front and the "domestic" home front? Is there *any* space, "domestic" or otherwise, that is not infiltrated by the masculinist discourse of war in Vietnam War novels or, for that matter, in post–World War II American culture more generally? Given that American historical memory of the Vietnam War has been mediated by electronic images that have seemingly brought the war home more im-mediately than any previous war, remembered connections—and discon-nections—between war front and home front have been complex, contra-dictory, and contested.[4] These (dis)connections have had implications not only for national identity but also for gendered identity; the political fall-out of the war has contributed to the reinforcement of gender categories that have marginalized women's representations of the Vietnam War and its "domestic" impact in the United States. In the following pages I exam-ine how *In Country* and a novel similarly concerned with cultural mythologies of war, Jayne Anne Phillips's *Machine Dreams*, each contest the early-1980s collective revision of the "Vietnam era" by foregrounding the gender politics of memory and amnesia, of home and homesickness. While dramatizing the electronic media's unprecedented role since the 1960s in the perception of war on the home front, those novels underscore how discourses of war construct gender, as they reconnect the Vietnam War to "domestic" narrative patterns of gendered social relations. They do so not through the recuperation of the dominant American narratives of post–Vietnam War national memory, however, but through their par-ody of the cultural myths with which American "involvement" in Viet-nam was rationalized—myths that have as much to do with the identifi-cation of "Americanness" with popular representations of the western frontier as with the United States' imperial interests in Southeast Asia.[5]

If the years immediately following the final U.S. military withdrawal from Vietnam were characterized by a "trance of collective amnesia" about the war,[6] by the time President Reagan officially accepted the Viet-nam Veterans Memorial in 1984 (two years after its dedication), popular print, film, and television representations of the Vietnam War were proliferating. The majority of popular American representations of the Vietnam War have been soldiers' stories, focusing on the horrors of combat and the corresponding sense of community among soldiers rather than on the broader social disintegration resulting from the national conflict over the war. Instead of the debates about international and domestic politics that informed debates about the war in the 1960s and the 1970s, in the 1980s greater attention was paid to the way the war was fought, the means of fighting rather than the ends. This emphasis on American soldiers' experience of the war is perhaps best exemplified by a film that has received both popular and critical acclaim, Oliver Stone's *Platoon*. The close-in, handheld camera view of the war in *Platoon* gives neither the soldiers nor the viewers any broader visual perspective; instead it conveys the soldiers' experience of fear and anxiety in a jungle that corresponds with their moral and political confusion, whether from their uncertainty about the enemy or differences in attitudes among themselves.[7] However, as Susan Jeffords has argued in her provocative study of Vietnam War representations, *The Remasculinization of America: Gender and the Vietnam War* (1989), there is one social category by which the Vietnam War has been more readily understood without such confusion: the category of gender, the difference of male and female defined by the masculine space of the war front and its feminine opposite, the domestic space of the home front.

As Jeffords's critical survey of Vietnam War narratives demonstrates, popular and academic representations of the war alike have appealed to "masculine bonding . . . as a basis for the regeneration of society as a whole," thus recuperating a conventional notion of masculinity defined in opposition to its repressed opposite.[8] For even those accounts of the war that most intensely convey its confusion through their narrative blurring of subject and object or of fact and fiction, "gender . . . is the single difference that is asserted as *not* participating in the confusion that characterizes other oppositions."[9] According to Jeffords, representations of the Vietnam War have recuperated a masculine collectivity that obscures hierarchical social difference analogously to the way commercial images of the domestic evoke a feminine collectivity: They "draw attention away from difference—both racial and class—by working within the framework of the apparently clearly structured difference of gender." War becomes "the functional equivalent of the domestic for the feminine in mass culture."[10] This opposition of war and the domestic, which relies on an exclusionary opposition of the public masculine sphere and the private feminine sphere, thus naturalizes patriarchal gender distinctions that have also made the "war novel" the province of male writers, especially writers who have experienced war firsthand, whether as participants or participant-observers.[11]

With its concern for the Vietnam War's devastating impact on American soldiers, *In Country* is in many ways similar to other 1980s narratives of the American involvement in Indochina. Its similarity to veterans' narratives of the return from war front to home front suggests why it has received more critical attention than *Machine Dreams*, which evokes the Vietnam War more obliquely. Both *In Country* and *Machine Dreams* present young female protagonists who do not experience the war firsthand; however, each protagonist is affected not only by the war's immediate fallout on her family but also by the pervasive masculinist discourse of warfare that reinforces hierarchical social relations. In revealing, and questioning, the gendered categories that differentiate war front from home front, *In Country* and *Machine Dreams* presume what John Limon has called the "home-front literariness of all writing on war," that is, the belatedness of representations of war.[12] More specifically, both novels reconnect the home front to the Vietnam War through parody of a masculinist national narrative that resonates throughout American literary history, including the history of the war novel. This narrative, which Nina Baym has defined as the "melodrama of beset manhood," explicitly opposes a feminine domestic sphere with the culturally privileged masculine sphere of the wilderness.

The "melodrama of beset manhood" posits an archetypal encounter of the (male Anglo- or Euro-) American self with "the promise offered by the idea of America," the promise of self-fulfillment offered by the unsettled wilderness, where the individual can "inscribe" his destiny.[13] This myth of the adventurous male, who departs the suffocating domestic world of family and village to be reborn in the wilderness, can be seen in canonical texts such as James Fenimore Cooper's *Leatherstocking Tales*, Henry David Thoreau's *Walden*, or Mark Twain's *The Adventures of Huckleberry Finn*. Whether as protagonists or as writers, women are mostly excluded from this cultural myth, which not only is premised on the traditionally male prerogative of mobility but also identifies the feminine with either the restrictive sphere of domesticity or the idealized "compliant and supportive" virginal wilderness landscape.[14] As Baym argues, by the twentieth century this myth is transformed by the recognition that "this supposed promise of America has always been known to be delusory."[15] This false promise is exposed in texts as different as Willa Cather's frontier narratives, F. Scott Fitzgerald's *The Great Gatsby*, and, as I will argue more specifically, Ernest Hemingway's post–World War I representation of war trauma, "Big Two-Hearted River." If this myth "has always been known to be delusory," its peculiarly discordant inflections during and after the Vietnam War—by politicians, military personnel, journalists, and writers of popular narratives—suggest the ideological power, and the deadly implications, of acting out "delusory" narratives.

In Country and *Machine Dreams* parody the American narrative tradition of "beset manhood" as it is ironically evoked in the post–World War I narratives of Hemingway and, more prominently, as it is absurdly but tragically evoked in soldiers' narratives of the Vietnam War. Both novels suggest their complicity with the post–Vietnam War displacement of unresolved political conflict into rituals of psychological healing. However, they both foreground their difference from dominant narratives of "beset manhood" by means of the conflicted perspectives of their female protagonists and by means of the transformation of conventional gender roles within their represented scenes of domesticity. With their female protagonists' mimicry of narrative roles conventionally coded masculine, and with their deconstruction of the opposition of home front and war front, both novels call into question the nostalgic narratives of "homesickness" that they evoke.[16] By locating the veterans' narratives of war within scenes of domestic discord, *In Country* and *Machine Dreams* both undermine the cultural authority of masculine representations of war, an authority based on the presumed immediacy of the eyewitness account. Foregrounding how their protagonists attempt to construct order out of the contradictory narratives that shape their experience, the novels reveal that access to history, even history as recent as the Vietnam War, is available only through representations of the past. Insisting on the critical interpretation of texts as performative and of cultural myths as ideological, these Vietnam War narratives do not represent the past nostalgically but instead critically investigate the ideological impact of nostalgic narratives; they thus not only counteract historical amnesia but also disclose the rhetorical processes conducive to such amnesia.

The most prevalent narratives of war in *In Country* and *Machine Dreams* are those available to their protagonists through the mass media. Each book dramatizes how discourses of warfare are disseminated in everyday life through such media as Hollywood films, television dramas, commercial advertising, and popular music yet are interpreted and deployed differently by male and female subjects. The epigraph of *In Country* introduces the unpredictable dialogue of popular culture with the revisionist transformation of the collective memory of the war taking place in the mid-1980s. The epigraph quotes Bruce Springsteen's "Born in the U.S.A.," a song whose reception exemplifies the contradictory possibilities of popular culture. "Born in the U.S.A." expresses a Vietnam veteran's bitter disaffection for his country. His war experience is recalled in starkly simple xenophobic terms: "Got in a little hometown jam so they put a rifle in my hand / Sent me off to a foreign land to go and kill the yellow man." As brutally ironic as Springsteen's narrative of depression, despair, and patriotic hatred is, the refrain of "Born in the U.S.A." nonetheless became a theme for both the Reagan and the Mondale presidential campaigns. Mason underscores the irony of this appropriation when the novel begins the narrative of Sam Hughes's summer of discontent: "It was the summer of the Michael Jackson *Victory* tour and the Bruce Springsteen *Born in the U.S.A.* tour, neither of which Sam got to go to. At her graduation, the commencement speaker, a Methodist minister, had preached about keeping the country strong, stressing sacrifice. He made Sam nervous. She started thinking about war, and it stayed on her mind all summer" (23).

This blending of an idiosyncratic personal memory with a contradictory but obsessive national collective memory of Vietnam in the mid-1980s characterizes Sam's thought processes throughout *In Country*; the example combines discourses of religion and national politics with popular cultural expressions whose titles themselves evoke anxiety about "keeping the country strong." Sam's quest to find out about the past of her father and her Uncle Emmett, who is usually silent about his Vietnam experience but is constantly fearful that he has been poisoned by Agent Orange, involves becoming a more informed, and more suspicious, interpreter of the contradictory messages conveyed by movie and video images, songs, and commercial and political advertisements concerning the war. Her quest involves, that is, not only the questioning of cultural myths that present themselves as "natural," but more specifically, the improvisational ability to piece together fragments of the consumer culture that shapes her knowledge of the war. She identifies this ability with the postwar domestic survival skills of her Uncle Emmett, but ironically, these domestic skills are analagous to Vietnamese military skills: "The Vietnamese used anything the Americans threw away—bomb casings and cigarette butts and helicopter parts and Coke cans. It was like Emmett rigging up things in the house. It was Vietnamese behavior, she thought, making do with what he could scrounge" (209).

Sam's quest to "make do" also involves an attempt to understand the American veterans' experience more immediately than mediately. But this quest frustrates her, as she is repeatedly confronted with either the discordant absurdity of the mass media narratives by which she understands these veterans' lives or her exclusion from *their* narratives of the Vietnam War. She becomes infatuated with the "homesick" veteran, Tom Hudson, a mechanic who repairs and sells her her first car, a rusty Volkswagen "bug." His ability to make something out of "unidentifiable, useless-looking objects," to "recreate beautiful cars out of a mess of greasy metal pieces and rusty pipes and screws" (76), is at first as mysterious and seductive as his recollections of the war later become for Sam. When she becomes romantically involved with Tom and goes home with him to his apartment after a veterans' dance at the local high school, she anticipates "that something was about to happen, like a familiar scene in a movie, the slow-motion sequence with the couple rolling in the sheets and time passing" (126). Although she "was aware of the slow-motion moves, the jump cuts" (127), she did not anticipate that the leading man would be impotent. It was not in her script.

If Sam's abbreviated romance with Tom causes her to rethink her script of the tragic Vietnam War veteran, another veteran she encounters immediately after sleeping with Tom suggests that her role in some postwar scripts is more delimited than she had imagined. This veteran, a man named Pete Simms who refers to her as "Sambo," does fulfill the Hollywood stereotype of the resentful crazed killer. He says that he misses the "'intensity'" of the war, "'what you went through together'" (134). But none of this really matters to "Sambo," Pete concludes:

> "You don't know how it was, and you never will. There is no way you can ever understand. So just forget it. Unless you've been humping the boonies, you don't know."
> "What's humping the boonies?"
> "That means going out in some godforsaken wilderness and doing what you have to do to survive. But I survived and I ain't going to waste it now." He laughed. "Now, if they want to get my wife in one of those counseling groups and beat some sense in her head, that would be all right with me. I wish they'd straighten her out." (136)

Although Sam is "sure that he was just shooting off his mouth" (136), the transition from "humping the boonies" to "beating some sense" into his wife's head suggests why Sam imagines the possibility of becoming pregnant in militaristic terms: "Her whole life could be ruined by some mischance, some stupid surprise, like sniper fire" (184). Excluded from the masculine collective memory of "humping the boonies," Sam might not be the subject of this Vietnam War narrative, but "Sambo" can certainly be the feminized, racialized object of its fallout.

Whereas *In Country* focuses on the domestic impact of the Vietnam War on the generation immediately following it, *Machine Dreams* traces the disintegration of a middle-class West Virginia family (consisting of mother, father, daughter, and son) over two generations, from World War II through the Vietnam War, contrasting the Asian wartime experiences of father (Mitch) and son (Billy). It begins not with one epigraph, but with a collage of quotes from a history of aviation, Greek legend, Hesiod's *Theogeny*, and Laurie Anderson's "O Superman." The first chapter begins with the memorable sentence "It's strange what you don't forget,"[17] and "what you don't forget" can be as mundane as a telephone number of a childhood friend, fragments of lyrics from popular songs, commercial icons, or old photographs and letters. In *Machine Dreams* memory often consists of the conflation of subconscious desires with objects of commercial fantasy; rather than a sense of personal identity and historical continuity, we experience the expression of a collective unconscious of which the Vietnam War is less an intrusion than a symptom of pervasive patterns of social relations in American culture.[18] But the meaning of memories nonetheless depends on how they are translated. More so than *In Country, Machine Dreams* structurally differentiates women's modes of recalling and narrating experience from men's. The contrast between the first two chapters alone, the mother's narrative, entitled "Reminiscence to a Daughter," and the father's, entitled "The Secret Country," establishes a pattern whereby women, by expressing their memories to each other, are able to sustain a sense of relatedness and continuity across generations, whereas the men, who repress those memories that are most disturbing, are more likely to fixate on their relations to machines—cars, trucks, trains, airplanes, and so on.[19] The final protagonist of the novel, Danner, the daughter of this marriage whose disintegration signifies a decline in traditional middle-class expectations about family and community, and the sister of a young pilot who is shot down in Vietnam, manages to persevere because she succeeds in negotiating between conflicting gendered codes of memory.

Throughout *Machine Dreams*, the dichotomy of affective female connectedness and stolid male solitude is disrupted *and* reinforced by the impact of war on family and nation. Traumatic war-front memories are mirrored by their domestic counterparts; as in *In Country*, the remembered war-front experience of home country frequently displaces the domestic experience of home. In "The Secret Country" Mitch relates how his return from World War II left him not only with a sense of homelessness but also with a loss of identity that is more sorrowful than liberating. As his hometown and the family farm where he had grown up had changed beyond recognition, he too was changed by the war years: "But out where the farm was—almost nothing. . . . Looking at it made me think I'd been asleep a long time and had wakened up in the wrong place, a hundred miles from where I lay down. Like I'd lost my memory and might be anyone" (53). When he later reflects on a haunting dream of his war experience in New Guinea, Mitch's alienation from the West Virginia home to which he had returned resembles Tom Hudson's "homesickness" for the memories of his "buddies": "He hardly ever thought of the bad things, although he thought of the men . . . and the base camp, alien the two years in New Guinea but now more familiar in memory than this house he slept in" (67). His fondest memory of New Guinea revolves around the military "machines" that return to him in his dreams. These "dozers and trucks," which the "black men" of Papua touch and name with "reverence" (67), are much like the improvised weapons that Sam Hughes associates with the Vietnamese: "built and repaired with scrap, metal welded in approximate versions of whatever parts broke down, the machines evolving further and further into jumbled mismatched puzzles that still worked. Worked and moved, groaned and rumbled according to some other logic of mechanics than what held in Cincinnati or Topeka or Wheeling" (67–68).

Not only do these improvised machines operate by "some other logic of mechanics," the Papuan men who put them together likewise contradict the sexual logic assumed by the American soldiers that distinguishes masculinity from femininity. The Papuan men are infantilized by the American soldiers because of their otherness, but they also resemble women to the Americans because of their dress. While the "women in the camp wore fatigues and boots . . . the native men had still worn grass skirts" (68). These skirts came to seem "natural on them rather than on the women, so that the outward things distinguishing men and women lost meaning" (68). As memories of the war evoke longing for a masculine collectivity apart from the domestic responsibilities of home and family, these memories likewise evoke a world "turned around," a world in which appearance violates conventional American gender codes, but a world in which men in skirts who speak in "strange mixtures of words whose cadences were backwards" (70) are easier for Mitch to communicate with than the women at "home."

Mitch's wife, Jean, has a dream that corresponds to Mitch's "machine dream." It takes place in a chapter ironically entitled "Anniversary Song: Jean, 1948," ironic because she is trying hard to convince herself that a "good wife" is "supposed to" remember anniversaries, even if her husband forgets (112). While reflecting on the coldness of her marriage on this New Year's Eve, however, the anniversary that she is remembering is the death of her mother, who died the same year she married Mitch. She drives to the cemetery to visit her mother's grave in the evening snow. While there, she falls asleep in the car and has a nightmare of visiting "an isolated house" as a child with her mother, a house in which an unspeakable act of domestic violence has taken place: "An old man bent down and said into Jean's face, 'Not a pretty sight, little girl, but history is made here today.' 'Imagine,' a woman's voice intoned, 'his own wife, his own children.' . . . 'When suffering seems reasonless,' her mother's voice said clearly, 'people come together and want to understand'" (115).

The man's impulse to create a spectacular "history" from the remains of destruction contrasts sharply here with the woman's impulse to "come together and want to understand." It is this remembered intimacy with her mother and her other female family members that Jean seeks but misses so much in her marriage: "There was no more talking, not really—no one whose past she knew, who knew her" (117). Her husband's silence is deathly, as *she* is buried alive in her marriage: "Mitch never spoke of his childhood, as most people did, or of the war" (119).

Mitch's silence about his war experience in *Machine Dreams*—like Emmett's silence in *In Country*—is reminiscent of Hemingway's post–World War I hero Nick Adams. Both novels echo the minimalist style of Hemingway's early fiction,[20] but their dramatic resolutions allude more specifically to his narratives of World War I, especially those that adapt the "melodrama of beset manhood" to postwar contexts. The masculine solution to domestic entrapment in Hemingway's fiction is exemplified by a well-known story that responds indirectly to the trauma of war, "Big Two-Hearted River," the conclusion of the post–World War I sequence of stories *In Our Time*. *In Our Time* juxtaposes the familiar American wilderness, Nick Adams's Lake Superior forests, with the moral wilderness of World War I Europe. From the opening words of *In Our Time* ("The strange thing was . . . ") until its final word ("America"), Hemingway's disillusioned White male American protagonists encounter cultural myths of masculinity that are devalued by deadly irony. *In Our Time* follows a perilous, labyrinthine road to the concluding "Big Two-Hearted River," the wilderness landscape where Nick seeks renewal. The road to recovery of this archetypal masculine identity is fraught not only with the minefields and gunfire of the "foreign" war, but with the threat of (feminine) domestication at home.[21] Only through constant renewals of women's cultural alienation, through the assertion of women's silence, marginality, and secondary status, does the American male retain his integrity in Hemingway's text. However, if "Big Two-Hearted River" represents the culmination of this process, the integrity of the solitary hero in the American wilderness is nonetheless revealed as a fragile construct.

The landscape of "Big Two-Hearted River" is hardly the virginal wilderness that Nick remembers; the charred remains of the village of Seney and its surrounding "hills of burnt timber" resemble the World War I battle ruins that he had presumably left behind in the "Old World."[22] It is only when Nick walks into the forest outside of the ruined village that he feels that "he had left everything behind, the need for thinking, the need to write, other needs."[23] When he sets up camp in the forest, then he feels he has left the past behind; his terms for having escaped the pressures of "civilization" are, however, curiously domestic: "There was something mysterious and homelike. . . . He was in his home where he had made it."[24] As content as he becomes in his self-made home, and as confident as he claims he is that he has left behind his "other needs," moments of introspective doubt interrupt the obsessive attention to exterior physical detail. Most notably, while fishing the next day, he dwells upon a gloomy nearby swamp, which he avoids because "in the swamp fishing was a tragic adventure." What is Nick's first response to these dark thoughts of "tragic adventure"? "He wished he had brought something to read. He felt like reading. He did not feel like going into the swamp."[25] As a refuge from self-doubt, the desire to read undermines the Adamic myth of self-sufficient satisfaction that Nick so desperately pursues in "Big Two-Hearted River." It is this undercurrent of uncertainty, based on a fragile yet imprisoning code of masculinity in which rituals of intense concentration on the physical work of the present repress painful memories of loss, that Mason and Phillips foreground in their female protagonists' response to trauma. Rather than desiring the modernist site of reading as an aesthetic refuge from introspective trauma, a site that even in "Big Two-Hearted River" is unattainable, these female protagonists have to decipher the various textual "melodramas of beset manhood" that exclude them as protagonists and situate them instead within the domestic sphere of home. They also have to brave the "tragic swamp" of texts that provide only glimpses of narrative insight into the trauma and deaths of male relatives too naive to recognize their predicaments.[26]

In Country's dramatic resolution revolves not around a desire for reading as escape but instead around a desire to escape an overabundance of textual representations. Most important are the two documents Sam's father had written in Vietnam, but which she reads for the first time. The first document is a packet of the letters he had sent to Sam's mother. One letter informs Sam of the disturbing news that her name was originally intended for a male child. Although Sam feels cheated that "Samantha was an afterthought" (182), the letters otherwise tell her little about her father's experience in the war. When her grandparents give her father's diary to her, however, what she finds is more disturbing, for both its blatant racism and its graphic violence: "The diary disgusted her, with the rotting corpse, her father's shriveled feet, his dead buddy, those sickly-sweet banana leaves. She had a morbid imagination, but it had always been like a horror movie, not something real. Now everything seemed suddenly so real it enveloped her, like something rotten she had fallen into" (206).

Sam's response to her repulsive discovery is to try to re-create her father's experience "in country." She decides to "hump the boonies" at Cawood's Pond—"the last place in western Kentucky where a person could really face the wild" (208)—to reenact the ordeal that her father, her Uncle Emmett, and other Vietnam veterans had experienced, to experience the wilderness as it "really" felt to them. Sam's journey into "the wild" parodies the very journey that Nick Adams enacts in "Big Two-Hearted River" and that soldiers like her father had imagined they were enacting in Vietnam.

Sam's journey to Cawood's Pond is thoroughly intertextual and also thoroughly inflected by her consciousness of gender difference. She initially questions whether gender differences can explain why men fight wars and women stay home:

> If men went to war for women, and for unborn generations, then she was going to find out what they went through. Sam didn't think the women or the unborn babies had any say in it. If it were up to women, there wouldn't be any war. No, that was a naive thought. When women got power, they were just like men. She thought of Indira Gandhi and Margaret Thatcher. She wouldn't want to meet those women out in the swamp at night. (208)

So much for gender difference as an explanation of war. Sam's frame of reference for "humping the boonies" is based primarily on texts by men, however. Her imagination of Vietnam is shaped most prominently by Hollywood movies such as *Apocalypse Now,* but she also recalls what to her are similarly absurd narratives of the "wilderness" from her high school English class, such as *Walden,* whose author/protagonist she dismisses as "paranoid" (210). In her anxiously intertextual free association, she conflates imagined fears of soldiers in Vietnam with fears about her own vulnerabilty—especially her fear of pregnancy.[27] Gender categories appear to disintegrate when Sam considers whether women have the potential to be as violent as men: "Soldiers murdered babies. But women did too. They ripped their own unborn babies out of themselves and flushed them away, squirming and bloody" (215). Sam's equation of abortion with soldiers murdering babies suggests how post-Vietnam discourses of war have affected women's consciousness of their bodies. And the subsequent events at Cawood's Pond show more thoroughly how such dehumanizing discourses inform Sam's image of herself as a young woman.

The conclusion of Sam's overnight camping trip suggests that her fears are specific to her gender. When she hears someone nearby in the forest, her immediate impulse is to fear that a rapist is approaching her:

> It couldn't be a rapist, she thought. Rapists didn't go out into the wilderness, where there weren't likely to be any women to rape. They were calculating. Sam was defenseless. She looked around for rocks and sticks. She felt inside her backpack for a weapon. She had the can of smoked baby oysters with a roll-key opener. Hurriedly, she worked to create a weapon with the sharp edge of the can. (216)

After fashioning this makeshift weapon and recalling what she had been taught about self-defense, she concludes: "What an idiotic thing to happen . . . to face the terror of the jungle and then meet a rapist" (217). The scene is absurd, especially when we find out that the imagined "V.C. rapist-terrorist" is Emmett; however, Sam's reflection on this absurdity itself leads to a sudden recognition of continuity with her mother, as she thinks that "maybe her mother would think the idea wasn't so ridiculous. Her mother had done braver things" (214). Sam's mock journey "in country" dramatizes the significance of difference, not only the difference of her father's Vietnam experience from her reenactment of it, but the gender difference that makes her journey dangerous indeed, even if it is in her own backyard.

After Emmett finds Sam and subsequently releases his pent-up grief about Vietnam, the "boonies" of Cawood's Pond begin "to seem like home" to her (224). And Emmett seems most like a father to her at the moment he is most vulnerable, as he proclaims his inadequacy as a parent. Despite this melodramatic scene of temporary domestic accord, however, Emmett contends that his war experience has little meaning for those growing up a generation later: "You can't learn from the past. The main thing you learn from history is that you can't learn from history. That's what history is." *In Country* itself contradicts Emmett, as its foregrounding of gender difference underscores the exclusionary nature of such master narratives as the Adamic individual in the wilderness that so often pass for American "history." If Emmett's eccentric domestic rituals only faintly resemble Nick Adams's carefully plotted response to trauma, the admitted limitations of his practical wisdom and of his ability to control his world echo the conclusion of "Big Two-Hearted River" remarkably closely: "'There are things you can figure out, but most things you can't.' He waved at the dark swamp. 'There are some things you can never figure out'" (226). It is ultimately Sam's role as interpreter that differentiates Mason's narrative from Hemingway's "melodrama of beset manhood." Emmett's Klingeresque mock femininity, which is mildly ridiculed throughout the novel as a sign of his deficiencies as a father figure, is now coded more affirmatively. As Sam observes Emmett walking through the swamp, "he looked like an old peasant woman hugging a baby" (226). If Sam can imagine her mother as a brave heroic figure in the wilderness, her image of the motherly Emmett suggests how boundaries between conventionally masculine and feminine spheres—the wilderness and the home—as well as boundaries between masculine and feminine identities are more absurd, and more improvisational, for Sam than they are for Nick Adams. Even the novel's conclusion at the Vietnam Veterans Memorial in Washington, D.C., which is often read as a recuperation of a national identity based on a masculinist collective narrative of the Vietnam War, foregrounds gender difference. When Sam touches her father's name on the wall, the name is represented in terms that foreground the arbitrariness of language and the interpreter's position in constructing meaning: "A scratching on a rock. Writing. Something for future archaeologists to puzzle over, clues to a language" (244). When she then "touches her own name" on the wall, the difference between name and identity suggests how gendered identity likewise seems to be arbitrarily constructed. But if "SAM A HUGHES" is *like* her name but not identical to her, her desire to be included among "all the names in America [that] have been used to decorate this wall" (244) confirms the lasting ideological power of monumental history to construct national identity, even as it absurdly underscores the gendered implications of this "decorative" history.

As does *In Country*, *Machine Dreams* reaches a point of resolution through its young female protagonist's comparative reading of written documents, in this case Danner's accounts of her brother Billy's disappearance in Vietnam. In a chapter entitled simply "War Letters," we are presented with a sequence of letters documenting Billy's entire military experience, many of which echo his father's World War II experience in New Guinea. The final two letters, however, are not written by Billy. The first letter is an official military document that states simply that Billy is missing in action. The second letter discusses the same event, but it is written by one of Billy's platoon members, a Black soldier from Los Angeles who speaks of Billy in the past tense and sends his family his condolences. The contrast of the cold bureaucratic language of the official letter with the colloquial but polite language of the soldier is striking. Danner's reaction to the second letter is equally striking: "The letter was a miracle. My first reaction was thankfulness and inordinate hope. I'm still thankful. No matter what happened when they got on the ground, he wasn't alone. . . . He hadn't been alone, that was it" (359).

Machine Dreams certainly contains many images of men alone in the wilderness, yet never with any hope for the satisfying solitude that Nick Adams seeks in "Big Two-Hearted River." The images are more likely to be associated with warfare in an alien environment. The most striking example of solitude, however, is the childhood memory Mitch recalls of Li Sung, a Chinese leper left in the West Virginia forest by his employer, the B&O Railroad. The first "Oriental" seen by most of the locals, Li Sung lives in extraordinary solitude: He has no hope of touching anyone or even speaking with them, because of the language difference. Li Sung's character evokes in an exaggerated way the otherness of the "Oriental," and his treatment foreshadows the protective but patronizing mind-set informing American military action in Asia. He also grotesquely exemplifies the emotional solitude of the stolid male characters who repress their feelings in *Machine Dreams*—except to release them through violence. For Mitch, the memory of Li Sung becomes emblematic of the "secret country" where his life story begins: "I never saw the inside of that shack. What did he do all day. No country, no family, no job. No one. Maybe he wasn't sure anymore who he was. He was a secret. . . . During the war I used to dream of him, walking toward me on one of the tarmac landing strips we laid in New Guinea. I'd wake up in a sweat" (53).

"No country, no family, no job": Li Sung's shack represents all that "home" is *not* to Mitch, but his homelessness also represents what a child of the Great Depression and World War II fears is imminently possible.

When Billy is in Vietnam, he writes to his father: "I don't know why I never asked you about the war you went to, I guess I thought I saw it in the movies" (330). This is the last letter Billy writes. If he is following in his father's footsteps by going to fight in Vietnam, he is doing so unconsciously. Billy's rationale for enlisting in the army (after receiving a high draft lottery number) is based on a code of masculinity that is remarkably unreasonable and remarkably passive. He says to his sister, "'Bad things can happen anywhere! ... You don't reason through these things. The best way to be lucky is to take what comes and not be a coward'" (302). He develops this code of masculine stoicism, ironically, in response to his parents' separation, which is depicted in militaristic terms: "Purposefully, Billy stayed out of the cross fire" (276). A conversation he has with his mother after he withdraws from school overtly conflates his family's domestic conflict with the conflict in Vietnam, as he reassures her: "'I don't think you made a mistake. You did what you had to do. I just wish you'd understand—I did, too. I'm in a bind like yours, in a way'" (298). Billy's identification with his mother, recognizing that each is "in a bind" that they presumably cannot control, makes his masculine stoicism seem especially hollow.

The "War Letters" chapter about Billy's military experience in Vietnam begins exactly as his father's "War Letters" chapter does, with an excerpt from a United States military propaganda pamphlet. This chapter differs from the World War II chapter, though, in that it juxtaposes South Vietnamese Liberation Forces (SVNLF) propaganda addressed to American soldiers with the U.S. propaganda materials. One of the SVNLF leaflets reads: "THE VIETNAMESE PEOPLE ARE FIGHTING FOR THEIR INDEPENDENCE AND FREEDOM THAT IS JUST WHAT THE AMERICAN DID IN 18TH CENTURY" (318). Such irony is lost on Billy. Although the war is "nothing like John Wayne" (324), fighting the Vietcong is "like cowboys and Indians, except the Indians are ghosts and they can't lose because nothing really kills them" (328). But it is not quite like "cowboys and Indians," because the enemy also includes women: "Women's Lib is real big with the NVA and the Cong—sometimes it's women trying to waste us" (328). Billy learns quickly that fighting in this war is hardly a matter of patriotic defense of his home country; it is simply a matter of survival. His "country" is the crew with whom he flies, as he writes to his sister: "These guys are the only country I know of and they're what I'm defending—I'm not stupid enough to think my country is over here" (329). This "only country" Billy knows is a multiethnic country; Luke, the chief of the crew, is part Osage, while the crew members with whom Billy "shares a hooch" are "Gonzalez (Texas) and Taylor, a black guy from LA" (326). It is the "black guy from LA" who writes the letter to Danner informing her that Billy and Luke were shot down. While Danner is relieved to discover firsthand testimony of what happened to her brother, her father's immediate reaction to Taylor's letter is "'You say this is a black fellow, from Los Angeles?'" (359). Whereas the multiethnic "country" that Billy defends is accepted matter-of-factly by his sister and him, his father lives in a nation where a Black man's testimony "is still hearsay" (359).

Danner's final narrative, "The World," begins with an explicit correspondence between her father at work and her father at war: "My father
owned a concrete plant. He wore khaki shirts and work pants, the same
kind of clothes he wore in wartime photographs when he was building
airstrips in New Guinea" (333). This correspondence between war and
work and between military conflicts and domestic conflicts is even more
explicit in Danner's description of her father's "makeshift office in the
basement of the house we'd moved to in Bellington" (334). This "office"
contains not only the expected office equipment but also "a single bed in
which [Danner's] mother slept the last few years of their marriage, boxes
of old toys, a washer and drier, and a discarded couch and chair from an
old living room set" (335). The contrast of this office with the concrete
plant is striking. This domestic office site makes Mitch's work seem more
feminine, but it does so amidst the signs of his wife's displacement.
Mitch's career had followed a descending path from his publicly prominent role as a self-employed builder to increasingly circumscribed "desk
jobs" to a desk in the very basement where his wife had taken refuge during the collapse of their marriage. If Mitch's "khaki" masculinity is buried
in the domestic refuse of a marriage whose disintegration coincided with
their son's departure to Vietnam, Jean likewise is not rejuvenated by her
independence. She spends her time creating "handmade cross-stitched
quilts"; however, this conventionally valued "women's work" is more of
an empty gesture than a meaningful social activity for her: She "makes
quilts in the long evenings when she is alone with the television set. *It
gives me something to do with my hands and keeps me from thinking,* she says"
(343). Even her stories about the past, stories that seem to connect mother
and daughter so strongly in the novel's beginning, are now pathetic to
Danner: "Her stories about the past seem to comfort her, but they sadden
me. After all, I'm in the stories. I'm here, relating the stories to the present
and to the future, and I'm always looking for hints" (344). Only when
Danner ultimately leaves the scene of this wrecked home to begin a new
life in northern California, where the land "seems foreign" (342) and
where she arrives "like a refugee" (367), is she able to find a perspective
from which to read these discordant stories. Only when she recognizes
that the domestic ideal of her childhood home is as distant, as ephemeral,
and perhaps as illusory as the national ideal for which her brother died
does she accept that the "hints" do not cohere into a comforting narrative.
For Danner, as for Sam Hughes, "home" can be constructed only from the
scraps of "homesick" narratives.

In a 1966 essay entitled "On Going Home," Joan Didion wrote:

Sometimes I think that those of us who are now in our thirties were born into
the last generation to carry the burden of "home," to find in family life the

source of all tension and drama. . . . The question of whether or not you
could go home again was a very real part of the sentimental and largely literary baggage with which we left home in the fifties; I suspect that it is irrele-
vant to the children born of the fragmentation after World War II. (165)

As Didion's Vietnam War narrative *Democracy* itself compels its readers
to acknowledge, postmodern American cultural myths of "home," and
the codes of femininity and masculinity that define "domestic" relations,
have more to do with the militaristic fallout of the Cold War than with the
specifically generational experience of either World War II or the Vietnam
War. However, *Machine Dreams* and *In Country* suggest that "the question
of whether or not you could go home again" *is* relevant to the "children
born of the fragmentation after World War II." With Danner's concluding
departure for California, *Machine Dreams* ironically replicates the wester-
ing pattern of the "melodrama of beset manhood." Yet she describes this
move not as an escape from "home" but as a recognition of the impossibility of such escape: "If I hated my government, shouldn't I go and live
in some other country? . . . But my parents are my country, my divided
country. By going to California, I'd made it to the far frontiers, but I'd
never leave my country. I never will" (368). Phillips's conflation of divided country with divided family accentuates the "domestic" impact of
the Vietnam War—and Cold War discourses more generally—in the
United States. As does *In Country*, *Machine Dreams* concludes with one
young woman's quest for the meaning of the Vietnam War, but this quest
opens into further questions about the cultural myths by which "Vietnam" has been commemorated. By foregrounding the gendered response
to representations of war, these "homesick" narratives suggest the cost of
locating Vietnam War narratives, or war narratives more generally, exclusively in terms of "beset" masculinity, even as they underscore the ideological force of the myths they invoke.

Notes

1. Bobbie Ann Mason, *In Country* (New York: HarperCollins, 1985), 79. Subsequent quotations from this work will be noted parenthetically within the text.
2. See Walter Capps, ed., *The Vietnam Reader* (New York: Routledge, 1991), for
contrasting perspectives on the aftermath of the Vietnam War in the United States,
especially in relation to the experience of Vietnam veterans. In contesting the late-
1970s translation of political conflicts about the war into psychological questions of
healing, the historian Frances Fitzgerald, the author of *Fire in the Lake* (1972), wrote:

Many vets have suffered—and continue to suffer—from a whole series of
emotions and existential disorders which they call "post-Vietnam syndrome." The word "syndrome" of course suggests a pathology, and by ac-

cepting the term, they have in effect accepted their victimization. They have accepted the displacement of responsibility from the sphere of politics to the sphere of individual psychology. And from this solipsism there is no exit. ("The War That Won't End," in Capps, *The Vietnam Reader*, 88)

3. See especially Fredric Jameson's opposition of postmodernist "nostalgia for the present" to historicism in his chapter on "nostalgia films" in *Postmodernism, or, The Cultural Logic of Late Capitalism* (Durham, N.C.: Duke University Press, 1991), 279–96.

4. Daniel Hallin provides a cogent critical overview of American mass media coverage of the Vietnam War in *The Uncensored War* (New York: Oxford University Press, 1986), whereas Todd Gitlin analyzes the impact of the mass media on the antiwar movement in *The Whole World Is Watching: Mass Media in the Making and Unmaking of the New Left* (Berkeley: University of California Press, 1980). For an especially lucid collection of essays on postwar American media representations of Vietnam, see John Carlos Rowe and Rick Berg, eds., *The Vietnam War and American Culture* (New York: Columbia University Press, 1991).

5. As John Hellman has delineated in *American Myth and the Legacy of Vietnam* (New York: Columbia University Press, 1986), Cold War foreign policy in Southeast Asia was shaped not only by the theory of containment of Soviet interest but also by cultural myths that can be traced to the Puritan idea of the redeemer nation. The nineteenth-century doctrine of manifest destiny viewed both the American west and Asia as symbolic landscapes in which "the westward course of empire" could progress. Under President Kennedy's "New Frontier" Vietnam policy, a policy informed by anxieties about potentially disastrous confrontations with the Soviet Union in Berlin and Cuba, the rationale for the escalation of American military force in Vietnam explicitly recalled nineteenth-century concepts of American national identity, as Hellman summarized:

Vietnam promised . . . the qualities of America's remembered frontier triumphs: remoteness from dangerous confrontation with a major European power, a savage enemy who could be righteously hunted down, a wilderness landscape in which the American could renew his virtues where the European had proved only his vices, and the Asian people America historically saw as the appointed beneficiaries of its destiny. (Hellman, *American Myth*, 51)

For detailed studies of how Vietnam War narratives variously evoke dominant cultural myths of American literary history, see also Philip D. Beidler, *American Literature and the Experience of Vietnam* (Athens: University of Georgia Press, 1982) and Philip H. Melling, *Vietnam in American Literature* (Boston: Twayne, 1990). Susan Jeffords critiques both Hellman and Beidler for their implicitly exclusive appeal to masculine bonding for the regeneration of American society. See *The Remasculinization of America: Gender and the Vietnam War* (Bloomington: Indiana University Press, 1989), 76–80.

6. Fox Butterfield, quoted in Michael Kammen, *Mystic Chords of Memory: The Transformation of Tradition in American Culture* (New York: Random House, 1991), 662.

7. See Jeffords, *Remasculinization of America*, 19–20, 50–51 on the cinematic strategies and effects of representing such confusion in *Platoon* and other Vietnam War films.

8. Jeffords, *Remasculinization*, 74.

9. Jeffords, *Remasculinization*, 53.

10. Jeffords, *Remasculinization*, 85.

11. Jeffords's critics, such as Lynne Hanley, have argued that her critical formulation of the "remasculinization of America" itself "perpetuates the privilege of the veteran to construct our memories of war by attending only to his account." Hanley, *Writing War: Fiction, Gender and Memory* (Amherst: University of Massachusetts Press, 1991), 124. See Hanley's critique of Jeffords's definition of war literature in *Writing War*, 123–24, and John Limon's critique of Jeffords's reading of *In Country* as a recuperation of the American veterans' masculinist perspective of the war in *Writing After War: American War Fiction from Realism to Postmodernism* (New York: Oxford University Press, 1994), 247–48.

12. Limon, *Writing After War*, 226.

13. Nina Baym, "Melodramas of Beset Manhood: How Theories of American Fiction Exclude Women Authors," in *The New Feminist Criticism: Essays on Women, Literature, and Theory*, edited by Elaine Showalter (New York: Pantheon, 1985), 71.

14. Baym, "Melodramas," 75.

15. Baym, "Melodramas," 72.

16. My argument about the critical function of parody is based on Linda Hutcheon's definition of postmodernist parody. Critiquing Fredric Jameson's distinction between (modernist) parody and postmodernist pastiche, Hutcheon argues that postmodernist parody is neither necessarily nostalgic nor dehistoricizing. Parody can instead serve a critical function in contesting the humanist notion of originality as well as capitalist notions of ownership and property. Parody furthermore foregrounds the politics of "re-presentation" by questioning which historical narratives are legitimized. See Hutcheon, *The Politics of Postmodernism* (New York: Routledge, 1989), 14–15, 34–38, 47–92.

17. Jayne Anne Phillips, *Machine Dreams* (New York: Washington Square–Pocket Books, 1984), 1. Subsequent quotations from this work will be noted parenthetically within the text.

18. Michael Clark argues this point persuasively in "Remembering Vietnam," in Rowe and Berg, *Vietnam War*, 192–93. Both Clark (192–98) and Joanna Price present comparative studies of *Machine Dreams* and *In Country* that examine the impact of consumer capitalism on the reception of the Vietnam War. See Price, "Remembering Vietnam: Subjectivity and Mourning in American New Realist Writing," *Journal of American Studies* 27 (1993), 173–86.

19. Phyllis Lassner elucidates the significance of the mother-daughter and father-son relationships for the narrative structure of *Machine Dreams*. See "Women's Narrative and the Recreation of History," in *American Women Writing Fiction: Memory, Identity, Family, Space*, edited by Mickey Pearlman (Lexington: University Press of Kentucky, 1989), 193–210.

20. Mason and Phillips are often associated with the minimalist literary style that John Barth, only slightly tongue-in-cheek, has labeled "post-Vietnam, post-literary, postmodernist, blue-collar neo-early Hemingwayism." Barth, "A Few Words About Minimalism," *The New York Times Book Review* 28 (December 1986): 2. Many explanations have been put forth for the 1980s prominence of an aesthetic characterized by terse, slightly plotted, extrospective, ironic storytelling, identi-

fied most often with the short stories of Raymond Carver. The popularity of this "postliterary" style has often been attributed to the overall decline of literacy among readers and writers alike; however, Barth's maximalist appellation for minimalist realism also points to the critical possibilities of such a style. Minimalist realism counters the manipulative abuses of language in advertising, both commercial and political, but as Barth suggests, this "period style" also evokes a more general "post-Vietnam" skepticism toward rhetorical uses of language, a skepticism resulting from the euphemistic misrepresentations of the war by politicians and by the media.

21. This confluence of war trauma and domestic entrapment is best exemplified in the story ironically entitled "Soldier's Home."

22. Ernest Hemingway, *In Our Time* (New York: Scribner's, 1929), 133.

23. Hemingway, *In Our Time,* 134.

24. Hemingway, *In Our Time,* 139.

25. Hemingway, *In Our Time,* 155.

26. My argument about the role of reading in *In Country* and *Machine Dreams* is influenced by Susan Schweick's incisive overview of women's conventional wartime roles as readers of war letters. See *A Gulf So Deeply Cut: American Women Poets and the Second World War* (Madison: University of Wisconsin Press, 1991), especially 85–170.

27. Sam's association of pregnancy with the Vietnam War begins earlier in the narrative when she finds out about her friend Dawn's unplanned pregnancy: "She was feeling the delayed stress of the Vietnam War. It was her inheritance. It was her version of Dawn's trouble. The pregnancy test had turned out positive" (89).

Works Cited

Barth, John. "A Few Words About Minimalism." *The New York Times Book Review,* 28 (December 1986): 1+.

Baym, Nina. "Melodramas of Beset Manhood: How Theories of American Fiction Exclude Women Authors." In *The New Feminist Criticism: Essays on Women, Literature, and Theory,* edited by Elaine Showalter, 63–80. New York: Pantheon, 1985.

Beidler, Philip D. *American Literature and the Experience of Vietnam.* Athens: University of Georgia Press, 1982.

Capps, Walter, ed. *The Vietnam Reader.* New York: Routledge, 1991.

Clark, Michael. "Remembering Vietnam." In *The Vietnam War and American Culture,* edited by John Carlos Rowe and Rick Berg, 177–207. New York: Columbia University Press, 1991.

Didion, Joan. *Democracy.* New York: Pocket Books, 1984.

———. "On Going Home." In *Slouching Towards Bethlehem,* 164–68. New York: Dell, 1968.

Fitzgerald, Frances. "The War That Won't End." In *The Vietnam Reader,* edited by Walter Capps, 87–88. New York: Routledge, 1991.

Gitlin, Todd. *The Whole World Is Watching: Mass Media in the Making and Unmaking of the New Left.* Berkeley: University of California Press, 1980.

Hallin, Daniel. *The Uncensored War*. New York: Oxford University Press, 1986.

Hanley, Lynne. *Writing War: Fiction, Gender and Memory*. Amherst: University of Massachusetts Press, 1991.

Hellman, John. *American Myth and the Legacy of Vietnam*. New York: Columbia University Press, 1986.

Hemingway, Ernest. *In Our Time*. New York: Scribner's, 1925.

Hutcheon, Linda. *The Politics of Postmodernism*. New York: Routledge, 1989.

Jameson, Fredric. *Postmodernism, or, The Cultural Logic of Late Capitalism*. Durham, N.C.: Duke University Press, 1991.

Jeffords, Susan. *The Remasculinization of America: Gender and the Vietnam War*. Bloomington: Indiana University Press, 1989.

Kammen, Michael. *Mystic Chords of Memory: The Transformation of Tradition in American Culture*. New York: Random House, 1991.

Lassner, Phyllis. "Women's Narrative and the Recreation of History." In *American Women Writing Fiction: Memory, Identity, Family, Space*, edited by Mickey Pearlman, 193–210. Lexington: University Press of Kentucky, 1989.

Limon, John. *Writing After War: American War Fiction from Realism to Postmodernism*. New York: Oxford University Press, 1994.

Mason, Bobbie Ann. *In Country*. New York: HarperCollins, 1985.

Melling, Philip H. *Vietnam in American Literature*. Boston: Twayne, 1990.

Phillips, Jayne Anne. *Machine Dreams*. New York: Washington Square–Pocket Books, 1984.

Price, Joanna. "Remembering Vietnam: Subjectivity and Mourning in American New Realist Writing." *Journal of American Studies* 27 (1993): 173–86.

Rowe, John Carlos, and Rick Berg, eds. *The Vietnam War and American Culture*. New York: Columbia University Press, 1991.

Schweik, Susan. *A Gulf So Deeply Cut: American Women Poets and the Second World War*. Madison: University of Wisconsin Press, 1991.

Chapter Thirteen

Domesticity and the Demon Mother: A Review Essay of Sorts

ANN DUCILLE

> *Always leave an inch of snow so it looks nice and white. Esthetics are very important in snow removal.*
>
> **—Blizzard advice from doyenne of domesticity Martha Stewart,** *Newsweek,* **January 29, 1996**

For years I've tried in vain to convince friends and family to invest in what I'm certain would be a successful venture: a snow-painting business. Freshly fallen snow holds a certain mesmerizing charm, even for a winter-hating, transplanted California sun goddess like me. But once the stuff has been on the ground for a while, its dingy, grimy presence becomes just another nasty discontent of this worst of all possible seasons. For reasonable fees, my company, Snowglow—the winter equivalent of Chemlawn—would use spray paint to revitalize dead snow. Options would range from basic snow jobs, a simple veneer of white paint sprayed over dirty lawns, to custom designer snow-blower jobs in an assortment of colors and patterns, including family crests, coats of arms, state seals, and presidential insignia. (What an account the White House would be.)

Despite its obvious potential as both a moneymaking enterprise and a valuable community service, Snowglow has not attracted investors. In fact, instead of being hailed as an entrepreneurial visionary, I've been laughed at and made fun of by friends and foes alike. Imagine my delight, then, when I read in a serious publication such as *Newsweek* that the lifestyle expert Martha Stewart, the ultimate authority on gracious living, had verified the aesthetic importance of proper snow maintenance and publicly attested to the rightness of whiteness. I'd been vindicated, and by none other than the supreme dragon lady of domesticity.

Domesticity. Now there's another word that nags the feminist critic.[1] Named by historians in the 1960s, "the cult of domesticity"—the social ethic that holds that women are the natural keepers of children, husband, home, and hearth—is generally considered part of prescriptive nineteenth-century ideologies of true womanhood and femininity.[2] Despite its association with days of yesteryear, however, the cult of domesticity remains alive, if not entirely well, on the cusp of the twenty-first century. In fact, Martha Stewart may be the best (or worst) evidence of just how au courant and internally fraught the cult of domesticity is. Our love/hate relationship with the woman *60 Minutes* called "Our Lady of Perpetual Perfection" may be emblematic of the ambivalence with which Americans greet this new ethos of domesticity that would have a Stepford wife in every custom-crafted kitchen and a chicken, or rather, a rum-basted Cornish game hen, in every French copper pot.

No mere happy homemaker, Martha Stewart stands at the helm of a $200 million multimedia empire that includes a monthly magazine, a nationally syndicated newspaper column—"Ask Martha"—and a television show, *Martha Stewart Living,* that airs six days a week on, appropriately, Lifetime, Television for Women. Her corporate empire, Martha Stewart, Inc., includes a direct-mail service—Martha by Mail—a line of designer linens and housewares exclusively for Kmart department stores, and her own Martha Stewart edition of Sherwin-Williams paints. Each of her videos, cookbooks, and other guides to gracious living has been a bestseller, from the first, *Entertaining* (1982), to the most upscale and pricey, *Martha Stewart Weddings* (1987), a glossy, coffee-table picture book that currently sells for a whopping seventy-five dollars. In addition to her own daily TV show, she has a weekly segment on CBS's *This Morning,* after a long run on *The Today Show* on NBC. She reportedly gets $25,000 a pop for personal appearances, which are almost always standing-room-only events, and devoted fans known as Martha Stewart wanna-bes not only wait in long lines to gaze upon their idol, they also pay money for the privilege of dining with her. Her success is partly responsible, I'm convinced, for the recent proliferation of TV home shows, including three cable networks devoted primarily and in some cases exclusively to gardening, cooking, decorating, sewing, building, and remodeling: TV Food Network, Home and Garden TV, and the Learning Channel.

But even as Martha Stewart is conspicuously consumed and imitated as the "guru of gracious living," she is also flagrantly mocked as the "dominatrix of domesticity." Joke books, tabloids, talk shows, and even a proposed ABC sitcom poke fun at her domestic domineering. In the pilot for the sitcom, a Stewartlike character, played by Kathleen Turner, orders a handyman cleaning out her duck pond to "polish the ducks before you put them back."[3] Riffing the movie *Mighty Aphrodite* along with the lifestyle queen, the cover of the August 1996 issue of *Spy* magazine featured a naked Martha Stewart look-alike as "Whitey Aphrodite," while the article inside presented the would-be angel of the home as a cruel, slave-driving demon whose staff performs most of the domestic wonders for which she claims credit.[4] Continuing the skewering, Jerry Oppenheimer's unauthorized biography, *Martha Stewart—Just Desserts* (1997), is less a life history than a scandal sheet, given over as it is to dishing the dirt on the "Queen of Pristine."

Whether she's being lampooned or lapped up, Martha Stewart is a study in contrasts: an icon of domesticity, on the one hand, and a corporate czar, on the other. Like the Barbie doll, perhaps the reigning icon of White femininity, Stewart seems to say, "We girls can do anything," in the corporation as well as in the kitchen, even as she defines woman's natural habitat as the spotless, tastefully decorated middle- to upper-class home. Reflecting precisely this contradiction, the November 1995 issue of *Martha Stewart Living* featured a ten-page spread on "the ultimate home office," including photos of Stewart's own New York City and East Hampton, Connecticut, "technologically state-of-the art" in-home workstations. (Her Connecticut home office had appeared previously on her weekly television show.) "What do most women want? A room of our own," the article asked and answered. But despite the seemingly feminist invocation of Virginia Woolf, the room of one's own that Martha Stewart advocates, especially for the working woman, isn't a private sanctuary in which she can create in solitude, but a "corner of the world to organize the multitude of notes and bills that define our lives" and "the piles of paper that running a household involves." "A home office," the article concluded, quoting Stewart, "should be integrated into your main living space, like the kitchen or family room, any place you feel comfortable."[5]

That women work outside the home appears to be a given of *Martha Stewart Living*, but so too is the assumption that running the household *well* is woman's real work, the kitchen or family room her rightful place. Such assumptions reflect both the standard by which men and women continue to live and work and the double duty women are still expected to perform, even after decades of feminist critiques of domesticity and the sexual division of labor.

This chapter makes three separate but related moves. First I review some of the mainstream feminist analyses of domesticity and the reproduction of mothering, including theories about the complicity of popular culture in what feminists such as Susan Faludi and Marilyn French insist is a postfeminist, profamily backlash against the women's movement, if not an all-out war on women who refuse domesticity. Next I explore the failures and surprising consequences of some of these critiques. Finally, I argue that White feminism's inability to tame down domesticity may be related to its refusal to attack it at its roots, to interrogate the cult of domesticity as a deeply historical national narrative that is finely raced as well as profoundly gendered.

Domesticity and the Rise of the Male Mother

From Barbie, G.I. Joe, and other toys that rehearse gender and maternity, to TV shows, movies, and political platforms that dictate family values, we are everywhere disciplined by domesticity—boys as well as girls, men as well as women, although the consequences of role training are and always have been different for the respective sexes. Real men may not eat quiche, but in the nineties they get a lot of points for baking them. Let a plane piloted by a woman crash, however, and the assumed cause isn't simply pilot error but flying while female. Domesticated men committed to coparenting get affirmative nods and special favors from male and female colleagues when they bring a baby to the office or rush out of a meeting to pick up the kids at day care. They are doing something extraordinary, above and beyond the call of masculinity. By contrast, women who bring children into the workplace are often perceived as behaving unprofessionally, bringing into the office what they should rightfully be doing in their own homes: mothering.

In the 1970s and 1980s, feminist scholars explored both the patriarchal standard that defines the home as woman's sphere and the sexual division of labor that reproduces male dominance. Studies by Nancy Chodorow, Jean Baker Miller, Carol Gilligan, Dorothy Dinnerstein, Adrienne Rich, and Jessica Benjamin, to name just a few, exposed motherhood as a self-replicating, socially constructed institution—if not the root cause of woman's oppression, the social instrument of it.[6] Revising and revamping Freud and other male theorists, these White feminists used psychoanalytical theory and, in Rich's case, personal experience to examine how the sexual division of labor dooms women to the domestic sphere and traps them into reproducing the very system that keeps them in bondage. Nancy Chodorow concluded, for example, that women mother because they have been mothered by women, and men don't "mother"— or at least their parenting capacities are reduced—precisely because they, too, have been mothered by women.[7] Her prescription for realigning both the oppressive sexual division of labor and the asymmetrical parental structure was to make men as well as women primary caretakers. "Equal parenting would not threaten anyone's primary sense of gendered self," she theorized, but "would leave people of both genders with the positive capacities each has" (p. 218).

Although her study, *The Bonds of Love* (1988), focused not on the mother-daughter relationship but on male-female, master-slave, subject-object patterns of domination and submission, Jessica Benjamin was similarly hopeful about the possibility of gender equality. And like Chodorow, she seemed to lay much of the responsibility for altering social relations at the feet of the "other," at the will of women who would be men's equals. "To halt this cycle of domination," she argued, "the other must make a difference. This means that women must claim their subjectivity and so be able to survive destruction. They must offer men a new possibility of colliding with the outside and becoming alive in the presence of an equal other."[8]

Groundbreaking in their day, these analyses and others like them may seem profoundly optimistic and decidedly race and class bound today. Neither Chodorow nor Benjamin believed, of course, that all of the age-old asymmetrical structures and their effects would be miraculously fixed by reordering the sexual division of labor within the family or by demanding equal rights. But the conclusion that it is mothers and their daughters who reproduce female oppression never seemed to me to go far enough or in the right direction. The story seemed to me to need another chapter, one that would take the discussion beyond the idea of women as interpellated subjects who, according to Adrienne Rich, "have learned to manipulate and seduce, or to internalize men's will and make it our own."[9]

When I first read these studies in graduate school, the extent to which they fingered the female, the mother, and the mother-daughter relationship seemed a little like blaming the victim. I was concerned that none of these analyses really considered race or class, but I was also surprised that few, if any, of them critically examined White male nationalism and the historical relationship between ideologies of domesticity and nation building. I wished for an analysis that focused less on women's complicity with patriarchy and more on domesticity as a metanarrative that has been inscribed in public policy as well as private practice at least since the eighteenth century.

Looking today at how society chews up, spits outs, ridicules, and punishes women who "claim their subjectivity"—Lani Guinier, Joycelyn Elders, Anita Hill, Geraldine Ferraro, Hillary Rodham Clinton—I am led back to my earlier desire for a different kind of analysis of the historical interplay between maternity, domesticity, race, and nation. The demand for equal subjectivity and coparenting that Benjamin and Chodorow called for has little changed the traditional power structure. Individual men and women may function differently as partners, as parents, and as professionals, but dominant, patriarchal ideology and its laws and cus-

toms have shifted only slightly and often in ways ultimately more beneficial to men than to women.

Indeed, as I suggested earlier, coparenting, flextime, family leave plans,
divorce-law reform, and other efforts to revise asymmetrical work and familial patterns may have done more for men in both public and private
arenas than for women in either. Women are still not hired for or promoted to certain positions because management fears what marriage and
motherhood might cost the company in maternity leave and child care.
Increasingly, single fathers enjoy a kind of favored-nation status in social
discourse and in popular culture, while single motherhood is patholo-
gized as aberrant. This last twist to feminist calls for equal opportunity
and coparenting—the masculinist privileging of male "mothering"—has
had dire consequences for women and children in divorce and family
courts. Martha Albertson Fineman, a law professor at Columbia, maintains that father-centered reforms have given men increased rights in
both divorce and nonmarital contexts, while devaluating "the concept of
Mother as a status worthy of any unique legal significance."[10]

Fineman views "the neutering of Mother" and the demonizing of single motherhood as patriarchy's attempt to maintain its historic control
over children and the family. One might emphasize here in addition that
Father Law is bent not simply on governing children and the family but
also on controlling women, harnessing female sexuality and keeping it in
its proper place: in the marital bed, within the heterosexual nuclear
household where it can serve its appropriate reproductive function. And
as I argue later, it's not just the nuclear family that patriarchy is bent on
preserving, but the nation.

It's fiction and of course only reflective of the real domestic dramas of
our times, but Sue Miller's novel *The Good Mother* (1996) weaves current
debates about parenthood, child custody, and female independence into a
deeply disturbing picture of Father Law's ability to discipline and control
both motherhood and female sexuality. After the breakup of her marriage, Anna Dunlap, the narrator and central consciousness of the novel,
begins a new life for herself and her four-year-old daughter, Molly—a life
that eventually includes a passionate affair with an artist named Leo Cutter. Despite his own remarriage, Brian Dunlap, Anna's lawyer ex-husband, seems almost immediately to resent Leo's presence in the family he
himself left for another woman. His resentment finds justification and instrument when innocent remarks from his daughter lead him to believe
that she has been sexually abused by Leo. In the custody battle that ensues, we watch the once nurturant married mother be transformed by
husband and court into the negligent single woman, from whose sexual
indiscretions the State (father, attorney, judge, court, and commonwealth)
must rescue the child.

But Miller offers more than an easy portrait of a good mother done wrong by patriarchy. As devoted to her daughter as Anna clearly is, her mothering is not beyond reproach. She has after all failed at marriage, already placing her child in jeopardy. Distracted by her impending divorce, she leaves Molly sleeping in the car while she goes into a building to have her divorce papers notarized. Molly awakens during her mother's absence feeling confused and abandoned. But however guilty Anna may feel about these and other infractions, her real maternal transgressions—the crimes for which she is so severely punished in the novel—are all sexual. She sleeps with Leo on the first date and soon permits him to stay overnight, even allowing him to baby-sit Molly while she works. A few months into the affair, she gets pregnant and has an abortion, because Leo thinks that having children is "a form of self-indulgence." On one occasion, she and Leo resume their lovemaking after Molly has gotten into bed with them and fallen asleep. She routinely lets her daughter see her naked body and Leo's as well. The loss of her daughter, then, is the price Anna must pay for her sins of the flesh. For the lawyer/father/ex-husband is able to make his case precisely because, once released from the moral strictures of her sterile marriage, the prim wife has become an improperly sensual unmarried woman, reckless enough to choose as her lover a less than gainfully employed artist.

Like almost every detail of this novel, Leo's profession—or lack thereof—is significant. In fact, we might say of Leo what the media theorist Elizabeth Traube says of Elden, the ubiquitous artist/housepainter on the TV sitcom *Murphy Brown*. In a brilliant reading of media images of White single motherhood that, unlike so many others, is finely concerned with race and class ideology, Traube argues that Elden, who became "mother" to Murphy's son during the 1992–1993 season, represents "the artist as natural man, enemy of bourgeois conventions (including conventional breadwinner masculinity)."[11] In his simultaneous rejection of middle-class convention and usurpation of the husband/father position, Leo Cutter indeed stands in threatening counterpoint to the displaced Father Law of Brian Dunlap. As her paramour of choice, Leo also demonstrates Anna's inability to choose appropriately, for displaying the moronic bad judgment of one insufficiently socialized or civilized, he assents to Molly's request to touch his penis when she sees him naked in the bathroom after a shower.

When Anna's lawyer asks Leo why he didn't just say no to Molly's request to touch him, he replies: "I didn't think that's what Anna—Mrs. Dunlap—would have wanted me to do. . . . I thought she'd want me to be relaxed, as natural with Molly, as she was. About her body and that kind of thing."[12] Leo is referring to Anna's attempts to treat sex and the body as natural—to raise her daughter to be less sexually inhibited than she was. But Leo's explanation can only make matters worse, for it demonstrates the distinction between Anna's permissive, aberrant single-female-headed household, where nudity and sex are taken as natural, and Brian's strict, normative nuclear family, where bodies are kept clothed and adult sexuality is kept hidden behind locked bedroom and bathroom doors.

Despite a court-appointed psychologist's finding that there has been some "very bad judgment" but no "pattern of abuse" in her household, custody is awarded to Brian and his wife Brenda. By the end of the novel, Anna, whose life has been reduced to trailing after her ex-husband and his growing family as they move from city to city, seems to agree that she was a bad mother, responsible, like Eve, for the original sin that drove her out of the garden and deprived her of the right to raise her child. Reflecting on the events that have left her effectively childless, homeless, and careerless, she thinks:

> There was no one I blamed as much as myself. I understood that what [Leo] had done was exactly what he would have thought I wanted. I could remember clearly the vision I'd had of the three of us in a kind of boundariless Eden, all part of each other. And I could see how that vision and my behavior had led directly, irrevocably, to Leo's letting Molly touch him, even to his getting hard when she did. It was a chain of events set in motion by me, by my euphoric forgetfulness of all the rules." (p. 280)

The rules, of course, are the rules of patriarchy, which both define and arbitrate proper maternal practice, and Anna didn't so much forget those rules as try to change them. By the end of the novel, she seems to have internalized not only the judgment that Molly belongs in a traditional, well-ordered patriarchal family but the judgment that she, Anna, belongs in one too. In what some critics read as a surrender to a "conservative pro-family vision,"[13] Anna thinks: "Brenda is pregnant again, and Molly is part of a family there. She loves being a big sister, she loves them—Brian and Brenda and Elizabeth, the baby. And sometimes when I imagine how it must be—the order, the deep pleasure in what happens predictably, each day, the healing beauty of everything that is commonplace—I yearn again myself to be a family" (p. 308).

What Anna longs for is her daughter, the right to mother her own child. Mothering Molly, the text makes clear, is Anna's true occupation. What she has internalized by the novel's end is the understanding that—whatever her own ideas about parenting—she could only be a "good mother" on patriarchy's terms.

A controversial best-seller, *The Good Mother* was made into an only slightly less controversial movie,[14] starring Diane Keaton, who has played the "deviant" single woman in a number of films, most notably

Looking for Mr. Goodbar. Some critics read *The Good Mother* as an antifeminist attack on single motherhood and female sexuality that works ideologically to deter women with children from making Anna's mistakes, from functioning as sexual beings outside the sacred institutions of marriage and family. Such an interpretation is invited by the text, to be sure, but I think that Miller's book can also be read as critiquing rather than advancing domestic ideals. For me, the text offers a scathing indictment of the patriarchal standards that define what the good mother is and punish those who don't conform. And while some readers lament Anna's lack of "feminist rage," I argue that the text rails against patriarchy in its depiction of the moral and legal vulnerability of poor, working, and even middle-class White women in a judicial system that makes a woman's sex life a legal issue but not a man's, not even his adultery. A female manifesto in which Anna Dunlap and a feminist pro bono lawyer fight the system and win Molly back would make for more uplifting reading, to be sure, but it would also represent a more utopian vision than the socioeconomic and legal position of women in our society supports.

Media, Motherhood, and the State

If we extrapolate from the plotlines of *The Good Mother* and other popular movies and television shows—*Kramer Versus Kramer, Mrs. Doubtfire, Mr. Mom, Three Men and a Baby* and its sequel, *Three Men and a Little Lady, Boyz N the Hood, Deep Cover, My Two Dads, Full House*—the actual upshot of feminist calls for male participation in child rearing may be the notion that not only do men mother, they mother better than women, especially women who work, divorce, date, or die. The ideological work that can be effected by means of mechanical media is one element that distinguishes the modern cult of domesticity from earlier versions. Female conduct books and other prescriptive literatures of the nineteenth century pale in their ability to alternately discipline and incite the masses when placed beside the incendiary potential of radio, television, film, and music videos.

In a world that seems increasingly out of joint, social, economic, and political discourse about family values, welfare mothers, career women, and the demise of western civilization figures White women and women and men of color as the cursed spites who have set things so wrong. From Senator Daniel Patrick Moynihan's assault on Black female-headed households to Vice President Dan Quayle's indictment of "unwed mother" Murphy Brown, women—categorized and racialized in conservative rhetoric as "Black welfare queens" and "liberal White feminists"— have replaced "the Reds" as the nation's number one foe. Corrupted by feminism, lured from the home by careers, and coddled by the welfare

system, American women have strayed too far from their essential natures as women (to paraphrase Marilyn Quayle, speaking at the Republican Convention in 1992) and in so doing have betrayed family, home, and
country.[15]

Nowhere is this message writ larger today, it seems, than in the movies,
where women whom patriarchy has failed to dominate and domesticate
are demonized as bad mothers who have left the home, psychotic career
women who would be kings (or at least CEOs), and femme fatales who,
like black widow spiders, lure unsuspecting, defenseless, married men to
their demise, if not their death. In the splendor of Technicolor, the demon
woman looms menacingly from the screen as a *Fatal Attraction*, as *The
Hand That Rocks the Cradle* to death, as *Poison Ivy*, and as a *Single/White/Fe-
male*, who in the *Final Analysis* is unable to control her *Basic Instincts*. Her
feminism and her careerism are *Bodies of Evidence* against her.

Of such films, *Fatal Attraction* is particularly noteworthy. Released by
20th Century Fox in 1987, it was one of the first contemporary films to
bring to the screen the demonic, unmarried career woman whose over-
wound biological clock has left her husband-hungry and baby-crazy.
Claiming to have been impregnated during a lost weekend of kinky sex
with a married man, Alex Forrest, a single/white/female career woman
(played by Glenn Close), lays claim to maternity with what is supposed
to be the unfulfilled career woman's lament: "I'm thirty-six years old! It
may be my last chance to have a child!"

Adrian Lyne, who directed the film, reportedly drew his portrait of the
archetypal unmarried career woman from the female Hollywood execu-
tives he saw around the studio—women he has described disdainfully as
man-eating "feminists" who "railroaded" and "walked all over" less successful and less powerful men in the most "unfeminine" ways.[16] Michael
Douglas, who plays Dan Gallagher, the wayward husband in *Fatal Attraction* (and in real life, if you believe the tabloids), is similarly contemptu-
ous of feminists, if not of women in general. (He has starred in a number
of antifeminist, antiwomen, antigay, antiminority films: *Basic Instinct*, *The
War of the Roses*, *Disclosure*, and *Falling Down*). He told a reporter that men
are in a "terrible crisis" today because of "women's unreasonable demands."[17] It's interesting to note that in *Fatal Attraction*, despite his adultery, the cheating husband gets out of his "terrible crisis" with nary a
scratch and without being villainized. It's the evil single, White, female
seductress who dies a demon's death and the innocent wife, Beth (played
by Anne Archer), who's forced to pull the trigger, to take a pregnant
woman's life, to save the domestic realm from both the pretender to the
hearth and the bastard child she carries.

But if we read the logic of the film closely, we could conclude that the
wife isn't entirely blameless. In fact, one could argue that by shooting the

pregnant intruder, Beth Gallagher is merely bringing to a close the tragic chain of events that she inadvertently set in motion when she denied her husband his conjugal rights earlier in the film. As Dan is getting undressed for bed and presumably sex, after the cocktail party at which he first meets Alex Forrest, Beth, alluring in the strapless, low-cut black dress she wore to the party, sends him out to walk the dog. He returns and heads immediately for the bedroom, grinning broadly and already unbuttoning his shirt, only to find that his wife has allowed the couple's young daughter into bed with her. The camera freezes for a few seconds on Dan in the doorway, as his face falls, his expression shifting in an instant from delight to disappointment, if not annoyance—a look to which Beth replies at once seductively and sweetly, "It's just for tonight, honey." Her body language, meaningful glances, and classically alluring pose—she's reclining among the sheets, her right arm raised and bent above her head—invite a response that the child in bed beside her belies.

In a catch-22 vaguely reminiscent of Anna Dunlap's dilemma, it is impossible for Beth to be at once the good mother and the good wife. Indulging her daughter means denying her husband. The child's presence in the marital bed may be "just for tonight, honey," but Beth knows that tomorrow night she'll be out of town, thus forcing her husband to go at least two nights without sex—unless of course he takes his pleasure elsewhere. In the very next scene, the morning after, we see Beth leaving home to visit her parents overnight and to shop for a dream house near them in the country—moves that open the door for another woman to take the place she has vacated. Beth is all the more at fault because she has been pressuring Dan to buy a house he fears he can't afford. The breadwinner anxiety brought on by his wife's house hunting makes him all the more vulnerable to the sympathetic arms of another woman.

Using *Fatal Attraction* as a case study, Susan Faludi, in *Backlash: The Undeclared War Against American Women* (1991), argued that Hollywood's portrayal of women in the 1980s typically set women against women: "Women's anger at their social circumstances was depoliticized and displayed as personal depression instead; and women's lives were framed as morality tales in which the 'good mother' wins and the independent woman gets punished." In this way, Hollywood, according to Faludi, lashed out at feminism, driving home the thesis that "American women were unhappy because they were too free; their liberation had denied them marriage and motherhood" (p. 113).

Although it too was a national best-seller, *Backlash* did not go unchallenged. One of its most scalding critiques came from Christina Hoff Sommers in *Who Stole Feminism: How Women Have Betrayed Women* (1994), in which she also took on Naomi Wolf's *Beauty Myth* (1992). Sommers described Faludi's approach as that of the "muckraking reporter," who manipulated the facts to fit her own conspiracy theory. Sommers then went on to detail Faludi's many misrepresentations, attributing to the author the malice aforethought of the backlash-mongering feminazi.[18]

Although I'm generally suspicious of conspiracy theories, I have been more inclined toward Faludi's argument, flaws and all, than toward Sommers's critique of it. Here again, though, it seems to me that Faludi didn't go far enough—and not just because she, too, focused on White media and White women, despite the fact that White patriarchy has a particular penchant for demonizing poor Black women. The media and the cinema don't simply absorb and reflect the trends of the times; they help produce them. As ideological apparatuses, they serve the interests of the State.[19] And the control of the masses, especially the gendered and racialized masses, is and always has been the business of the State. Priorities, targets, and even seats of power surely shift with the times, but the cinematic demonizing of independent women may be less a matter of a new conspiracy against feminists than business as usual.

That is to say, the construction of women as menaces—as enemies of the State—is nothing new. Nor is the idea that feminine wiles and female sexuality lead to the downfall of men and nations. Think of Helen of Troy, the face that launched a thousand ships. And Cleopatra. And Shakespeare's Lady Macbeth. Consider how legend credits Lady Guinevere with coming between King Arthur and his bravest knight, Sir Lancelot, and helping to bring down Camelot. Arguing for the ratification of the U.S. Constitution, Alexander Hamilton warned his countrymen against the State's vulnerability to the wiles of women, citing Pericles' follies at the bidding of a prostitute and the civic upheaval wrought in France and England by the likes of Madame de Maintenon, the Duchess of Marlborough, and Madame de Pompadour.[20] (Today he would no doubt include Princess Diana and her rival Camilla Parker Bowles.) In the Judeo-Christian tradition, we can go back to the beginning of time. In the beginning, God created the heavens and the earth and made man in his own image. And God took man and put him in the Garden of Eden, where the living was to be easy for all time. But then God created woman and, with a little help from a sexy serpent, she got man and mankind kicked out of Paradise.

Contemporary politics and popular culture present a number of other examples. The film *The American President* (1995), for instance, offers a thoroughly modern yet profoundly old-fashioned rendition of the woman-as-menace theme. It features the ubiquitous Michael Douglas as Andrew Shepherd, the handsome, young Kennedyesque president of the United States. As the film opens, Shepherd, a Democrat and a widower, is up for reelection, but he's not worried because he has a 63-percent approval rate among the American people, good character, and a clean record. Not only is he a fine and fearless leader and a sensitive, erudite friend of the people and the environment, but he's also a good father to his motherless daughter, who adores him, as does his staff. Then—against the advice of his aids—he falls in love with Sydney Ellen Wade (Annette Benning), an environmental lobbyist, and the walls come tumbling down.

No matter that she saves a State dinner by schmoozing with the French ambassador and his wife *en francais* and corrects the president when he calls the China Room the Dish Room, she's a liability. He drops a bomb on Libya, but all the press wants to know is who's the broad in the president's bed. She's constructed as a flag-burning whore by the opposition; her boss tells her "I hired a pit bull, not a prom queen," when he sees front-page pictures of her dancing at the White House; and the president's approval rate plummets 22 percentage points almost overnight. The election, once a sure thing, is in serious jeopardy—all because of a woman. But it's Hollywood, so it all comes out right in the end. Presumably the president and his first lady elect will marry and live happily ever after in the White House—or at least for another four years.

In real life, domestic affairs haven't been settled quite so simply for President Bill Clinton and his first lady. A smart, outspoken activist with a law degree, a career, and a life beyond the roles of wife and mother, Hillary Rodham Clinton has been a bigger liability to the president than draft dodging, pot smoking, and bimbo bedding. The moral majority notwithstanding, this is still a boys-will-be-boys kind of country, and Gennifer Flowers, Paula Jones, et al. are merely indicia that Clinton is a real man, even if he didn't go to war. But Hillary—well, as a cover story in *Spy* magazine suggests, she's no lady, first, last, or otherwise; she has balls. The cover graphic depicts a Hillary look-alike in the famous Marilyn Monroe pose, with her billowing skirt exposing not lace panties but white jockey shorts that just barely restrain a bulging penis. The caption reads "Hillary's Big Secret," while the article inside promises a peek "under Hillary's skirt to find out who *really* wears the, um, pants, in the family."

Like the *Spy* cover story, attacks on Hillary Clinton in the media and in popular culture often hit below the belt, suggesting that she's more man than woman or that, as Adam Sandler's character Opera Man sang in a segment on *Saturday Night Live*: "Bill Clin-tin-o ez puss-y-whip-o." What accounts for the voluptuous, mean-spirited, witch-hunting, bitch-burning character of anti-Clintonism that pillories Hillary? In a perhaps tongue-in-cheek comparison of Hillary Clinton and Elizabeth Dole, *Newsweek* may have hit upon the answer. Noting that, unlike "Mrs. Dole," Hillary Clinton would never allow her husband to make a major political decision without her, *Newsweek* concluded that "for all of Mrs. Dole's accomplishments . . . no one would mistake her for his equal. . . . A North Carolina native and devout Methodist, she was taught to defer to men, even beguile them, but rarely challenge them."[21]

Written of as the good wife, Elizabeth Dole—referred to throughout the article as "Mrs. Dole," her preferred manner of address—not only defers to the man who would be president; she also "humanizes her dour husband," a classic wifely function. If she doesn't quite hide her own light under a bushel, she is most certainly committed to making his little light shine. Hillary Clinton, by contrast, defies the role of "Mrs." and the entire discourse of female deference, even for a long time refusing to take her husband's last name. Although Elizabeth "Sugar Lips" Dole is a forceful politician in her own right, she knows how to sweet-talk her way around the man's world in which she operates, unlike the "strident," ball-busting Hillary Clinton. No, Hillary hating isn't just politics as usual; it's unusual politics, or rather, it's a hypertraditional response to the nontraditional nature of the Clintons' domestic politics and the too-awful-to-contemplate possibility of a female head of state. A woman with power who, unlike "Mrs. Dole," does not defer to male authority is a serious threat to national *in*security.

Not long after Bill Clinton assumed the presidency, it was widely reported that when Chelsea Clinton got sick at school, she told the nurse to call her father because her mother was "kind of busy." Instead of pointing an admiring finger at Bill Clinton for being a good father, recognized by his daughter as an active coparent, Rush Limbaugh and much of the media pointed an accusing finger at Hillary Clinton for being a bad mother. And bad mothering is not only a crime against the child and the family, it is a crime against the State.

Martha by Male

If indeed a war on women is being waged in the media, in popular culture, and in public policy today, it cannot be understood as separate and distinct from the larger historical narratives of domesticity and race on which the nation turns. To see how ideals of gender, domesticity, sexuality, and nation are both closely intertwined and finely racialized, we would do well to examine not only White male–authored documents such as the Declaration of Independence and the Constitution, but also articulations of American identity as diverse as White female–authored captivity narratives dating back to the seventeenth century and the variety of home-and-hearth discourses being mass-produced today.

The classic Anglo-American captivity narrative tells the story of the White woman's abduction by and confinement among Indians and documents what Nancy Armstrong and Leonard Tennenhouse describe as the lost daughter's "single-minded desire to return home," unsullied by native hands. According to Armstrong and Tennenhouse, these narratives "described an experience that people of 'the middling sort' in England could not have imagined were it not for the colonial venture; it asked its readers to imagine being English in America."[22] I would add that in addition to advancing Englishness, these narratives also constructed Whiteness; that is, they figured national identity as White, where what the good White woman does is give her body over to building the new nation by bearing White children and reproducing the White household.

Domesticity, then, and good motherhood have been and remain the cornerstones of nation building, the fertile ground on which White patriarchy reproduces itself. The big-busted, thick-lipped, broad-lapped Black mammy may be the archetypal earth mother in the plantation tradition, but the quintessential good mother in the national romance is the true woman/White daughter. Perhaps this is why the reigning queen of domesticity, Martha Stewart, has gone to such great lengths to construct herself not simply as the grand dame of gracious living, but also as the good daughter, the ideal wife, and the model mother, inventing for herself a perfect childhood, a perfect marriage, and perfect offspring.

The myth of the perfect White superwoman has made Martha Stewart a multimillionaire and an icon of the *American* way. "She's America," Kmart executive Barbara Loren-Snyder concluded the first time she came across Martha Stewart's beautiful blond image on the dust jacket of a cookbook. "Just seeing her picture," Loren-Snyder decided to recruit Stewart to become Kmart's national spokesperson and home consultant. "I looked at the book, and I thought, 'She's extremely attractive, the right age, a wife, a mother.... She's America.' "[23]

What the savvy Kmart executive undoubtedly saw, but doesn't say, is that Martha "Mother Mary" Stewart was not only of the right age and marital and maternal status, but also of the right race to be America. What Loren-Snyder didn't know at the time, however, is that her chosen Mrs. America's perfect past, perfect marriage, and perfect motherhood are, by all reports except Stewart's, shameless shams. But then, if we believe her detractors (who include many of her friends and relatives), almost everything about Martha Stewart is a sham. Even as Kmart was signing her up as the world's leading expert on home, hearth, and family values, Stewart's own long-troubled marriage was crumbling. Her critics, especially her would-be biographer Jerry Oppenheimer, delight in pointing out that not only did her husband of twenty-six years leave her and file for divorce while she was on tour promoting, ironically, *Martha Stewart Weddings*, dedicated to him and their daughter, but he also took out a restraining order to keep her from harassing him, after she burst into his Manhattan office screaming and threatening to throw his "shit out the window."[24]

Counting relatives, childhood friends, neighbors, business associates, and employees among its Deep Throats, Oppenheimer's unauthorized biography paints a 360-page portrait of a petty, humorless megalomaniac who bullied, manipulated, and lobster-clawed her way from poor little Polish girl to millionaire corporate czar, leaving in her wake betrayed friends and relatives, exploited coworkers, a henpecked husband, and a neglected daughter. *Spy* and other sources are equally ungenerous in their depictions of the *real* "Martha Dearest." Calling her a "home-and-hearth charlatan," *Spy* advises, "If you respect Martha Stewart, respect her because she knows there's a sucker born every minute. Don't respect her because you're one of them" (p. 52).

If the husband I made a millionaire divorced me and took up with my much younger former assistant, I might threaten to throw *him* out the window. Though I have my own bones to pick with the unrelenting Whiteness and elitism of Martha Stewart's kind of living, I don't want to point out that the nasty things said about her—some of them anyway—are the same kind of things said about Leona Helmsley, Hillary Clinton, and other powerful women, even the hugely popular Oprah Winfrey. The sins of oppression for which Martha Stewart and other successful women are condemned are often the same virtues of aggression for which men are praised, prized, and promoted. Single-mindedness, subterfuge, ruthlessness, manipulation, even deceit are the stuff of which CEOs and heads of state are made. Society calls such authoritative men movers and shakers, leaders, tycoons, good old boys; such women it calls bitches.

Where No Woman Has Gone Before

Strong, independent, single women seem to thrive only in the realm of the imaginary: Wonder Woman, Xena, Buffy the Vampire Slayer. Indeed, if past and present narratives of nation leave us little cause to celebrate women's liberation from the cult of domesticity, science fiction and fantasy have sometimes offered a more hopeful vision of future race and gender relations. The imagined communities of the *Star Trek* television series, for example, particularly in its more recent incarnations—*Next Generation, Deep Space Nine,* and *Voyager*—appear to offer some relief from both male dominance and the traditional division of labor in their portrayals of intergalactic domesticity. Many-nationed, multispecied, mixed-race crews fly through the galaxy, if not with the greatest of ease, at least with enough accord to operate as a federation. It's not quite clear who changes diapers in the inner spaces of outer space, but as an equal opportunity employer, Star Fleet provides on-site day care, and sophisticated computers called replicators do the cooking. The glass ceiling has been shattered to the point that women routinely serve as officers, even rising to the rank of admiral.

It's worth noting, though, that in most of these outer-space adventures, female officers are addressed as "sir," terminology that may suggest that in the twenty-fourth century, species have advanced beyond the gender gap, but everyone is male. And while everyone is no longer White and the "N word" is never spoken, racial and ethnic stereotypes that have traditionally been associated with certain groups—Blacks and Jews, for instance—are reproduced in the uncivilized, animalistic, dark, and swarthy Klingon warlords and the miserly, double-dealing Ferengi merchants.[25]

In the latest *Star Trek* series, Captain Katherine Janeway (Kate Mulgrew) commands the starship *Voyager*. Hers is the first female-headed craft to fly through prime time, even on a cable network. Hers is also the first starship in a leading role to be permanently lost in space, having been transported into another quadrant, 70,000 light-years from Earth. And although she clearly displays the captive daughter's "single-minded desire to return home," in three seasons Janeway hasn't managed to find the way back, something Kirk or Picard or even Sisko, the Black captain in *Deep Space Nine*, would have accomplished in a single episode—two at most. I realize, of course, that if *Voyager* made it back to Earth, the show would be bereft of plot, but what does it mean that a woman is cast as captain for the first time in a series whose success depends on her failure? As the captain of the *Enterprise*, James T. Kirk could always depend on the mechanical wizardry of his chief engineer Montgomery "Scottie" Scott to beam him up or warp him out of harm's way. Mechanical engineering having failed, perhaps what Janeway needs is a little domestic domineering. If I were in her combat boots, I'd beam up Martha Stewart and have her whisk us the heck home. It's a good thing.

Notes

1. With apologies to Mary Helen Washington, who wrote: "Tradition. Now there's a word that nags the feminist critic." See "'The Darkened Eye Restored': Notes Toward a Literary History of Black Women," in Mary Helen Washington, ed., *Invented Lives: Narratives of Black Women, 1860–1960* (Garden City, N.Y.: Anchor, 1987), p. xvii.

2. According to the historian Nancy Cott, the phrase "cult of domesticity" was introduced by Aileen S. Kraditor in her introduction to *Up from the Pedestal: Selected Writings in the History of American Feminism* (Chicago: Quadrangle Books, 1968).

The feminist historian Barbara Welter identified and named the "cult of true womanhood" in 1966. See Barbara Welter, "The Cult of True Womanhood," *American Quarterly* 18 (1966): 151–74, reprinted in Welter, ed., *Dimity Convictions: The American Woman in the Nineteenth Century* (Columbus: Ohio University Press, 1975).

3. The tabloids are particularly prone to Martha Stewart bashing. See the *Globe*, May 21, 1996, p. 35, and the *National Enquirer*, April 23, 1996, p. 8. The *Enquirer* describes Stewart as a power-hungry media executive with a master plan to control

people's minds, "from America to Zanzibar," via the Internet. See also parody magazines by Tom Connor and Jim Downey, *Is Martha Stuart Living?* (New York: HarperCollins, 1994) and *Martha Stuart's Better Than You at Entertaining* (New York: HarperCollins, 1996).

4. Greg Easley, "The Divine Myth Stewart," *Spy,* July/August 1996, pp. 50–57.

5. "The Ultimate Home Office," *Martha Stewart Living,* November 1995, pp. 90–99.

6. See Jessica Benjamin, *The Bonds of Love: Psychoanalysis, Feminism, and the Problem of Domination* (New York: Pantheon, 1988); Nancy Chodorow, *The Reproduction of Mothering: Psychoanalysis and the Sociology of Gender* (Berkeley: University of California Press, 1978); Dorothy Dinnerstein, *The Mermaid and the Minotaur* (New York: Harper and Row, 1976); Carol Gilligan, *In a Different Voice: Psychological Theory and Women's Development* (Cambridge, Mass.: Harvard University Press, 1982); and Adrienne Rich, *Of Woman Born: Motherhood as Experience and Institution* (New York: W. W. Norton, 1976; reprinted 1986).

7. Chodorow, *The Reproduction of Mothering,* p. 211.

8. Benjamin, *The Bonds of Love,* p. 221.

9. Rich, *Of Woman Born,* p. 68.

10. Martha Albertson Fineman, *The Neutered Mother, The Sexual Family, and Other Twentieth Century Tragedies* (New York: Routledge, 1995), p. 101.

11. Elizabeth Traube, "Family Matters: Postfeminist Constructions of a Contested Site," *Visual Anthropology Review* 9(1) (Spring 1993): 56–73. Traube also suggests a link between the "'beat culture' evoked through Elden and African American street cultures" (p. 71, n. 24). Again, much the same might be said about Leo Cutter.

12. Sue Miller, *The Good Mother* (New York: Delta, 1986), p. 178.

13. Deborah Rosenfelt and Judith Stacey, "Second Thoughts on the Second Wave," *Feminist Review* 27 (1987): 77–95; quotation from p. 81.

14. The film omits the detail that Leo began to get an erection when Molly touched him, and it has a somewhat more hopeful ending, since it doesn't depict the nomadic, impoverished life Anna lives to see Molly.

15. In her contribution to the Republican attack on feminism in general and Hillary Clinton in particular, Marilyn Quayle opined: "I sometimes think that the liberals are always so angry because they believe the grandiose promises of the liberation movements. They're disappointed because most women do not wish to be liberated from their essential natures as women."

16. Susan Faludi, *Backlash: The Undeclared War Against American Women* (New York: Doubleday, 1991), p. 121. According to Faludi, Lyne described these "unfeminine," man-eating sharks as feminists who talk "about fucking men rather than being fucked."

17. Joan Smith, *Misogynies: Reflections on Myth and Malice* (New York: Fawcett, 1989), pp. 31–32; quoted by Faludi, p. 121.

18. See Christina Hoff Sommers, "The Backlash Myth," in *Who Stole Feminism? How Women Have Betrayed Women* (New York: Touchstone, 1994), pp. 226–54.

19. Of course, not everyone would agree. As Elizabeth Traube and other media theorists have shown, conservative forces argue that it's liberals who control the media; they blame mass communication for society's moral breakdown. Traube

explores this point in a particularly interesting way, noting different responses to the televisual pregnancy of the character Murphy Brown: "For in a sitcom which a frustrated feminist of the second wave might have seen as one more foray in a campaign to redomesticate independent women, Quayle found an attempted subversion of patriarchal order consistent with and partly responsible for the upheaval in Los Angeles over the Rodney King verdict." See Elizabeth Traube, "Family Matters," p. 56.

20. See *The Federalist Papers, No. 6.*

21. Eleanor Clift, "The Steel Magnolia," *Newsweek*, May 27, 1996, p. 33.

22. Nancy Armstrong and Leonard Tennenhouse, *The Imaginary Puritan: Literature, Intellectual Labor, and the Origins of Personal Life* (Berkeley: University of California Press, 1992), p. 205.

23. Jerry Oppenheimer, *Martha Stewart—Just Desserts* (New York: William Morrow, 1997), p. 261.

24. Oppenheimer, *Martha Stewart*, pp. 284–5.

25. I'm grateful to Rhett Gambol for sharing his thoughts about the racial politics of *Star Trek*.

Part Four

Bringing Down the House: Dreaming, Revising, Burning

Chapter Fourteen

Feminists Are Modern; Families Are Indian: Women's Magazines and the Politics of Modernity

K. SRILATA

Some women feel that their wifely duties cease at being a good cook and a house-keeper. No, it does not. The modern husband is much more demanding.

He wants an intelligent, beautiful and smart mate who will walk proudly by his side, take interest in his work and share his interests.
—Podder, Woman's Era, March 1, 1992

Why, for instance, is the Barbie doll sold in India but not the cabbage patch doll? Why did the Indian Mattel affiliate choose to market Barbie dressed in a sari while Ken remains dressed in "American" clothes? Why is Barbie dressed in a sari (universalizing/nationalizing a regional mode of dress) and not in other women's styles of dress? Which class buys these dolls and how do children play with them in different locations?
—Grewal and Kaplan, 1994, 12–13

Culture as Tradition, Culture as Modernity

The figure of Barbie dressed in Indian clothes signals for me important ways of thinking about culture outside the familiar binary of "tradition" and "modernity." In India, as elsewhere, culture is a contentious terrain. It is a terrain where battles regarding caste, nationality, and gender are fought. The air over the battlefield of "Indian" culture is thick with the dualism of tradition and modernity as family and feminist politics, even marriage and romance, are pitted against each other. By a process of strict affiliation, these elements are placed under one of the two major signs, tradition or modernity. What I wish to point to is the mutual constitution of tradition/modernity discourses at different moments in Indian history and the stakes involved in masking them as separate.

As Kumkum Sangari and Sudesh Vaid (1989) tell us, both tradition and modernity are colonial constructs that have operated within the Indian context as carriers of patriarchal ideologies. Within colonial discourse, the dualism of these constructs was useful in framing the "native" in particular ways, in placing him or her within the frozen fixity of the "past." Modernizing movements, such as the social reform movement of the late nineteenth and early twentieth centuries, are underwritten by a desire to "progress" to the modern or contemporaneous moment, so that the "native" can occupy a space close to the colonizer. More recently, with the resurgence of a Hindu fascist movement under the leadership of the BJP-VHP-RSS combine, a Hindu-Aryan past has been discursively created and rewritten under the sign "tradition." Tradition, then, serves as a guise and a natural explanation for caste and gender inequalities occurring even in the present. By *tradition*, I am also referring to its construction as the ageless essence of Indian culture: "The dominant culture obscures by its homogenizing gesture the historical complexity of our cultural/ideological formations. The very perception of tradition as unchanging is a misrecognition that denies the historicity of tradition, the ways in which it is continually invented, constructed and improvised" (Niranjana, Sudhir, and Dhareshwar 1993, 6).

Modernity has been constructed within the Indian context as a set of practices either indicative of "westernization" (and therefore, according to modernity's detractors, morally unsound) or signifying (for modernity's supporters) the liberatory and the progressive.

The Tradition/Modernity binary, however, does not account for *multiply* constituted identities produced across different cultural locations. Perhaps, seeing culture in terms of transnational flows, as an effect of "scattered hegemonies," is a useful way of breaking down what seem to be dualistic and mutually impermeable categories. *Scattered hegemonies* is a term used by Inderpal Grewal in referring to "the effects of mobile capital as well as the multiple subjectivities that replace the European unitary subject" (Grewal and Kaplan 1994, 7). I deploy it here to unsettle the Tradition/Modernity binary as it relates to another binary, western/non-western or western/Indian. "Scattered hegemonies" is a useful shorthand for the *mutual* historical constitution of the Traditional/Indian and the Modern/Western. The term's reach extends beyond its more obvious connotations of the transnational economic and cultural flows of the multinational present. One could read as *scattered hegemonies* the links between British colonial intervention through legal reform or land revenue settlements and the patriarchal practices of the local Indian elite. Readings of the social reform movement of the late nineteenth and early twentieth centuries reveal the continuities between Victorian ideologies and the ideologies of middle-class Indian male social reformers, which coalesce around the "woman" question. In stressing the collusions between what appear to be unrelated sets of ideologies, I attempt to unsettle the mutual exclusivity of Tradition/Modernity discourses as they relate to the western/nonwestern binary. Speaking visually, then, Tradition and Modernity can never have entirely separate forms because they are constantly jostling against and melting into one another. Both have equal claim to the contemporary moment; there is no position outside of modernity.

The terms *Tradition* and *Modernity* are always value loaded; one has to contend not with two but with *four* umbrella categories—Good Tradition and Bad Tradition, Good Modernity and Bad Modernity. Formations such as family, feminism, marriage, romance, and caste, which one finds placed under one or the other of these four categories at any given point in time, are constantly traveling from one category to another. I map this travel by means of an examination of three major moments in Indian history. The first of these moments is the late nineteenth and early twentieth centuries, best exemplified for me by the social reform movement that swept parts of India at that time. The second is the postindependence moment, characterized by the discourse of secularism, which was tied to Modernity. The third moment, perhaps the hardest to describe, is the present moment, the 1980s and the 1990s—the moment of postliberalization, anti-Mandal, and Hindutva discourses.[1] I use the word *moment* rather than *historical period* to allow myself the freedom necessary to analyze discourses that circulate, linger, and dovetail into each other. This choice of word enables me, for instance, to read the continuous and common structures of feeling that link the constructions of caste, class, and gender during the period of social reform to constructions of the same formations in a contemporary women's magazine such as *Woman's Era*.

The women's movement in India has constantly had to struggle with "commonsensical" perceptions about women as natural caregivers and nurturers of families. These perceptions, as I demonstrate in detail, are shaped by the emergence of a middle-class culture during the social reform movement. This movement marks a shift toward the *gendered* separation of the public and private spheres and a construction of women based on notions of their domesticity. The collapsing of women's interests with the interests of the family, the children, the husband, and the home can be traced back to this historical period. The family as an institution that reproduces national culture through the bodies of women emerges with the consolidation of the middle classes during the early decades of the twentieth century.

Through readings of *Woman's Era* against and with some of the literatures of the social reform moment, I examine the continuities and the discontinuities, the circuits of travel and the kaleidoscopic shifts that have occurred within the mutually constitutive discourses of tradition and modernity and the resonances that these shifts have for gender construction. In mapping these circuits of travel, I use a circular mode of analysis rather than a chronological one. I begin, then, with postindependence and more recent narratives that construct tradition and modernity, studying them in relation to the social reform movement.

The Secular Modern Mood of Postindependence India

Secular modern discourse was, and in some senses continues to be, hegemonic in postindependence India. It is linked in interesting ways to the more recent growth of Hindu nationalisms and the pro-upper-caste anti-Mandal agitations to which I return in the following section. The vision of a newly independent India necessitated a sometimes subtle, sometimes drastic shift in the valences attached to tradition and modernity, to the formations that make up the chart of these discourses. The secular modern mood of postindependence India was accompanied by an erasure or repression of categories such as "caste" and "community." These categories became effectively unavailable as categories for critical reflection. As Vivek Dhareshwar tells us:

> It was not that caste was ignored, but a certain opacity was nevertheless attached—no doubt still is—to it; its use was always surrounded by embarrassment, uneasiness, ambivalence and, sometimes, even guilt. . . . A large part of our intellectual discourse has in fact been an autobiography of the secular (read upper-caste) self, its origin, its conflict with tradition, its desire to be modern. (Dhareshwar 1993, 115)

Dhareshwar links this historical erasure of caste to the use of English by the Indian elite, especially in the public sphere. He argues that English functions as a semiotic system signifying modernity:

> When the metropolitan subjectivity constitutes itself in English, caste has to be approached at one remove, as it were, as an experience-distant concept. At one level, English as a sign of modernity seems to remove or mark out the elite from the active traces of social conflict. . . . To speak about caste, or to theorize it, in English, in the political idiom, however eclectic it may be, that English makes available, is already to distance caste practice as something

alien to one's subject position. It is as though in English one only engages, as it were, in second order discourse about caste, that discourse itself being seen as discontinuous with caste practices. Caste, then, becomes repressed by being driven into the private domain—a domain, significantly enough, where very often the vernacular is deployed. . . . Those who appropriated English could claim a subject position which was free from caste marks, especially in the public sphere—which by definition was secular. . . . In the private domain . . . seen as the domain of the vernacular—caste practices could be reiterated or reinvented. (Dhareshwar 1993, 117–118)

For secular liberals as well as leftists, class replaced caste as a category of analysis. Caste was distanced as belonging to Bad Tradition, while class came to be perceived as Good Modernity.

The Present Moment

The narratives of self and nation are being reconfigured in the wake of economic liberalization, the right-wing Hindutva fundamentalist movement, and the antireservation stir by upper-caste youth. The secular modern mood was subtly unsettled when caste was forced into the consciousness of the secular self by the Mandal commission in what Dhareshwar described as a return of the repressed. On August 7, 1990, then Prime Minister V. P Singh announced the implementation of the Mandal commission's recommendation for reservations (quotas) of up to 27 percent for the "backward" castes, apart from the 22.5 percent reservation for the scheduled castes and the scheduled tribes, in government service and in the public sector. This sparked major riots and protests, especially in parts of North India, where upper-caste college youth participated in large numbers. While the most dramatic of these protests involved self-immolation by some youth, other modes of protest were equally compelling and visible. Some students sat by the curbside polishing the boots of those passing by, while others swept the streets of cities or offered their services as porters in railway stations. The point of these modes of protest, which relied heavily on the discourse of secular merit, was to indicate to the people that the Mandal commission's recommendations would "reduce" deserving upper-caste youth to such "menial" tasks, which have historically been performed by the lower castes. Upper-caste youth who perceived the commission's recommendations as giving them a raw deal in terms of educational and employment opportunities chose to ignore the fact that at the time of the Mandal announcements, the private sector was expanding rapidly (and was outside the purview of the recommendations). The agitators argued that class rather than caste should be the category used in reservation policies. A question frequently articulated in many different ways was "What happens to *poor* Brahmans?" Such a question was the result of a refusal to acknowledge two factors: one, that caste and class differences often overlapped, and two, that the *poor* Brahman made up in terms of cultural and educational capital what he or she lacked in terms of economic resources.

Despite the force with which Mandal put caste back on the nation's agenda, members of the upper castes, many of whom are formed by postindependence secular modern discourse, continue to distance themselves from the practice of caste. Dhareshwar points to the systemic slippage that equates caste exclusively with the lower caste:

> The upper castes do not, or so they claim, experience caste; it is not a subjective reality for them; but they would admit to its facticity—an objective given. Whereas the semiotics of caste has been imposed upon the lower-castes. They are "locked" into their identities. The repression or disavowal of caste by the secular self, then, has the seemingly paradoxical consequence of producing an excess of identity for the lower-castes. The double semiotic of caste and class has allowed the "upper-castes" considerable mobility of identity. (Dhareshwar 1993, 121)

Just as the upper-caste self remains unburdened by his or her caste identity and is therefore securely modern, the Hindu is similarly unmarked, coded in fact as secular. The Hindu right has repeatedly mobilized and constructed an exclusionary Indian (read upper-caste, Hindu) past and tradition as part of its sustained campaign to target religious minorities, legitimizing inequalities of caste and gender as the essence of Hindu culture. Once the normative Indian subject is coded by processes of othering/differentiation, (the "others," in this case, being Muslims and the lower castes), the processes themselves become invisible. The Muslim becomes the religious fanatic, the destroyer of Indian culture, the dangerous Other, the bearer of religious and communal identity.

A rapidly globalizing Indian middle class, partly the result of the Indian government's economic policy of "liberalization," has only strengthened this coding of the upper-caste Hindu as the secular modern self. The congress-government-promoted program for globalization of the Indian economy includes a liberalization of controls and integration with the world market instead of protection and import substitution, the expansion of the private sector, and the opening of the economy to foreign capital. As I have already noted, the expansion of the private sector favored the upper-caste, English-speaking elite. The cosmopolitan consumer of the "global" middle class, whom Satish Deshpande aptly termed the new "darling of the national imagination," is even further distanced from "antimodern" caste and "communal" discourse:

> The figure of the cosmopolitan is the unexpected or the "new" term, one that is relatively unprecedented in Indian ideological history. Its clearest repre-

sentative is perhaps the ubiquitous figure of the Non Resident Indian, the closest approximation to a modern mythological hero that the Indian middle classes possess. The cosmopolitan is a more inclusive term, however, and refers to all those Indians (whether resident or not) who can and do consider themselves to be citizens of the world. For obvious reasons, this tribe is restricted to the "creamy layers" of the urban middle and upper middle classes, and is thoroughly "modernized" (perhaps "globalized" would be more accurate) in its outlook. For this group, economic challenges are not confined to the Indian economy, whether these involve decisions on the income/production or the expenditure/consumption side. This group, which consists of the Indian middle class elite, may be said to have joined the global middle class. (Deshpande 1993, 27–28)

The New Woman of the Liberalization Era

What has specific resonances for the gender question during the postliberalization era, however, is the recasting of the earlier figure of the educated and hence "emancipated" middle-class woman, who, as I argue in the following section, is a legacy from the social reform movement. The ideal of womanhood in the context of a globalizing economy has shifted from the social reform's educated-yet-traditional woman to a distinctly different figure, the urban, English-educated, upper-class New Woman. As a member of the modern global upper middle class, this New Woman is distinct from the middle-class urban working woman or housewife. The middle-class woman, constructed through the discourses of the social reform movement, followed a set of practices deemed as Good Tradition to attain a Good Modernity. Her modernity (of which her education was an important marker) was coded as good because it was pressed into the service of tradition. Much of what went under the name of Bad Modernity (such as romantic love and the wearing of western clothes) was out-of-bounds for her. What was tabooed as Bad Modernity for the woman of the social reform movement is recast as Good Modernity in the present context. The New Woman has a more easy relationship with modernity. She is English educated and comfortable with technology both inside and outside the home. She may live in Levi's but still occasionally sport "ethnic" Indian clothes (the ethnicity of the Levi's themselves, of course, remains unmarked). Like Barbie, she can don her ethnicity on demand. She is pan-Indian and remains peculiarly unmarked by caste, linguistic, and religious difference. Her defining identity is in fact her innocent upper-class status. Her formation is thus linked to the secularizing projects intrinsic to the making of the global middle class of the last two decades. She is above all an *individual* with agency that is about being publicly visible (even feminist) and falling in love.

The New Woman and the Middle-Class Woman

The liberal, modern figure of the New Woman haunts the construction of the middle-class woman today. The New Woman's agency, expressed in terms of her public visibility, the clothes she wears, and her participation in the discourse of "free choice" and its corollary, romantic love, is especially seductive. This agency is at least potentially more easily available to the middle-class woman, who, unlike her predecessor in the days of the social reform movement, often studies or works outside the home. Both the college woman and the "working" woman of today have a more comfortable relationship with public visibility. Despite what many middle-class women jokingly refer to as "curfew" rules imposed on them by their families, it seems that the battle to leave the domestic space is at least partially won.

In fact, as Susie Tharu and Tejaswini Niranjana tell us, "suddenly, women are everywhere" (1994). They argue that across the political spectrum, in left-wing as well as right-wing politics, middle-class women have been increasingly visible:

> Over 1991–92, for instance, upper-caste women thronged the streets in the anti-Mandal protests; the BJP identified women and dalits as the principal targets of their next election campaign; women shot into prominence as leaders in the Ramjanmabhoomi movement. The People's War Group of the CPI-ML found themselves drawn increasingly into popular women's campaigns against sexual and domestic violence, dowry and the sale of arrack [country liquor]. Film after film features the new woman as active, critical, angry— she also figures prominently in Doordarshan [public television] programs. In overwhelming numbers women have joined the literacy campaigns in Pondicherry and parts of Andhra Pradesh.[2] (Tharu and Niranjana 1994, 93)

Attempting to read these phenomena, Tharu and Niranjana argue that "women" seems to stand in for the subject of feminism itself and that the newly visible and so "public" woman is perhaps one who might be regarded as feminist. Analyzing the participation of women in the anti-Mandal agitation, they point out:

> The fact of women "taking to the streets" became in the hegemonic culture iconic of an idealism that recalled the days of the freedom struggle. The marking of "women" as middle class and upper caste has a long genealogy which, historically and conceptually, goes back into nationalism as well as social reform. Marked thus, "women" are seen as morally pure and uncorrupted; hence the significance of their protest, which becomes a "disinterested" one, since they have no place in the organised political process. However, as a powerful strand of nationalism asserted, it was women who were entrusted with the task of saving the Nation. In fact, the nation was fre-

quently imaged as "woman" (*Bharatmata*, Mother India). (Tharu and Niranjana 1994, 99)

This public visibility of middle-class women and their very "feminism"
are acceptable because both are coded as arising out of their love for the
Indian nation. This particular brand of feminism therefore avoids being
compared with the Bad Modernity of western feminism. Tharu and Niranjana caution that this visibility of women in the politics of the anti-
Mandal agitation, as well as in other upper-caste and Hindu resurgence
politics, is deeply problematic, given that these projects, even as they
seem to extend feminist demands, are linked to initiatives that would be
unacceptable to an egalitarian feminism. In all these struggles, the subject
of feminism remains the middle-class, upper-caste woman.

Woman's Era: A Repressed Desire for Modernity

I argue that the late 1980s and the early 1990s mark a split in the kinds of
literature available to non-lower-class, non-lower-caste women and that
the split reflects the ways in which the upper-class New Woman and the
middle-class woman are differently constructed in relation to questions of
tradition and modernity. *Woman's Era* (a fortnightly magazine in English
published in India) is representative of a popular literature that interpel-
lates the middle-class woman, while *Femina* and *Savvy* are specifically
coded as magazines for the upper-class New Woman.

Woman's Era, advertised as India's "largest selling woman's magazine in
English," is part of a chain of magazines for women and children published
in English and Hindi. A publisher's blurb describes it as a magazine that
"carries women-oriented fiction, articles of general interest as well as on
family affairs, exotic food recipes, latest trends in fashion and films."
Within the internal hierarchies and politics of the magazine industry in India, *Woman's Era* is a relatively down-market magazine—in relation, that is,
to other English-language magazines for women, such as *Femina* and
Savvy. In a survey conducted in Madras in 1994 among two groups of middle-class women—college-going women ages eighteen to twenty-two and
housewives ages thirty to fifty—I found that the former preferred *Femina*,
Savvy, and the Mills and Boon, Harlequin, and Silhouette romance novel
series to *Woman's Era*, which they repeatedly described as "boring" and
"conservative," even pointing to its bad English.[3] Thus, issues such as language usage and the age of its readers determine a magazine's status vis-à-
vis modernity.[4] Price and packaging also matter. With their glossy pages,
Femina and *Savvy* are automatically coded as magazines for the upwardly
mobile; they are also priced to suit the pockets of the upper middle class.
Femina is priced at eighteen rupees per copy, as against *Woman's Era*, which

costs only twelve rupees (1995 prices). And lastly, but perhaps most interestingly, *Woman's Era*'s modernity is down-market also because of its unsubtly antifeminist stance. Many of the college-going respondents to my survey spoke of the magazine as "conservative." Some even pointed to its antiromantic discourse as "antifeminist."

Woman's Era, however, sells a different kind of modernity, one accessible to its audience of lower-middle-class and middle-class housewives ages thirty to fifty.[5] A call to readers (specifically, to parents of young men and women) inviting them to place advertisements in the magazine's matrimonial columns as well as in those of its counterpart in Hindi, *Sarita*, perhaps best epitomizes *Woman's Era*'s repressed desire for the New Woman style of modernity:

> Searching for brides and grooms? The traditional priest and the family barber have become out of date and a thing of the past. Matrimonial columns in *Woman's Era* and *Sarita* provide you with an opportunity to establish contacts all over the country for brides and grooms for your sons and daughters and other relatives.
>
> Being essentially upper class magazines, *Sarita* and *Woman's Era* are widely circulated all over India among the intellectual and affluent classes. (*Woman's Era*, June 2, 1992, 67)

In coding the "traditional priest" and the "family barber" (both caste-specific occupations) as "out of date and a thing of the past," *Woman's Era* represents caste as nonmodern. It proceeds, then, to replace caste with class; the message of the advertisement is that class rather than caste is the category that should concern one in arranging a marriage. Notice that in proclaiming its fitness for the task of a marriage broker, *Woman's Era* describes itself as an upper-class magazine. *Woman's Era* plays high priestess of both Good Tradition and Good Modernity.

It is interesting to reflect not only on the constitution of caste as a nonmodern category but also on what gets constituted as its flip side, class as a modern category. The college students who participated in my survey emphasized that they preferred to read Mills and Boon, Harlequin, and Silhouette romance novels because the heroes of these novels were "classier" (and hence more desirable) than those of the *Woman's Era* stories, whom they described as "ordinary." The fact that these novels are written and published in the west, and packaged therefore as "English" or "American," automatically positions them within the modern. The narratives of these novels are "ideal" romance stories in the eyes of the "liberal" middle-class Indian reader because of the absence of caste, religious, linguistic, or any other "ethnic" markers. The characters of these novels, by virtue of being White, appear to be ethnically unmarked. The hero's upper-class status is a necessary condition of his desirability, a vital ingredient for the plot of the romance. In response to my question about what they rated as important in a hero, many of my survey respondents mentioned that he must be "rich." Despite the fact that most romance novel heroes are White, wealthy, successful capitalists, whereas the heroines are White and middle-class, the middle-class Indian reader seems to miss the fact that the characters' racial and class positions are important preconditions for the romance plot. Even when readers notice that the success of the romance plot and the desirability of the hero are directly proportionate to the latter's class position, they rationalize "class" as a modern category. As one student told me in response to my survey, it is "understandable" that people from very different class backgrounds will not be attracted to one another because "class is important," but societal and parental disapproval of intercaste romantic relationships and marriages was "irrational and backward." Class, as I argued before, is constituted as a modern category.

Woman's Era also deploys fashion and beauty care as easy and obviously recognizable signs of its modernity, presenting both as accessible to the "ordinary," "average" middle-class reader. Such a modernity is also carefully and deliberately distanced from the undesirable "excesses" of modernity, such as feminism. For instance, by encouraging the use of "kitchen cosmetics," such as turmeric paste, cucumber, and so on, and promoting ethnic Indian clothes as well as western clothes worn with Indian accessories, *Woman's Era* packages beauty care and fashion to suit lower-middle-class incomes and lifestyles.[6] The magazine also emphasizes the *work* behind beauty care, as in the following quote: "Skin care is a bit like housework; it is tedious and repetitive, it takes time and energy and also, like housework, it only shows when you don't do it. . . . The best beauty treatment for your skin doesn't lie in a jar, or a bottle, or a facial sauna, or even in a diet of the purest vitamins" (Singh 1992, 102). While for *Femina*, being well-groomed and well-dressed is often part of the larger liberal project of boosting the modern woman's self-confidence, *Woman's Era* tames fashion's potentially dangerous modernity (just as the social reform movement sought to contain women's education) by representing it as a "woman's duty towards her husband." Fashion, then, comes to exist in harmony with Good Tradition:

> Some women simply let themselves go after having children. They put on weight and become unrecognizable from the pretty women they once were.
>
> This is something a wife must avoid if she wants to retain her husband. A man meets so many attractive, poised and intelligent women outside his home that he is likely to compare his wife with these women at some stage or the other. . . .
>
> Some women feel that their wifely duties cease at being a good cook and a housekeeper. No, it does not. The modern husband is much more demanding.

He wants an intelligent, beautiful and smart mate who will walk proudly
by his side, take interest in his work and share his interests. (Podder 1992, 13)

A wife therefore has to both look like and be an ideal companion for her
"modern" husband. Notice that an Indian man's relationship with
modernity is smoothed out and has none of the tensions that have,
throughout history, marked the Indian woman's positioning within its
discourse.

Woman's Era's attempts to contain its middle-class reader's desire for
the "more modern" modernity of the New Woman are also obvious in
some of its short stories about marital relations. Amita Tyagi and Patricia
Uberoi (1990) dub these tales "post marital romances" or "romance after
marriage" stories. The stories begin with the problems a married couple
face in their relationship. After the occurrence of some dramatic event or
through the efforts of a mediator, the couple is happily reconciled and
back to "being in love." Woman's Era treats romance before marriage as
morally suspect, as something that is not part of Good Tradition. These
stories, then, surround a preexisting relationship of marriage (often family arranged and therefore between people who belong to the same class
and community) with the halo of a romance, achieved toward the end of
the narrative and with some difficulty. The protagonists of this kind of
narrative lay claim to Good Tradition by marrying in the traditionally approved fashion. Through their affirmations of "being in love," they are
also contestants for the Good Modernity of the New Woman.

Woman's Era's construction of the middle-class woman as "modern" yet
"traditional" draws heavily on the rhetoric of female emancipation employed by the social reform movement, even as it contains its middle-
class reader's desire for a New Woman–style modernity. The social reform and patriarchal nationalist movements' figure of woman as
emancipated yet traditional or, rather, emancipated enough to be trusted
with tradition, family, children, and therefore the nation and its future has
not vanished from the present. As my analysis of Woman's Era demonstrates, present discourses on gender are strongly informed by the discursive moments of the social reform movement. Perhaps it is important to
remember that even as the social reform movement worked within notions of traditional womanhood, partly to maintain a rigid division between the public and the private spheres, it was played out as a modernizing movement. The movement was built on a selective appropriation of
the past to modernize the present, to "improve" the status of women, to
prevent "social evils" such as child marriage and so on.

The upper-class New Woman, who is represented as authentically
modern, is too close to the present to be affected by social reform discourse. However, the middle-class Indian woman of the 1980s and the

1990s, like her nineteenth-century predecessor, is expected to take the social reform version of Good Tradition seriously, to care for home and
hearth, to please her husband and her in-laws, and to work within the
rules of her community. To analyze the present moment, then, it becomes
necessary to go back in time to the late nineteenth and early twentieth
centuries, to the social reform movement of preindependence India.

The Social Reform Movement and the Construction of the Middle-Class Woman

Uma Chakravarti (1989) argues that in the interaction between colonialism and nationalism, the idea that the golden age of Indian womanhood
was located in the Vedic period and that the upper-caste Aryan woman
best represented it came to assume the status of a revealed truth for
Hindu liberals as well as conservatives. Reform organizations such as the
Arya Samaj often found common ground with the colonial regime in reinforcing certain local patriarchal customs (such as a form of widow remarriage known as *karewa* that ensured male control over inheritance and
property) as Vedic practices. In turn, the British codified the customs and
practices of dominant indigenous groups, freezing them into law. Certain
upper-caste Hindu patriarchal norms regarding marriage, succession,
and adoption, for instance, were privileged over customary law and codified as Hindu law, to the disadvantage of all Hindu women. Sangari and
Vaid (1989) point to the links between colonial intervention (in the form
of legal reform and apparently gender-neutral land revenue settlements)
and the already existing local patriarchal practices. They argue that land
settlements by the British resulted in many interrelated transformations,
including a reconstitution of patriarchal practices. Former landowners
were reempowered within the new context of individual ownership of
property, resulting in a further impoverishment of women from the laboring and tenant classes. Secondly, because individual property rights came
to rest primarily in the hands of men, women continued to be excluded
from ownership and control of the means of production (just as they were
within precolonial agrarian structures). Even where matrilineal systems
did exist, they were changed to suit patrilineal patterns of succession.
Women had extremely restricted access to the colonial legal machinery
and bureaucracy, which came to be cast as "modern"; they were placed,
then, outside the modern. Matrilineal systems and customary law (which
was more accessible to women) were framed within the past, within a
not-so-progressive "tradition."

Orientalism and utilitarianism came together in the work of the early
nationalist writers, who constructed the image of a glorious Indian womanhood in the lost past as a contrast to the visibly low status of women in

the present. Orientalist notions about ideal womanhood fed directly into the formation of the middle class during the social reform movement of the late nineteenth and early twentieth centuries. As a result of middle-class ideologies, a differential construction of the private and public spheres emerges in the colonial period. Eligibility for the subject position "woman" comes to be awarded only to those women who stay within the confines of a home, who occupy the sphere of the private in all ways. Consequently, women from the lower classes who could not afford to withdraw from the "public" sphere of work outside the home (which, incidentally, came to be marked as the only kind of "work") are barred from occupying this particular subject position. The identities of middle-class women are now defined in contrast to those of women from the lower economic strata, who do not adhere to the seclusion of the private sphere. The middle-class woman modeled on the Vedic woman is thus literally "built upon the labour of lower social groups and is also a mark of distinction from them" (Sangari and Vaid 1989, 10).

The setting up of a rigid divide between middle-class women and women from the lower social groups had important effects on women's popular culture. Referring to the cultural homogenization of the urban Bengali middle class, called the *bhadralok* (literally, the respectable, good people), Sumanta Banerjee (1989) argues that the appeal of popular genres of nineteenth-century Bengal, composed and performed mainly by women of the lower castes and classes, cut across economic divisions among Bengali women. The street culture of songs, dances, doggerel, and theater performances brought into Calcutta by immigrant Bengali villagers represented a partially shared idiom among all Bengali women. However, with the social reform movement's foregrounding of education and book culture as the sites of women's emancipation, this street culture was effectively displaced from Bengali middle-class society. The construction of gender cannot be studied outside of the deployment of formal education in the construction of middle-classness. The family and the private sphere, both of which are nation- and gender-producing machines, emerge with the formation of the educated middle-class. The nation is literally reproduced by the educated middle-class woman through the apparatus of the family. In fact, the 1949 report of the Indian government's University Education Committee noted:

> The underlying habits of men and women are largely fixed in the early years, and these years are spent chiefly with the mother. If she is open-minded, inquiring and alert, looking behind rumour and tradition to find the facts, concerned with the course of events, informed about the nature of the world around her and interested in it, and acquainted with history and literature and enjoying them, then her children will learn these interests and attitudes from her. The educated, conscientious mother who lives and works with her

children in the home is the best teacher in the world of both character and intelligence. (University Education Committee, 1949, 392)

Under colonial influence, the *bhadralok* began to frown on street culture
as low and obscene, as exposing women to wantonness and vulgarity, as
representing their "natural" tendency toward depravity. Educated Bengali men attempted to wean their wives and daughters away from popular culture practiced in public spaces—the street, the marketplace, fairs,
and festivals. From the late eighteenth to the end of the nineteenth century, both missionary and administrative literature is full of horrified
descriptions of the so-called abandonment that characterized women's
popular culture. Banerjee points out that, influenced by Victorian interpretations of Hindu religious mythology, some of the *bhadralok* turned to
Christianity, while almost all of them disowned forms of popular culture
that made fun of the Hindu divinities.

Vital to the self-definition of the middle class, then, was the coming into
being of a distinctly middle-class culture. Banerjee points out that from
the end of the nineteenth century, the "emancipated" women of the Bengali middle class who allied themselves with educated men replaced
older forms of women's popular culture with their "cultivated" writings," especially in women's magazines. However, proficiency in the new
literary forms was not the only requirement for entry into the world of
the *bhadramahila*, the respectable middle-class woman. A woman hoping
to enter this world was expected to be totally homebound and dependent
on the male head of the family. Her literary activities arose from within
the framework of a strictly defined domestic role. The *bhadramahila* was
obliged to practice a certain refinement, to cultivate tastes that appealed
to her husband. However, the economic self-reliance and nonconformity
to the morals of *bhadralok* society allowed the Vaishnava women of the
marketplace a greater freedom, which predictably enough came in for a
lot of censure.[7] As Banerjee argues, they became targets of attack because
they represented a literary as well as a social tradition that was threatening to the founding principles of *bhadralok* society. Vaishnava women
were gradually but firmly eliminated from the secluded world of the *an-
darmahal* (the inner spaces of the home), to which the women of rich and
middle-class families were seen as belonging. The rise of *bhadralok* literary
culture and of a certain construction of middle-classness thus tied in with
the notion of a segregated domestic space over which the newly emancipated *bhadramahila*, a woman with the leisure to read and write, seemingly reigned. The street performer, the courtesan, and the *devadasi* (temple dancers) who made a living outside the domestic space suddenly
found themselves recast as "loose women" or as prostitutes. In occupying
a space outside of the domestic, they were literally in a no-woman's-land,

for they were not "emancipated" in the sense that their middle-class sisters were, nor were they the figures of Tradition and Culture (living as they did outside of patriarchal, familial norms).

The Traditional Indian woman was also constructed in opposition to the "Bad" Modern western woman. The latter was perceived as active in the public sphere, fighting for her "freedom" and her "rights." C. S. Lakshmi cites an issue of the Tamil magazine *Chakravartini* (named, incidentally, after Queen Victoria), started in 1905 for the "betterment" of women, which carries a lengthy editorial by C. Subramania Bharathi on issues of freedom and political rights for women :

> Regarding political rights for women the editor had an interesting angle to take. Women abroad who wanted these rights were mostly unmarried, he said. . . . In countries like America there was no limit to the freedom they demanded, he complained. Political rights have not been granted to these women because these ideas were not their own, he said. Due to their ugliness and other reasons they were unable to marry and so they listened to men and repeated what was told. A home-loving woman devoted to her children will not bother much about parliamentary rights, he was very sure. . . . Women had all the freedom at home. Women were kept indoors because India was a hot country and women would suffer if they moved around a lot. It was climate also that determined these things, he said. (Bharathi 1907, cited in Lakshmi 1984, 50–51)

Along with the Bad Modern western woman and "Western Feminism," the discourse of romantic love also came to be represented as false consciousness, as a threat to family and culture, as Bad Modernity. For instance, in an article by Mahalinga Sastrigal in the journal *Bharata Mani*, a woman advises her daughter that while "love" is a western concept, "liking" and "affection" are Indian (Sastrigal 1945, cited in Lakshmi 1984, 44).

Educating Women:
Women as Objects of Reform and Advice

The effects of the social reform movement in terms of the differential construction of the private and public spheres and the formation of a literary middle-class culture were not restricted to Bengal alone. Susie Tharu and K. Lalitha (1991) describe the furor that followed when a learned courtesan, Bangalore Nagaratnamma, got the eighteenth-century Telugu poet Muddupalani's work *Radhika Santwanam (Appeasing Radhika)* reprinted in 1910. Muddupalani's work, which refers to Radhika's frank sensuality, was ultimately banned by the British government, convinced that the book would corrupt its Indian subjects. The ban order was removed only in 1947. Novels and journals were commonly used as a platform of social reform during the late nineteenth and early twentieth centuries in what is today the state of Tamil Nadu. Not surprisingly, much of this literature, often authored by men, was "advice" literature, which interpellated women as the objects of social reform. The advice columns and many other articles in *Woman's Era* are clearly part of the same genre. C. S. Lakshmi cites extensively from popular journals and novels in Tamil published both during this period and immediately after that advise women on questions of morality and conduct as part of their middle-class progressive politics. For instance, Vedanayakam Pillai, in his historical novel *Suguna Sundari Charitram*, speaks of the importance of hygiene for women and the evils of social customs such as child marriage (Pillai 1950, cited in Lakshmi 1984, 35–36). A women's column in the weekly *Ananda Vikatan* carries an article by an upper-caste, Brahman man advising women to read books with high ideals, play the "traditional" games women play at home, converse in a pleasing tone, and avoid gossip (Aiyer 1930, cited in Lakshmi 1984, 44). Sometimes, male writers of such articles took on female pseudonyms, perhaps to provide a greater measure of legitimacy and valency to their authorial voice. The male writer Thumilan, who wrote for the highly misogynist "women's" column titled "*Anthapura Pechu*" ("Conversations in the Harem") in the journal *Kalki*, used a woman's name, Anasuyai, as his literary pseudonym. The early decades of the twentieth century were also marked by the emergence of the genre of the middle-class women's magazine in Tamil Nadu. Prominent among these magazines, which shaped middle-classness through a valorization of education, were *Hitkarini*, started by Pandit Visalakshi Ammal in 1909, and *Penn Kalvi* (which translates literally as *Women's Education*), started in 1912 by Revu Thayaramma.

Questions of female literacy were invariably linked with the construction of the "emancipated" yet traditional and homebound middle-class Indian woman. According to the social reform model, the main purpose of educating women was to make them more capable of fulfilling their traditional roles in society as wives and mothers. This was reflected much later, in postindependence official policies on women's education and in the ways in which syllabi were designed. For instance, the report of the University Education Committee (1949) suggests that women be taught to cope with marital problems effectively and that they receive training in home management:

> Women have demonstrated their ability to think and work alongside of men. Why not take that ability for granted and begin to recognize the ways in which the education of women can well be differentiated from that of men? It is time to realize that the finest family relations result from the association of a man and a woman who have had much of their education in common,

but each of whom has developed according to his or her own nature, and not in imitation of the other. . . .

A woman should learn something of problems that are certain to come up in all marriages, and in the relations of parents and children, and how they may be met. Her education should make her familiar with problems of home management and skilled in meeting them. (University Education Committee 1949, 394)

The opposition of the orthodox conservatives to female education was thus countered by the argument that women's education would strengthen the bonds of tradition and family. Thus the social reform model of female emancipation, played out largely in the sites of culture and education, created and gendered afresh the private sphere, the family and tradition. As part of the nationalist struggle, the social reform movement depended crucially on a certain framing of the women's question that today we might read as antifeminist. This antifeminism is reflected in the exclusions that were woven into the model, in the ways in which the normative traditional, middle-class Indian woman was constructed in opposition to the lower-class/lower-caste woman.

Three distinct configurations emerge from within the tradition/modernity discourses surrounding the social reform movement—Bad Tradition, a selective tradition signifying Good Modernity, and thirdly, Bad Modernity. The configuration of Bad Modernity comprised "western feminism" and romantic love, while that of bad tradition is constituted by "the superstition of the natives" and their "evil customs," such as widow burning, or sati, child marriage, the *devadasi*'s "prostitution," and street performances by lower-caste women. Good Modernity, a semiotic field that the social reform movement shares with *Woman's Era*, was to be attained by adhering to a set of practices that qualified simultaneously as Good Tradition. The figure of the educated, cultured, and therefore emancipated middle-class woman whose domain was the home and the family ideally fitted this particular slot, which called for enormous skill and, one would assume, ideological self-control. This middle-class woman's "culture" and "education" (signs of her emancipation and therefore her modernity) were channeled toward making her a "pleasing companion" for her husband, a skilled housekeeper, and a good mother. Her modernity was therefore obviously constituted and controlled by the patriarchal gaze.

In the Interests of Women:
Woman's Era Stories on Marriage and Divorce

In claiming to publish "women-oriented fiction" and articles about "family affairs," *Woman's Era* clearly marks itself as apolitical, as outside ideology (for isn't the space of the "domestic" that women and the family occupy always represented as outside politics?). In fact, the magazine's construction of gender is inseparable from its construction of the family. A fine slide occurs between "women's" interests and the welfare of the family, and what get constructed as "women's issues" are, typically, cooking and housekeeping, child care, marital harmony, maintaining a good relationship with one's in-laws, and so on. It is almost as though the magazine is carrying out the agendas of the 1949 report of the University Education Committee regarding the reform and education of women. Women are simultaneously blamed for and called upon to repair problems within the family. As one editorial on "Women and Population Control" notes: "Men are often careless; it is for women to plan for the happiness and future of their families" (*Woman's Era*, June 2, 1992, 7).

Even as they are exhorted to preserve "family life," women are also entrusted with the tasks of reproducing culture and tradition and preserving these from the onslaughts of westernization and feminism. *Woman's Era*, for instance, regularly carries articles advising women to get married instead of having a relationship outside of marriage. Marriage is naturalized as Good Tradition:

> Marriage may be termed old-fashioned by the feminists, but it is the basis of a stable social life. . . . Some people influenced by Western ideology would claim that marriage is not absolutely essential. Feminists and several women's groups also claim that there is no need for people to get married and to lead settled lives. In America and several European countries, many couples do not get married legally and with a wedding ceremony, but just stay together in a live-in relationship. . . .
>
> These relationships flourish in Western countries, but in India, such an attitude would only be looked upon as very "loose living" with no values and meaning. India is a country steeped in traditional beliefs, culture and tradition, where marriage is looked upon as the only mode of adults living together. (Nawaz 1991, 83)

Nawaz goes on to caution readers that children born out of wedlock and children of divorced parents suffer emotional and mental problems. Feminism, "Western ideology," "live-in relationships," and divorce are invoked and constructed as the dangerous, interlinked Others of the family and Indian tradition, as threats therefore to women themselves. This echoes C. Subramania Bharathi's evocation of the Bad Modernity of the western woman and her feminism.

Even columns in *Woman's Era* that are not explicitly part of the advice genre often contain powerful warnings or an obvious "moral of the story" through which women are advised. For instance, the column titled "I Am a Divorcée" uses first-person narratives by divorced women to construct divorce as the natural result of a dangerous and antiwoman feminist agency. Inviting contributions to this column, the editor writes:

> Are you a divorcée . . . and wish you'd not gone into it? *Woman's Era* would like to publish your story. . . . This series, which is open to both men and women, aims at presenting before the readers the causes that lead to the breakdown of marriage and divorce, so that they can take care of their own lives and ensure a happy married life. (*Woman's Era*, June 2, 1992, 81)

Notice that the editor shows no interest in soliciting "happy" divorce stories. In one particular divorce story, the narrator's husband resents her friendship with other men. Haunted by the pain of being neglected by his mother in childhood, he also insists that she resign her job to look after their baby. The narrator, who claims to have been a "staunch believer in women's liberation" in the past, refuses to do his bidding, and her son dies owing to the carelessness of the nurse. Her husband is furious and sues for divorce. The narrator writes: "Even today, I often think about my wrecked marriage. And I ask myself whether my pride and my beliefs were more valuable than my home and my baby. Every time I get the answer: "No!" . . . I sincerely hope that nobody else will ever make the horrible mistake I made" (*Woman's Era*, March 2, 1992, 78).

Stories such as the one above, which are obviously used (even fabricated, as some critics of popular culture might point out) to illustrate a particular moral, clearly carry the power of truth because of the "true life" story, personal-confession mode that they employ. The "I Am a Divorcée" column is framed in a way that allows the telling of only one particular kind of story, a story that maps the divorced woman's pain and loneliness, the economic ruin that invariably follows her divorce, and her regret at having attempted to travel outside the comfortable confines of family and tradition, egged on by her stubborn and misplaced faith in feminism. It is, however, not difficult to read between the lines (or against the grain) of the narrator's regretful voice for other stories, to recognize the reasons for her dissatisfaction with the marriage. The stories rely heavily on a rhetoric of "experience," "common sense," and "old-fashioned wisdom," suggesting that a divorced woman's life is never easy.

Woman's Era also carries "success" stories, which contrast with the stories of failure in the column just analyzed. One obvious example of a column that is framed to tell success stories is called "How I Saved My Marriage." Asking for contributions, the editor writes: "Does your husband (or wife) have an infuriating habit, a hot temper, miserly ways, a roving eye or a lazy disposition? But still, since he is your husband, you have learnt to cope with the situation and keep your marriage and home safe and happy. How did you manage this?" (*Woman's Era*, November 2, 1993, 44).

For *Woman's Era*, premarital romance usually works against the ideal of a "happy married life." The magazine participates in a consciously antiromantic discourse, writing against any possible fascination or desire that its middle-class reader might have for the New Woman's cultural capital, which, as I said before, is constituted partly by her participation in the discourse of romantic love and partly by her feminism. Important sites for the constitution of the New Woman, romantic relationships and marriage represent the conflicts and play of meaning between tradition and modernity in the Indian context. The romantic relationship leading to a so-called "love marriage," a self-arranged marriage that follows a period of courtship, has come to be regarded within liberal, middle-class discourse as the secular modern alternative to the family-arranged marriage, or the "arranged marriage," as it is popularly known. The arranged marriage is understood to be symptomatic of traditional patriarchal structures in that it removes all freedom of choice and agency from the couples concerned, and women, we are told, are the worst sufferers under this system. Horror stories are freely exchanged about both men and women "forced" into incompatible, unhappy marriages. Also, because families concerned arrange for the marriages of their children only with those who belong to the same community, arranged marriages are coded as nonsecular, perceived as reinforcing caste, class, regional, linguistic, and religious divides. Romantic relationships leading to love marriages, however, are placed in binary opposition to arranged marriages and are seen as inhabiting a secular space, a space of freedom, choice, and modernity, a space, therefore, that is sometimes also understood as feminist.[8] The discourse of romance and love marriage is enabled simultaneously by a secular and nationalist disavowal of factors such as caste and class, and the workings of transnational cultural flows, both of which grant the subject his or her modernity. Romance is caught within what Madhava Prasad (1993) describes as the "naturalization of the ideological conflict between tradition and modernity" (79). Outside liberal discourse, romance comes to be perceived as a threat to Indian tradition and is placed carefully outside its borders and within the space of the modern.[9]

Articles and stories suggesting that romance is an expression of transient sexuality, that it is bound to lead to societal and parental disapproval, are commonplace in *Woman's Era*. In her article titled "Why Marriage?" Heera Nawaz argues: "Since marriage is essential, if one opts for a love marriage, all the positive thinking will not work if one has made a bad selection, or, one has been tempted by plain good looks, sexuality (which is usually not long lasting) or just "love at first sight" which is usually transient and not permanent" (1991, 84).

A short story titled "A Change for the Better" by Valsala Balakesari revolves around the discord that threatens the interreligious love marriage of Suruchi, the only daughter of a well-to-do Hindu family, and George, the eldest son of a middle-class Christian family. A counselor figure, in the form of Suruchi's college mate, Meena, who is described as the "only person in those old days who had not been carried away by romantic notions and had urged Suruchi to think carefully before taking the plunge," saves the marriage by advising Suruchi to go back to her husband (Balakesari 1991, 16). In accusing Suruchi of not really loving George when she married him, Meena implies (as did Heera Nawaz, cited previously) that romantic love is "false":

> "No you did not [love George]. Because if you had loved him, the question of religion would not have risen. You were carried away by all his adulation and worship and you only wanted to prove that you were a rebel, by marrying George. It was a matter of pride and prestige to you. . . . If you love him now, think of him only as a man and a human being, not as a Christian or a Hindu." (Balakesari 1991, 18)

Let us for a moment place this story beside the article by Mahalinga Sastrigal (1945) in the journal *Bharata Mani*. In Sastrigal's article, we have a woman informing her daughter that "love" is a western concept, whereas "liking" and "affection" are Indian. On the other hand, despite its consciously antiromance stance, the *Woman's Era* story affirms a certain "pure love" discourse. In this discourse of pure love, the subjects concerned are assumed to be free from the mediating factors of culture and society. According to "commonsensical" perceptions, people who are really in love are oblivious to their particular historical and social situations. Its participation in the discourse of pure love makes the *Woman's Era* story discontinuous from the discourses of the social reform movement. In Meena's upholding of the human being, "not the Christian or the Hindu," the story is consciously "modern." In its explicit coding of George as a Christian and Suruchi as a Hindu and in its emphasis on the class difference between the two, the story offers an advance, ready-made reason for their marital problems. Suruchi is fated to misread George as a Christian, to miss his essential humanness. It takes Meena's extraordinary wisdom and insight to point this out to Suruchi. The story, however, is about the misreadings and the mistakes that ordinary people, ordinary women, are bound to make. The implicit moral is not about accepting everyone as human; it is, rather, a warning to ordinary women to tread the murky waters of religious and class differences carefully, to avoid them if we can. This implicit moral provides the linkages between this story and the article in *Bharata Mani*.

Conclusion: Forging a Second Position for Progressive Politics

Though perhaps not in as startling and obvious a fashion as the sari-clad Barbie, *Woman's Era* helps us see contests around culture as occurring *within* the position of modernity. This might lead us to critically reflect on the "modernity" not merely of culture (as we generally understand it) but also of "progressive politics," even that of the social reform movement, which is seemingly centered around the valorization of a selective tradition.

One has to be aware of strategic namings, of the processes that naturalize certain formations (such as caste, family, and arranged marriage) as traditional and Indian, and certain others (class and feminism) as modern and western. It is important to ask why women have had to bear the marks of tradition even in a world that has taken up with great passion the project of modernity, to ask why Barbie wears "ethnicity" in wearing a sari while Ken does not, to question the modernity of feminism. It is important to use cultural analyses in working toward a second position for progressive politics, a kind of contaminated space that exists outside the pale of binaries.

Notes

I would like to thank Rosemary George for making me feel that this was a worthwhile project. I am especially grateful to Donna Haraway and all the participants in the Feminist Theory writing workshop at the History of Consciousness Program, University of California–Santa Cruz, for their extremely useful feedback. This chapter was made possible by their painstaking attention to earlier drafts. As always, my thanks to Tejaswini Niranjana and my friends at the University of Hyderabad for fashioning the crucial critical and political contexts without which this work would never have been possible.

1. The Mandal Commission was a government-appointed body charged with recommending changes that would result in a more equitable assignment of government and public-sector jobs between caste groups. The commission's report, released in 1990, called for more job "reservations" for "backward castes and scheduled castes/tribes." Anti-Mandal responses to the commission's report are discussed in greater detail later in the chapter. *Hindutva* refers to right-wing Hindu nationalism.

2. *BJP* refers to the Bharatiya Janata Party (Indian People's Party)—a Hindu chauvinist political party. *Dalits* are oppressed groups below the lowest caste. *CPI-ML* refers to the Communist Party of India—a Marxist-Leninist group.

The Ramjanmabhoomi movement is a political movement that takes its name from the project to reclaim the birthplace of the Hindu deity Ram. The movement gathered momentum in the late 1980s and peaked with the destruction of Babri Masjid, a sixteenth-century mosque in Ayodhya, Uttar Pradesh state, alleged to occupy the site of Ram's birth. See *Politics After Television: Religious Nationalism and the Retailing of "Hindu-ness,"* by Arvind Rajagopal (forthcoming from Cambridge University Press) for more on this movement and its repercussions.

3. Survey conducted in January 1994 at Stella Maris College, Madras, a private college for women, and in a housing colony at Ashoknagar, Madras.

4. See Madhava Prasad (1995) for an analysis of the politics of language hierarchy in the Indian context.

5. Ipsita Chanda (1991) makes a similar argument about two Bengali women's magazines, one of which she says is more sophisticated and up-market than the other.

6. Using the visual impact of fashion and fashion photography to appear "modern" is a common enough strategy employed by television advertisements and serials, films, and magazines. But often, the upper middle class regards particular kinds of obviously modern fashions as representing the crass culture of the nouveau riche. One student I spoke with during my survey pointed out that western clothes like trousers and skirts clash with plaited hair, *bindis* (the dot, usually red but also other colors, worn on the forehead by some South Asian women, and on occasion some South Asian men, for a variety of reasons), and Indian costume jewelry—that is, with bodies marked as traditional Indian.

7. According to Sumanta Banerjee, "the Vaishnava religion in Bengal, with its stress on the equality of man and woman among other things, provided room for Bengali women from different segments of society" (134). Banerjee notes that this religious cult accommodated widows, older prostitutes, abandoned women, the physically handicapped, and other social outcasts. Many Vaishnava women spent their days singing in the streets and begging alms from door to door.

8. See Tejaswini Niranjana's 1995 paper, in which she analyses the popular Indian film director Maniratnam's film *Bombay*. The film, released in early 1995, was produced in Tamil and Telugu and dubbed into Hindi. It narrativizes the love of Shekar, an upper-caste Hindu working for a newspaper in Bombay, and Shaila Banu, the daughter of a Muslim brick maker. After the couple get married, the Hindu-Muslim Bombay riots of January 1993 take place. Amidst scenes of rioting shot in documentary fashion, Shekar pleads with the rioters to stop their senseless violence. In response to his pleas, rioters from both the Hindu and the Muslim communities relinquish their weapons and hold hands. Niranjana argues that in *Bombay*, the capacity for romantic love is not only a significant marker of modernity, it is also seen as the highest form of secularism (20).

9. See also the introduction to Inderpal Grewal and Caren Kaplan (1994) for a discussion of modernist modes of representation.

Works Cited

Aiyer, V. V. S. 1930. "Penn Makkat Pagudi." *Ananda Vikatan*, December 15.

Balakesari, Valsala. 1991. "A Change for the Better." *Woman's Era*, October 1.

Banerjee, Sumanta. 1989. "Marginalization of Women's Popular Culture in Nineteenth Century Bengal." In Kumkum Sangari and Sudesh Vaid, eds. *Recasting Women: Essays in Indian Colonial History*. New Brunswick, New Jersey: Rutgers University Press.

Bharathi, C. Subramania. 1907. *Chakravartini*, April.

Chakravarti, Uma. 1989. "Whatever Happened to the Vedic *Dasi*? Orientalism, Nationalism and a Script for the Past." In Kumkum Sangari and Sudesh Vaid, eds. *Recasting Women: Essays in Indian Colonial History*. New Brunswick, New Jersey: Rutgers University Press.

Chanda, Ipsita. 1991. "Birthing Terrible Beauties: Feminisms and 'Women's Magazines.'" *Economic and Political Weekly*, Vol. 26, No.43: WS67–70.

Committee on the Status of Women in India, Government of India, 1974. *Towards Equality*. New Delhi.

Deshpande, Satish. 1993. "Imagined Economies: Style of Nation Building in Twentieth Century India." *Journal of Arts and Ideas*, Nos. 25–26: 5–35.

Dhareshwar, Vivek. 1993. "Caste and the Secular Self." *Journal of Arts and Ideas*, Nos. 25–26: 115-26.

Grewal, Inderpal, and Caren Kaplan, eds. 1994. *Scattered Hegemonies: Postmodernity and Transnational Feminist Practices*. Minneapolis: University of Minnesota Press.

Lakshmi, C. S. 1984. *The Face Behind the Mask*. New Delhi, India: Shakti.

Nawaz, Heera. 1991. *Woman's Era*, October 1.

Niranjana, Tejaswini. 1995. "Nationalism Refigured: Gender and Contemporary Popular Cinema." Draft of paper presented at Subaltern Studies Conference IX, June 1995.

Niranjana, Tejaswini, P. Sudhir, and Vivek Dhareshwar, eds. 1993. *Interrogating Modernity: Culture and Colonialism in India*. Calcutta, India: Seagull.

Pillai, Vedanayakam. 1950 (later edition). *Suguna Sundari Chartitram*. Madras, India.

Podder, Tanushree. 1992. "The 'Other Woman' Syndrome." *Woman's Era*, March 1.

Prasad, Madhava. 1993. "Cinema and the Desire for Modernity." *Journal of Arts and Ideas*, Nos. 25–26: 71–86.

———. 1995. "Teaching Capitalism as a Native Language." Paper presented at national seminar entitled "New Directions in English Studies," Department of English, University of Hyderabad, February 1995.

Sangari, Kumkum, and Sudesh Vaid, eds. 1989. *Recasting Women: Essays in Indian Colonial History*. New Brunswick, New Jersey: Rutgers University Press.

Sastrigal, Mahalinga. 1945. "Kadalam Kadalaradal." *Bharata Mani*. Madras, India.

Singh, Chandra. 1992. "Skin Care." *Woman's Era*, November 1.

Sunder Rajan, Rajeswari. 1993. *Real and Imagined Women: Gender, Culture, Post-colonialism*. London: Routledge.

Tharu, Susie, and K. Lalitha, eds. 1991. *Women Writing in India*, Vol. 1. New York: Feminist Press.

Tharu, Susie, and Tejaswini Niranjana. 1994. "Problems for a Contemporary Theory of Gender." *Social Scientist*, Vol. 22, Nos. 3–4: 93–117.

Tyagi, Amita, and Patricia Uberoi. 1990. "Adjustment Is the Key: Post Marital Romance in Indian Popular Fiction." *Manushi*, Vol. 61: 15–s21.

University Education Committee, Government of India. Report, Vol. 1, December 1948 to August 1949.

Woman's Era, June 2, 1992.

Woman's Era, November 2, 1992.

Chapter Fifteen

In a Neighborhood of Another Color: Latina/Latino Struggles for Home

SUSAN SÁNCHEZ CASAL

Those who don't know any better come into our neighborhood scared. They think we're dangerous. They think we will attack them with shiny knives. They are stupid people who are lost and got here by mistake.

All brown all around, we are safe. But watch us drive into a neighborhood of another color and our knees go shakity-shake and our car windows get rolled up tight and our eyes look straight. Yeah. That's how it goes and goes.
—**Sandra Cisneros,** *The House on Mango Street*

I am a light-skinned Latina who grew up in the Borderlands of southern California. My father's parents come from Asturias, a region in northern Spain, and immigrated to the United States in the 1920s. My paternal grandparents came to this country in economic exile, not searching for the American Dream as it is represented in national, stereotypical images, but seeking the opportunity to see their dream grow in America. My mother was born in Puerto Rico and lived the first six years of her life there. When my mother was two years old, her parents left their Caribbean island for New York, in search of greater economic opportunity. My mother was left behind with her grandmother and would not arrive in the South

Bronx, New York, for another four years. Both families eventually made their way to southern California, with the dream of becoming ranchers.

I was born in Wilmington, California, a barrio of southeast Los Angeles. Growing up in a community of people who came in hundreds of shades of brown, I was *"la güerita,"* the light-skinned one. It was not until my family edged closer to the White/Anglo community that I began to understand how I was *raced,* or *racialized,* by White people. I remember the exact moment we crossed the racial/ethnic border and how in that crossing I *became* a person of color.

When I was still a child, my family moved from our Mexican/Chicano/Latino neighborhood to Compton, California, which at that time was predominantly White. I remember our neighbors, the Zeislers, coming out to greet my parents. During the course of the conversation I watched something change in my father's face as Mr. Zeisler said, "We're so relieved now that we've finally met you; when the realtor told us that the new family moving in was named Sánchez, we almost put the house up for sale!" Like the Cordero family in Sandra Cisneros's *The House on Mango Street,* the Sánchez family's entrance into "mainstream" America brought us face-to-face with the hegemony of Whiteness. Although Mr. Zeisler was acting friendly, smiling and congratulating us for being light skinned and "looking like any other family on the block," his evaluation of our racial and social acceptability was complicated and insidious. My father's reaction was also complicated. His smile was a gesture of humility, an act of submission, a disguise. I'm sure my father was relieved at Zeisler's gesture, relieved that we wouldn't be ostracized or blamed for the neighborhood "going to hell," but what I remember most was the look of shame I recorded on his face. As Cherríe Moraga has said about her own experience as a Chicana lesbian, I found out quite early in life that "I was born into this world with complications" (Moraga, 1984, ii).

Although my family's light skin earned us race privilege, redeeming us in the eyes of our neighbors and many times allowing us to pass undetected, the name Sánchez was a racial marker that stubbornly announced our identity as undesirable ethnic and racial outsiders. I would learn to despise that name, to fear its repercussions, and to envy other light-skinned Latinas and Latinos whose names were less "incriminating." What we learned from Zeisler that day was that we were perceived as trespassers on White land. Intruders. And this was our new *home.* We soon learned, however, that taking up residence in White southern Californian suburbia would require some fancy footwork. So we put ourselves to the hideous task, working daily to chisel away the signs of our difference, oh so careful not to stand out among the model of Whiteness we were just beginning to understand. We refashioned ourselves according to the obstinate dictates of the gringo. We learned not to speak Spanish (to this day I can still hear my father's "Speak English!" ringing in my ears),[1] not to yell or laugh too loud, not to play Latin or Spanish music, not to dress Latin, not to have too many Latino people over at once. My struggle for self-definition began in that border crossing, when I first confronted Latino ontologies formed by the dominant race: as Latinas and Latinos in the Borderlands, our social value is proportionate to the degree that we don't resemble *what we are*.

As a middle-class Latina who grew up in a neighborhood of another color, I carry both the privilege and the burden of my light olive skin. I know that my skin color and middle-class status have opened doors for me that remain closed to the majority of Latinas who are dark skinned and survive at or below the poverty level. I have enjoyed my race and class privileges and know that they have helped me get where I wanted to go; I won't deny it. I know what it's like to be rewarded by dominant society for my exceptional, light-skinned performance in a Latina role. When I stand to hail a taxi in New York, the driver doesn't see a Latina. He sees a woman. When I sit in airplanes, White people sometimes tell me racist jokes. They don't see *me*. Once I was on a plane, and the White man sitting next to me told me he was leaving southern California for Pennsylvania. "Too many Blacks and Mexicans," he said; "*you know what I mean.*" So when he asked me how I liked living and teaching in a small town in central New York, I said, "Oh, it's OK, but I'm Latina, so it's really hard for me to be in a place where there are so few people of color." He looked at me like he was waiting for the punch line, so I said, "*You know what I mean.*" He knew exactly what I meant, because after our little "talk," he gulped down three glasses of wine and didn't look my way for the rest of the flight. My Latina identity is something I carry inside, something I can pull out and surprise others with. Something I use like a weapon when the dominant seek the complicity of my light skin. Something I could hide, if I wanted to.

Some Latinas and Latinos hate the light-skinned among us because they say we have a "choice." But as Ana Castillo says, "An Anglicized brown woman always walks a delicate tightrope. Denial of her mestizaje does not change *what she is*" (my italics; 1994, 171). I know what Castillo means, because there was a time in my life when I tried desperately to change what I was. As a Latina child growing up in the White suburban landscape of southern California, I was taught a million times to hate my Latinaness. I remember one year—I must have been ten years old—I was playing in the Bobby Sox softball league (my childhood passion). One of the team mothers was hateful to me and repeatedly tried to get me taken off the starting lineup. I was hurt and afraid of her and, above all, confused. Two of her daughters were my teammates. One day I asked one of the girls why her mother hated me so much; what had I done wrong? The girl replied coolly, "She doesn't hate *you*, Susan; she just hates all Mexicans." After being told so many times by White childhood friends that I couldn't come to their houses to play (nor they to mine) because I was "Mexican," or that their parents didn't like me "because I was Mexican," I finally got the message.[2] So I tried to move to their side of the street. I tried to be White. I "passed" whenever and wherever I could.[3] I used to race my grandmother to the phone, terrorized that her thickly accented "hello" would blow my cover. I even started lying to people, telling them that my dad was Mexican but my mom was White, feeling that any claim to Whiteness, however small, would allow me to "cross the border" (I had, by then, given up the futile attempt to explain to people that my father was Spanish, not Mexican). I vividly remember a classmate—ironically, the only one who believed I was Puerto Rican—explaining why I couldn't come to her birthday party: "You can't come to my party because my mom says that all Puerto Ricans are Black." When I explained my classmate's comment to my anglicized, light-skinned Puerto Rican mother, she started yelling, "We're Caucasian! We're as Caucasian as anybody else!" *Híjole mano*, I was confused. But as Castillo says, even if I *could* have hidden my ethnicity from people who despised it in me, it didn't change *what I was*. In fact, after years of swallowing the jagged racism that White society delivered to me in so many doses, after years of "choosing" to be White, hiding my brownness and silencing the Puerto Rican voices of my grandmother and my mother, I rebelled. In my twenties, I joined MEChA (Movimiento Estudiantil Chicano de Aztlán), the Chicano student association. I started to read everything and anything written by Latin Americans and Latinos and Latinas. I began to see the name Sánchez everywhere: protagonists, authors, historical figures. It was the first time I had ever seen my last name displayed with dignity, and I began to assume my Latinaness with a defiant vengeance. *¡Que viva la raza Latina!* I was angry—angry with the White world that made me experience my Latinaness as something filthy, angry with myself and with my parents for having accepted and internalized its filthy judgment.[4]

Because I am a light-skinned Latina, the racial and ethnic borders I cross have complicated my struggle for identity. I know what it's like to be rejected and suspected not only by dominant society, but by my own people as well. I know the pain of feeling "neither/nor." I know how it feels to walk in the shoes of the eternal impostor, to be submitted to the Latina "test" over and over, to apologize continually for my privilege of being able to "pass," constantly feeling the need to prove my ethnic loyalty. When I'm around other Latinas and Latinos who look more "mestizo," I worry about my light skin, about the "uncoolness" of my awkward, educated Spanish, about the shifting borders of my Latina identity. In the Southwest, Mexicans and Chicanos hear the Puerto Rican inflection in my Spanish; in the East, Puerto Ricans and Dominicans hear the Chicana in me. I never stop being an outsider. I have trouble accepting the "Whiteness" in me, although its signs are a dynamic part of who I am and who I have been. Within the context of our racist society, the heterogeneity of Latino *mestizaje* works against us. The fact that society has rewarded me for my light skin and class status has privileged me over other Latinas. I have been admitted to rooms where other Latinas who don't look or sound like me have been denied. Does this make me a betrayer of my race? Does this disqualify me from claiming full-fledged Latina status? How do I legitimately claim community with other Latinas and Latinos whose lives and experiences do not resemble mine?

I still struggle to get to the truth about myself, about what being a Latina means and has meant to me in the context of the racist politics of this country and my own personal history. What I have learned so far is that I do have "choice," but not about my racial and ethnic identification. In my conflictive struggle for identity, I have chosen to transform a reductionist politic of identity into one that dialogues with the specificity of my experience. I reject the monological idea that I must be "either this *or* that"; my identity as a Latina has emerged from the dynamic tension of my own heterogeneity and from my struggle to include and accept all of it. I am a woman of color whose *mestizaje* spills out from the chaotic corners of personal and political experience and struggle: I was born Puerto Rican, but I speak Spanish like an educated Chicana from the Southwest; most of the time I feel more at home in English than in Spanish; some days I'm both Chicana and Puerto Rican (I put *chipotle* on my *picadillo*, for example); Latin Americans have told me that I'm a "gringa," White people prefer to see me White, and brown people may not recognize me as one of their own, but I am brown inside.

I am a politicized mestiza of the Borderlands of the United States whose path has extended from the Latino barrio of Wilmington, California, to the white picket fences of upstate New York. I cannot say that I feel "at home" in my present location, but I can say that it has been within my struggle to find "home" that I have begun to discover who I am and *who I can be* in this world. In this chapter I provide a way of thinking about the conflictive processes by which Latinas and Latinos claim "home" in the United States—at the national level, within our own communities, within academia, and within our varying shades of skin.

Difference and Visibility

Although the majority of Latinas and Latinos living in the Borderlands share a common historical and social experience, Latinos remain a heterogeneous group, both racially and socially. Our *mestizaje* includes indigenous, African, European, Islamic, Jewish, and Asian ancestors. Sharp demographic differences also exist among Latinos: in general, among the three largest Latino groups, Mexicans and Puerto Ricans are the poorest (Puerto Ricans in the United States are poorer, on the whole, than African Americans); Cubans are the most economically privileged Latinos, although considerable stratification exists within the Cuban community in Florida (Rodríguez, 1994, 7). The arrival of more recent immigrants from Central and South America and the Dominican Republic is causing great tension in previously Mexican and Puerto Rican communities, partially due to the fact that employers are replacing Puerto Ricans with Dominicans and other recent Latino immigrants whom they now prefer to exploit as a cheaper labor force. Class differences within the Latino community are especially apparent in the case of Cubans and Cuban Americans living in the United States. The first major wave of Cuban immigrants to the United States followed Fidel Castro's overthrow of the Batista regime in 1959. Although the majority of Mexicans, Puerto Ricans, Dominicans, and recent Central and South American immigrants are dark skinned and of the rural peasant or urban working class, first-wave Cuban immigrants included mostly the light-skinned upper classes of Cuban society and its most highly skilled labor force. Furthermore, because first-wave Cubans were fleeing a government obstinately opposed to U.S. neocolonization of Latin America, the U.S. government responded generously by funding and implementing programs to assist in their relocation: retraining of workers, medical benefits, welfare, and tuition assistance. Many Cubans don't consider the United States their home or identify themselves as Latinos. As political exiles, they continue to wait for the fall of Castro's government, hoping someday to return home to Cuba.

Latinas and Latinos in the United States are often perceived and represented as newly arrived or illegal immigrants.[5] The sweeping notion of Latinos as foreigners who steal jobs from U.S. citizens fuels exaggerated ideas about the threat of Latin American illegal immigration to the United States. When "average Americans" think "illegal alien," they immediately see a Mexican or a Central American face, yet outside the border areas, Mexicans and Central Americans make up less than half of the illegal immigrant population. In fact, in 1995 the *New York Times* reported that slightly more than half of the nation's illegal immigrants (from Italy, Poland, Ireland, Canada, France, Sweden, and other non-Latino countries) enter the country effortlessly, as tourists, students, or businesspeople, and then simply overstay their visas. Although the Immigration and Naturalization Service spends millions to patrol the United States' southwestern border, the agency virtually ignores those light-skinned illegal immigrants who walk in through the nation's front door. Yet in spite of these statistics, as Cecilia Muñoz, deputy vice president of the National

Council of La Raza, reports, 99 percent of immigration enforcement efforts are directed at Latinas and Latinos (Dunn, 1995, 5).

But many of us never crossed a geographical border, and because of the colonial relationship between the United States and Puerto Rico and the neocolonial relationship between the United States and Mexico,[6] our experience cannot be read through the history of White immigration in America. Latinas and Latinos, even those born in the United States, are often reminded of their status as "foreigners." Unlike the legacy of slavery, which explains both the presence of African Americans in the United States and their history of resistance to slavery and internal colonization, no analogous historical marker exists for Latinos. Our reason for being here is not understood as the *effect* of the colonialist and neocolonialist history of our nation. "So when are you going back to your country?" is a question often posed not only to recent Latin American immigrants but also to United States–born Latinas and Latinos, longtime Latina/Latino residents, and naturalized citizens of the United States. The darker the skin, the lower the wage, the more we're asked.

Although Puerto Ricans were granted U.S. citizenship in 1917, our right to claim a home here is challenged by dominant society. In the collection of short stories *El Bronx Remembered* by *Nuyorican* Nicholasa Mohr, Vickie, a thirteen-year-old Puerto Rican born in New York, meets with an attorney because her mother has been picked up for running numbers. The attorney greets her in Spanish:

"¿Cómo estás?" Mr. Crane laughed softly. "See, how's that? I love Spanish and I love your country. My family and I were in San Juan last winter. What an island of paradise! You should be proud of your country Victoria. I know many, many Puerto Ricans. They visit us and we visit them"(1975, 41).

Whereas Mr. Crane sees Puerto Ricans as "visitors" who will, like all visitors, go back "home" someday, the narrator steps in to inform the reader that "Vickie and her younger sisters and brother were born in New York and had seldom left the Bronx. Every morning in school they pledged allegiance 'to the flag of the United States of America, and to the Republic for which it stands.' She had never thought of Puerto Rico as her country"(40). Puerto Ricans, whose Caribbean island was invaded and colonized by the United States in 1898, continue to be seen as "outsiders" in America and often find themselves "proving" to others that they belong here. Around White Americans the Latino "becomes" *less than*, yet in the Latin American or Caribbean countries that we are told we belong to, we are often rejected as outsiders, traitors, even delinquents. "*Ni de aquí ni de allá*,"[7] Latinas and Latinos are defined according to hegemonic models that push them to the borders of national identity. Self-definition becomes an act of defiance.[8]

Racist attitudes and ignorance about New York Puerto Ricans are not restricted to the "mainland," however. Many Puerto Ricans on the island are ashamed of *Nuyoricans,* seeing them as national "traitors" and troublemakers. They fear that the "bad reputation" *Nuyoricans* have acquired in the United States will tarnish the names of Puerto Ricans everywhere. And they have reason to fear. While I was in Peru last summer, a Peruvian taxi driver started talking to me about the States. "I have a cousin who lives in New York," he said. "He loves your country, but it's not easy for him there. It's too bad there are so many Puerto Ricans in New York. They ruin everything. They make it hard for Latin Americans to be accepted." After intervening to tell the taxi driver that I was Puerto Rican, sparing myself any more "insight" on his part, I started thinking about borders, about how the crossing of the U.S. border, for the Latin American, requires a "splitting of self." The Latin American immigrant—like the U.S. Latina or Latino child who experiences race hate—sees him or herself being seen by dominant society as the degraded "other" and tries to establish distance from those rejected in White consciousness. What the Peruvian taxi driver's cousin doesn't understand is that—within the context of racialization in the United States—Latin American national identity is flattened and subsumed into a diasporic notion of Latino nation. In the United States his cousin loses his Peruvian national status; he *unbecomes* Peruvian and becomes Latino. Regardless of their racial composition, the great majority of Latin Americans in the United States *become* people of color. And as people of color, their fate in this nation is tied to the fate of all Latinos.

Let Me Speak!

Not me sold out my people but they me. So yes, though "home" permeates every sinew and cartilage in my body, I too am afraid of going home.
—Gloria Anzaldúa, *Borderlands: La Frontera,* 21

Latinas and Latinos have actively resisted colonization in the United States. In the last thirty years, Chicano/Latino political movement has fueled the struggles of Cesar Chávez and Mexican/Latino farmworkers, the Chicano Moratorium against the Vietnam War, and the Chicano and Puerto Rican Civil Rights Movements of the 1960s and 1970s. Although Latinas and Latinos have struggled together against racist institutions and politics, in our own communities the historical experience of the Latina woman and the social and political conditions of her life remain largely invisible and unquestioned. We can assume that of the estimated 23 million Latinos in the United States, about half are women. One million households are headed by Latina women, who comprise the lowest-paid labor force in the country. Fifty-two percent of those households survive below the poverty level (Castillo, 1994, 37). Latina feminists have

actively engaged in theorizing the Latina/Latino experience, in redefining our histories—both in the United States and in the indigenous,
African, and European cultures of our ancestors—and in fighting racist
and sexist institutions, struggling for reproductive rights, battered-
women's shelters, rape crisis centers, welfare advocacy, health and self-
help clinics, voter registration, and labor regulation (Moraga, 1984, 106).
In the 1970s Latina feminists and other feminists of color exposed and
fought against the U.S. government's sterilization of nonconsenting poor
women and in this struggle made known the fact that during that period
one-third of the female population of Puerto Rico was permanently steril-
ized (Castillo, 1994, 35). But in spite of the fact that Latinas have fought
both the effects and the structures of racism alongside Latino men and
worked to create a supportive infrastructure in our communities, politically engaged Latinos (and antifeminist Latinas) have accused us of dilut-
ing the struggle for collective liberation for all Latinos by acknowledging
the antisexist imperatives of third world feminist struggle.

In response to those who would silence us, Latina feminists pose a
compelling question: how can a liberation struggle that articulates the
historical grievances of an oppressed people ignore the specific conditions of external and internal oppression of half of its population? As
Latina feminists, we have never abandoned the imperatives of antiracist
struggle; on the contrary, it is we who have been abandoned in our struggle to acknowledge and change external and internal conditions that create and reproduce woman's social inferiority. Latina feminists understand that the systems that support racism, sexism, and homophobia are
inextricably linked, and we therefore struggle for the eradication of all re-
lational oppressions. Those of us who are shoved to the margins of national and cultural experience by more than one "ism" know through experience that suffering multiple oppressions makes us *more* likely to
become politicized, something that supports all Latino movement for social justice (not detracts from it). But because "women's issues" are trivi-
alized and continue to be seen as a "special," peripheral category, Latina
feminists who struggle on the front lines for social justice for all women
of color are charged with treason. Norma Alarcón argued that the charge
of betrayal is wielded upon women to silence us and stall feminist consciousness and movement. She stated:

> The charge [of betrayal] remains as a clear image imprinted on Chicanas
> (and I believe most Third World women, in this country or outside of it) by
> men. It continues to urge us to make quantum leaps towards a male ideolo-
> gized humanism devoid of female consciousness. The lure of an ideal hu-
> manism is seductive, especially for spiritual women such as we have often
> been brought up to be; but without female consciousness and envisioning
> *how as women we would like to exist in the material world*, to leap into humanism

without repossessing ourselves may be exchanging one male ideology for another. (emphasis added, 1981, 188)

For Latinas, the key word in Alarcón's analysis is *envisioning*. She is arguing that we must bring the quality of vision, of imagination, into our struggle, so that we know not only what we are fighting against, but what we would like to see put in its place. "Repossessing ourselves" means cultivating imagination, political consciousness, and social practice outside the bounds of conventional patriarchal logic. We must engage feminist vision and practice to envision new homes for ourselves, spaces that reflect how we would like to exist in the world. But reimagining ourselves and our surroundings is a difficult thing for Latinas to do, since we have been trained to submit quietly to authority, shamed into lowering our eyes in the face of male power, threatened into not questioning the order of things. The Latina who dares to question is seen as a sellout to White society and may find herself terrorized by the words *"Te estás poniendo muy gringa"* ("You're starting to act like a White woman"). So when *do* Latinas earn the right to criticize those ideological bases of our oppressed cultures that oppress *us*? Our voices and our vision are welcome when we support male practice and ideology but discounted when we insist on seeing and speaking ourselves.[9] Gloria Anzaldúa turns the charge of betrayal on its head, by working to identify and reject those customs and values of our cultures that betray us:

> No, I do not buy all the myths of the tribe into which I was born. . . . My Chicana identity is grounded in the Indian woman's history of resistance. . . . I feel perfectly free to rebel and rail against my culture; . . . and if going home is denied me, then I will have to stand and claim my space, making a new culture—una cultura mestiza—with my own lumber, my own bricks and mortar, and my own feminist architecture. (1987, 22)

Latinas have fought racism and classism alongside our men, with them and for them; as Latina feminists, we challenge our communities to make a home for our struggles, to support us in feminist awareness and movement, to fight sexism and homophobia with us and for us.

Free the Daughters

Todavía soy la hija de mi mamá *["I am still my mother's daughter"]. Keep thinking, it's the daughters. It's the daughters who remain loyal to the mother. She is the only woman we stand by. It is not always reciprocated. To be free means on some level to cut that painful loyalty when it begins to punish us. Stop the chain of events.* La procesión de mujeres, sufriendo *["The procession of women, suffering"]. Dolores my grandmother, Dolores her daughter, Dolores her*

daughter's daughter. Free the daughter to love her own daughter. It is the daugh-
ters who are my audience.[10]

—Cherríe Moraga,
Loving in the War Years: Lo que nunca pasó por sus labios

Latinas, like other women of color in the United States, experience simultaneously the triple jeopardy of racism, sexism, and classism. Like all
women, we are the consistent victims of male violence: rape, battering,
emotional abuse, confinement. Resisting male dominance and abuse is
particularly challenging for Latinas, since we are taught from childhood
that submission and silence are the highest degree of femininity. Prescribed notions of Latina femininity are deeply rooted in the family and
in Catholic mythology, in which female subservience to male authority is
issued from the pulpit on Sundays. One of the fiercest historical bases of
Latina subjugation is the Latin American cult of the Virgin Mary—known
as *Marianismo*—which proclaims the superior moral and spiritual qualities of woman while simultaneously demanding her social inferiority.
Marianismo inauthentically "exalts" the figure of woman, mystifying her
essential nature as semidivine and, consequently, narrowing her range of
human complexity and potential.

The process of *Marianismo* in our cultures is complex: the socially sanctioned moral superiority of the Latina allows her to exercise considerable
power in the domestic sphere, especially with regard to the rearing of
children. It also creates a space in the Latino imaginary for the "strong, capable, insightful woman," something that might explain why there have
been women presidents in Latin America (something we have yet even to
propose in this country). The limitations imposed (and self-imposed) on
women by the tenets of *Marianismo* are compelling, yet the existence of a
divine female icon also works *for* women, as long, of course, as their actions do not defy the power of men. As long as the Latina submits to *Marianismo's* prescription of abnegation and submission, she is esteemed in
the eyes of the community. In all of her traditional roles, the Latina continues to exist for men, chastising herself for "selfishness" if she struggles
for her own desire and freedom and in the process fails to please her man.
Those who dare to subvert this model are pushed to the borders of the
Latino community, where we struggle to reimagine the feminine. Virgins,
martyrs, renegades. And not much in between. Latina lesbians and feminists rail against these limitations, battling fiercely to free ourselves from
this imposed reduction of who we can be.

Latinas who subvert traditional models of womanhood risk alienation
and rejection from our families, our churches, and our communities. Home
and family nurture and support us, yet for the Latina, home and family can
be threatening structures that imprison us, compromise our integrity and

potential as women, and deny us access to the outside world. Consequently, Latina feminists are actively searching for ways to leave the patriarchal home and, in Gloria Anzaldúa's words, to "enter the world":

> The culture expects women to show greater acceptance of, and commitment to, the value system than men. The culture and the Church insist that women are subservient to males. If a woman rebels, she is a *mujer mala* [bad woman]. If a woman doesn't renounce herself in favor of the male, she is selfish. If a woman remains a *virgin* until she is married, she is a good woman. For a woman of my culture there used to be only three directions she could turn: to the Church as a nun, to the streets as a prostitute, or to the home as a mother. Today some of us have a fourth choice: *entering the world* [my italics] by way of education and career and becoming self-autonomous persons. (1987, 17)

For politically conscious Latinas, the price for "entering the world" and becoming the women we want to be can be domestic exile. Cherríe Moraga reports that the questions she is most often asked by students, the majority of them Chicano and Chicana, are "Can you go home? Do your parents know? Have they read your work?"(1984, iv). "It's as if they're hungry to know if it's possible to have both," Moraga states, "your own life and the life of the familia"(1984, iv). The real question, I believe, is not whether we can go home again or not, but what the "going home" will mean to us, what it will "cost." As radical Latinas we often feel like outsiders in our own families, so much so that "going home" is both a literal and an imaginal process. We look for soulful ways to negotiate our differences so that we *can* go home, so that the supportive community that we share in our families continues to thrive, yet we know that the family home cannot reflect back to us the kind of women we are, nor how we exist and would like to exist in the world. Too much gets left at the doorstep. So the answer to the question is, "Yes," I can have my own life and the life of the family, but in some significant ways, the two will always stand apart. I am always welcome but seldom *at home* in my parents' house. I am the bridge where the woman and the daughter face each other in loving confrontation.

Latinas who do go home walk a tightrope of gender loyalty. Most of our mothers and grandmothers had few ways of leaving the patriarchal home, few "worlds to enter into," and therefore resigned themselves to the rigid codes of femininity spelled out for them in our cultures. They learned to serve, to please, to endure, to yield, to whittle themselves down to the limitations of *Marianismo*. Cherríe Moraga tells this story about her mother:

> When my mother had been our age, over forty years earlier, she had waited on her brothers and their friends. . . . They'd come in from work or a day's drinking. And las mujeres, often just in from the fields themselves, would

already be in the kitchen making tortillas, warming frijoles or pigs feet, albóndigas soup, what-have-you. And the men would get a clean white tablecloth and a spread of food laid out before their eyes and not a word of resentment from the women. (1984, 91)

Our mothers did what they were supposed to do and much more, convinced that their place in Latino patriarchy was the natural and divinely sanctioned order of things. (Although I'm sure I speak for most Latinas when I say that our mothers were anything but passive or sad women.) But the self-sacrifice implicit in conforming to the dictates of Latino patriarchy has robbed our mothers of choice and filled them with remorse. In *The House on Mango Street* Esperanza Cordero's mother sighs as she tells her daughter, "I could've been somebody, you know?" As Latina daughters of women whose options were limited or fixed by others, we experience "home" as an ambivalent, threatening space that punishes women and compromises their freedom to act. It is the witnessing of our mothers' lives that makes us think to ourselves growing up: "I don't want a life like hers." Our first move as budding Latina feminists is a negation; we know what kind of a life *we don't want*. Yet we ask ourselves: since I consciously decide not to follow the model of subjected womanhood provided for me by my mother, how do I reimagine myself as a Latina daughter struggling to define her mission in life, while still honoring the history and process of all of the *mamás* and *abuelas* (grandmothers) whose mission was decided for them? How do I question traditional models and functions of womanhood *without questioning the women* who came before me and devaluing their experience? How is communication and community possible between Latina women of different generations whose lives barely resemble each other's?

In my house, when I was growing up, my sister and I were expected to serve the men in the family, especially our father. When it occurred to me that my father asked only my sister and me to make him his endless cup of coffee, I asked him why he never asked my brothers for service. His reply was "Because the boys don't know how to make coffee like you do!" This was true, but the only reason they didn't know how was because no one ever asked them to do it. But I was in daughter/wife training and knew exactly how my father wanted his coffee—strong, with a little milk and exactly one teaspoon of sugar. When my brothers married, they wouldn't need that training; their wives would be making the coffee. My sister and I were also expected to do the boys' chores when they had more exciting activities—sports mainly—to attend to. When we objected to this double standard, seeing no reason in the world why our lazy brothers had earned the right to special treatment, my *abuela* would laugh and tell us not to waste our time getting upset. "It's easier just to give them what they want so they'll get out of here and leave us alone!" she would say and laugh. I grew up in the kitchen, with my mother and grandmother and my little sister, listening to my *abuela's* stories about life in Puerto Rico, laughing at her raunchy jokes (I can still hear my offended mother pleading with her to stop: *"Mamá, ¡por favor!"*). It was there, in the traditional Latina kitchen, that I first heard the ambiguous rumblings of female resistance to male power. If I could paraphrase my grandmother's attitude—an attitude frequently exhibited in Latina kitchens—about woman's relationship to man, it might sound like this:

> Men are a nuisance and certainly not what they pretend to be, but it's our job not to let them know how silly and annoying they are to us. We do what tradition asks of us, we even accept that men are the chosen ones, but secretly, to ourselves, we're always looking down on them. They're not as strong as we are. They stand and stick their chests out like proud roosters, when really, they're just like children who need a mother. We can live without them, but they can't live without us.

The dynamics of *Marianismo* are transparent in this example: Latina women assume the pedestal by believing that they are morally superior to men, yet they understand that the only way they may remain on the throne is by hiding their feelings from men and not acting on what they know. Powerful, but closeted, female subjectivity: the queen must assume the posture of the servant to preserve her title. Latina daughters are increasingly unwilling to assume that posture, although the road back home can be filled with mindful compromise, as Moraga reports:

> When my sister and I were fifteen and fourteen, respectively, and my brother a few years older, we were still waiting on him. I write "were" as if now, nearly two decades later, it were over. But that would be a lie. To this day in my mother's home, my brother and father are waited on, including by me. I do this out of respect for my mother and her wishes. (1984, 90)

From Remorse to Resistance

In *The House on Mango Street* Chicana Sandra Cisneros writes about a young Latina girl's desire to leave home and enter the world through education, writing, and self-exploration. This text forms part of the growing body of Latina literature that defiantly and lovingly criticizes the Latina experience from within. *House* tells stories about Latinas who are full of desire and potential but cannot escape their confinement and abuse in the houses of fathers and husbands. Although *House* creates positive, dynamic Latina characters, the text focuses on the oppression of Latinas by repeatedly employing the metaphor of women sitting by the window, tragically staring at the world outside that they cannot engage. The figure of the caged, frustrated Latina shapes Cisneros's text, establishing an opposition between traditional Latinas who "cannot out" and Esperanza, the new, subversive Latina daughter who dreams of leaving the patriarchal home.

Although *House* does more than produce a criticism of the gendered politics of Latino homes, the text is mainly concerned with Esperanza's growing feminist awareness and her desire to dismantle the patriarchal logic that rules Mango Street. At first, her desire to have "a real house," one she "can point to," is motivated by the shame of internalized classism. In the first story, Esperanza tells us that the house on Mango Street "is not the house we'd thought we'd get." Both Esperanza and her parents dream the elusive, White American Dream: "Our house would be white with trees around it, a great big yard and grass growing without a fence. This was the house Papa talked about when he held a lottery ticket and this was the house Mama dreamed up in the stories she told us before we went to bed" (1989, 4).

But Esperanza's dream to leave Mango Street soon diverges from her parents' and becomes all her own, as she begins to examine the conditions of her own life and those of the women around her. Leaving Mango Street and finding a new home becomes a political project inspired by feminist desire. Esperanza doesn't want a house where she will continue to exist as the traditional Latina daughter and wife. She wants a house of her own, a woman's house: "Not a flat. Not an apartment in back. Not a man's house. Not a daddy's. A house all my own. With my porch and my pillow, my pretty purple petunias. My books and my stories. My two shoes waiting beside the bed. Nobody to shake a stick at. Nobody's garbage to pick up after. Only a house quiet as snow, a space for myself to go, clean as paper before the poem" (108).

Esperanza dreams of a home that serves as refuge and sanctuary for female autonomy. Although she does not—unlike the majority of female characters in the text—directly experience male violence, Esperanza begins to rebel against the double standard for men and women that exists in her home. In questioning the order of things, she questions and resists not only her own father's hegemonic position, but all the institutional bases that support the practice of coercive male power. Esperanza dreams of a house where the bounds of female experience are unlimited, a house where she can leave her plate on the table if she feels like it, a house that defies female servitude, a house she won't get stuck or trapped in. Esperanza loves her mother and her grandmother, but she rejects their resigned space at the window, finding in their frustrated gaze the seeds of her own resistance. It is Esperanza's ability to see and interpret her own reality through subversive eyes that moves her toward Latina feminist consciousness. "I have begun my own quiet war," she says. "Simple. Sure. I am one who leaves the table like a man, without putting back the chair or picking up the plate"(89).

Unlike her friends Sally, Minerva, and Rafaela, who remain trapped in the conditions of their oppression by choosing a "false exit" to Mango Street (marriage), Esperanza struggles to escape the double oppression of ethnicity and gender authentically; she will not remap the location of woman's oppression from father's to husband's house, but will create a new, subversive space of her own. Esperanza confronts the mythologies of Latina femininity by imagining a new way of being. She understands that escaping the family home is not enough; one must leave by the right door. Esperanza, the daughter, the new Latina, asks the question that never made it to our mothers' lips: *What kind of life do I want to lead? What kind of woman do I want to be?*

In Spanish *esperanza* means "hope." But it also means "waiting." The Latinas who populate *House* are more patient than hopeful, something that Esperanza refuses to be. She has inherited her name from her great-grandmother, "a horse woman" who refused to marry until she was forced to: "And the story goes she never forgave him. She looked out the window her whole life, the way so many women sit their sadness on an elbow. I wonder if she made the best with what she got or was she sorry because she couldn't be all the things she wanted to be. Esperanza. I have inherited her name, but I don't want to inherit her place by the window" (11).

In *House,* women's desire is usually expressed in negation or condition—"I would have been," "I could have been," "she couldn't be," "I don't want." The new has not yet emerged, but the old is full of soulful stories of Latinas' frustrated desire. This conditional discursive world has sometimes been interpreted as a sign of Latina resignation and remorse, a static rehashing of past grievances. But I challenge those who see this text as "pessimistic" to examine the racist and sexist underpinnings of that evaluation. Since the real conditions of Latinas' lives have hardly been examined or questioned, it is essential that we unearth and examine what has been buried so that we may transform and redirect it into the flow of feminist movement. Our mothers' stories are old, but their function in this text, and in our lives, is new. What is new about this chronicling of the remorse of our mothers and grandmothers is the text's organization of those shadow stories into a feminist knowledge base that creates Esperanza's liberating consciousness. As Esperanza thinks and feels through the experience of other Latinas—even and especially those unlike her—she begins to understand that her political location as a Latina daughter is not part of a natural geography. Esperanza's exceptionality and individual action are possible because she does not distinguish herself from the collective experience of Latinas; instead she assumes their histories in her own struggle for change.[11] With clear political imagination, Latina daughters struggle to transform our mothers' and grandmothers' and great-grandmothers' regret into feminist desire and movement.

As women of color who advocate and participate in third world feminist movements, returning to the family home means confronting our "otherness." I have enjoyed privileges that were altogether denied to my mother, who is also light skinned but grew up poor in the South Bronx. When my feminist consciousness was ready to be raised, a radical movement of women of color—which did not exist for her—challenged, supported, nurtured, and educated me. I have achieved an autonomy that has made my mother proud but also envious and sometimes resentful of me. My mother, like Esperanza Cordero's, "could've been a contender" too. She has often told me stories of remorse, of how she wanted to be a lab technician, but her father refused to let her continue her education. About how, when she was born, her father was so furious that she wasn't a boy that he refused to look at her for a week! About how she too would have liked to become a professor or a writer, if only she'd had the chance. In her late fifties, after all five kids had left the house, my mother enrolled in courses at Cal State Long Beach and four years later graduated with honors with a B.A. in anthropology. But even this accomplishment was tinged with sadness and remorse, because she felt it was too late for her "to do anything with it." I believe that my mother didn't try to use her degree professionally because she was socially intimidated. Because of the disempowering consequences of racism, classism, and sexism, my mother did not feel ready to leave home and "enter the world." The words of Mitsuye Yamada about the relationship of her mother's life to Yamada's own movement toward feminist consciousness may apply to all third world feminists:

> I, a second generation Asian American woman who grew up believing in the American Dream, have come to know who I am through understanding the nature of my mother's experience: I have come to see connections in our lives as well as the lives of many women like us, and through her I have become more sensitive to the needs of Third World women throughout the world. (1981, 74)

Assuming the historical oppression of our mothers supports us in the struggle for the liberation of all women of color. Although we cannot change their external conditions nor use their experience of traditional womanhood as a model for our own, we *can* make their conflictive situations the loving source of our movement for social change. We cannot "free" our mothers, nor insist that they free us, but we can work to free ourselves, the daughters, to love the daughters who come after us.

Straightening Up the Master's House: The Multicultural Academy

The need for broad-based political coalition among all peoples of color has never been more urgent than today. Reminding us of the retro-politics of Reaganomics, the Republican Congress that came into office in 1994 announced its blatantly racist platform by proposing systematic assaults on people of color. Newt Gingrich's "Contract *on* America," as people of color commonly refer to it, supports the slashing of all forms of public assistance and educational funding to those living the violence of poverty. His calls for building more orphanages and prisons to house those who have been most punished by racist capitalism constitute a new and more vicious policy of disenfranchisement of all poor people and of the majority of peoples of color in the United States. By spring 1995 in "post–Proposition 187" California, twelve pieces of apartheid legislation were introduced, all aimed at depriving the American-born children of undocumented Latina/Latino workers the rights to public assistance, health care, school lunch programs, and federal funds for higher education. In New York in 1995, Republican governor Pataki proposed the elimination of Equal Opportunity funds, threatening in one stroke the fate of most students of color in New York's higher education system. Police brutality against Latinas and Latinos and African Americans has increased dramatically since 1990.[12] Racism is on the rise.

But in the academy, it's multicultural time, although few of us are really sure what a multicultural agenda is all about. Because the academic institution is multiculturalism's "home base," I would like to explore the question of who is "at home" and "safe" there. What are the real conditions of life for Latina/Latino students and faculty and other students and faculty of color? Does multiculturalism have anything to do with antiracist work? If in its present form multiculturalism does little in the way of changing racist conditions of life for professors and students of color, who, then, does it benefit?

While multiculturalism has become a new marketing handle whose jargon permeates the academic institution, proponents of real institutional change are met with fear, disdain, and silence. Outspoken opponents of multicultural education such as George Will claim that America's future is at risk because of the new "dictatorship of multicultural virtue." Will has even argued that cultural institutions in the United States have fallen into the hands of people "who despise America." The complaint heard most often from multiculturalism's opponents is that unauthorized, disgruntled "minorities" are silencing and threatening the dominant and rewriting American history from the location of mystified victimization. This is the antinomy of the debate over multiculturalism: while George Will and company rage about the intellectual paucity of the histories of domination and oppression, academic institutions that have their eye on the market are busy commodifying diversity. Meanwhile, somewhere in the academy, politicized voices are calling for real change.[13] But our attempts to question seriously and substantively are met with massive resistance. And the band plays on.

Although multiculturalists have been accused of being humorless, I have to object to that, because Latinas and Latinos happen to be very funny people. Sometimes we use humor as catharsis, to alleviate the pain of institutional, multicultural distress. Among Latino faculty—the most underrepresented group in the academy, comprising one-hundredth to one-fortieth of a percent—there is widespread multicultural distress syndrome. This syndrome is opportunistic and strikes when the untenured Latina discovers that she is working harder for the money. As faculty of color in small liberal arts colleges that are not prepared to accommodate the needs of Latina/Latino students, Latina/Latino professors are automatically thrown into the demanding role of multicultural administrators. We are expected to take part in the formal advising of Latino student groups, in addition to our regular advising responsibilities, and the informal advising of our entire Latino student constituencies. We are appointed to any and every task force and committee that plans to "discuss" multicultural options, from ad hoc committees on "community relations" to "residential life task forces" to "prejudice-reduction workshops." We are expected to participate in recruiting students, faculty, and administrators of color. And the list goes on. Those extra multicultural duties—the great majority of them shouldered by women—do not relieve us of the other duties that regular pretenured faculty are expected to assume. And none of these extra assignments get us tenure. In fact, *Black Issues in Higher Education* recently reported that the tokenization of faculty of color in "multicultural agendas" contributes to the high rate at which we are denied tenure.[14]

Latinas and Latinos and other faculty of color find ourselves in a bind. We are committed to our students and willingly mentor them and participate actively in their academic and personal development; we rush to their defense when they find themselves compromised by the racist politics of our institutions; we laugh and cry with them; we break bread together; we revel in their spirit of discovery and accomplishment; we get mad at them; we give them a good "push" when they need one. They are part of our families in the academy. But because there are so few of us, we find ourselves unfairly burdened with administrative multicultural work. When we say "no" because we cannot give another inch, we worry that no one will speak or act for students of color. So we don't say "no." Unfortunately, in the academy, multiculturalism says what it won't live up to: whereas universities and colleges agree that they need Latina/Latino presence in all of these institutional arenas, that need is not translated into the *hiring* of more Latina/Latino bodies. This means that one of the effects of commodifying multiculturalism is the creation of a two-tier system of academic service, in which the burden of supporting an imagined multicultural community falls on an underrepresented and overworked faculty of color.

Multiculturalism is the cause for much conversation and much silence among academicians. Although the desire for conversation is articulated in the workshops sponsored by the National Coalition Building Institute and the National Endowment for the Humanities initiative "The National Conversation," real multicultural dialogue has been stalled. These types of workshops aimed at "prejudice reduction" and "sensitivity training" are popular among dominant groups, but without real structural and institutional changes, their effect is merely cosmetic. Even with the best intentions, a bunch of White folks sitting around discussing texts written by people of color does little in the way of changing the institutional systems and conditions of life at the academic institution. Multicultural conversations like these create a "smoke screen" that hides the real imperatives of structural diversity. But because of administrative refusal to speak to those profound issues, the burden to speak falls on those who have lived "difference," and in assuming that burden, we become undesirable.

In the academic neighborhood, "passing" is not a question of skin color, but of politics. Faculty of color are invited to "pass" by distinguishing themselves from the radical voices that make visible the institution's role in maintaining the racist status quo.[15] When Latina/Latino and other faculty of color struggle for institutional commitment to structural diversity—the development of multicultural curricula and student development programs and the recruiting, admitting, and retaining of students, faculty, and administrators of color—we are seen as essentially "angry," "aggressive," and "uncooperative" people. We are called these things in conversations that take place *outside* the NCI workshops, where the dominant collapse real political differences into the abnormal psychology of people of color. Reaching into the bag of national mythologies, the powerful opponents of structural multiculturalism reinvoke the binary opposition of White rational virtue and the instinctual dark savage.

A controversy is growing at institutions across the country about whether or not to allow students of color to "segregate" themselves in multicultural housing. When this question comes up in the academy (and it comes up routinely, both at my institution and at others where I have been invited as a consultant), there are always White colleagues who argue that if Latina/Latino students (or African American or Asian American or "international" students from the third world) are allowed to "segregate" themselves, they won't be *contributing* their multicultural treasures to the rest of the student community. When confronted by these situations, I challenge my colleagues with the following question: "What are White students asked to *contribute* to students of color on this campus?" Why are Latina/Latino students and other students of color expected to "educate" and "share themselves" with White students? In "The Master's Tools Will Never Dismantle the Master's House," Audre

Lorde exposes the racist patriarchal foundation that supports those kinds of attitudes in the dominant:

> Women of today are still being called upon to stretch across the gap of male ignorance, and to educate men as to our existence and our needs. This is an old and primary tool of all oppressors to keep the oppressed occupied with the master's concerns. Now we hear that it is the task of Black and third world women to educate white women, in the face of tremendous resistance, as to our existence, our differences, our relative roles in our joint survival. This is a diversion of energies and a tragic repetition of racist patriarchal thought. (1981, 100)

In the face of tremendous resistance, students of color are asked to educate White students about their lives and their struggles in the White academic neighborhood. This expectation reflects not only unchecked racist thought, but also the economic and racial inequality of White students and students of color who exist under the same academic roof. In the multicultural academy, students of color, most of whom rely on financial aid from the institution, are asked to *serve* the master's children. By ignoring the real conditions of life of students of color in White institutions, faculty and administrators in the academy exotify and trivialize racial, ethnic, and cultural difference, collapsing real political and social conflict into a neutralized "multiculturalism."[16] This kind of static multiculturalism works against students of color, since it gives the false impression that if only they would share themselves with White students, their difference would be accepted, understood, and "appreciated." Are we to believe that White students are sitting around hoping that folks of color will come and hang out with them?[17] Even when the races interact—which is rare—whether in the classroom or on the sports field or in student government, the student of color always walks home alone. The truth about the conditions of life of our students in the academy is that they find themselves living in racially segregated neighborhoods. This is not because they refuse to live with White students, but because the great majority of White students refuse to live or share their lives with students of color. Students of color know where they're living, and their desire to live under the same roof with others who are excluded from the "centers" of campus life is an attempt to *integrate* themselves and their specific experiences in the master's house within an empowering and supportive neighborhood of their own color.

While the institution continues to commodify diversity, making public claims about its commitment to multiculturalism, it remains unreflexive about its own role in reproducing antimulticultural agendas: hegemonic Eurocentric curricula; unqualified academic and administrative advising;[18] lack of commitment to the recruitment of students, faculty, and administrators of color; the deficiencies of in-house equal opportunity programs that often create a two-tier system of student academic support that penalizes students of color; residential housing that—with rare exceptions—provides no opportunity for students of color to group together in a collective and supportive living space; lack of support for third world cultural spaces; the lack or poor quality of retention and development programs; and underfunded, understaffed departments that offer multicultural curricula.

One of the most notorious examples of institutions' refusal to support real multiculturalism is their current policies toward Spanish departments (and Spanish programs housed in literature departments). These academic departments and divisions—which not only teach the Spanish language, but often house Latino Studies programs and offer courses in Latin American and Latino literatures and cultures—are in crisis. The "problem" is simple. Students are enthusiastically pounding down the doors in Spanish divisions, overfilling classrooms, and requesting administrative advising on programs and internships in Spanish-speaking countries. Although colleagues in Spanish divisions across the nation are ecstatic about this burst of interest, we cannot possibly accommodate student interest with our present staffing. Although the student-generated demand for the study of Spanish continues to skyrocket,[19] academic institutions have made little attempt to support substantively this movement toward growth, preferring instead to contain the "problem" by relying on inadequate or nonpermanent staffing of these departments. In other words, after having been marginalized in Romance Language departments for decades, Spanish departments are being refused this long-awaited opportunity to take the lead, to grow. The academy, by seeking to stall this growth, betrays its investment in preserving the antimulticultural status quo. Administrators at some institutions have even suggested that Spanish departments begin to limit enrollments in their most attended classes, so that students will "spill over" into sparsely populated French classes.[20] Arguing that the current boom in Spanish divisions represents a "trend" or a "fad" that will dissipate as quickly as it appeared, the academy is systematically promoting the "ghettoization" of Spanish divisions all over the country, resulting in overcrowded classrooms, nonpermanent and last-minute "emergency" staffing (something that makes impossible the retention of high-quality, committed educators), limited curricula, overworked and demoralized faculty and staff, and frustrated students. Whether conscious or unconscious, these policies function to limit the population of "alien" Spanish divisions, guarding and securing the well-established Eurocentric borders of the academy.

Those of us who work in Spanish departments understand that the dramatic rise in the demand for the study of the Spanish language and its related fields of study—Spanish, Latin American, and Latino cultures and literatures—issues from the political history of the Spanish language in the United States and current and future consequences of that history. It is estimated that by the mid–twenty-first century, half of the United States will be Spanish speaking.[21] Although the astounding growth of both Spanish and East Asian language and literature divisions is undoubtedly related to the growing international economy, the fact that droves of U.S. students are crossing the border into Spanish territory reflects the growing reality that Spanish is a language "native" to the United States. In other words, students want to speak Spanish because Spanish is a language that is spoken *here*.

To speak Spanish in the context of the racist politics of our country is an act of resistance. Beginning with the U.S. conquest of Mexico and the colonization of Puerto Rico, the violent campaign to steal the tongue of Spanish speakers has been systematic and institutional. Academic support for Spanish departments would contribute to the critical movement toward cultural decolonization, toward the reclaiming of what has been distorted and deformed in national consciousness. Institutional support of Spanish divisions would not only encourage the growth of multicultural curriculums, but also directly aid in the process of recruiting and retaining students of color, especially Latinas and Latinos. The dramatic increase in the number of students who would like to study Spanish at the college level represents an opportunity for the academy to live up to its discourse on diversity and multiculturalism. If the academy is really interested in promoting diversity, shouldn't it support and encourage multiculturalism when it comes knocking at the front door? For Latina/Latino faculty, the institution's unwillingness to "put its funding where its marketing is" constitutes an unethical and demoralizing response to what should be considered an opportunity—not a "problem." We are expected to contribute our precious time and energy to the academy's marketing of "multiculturalism" while at the same time being punished daily by its stubborn refusal to support organic manifestations of multicultural growth.

Without ethical motives and a direct connection to antiracist work, multicultural agendas are meaningless. Even worse, they become a facade that protects and defends the White order of things. In spite of its potential for challenging the racist dynamics of the academy, in its present, disembodied form, multiculturalism functions as a new tool of the master that "co-opts" and neutralizes a potentially radical movement toward the dismantling of White, Eurocentric academic power.

In the academy, as in society, those of us committed to antiracist imperatives will continue to struggle for social justice, in spite of our fears and the real risks to our livelihood and our lives. We will continue to strive to

take back and transform what has been taken from us, to reclaim, to reoc-
cupy, to decolonize conquered intellectual, spiritual, and psychological
territory. We will continue to mount spirited, organized resistance to institutional racism; we will continue to demand justice for all people of
color, even if the odds seem insurmountable.

As poet, novelist, journalist, and community peacemaker Luis J. Rodríguez has argued, for Latinas and Latinos in the Borderlands—who will
be the largest population group in the United States by the year 2060—*the
threat of apartheid is real.* We must, now more than ever, continue to act, to
raise our voices, to engage our minds, our hearts, our arms, and our legs
in defiance of the racist systems of the United States and its institutions,
for what we do each day determines the future of all Latinas and Latinos
struggling for home in the Borderlands. But let us remember that uniting
against a common enemy is never sufficient grounds for coalition. As
Latinas and Latinos move toward the end of the millennium, our work
must be inclusive. Light-skinned, dark-skinned, lesbian, gay, straight,
men, women, adults, children, old, young, rich, middle-class, poor—collectively, we must make intelligible and political our common experiences as colonized peoples of the United States, so that we may begin, in
Audre Lorde's words, to "transform silence into language and action." I
empower myself when I choose to link my history to the experiences of
all peoples of color, so that in finding my voice, I do not silence those who
would speak *with* me and *for* me. ¡Fuerza a la raza latina!

Notes

I would like to thank my soul sisters Jacqui Alexander, Chandra Talpade Mohanty,
and Amie Macdonald for their inspiration, instruction, and support during the creation of this chapter. I am indebted to Jacqui, whose brilliant and moving speech at
the Sisters of Color International Conference held at Hamilton College in April 1995
greatly inspired the theory and the passion of this piece; Chandra was instrumental
in helping to bring this essay to publication; Amie (as always) volunteered much
precious time to help me think through and edit my ideas. Finally, I would like to
thank Rosemary Marangoly George for her thoughtful editorial suggestions.

1. In my family, as in many Latino families, we were not allowed into the
"Spanish-speaking room." Although my grandmother and parents spoke Spanish
to each other daily, if we (the kids) were heard speaking Spanish with my grandmother, my father's cajoling "Speak English!" would boom across the room. At
age five I thought I was so special because I could speak Spanish. By age ten the
language had been stolen from me, and I was ashamed to be associated with it.

2. As amazing as it seems, I spent my childhood trying to explain to confused
White people in southern California that not all Spanish-surnamed people are
Mexican.

3. "Passing" for a White woman is something that has happened to me both with and without intent. Although I was once asked to prove my citizenship by a U.S. immigration official (a Chicana) at the Californian/Mexican border at Tijuana, my skin color ensures that I will never be pulled over and beaten to a pulp by police officers who suspect me of being an illegal immigrant.

4. I wasn't the only angry one, either. The first time my parents heard me proudly announce that I identified myself as a *Chicana-riqueña*, a term that my friends and I coined to characterize my hybrid Latina identity (Puerto Rican born, Chicana identified), my parents hit the roof. "You're not a Chicana!" they said, exasperated. "Why do you want to undo everything we have done for you?" Although they knew me well enough to know that I wouldn't be swayed by their disapproval, it took them many years to accept it. But then a remarkable thing happened. After having been denied the choice to communicate with my father in Spanish, I picked up the phone one day to hear his jovial voice greeting me with "*¡Susana! ¿Cómo estás, hija?*" As the years have gone by, both my parents have reclaimed a long-lost pride in their once-rejected ethnic identity. I have joked to my mother that I consider my family "recovering Latinos," people who have come to ontological sobriety after long, dark years of denial.

5. A good example of this is Hollywood, which not only continues to use White actors to portray Latinos—especially in the rare case that the Latino character is not a "field hand," a drug dealer, a thief, or a gang member—but also insists on representing Latinas and Latinos as nonindigenous to the United States. As a rule, Hollywood reduces the possibilities for Latino characters to criminals or illegal immigrants (mostly female domestic employees). In both cases, Hollywood reproduces the distorted stereotype of the Latina/Latino "threat" to the White neighborhood, both at the community and the national level.

6. The U.S. conquest of the Southwest began in the 1800s, when Anglos illegally entered and settled on Mexican land. Mexico declared war against the United States but lost, and almost half their land, what is now Texas, New Mexico, Arizona, Colorado, and California, was annexed to the United States. Almost overnight, Mexicans mutated from landowners to landless. The land that remained in the hands of conquered Mexicans on the United States side of the border was eventually swindled by Whites, and the institutional theft of the Spanish language—the origin of today's "English Only" movement—was launched, prohibiting the use of Spanish in schools, work sites, and public places. The U.S./Mexican border was created in 1848 with the signing of the Treaty of Guadalupe Hidalgo. Although the treaty promised to allow Mexicans both their land and their language, it was dishonored by the United States.

7. "From neither here nor there."

8. When I presented an earlier version of this chapter at a conference in the spring of 1996, I was criticized—aggressively—by a light-skinned, island-born-and-raised Puerto Rican colleague from a prestigious liberal arts college, who protested that my representation of the Puerto Rican as the mere object of homogeneous White perception was extremely problematic. I would like to speak to her objection by qualifying my analysis of the U.S. Latina and Latino's struggle for self-definition in relation to White society. First of all, I understand that the dynamics of race, class, gender, and sexuality have created more than one "White

community" in the United States. Furthermore, Latino communities in the United States are themselves extremely diverse, something that of course creates the possibility of more than one potential Latino response to the oppression of racism. The analysis I am attempting to construct in this chapter addresses the general claims and experiences of the majority of U.S. Latinas and Latinos who—because of their particular configurations of race, class, gender, and ethnic identity—have experienced racism in the United States. As Franz Fanon, Paolo Freyre, and others have argued, one of the most devastating effects of racist violence on its victims is the internalization of oppression, which results in self-loathing. For me, as for most Latinas and Latinos, these are not mere theories, but historical and political truths, since the memory of racist experiences and its effects on us have shaped our struggle to free ourselves from our own internal oppressor. I am not trying to reduce the Latino experience to that of the object of oppression, but I am trying to discuss and analyze the effects of that oppression, because I believe that to build coalition in our communities, we must work to change both external and internal racism. It is the effects of racist experiences that invite Latinas and Latinos to feel less than Whites. Light-skinned, upper-class Puerto Ricans and Latinas and Latinos whose privilege has sheltered them from these kinds of experiences—and made them ignorant of the social and psychological realities of the majority of Latinas and Latinos—have much to learn about our struggles in the United States.

9. The discounting and devaluing of Latina experience and analysis comes from White society as well. While teaching a course on the Latino Experience, a White male student complained to me that he wasn't getting what he wanted from the class. "I took this class to understand something about Latino culture," he said, "but so far all we've done is talk about women." What really impressed me about his missive—aside from his glaring patriarchal obstinance—was the idea that I was betraying the class by sneaking in Latina experience and feminist criticism where Latino male history and perspective was supposed to be. I was betraying the authority of men, both Latino and White, by telling women's stories.

10. In Spanish, *Dolores* is a woman's name. But literally, *dolores* means pain and suffering.

11. The fact that Esperanza has no female role models is a textual problem that remains unresolved. Lacking the experiences of other subversive women from which to draw her own strength, Esperanza distinguishes herself from all other women in the text, something that might suggest individualistic exceptionality. However, I argue that this exceptionality is the consequence of the effectiveness of *Marianismo*; the fact that this textualized Latina daughter has no role models suggests not her unique supremacy in relation to other women, nor the absence of female desire, but the real effects of the iron hand of patriarchal power in Latino communities.

12. As I write this paper, a chilling repetition of the Rodney King "incident" has been played out in the suburban Los Angeles area on the bodies of a Mexican man and woman. The videotaped police beating of these "suspected illegal immigrants" by two Riverside County sheriff's deputies has sparked outrage in southern California's Chicano/Latino community.

13. When I think about the voices calling for institutional change, I hear the voices of the women alongside whom I have struggled: lesbians of all colors, Lati-

nas, African American and Asian American women, third world feminists, Jewish feminists, radical White feminists.

14. Overassignment in multicultural service agendas is, of course, not only the burden of Latina/Latino faculty, but also African American, Asian American, and to some extent, all faculty of color.

15. Skin color does, however, complicate the picture. As a light-skinned Latina, I have found myself submitted—by White colleagues—to the "race loyalty test" on more than one occasion. When darker-skinned sisters have raised their beautiful, courageous voices in sharp criticism of the institution's racist systems, I have been approached—privately—by White colleagues who have falsely assumed that my position will be more "reasonable." Although my politics have been made quite clear to them, these colleagues apparently seek the complicity of my skin color as a way to bridge the real political differences that divide us.

16. Unfortunately, in the academy, Latino "culture" is often conflated with eating burritos and learning Latino dance steps. Mexican, Chicano, and Latino histories are reduced to celebrations of a distant, mummified culture: the annual "ballet folklórico" festival, a salsa and merengue dance, a Cinco de Mayo celebration. While these celebrations provide a space for the public representation of Latino cultures, they are disembodied from the Latino experience in the United States. In fact, in the absence of any real education about and for Latinos, these kinds of events become metaphors of colonization. Californians who show up for Ballet Folklórico or drink a margarita at a Cinco de Mayo party probably don't even know that the land they're standing on was once Mexican. Latino history is substituted by mainstream consumption of salsa and merengue, Tex-Mex music, tacos, fajitas, beer, and tequila. Tourist multiculturalism. Latino culture reduced to what we can sell and what we can entice White "America" to consume.

17. The idea that Whites actively seek the company of students of color is false. Those of us who teach in the academy have experienced firsthand the systematic self-segregation of White students. The Hispanic Outlook in Higher Education (September 15, 1994, 4) states that "contrary to the appearance of self-segregation, students of color are more likely than Whites to interact with students from different racial groups."

18. A tragic example of unqualified and racist advising of Latina and Latino students involves study of the Spanish language. It is commonplace for academic advisors to discourage Latina/Latino students from taking up the formal study of the Spanish language or the literatures of Spanish-speaking countries, because, they argue, these students "already know the language." In the first place, many Latina/Latino students do not speak Spanish at all, and others have some knowledge of the language but, like me, were discouraged or prohibited from speaking it and were therefore "robbed" of the tongue. Others are fluent speakers but cannot read or write in Spanish. Most Latina/Latino students have never had the opportunity to study Latina/Latino and Latin American literatures, the result of the erasure of their histories from public school curriculums. Furthermore, advising a Latina or Latino student to avoid study of Spanish is tantamount to telling White students that they should avoid courses in the English department, "since they already know that language." The fact is that most institutions not only recommend, but require, that students study English at the college level (after taking

four years of it in high school). Apparently an English speaker can never take enough courses in an English department, but a Spanish speaker has no reason to take even one course in a Spanish department. It's infuriating. When we turn this equation on its head, the implicit racism and devaluing of the Spanish language and its related cultural fields is glaringly evident.

19. Enrollments at my institution have increased almost 50 percent in the last four years.

20. This suggestion is outrageous. In the history of the academy in the United States, the Spanish language has been considered a "lesser" language than French, whose cultural value corresponds to the perceived superiority of continental French culture. Until recently, Spanish was the least-populated and staffed division in romance language and literature departments. This situation was never questioned by the academy or seen as a "problem," and it was certainly never suggested by administrators that French divisions limit their class enrollments to encourage students to take Spanish.

21. At last, the reconquest of the Spanish language *(la revancha)*! That the Spanish language has not only survived but flourished in hostile conditions is a beautiful testament to the cultural resistance of Latinas and Latinos and the magic of the language itself. It is encouraging, empowering, and I admit, supremely satisfying to witness the powerlessness of "English Only" campaigns to silence the melodic, joyous rhythms of the indigenous Spanish language. *¡Que viva y que crezca la lengua española!*

Works Cited

Acuña, Rodolfo. 1972. *Occupied America: The Chicano's Struggle Toward Liberation.* San Francisco: Canfield Press.

Alarcón, Norma. 1981. "Chicana's Feminist Literature: A Re-vision Through Malintzin/or Malintzin: Putting Flesh Back on the Object." In Moraga and Anzaldúa (1983).

Anzaldúa, Gloria. 1987. *Borderlands: La Frontera.* San Francisco: Aunt Lute Book Company.

Castillo, Ana. 1994. *Massacre of the Dreamers: Essays on Xicanisma.* Albuquerque: University of New Mexico Press.

Cisneros, Sandra. 1989. *The House on Mango Street.* New York: Random House.

de Lauretis, Teresa. 1986. *Feminist Studies/Critical Studies.* Bloomington: Indiana University Press.

Dunn, Ashley. 1995. "INS Virtually Ignores Thousands of Tourists Who Remain Illegally." *New York Times* (January 5, 1995).

Falcón, Luis M., and Dan Gilbarg. 1992. "Latinos in the Labor Market: Mexicans, Puerto Ricans and Cubans." *Latino Studies Journal*, v. 3, n. 3 (September 1, 1992).

hooks, bell. 1984. Feminist Theory: From Margin to Center. Boston: South End Press.

Lorde, Audre. 1979. "The Master's Tools Will Never Dismantle the Master's House." In Moraga and Anzaldúa (1983).

Mohanty, Chandra Talpade, and Biddy Martin. 1986. "Feminist Politics: What's Home Got to Do with It?" In de Lauretis (1986).

Mohr, Nicholasa. 1975. *El Bronx Remembered*. New York: HarperCollins Publishers.

Moraga, Cherríe. 1984. *Loving in the War Years: Lo que nunca pasó por sus labios*. Boston: South End Press.

Moraga, Cherríe, and Gloria Anzaldúa, eds. 1983. *This Bridge Called My Back: Writings by Radical Women of Color*. New York: Kitchen Table Press.

Morales, Aurora Levins, and Rosario Morales. 1986. *Getting Home Alive*. New York: Firebrand Books.

Rios, Denice A. 1994. "Segregated Student Housing—By Choice." *Hispanic Outlook in Higher Education*, v. 5, n. 2 (September 1994).

Rodríguez, Luis J. 1993. *Always Running; La Vida Loca: Gang Days in L.A.* New York: Touchstone Press.

_____. 1994. "Who We Are." *Hungry Mind Review* (Fall 1994).

_____. 1996. "Steal This Book." *Hungry Mind Review* (Spring 1996).

Takaki, Ronald. 1979. *Iron Cages: Race and Culture in 19th Century America*. New York: Oxford University Press.

Torres, Lourdes. 1991. "The Construction of the Self in U.S. Latina Autobiographies." In Chandra T. Mohanty, Ann Russo, and Lourdes Torres, eds., *Third World Women and the Politics of Feminism*. Bloomington: Indiana University Press.

Yamada, Mitsuye. 1981. "Asian Pacific American Women and Feminism." In Moraga and Anzaldúa (1983).

Chapter Sixteen

Home, Houses, Nonidentity: Paris Is Burning

CHANDAN C. REDDY

While audiences of Jennie Livingston's *Paris Is Burning*[1] view a pho-
tomontage of European models on the cover of fashion magazines, advertisements for million-dollar condominiums, and a magazine story on the
quintessential eighties Hollywood "family," the Carringtons from *Dynasty,* the husky voice of Octavia Saint Laurent provides the viewers with
the caption to the montage: "Seeing the riches, seeing the way people on
Dynasty lived, these huge houses, and I would think, these people have
forty-two rooms in their house, oh my God, what kind of house is that,
and we've got three. So why is it that they can have that and I didn't? I always felt cheated. I always felt cheated out of things like that."

The ironic pathos of Livingston's documentary, effected by contrasting
the fantasy of equal opulence with the grave disparity between Hollywood set and New York tenement, is repeated in another cut of Octavia
later in the film.

Striking a pose of iconic femininity, standing on a platform raised
above the level of the camera, dressed in a two-piece yellow bathing suit,
Octavia interrupts her "form" by announcing, "I don't think the world
has been fair to me. Not yet anyway." While submitting to the interpellative demand for a normative and idealized femininity that "recruits" subjects who both "internalize" and "speak" its ideologies, Octavia equally
voices her material nonequivalence to that demand, forcefully articulating a contradiction. Her identification with an ideal concept of femininity,
demanded by herself and the fashion industry, is simultaneously troubled by a persistent contradiction.[2] Lisa Lowe eloquently formulates this
contradiction as inherent in all interpellations in which the ideological
demand for identification is in tension with the "contradictory material

conditions within which that demand is made."[3] The logic of identical equivalence, that each thing or person is formally identical with another, governing every articulation of identity, is interrupted and contradicted by Octavia's voicing of material strata (her cramped "home"), inequity ("I always felt cheated"), and utter nonequivalence (corporeal difference) between herself and her feminine ideal.

I open with these two moments of subjective contradiction, in which the interpellative fantasy of formal equivalence and identity is disrupted by the demand for material strata, racial formations, and gendered differences required to build and maintain the opulent American "Dynasty" home, because it situates this chapter's route to thinking about (White) American domesticity. Much of Marxist literature, concerned with the contradictions of "modern" European and American capitalist economic processes, has explored the domestic, the home, and the family only to the degree that it considers these sites as ideological locations or "Ideological State Apparatuses" that interpellate and socialize subjects for the State and modern national economies. Yet if we rethink the (White) American "Home" from the standpoint of racialized gendered subjects, it becomes clear that the White Home and its private sphere are not simply sites adjacent to modern public life, or a historically anterior site of a simpler economy that serves solely an ideological function. Rather, that standpoint forces a reconsideration of the White U.S. Home as a social location whose *material* reproduction and maintenance require the forms of social division and organization (the racial formation of domestic labor, the gendered division of labor, and the colonial differential of the wage scale) instantiated and sustained by the modern U.S. State and its public culture.

This chapter explores this standpoint from the material and cultural position of "queers of color." Specifically, I take up the relation established between "home" and "houses" by the documentary subjects of Livingston's *Paris Is Burning* to extend that standpoint to bear upon inquiries into subjective social and self-formations. I begin my examination of the "houses" of the ball circuit captured in the documentary *Paris Is Burning* with a genealogy of racial/ethnic[4] people's history in the United States, focusing on the paradox by which racial/ethnics were excluded from the "home" of the nation exactly at times when their "labor" was central to its constitution, maintenance, and reproduction. Unaccounted for within both Marxist and liberal pluralist discussions of the home and the nation, queers of color *as people of color*, I argue, take up the critical task of both remembering and rejecting the model of the "home" offered in the United States in two ways: first, by attending to the ways in which it was defined over and against people of color, and second, by expanding the locations and moments of that critique of the home to interrogate processes of group and self-formation from the experience of being expelled from their own dwellings and families for not conforming to the dictation of and demand for uniform gendered and sexual types. The "houses" that make up the units of the ball circuit are sites of critical importance, not only because they form counter-cultures and alternative social formations that provide both support and community for the urban queers of color interviewed in Livingston's documentary, but also because the "houses" never replace the "home." Put otherwise, the documentary subjects interviewed in Livingston's film never replace the original home from which they were often brutally expelled with the "houses" of the ball circuit. The "houses" are, rather, the site from which to remember the constitutive violence of the home, and the location from which to perform the pleasures and demands of alternative living, while at the same time functioning as an "interlocutionary device" between homes and queer subjects. These "houses" are collectivities that form precisely to supplement the often violent and constitutive experience of the home—collectivities whose potential lies not in rearticulating an idealized alternative domesticity, but rather in forming shared sites that enable each particular subject to collectively remember the home as a site of contradictory demands and conditions.

*   *   *

In his 1970 essay "Ideology and Ideological State Apparatuses," the Marxist philosopher Louis Althusser built upon Marx's assertion that the most important component of the conditions of production in any capitalist society is the reproduction of the conditions of production. Separating out the "capitalist" process from other economic processes, such as slavery and feudalism, Althusser suggests that what distinguishes the modern capitalist era from other economic eras is that the reproduction of both the means of production (gaining "skills" for work and maintaining a "healthy" population of laborers as labor power) and the relations of production (the formation of subjects who "accept" their position) occurs not within the social relations of production, but rather in sites and spheres "outside" the capitalist relations of production. As Stuart Hall explains, the reproduction of the conditions of production occurs "in the domain of the superstructure: in institutions like the family and the church."[5] Althusser names these institutions "Ideological State Apparatuses" to emphasize their role, like that of the State in general, in reproducing the social formation. These Ideological State Apparatuses[6] as *material* locations are hybrid, impure, and nondiscrete, with a particular apparatus often attaching itself to other material apparatuses adjacent or historically anterior to it. Yet each apparatus remains distinct from others; each has heterogeneous historical origins and conditions, often producing, as Lowe suggests, important "conflicts and noncorrespondences be-

tween hailing apparatuses."[7] What establishes a "complex unity" among
these apparatuses is that they all have the function of "hailing" individuals and transforming them, although always only partially, into formal
subjects. Often, hailing apparatuses build upon the logic or fantasies of
equivalence and identical repetition found within the functionings of
other Ideological Apparatuses. Yet, as Lowe suggests in discussing *Dictée*,
a cultural text that itself thematizes the relation between an individual
subject and a variety of hailing apparatuses (educational, religious, colonial, and citizenship): "*Dictée* is more specific about multiple hailings,
particularly about the conflicts and noncorrespondences between hailing
apparatuses; while they may intersect or coexist, or be linked through the
use of similar modes and logics, these apparatuses are often at odds with
one another."[8]

Equally, Ideological Apparatuses produce contradictory interpellations, not only because they might conflict with an adjacent or previous
interpellation, but because each apparatus is itself a *material* institution.
The forms of strata, division, and "difference" found within that material
site and required for its maintenance and reproduction are often the
ground for negating the fantasy of equivalence or identity lodged in any
hailing.

This segment of the chapter examines the rhetoric of the "family wage"
and the "American Standard of Living" during the early twentieth century as an important illustration of the forms of contradiction found between interdependent hailing apparatuses—in this case the Family and
Citizenship Apparatuses—and the contradictions that emerge internally
in any distinct apparatus from the standpoint of its need to function materially and reproduce. I begin with an exploration of home and housing
in the United States to set up a genealogy in which to situate the relation
between racial/ethnic people and national rhetorics of the home. While
this might seem like a long detour on the way to discussing the cultural
practices of late-twentieth-century ball culture, I maintain that a powerful
critical thematic emerges from "queer of color" cultural production when
contextualized within the problematic relation between racial/ethnic
people and home and housing in the United States. In the following discussion I track the rhetorical uses of "the home" and "the family wage" as
it was used at the turn of the century in socializing subjects for the State. I
contrast this to the material differences between racial/ethnic people and
"Whites" during that period to suggest that this exact ideology produced
a contradiction for racial/ethnic people. My examination begins with an
overview of Marxist sketchings of the home. Whereas Althusser's essay
examines Ideological State Apparatuses only with respect to how they
take up many of the responsibilities and functions of the State in reproducing the social formation, I argue in this chapter that in the United

States, the *modern* State was, and continues to be, central in producing the racial and gendered relations upon which the material existence of the U.S. Home is predicated. In this way I seek a more reciprocal dynamic to describe the relationship between Ideological Apparatuses and the State. Secondly, I argue that while at one point the State and national public culture attached themselves to the heterosexual, patriarchal "home"—as a form in which to narrate national history—at other moments, the "home" signified a discursive and material location that existed before State society and outside of its regulatory jurisdiction, allowing for forms of racialized and gendered labor to be unaccounted for and ignored during the exact period when the State suppressed dissent from organized labor through rhetorics of formal political, cultural, and national equivalence. The "home" does not have a univocal meaning or rhetorical purpose in relationship to cultural and political narratives of nation and modernity. It remains an unstable ideological site, due to its noncorrespondence with concepts of both nation and modernity. At the same time, the U.S. home is a specifically modern home, in the sense that it is embedded within larger relations of production and reproduction for its existence. As the contemporary history of the Federal Housing Administration (FHA) shows, housing in the United States is one site in which the State and the capitalist "market" produce and maintain "racial formations." Although the home serves within traditional sociology as the location in which culture and racial and ethnic identity are vertically transmitted, the history of housing in the United States—redlining, racial discrimination in loaning practices, and unequal levels of wealth—suggests that "race" is equally the product of State and market practices. I conclude this chapter by suggesting that through the cultural practices and emergent subjectivities of "queers of color," a subjective location may open up from which to remember and practice this contradictory formation. That is, "queers of color" might be the subjective location from which to interact, remember, and practice the contradictory relations of people of color to home and housing in the United States.

By the turn of the century in the United States, the "home" and domesticity had become central discursive sites in resolving the contradictions that the changing political nation (with the abolition of slavery, the shift to wage labor, and the political emphasis on "White" citizenship) and its new economy brought forth. The home became embedded within the social relations and material practices that defined the modern nation. And as the following discussion of the family wage and the "American Standard of Living" makes evident, the American "home" was defined as exclusively White.

By the late nineteenth century, organized labor in the United States rallied around the rhetoric of the "living wage" and the "American Standard of Living." Earlier, producerist republicanism had equated "wages" and "slavery," reserving "freedom" as a feature to be enjoyed only by individuals with jobs that were not on the wage system. By as soon as the mid-1880s, such an equation failed to signify, and instead the idea of a wage economy became coupled with notions of "progress," indexing the advances of the nation and the modern capitalist economy. Lawrence Glickman neatly summarizes this shift:

> With living wages—defined by most male breadwinners as sufficient earnings to meet the ever-expanding consuming needs of their families—slavery could be avoided and its opposite, republican freedom, gained. . . . Rather than counterposing wage work with freedom, workers began to equate the two. The new slavery, in this context, was not wage labor but low standards of living; by the same token, republican freedom became equated with the American Standard of Living.[9]

The "American Standard of Living" not only marks the transition toward a wage economy; it also highlights the fact that by the end of the century in the United States, organized labor—citizen, male, and "White"—increasingly was defined against the "unorganized" and "informal" segments of labor, which were female, noncitizen, and non-White.

By providing a measure of equivalence by which each worker was said to be identical to the other due to a shared or common standard of living, the discourses of the "American Standard of Living" and the "family wage" that gripped the United States in the early 1900s demonstrate well the role of ideologies and ideological apparatuses in transforming individuals into subjects as equivalent units of abstract labor. Yet, in the United States, both capital and (organized) labor defined this subject as exclusive of racial, immigrant, and female populations.

Although the concept of the "family wage" purportedly raised the wages earned by a male worker, in order that his wages might support the entire family, it also had the specific effect of depressing women's wages by defining women as secondary earners and defining the male as the breadwinner. The "American Standard of Living" was said to be a national and culturally specific standard acknowledged to be higher than the "European Standard of Living," which was itself higher than the "Oriental Standard of Living."[10] Ordered in a hierarchy of standards, this rhetoric of national equivalence recognized from the outset a tension and, more specifically, a contradiction between an ideological apparatus that generated national political and social equivalence and the need for a stratified and racialized labor force. Because the demand for "informal" labor existed precisely at that moment when there was a drive toward "organized labor" within a modern economy—displaying a formal link and constitutive relation between "organized" and "informal" labor in a modern capitalist economic process—both labor and capital justified their exclusion of racialized labor within the cultural sphere. Hence, the universality of the American Standard of Living—as well as the "family" it called into existence—can be negated from the perspective of people of color, both for the ways in which it justified a family wage that depressed the wages of women and people of color and simultaneously for the ways in which it served as a cultural narrative of ordered and stable levels of progress and development that masked the demand by capital for "informal," unstable, and specifically *racial* labor.

The family wage in the United States defined the "home," which it cited as cause for higher wages, as exclusively White and American. The American standard of living demanded that male American workers get paid higher wages to meet their living standards. Lower wages meted out to racialized gendered workers by employers and the State were the result of their lower cultural and "human" needs. Cultural discourses about the limited desires of Asian immigrants for housing, nourishment, and family not only rescripted the living conditions of Asian workers, but more specifically disavowed the conditions under which Asian immigrants were barred from forming family structures in the United States precisely because of political and citizenship exclusion. Instead, as Glickman notes:

> If the American Standard enabled white male workers to fashion themselves as wage-earning citizens, it gave these same workers a means to declare others unfit for membership in the polity. In 1880, an article in the Journal of United Labor argued that the Chinese acted in direct opposition to "white Christian" labor's economic and political understandings. The article decried the Chinese as anti-republican, uninterested in freedom, and ignorant of the meaning of citizenship. . . . According to this argument the Chinese worked for less because they were willing to spend less, not vice versa.[11]

Glickman also remarks that often the justification for lower wages was rendered in terms of consumption. While these narratives suggested that Chinese workers consumed too little, justification for the asymmetry of African American wages was often based not on their minimal consumer needs but on their erratic and mindless consumption of purchased goods. Finally, Glickman exposes how the "home" functioned as a regulatory locus for consumptive desires, proscribing consumption in brothels or other disreputable places. Summing up the logic of an 1898 labor leader, Glickman wrote, "Gunton argued that the home, not the salon or the whorehouse, should be the 'focal' point of consumption."[12]

By the turn of the century in the United States, family, labor market, media, literature, and State came to articulation, interpellating certain groups of people as national subjects and simultaneously racializing others in relation to these diverse social sites, of which the family or the home is just one instance.[13] Yet the rhetorical force of the family wage and the heterosexual nuclear unit that it performatively cited resulted not only because the family wage fulfilled a crucial function in interpellating individuals as state subjects but also because it served ultimately to provide a discourse of "development," progress, and stability to shifts in the capitalist economic process that were uneven and unstable and dependent on "racial" nonequivalence.

I highlight this moment in U.S. history firstly because it exposes how these cultural narratives refigured and rearticulated the "home" as an idealized zone that "focused" and "domesticated" unruly capitalist economic upheavals and inconsistencies; the "home" became a discursive site that fulfilled the demand of the modern political nation for a stable and developmental narrative of progress. Secondly, as this moment makes evident, the American "home" has historically served, as Althusser suggested, the function of an Ideological State Apparatus that contributes centrally to the reproduction of modern life. Yet to the extent that the White "Home" is also a material location that both appropriates women's labor and relies on its differentiation from the racialized work and dwellings that are, in part, instantiated by the conditions produced by modern state activity, the "home" remains a contradictory apparatus. That is, the American "home" is a social location that dynamically interacts with and is deeply embedded within modern "public" culture and economy, requiring the forms of racial differentiation and social strata found in those sites for its material maintenance and reproduction; due to this condition, the home remains a contradictory apparatus of subject formation.

This history of the family wage and the "American Standard of Living" demonstrates the important position advanced by Althusser on the ideological function of the "family" in reproducing the relations of production. Yet the family wage, a rhetoric that interpellated individuals as national political equivalents, required and justified the depressed wages and living conditions of people of color and the appropriation of gendered labor in the home. This ought to serve as a reminder that any ideological apparatus, and specifically the Family Ideological State Apparatus, is always also a contradictory apparatus or technology precisely due to the material heterogeneity and conditions on which interpellating apparatuses are founded.

The White home in the United States at the turn of the century was rhetorically and materially defined by its exclusion of racial/ethnic people. As an Ideological State Apparatus, it served paradoxical ends. On the one hand, it became the site that "resolved" the tensions within a capitalist classed society by fulfilling the political demand of the nation for abstract equivalence. On the other, it became the site that excluded racial/ethnic people from being a part of that equivalence, announcing them to have other "national" standards of living, such as the "Oriental Standard," the "Negro Standard," and the "Immigrant Standard." If the American home and the standard of living it was predicated upon were an Ideological Apparatus that secured the relations of exploitation by "resolving" economic contradictions within the spheres of politics, public culture, and the "private" home, then for racial/ethnic people, that "home" articulated a contradiction between its function as a representation of national equivalence and its role within a racial discourse that positioned racial/ethnic people both ideologically and materially outside the national home.

The "home" as a discursive production figured dominantly within political speeches and public cultural texts during the early parts of this century, gaining a public life that was unprecedented. Yet the home as a site of lived relations, material practices, and productive and reproductive labor remained excluded from the discourse. During the New Deal era, the rhetorics of "home" and citizenship became significantly linked, albeit differently from in the earlier period. Eileen Boris delineated the link between racialized gendered workers and the "American home": "But as workers, African American women also could be invisible to the law, as when New Deal labor standards excluded domestic service and agricultural labor, work dominated by women and men of color that easily became collapsed into household or family labor."[14]

Not only was the American "home" defined in racially exclusive ways, but the forms of labor located "within" it were artificially demarcated as outside the State's regulatory reach. Although Roosevelt's New Deal inaugurated federal social citizenship, it unevenly distributed the properties of citizenship along racialized and gendered lines. Building on the previous era of the family wage and the American Standard of Living that posited the concept of the male breadwinner, the WPA, one of the most important New Deal institutions, hired only "heads of households," often excluding female labor. Building upon earlier exclusions, the federal government defined, implemented, and reproduced a welfare state that directly, if "inadvertently," excluded racial/ethnic workers and communities. It might also be noted that the Fair Labor Standards Act and the provisions allocated in the New Deal Welfare State did not extend to the colonial territories of the United States, such as Puerto Rico.[15] And as George Lipsitz's records in his appropriately titled "Possessive Investment in Whiteness," "The Federal Housing Act of 1934 brought home ownership within reach of millions of citizens ... but overtly racist categories in the Federal Housing Administration (FHA) ... channeled almost all of the loan money toward whites and away from communities of color."[16]

Lipsitz argues that throughout the twentieth century the FHA developed policy and distributed monies that more than any other state organ widened the gap between the resources available to Whites and those available to aggrieved racial communities. Lipsitz suggests that "during the decades following World War II, urban renewal helped construct a new 'white' identity in the suburbs. . . . This 'white' unity rested on residential segregation and on shared access to housing and life chances largely unavailable to communities of color."[17] Even after the important movements for civil rights by people of color, housing discrimination persisted by taking an alternate form. Although the State declared itself to be formally nonracial, mandating "color-bind" housing policy, it refused to enforce many of the antidiscrimination clauses written to protect minorities, which resulted in gross discrimination in the private sector. The "color-blind" State strove to "resolve" the persistence of racially segregated communities, in part through an official multiculturalism that sought to give "cultural" explanations of ethnic contiguity for racially divided housing. The State also relied on "market forces" to fulfill the promise of Whiteness after formally declaring itself color-blind. By means of redlining, destruction of housing as part of "urban renewal" programs, and racial discrimination in federal and private lending institutions, the "market" helped to define the representative American home as still essentially "White."

The history of housing discrimination at the level of the State, the private sector, and civil society is continuous with the earlier periods I discussed in this chapter. The American Home and its representative family continue to be defined by their "Whiteness," a "Whiteness" that is not only a cultural identity, but a collective experience of structural advantage and state "assistance" in a racially defined national terrain. If the United States sought to gain consent for its imperialist wars and racist activities, both domestic and foreign, in part by interpellating its citizenry as politically equivalent abstract citizen-subjects who had equal access to state representation, a concept embodied in the architecture and establishment of suburban housing for which the federal government channeled aid, then its practices engendered a contradiction for racial/ethnic citizens and immigrants systematically robbed of their property and denied adequate housing by that same State.[18] This is, in part, why fair housing and antidiscrimination rights were so forcefully staked out within the demands of the Civil Rights Movement.[19] It also suggests that the forms of housing and community generated by people of color in the United States can be seen as locations of collective endurance against the history of inequality and state disenfranchisement. Queers of color, with their experiences of homophobia and engagement with the home as a material, ideological, and formative site, can resignify those forms of housing and community not as static objects found throughout historical time, but as contemporary sites of change and transformation, interfacing with home and community at their points of historical movement and dynamic transformation. The following discussion explores three different critical models of evaluating the "home" within larger discussions of the political nation and capitalist formations—Marxist, Marxist feminist, and "women of color." I conclude by laterally connecting the historically previous and contemporary enterprise of "women of color" critical and cultural production with queer of color cultural practices, linking together the different subjects elaborated by each for their shared interest in an alternative framework—although founded within and constituted by different types of contradiction and antagonism to the home and patriarchy—for thinking about the home and its dwelling subjects.

*   *   *

Marxist models that took for granted the male as the typical worker and that were unable to link waged labor to unwaged labor in the home developed critical models of the social formation that failed to incorporate the contemporaneous history of the domestic sphere and the patriarchal home in the "modern" era.[20] Marxist feminism located this lacuna and figured new critical models and methods from the standpoint of "woman," such as dual systems theory that analyzed capitalism and patriarchy as separate and dynamic yet interrelated and mutually constitutive forms of subordination and social hierarchy.[21] Additionally, Marxist feminism disputed and displaced the concept of the home as a site that expressed unitary interests. By analyzing the "home" from the standpoint of "woman," Marxist feminism suggested that the sense of the home as a site of unitary interests disavowed the conditions of a sexual division of labor, which contradicted the concept of the home as a unitary site. They rewrote the "home" as an important location of struggle against both violence and the appropriation of women's labor and reproductive rights. Yet to the degree that Marxist feminism failed to consider heterogeneity within the category of "woman" by race and national difference, it was unable to articulate the ways in which the modern state as a racialized gendered state or as a colonial state often produced the forms of society required to support White patriarchy.[22] Evelyn Nakano Glenn, writing from the historical standpoint of "women of color," has articulated one of the most crucial critiques of the Marxist feminist model. She concludes that the history of White women and women of color in the United States is not only different because of the added axis of race, but that women of color, located at the intersection of race and gender, have a dialectical re-

lation with White women. "Race, gender, class interact in such a way that
the histories of white and racial/ethnic women are intertwined. . . . The
situation of white women has depended on the situation of women of
color."[23] Glenn suggests that both dual systems theory and the "internal
colonialism model," which abstracts men of color's experiences for explaining racial subordination in the United States, are inadequate to the
task of thinking about racial and gender relations in the United States.

From the historical standpoint of "women of color," Glenn makes the
important distinction between U.S. racial/ethnic homes and "White"
homes. She excavates alternative forms of "home" and "housing" established by racial/ethnics in response to and often against the racial and
gender forces of production. These include informal extended kinship
networks among the Chinese "bachelor" workers, whose exclusion from
citizenship and the right to bring family members to the United States demanded new forms of "private" collectivity; collectivity and horizontality
established through practices such as "wage pooling"; shared and group
child rearing due to racial/ethnic mothers' high levels of labor force participation; and the collapse of the public/private distinction in the
racial/ethnic home, which can be attached to family businesses such as
laundries or the site of urban homeworking or petty commodity production to augment the depressed wages of the racialized or absent "primary" worker. Due to the organization of these extended "families" for
whom the nuclear model was invalid and materially impossible and their
historical exclusion from "equality" within the State, then, racial/ethnic
homes can be sites for the emergence of counter-knowledges of how social relations might be imagined and practiced differently from the form
demanded by White patriarchal domesticity and the racial and gendered
State that supports it. In this way, racial/ethnic "domesticities" can be
sites that not only are in contradiction with, but also run counter to the
function of an "Ideological State Apparatus." This is true, in part, because
of the social, economic, and political location of racial/ethnic homes as
demanded by and enforced by precisely that State entity that might otherwise—as it does with "White" homes—imagine and recruit them as
"apparatuses" that can provide a crucial ideological function that "services" the State.

Returning to the work of Lisa Lowe, we can better understand the significance of the asymmetry, nonequivalence, and nonidentity between
racial/ethnic homes and White homes. Lowe reviews the work of Stuart
Hall, in which he suggests that social formations produce their own
forms of antagonism that subjects and groups can organize around. He
gives the example of the discursive category "Black" in England, suggesting that any ideology or ideological site is both the articulation of domination and its simultaneous rearticulation by minority or counterhege-

monic groups. Hall writes, "'Black,' then, exists ideologically only in relation to the contestation around those chains of meaning, and the social
forces involved in that contestation. . . . Social reproduction itself becomes
a contested process."[24] Lowe's reading of Cha's *Dictée*, however, extends
this notion a bit further by suggesting that in addition to the strategic and
necessary attacks on the prevailing form of domination in terms of that
domination, it may also be interventions from the standpoints of alterity
to the structure in dominance that enable the displacement of that dominance.[25]

This chapter concludes by examining the "houses" of queers of color as
locations whose potential for transformation lies precisely in their "alterity" to the racial and gender "structure in dominance," which is nonetheless a determining condition. These are "houses" nonidentical with domesticity, opening up a subjective critical space that remaps the
"location" of the home. Within such spaces the "home" is rendered not as
a site of singular privacy, but as a crucial vector of living and subjectivation that is embedded within, requires, and transforms other vectors in
the social formation.

*   *   *

The final section of this chapter argues, through a reading of *Paris Is Burning*, that the social grouping "queers of color" can engender subjective
formations based on cultural logics analogous to the standpoints developed by mapping the critical genealogy of the U.S. "home." That is, if it is
through a genealogical excavation of the American home from the standpoint of racial/ethnic people and labor that we are able to produce
methodological paradigms that break with conceptual models of the
home that investigate it in isolation, in its "privacy" from other processes
such as modern State and "market" racializations, then it may be the subject formation of "queers of color"—with their history of the home as a
contradictory location that is open and hybrid—that can remember the
interaction between the "structure in dominance" and the "home," enabling other subjective logic and mappings of the "home." Queers of
color, as subjects located at the intersection of multiple hailings, thema-
tize the ways in which the conflicting, noncorrespondent, and overlapping constitutive interpellations of race, gender, and sexuality form cultural subjects whose potential lies precisely in their "confusion" or
"fusion" of more than one determination within a singular subject. The
subjects of *Paris* perform such "con-fusions" throughout the film, such as
when Venus Xtravaganza plays with the fantasy of White suburban domesticity, imagining and desiring a different conjuncture of racial, sexual,
gender, and class subject formation than the arbitrary intersection she
must live out. The subjects of *Paris*, though, not only perform the con-

fusion of social identities, they produce cultural formations that fail to separate cultural productions from material circumstances and political representation, producing powerful confusions of culture, politics, and economic circumstances that engender contradictory subjectivities.

One of the paradoxes of speaking about the subjectivities of "queers of color" through a reading of *Paris* is that those subject positions become available to the viewer only through the documentary form that "records" them.[26] The documentary is a form that has its historical origins in colonialism and anthropology and has been a crucial technology in "racializing" and exoticizing its objects, separating them from their historical context and the filmmaker and distancing the viewer from the locations depicted on screen, no matter how "nearby" that ethnography might take place.[27] The documentary is a form deeply entrenched within ethnography that persistently justifies egregious acts of White violence by rendering people as exotic others that require "western" cultural development, usually in the form of colonial penetration. There are ways in which Livingston's own film is mired in some of these precise tropes. For example, in a few instances, the audience gains a sense of location within Livingston's film. Except for the captions, which provide the viewer with, for example, "New York, 1987" or "New York, 1989," the location of the subjects' lives goes unaccounted for. In viewing talking heads and other tight shots, the viewer loses the sense of place within which these subjects live. That loss of locational specificity is a dramatic method of constituting the documentary subjects as hidden from, distant, or unlocatable to the audience.

Yet the subjects of *Paris* seem to know precisely the paradox of their entry onto the screen. They are left with the difficult situation of having to seize precisely the apparatus that constitutes their otherness to achieve representation. What is most instructive to the viewer is the way in which the subjects of *Paris*, cognizant of the paradox, embrace, by playing up to the camera (and to Livingston), the fundamental impurity of their entrance into representation. Rather than accept a falsifying logic that suggests that representation can mimetically re-present social reality, they approach "social reality" as a contradiction. The subjects of *Paris*, skilled in the arts of mimesis, expose that at least one reason why representation veers away from so-called "reality" is that a field of power is located in the divide. As racialized, poor, and sexual minorities, they maintain a standpoint that suggests that both social reality and public representation are sites that must disavow this field of power to legitimate the exclusion of racial, class, gendered, and sexual others. While no representation mimetically re-presents its supposed prior reality, in *Paris* the critique is offered from the more specific avowal that both normative representation and social reality are forceful sites of exclusivity that must refuse other forms of representation and the unique histories they "contain," histories that emerge from disenfranchized racial and sexual communities.

As Dorian Corey proclaims, "I'm not trying to look real."[28] What might be at stake in the policing of social reality and normative representations of the subject is not only the cutting off of access to histories of exclusion and subordination that give the lie to discourses of free democratic national public life, but equally the suppression of forms that give marginalized subjectivities and subjugated histories their "shape"—their syntax, rhetoric, and morphology. Marginalized subjects might produce narratives and subject positions that record reality as a series of contradictions, paradoxes, gaps, and incoherences, which social reality must smooth over, producing representations of the subject on the model of univocality, development, and synthesis, instituting the rational agent at its center.

Livingston herself partakes in this reformulation, through a reconceptualization of the documentary. As Rabinowitz writes, "Livingston's film is hardly seamless; she breaks both the composed interviews and the spontaneous *vérité* shots of the balls and the streets with inter-titles highlighting ball vernacular . . . and with the names of the houses."[29] Due to both Livingston's filmic methods and the interviewed subjects' penchant for hyperbole, fantasy, and melodrama, the film is always on the verge of breaking down, losing precisely those formal traits that distinguish it as a documentary from other cinematic forms such as realism and classic cinema—namely, the objectivity of evidence and the moral imperative for truth. Rather than considering *Paris Is Burning* an anomalous piece in its generation of a crisis of form, I maintain that this crisis is true of all documentary; an inevitable contradiction exists between the moral imperative for truth and fidelity to "reality" and the dramatic and narrative techniques necessary to represent that "reality." "'Realness' exposes realism and even reality as yet another guise dependent upon simulation and consent."[30] Realness is not a category of living or representation; it is, as Judith Butler suggests, "a *standard* that is used to judge any given performance within the established categories"[31] [emphasis added]. Realness functions in the film not as an alternative to social reality, but as the aesthetic basis by which to negate and contradict "reality." Jackie Goldsby eloquently renders this relationship: "The critical term here is 'realness,' which is the aesthetic imperative defining the ball and its culture. . . . The trope of 'realness' derives its charge from the gesture of erasure precisely because the marks of race, class and sexuality limn these image(s) indelibly and cannot be suppressed no matter how hard the children try."[32]

Rabinowitz's own reading of *Paris* situates the film within and against the continuing interaction between domesticity and the documentary form. The documentary and the docudrama, Rabinowitz argues, have been central to public constructions of American domesticity. And "Livingston's entry into the houses constituting the ball community owed as much to Craig Gilbert's seven-month stay with the Louds [in *An American Family*] as it did to Alex Haley's search for his ancestors [in *Roots*]."[33] Yet, as the film declares through the voice of one its documentary subjects, "This movie is about the ball circuit and the gay people that's involved in it and how each person's life brought them to this circuit." Within the course of the film, that circuit ranges from living in conditions of impoverished housing to turning tricks on the corner; from creating forms of mutual support to throwing forms of fierce shade; from moving into the center of national public fame to collective mournings of lost "children."

Paris Is Burning references domesticity and the "home," yet it does so only from a position of eccentricity. While much of the subjects' lexicon and language is "mopped" from the annals of domestic life, domesticity is not the center of the documentary's dramatic structure. Rather, the film is organized around the ball circuit, the houses that sustain it, and the members who walk the floor. Domesticity is the absent presence that punctuates the life narratives of many of the interviewed subjects. Homes and domesticity in *Paris* are constitutive, yet absent. As Pepper LaBeija proclaims, "I fill the void these kids have without parents." While domesticity in *Paris* is an intimate experience unique and particular to each subject, the "circuit" is the occasion at which each subject's experience is collected and shared through lateral and vertical relations with "brothers," "sisters," and "mothers."

Paris collects testimony from many of its central documentary subjects, Pepper LaBeija, Dorian Corey, Venus, and Angie Xtravaganza, on the absence of home, following it up with a series of clips and interviews organized around the linguistic cue "House." Within the dramatic sequencing of the film, then, "houses" are suggested as explicit responses to and impermanent structures built for, in part, the experience of domestic loss, evacuation, ejection.

Although at first it seems as though both Livingston and the documentary subjects posit these "houses" as possibly more accommodating homes, fulfilling the ideal promises of a universally incorporative loving domesticity, a more complicated architecture of the "houses" emerges. Dorian Corey initially responds to Livingston's question with "A house? They are families. You could say that. They are families." Yet, already intonating a failed metaphor of "houses" and "family," Corey continues: "Houses are families for a lot who don't have family. It's not a man, a women, and children, which we grew up knowing is a family. This is a new meaning of family. It's a question of a group of human beings in a mutual bond." As though exhausted by the length of her own answer, she quips, "A house? I'll tell you what a house is. A house is a gay street gang." In Corey's commentary, "houses" shift from establishing identity with family, to reformulations of the family model, to, finally, an analogy with a street gang. Corey's own definition of the "houses" is unstable, moving from rearticulations of domesticity to, ultimately, an analogy with other formations of recalcitrant "counter-public" collectivities (street gangs) that cannot replace the constitutive violence of "home" yet must supplement it. Pepper LaBeija's own explanation for why she filed suit against Livingston and Miramax for a share of the film's profits is possibly most telling of the distance and nonanalogy between "home" and "house": "I really just live in the Bronx with my mom. And I am so desperate to get out of here! It's hard to be the mother of a house while you're living with your own mother."[34]

Harassed in or expelled from their homes for their sexuality or gender transgressions, the subjects of *Paris* rely on the houses for support, pleasure, and recognition. Corey's own discussion of the houses in the film, for example, is set to visual shots not of any of the subjects' homes, but of queer of color "counter-publics" such as the Christopher Street Pier and the small parks that dot Greenwich Village. Contextualizing the "houses" of *Paris* within scenes of group discussion on park bleachers and chats on the pier, the film demonstrates that these "houses" are nonidentical to the "home." The houses in *Paris* are not only materially distinct from the home (sometimes functioning as a network of support and not a physical dwelling), their existence is, in part, due to conditions founded in the home, generating cultural formations whose function it is to recognize subjects who are made unintelligible or abject within their own homes and the large social formation. As cultural and social sites, the houses in *Paris* dramatically destabilize the concept of the home or any other single determining apparatus as the subject's singular site of development and self-formation. The houses in *Paris* attest to the shifting, changing, and incoherent history of self-formation, not figuring subjects who are predicated on a linear model of development or statically or singularly constituted, but rather imagining subjects who are always in the process of change and transformation, responding partially to changing material and corporeal conditions.[35] Most of all, the houses of *Paris* are crucial collectivities that respond to violences and subordinations generated in the home *and* in public life, exposing nodes of affinity and identity between the two locations.

This is tragically dramatized in the interview with Angie Xtravaganza after the death of Venus Xtravaganza. Angie recounts to the camera that when she found out about Venus's death, she was at a Christmas show she had booked for her "house." She recollects going to the State morgue to "claim" Venus's body, which was found three days after her murder in a motel room. "They were about to cremate her because nobody came to claim her body." In this stark example, it is literally Angie's recognition of

Venus that transforms her from an anonymous corpse, unaccounted for and identical to the rest, into a subject not only of the State, but of a counter-collectivity that gives her history and remembers her "legend." Ironically, it is Angie, mother of the house of Xtravaganza, who must inform Venus's family of her death.

"Houses" in *Paris* are not new domestic ideals. Rather, they are needed collectivities giving financial support, temporary living space, advice, and pleasure. As Jackie Goldsby declares, "In the world of *Paris Is Burning*, a house is not a home."[36] In Goldsby's reading, the houses of *Paris* are most important for how they "fail" to reproduce the structure of the home. They are social collectivities that disunify the simple trinity of "family," "community," and "nation" that undergirds the logic of many cultural nationalisms. Simultaneously, the subjects of *Paris* refuse to disengage the home as a crucial location within oppositional and minority communities or within public life.

The "home" is remembered as a founding condition for the house. The home is not duplicated through the practices of the house; rather, the house acts as the home's nonidentical supplement. For Goldsby, "'Home' no longer stands as the unproblematic site of Black cultural salvation it represented for DuBois; it is, instead, a fount of homophobia that damns difference and sponsors rejection, which, in turn, inspires the rebirth of the 'house.'"[37] The radical gesture in declaring a nonidentity between the home and the house is that it suggests that the house can never replace the home. The home is a location crucial to another moment and condition of the subject's formation. Rather than substituting for, replacing, or rearticulating the home, the houses are sites whose cohesions are founded in subordinations and violences that are explicitly avowed, only some of which stem from the home. As Angie remarks of Venus's death, "That's part of life, part of being a transsexual in New York City."

Houses are locations that presuppose each subject as the product of an earlier interpellation, an interpellation whose contradiction elaborates itself as damage to subjects who inhabit that contradiction—a damage that, in relationship to Black social formations, Goldsby locates as equally found within assimilationist and nationalist responses to racism.[38] "The fact of the matter is that black heterosexual culture—from assimilationist to nationalist—exercises the power and privilege to exclude and silence its (queer) own."[39] Yet it is precisely this damage and the subjects who bear its traces that can become the site for the formation of collectivities that collect unlike individuals and imagine a different sense of community.

The houses of *Paris* are collectivities that place into community heterogeneous subjects—transgenders, preop transsexuals, gay men, postop transsexuals, and other young queers of color—who are not "unified" by a prior identity that transcends these heterogeneities. Instead, the houses are explicitly locations that "unify" heterogeneous subjects by avowing and founding their cohesion on the damage produced by the demands and dictations for uniformity within a heterosexual matrix of gender and sexuality. And rather than succumbing to the logic of privacy, whereby the heterosexual demand for the sexual as "private," which heterosexuality itself institutes, can further isolate queer subjects, the subjects of *Paris* form important collectivities by which each "private" ejection from the home, whether imposed or "chosen," is brought together. The houses are locations that refuse "privacy" as a concept that is in part heterosexist and racist, and they simultaneously negate the demand for identity, embracing collectivities founded precisely on heterogeneity and nonidentity, since it is the subjects' refusals to conform to the proper family type that originally founded their condition and need for collectivity. In other words, the "houses" are, in part, sites that are established by queers of color in antagonism to the ideologies and material exclusions of the home, whose central purpose is not necessarily, in the case of racial/ethnic homes, the reproduction of state racism. Yet, because queers of color are part of the political formation "people of color," it is these collectivities, in alterity to forms of antagonism articulated "directly" against racial subordination— which are nonetheless central, as the history of racially discriminatory housing in the United States makes evident—that might found an alternative logic or mapping of subjectivity that can extend our movement in the fight against the State and cultural "structure in dominance."

Notes

I would like to thank Gayatri Gopinath, Eleanor Jaluage, and Victor Bascara for their support and encouragement with this project. My discussions with Sonali Perera and Amie Parry have influenced my thinking tremendously; this chapter is an index of those conversations. The chapter began under the guidance of Judith Halberstam, and her mentorship and teaching have guided the entirety of the project. David Blackmore made sure I finished and gave the chapter an invaluable reading. As this essay clearly exposes, the teachings and intellectual work of Lisa Lowe made writing it possible. Lastly, my thanks must go to one other person. Rosemary George's discussions and generative suggestions around domesticity and *Paris Is Burning* gave this chapter its direction and focus. Her editorship has been invaluable.

1. *Paris Is Burning*. Videotape. Directed by Jennie Livingston. Academy Entertainment, 1991. 76 min.

2. See Louis Althusser, *Lenin and Philosophy*, trans. Ben Brewster (New York: Monthly Review Press, 1971), pp. 127–86.

3. Lisa Lowe, "Unfaithful to the Original: The Subject of Dictée," in *Writing Self Writing Nation*, eds. Norma Alarcón and Elaine H. Kim (Berkeley: Third Woman Press, 1994), p. 55.

4. I use the term "racial/ethnic people" to designate a heterogeneous social grouping composed of different sets of racialized populations. The term does not signify a homogenization of the important differences and heterogeneities within the category but rather marks the explicit history of State racialization—a historically situated force that galvanizes different populations with their unique experiences of racialization in relation to a common repressive State. Maxine Baca Zinn and Bonnie Thornton Dill have provided one definition of "racial/ethnic people":

> The term racial-ethnic refers to groups that are socially and legally subordinated and remain culturally distinct within U.S. society. It is meant to include (1) the systematic discrimination of socially constructed racial groups and (2) their distinctive cultural arrangements. Historically, the categories of African American, Latino, Asian American and Native American were constructed as both racially and culturally distinct. In this book we use such terms interchangeably because they are currently used in both popular and scholarly discourse.

I would add that it is the role of multiculturalism to imagine cultural formations that are pure and closed and rendered discrete from one another. Racial/ethnic cultural history might rethink cultural formations as heterogeneous, impure, and unclosed. Also, while the State and pluralist multiculturalism might level important differences between ethnic groups within a single racial classification, racial/ethnic culture is the site that articulates and investigates the history of coalition and linkage between distinct social groupings in order not to recapitulate the logic of either an undifferentiated homogeneity of a racial grouping demanded by state multiculturalism or an essential uniqueness and difference of ethnicity demanded by cultural nationalist models. See Maxine Baca Zinn and Bonnie Thornton Dill, "Difference and Domination," in *Women of Color in U.S. Society*, eds. Maxine Baca Zinn and Bonnie Thornton Dill (Philadelphia: Temple University Press, 1994), p. 12.

5. Stuart Hall, "Signification, Representation, Ideology: Althusser and the Post-Structuralist Debates," *Critical Studies in Mass Communications*, Volume 2, Number 2 (June 1985), p. 98. I have learned greatly from this essay, not only about what is valuable in Althusser's essay, but also about what parts of his essay need significant elaboration and reformulation from the standpoint of people living within a racial national society such as Britain in the 1980s.

6. Hall takes issue with the naming of these private and civil institutions as "Ideological State Apparatuses" because it simplifies the more complicated and urgent questions under liberal capitalism of how it is that even when "civil society" is granted a level of "autonomy" from the State, it nonetheless reproduces ideologies that reproduce State concepts or support forms of capitalism autonomously. Hall writes:

> His [Althusser's] nomenclature does not give sufficient weight to what Gramsci would call the immense complexities of society in modern social formations—"the trenches and fortifications of civil society." It does not begin to make sense of how complex are the processes by which capitalism must work to order and organize a civil society which is not, technically, under its immediate control. These are important problems in the field of ideol-

ogy and culture which the formulation, "ideological state apparatuses," encourages us to evade.

See Hall, p. 101. For this reason, I have varied my naming of these institutions, sometimes referring to them as "Ideological State Apparatuses" and other times simply as "Ideological Apparatuses." Any apparatus can fulfill the function of both directives, interpellating subjects for the State, as does the Educational Apparatus (including both public and private schools), for example, and at the same time aiding in the reproduction of an "autonomous" civil society. The "Family" Apparatus is one of the most important institutions in making "good" subjects for the State. At the same time, in the contemporary period, for some racial/ethnic or "third world" women workers located in export manufacturing zones, offshore production ports, and the "informal" global economy, the family can be the apparatus that aids in making *specifically* gendered working subjects not for the State, but for a postfordist "global" economic labor chain. See the essays compiled in Edna Acosta-Belen and Christine Bose, *Women in the Latin American Development Process* (Philadelphia: Temple University Press, 1995). Also, by calling the family an "Ideological Apparatus," I do not intend a dyadic opposition between ideology and "freedom" or "liberation," implying that if one only exited the site of that apparatus, he or she would be outside its capture. Rather, ideologies can be as much the interpellative ideas of submission, hierarchy, and individual subjectivation as they can be the critically important ideas of antagonism, collectivity, and dissent.

7. Lowe, "Unfaithful," p. 56.

8. Lowe, "Unfaithful," p. 56.

9. Lawrence Glickman, "Inventing the 'American Standard of Living': Gender, Race and Working-Class Identity, 1880–1925," *Labor History*, Volume 34, Numbers 2–3 (Spring/Summer 1993), p. 223.

10. In his essay on the Ideological State Apparatus, Althusser points out that the Guaranteed Minimum Wage needed for the reproduction of labor power is a historical minimum, variable upon national location: "Marx noted that English workers need beer while French proletarians need wine." He defines this minimum as doubly historical because the variable minimum is established not only by a "recognition" of the needs of the working classes by the capitalist class, but also by the historical needs imposed by the proletarian class struggle. The specific history of the United States focuses this idea further by exposing that the capitalist class didn't just "recognize" the needs of the working class across the board, but also specifically "recognized" a White working class different from racial/ethnic workers. See Althusser, p. 131.

11. Glickman, "Inventing," pp. 231–2.

12. Glickman, "Inventing," p. 232.

13. By "articulation" I mean to employ the definition given to the term by Stuart Hall. Hall suggests that it is true that within any national location the State cannot be thought of as a kind of single object. There are many different social contradictions with distinct origins that converge within any historical formation. The State itself is the expression of contradictory social classes and is multidimensional. Yet Hall reminds the reader that the State remains one of the crucial sites in a modern capitalist social formation, "where political practices of different kinds

are *condensed."* Hall continues, "The function of the State is, in part, precisely to bring together or *articulate* into a complexly structured instance, a range of political discourses and social practices" (emphasis added). Equally, though, subjugated people, unevenly determined by that range of discourses and practices, simultaneously organize around and through the exact terms of domination and force a rearticulation. See Hall, p. 93.

14. Eileen Boris, "The Racialized Gendered State: Constructions of Citizenship in the United States," *Social Politics* (Summer 1995), p. 166.

15. This is an important note because the cultural and political formation "people of color" or "racial/ethnic people" of which this chapter speaks includes social groupings that not only have a racial history in relation to the United States *in* the United States but also retain their *specific* history of "racial" formation in relation to the United States as an imperial and colonial State in their "homelands." For example, the Welfare State of the 1930s did not extend to the people of Puerto Rico, who have nonetheless been forced to live under U.S. colonial tutelage since 1898. Although women workers in the tobacco and needlework industries militantly demanded that the Free Labor Federation (FLT) advocate to include Puerto Rico in the minimum wage legislation passed under the Fair Labor Standards Act, the FLT and the United States failed to recognize these demands. When provisions associated with the Welfare State did arrive in Puerto Rico, they were meted out in specifically colonial ways, perpetuating local dependence. For example, food stamps, a program begun in the 1970s, reached over half the Puerto Rican population in the 1980s. These "welfare" provisions, know as transfer payments, are specific ways in which the "modernizing and neocolonial" State aids industry and capital in supplementing workers' means of subsistence and reducing their actual wages—supporting, engendering, and sustaining a colonial or neocolonial economic formation. As Helen Safa states, "While seen as subsidies to workers, these transfer payments are also aids to low-wage industries like apparel that do not pay an adequate wage and might otherwise leave the island." See Helen Safa, *The Myth of the Male Breadwinner: Women and Industrialization in the Caribbean* (Boulder: Westview Press, 1995), p. 17.

16. George Lipsitz, "The Possessive Investment in Whiteness: Racialized Social Democracy and the 'White' Problem in American Studies," *American Quarterly,* Volume 47, Number 3 (September 1995), p. 372.

17. Lipsitz, "The Possessive Investment," pp. 373–4.

18. See Lipsitz, pp. 372–4. "By 1993, 86 percent of suburban whites still lived in places with a black population below 1 percent." Lipsitz, p. 374.

19. See Kimberlé Crenshaw, "Race, Reform and Retrenchment: Transformation and Legitimation in Anti-Discrimination Law," in *Critical Race Theory: The Key Writings That Formed the Movement,* eds. Kimberlé Crenshaw et al. (New York: The New Press, 1996), pp. 103–22. Crenshaw's article is an important one from which I have learned much. She asserts that whereas Marxist readings of the law suggested that the law was a legitimating apparatus that stymied dissent and "resolved" political and economic contradiction within the juridical sphere, for racial/ethnic people with their historical experience of exclusion from the law and citizenship, the law functioned not as a legitimating apparatus or state technology, but as an important contradiction that contributed to a "racial" overdetermination of the social formation.

20. See, for example, Althusser, *Lenin and Philosophy*, pp. 127–86.

21. See Heidi Hartmann, "The Unhappy Marriage of Marxism and Feminism: Towards a More Progressive Union," in *Women and Revolution: A Discussion of the Unhappy Marriage of Marxism and Feminism*, ed. Lydia Sargent (Boston: South End Press, 1981), pp. 1–41.

22. Evelyn Nakano Glenn, "Racial Ethnic Women's Labor: The Intersection of Race, Gender and Class Oppression," *Review of Radical Political Economics*, Volume 17, Number 3 (1983), pp. 86–108. See Bina Agarwal for an exploration of the role of the colonial state and the "modernizing" state in the formation of gendered subjects and the home. Bina Agarwal, "Patriarchy and the 'Modernizing' State: An Introduction," in *Structures of Patriarchy: State, Community and Household in Modernizing Asia*, ed. Bina Agarwal (New Delhi, India: Kali for Women, 1988), pp. 1–28. Also see Rosemary George's chapter in this book for a history of the colonial home and a reevaluation of the (White colonial) subject posited by American and British feminisms.

23. See Glenn, "Racial Ethnic Women's Labor," p. 105. Glenn's critique is powerful and illuminating; I have provided only one segment of it.

24. Quoted in Lowe, "Unfaithful," p. 57. See Hall, "Signification," p. 113.

25. Lowe, "Unfaithful," p. 57.

26. Important critiques of the filmmaker, the documentary form, and the reception of the film within White, straight national audiences are available. See Phillip Brian Harper's essay on the constitutive contradiction of the documentary form as one that transforms Jennie Livingston into a creative agent, or filmmaker, while it robs the documentary subjects of any claims to the film's creative and economic capital, reducing their legal and subjective status to that of an object. Harper subtly concludes that this is a "structural condition" of the documentary form that forces a reconsideration of the proclamations of "transgression" and "subversion" made by White liberal critics of the film. Harper writes, "As Livingston herself noted some two years after the film's release, 'I am a film maker . . . And that's something I wasn't before'; at the same time, to quote from Jesse Green's *New York Times* article, in which that self-characterization appears, those presented in *Paris Is Burning* 'remain[ed], at best, exactly where they were when filmed.'" See Phillip Brian Harper, "'The Subversive Edge': *Paris Is Burning*, Social Critique, and the Limits of Subjective Agency," *Diacritics*, Volume 24, Numbers 2–3 (Summer/Fall 1994), p. 99. For lack of space, I have omitted a review of those critiques, yet my reading is cognizant and contoured by them. See also bell hooks, *Black Looks: Race and Representation* (Boston: South End Press, 1992), pp. 145–56.

27. Paula Rabinowitz writes, "Documentary is a modern term, coined in 1926 by the filmmaker, John Grierson, to describe the 'value' of Robert Flaherty's visual account of the daily life of Polynesian Islanders, *Moana*." While Rabinowitz places the documentary as originating in an earlier moment, through still photography in the late nineteenth century, it remains true that its generic origins are firmly within colonialism. Documentary is not only a central technology of colonial representation, as Rabinowitz's work makes clear, it is equally a technology that constitutes the gendered division of the "public" and the "private" exactly by constantly shuttling between the two performatively constituted locations. Yet to the degree that no genre is univocal, Rabinowitz's book explores the form as a hetero-

geneous genre that has enabled both repressive or regressive and radical or feminist projects. I have relied heavily on the work of Paula Rabinowitz in shaping my thinking about the documentary. While I can only inadequately index this in this chapter, her book has helped me conceive this portion of the chapter. See Paula Rabinowitz, *They Must Be Represented: The Politics of Documentary* (New York: Verso, 1994), p. 5.

28. Quoted in Jesse Green, "Paris Has Burned," *New York Times*, April 18, 1993, section 9, p. 11.

29. Rabinowitz, *They Must Be Represented*, p. 132.

30. Rabinowitz, *They Must Be Represented*, p. 131.

31. Judith Butler, *Bodies That Matter: On the Discursive Limits of "Sex"* (New York: Routledge, 1993), p. 129. This text is far too rich to summarize in any one article, so I have absented myself from the task. Particularly important for my thinking is the way Butler reinvents the category of "gender" within the context of the fantasy of Venus Xtravaganza to be the *vehicle* for Venus's race and class desires. Butler's reading of kinship is provocative in many ways. This essay deviates, though, from considering the houses as resignifications of kinship, to thinking about them as supplements to racial/ethnic homes, sites that can remember annihilations both within domesticity and from White public culture.

32. Jackie Goldsby, "Queens of Language: *Paris Is Burning*," in *Queer Looks: Perspectives on Lesbian and Gay Film and Video*, eds. Martha Gever, John Greyson, and Pratibha Parmar (New York: Routledge, 1993), p. 110.

33. Rabinowitz, *They Must Be Represented*, p. 131.

34. Green, "Paris Has Burned," p. 11.

35. Certain anthropological writings and English literatures posit the subject's entrance into adult sexuality as the period when the subject's constitution is complete. Anthropological discussions of "rites of passage"—particularly the movement from puberty to adulthood—tend to predicate the subject's development on models of linearity. In English literature the bildungsroman narrates the development of the protagonist from youthful innocence to mature adulthood. Adulthood resolves the inconsistencies, chaos, and confusion of childhood and marks the subject's completion into stable identity. Often this is marked by heterosexual marriage as the *leitmotiv* of stability, synthesis, and identity. Even psychoanalysis, because it evaluates the subject's history from the standpoint of sexual difference as the original and primary axis of differentiation and constitution, has historically been mired in a less dynamic, hybrid, and multiply constituted subject. To the degree that queers of color record their entrance into sexuality as a destabilizing moment, when other forms of difference cross social relations and the arbitrary "beginning" of the subject's multidimensional history, in which gender, race, and class overlap, unevenly yet simultaneously determining the subject's forms of object choice and self-identity, these other models of development are thrown into question, and a more complex model reformulated.

36. Goldsby, "Queens of Language," p. 109.

37. Goldsby, "Queens of Language," pp. 113–14.

38. For more on the concept of "damage" and its relation to the colonial subject, please see David Lloyd, *Anomalous States: Irish Writing and the Post-Colonial Moment* (Durham, N.C.: Duke University Press, 1993). See also his chapter in this

book. Within a U.S. queer context, Ann Cvetkovich has argued not to disavow forms of sexual and violent trauma, but to explore their difficult history within the context of "adult" or contemporary queer culture. Cvetkovich suggests that the connection, no matter how immediate or distant, is never direct. A queer contribution to notions of trauma and healing comes, Cvetkovich argues, in the form of a complication in which "trauma is a far from straightforward experience, and no simple prescription, whether therapeutic or political, or both, can heal it." See Ann Cvetkovich, "Sexual Trauma/Queer Memory: Incest, Lesbianism, and Therapeutic Culture," *GLQ*, Volume 2, Number 4 (Fall 1995), p. 373.

39. Goldsby, "Queens of Language," p. 114.

Chapter Seventeen

The Squat, the Tearoom, the Urn, and the Designer Bathroom: Citing Home in Ken Loach's Riff Raff

MAURIZIA BOSCAGLI

In 1990 *Riff Raff* marked Ken Loach's return to the screen after almost ten years of absence. With this film, the British director once again took up the analysis of and politically committed commentary on contemporary British society that had characterized his production since the 1960s—for instance, with such films as *Poor Cow* (1969) and *Family Life* (1972). In *Riff Raff*, a film produced after much hesitation by the BBC's Channel Four, Loach turns the camera's eye on the bleak scenario of unemployment and working-class uprootedness left behind by more than a decade of Thatcherism in England. Through the realist formulas of docu-fiction, *Riff Raff* portrays a group of casual workers employed by a construction firm in North London to transform a decayed former hospital into luxury condos; the ex–Prince of Wales Hospital is being "restored" by "London Heritage Homes." All coming from the periphery (Bristol, Glasgow, Liverpool, as well as Africa), and in most cases clandestines in order to retain their welfare subsidies, the workers come together to form a volatile group, which will necessarily dissolve at the end. However aware they are about the chief element that keeps them together as a community— their shared condition of exploited labor—they remain unable to effectively respond to it, instead lashing out in the angry gesture of revenge that concludes the film after a fatal work accident.

As a proletarian drama tenuously and bitterly filtered through comedy, *Riff Raff* is first of all a fierce and uncompromising critique of the British government's welfare politics at the time of the 1990 Maastricht Conference. At Maastricht the attempt of the countries of the European Community to elaborate a common welfare system aimed at regulating and protecting labor through shared legislation was opposed by Britain, which chose instead to "opt out." As a result, the question of social policy became one of the lowest priorities in the final text of the treaty, to forestall a conflict between Britain and the other EC members. The norms regulating labor in Europe were finally negotiated only among the other eleven member states; Britain chose to remain excluded from the new legislation and instead to continue Thatcher's program of deregulation in favor of the market's needs.

Produced in this climate, *Riff Raff* is explicitly a film of social denunciation, whose plot and tone mark it as a highly charged political and "public" text. Unexpectedly, however, its portrayal of exploitation and class antagonism is centered upon the image and the problematic of the home, a space traditionally signifying domesticity, familial privacy, and the personal. During the 1980s, "home" had become a highly charged term in the British national imaginary, specifically in the imaginary that Thatcherism tried hard to hegemonize and shape through the ideology of country, nation, and family. While class was continually downgraded as a category of social cohesiveness both in political discourse and in social theory debates, the rhetoric of home became even more ubiquitous in conservative discourse, to the point of dominating all notions of the social. Hence one of Margaret Thatcher's most notorious catch phrases: "There is no society, there are only individuals and their families."[1] Domestic space as imagined in Thatcherite ideology was deeply inflected with ideas of order, Englishness, and gender hierarchy. Far from representing such space as the sheltering milieu of bourgeois privacy, in *Riff Raff* Loach balances the inversely proportional relationship between class and home, the political and the private, to read Thatcherite representations of the home against the grain. In *Riff Raff*, therefore, the newly dislocated space of home in fact functions to foreground the social; in particular, it contradicts Thatcherite representations of society as an idealized corporate entity organized around principles of cooperation rather than class-based antagonisms.

In Loach's film the issue of class identity, of how a group of disaffected and exasperated proletarians can acquire a consciousness of themselves as a class and therefore try to conquer a measure of political and social currency, is shown to hinge on the question of their visibility. As workers or producers, they are the hidden reality behind the glamorous spectacle of London's gentrification. Making them visible, then, relies on the possibility of representing the local—that is, of telling a story capable of contradicting the view of reality produced by the global interests of the market, which the hegemonic discourses of Thatcherism celebrated.

The social invisibility of Stevie, Desmond, Larry, Fiaman, and the other workers shown in the film is a structural effect of the spatial and economic restructuring and dislocation of labor that characterizes the current postfordist stage of capitalism.[2] The multinational organization of postindustrial capitalism has managed to put "out of sight" production and its social costs by relocating both as much as possible at the peripheries, often away from the core countries; the effect of the international division of labor of the postfordist moment is the partial displacement of the class divisions previously situated within the industrial metropolis onto the dislocation between first and third worlds. This general trend, then, leads to the fiction of the disappearance of productive labor altogether in the core countries, which in turn feeds into the Thatcherite mythology of the end of the class system and of class antagonism, and the representation of *all* British citizens as consumers. But productive labor, even if rendered less and less visible, has by no means disappeared even in the first world. In fact, postindustrial economy heavily depends on its productive power both in the periphery and in the core countries.

By focusing on the local and on the home as sites of consumption where production is comfortably forgotten, Loach clearly asserts this fact and implicitly affirms that the real globalism of capital is a story of globally shared abuse and exploitation of laborers of all nationalities. However, the film neither triumphantly affirms the visibility of class nor situates it automatically within the space of home. Rather the characters shown working on the building site in *Riff Raff* are lumpen proletarians, whose survival depends precisely on their uprootedness and on their explicit renunciation of any avowed locality of home, family, or class and ethnic communities. These are displaced individuals, both migrants and casual workers, attracted to London by its burgeoning building industry. Instead, the question of class identity is situated "inside" the domestic space by the crucial and bitter paradox that sets off the narrative: Loach's defamiliarizing parable of home in *Riff Raff* is told as the story of homeless and dispossessed people building a house that will never be home for them. Given the bitter truth that this "house" will never be lived in by the workers who build it (and, by extension, that England as a pastoral fantasy of corporate nation and allegedly classless national heritage will never be home to them either), it is imperative for Loach's workers to search for another "home" and another kind of homeland. Loach shows them engaged in this search, contesting the terms on which hegemonic discourses of domesticity and family are formulated.

In *Riff Raff*, the London Heritage Homes project is, literally, the structure on which the discourses of domesticity, affect, citizenship, and social visibility as Thatcherite discourse produced them are contested. Hence, it is crucial, in order to redefine the domestic as a space capable of guaranteeing visibility to those who, as the characters in *Riff Raff*, are denied access to the master's house rather than in a subaltern and marginal position, to represent home "citationally," as a displaced quotation of an impossible, a nonexistent real thing—that is, as a catachresis. A catachresis, as Gayatri Spivak explains in her discussion of Nietzsche's and Derrida's appropriation of "woman," is a concept and metaphor "used in such a way that I cannot locate an adequate literal referent for the word" (Spivak, 126). "Home" as a catachresis, therefore, is a signified that cannot be given up but that, because of its colonization by the conservative camp, refuses to have a fixed referent and rather acquires new meanings by its multiple, continual displacements. The itinerant, fragmentary, and citational notion of home in *Riff Raff* points to its catachrestic quality: never once and for all spatially stabilized or safely centered on the image that most traditionally defines the domestic space, the maternal body, home is represented as an impossible space, "cited" by the approximation through unexpected locales. By examining four of these unusual rewritings of home—the squat where one of the workers lives, the tearoom where they eat lunch and chat, the urn that significantly contains the ashes of the maternal body, and a newly built designer bathroom—this chapter shows how an ex-centric notion of domesticity and privacy can become the ground for a reformulation of the social and, in turn, how it can function to tear apart the phantasmally seamless British national identity that the Thatcherite discourse of "heritage" asserts, instead bringing the notion of class antagonism to the forefront.

Athens Without the Slaves: The Squat/The Tearoom

The social invisibility of Loach's workers is produced on the one hand by the structural dislocation of labor that characterizes postindustrial capitalism and on the other by the privileging of consumption in the cultural analysis of postmodernity that such spatial restructuring allows. By focusing exclusively on consumption (what remains visible once production takes place offshore, in faraway places), theorists as different as Daniel Bell, Jean Baudrillard, Henri Lefevre, and Andre Gorz, among others, have contributed to a classless representation of postmodern society, which disregards traditional and multilayered class stratification to recognize only a managerial technocracy (inhabiting by right the information society) and an undistinguished mass of disenfranchised marginal individuals, underemployed and unemployed.[3] The claimed obsolescence of the working class and the idea that contemporary western societies are more or less homogeneously constituted by technocracies of nonmanual workers seem to be supported also by the technological progress that has characterized postfordism, as it is bolstered up by an enormous faith in the liberating power of the technologies of the information age. This faith appeared full-fledged in the words of Thatcher's then energy secretary Peter Walker, who, in an interview in 1983, attempted to give a classical humanist gloss to the narrative of contemporary unemployment by turning to the thoroughly modernist rhetoric of the machine: "It is a whole new concept of life that the information society is going to provide. We have the opportunity of creating Athens without the slaves, where the slaves will be the computer and the microchip, and the human race can obtain a new sense of enjoyment, leisure and fulfillment."[4] Considering Walker's profession of faith in the light of the last decade of British sociocultural history, it is clear that the Thatcherite project of replacing Britain's fading manufacturing industry with the global digital highway has not freed people from toil. Instead, the global spread of corporate culture along with the "infobahn" has had as one of its main social and cultural consequences the demise of a sense of the local, "not just defined by geography," as the artists Peter Dunn and Loraine Leeson affirm, "but as the specificity of what it is like to be working class in this society, or a woman, or black, or gay, or to be differently abled" (Bird et al., 143).[5] It is this specificity that Walker's discourse of leisure without production, inscribed in the utopia of "Athens without the slaves," implicitly denies.

The setting of *Riff Raff*, the London building site, reinscribes with particular poignancy this dialectic of global and local, visibility and invisibility, by directly representing the capitalist spatialization of production and consumption at the center of the western city. During the 1980s London became the site of grand schemas of urban renovation aimed at gentrifying and revitalizing decayed neighborhoods and individual buildings. In most cases these transformations took place through the privatization of public state property and a savage deregulation of urban planning, explicitly supported by the conservative government. In 1981 the UDC (Urban Development Corporation), an organization directly appointed by the secretary of state and representing business and property interests, was given the power to grant planning permission without any consultation with or investigation by the local authorities.[6] Thus the "urban revitalization" that the UDC had championed promoted free-market interventions in what had previously been the territory of the local authorities (specifically the Labour Councils) and of the communities of people that lived in the areas in question. The areas that the UDC helped insert into the circuits of international finance and global enterprise, therefore, were often converted either from spaces of public and social service or from the historical home ground of ethnic and working-class communities. Thus *Riff Raff*'s focus on a hospital (suggestive of the gutted British National Health Service) being rebuilt as expensive apartments is particularly apt. The most famous of these transformations into the visually and architecturally homogenized spaces of "sanitized" business, decked out with the trappings of leisure and consumption, has been the massive rebuilding of London's "Docklands." Since 1981 the London Docklands Development Corporation has overseen the transformation of a blighted working-class sector of the city into, as Jon Bird describes it, "the global postmodern as a building site" (Bird et al., 124), a space not only where, despite the developers, affluence and poverty continue to rub elbows together but where the social and ethnic fabric of a closely knit neighborhood has been torn apart by a rampant architectural and economic postmodernization. The economic shift that turned the former docks into a urban wasteland in the first place is also accountable for the attempt to delete the presence of the workers who had lived and worked there for years: "This time the labor was not needed in the new port; moreover, the physical presence of their communities was both an inconvenience and an embarrassment. It was not enough that they were dispossessed and politically disenfranchised, but they had to be rendered invisible too" (Dunn and Leeson, 138). Once the old docks had been closed and the once powerful labor force of dockers was no longer needed, the area was ready to be transformed into the center of a new economy, one that implicitly turned the previous workers into part of the unsightly decay of the place.

Riff Raff photographs with acute precision the modalities of this making invisible of manual workers by placing the contemporary "slaves," to use Peter Walker's paraphrase of Aristotle's *Politics*, in the middle of the "cleaned up" space of the core city. Situated in the midst of the Thatcherite project of privatization and globalization of social and urban space, these workers exist as a submerged, unofficial, and even illegal presence, but they are "there" nonetheless, exactly because they represent cheap labor for capital (the infobahn and its technocracy cannot lay bricks, after all).

Not only are the workers situated in the midst of the revitalized urban space, but as their representation in the film makes clear, their visibility is regulated according to the principles of shock (and pleasure), disgust (and desire), that had defined the presence of the abject in the modern industrial city.[7] But this time, in the deregulated space of the postmodern metropolis, the material and metaphorical barriers between the slums and the residential quarters that had regulated the physical and spatial proximity between the bourgeoisie and the working class—barriers designed, as Friedrich Engels wrote, "to conceal from the eyes of the wealthy men and women of strong stomachs and weak nerves the misery and grime that forms the complement of their wealth"[8]—have been weakened, so that the contemporary workers are once again situated at the center of the revitalized urban space, only to have it made clear that there is no space there for them.

The anonymity and placelessness of the workers is made evident from the very beginning of *Riff Raff*. From the opening scene, centered on the image of rats, the abject and parasitical animals associated with disease, dirt, and contamination that came to symbolize all that was lamentable in the proletarians and their unsightly slums in the nineteenth century, the camera pans to the rats' contemporary human equivalent, the homeless. We are then shown an animated and commercial city street early in the morning, with a group of people sleeping huddled in a nook of the sidewalk. They are the riff raff of the film's title, part of a population of vagrant homeless, "parasites" who in Thatcherite lore do not contribute to the national firm, but rather "scrounge,"[9] benefiting from other people's efforts.

One of these homeless, one forgettable body among other forgettable and implicitly forgotten bodies, is Stevie, the character whose story is central to Loach's narrative. Stevie's anonymity continues when he reaches the building site of London Heritage Homes, asking for a job, and ceases only once he joins the other workers at the "orientation" meeting in the tearoom. Yet, when interpellated as a subaltern by the corporation via the foreman's words, once again Stevie becomes the faceless subject that he had been as a homeless person.

The foreman's harangue to the new and old workers consists of a few, basic statements, which make clear the precariousness of these workers: "Thursday paying day—and sacking day. We don't allow thieving. Signing under a name. A casual approach to work. Laziness and fucking foul language. No pissing in corners." When asked comically by one of the workers to give his opinion on the ozone layer, the foreman, in a perfect rehearsal of the Thatcherite discourse of the free market, answers: "I'll turn a blind eye on it as long as it doesn't interfere with the job." This self-serving blindness becomes more than metaphorical when any suggestion to their right to accident insurance is made by the workers. As Gus, the foreman, explains, "Tax is paid for by us, but . . . you pay your own insurance. You are self-employed." The elusiveness of the corporation when dealing with the workers' rights on the one hand propels the narrative to its dramatic finale (the fateful accident) and on the other creates the setting for the enunciation of the illegal fiction (the workers as self-employed), which constructs them all, in a grotesque reversal of roles, as the dynamic entrepreneurs whom Thatcherite culture values highly and which in fact the workers are not. In other words, by the illegality of their position, and by the illegal conditions of their labor, the workers in *Riff*

Raff are paradoxically, and only nominally, each turned into the type of citizen that Thatcherism desires, "the self-sufficient . . . respectable, patriarchal, entrepreneurial subject," as Stuart Hall puts it (Hall, 10), a subject self-identified in national terms through the exclusivist logic of inside-outside shape by the conservative rhetoric of home.

By questioning the "commonsense" definition of home as the space of safe privacy and national heritage, Loach also questions the identity that such milieu is supposed to produce. The workers' simultaneous interpellation in and exclusion from the terrain of home function to expose the claimed universalism of this particular rhetoric of location, by showing how those who are materially building the dream house of Englishness do not belong to it and are in fact homeless. At the same time, they cannot give up their *right* to have a home and, implicitly, a place in society; this double bind is signified in the film by the splintering of home into provisional spaces where the workers can survive as social and individualized subjects. As alternative spaces where their dignity can be at least temporarily reconquered, Stevie's squat and the workers' common room (the tearoom) are complementary to each other, each housing a function of the domestic space—physical and social reproduction and affective contact with others—which are impossible to renounce even if their characteristic site is unavailable. The tearoom, where the radio is played, food is cooked, stories and jokes are shared, is a space of recreation and solidarity, where bourgeois privacy is supplanted by a form of volatile community and, on occasion, of public intimacy. Yet it is not home: the workers must leave the building site at night and find their own accommodations. Thus "home" for Stevie is the squat in a housing project that Shem, Moe, and Larry find for him. Although the squat provides the material shelter of walls and a roof, it is entirely devoid of the familial and domestic connotations that the tearoom possesses; Stevie's solitude in a squalidly empty interior when his friends leave is thus another bitterly parodic portrayal of bourgeois privacy.

Far from being an instance of the pastoral, a space where, as Kathleen Biddick affirms, "contradictions are projected out and contained,"[10] home is represented as a paradigmatic nonsite where social contradictions become instead visible and irreconcilable. In this sense, both the tearoom and the squat are displacements and reenactments of domesticity aimed at puncturing and deconstructing any ideological seamlessness that the notion of home may embody. If both the squat and the "heritage home" itself are uninhabitable, Loach is not romanticizing the tearoom as a domestic surrogate; the film is careful not to represent the togetherness and the sense of community that this space provides for the workers as the happy, if improvised, solution to their precarious status, their exploitation, and their lack of identity. Although the humor and the solidarity of the tearoom under such conditions may be, as both Loach and script cowriter Bill Jesse declared, a means of survival,[11] they are at the same time the scenario of an urgent social critique, aimed at reconstructing the workers' identity as a class.

"Depressions Are for the Middle Class": The Squat/The Urn

While hooking up the electricity and the gas in Stevie's squat, Larry reconstructs in a few, concise points "how we got here"—that is, how the free-market politics favored by the conservative government managed to exploit and interpellate at the same time masses of people, "by forging," as Stuart Hall affirms, "new discursive articulations between the liberal discourses of the 'free market' and economic man, and the organic conservative terms of tradition, family and nation" (Hall, 2). As usual, Shem and Moe refuse to listen to what they consider "a bleeding parliamentary debate," thus demonstrating how the language of social awareness and mobilization has lost currency among the workers at large. In turn, it is their disinterest, their passive and disengaged attitude, that prompts Larry to address them as "lumpen proletariat": "Everyday people are having their electricity cut off and their gas 'cos they can't pay. I know I go on! They had you in mind when they invented the saying!" When Larry addresses his friends in these terms, evoking the image of "the whole, indefinite, disintegrated mass, thrown hither and thither" that Marx describes in *The Eighteenth of Brumaire of Louis Bonaparte*, he is directly pointing to one of the central issues articulated by the film: the workers' incapability to represent themselves as a class.

As the British social theorists Alex Callinicos and Chris Harman sustain, the question of how a class-based politics might continue to be articulated has been one of the central political issues of the 1980s. During the period of a massive weakening of the welfare state and of the demise of the power of unions and labor movements—and when social antagonisms continued to emerge not only and not merely in terms of class, but along lines of race, gender, and sexuality—the Marxist construction of the working class as the carrier of a homogeneous consciousness and as the chief agent of social change has increasingly come to seem obsolete. In Britain the theoretical discussion on class and class antagonism has split into two camps: on one side are the supporters of the thesis of the decline of the working class, proposed by Andre Gorz in *Farewell to the Working Class*, translated into English in 1982, and promptly incorporated by the historian Eric Hobsbawm in his journal *Marxism Today*. On the other are the detractors of this very thesis, such as Alex Callinicos, Chris Harman,

and Eric Olin Right, among others, who refuse the idea of the end of the
working class as a social and political force.[12]

Although *Riff Raff* is not neatly situated in either camp, it nonetheless
addresses the same questions about the validity and the possibility of a
cohesive image of the working class as Callinicos and Hobsbawm have
debated. On the one hand, the film's narrative seems to testify to the crisis
of the representation of the working class as homogeneous and fully antagonistic to capital. On the other, particularly through the figure of a
class-conscious and politically aware figure among the workers, Larry,
the film seems unwilling to renounce the notion of class consciousness,
particularly since the characters are exploited exactly in terms of class. If
the workers at the Prince of Wales Hospital are exploited as labor by being underpaid and expected to work without security of employment,
health or accident insurance, and adequate safety precautions, they
should, the film constantly implies, be capable of recognizing the terms of
their exploitation. *Riff Raff* suggests that even though class should not
stand as the master category of the workers' social identity, the element
that explains all, it should nonetheless be maintained as a category that
can partly, and necessarily, contribute to their self-representation as
overdetermined social subjects, while they simultaneously partake in
multiple categories of subjective identification.

Loach's antinostalgic handling of class is visible in his depiction of a
heterogeneous lumpen proletariat. It includes migrant workers, laborers
by trade (such as Moe and Larry), and "temporaries" who, like Stevie, are
just out of prison and plan to "labor" only for a while before embarking
on some new venture or who, like Jo, need some extra money to continue
their studies. Such a variegated panorama is no guarantee of any homogeneous and "predetermined" working-class consciousness; rather, it acknowledges that consciousness is contradictory and that on the basis of
such contradictoriness an individual can be ideologically interpellated in
different, even antagonistic, directions. Thatcherism's cultural hegemony
was founded, and its interpellative power based, as Hall points out, precisely on the clever management and articulation of the contradictory
character of consciousness:

> We underestimate the degree to which Thatcherism succeeded in represent-
> ing itself "on the side of the little people against the big battalions." Ideolog-
> ically, it has made itself, to some degree, not only "one of them," but, more
> disconcertingly, "one of us"; it has aligned itself with "what some of the peo-
> ple really want," while at the same time continuing to dominate them
> through the power bloc. (Hall, 5)

It is by virtue of this contradictory character of consciousness that
Thatcherism as a populist ideology of national cohesiveness hinging on

the image of a self-sufficient, entrepreneurial model of subjectivity has succeeded in interpellating and including in its political and economic project masses of people who had no purchase in it and who in fact were eventually damaged by it.

Part of the narrative of *Riff Raff* makes clear also how Thatcherism, by speaking an interclassist language of corporate nationalism, has managed to spread the conviction that any one of "them" could become part of the "big battalions" of privilege, status, and money, that anyone could become an entrepreneur, at least at the level of fantasy. It is such a fantasy that contributes to the pathos of Stevie's overdetermined and schizophrenic self-perception as temporary laborer and future businessman (he has a dream of selling boxer shorts), a fantasy that metonymically points to the incapability and refusal of the working class to narrativize themselves as class.

Stevie's aspiration to a better social status and a respectable and successful job emerge in the course of his first encounter with Susan, a young woman with whom he later embarks on a romance and who shares the squat with him for a while. When Stevie goes to Susan's house to return her stolen bag, which he had found by the building site, he is reticently invited in for a cup of tea. Susan, who is from Dublin, introduces herself as "a singer," immediately explaining in a befuddled tone that actually she is only singing in pubs, that, in other words, she's only trying to become one. The same self-representation is projected by Stevie, who, when asked what his occupation is, answers: "I'm into merchandising; that's where I am heading. . . . Boxer shorts, good money in it, you know. . . . Big demand for them in the markets. I got plans, if I can only get started. Maybe open up a small shop. Maybe selling from a van or a market stall. This laboring is only temporary, you know. . . . It's crap." Ironically, the only one of the two who actively pursues her dream and tries to become the persona through which she represents herself to herself is crushed at the end: Susan, who believes in astrology and copes with life by doing drugs occasionally and the I Ching daily, auditions whenever she can, never loses hope, and sings even in the subway, while Stevie's aspirations never seem more than daydreaming or a hypothetical intention. Yet it is Susan who, mostly through Stevie's perspective, is constructed as a weak and parasitic figure, whose emotional ups and downs are presented as a vacuous luxury (the luxury of desperation, one could say) and as decadent and implicitly bourgeois nonsense.

The discourse of class and class identity is suddenly reintroduced in the film during an emotional exchange between the two characters, once Susan, after many hesitations, moves in with Stevie. When she expresses her desire for their relationship to work, she also confesses that in the past, at the height of a period of depression, she attempted suicide. When asked if he ever gets depressed, Stevie harshly and unexpectedly replies: "Depressions are for the middle classes. The rest of us have an early start in the morning." With these words he seems to reclaim a proletarian identity (and a class ressentiment), which, like Susan's depression, has not yet emerged. Nonetheless, the harshness of his reply is mitigated by Stevie's awareness that both are survivors, that both in some way or another made it, and that their "being there" testifies to their survival. ("I'm still here. You are still here. We made it. It's going to work out. Your furniture is here.") In the end the stability and safety that Susan's few flimsy items of furniture as a signifier of domesticity seem to guarantee to their menage and to the newly "domesticated" scenario of the squat turn out to be more fictitious and volatile than Stevie thought. Their relationship will fail and dissolve exactly because of their different understanding of "being there," or perhaps because of Susan's inability to redeem herself into the ethics of labor, to commit herself, that is, to the hard bedrock of reality-as-labor experienced by all those who, according to Stevie, have an early start in the morning.

At this point in the film, the discourse of the proletarian work ethic becomes for the protagonist a means of survival, a discourse of sacrifice and moral integrity providing him with a form of stable and acceptable identity that his status as "riff raff" otherwise denies him. And yet this upright proletarian antihero steals a tool from the work site to sell, after promising Susan that he would not do so anymore. The figure of the worker "thieving" after his early start in the morning seems to complicate the meaning of "being there"—Stevie's claim to be self-present, aware, and accepting of his own position within the social whole and, in particular, within the relations of production. The dutiful (and resentful) attachment to work, in which Stevie seems to find a viable identity, are the same qualities that the Thatcherite social credo of cooperation and efficiency demands. To disavow the way Stevie's loyalty to labor and his reliability as a worker juxtapose with the expectations of capital, Loach needs to depict his proletarian characters as disaffected and antagonistic. The protagonist of *Riff Raff* gets up early in the morning *and* steals the kango from the work site, and in the end his dissent and discontent manifest themselves even more as a direct attack on property.

When Stevie says that "depressions are for the middle class," he claims to "be there" more than Susan and affirms a sense of belonging and of responsibility that she doesn't seem to have. Nonetheless, between her fantasies of success and the reality of her singing Irish ballads in the subway, Susan runs the same distance that separates Stevie's early mornings from his own entrepreneurial dreams. If Susan escapes reality and refuses to "be there" to follow her delusions, "walking in a daze, waiting for the party to begin," as Stevie brutally points out, so does he. In fact, through his alleged claim to a stable class identity, he makes clear at all turns his sense of transience and social homelessness. It is, ironically, the misrecognition of the similarity of their condition that drives them apart. Notwithstanding the family scene taking place in the squat (Susan decorating its space with flowers, sparse furniture, and posters, Stevie boiling water to make tea in the morning, Susan presenting him with a cake for his birthday), their relationship, as an attempt to find and found a home, fails.

The bankruptcy of a traditional definition of home centered upon the solid presence of the female figure and around notions of privacy, order, hierarchy, and consumption that Stevie's and Susan's story dramatizes is poignantly reiterated during one of the chief moments of comic relief (albeit in the tone of black humor) in the film, the scene of the funeral of Stevie's mother in Glasgow. The funeral marks the moment of the symbolic explosion of the notion of home through the pulverization and dispersal of the female body. After a dismal journey through Glasgow's urban and suburban desolation, Stevie and his family come to the cemetery where his mother's body will be cremated. Here, in the eerily pastoral world of the cemetery (the scene of the scattering of the ashes is dominated by the green of the grass and ancient, huge trees), "home" as a space is once again cited and symbolically reappears in the image of the urn containing the ashes of Stevie's mother. But, as already happened with the squat, the urn, too, as a catachrestic image of home, reveals itself to be dysfunctional: The female, maternal body, around which the pastoral, nostalgic fantasy of home solidifies, is absent, "not there," and once again refuses to be confined to an enclosed space. At the climactic moment of the ceremony, after a squabble about which of the siblings is going to scatter the ashes, Stevie's inept sister scatters them all over the mourners, who almost hysterically try to shake "their mother" off their Sunday best. The family is finally dispersed and sent away by the angry undertaker, spluttering at their inappropriate behavior and the disorder they caused (after the unsuccessful dispersal of the ashes, everybody started loudly and comically to fight with each other). With this counterpastoral representation of the family, Loach stages a final reversal of the Thatcherite ideology of the domestic as the medium of social and interpersonal order.

Upon his return from Scotland, Stevie surprises Susan injecting drugs in their bedroom (another female body in the process of self-unmaking and drifting away from life) and orders her out. When he comes back from work that evening, "home" has turned once again into the squat; Susan's furniture is gone, and with it any trace of intimacy and family life. Susan's departure, signaling the end of any figuration of domesticity, of any possibility of "home" for Stevie and his companions, is anticipated by the departure of the single potential parental figure in the film, Larry. As the most mature member of the group of workers, he is always represented in a mediating, paternal position. ("Watch your manners. . . . I have children your age," he tells his superior, the foreman.) Above all he represents the consciousness, in particular the class consciousness, of the group, the voice of reason and class solidarity that tries to keep them together at all costs ("Don't fall out over a few pounds!" he warns Fiaman and the others during a fight) and to mobilize them as exploited labor, inviting them to join the union and protest against the unsafe conditions of the work site.

Although during a discussion in the tearoom everybody agrees "to stick together for security," as Fiaman puts it, Larry goes to the foreman's booth alone to protest, and the next Thursday ("paying day and sacking day," as Gus the foreman had warned at the beginning), he is fired. He accepts the news with resignation and leaves defeated, guilty of, as he says, "having opened my big mouth once again." He bids good-bye sadly to the others. Without really being backed by the other workers, at the mercy of their employer, Loach's characters cannot interpret solidarity as anything more than this sad good-bye to Larry. His departure leaves behind a bleak scenario of disenfranchised and resigned individuals, homeless and without rights. What is left for Stevie, Moe, Shem, and the others is only suppressed anger and the desire to escape, with nothing to lose.

Going Back to Where One Has Never Been: Away/Abroad (the Designer Bathroom)

By the end, the narrative of *Riff Raff* comes full circle and closes as it began, with the image of the out-of-placedness and lack of connection among the workers. Toward the conclusion, the film's politics of location take an unexpected turn, so that the characters' attempt to resist their imposed invisibility through the displacement and reconfiguration of "home" becomes more and more interspersed with the desire of "not being there," of going away or at least dreaming of a better place to live. These escapist fantasies (and actions) are directly related to the characters' full awareness of the material and metaphorical uninhabitability, for them, of the house they are building. If home, as the space of affective and material reproduction, cannot be given up by these dispossessed subjects and is continually reimagined, at least as a utopia, the house (representing a complex constellation of the public sphere, England, legality, the state, and the nation) can in no way be appropriated and remains an alienating and excluding space that cannot be dislocated or changed.

The uneasiness and out-of-placedness of the workers inside the house become fully visible in two scenes, Larry's visit to the model apartment and Desmond's death when he accidentally falls from the scaffolding. When the workers' portable toilet breaks down, Larry climbs up to the fourth floor and steals into the model apartment through an open window to use the bathroom. By assuming Larry's point of view, the spectator is made to look at the apartment through the defamiliarizing gaze of the subaltern, a mixture of awe, the fear of being caught, and the awareness of being off-limits. In the next scene, the camera pans on a Rolls-Royce entering the gate of the London Heritage Homes work site; while the agent and four women in chador move toward the front entrance of the building, Larry has decided to allow himself the luxury of a bath in the privacy and "foreignness" of the bathroom. By the time the visitors reach the fourth floor, it's too late for him to leave. The spectacle of the designer bathroom as a consumable view for the prospective buyers is irreparably marred by Larry's no-brand naked body, as he holds in front of his genitals the unequivocal sign of his lower status, the worker's hard hat. Chased out of the apartment by five screaming women, he steals back out the window and down the scaffolding, like a criminal. This scene punctually reinscribes both "a characteristically bourgeois mode of perception" (Kester, 73), founded on the exclusion of the sight of the proletarian, and the organizing principle of this perception, the logic of the reified commodity fetish. In this instance, the designer bathroom assumes "the mystical character of the commodity," so that any trace of its material conditions of production (of which Larry is an extremely visible memento) must be eliminated. Even more in this scene, the image of traditional domesticity that the Heritage Homes evoke is once again displaced. With the image of the woman in chador, the female figure is once again placed at the center of the home, but paradoxically, in this instance "Englishness" comes to be signified by an un-English and foreign body. At the same time, Larry, who is English "by blood," but proletarian, is excluded from the national domestic space. At this point it becomes clear that "national heritage" is in no way the property of the body; rather, it is a salable commodity, available to whomever can pay its price.

Back on the safe ground of the tearoom, Larry is able to turn his misadventure "abroad" into a tall tale for his friends. In his version of the story, he is seduced by the women, who don't want to let him go, so that instead of being thrown out of the apartment, he has to run away. Larry's encounter with the exotic buyers triggers a discussion of faraway places; Africa, in particular, is always on the mind of Desmond, one of the Black workers. For him, born in England and never having been to Africa, the dream of Africa fulfills, in one stroke, the double desire for home and a faraway heterotopia, for "being there" and going away.

Desmond's desire for Africa, apparently predicated on the "authenticity" of the discourse of "roots," is unconsciously filtered, for him, by the discourse of western tourism, as the dialogue with Jo, one of the workers from Africa, shows: "I hear you lot still live in huts." Jo: "In Peckham . . . my father's "hut" has two floors and fitted carpets. I study the law. . . . "

At this point, Desmond's desire for the pastoral has much the same meaning as the discourse of "heritage" represented by the "revitalized" Prince of Wales Hospital; in fact, he's seeing Africa almost through the lenses of White colonial nostalgia. Desmond's utopia and his desire to know "what it's really like there" are both nurtured and debunked by Jo and Fiaman, both emigrants from Nigeria. In their descriptions and reminiscences, Africa becomes split into an image of the earthly paradise, a world of abundance featuring endless parties, uncontaminated nature, food, and beautiful women (a tourist's vision or the romanticizing, nostalgic view of the emigrant) and an image of the troubled country in need of material help, where holidays are only for foreigners. Jo: "You want to discover your roots?" Desmond: "Yes, among other things." Jo: "It's not so simple. What can you do? Are you an engineer? . . . Are you an accountant? Do you have any skills?" In the course of this dialogue, the romanticized representation of "home" as a protective shelter fades away. The scene implicitly evokes the moment when Larry is excluded from the space of Englishness, symbolized by the designer bathroom in the Heritage Homes, because of his social status. Also, in Desmond's case, his national and racial claims to Africa as home are not enough; as Larry has been ousted from his national heritage by the women in chador (possibly postcolonial subjects), the first world expert, engineer, doctor, or accountant takes precedence over Desmond in acceding to Africa.

Jo's and Fiaman's two versions of Africa become even more irreconcilably split in another point-counterpoint exchange in which their voices almost juxtapose. Fiaman: "I went to a party that lasted two weeks, man!" Jo: "What is he going to eat?" The idea of the homeland as pastoral fantasy is once and for all crashed against the image of an irrevocable materiality. The question of the uninhabitability of home, particularly for those at the margins of the circuit of social and economic privilege, is fully brought into focus by the discussion of Africa. Home, as a recognizable, fixed location to be desired nostalgically, does not exist. Going back home means returning to a place where one has never been, as another fragment of the dialogue between Desmond and Jo makes clear: "I am seriously thinking of going back." "You have never been."

Loach uses the ex-centric discourse of Africa as "lost homeland" to expose the romanticism and false universalism of any prepackaged discourse of home. Like the Britain signified by London Heritage Homes, Desmond's Africa exists only in the travel brochure he continually studies. In Jo's, Fiaman's, and Desmond's narrative, Africa as home becomes spliced between the view of exotic huts featured in the brochure and the two-story carpeted "hut" where Jo's father lives in Peckham, between the Edenlike image fantasized about by Fiaman and a place that is still, literally, in the process of being constructed.

This necessary liminality of home finally spells out the politics of location that *Riff Raff* has throughout dramatized. The image of home that ultimately results is suspended between "being there" (at the work site, in the squat, in Africa) and being denied access to the house and thus having to fight to find a location, to inhabit the house, to be granted social recognition and a physical and affective space to live in.

This struggle is further dramatized when Desmond, the one among Loach's characters who, more than any other, dreams of leaving the house to find a home, dies the victim of the unsafe conditions of the building site. Notwithstanding Stevie's and Moe's desperate attempt to save him, the scaffolding on which he leans yields, and he falls to the ground from the fourth floor, to die at the hospital. The scene at the hospital reiterates and makes even more evident the invisibility of the subaltern. When Stevie asks the receptionist for news of his friend Desmond Harris, he discovers that his real name is Leroy Winston. When asked by the woman about his own identity and name, he leaves. However painful and inhuman it is for Stevie to abandon his friend in the hospital, giving his own name means to risk his job and perhaps even his freedom.

Just as Larry leaves the work site alone, after having been fired, Desmond is left to a solitary death by the "illegality" and facelessness of his coworkers. With this death, the tenuous ties of worker solidarity, friendship, and community that, beyond any fixed spatiality, have functioned to define "home" in the film, are lost. At this point nothing is left to the survivors but to take their revenge, and they take it by destroying the tangible symbol of the power that produced their invisibility, the newly built house. At night Moe and Stevie return to the work site and set the building on fire. Sitting on a high wall nearby, they watch the spectacle of the flames and exchange a knowing smile before jumping down and disappearing into the darkness behind. In the last scene, in a symmetrical repetition of the beginning, the rats appear at the center of the frame, swiftly moving to escape the flames, the dirt, and the debris of more urban desolation.

Has the subaltern spoken? What does the fire, a gesture of class revenge as closure, accomplish in the narrative economy of the film? For Stevie and Moe it is certainly an act of revenge, but both for them and for the audience, it has no cathartic quality. Once the language of negotiation, reclaimed rights, and labor mobilization spoken by the unions has been validated, as Larry's figure shows, what other language is left? The final burning down of the house reminds the viewer of several moments of civic upheaval that punctuated the British history of the 1980s, starting with the Brixton riots of 1981. Yet the resemblance is not perfect; a *civic* upheaval implies a choral action, a communal rebellion, rather that the actions of isolated individuals.

The fire is a gesture of revenge, but not of victory. Stevie and Moe "lose" their battle, so to speak, not simply because their gesture is violent and destructive, but because, like Larry at the moment of his departure and Desmond at the moment of his (very political) death, they are alone. With their final jump in the dark, the discourse of commitment (the fight for one's rights and the attempt to reconstruct a sense of class consciousness via the domestic space) that the film has tried over and over again to articulate seems to evaporate. The conflict between Stevie's claim to "being there" and his final getaway (to prison? to another casual job? to his selling van?) is not resolved. With this irresolution, the notion of home, until now nomadically displaced, redefined, critiqued, and intermittently recuperated, is also eclipsed.

All we know and all we see is that the master's house, materially represented by the speculative building project of the Prince of Wales Hospital, and its economic investment in myths of homeliness are finally destroyed, but the conclusion of Riff Raff provides nothing that can stand in place of its ruins. The violent destruction of the house is the only way that the subaltern can be made visible in this context, but subalternity cannot "rescue" and find for itself any viable form of representation. The volatile sense of community that being a subaltern seems to spontaneously generate in the workers' tearoom never coheres in a more substantial and solid self-awareness of one's own exploitation. Rather, Loach's workers remain throughout structurally isolated free players. From this perspective the last scene portrays an act of exasperated and desperate resistance. On the one hand, burning down the house changes nothing in the life of these workers; on the other, for lack of another language, it's a gesture of impotence, albeit a powerful one. And when the flames rise high in the night, one regrets that the spectacle watched by Moe and Stevie remains a private one.

Notes

1. Quoted in Stuart Hall, The Hard Way to Renewal: Thatcherism and the Crisis of the Left (London: Verso, 1988), p. 12.

2. On the effects of postfordism and the spatial reorganization of labor, see David Harvey, The Condition of Postmodernity (London: Blackwell, 1989); Stuart Hall and Martin Jacques, eds., New Times: The Changing Face of Politics in the 1990s (London: Lawrence and Wishart, 1989); John Urry, "Class, Space and Disorganized Capitalism," in Keith Hoggart and Eleanor Kofman, eds., Politics, Geography and Social Stratification (Kent: Croom Helm, 1986); Doreen Massey, Spatial Divisions of Labor: Social Structure and the Geography of Production (Oxford: Blackwell, 1984); Edward Soja, Postmodern Geographies: The Reassertion of Space in Critical Social Theory (London: Verso, 1989); and Richard Peet and Nigel Thrift, eds., New Models in Geography: The Political Economy Perspective (London: Unwin Hyman, 1989).

3. For a more extended discussion of the collusion of different critiques of post-modernism, see Grant H. Kester, "Out of Sight Is Out of Mind: The Imaginary Space of Postindustrial Culture," *Social Text*, Vol. 35, Summer 1993, 72–93; and Neil Lazarus, "Doubting the New World Order: Marxism, Realism and the Claims of Postmodernist Social Theory," *Differences*, Vol. 3, No. 3, Fall 1991, 94–139.

4. Quoted in Brian Deer, "How Leisure Disappeared from Our Crowded Hours," *The Sunday London Times*, December 11, 1994, p. 12 of the "Culture" section.

5. Peter Dunn and Loraine Leeson are two artists who, during the 1980s, coordinated the Docklands Community Poster Project, an agitprop movement aimed at mobilizing the public opinion in favor of the local community of the Docklands against the project of redevelopment that the area was undergoing at the time. Their collages (figuratively and ideologically close to the denunciatory tone of 1920s Berlin dada), publications, leaflets, and banners stand as a unique example of "local" organized urban resistance. See Peter Dunn and Loraine Leeson, "The Art of Change in Docklands," in Jon Bird, Barry Curtis, Tim Putnam, George Robertson, and Lisa Tickner, eds., *Mapping Futures: Local Culture, Global Change* (London: Verso, 1993), pp. 136–50. For a feminist discussion of the politics of location and the importance of the local, see Elspeth Probyn, "Travels in the Postmodern: Making Sense of the Local," in Linda Nicholson, ed., *Feminism/Postmodernism* (New York: Routledge, 1990), pp. 176–90.

6. Jon Bird gives a full explanation of the functioning of the UDC in "Dystopia on the Thames," in Bird et al., *Mapping Futures*.

7. See Peter Stallybrass and Allon White, *The Politics and Poetics of Transgression* (Ithaca: Cornell University Press, 1986).

8. Friedrich Engels, *The Condition of the Working Class in England* (Moscow: Progress Publishers, 1980), p. 78.

9. "The essence of the British people was identified with self-reliance and personal responsibility, as against the image of the overtaxed individual, enervated by welfare state 'coddling,' his or her moral fibre irrevocably sapped by 'state handouts.' This assault, not just on welfare overspending, but on the very principle and essence of collective social welfare . . . was mounted not through an analysis of which class of the deserving made most out of the welfare state, but through the emotive image of the 'scrounger': the new folk-devil" (Stuart Hall, p. 47).

10. Kathleen Biddick discusses the family as a pastoral space in the context of the conservative ideology of the past in medieval studies in the paper "English America: Curricular Masks/Imperial Phantasmatics," presented at the conference "Rethinking Britain," University of California–Santa Barbara, October 21–23, 1994.

11. See Renzo Gilodi, "I proletari di Loach," *Cinema Sessanta*, No. 5/6, settembre/dicembre 1991, 5–7.

12. See Andre Gorz, *Farewell to the Working Class*, trans. Michael Sonenscher (Boston: South End Press, 1982) and Alex Callinicos and Chris Harman, *The Changing Working Class* (London: Bookmarks, 1987).

About the Editor
and Contributors

Nancy Armstrong is the Nancy Duke Lewis Professor of Comparative Literature, English, Modern Culture and Media, and Women's Studies at Brown University in Providence, Rhode Island. She is the author of *Desire and Domestic Fiction: A Political History of the Novel* (Oxford University Press, 1987) and *The Imaginary Puritan: Literature, Intellectual Labor, and the Origins of Personal Life*, coauthored with Leonard Tennenhouse (University of California Press, 1992).

Maurizia Boscagli is associate professor of English at the University of California–Santa Barbara, where she teaches gender studies, modernism, and cultural theory. She is the author of *Eye on the Flesh: Fashions of Masculinity in the Early Twentieth Century* (Westview Press, 1996). Her work on the body, on gender and the rhetoric of emotions, and on contemporary American culture has appeared in *differences, Discourse,* and *College Literature.*

Ann duCille is professor of American and African American literature at the University of California–San Diego. She is the author of *The Coupling Convention: Sex, Text and Tradition in Black Women's Fiction* (Oxford University Press, 1993) and *Skin Trade* (Harvard University Press, 1996).

Rosemary Marangoly George is an assistant professor of literatures in English and cultural studies at the University of California–San Diego. She is the author of *The Politics of Home: Postcolonial Relocations and Twentieth-Century Fiction* (Cambridge University Press, 1996). Her work on postcolonial literatures, British imperialism, and diaspora studies has appeared in *differences, NOVEL, Cultural Critique, Diaspora,* and *MELUS.*

Gayatri Gopinath is a doctoral candidate in the department of English and comparative literature at Columbia University, New York. She is working on a dissertation on queer diaspora and South Asian popular culture. Her work has appeared in *Diaspora* and the anthology *Asian-American Sexualities*, edited by Russell Leong (Routledge, 1995).

David Lloyd was born in Dublin in 1955 and studied in Belfast and Cambridge, England, receiving a doctorate in Anglo Irish literature from King's College–Cambridge in 1982. He currently holds the Hartley Burr Alexander Chair in the Humanities at Scripps College, Claremont, California. He has published *Nationalism and Minor Literature: James Clarence Mangan and the Emergence of Irish Cultural Nationalism* (University of California Press,1987) and edited *The Nature and Context of Minority Discourse* (Oxford University Press, 1990) with Abdul Jan Mohammad. He has also written numerous essays on Irish literature, on aesthetics, and on cultural politics. His most recent book is *Anomalous States: Irish Writing in the Post-colonial Moment* (Dublin: Lilliput Press and Durham, N.C.: Duke University Press, 1993). Other works include *Other Circuits: Intersections and Exchanges in World Theory and Practice*, coedited with Lisa Lowe (Duke University Press, 1997) and *Culture and the State*, with Paul Thomas (Routledge 1997).

John Lowney is assistant professor of English at Saint John's University in New York. He is the author of *The American Avant-Garde Tradition: William Carlos William, Postmodern Poetry and the Politics of Cultural Memory* (Bucknell University Press, 1996).

Katharyne Mitchell teaches in the department of Geography at the University of Washington. Her recent articles about the transnational flows of people and capital in the Pacific Rim have appeared in *Transactions of the Institute of British Geographers, Economic Geography*, and the edited volumes *Global/Local* and *Edges of Empires*. Her book *Diaspora and the Politics of Space* is forthcoming from the University of California Press.

Amie Parry is an associate professor of foreign languages and literatures at National Chiao Tung University in Hsinchu, Taiwan. She is currently finishing a book on literary modernism in the Taiwan and U.S. contexts, forthcoming from Duke University Press.

Chandan C. Reddy is pursuing his doctorate at Columbia University, New York, in the department of English and comparative literature. His chapter in this collection is part of a larger project on the critical emergence of "queers of color" subjectivities within the social grouping "people of color" in the United States. His research includes comparative studies of U.S. and British colonial projects and liberal pluralisms in the late nineteenth and twentieth centuries.

Aparajita Sagar is an associate professor at Purdue University, Indiana, where she teaches postcolonial literature and cultural studies. She has edited a *Modern Fiction Studies* special issue on South Asian literature and published articles on Caribbean fiction. She recently completed a book manuscript titled *The Caribbean Palimpsest: Women, Writing, and Postcoloniality* (forthcoming from Duke University Press, 1998).

Dayana Salazar is an assistant professor in the urban and regional planning department at San Jose State University, California. She is currently working (in collaboration with the Santa Clara County School District) on a series of community-based urban design projects concentrated on Hispanic immigrant neighborhoods throughout the Silicon Valley. Salazar is also researching the use of computer-aided visualization as a tool to facilitate citizen participation in community design processes.

Susan Sánchez Casal is assistant professor of Spanish in the Department of Romance Languages and Literature at Hamilton College in Clinton, New York, where she teaches literature and women's studies courses on contemporary Latin American and Latina/Latino narrative. Her published articles include "Testimony as Writing: Criticism, Representation, Reception" (1993) and "I Am [Not] Like You: Ideologies of Selfhood in *I, Rigoberta Menchú*" (forthcoming). Professor Sánchez Casal is currently coediting a critical anthology of interdisciplinary essays entitled *The Feminist Classroom for the Twenty-first Century: Pedagogies of Power and Difference* (Garland Publishing, forthcoming in 1999). In her teaching, her writing, and her life, she is committed to feminist, antiracist criticism and pedagogies.

Siobhan Somerville is an assistant professor of English and women's studies at Purdue University, Indiana. Her book, which explores intersecting constructions of race and sexuality in late-nineteenth-century sexology, fiction, and film in the United States, is forthcoming from Duke University Press. Her articles have appeared in *Journal of the History of Sexuality* and *American Literature*.

K. Srilata is a doctoral candidate in the department of English at Central University in Hyderabad, India. Her dissertation studies popular literatures for women in the contexts of language politics and debates around modernity in contemporary India. She has presented her work on romance, caste, gender, and language use at scholarly conferences and has published an article on romance, post-coloniality, and popular culture in *The Indian Journal of American Studies*.

Kimberly Wallace Sanders is an assistant professor of women's studies and assistant director of the Women's Research and Resource Center at Spellman College, Atlanta. She has worked extensively on Black motherhood and the Black mammy figure in U.S. cultural texts. She is currently compiling a collection of essays on the Black female body.

Index

Abdel Kader, Soha, 175, 184(n3)
Abortion, 269
Abraham, Julie, 100(n18)
Adorno, Theodore, 1, 8, 17(n1)
Advertising. *See* Aunt Jemima
Africa, 5–7, 65, 394–395
African Americans
    class distinctions among, 221–223,
        241, 248–249
    homosexuality among. *See also*
        Contending Forces; Homosexuality,
        among people of color; *Paris is*
        Burning; Women, African
        American
    and marriage, 233–234, 246–248,
        251–252, 254(n10)
    racism against, 94, 217, 220–224, 287,
        290, 293
    in Stein's "Melanctha," 94
    See also Aunt Jemima; Racism;
        Slavery; Women, African
        American
Alarcón, Norma, 334–335
Althusser, Louis, 357, 358, 362,
    372(nn 5,6), 374–375(n6), 375(n10)
Altman, Dennis, 118
America. *See* United States of
    America
American Dream, 219, 326
American President, The (1995), 290–291
American Standard of Living, 359–363
Anthropology
    documentary form and, 368,
        377(n26), 377–378(n27)
    sexuality and, 109–116
Anzaldúa, Gloria, 335, 337
Arabic language, 178, 183

Architecture
    architectural style as scapegoat for
        racial tensions, 196–197, 210(n24)
    modern/international style, 143,
        149(n53)
    neoclassic, 128, 130–131, 133,
        134(figure), 143
    postmodern, 197
    refugee housing in Dekaokto,
        Greece, 132–140, 134(figure),
        136(figure)
    traditional British styles, 198–199
    See also Monster Houses
Armstrong, Nancy, 49, 233, 236, 292
Arnold, Matthew, 91, 99(n3), 155,
    167(n6)
Articulation, 361–362, 375–376(n13)
Aryan Model of western history,
    146(n19)
Assimilation
    Greek refugees lack of, 128–129,
        145(nn 10,12)
    narratives of, 33, 35, 40–41
Athens, 131–132, 147(n25)
Aunt Jemima, 14, 215–229,
    229–230(n14), 230(nn 15,16,28)
    advertising, 215–217, 219–220,
        224–228
    company ownership, 229(n5),
        230(n15)
    official representatives for, 218,
        220–223, 228, 229(n12),
        229–230(n14)
Authoritative self, 47, 48, 50

Badran, Margot, 175
Baker, Houston, 243